Opinions and Reflections

A Free Mind at Work
1990-2015

Paul Monk

BARRALLIERBOOKS

First published in 2015 by Barrallier Books Pty Ltd,
Registered Office: 35-37 Gordon Avenue, West Geelong, Victoria 3220, Australia.
www.barrallierbooks.com

Copyright © Paul Monk 2015

National Library of Australia cataloguing-in-publication information:

Creator: Monk, Paul M., author.

Opinions and reflections : a free mind at work, 1990-2015/Paul Monk.

ISBN: 9780994281159 (hardback)

Notes: Includes index.

Subjects: Australian essays.

Dewey Number: A824.4

Set in Garamond Premier Pro 12/17 and Fragrance

Cover image: *Shell*
Jörg Schmeisser

Portrait of the author by John Spooner, March 2015

For my mother, who first encouraged me to read; and for Claudia, who requested this book specifically

Contents

Preface: What it means to be a public intellectual and how I became one ... xi

Part I: Late 20th century pieces

Section 1: 1990-91
1. The collapse of the Soviet bloc in Eastern Europe in 1989 ... 5
2. Bread, circuses and classical scholarship ... 10
3. The genius of Ludwig Wittgenstein ... 12
4. The Western as a film genre ... 16
5. Charles De Gaulle as an epic hero ... 18
6. Israel's secret wars ... 22
7. Indonesia's bloodletting of 1965-66 and the US ambassador ... 25
8. James Jesus Angleton and CIA counter-intelligence ... 29
9. Strategic bombing and the genocidal mentality ... 34
10. A dubious prophesy of US war with Japan ... 38

Section 2: 1991-92
11. Noam Chomsky's critique of American democracy ... 42
12. Israel, the bomb and a conspiracy of silence ... 45
13. The Cambridge spies and the dark side of the force ... 48
14. Oliver Stone, JFK and conspiracy theory ... 52
15. The strange persistence of anti-Semitism ... 59
16. Alienating Russia at the end of the Cold War ... 63
17. Hector Bywater and the coming of the Pacific War ... 68
18. Charles De Gaulle and the grandeur of France ... 71
19. J. R. R. Tolkien's works at the centenary of his birth ... 74
20. International economic competition before China's rise ... 79

Section 3: 1992-93
21. Australia and the wars in Southeast Asia ... 84
22. The last Tsar and the fate of his family ... 89
23. Anti-Americanism and political rationality ... 92
24. A fatuous potboiler on war in Asia ... 96
25. George F. Kennan as an American elder statesman ... 99
26. Pol Pot and the genocide in Cambodia 1975-78 ... 102

27. The shape of things to come in the 21st century	105
28. Werner Heisenberg and the atomic bomb	109
29. Premonitions of the end of Hong Kong	113
30. Allan Bloom on love and friendship	116

Section 4: 1994-97

31. The evolution of 'total war'	121
32. China as the next economic superpower	125
33. Henry Kissinger and power politics	129
34. The looming danger to Hong Kong's liberties	133
35. Keeping the rise of China in perspective in 1995	137
36. Hidden aspects of Nazi eugenics	141
37. The rise and fall of totalitarianism	145
38. The August 1945 communist revolution in Vietnam	149
39. Contemplating the end of the world	153
40. Tales of Holocaust survival	157

Intermezzo: Seven turn of the century essays (1998-2001)

1. Kim Jong-Il's paranoia	163
2. Looking back at the 1960s	172
3. *Habemus Papam*: an appreciation of Pope John Paul II	183
4. Christianity and the cathedral of the mind	196
5. Atlantis and the science of archaeology	208
6. Secret intelligence and escape clauses	219
7. The allure of Mary McCarthy	253

Part II: Early 21st century pieces

Section 1: 2007-08

1. Integrity, secrecy and the public interest	262
2. Silencing even the hint of dissent in China	264
3. Iraq and Vietnam: three analogies	266
4. Wake up and ban the bomb	268
5. The children of democratic principles foil Hugo Chavez	270
6. The death of Suharto and the nature of our judgement	273
7. Beware China's emerging naval ambitions	275
8. Open the book on Cold War spies	277
9. Iran, the bomb and the war of ideas	279
10. Stalin, Trotsky and the Soviet archives	281

Section 2: 2008-09

11. Freedom is the name of the game	288
12. Balibo: theatre and history	291
13. Perfidious Albion and the merits of Zionism	294
14. Overthrowing Rudd: the system worked	296
15. The climate debate: more heat than light	298
16. Michael Scammell on Solzhenitsyn and Koestler	306
17. Latin America and the Washington Consensus	312
18. Conspiracy theory vs learning: Assange and Ellsberg	317
19. On challenging the scientific consensus	319
20. Galileo, science and religious authority	322

Section 3: 2009-10

21. Why democratization would be good for China	326
22. Six true heroes of modern China	328
23. Politics, reason and gay marriage	331
24. Meaning, secular nihilism and the work of Hubert Dreyfus	333
25. Ishmael's house and the origins of Israel	336
26. Jose Saramago's Cain mutiny	338
27. Efraim Karsh's *tour de force* on Palestine	340
28. The end is NIE: divergent assessments of the nuclear peril	344
29. Is China an autistic dragon?	347
30. If current trends continue ...	350

Section 4: 2010-11

31. Love among the ruins of Stalinism	354
32. Constraining Iran's nuclear ambitions	356
33. Daniel Kahneman on thinking fast and slow	358
34. Roman Krznaric's wonder box	361
35. The soloist and the chorus	363
36. *Mississippi Burning* in Tibet	366
37. Two funerals and an anniversary	369
38. The epic life of Ariel Sharon	372
39. The task in front of Barack Obama	375
40. Neuroscience and the new atheism	378

Section 5: 2012-13

41. Massive Chinese espionage afoot	382
42. Don't cry for me, Venezuela: the death of Hugo Chavez	384

43. Zionism, peace and illusion — 387
44. Miscavige of justice: indicting the Church of Scientology — 391
45. A calm and humane eye cast over China — 395
46. The puzzle of why nations fail — 398
47. Beyond Benedict: the Papacy and bridge-building — 400
48. Keating's confusion in regard to Indonesia — 403
49. Abraham Lincoln and the great task remaining before us — 406
50. Making democracy work — 408

Section 6: 2013-14

51. You call that a leaders' debate? — 414
52. Syria and the next defence white paper — 416
53. Edward Snowden: peering into the stateroom — 418
54. 'Suzie' and the fate of China — 421
55. Stuffing up a conspiracy theory — 423
56. A young Hazara woman off a boat — 429
57. Stan Wawrinka at the Australian Open — 432
58. Dog days punditry and the mining boom — 434
59. Cancer as a cellular atavism — 437
60. *Duty*: the Pentagon memoirs of Robert Gates — 440

Section 7: 2014-15

61. *Noah*: a fatuous cartoon — 446
62. Malcolm Fraser's rejection of the US alliance — 448
63. August 1914 and our time — 450
64. Getting perspective on Gaza and Hamas — 453
65. Eichmann and the caliphate: grappling with evil — 455
66. Israel as an occupying power — 458
67. Euthanasia: give us good choices, not fearful bans — 462
68. Xi Jinping and the denial of historical facts — 464
69. Cosmology and 'intelligent design' — 466
70. Palmyra, ISIS and the Crisis of Islam — 469

Acknowledgements — 473

Index — 476

Cover image from the author's first academic monograph, *Truth and Power: Robert S. Hardie and Land Reform Debates in the Philippines 1950-1987*, published in 1990. The cartoon originally appeared in the *Manila Daily Mirror* on 3 January 1953.

Preface: What it means to be a public intellectual and how I became one.

I am what is known as a public intellectual. This is a role I have carved out for myself over the past 25 years with an independence of mind that I have never been willing to surrender to any camp, ideology or institution. I am not a 'boffin' in the 'ivory towers of academe'; I am not the spokesman or lobbyist for a political party, a business corporation, a trade union, a religious sect or church. I am, instead, simply a person who freely expresses his opinion on matters of public significance, contributing in an uninhibited way to the wider debate on those matters in what we like to call 'civil society'. The writings gathered together here show the evolution of that freedom of expression. Together, I would like to think, they provide a kind of template for the role of the public intellectual in civil society, if that is not too bold a claim to make.

Opinions and Reflections is not, in other words, a book *about* freedom of expression. It is a book which *exhibits* freedom of expression. Had I lived in the Russia of Vladimir Putin, contemporary China under the Communist Party, Iran under the mullahs, Turkey under the more and more dictatorial Recep Tayyip Erdogan, or any number of other countries with illiberal and authoritarian regimes, from North Korea, Vietnam and Cuba, to Venezuela, Syria or Zimbabwe, I could not safely have written in this manner. I would not have been permitted to publish across such a wide range of topics with the freedom I have enjoyed as a result of being the citizen of an Anglo-Saxon constitutional democracy. That liberty has not been easily won even in the Anglophone world; it is far from being universally established; and yet it is too easily and too often taken for granted, or even dismissed as somehow unreal by those who benefit from it. I cherish it and live by it.[1]

---

1 I do not subscribe, as these opening remarks surely make clear, to the bizarre notions of the likes of Louis Althusser (1918-1990) or Noam Chomsky (1928-), that the public sphere in the Western democracies somehow obscures a totalitarian hegemonic conspiracy to 'manufacture consent'. Nor do I subscribe to the notions of Antonio Negri (1933-) or Slavoj Zizek (1949-) that we in the West constitute an insidious 'Empire' or live under a subtle version of domination comparable to, if not worse than, that which existed under the old Soviet order (and, in important and demonstrable ways, still exists in China under the Communist Party in the era of Xi Jinping). In other words, my writing is more than a liberal manifesto; it is *proof* that there is not a totalitarian hegemonic order in Australia. Moreover, the fact that there is not such an order has everything to do with the liberal and utilitarian, parliamentary and civil conventions which we, as a nation, inherited from the British colonial order and have continued, modified and upheld in more than

These opinion pieces and reflective essays include trenchant criticisms of current or former top political figures, powerful religious organizations, intelligence agencies and foreign governments. They include reflections of an independent character on the climate debate and the nature of science, gay marriage, refugee policy, euthanasia, terrorism, the leaking of state secrets, genocide, macro-economic policy, Israel and Zionism, Islam, anti-Semitism and repression in China, among many other topics. They have not been written to serve the interests of any political, religious or business group; nor have they been constrained by fear or favour. They are, quite simply, my own expressions of opinion over the past twenty five years. They are the work of a public intellectual in civil society. They have been possible because I *live* in a civil society, not an authoritarian or sectarian one.

How I came to be the kind of person who was both able and willing to write so freely on so many things I shall recount presently, but it seems good to begin by stating that this collection has been brought together now by way of championing the intellectual liberty that it embodies. Freedom of expression flared up, as a hot topic of debate, in the wake of the Islamist shooting of twenty three journalists (twelve of them fatally) at *Charlie Hebdo* in Paris in the first week of January 2015. Clear memory of that massacre will soon fade, but when Islamic terrorists armed with Kalashnikovs stormed the offices of *Charlie Hebdo* and shot down its editor and many other staff in the name of religion, freedom of expression was being directly and savagely challenged. This book is my way, if you prefer, of declaring '*Je suis Charlie*'. It does not centre on Islam, but it is a kind of manifesto for freedom of expression in general.

My response to that brutal Islamist assault on a satirical magazine and its staff is unequivocal. There must be zero tolerance for this kind of physical assault on people for what they write or draw. Religious belief is not a legitimate pretext for such violence. The discourse about freedom of expression that followed, however, seems to me to have been diverted to a preoccupation with the 'right to offend'. That should *not* be our banner. It smacks too much of taunting, reckless obscenities and exchanges of vitriol. The right to engage in critical analysis, *whether or not* that offends powerful or interested parties, is the more important cause. Deliberately 'offending' is a sub-text. Again and again, in the pages of this book, the reader will find critical analysis, some of which might 'offend' various parties. But the key to the book is not any presumed right to *offend*. It is the openly exercised right to *criticise, challenge and confute*, based on reason.

---

a century since Federation. These are somewhat unfashionable views, but ones for which I make no apology. They are the conditions which have made possible what this book embodies.

Those, rather than satire or the deliberate giving of offence, are what I take to be the primary functions of public intellectuals. They provide a service because the writer publicly thinks through ideas that others might prefer were left unchallenged or which they (as citizens) feel uneasy about but lack the means to challenge. I have simply exercised such 'rights' over an unusually wide range. Let me be clear: I enjoy satirical cartoons and have no hesitation in championing the freedom of cartoonists and lampoonists to mock the pretensions of the ostentatious, the powerful, the self-righteous, the pompous and the thuggish of all stripes. I do not believe for a moment that any religion should be considered immune from mockery or criticism, least of all on account of threatened violence against its critics.[2] All too often religious authorities or religious superstitions simply cry out to be mocked. Our liberties would soon shrink to the vanishing point if we accepted and succumbed to threats of violence against anyone who offended on these points. Let those who fear or resent being caricatured look to how they occur in the eyes of others.

The assertion that such figures as Jesus, Mohammed or, say, Joseph Smith or L. Ron Hubbard, for example, should not be mocked is one we should reject. There is nothing other than institutionalized mythology and prejudice that makes such figures any more 'sacred' or above criticism than other thinkers, be they philosophers, economists, poets or political leaders—such as dictators or old style absolute monarchs. Freedom from the constraints of piety in regard to such figures is part of what it means to live in an *emancipated* society. Given the variety of religious beliefs, it cannot be left to religious believers of any particular kind to insist that their icons and beliefs be treated as sacrosanct. The more vehemently they insist on this, paradoxically, the more open they leave themselves to satirical mockery. That's what the violent Muslims have been doing.

---

2   While, in terms of social and political philosophy I am strongly inclined towards liberal utilitarianism in the tradition of John Stuart Mill, there is many a thinker of a different cast of mind who has had insights well worth pondering. On the question of religion and satire, I have long been impressed by two aphorisms, one by Arthur Schopenhauer and one by Friedrich Nietzsche, neither of them exactly a liberal or utilitarian. Schopenhauer wrote, almost two centuries ago:

> *What a bad conscience religion must have is to be judged by the fact that it is forbidden under pain of such severe penalties to mock it.*

Half a century later, Nietzsche wrote:

> *Objection, evasion, happy distrust, pleasure in mockery are signs of health. Everything unconditional belongs in pathology.*

It is noteworthy that both thinkers had Christianity more in mind than Islam. In our time, however, Islam is by far the greater cause for concern in this regard and needs rather badly to be brought under secular discipline and taught a certain humility under the law, as Christianity has been since the Enlightenment.

Now, religion has been a human universal and impiety has been frowned upon in most societies, especially if it seemed deliberate or aggressive. It has very often been persecuted, even where the 'impiety' in question consisted of serious and intelligent questioning of traditions, rather than open mockery of them. The single most famous such case in the West, at least, is that of Socrates, who was famously condemned to death for impiety in 399 BCE.[3] He was, in a sense, the West's first real public intellectual. To this day, the label 'Socratic dialogue' is used to refer to close questioning of assumptions and opinions, even though our means for critical analysis have far outgrown those available to Socrates. Crucially, however, he was concerned with the relationship between politics, virtue and religion—and this led to his arrest and condemnation.

Where complex argument and deeply held pieties or assumptions cannot readily be brought into the open and debated, theatre and humour have often been resorted to. But they require a degree of licence. It has always been dangerous to lampoon the powerful, where there are no legal protections or conventions of what might be called 'the rights of the clown'. And long after civil liberties began to find a more secure footing under English law, even in the 19th century and to a lesser extent well into the 20th, the powers that be would again and again seek to shut down the expression of opinions or the publishing of information that it was inconvenient for them to have in the public domain. The role of cartoonists emerged in such a context to pour scepticism and ridicule upon the pretensions and mendacities of those in political office.

Satirical cartoons can play a healthy role in this regard. Some sixteen years ago, when I was lecturing in Chinese politics at one of our universities, I brought into the class a wonderful satirical cartoon about Jeff Kennett, the Liberal premier who had just lost the state election in Victoria. One of his supporters had declared on radio during the lead-up to the election 'Jeff fucking rules!' The cartoon showed a massive plinth in a public park surmounted by two feet

---

3   For two different and stimulating modern accounts of the trial and death of Socrates, see I. F. Stone *The Trial of Socrates*, Jonathan Cape, London, 1988; and Bettany Hughes *The Hemlock Cup: Socrates, Athens and the Search for the Good Life*, Jonathan Cape, London, 2010. Wrote I. F. Stone:

> *The more I fell in love with the Greeks, the more agonizing grew the spectacle of Socrates before his judges. It horrified me as a civil libertarian. It shook my Jeffersonian faith in the common man. It was a black mark for Athens and the freedom it symbolized. How could the trial of Socrates have happened in so free a society? How could Athens have been so untrue to itself?*

> But, of course, Athens was far from being the ideally free and rational society we sometimes imagine it to have been. We tend to focus on the key figures, including Socrates, whom we most admire and forget that they were always a small minority in a substantial population. There was only one Aeschylus, one Sophocles, one Euripides; there was only one Thucydides and he wrote his great work in exile. Aristotle —a sympathizer with the Macedonian court—left Athens at the end of his life, as he himself recorded, lest he be treated in the same manner as Socrates.

cast in bronze but snapped off at the ankles. Inscribed on the side of the plinth were the words 'Jeff *%$#@*^ Rules'. A father stood in front of it saying to his little boy, 'Well, his first name was Jeff and his last name was Rules and that's really all we know about him, son.' Such a cartoon, I suggested to the class, *embodies* the political liberties and freedom of expression we have in Australia—in stark contrast with the repression and censorship in China under the Communist Party, both under and after Mao Zedong.

Whatever one thought about Jeff Kennett as a person or as a premier, the cartoon was bitingly clever, very funny and completely free of any kind of censorship or retribution. So it should be, just in so far as we cherish our liberties. Is it even conceivable that we would have made any excuse or felt the slightest empathy for a group of Young Liberals had they stormed the offices of *The Age*, where the cartoon appeared, and shot down numerous staff, including the cartoonist, on the basis that they felt *offended* at this satirical cartoon? The likes of Erdogan in Turkey or the Ayatollah Khamenei in Iran positively scream out to be lampooned in this manner, but try doing so in Turkey or Iran and you are likely to find yourself beaten up or jailed or both. Just because such extravagant claims are made for their immunity from criticism, Erdogan, the Ayatollahs or Mohammed himself are badly in need of being brought down to Earth in the manner of Kennett.

Yet the Kennett cartoon would have made no *sense* had there not been a context of shared understanding in which the premier was seen as arrogant and in which it was also taken for granted that once defeated in the election he would be gone from office without so much as a protest. That context is what we should pay the most attention to, not simply the wry humour of a given cartoon. Thus, when Mohammed is lampooned, the context is one in which Islam is widely seen as a reactionary religion, whose practitioners in many countries hold violent and dogmatic views that occur to others as barbarous, unjustified or at best anachronistic. This is not just a matter of ISIL or Boko Haram, but of Saudi Arabia and Pakistan, the Taliban in Afghanistan, the mullahs in Tehran and the fanatics of Hezbollah. That context of shared understanding alone makes sense of a satirical cartoon. In circumstances where Islam was generally seen as a religion of reason, progress and humane values, such satire would *not* make sense to most people and would, in fact, be unlikely even to occur.

For these reasons, my own practice has been always to seek to create *a sense of context for judgments* and to do so from the point of view of shared understanding, not any partisan agenda. Naturally, on any given occasion, there will be those who will disagree with my judgments. There are some judgments which, looking back, I would make differently in hindsight, but which I have left unaltered to reflect accurately what I thought at the time. The crucial thing is that I have been free to form opinions, think about them without fear or pressure and get them published in the nation's serious newspapers and magazines. This has made them a contribution to that broad flow of discussion, formation and *revision* of opinion of which civil society, when it is free and flourishing, chiefly consists. The point is not that my opinions are the only correct ones. Rather, it is that I have had and have exercised the freedom to *hold* dissenting opinions, to *express* them with complete freedom and to *change* them at my own discretion.

Have I offended anyone in the writing I have done over the past twenty five years? It's quite possible that I have; but offending was not the intention—*argument* was always the intention. This is not to say that I have fastidiously attempted to avoid offending anyone. Where ridicule seemed appropriate, it has been served up. More than twenty years ago, I labelled a book by Simon Winchester on war in Asia 'a fatuous potboiler'. Just last year, I flared out at David Aronofsky's film *Noah,* describing it as 'a fatuous cartoon'. If either of them even noticed my expression of opinion, they might conceivably have felt offended. In neither case was there any aggrieved response. But on more serious subjects, I may well have caused 'offence' to the governments of China, Venezuela and Iran; to anti-Semites or militant anti-Zionists; to partisans of Hamas or ISIL, to Scientologists or to opponents of euthanasia or gay marriage by what I have written. In all the circumstances, I'd be disappointed had I *not* done so. The point of my writing, however, was not to *cause* offence, but to write with unsparing candour on important and sensitive topics.

A decade ago, when my book on China, *Thunder from the Silent Zone: Rethinking China*, had just been published, I rang the Counsellor at the Chinese Embassy in Canberra, Ms Ou Boqian, with whom I was acquainted. I announced that I had a book out and she responded, 'Yes, so I understand. You should know, of course, that not everybody in the Chinese community approves of what you write about China.' 'I'd be disappointed if they did,' I replied. I offered her a copy of the book, which she was delighted to accept and when I was next in Canberra we met for a coffee in the lobby lounge of the Hyatt opposite the Embassy and I presented her with the pristine publication. Her face radiated pleasure in receiving the book, but then she opened it and saw the dedication. The exchange that followed tells a pointed story about candour, offence and freedom of expression.

The dedication has two parts. The first part reads:

> To the tens of millions of victims of Communism in China: those executed, tortured, starved to death, set to forced labour, imprisoned, abused and deprived of the most elementary human rights, all in the name of 'revolution'.

She read that far, paused and exclaimed 'Tens of millions?! That's not true! That's a complete exaggeration!' I responded calmly, 'Well, we can step through the data, if you like; since the figures are now quite clear.' She let that pass, as she absorbed the second part of the dedication, which reads:

To Wei Jingsheng, Peng Mingmin and Martin Lee Shuming. May their cause prevail.[4]

'Ah!' she declared emphatically, as if she had made a great discovery. 'I see that you got your information from those three liars!' 'No,' I responded, 'I've met all three gentlemen and I do not consider any of them to be a liar, as you put it; but they were not the source of my information. It comes from the best scholarly sources, both English and Chinese.' 'Well,' she said rather primly, putting the book to one side, 'I will read your book and I will respond; but I will be very frank.' 'Splendid!' I returned. 'As you can see, the book itself is very frank.'

I never heard further from Ms Ou. Some years later, however, when I was about to visit China

---

4   Wei Jing sheng (born in 1950) was in the late 1970s a leader of the Democracy Wall Movement, which was suppressed by Deng Xiaoping in 1979. I met him more than once in the 1990s, after his release from prison in China and his exile to the United States. He was put on trial and sentenced to fifteen years in prison and three years without any political rights after his release for his open defence of what the trial judge derided as 'so-called freedom of speech'. He made a spirited speech in his own defence at his trial, in October 1979, basing his defence on Article 45 of the Chinese constitution, which states, as he recited it to the court: 'Citizens enjoy freedom of speech, correspondence, the press, assembly, association, procession, demonstration and the freedom to strike and have the right to speak out freely, air their views fully, hold great debates and write big character posters.' His experience demonstrated that none of this was true. Such has been the lack of progress in this regard in China that, to this day, his speech remains a clarion call. The imprisonment of Liu Xiaobo and others for creating and promulgating Charter 08 made this abundantly clear. Liu remains in prison as of this writing.

Peng Mingmin (born in 1923) was for decades one of the leading figures in the Taiwanese democracy and independence movement, struggling against the dictatorship by the Guomindang, under first Chiang Kaishek and then his son Chiang Chingkuo. He was imprisoned in 1964, moved to house arrest in 1966 and in 1970 escaped and fled to the United States. When the DPP won the presidency more than decade ago, he became a personal adviser to President Chen Shui-bian. His book *A Taste of Freedom: Memoirs of a Formosan Independence Leader*, first published by Holt, Rinehart and Winston, in New York, in 1972, was republished in Taipei in 1994, after President Lee Teng-hui had come to office and expanded on the political liberties first opened up by Chiang Chingkuo in the late 1980s. I met him at the Presidential Palace on a visit to Taiwan in November 2002.

Martin Lee Shuming (born in 1938 in Hong Kong and raised in Guangzhou) is the son of a former Guomindang major general, who fled China to escape the Communists in 1949. He is a prominent Hong Kong lawyer and leader of the democracy movement there, as he has been for many years. I met him in Canberra when I was still working for the Defence Intelligence Organization. That was before the handover of Hong Kong to China in 1997. He was the founding chairman (1994–2002) of the Democratic Party in Hong Kong and was still active in 2014 in the Occupy Central Movement calling for China to refrain from interference in Hong Kong's internal politics and to honour its commitment under the Basic Law governing the handover of Hong Kong to allow the emergence of a universal franchise in the city. He has long been denounced by the Chinese Communist Party as a traitor and a running dog of the colonialists.

to see Beijing again and to spend some time with friends who were working there, acquaintances here in Australia would say to me, 'Are you sure you want to go to China? They might not let you out again.' I assured them that either the Chinese authorities would not allow me *into* the country in the first place or they would let me both come and go. Had I been of Chinese origin, the story might have been different. In the event, I spent a very stimulating few days in Beijing, moving around the city freely and marvelling at its transformation since I had first visited it in 1994, on government business. Did the Ministry of State Security think that I was still working in some capacity for the Australian government? Did they think that I had a hidden agenda in visiting China again? Or did they take no real notice of me, in the belief that I was simply that *rara avis*, a foreign intellectual who worked for no-one and had no agenda other than living freely? I have no way of knowing.

The last of these is, however, the truth of the matter. As a public intellectual, one is necessarily something of a rare bird. If you are not a lobbyist for some interest group or other, or a spokesperson for some ideological camp, in short someone whose views are pretty predictable and can be attacked or dismissed by opposing camps on that ground alone, you are at serious risk of becoming isolated and marginal, due to the simple fact that your reasonings serve no-one's direct interest. I have always felt 'marginal' as a writer for this reason. Yet there is an element of what Hannah Arendt called 'public happiness' in playing such a role. The task is not to win an election, win a prize or win the applause of some partisan assembly, but simply to exercise liberty and express opinions with complete freedom of spirit. Perhaps it is eccentric in me, but I have never seriously contemplated doing otherwise. If there was wisdom in doing so or profit to be had from offering my pen in service, it is much too late in the day for that now. If I declared that I was available for hire, no one, I like to think, would believe me. I would not be trusted to lie for the sake of either lucre or preferment.

What difference does such writing make? There are times when Australia seems to be an anti-intellectual country and the very attempt to be well-informed and articulate almost feels like a cultural heresy or at best a personal eccentricity. I have at times felt and said to close friends that I felt rather like a Jew in a Muslim or conservative Christian country. Even where intellectual life is taken seriously, it often feels as though being a public intellectual in Australia is rather like being one in, say, Iceland or Colombia or the Philippines. Who will actually take any notice in places where the world is moved and shaken? Henry Kissinger is said to have told the Chilean Foreign Minister in 1969 that history ran on an axis beginning in Moscow, running through Berlin and Washington and finishing in Tokyo, making Chile of no consequence. If he did say that, he was being extraordinarily arrogant. The question is, however, if you are Chilean or Australian, with an interest in the large affairs of the world, what can you seriously hope to achieve? Don't you have to be published in New York and London to even make the short list of 'influential' intellectuals?[5]

I confess that, at times, I have succumbed to this 'cultural cringe' and lamented that I did not long ago do what many Australian intellectuals have done—move to the metropolitan centres and seek to make an impression from there. Yet, *wherever* you are, the fundamental issue is the same: intellectual integrity and freedom of expression. Think of the leading figures in Ibsen's plays, not least *An Enemy of the People*. Ibsen was Norwegian, not English or German or American. Socrates himself was the citizen of a city of only 100,000 people on the margins of what many in the East would have considered the civilized world. The delusions of global or cosmopolitan celebrity and of running with some allegedly clever crowd or other are no substitute for integrity and freedom. The hope of one day in some way being able to make a 'decisive' contribution in the corridors of power or in the halls of academe can warp those values. I have enjoyed access to all the best that is being written in the world, outlets for expressing opinions or offering reflections on a wide range of these things and freedom from all hierarchies of authority or peer pressures for consensus or political correctness. This has given me an untrammelled freedom unavailable to those who serve a church, a political party, a corporation, a division of the civil service or even a university. I cherish that freedom.

I didn't always think quite this way, of course. I became a public intellectual step by step because I would not pull my head in or bow to 'conventional' (including conventional 'radical') opinion. My dream, when I was a younger man, was to understand enough of history and world affairs, philosophy and economics to become some combination of merchant banker, political adviser and writer. Malcolm Turnbull is a reasonable facsimile of how I hoped to turn out at that point in my life—but he is caught, clearly, by his membership of the Liberal Party and is not at liberty to speak his mind. I am under no such constraints, never having become a party man. Whenever I have encountered a point of view, religious or political, historical or philosophical that I did not understand or could not believe, I have been constitutionally unable to let it pass and concentrate on my immediate, practical interests.

This has not served me well in worldly terms—any more than it did Socrates - and it plainly is not what the vast majority of people do. I felt a compulsion to inquire, read, question and reflect, while most of my peers got on with developing a career, finding a partner and taking out a mortgage. That's the real origin of both the liberty and variety of opinions you

---

5 A model for the kind of intellectual I have in mind here would be the late Tony Judt, a posthumous volume of whose essays has just been published, in early 2015, under the title *When the Facts Change*.

will find in this book: an incorrigible inclination to question, inquire and seek to develop an informed opinion on—well, almost everything. It began at Catholic secondary school, when I persistently asked questions about religious doctrine that the Christian Brothers who were teaching me found challenging. It never ended. After my school days, I began relentlessly to build up a library and to read while others partied, worked, courted, played sport and watched television. Reading became my life; with the objective of developing a synoptic understanding of the world. Unfortunately, it was very difficult to find teachers or mentors who were willing or able to help me do this.

I remember well feeling scandalized by an incident in the opening session of an honours stream philosophy seminar, in second year university, in which the then chairman of the Philosophy Department at the University of Melbourne, Len Goddard[6], asked the class whether we had any questions of a general nature which we would like to discuss before we settled into reading and analysing Willard Van Orman Quine's classic work *Word and Object*. I raised a hand and asked could we spend a little time discussing the *history* of philosophy, in order to get some perspective on what philosophers since the pre-Socratics had been trying to do and what progress they had made. Goddard rather coolly responded: 'What kind of perspective do *you* suggest?' 'Well,' I offered, 'the American philosopher Walter Kaufmann has suggested that the history of philosophy since Descartes consists, for better or worse, in emancipation from organized religion.' 'That's all very well,' retorted the chairman of the Philosophy Department rather tartly, 'but I don't happen to agree. Does anyone else have a question?'

I have never quite recovered from the shock of the chairman of a Philosophy Department dismissing an honest question on the basis that he did not *happen to agree*. I walked out of his Quine seminar and did not return. I abandoned the formal study of Philosophy at the University of Melbourne and changed to the study of History. Among the many subjects I then studied were Reformation History, Origins of the Marketplace Society, Changing Concepts of Women's Place in Western Society and Thought from 1800 to the Present and Classical Social Theory. I also studied Russian

---

6   Goddard was an undergraduate at St Andrews after the Second World War and a graduate student at Cambridge. He left Britain for Australia in 1956 to take up a lectureship and then the Chair of Philosophy at the University of New England. He returned to St Andrews, to the Chair of Logic and Metaphysics, in 1967. He returned to Australia in 1977, to the Boyce Gibson Chair of Philosophy at the University of Melbourne, which is where I met him, the following year. I had no idea of his background and never had a personal conversation with him. To this day, I do not know what if any his religious beliefs were. It's quite possible, of course, that had I done so, we might have reached a more amicable understanding on the matter of philosophy and organized religion. His main work was in logic, significance and the work of Wittgenstein. He retired in 1990 and died in 2009, having lived out his life in Melbourne.

History from the Emancipation of the Serfs to the Great Terror. I was astonished one day to hear my professor, S. T. Leong, in a lecture on the origins of Marxism in Russia, declare to the class that he had never read Marx's *Capital*, because he found it 'impenetrable'. I had already read all three volumes and did not think them 'impenetrable' at all. In fact, at many points I found them very interesting and well written.

I studied French History from the Paris Commune to the Popular Front. I was intrigued by the myriad stories of French intellectuals disillusioned with the Socialist International flocking to the Communist International and then departing again in droves in diverse directions out of disappointment with Lenin and Stalin. I was learning a great deal in these subjects, at every step, but it was not a *doctrine* I was imbibing. I was learning, rather, about political complexity, historical tragedy and the nature of humanity. This has remained my outlook. I don't write from a doctrinaire perspective, but as a student of complexity, tragedy and humanity. I would like to think that that, above all, is what readers of this book will imbibe from it.

In order to drive my inquiries home, I chose to undertake, for my History honours thesis, a study of the general strike and student rebellion in France in May 1968. It is an indication of the scope of what I was attempting in my Arts degree that, at the same time, I took a seminar in Roman Historiography and wrote three 8,000 word research papers: one on Edward Gibbon and the decline and fall of the Roman Empire; one on Theodor Mommsen and the history of the Roman Republic; and one on Mikhail Rostovtzeff and the third century crisis of the Roman imperial order. Historiography being a study of how history itself is written, it was very instructive looking, in turn, at the work of an 18th century British historian of Rome, a 19th century German historian of Rome and a 20th century Russian historian of Rome.

I lamented only that I could not, also, have done research papers on the Italian Machiavelli as a sixteenth century historian of Rome and one on the New Zealander Ronald Syme's magisterial work on the Roman revolution and the historiography of Tacitus. Others wrote and delivered such papers to the small seminar, however, as well as papers on such fascinating subjects as Rodolfo Lanciani and the archaeology of ancient Rome and the 18th century etchings by Giovanni Battista Piranesi inspired by the ruins of Rome.[7] All *this* was an education,

7   Marguerite Yourcenar's essay 'The Dark Brain of Piranesi', taking its title from an allusion by Victor Hugo to Piranesi's famous 'imaginary prisons', tells the story of this imaginative and gifted Venetian who, after entering Rome for the first time at the age of twenty, in 1740, as a draftsman attached to the household of the Venetian ambassador, found in Rome the inspiration for the rest of his life. He spent thirty eight years creating an unprecedented portrait of its ancient ruins long before modern archaeology had begun to retrieve any of them from secular decay. He overworked himself in this labour and died at the age of 58 after a prolonged illness brought on by his self-imposed privations. He was, Yourcenar remarked, 'a man of passionate feelings, intoxicated by work, careless of his health and

the like of which fewer and fewer young people appear to be getting. Given time and good health, I hope, in the not too distant future, to write a book called *Reflections on an Education*, which will delve more deeply into this problem of liberal education for our time.

Alongside this classical element of my education, the inquiry into the rebellion against capitalist modernity, modern education itself and the structures of industrial society in 1968 was instructive in a whole other way. I had a keen interest in modes of rebellion at that age, being still young and charged with restless hormones and uncertain ambitions. But even then, in 1981, I was sceptical of Marxism, having read about its catastrophes from a young age[8] and reflected on them in a more formal manner during my History degree. I was groping for an understanding of what forces and tensions were shaping the world in the late 20th century and this subject

---

his comfort ... '. He left behind 'countless representations of ancient monuments', including what she describes as 'his great polemical study *Della Magnificenza ed Architettura de' Romani*'.

The place of Piranesi (1720-1778) in Roman historiography is beautifully captured by Yourcenar in her citation of his own observation:

> *When I realized that in Rome the majority of the ancient monuments were lying forsaken in fields or gardens, or even now serving as a quarry for new structures, I resolved to preserve their memory with the help of my engravings. I have, therefore, attempted to exercise the greatest possible exactitude.*

She added:

> *There is already something Goethean about this sentence in its assertion of a modest desire to be useful. To grasp the importance of this rescue work, we must recall that at least a third of the monuments drawn by Piranesi have since vanished; and that what remains has most often been despoiled of the surfacings and stuccos then still in place, or again modified and restored, sometimes clumsily, between the end of the eighteenth century and our own time. Nowadays, when artists believe they are liberating themselves by breaking the links which connect them to the outside world, it is worth noting what a precise solicitude for the object contemplated is at the source of Piranesi's almost hallucinatory masterpieces.*

It need hardly be said that this same observation can be applied to our intellectual culture more broadly, after the ravages of various fashionable ideologies have contrived or conspired to suggest that neither philosophical nor historical objectivity is possible and that all dispassionate opinion—except, apparently, the ideological nostrums of those advancing these notions—is a façade or an imposture. It is, of course, the other way around. There is so much imposture in those often French ideologies and their derivatives, which have exercised an obscurantist and nihilistic influence on Western cultures and other cultures around the world since the mid-20th century. Their *reductio ad absurdum* was the genocidal utopian mania of the Paris-educated Marxian Khmer Rouge in the late 1970s.

8   I played truant from sixth grade in 1968 to read Stuart Schram's biography of Mao Zedong and prevailed upon my parents to give me, for my twelfth birthday, a copy of Isaac Deutscher's biography of Stalin, which I then read avidly during the summer vacation.

seemed to me, by early 1981, to be a fruitful way to focus my efforts in that general direction. It proved to be a good choice. I was able to establish that there had been basically three kinds of interpretation of what had happened in France in May 1968 and that none of them had quite got it right. Looking back on that piece of work, I am chiefly impressed by how much critical thinking I did in *not* subscribing to any of the dominant ideological interpretations available in the literature—conservative/liberal, Stalinist or New Left.[9]

In summing up my argument, I wrote:

> *I have not attempted to force the May events into the frame of a political philosophy for the 'real world'—of Aron's liberal realism, which sees May as madness, of the Communist Party's dismissal of it as pre-Marxian utopianism; or of Singer's Neo-Marxist historicism, which sees May as a prelude to socialist 'revolution'. I think the most interesting thing about May is the extent to which much of what happened simply lit up latent human yearnings for community, discourse, expression, autonomy which conceivably no currently available industrial regime could satisfy, but which will not for that reason go away or cease from placing question marks against the orders of 'progress' that technocrats build. As for violent revolution, I do not regret its failure to occur in 1968. It may have availed little. It may have made things worse. There are more options than two, I think. There are many shades of grey.*

Looking back, I would more emphatically reject the idea of violent revolution, especially against Charles De Gaulle's orderly and effective Fifth Republic. But I would not otherwise alter my assessment of the significance of the upheaval that did take place.

With all this behind me, what should I have done next? As I finished my History degree, I judged that it was now time to head into the mainstream and get some law and economics under my belt, so that I could become the 'man of the world' that I aspired to be. I had the good fortune, at that time, to encounter Professor Robert Meagher, a lecturer in International Law from the Fletcher School, in Boston, who was visiting Ormond College, where I spent my honours year. He pointed me in the direction of the Master of Arts in Law and Diplomacy that the Fletcher School offered—as it still does—and sent me their catalogue on his return to Boston. It lit up my imagination as nothing else had ever done. I sat the exam one needed to take in order to qualify for graduate studies in the United States and did so well that I received unsolicited offers

---

9   I was quite strongly influenced in how I approached this subject by a close reading of the work of Jürgen Habermas on communication, legitimation and modern society; but also by the writings of Lewis Mumford on technology, the city in history and the nature of organizational power. But there were many other influences, not least Simone Weil and Richard Sennett. It was Habermas, however, who kept open the door to philosophy, pointing me in the direction of the American pragmatists and encouraging me to see critical inquiry and the conditions under which reflective discourse and public policy debate actually occur as vital subjects that demanded my attention. This would surface not only in my honours thesis but even more in my PhD dissertation and then in my approach to intelligence analysis in the 1990s. As an undergraduate, however, I was simply reading everything I could lay my hands on and digesting it as best I could.

from both Harvard and Princeton Universities, as well as the Fletcher School. There was just one catch, a kind of Catch-22: in order to take up any of the offers, I would have to find $US20,000 to pay for my first year. I could think of no way to raise any such sum and had to accept that taking up these exciting offers from some of the best tertiary institutions in the United States was simply beyond my means.

That was sobering and has long convinced me of the need for a scholarship system which would make money alone no barrier to academic progress. At the time, however, there was no scholarship here or in the United States that I could even apply for and which would cover such expenses. I had, therefore, to turn elsewhere. After some thought, I opted to accept the offer of a Commonwealth scholarship and undertake a PhD in International Relations at the Australian National University. When I arrived in Canberra, Professor J. D. B. Miller, a well-known and influential figure on the campus in the 1980s[10] and chairman of the Department of International Relations, made me welcome and advised me to spend two or three months thinking about what I would like to take as my dissertation topic, before plunging into concentrated research. I was interested in at least three broad areas of inquiry: world food supply as reflected in global grain trade; the Vietnam War as a matter of public policy debate and contention; and war, more generally, as a problem in human affairs. For several months, given free rein by 'Big Miller', I read widely within these general parameters

It was in early April 1983 that I chanced upon the precise line of inquiry I would pursue. I was reading a book called *The Challenge of World Poverty*, by the émigré Ukrainian Jewish agricultural economist, Wolf Isaac Ladejinsky, which sat close to the intersection of all my areas of interest. In a footnote to it, I stumbled upon his remark, in 1950, that if the United States wished to head off Communist-led peasant rebellions across the 'Third World' of the kind which had just led to the Communist seizure of power in China, then it would have to export 'the American agrarian tradition of forty acres and a mule, or an Asian variant of it'. I pounced on this and instantly wrote out my research program in the form of a set of questions:

> *Was 'forty acres and a mule' actually the 'American agrarian tradition'?*
> *If it was, could it be exported, even in principle, to the Third World in the Cold War context?*
> *Assuming that it was possible in principle, had it actually been seriously attempted and, if so, with what results?*

---

10 John Donald Bruce Miller (1922-2011) was one of the last of the old academic mandarins, who made his career before the era of diploma mills and endless numbers of PhDs. He once assured me that I need not worry about the utility of my PhD by research, since he had never even done a PhD and yet had ended up Professor of International Relations at the Australian National University. That had been in another era, of course. My own experience was to prove rather different.

> *Suppose, on the other hand, that it was not the American agrarian tradition? Where would that leave land reform proponents such as Ladejinsky and with what implications for the anti-Communist foreign policy agenda of the United States?*

Without hesitation, on the back of these questions, I drew up a design for how I would address them. I would have to look at modern revolutions and their relationship to peasant land tenure grievances. I would have to learn a lot about American agrarian politics. I would have to develop an understanding of United States foreign policy and counter-insurgency thinking. I would need a set of case studies and these should begin with Ladejinsky's own experience as the architect of land reform in post-Second World War Japan. They should include Vietnam and, I rapidly decided, the Philippines and El Salvador, since civil wars were at that time under way in both countries, with Communists leading peasant rebels against conservative, land-owning elites. These three case studies also had the merit of spanning, between them, the whole Cold War era, from the late 1940s to the mid-1980s.

That was an enormous amount to take on from scratch. One senior scholar at the ANU remarked to me that what I was proposing was 'not a PhD dissertation, but a life's work'. Nonetheless, Big Miller gave it his seal of approval and I launched into it. The work ended up taking six years and left me both penniless and ill from glandular fever, but I learned a colossal amount along the way. One American examiner of my thesis declared that the research in my dissertation was 'staggering' and that it was a pity that more PhDs could not be written 'at the level and standards of this one'. Another commented that the opening chapter on modern revolutions was 'just what you would expect from the brightest (by far) graduate student in the class'. From an intellectual point of view, therefore, the exercise was a triumph. From a *practical* point of view, it turned out to have served no purpose at all. Financially, I went backwards during those years, painstakingly developing knowledge and intellectual independence that would, as it turned out, render me virtually unemployable in Canberra in the years that followed. Never guessing that that would be the case, I persevered year after year and spent many months in US archives, in Central America and in the Philippines on field work. Above all, I learned a great deal about how American foreign and security policy worked and about the logic and destructiveness of the Cold War.

As with the honours thesis, so with the PhD: I did not start with or finish with an ideological frame of reference that overdetermined my findings. I started with my set of questions and I developed my understanding as I went. That understanding came, finally, to centre on a number of *cognitive* issues that transcended the ideologies at stake in the Cold War. I discovered, to my fascination, that, even as a graduate student eighteen months into so large a field of inquiry, I again and again interviewed bureaucrats, diplomats and military officers who knew *less* than I did about the history of the very things they had been engaged in addressing, on behalf of the United States government. This had not been my expectation at all. To be sure, they could, without significant exception, tell me much that I did not know about their *personal* experience or immediate policy involvement. What they did *not* know, equally without significant exception, was the history of the problems in question going back much *before* their personal involvement. In short, there was an almost complete *lack of institutional memory* in the US bureaucracies. As a young historian, I found this both surprising and disturbing.

The lack of institutional memory, I soon realized, had nothing to do with ideology, capitalism or 'imperialism'. It had to do with the logic and functions of government or corporate organizations.[11] Whether I was inquiring about foreign aid programs or counter-insurgency experience, about Vietnamese, Philippine or Central American affairs, or for that matter—as an aside—American relations with Iran, I found the same pattern of institutionalized amnesia and the endless reinvention of 'wheels'. Had I been able to find a straight path to a post-doctoral program, this would almost certainly have become my chief area of interest and research. That did not happen, but in the interim my grasp of the problem was enormously facilitated by reading Daniel Ellsberg's *Papers on the War*,[12] a volume of essays about his experience as an analyst of strategic affairs at the Rand Corporation and the Pentagon in the 1960s, dealing chiefly with his slow and painful education about the challenge the United States had taken on in Vietnam.

The single most compelling paragraph in *Papers on the War* and one which I have cited again and again, to various audiences, in the past thirty years, since I first read it, is the following:

11   I had learned to appreciate the sociology of Max Weber while studying Classical Social Theory in 1979 under the guidance of the wry and complex Frank Knopfelmacher. Weber's work on social systems, bureaucracies, parties, castes and the 'iron cage' of modern capitalism had made a profound impression on me. It certainly seemed to me far more interesting, because more complex, detached and attuned to organizational and psychological, political and cultural variables than anything in Marx and Engels, to say nothing of the gross philistine Vladimir Lenin. From 1985, it helped me to think of the cognitive deficiencies I was finding in the US departments of state as interesting and important problems in their own right, which could not be reduced to any reductionist Marxist formulas about capitalism or bourgeois hegemony.

12   All the papers in question, as Ellsberg remarked in his Introduction, 'were written prior to June 13, 1971, when the *New York Times* began publishing documents from the McNamara Study ... all of the pieces were written after the fall of 1969, when I completed reading the Pentagon Papers.' Many years later, Ellsberg wrote a memoir, which enlarged upon the essays of 1969-71: *Secrets: A Memoir of Vietnam and the Pentagon Papers* (Viking Penguin, New York, 2002). In 2009, Judith Ehrlich and Rick Goldsmith produced an outstanding film documentary titled *The Most Dangerous Man in America: Daniel Ellsberg and the Pentagon Papers*. Both books and the documentary are still eminently worth studying.

> *The urgent need to circumvent the lying and the self-deception was, for me, one of the 'lessons of Vietnam'; a broader one was that there were situations—Vietnam was an example—in which the US Government, starting ignorant, did not, would not, learn. There was a whole set of what amounted to institutional anti-learning mechanisms working to preserve and guarantee unadaptive and unsuccessful behaviour: the fast turnover in personnel; the lack of institutional memory at any level; the failure to study history, to analyse or even record operational experience or mistakes; the effective pressures for optimistically false reporting at every level, for describing 'progress' rather than problems or failure, thus concealing the very need for change in approach or for learning. Well, helping the US Government learn—in this case learn how to learn—was something, perhaps, I could do; that had been my business.*[13]

Ellsberg's knowledge and experience were largely confined to the United States, but I knew even in the 1980s that this inability to learn and the disastrous consequences it can have were anything but a peculiar defect of American governmental institutions. This was an issue that pointed directly at radical and fundamental problems of governance, authority, epistemology and the whole idea of modern emancipation. Seeing it at work, seeing it highlighted by as bright and reflective an individual as Ellsberg, seeing it replicated in my other case studies, seeing it instantiated in the very people I was interviewing, threw into high relief the real problems that were at stake, as distinct from the ideological fixations which circumscribed so much thinking during the Cold War.[14]

Where do you go, once you have absorbed insights of this nature? I ran up at once against the same constraints that had prevented me from doing graduate studies in the United States six or seven years earlier: I had no money and the years were passing swiftly. I would very probably have been better off, in retrospect, finding a decent American university at which to do a post-doctoral program and deepen my understanding of these cognitive issues and their implications. However, I gave priority to earning an at least basic income and recovering from exhaustion. I decided that the most natural way to do this would be to seek work in Canberra in either the Department of Foreign Affairs and Trade or the Department of Defence, perhaps in the intelligence organizations. I had met Paul Dibb at

---

13 Daniel Ellsberg, *Papers on the War*, (Simon and Schuster, New York, 1972), p. 18.

14 A decade after I read Ellsberg and after I had already left government service and was teaching Chinese politics, I had the good fortune to discover Dali Yang's brilliant study of the cognitive impact on the Chinese Communist Party leadership of the calamitous famine caused by the Great Leap Forward between 1959 and 1961: *Calamity and Reform in China* (Stanford University Press, 1996). Yang had zeroed in on exactly the cognitive issues that I had stumbled upon in my doctoral dissertation, but in an utterly different context: that of 'revolution' and ideology in the China of Mao Zedong. America's war in Vietnam cost several million (mostly Vietnamese) lives. The famine Mao caused in China resulted in the deaths by starvation in peace time of some 35 to 40 million people; by far the worst famine in recorded history in terms of absolute mortalities.

the ANU when I first arrived there in 1983[15] and he had invited me for a drink a couple of years later. Over a beer in the famous Cellar Bar of University House, he suggested that I might consider working for the Joint Intelligence Organization when I completed the PhD.[16] This now seemed like a useful and perhaps fruitful next step after my doctorate. I therefore applied, in late 1988, to work for the Department of Defence, with a view to progressing onto JIO or moving across to DFAT once the PhD had been passed.

Things did not quite work out as I had hoped. I was initially refused a Negative Vetting clearance on the absurd and totally unexpected grounds that I was 'pro-Soviet, pro-Communist and pro-terrorist' and had 'a library full of books about Communism and terrorism'. But before telling that tale, it is worth pausing to recall that, only a month or so prior to that strange judgment, I had been told by Verity Burgmann in the University of Melbourne, for whom I had worked as a tutor in Australian politics in 1988, that there was 'no possibility' of my retaining the job in 1989. We were not well aligned, she and I. At the beginning of the academic year, she and her senior tutor had informed the small group of other tutors that 'our objective in this course is to radicalize the students'. It had quickly become clear that this meant indoctrinating them in Marxist-Leninist ideas. The first lecture was delivered by the near blind Lloyd Churchward, a veteran member of the Communist Party of Australia and Emeritus Professor of Politics, whom Verity Burgmann introduced in reverential terms. He proceeded to tell the first year students that he had always struggled to understand Max Weber's work 'even in English' and that Marx and Lenin were the ideal models of social analysis and political practice, respectively.

My first tutorial immediately followed the lecture. I remarked tersely to the students as soon as they were seated: 'That lecture was a disgrace! Any Emeritus Professor of Politics who says that he cannot understand the writings of Max Weber in English should have lost his job thirty years ago. Let's start again, shall we?' That set the stage for a long series of countermandings of

---

15 I will always remember being shown into the Reading Room of the Department of International Relations and the Strategic Studies Centre by the late Coral Bell (1923-2012) to find Paul Dibb sitting on the edge of the coffee table. Coral introduced me to him and he remarked with a gleam in those pale blue eyes of his: 'So, this is the young man with a library of three thousand books!' My reputation had preceded me, clearly. I happen to have mentioned in my application to the ANU that I possessed such a library. It has not grown in size since, because I weed it like a garden or prune it like a tree. Countless books—as it happens, including most of the work of Marx, Engels, Lenin and Gramsci—have been sold off or given away to second hand book dealers and replaced by new and better books over the years.

16 Little did I suspect, in the early to mid-1980s, that these meetings with Paul Dibb would ever be held against me by Defence Security. It transpired, however, that there were individuals dug into Defence Security in those days who regarded Dibb as a Soviet mole, no less. I did not discover this until 1989, but by then the 'damage' was done. Those same people suspected that I might have been recruited by Dibb to penetrate the intelligence service (as he had supposedly done) and serve the Soviet Union.

the set readings and lecture declarations throughout the course, which can hardly have endeared me to Verity and her offsider. I was not, therefore, surprised when she informed me at year's end that I would not be re-employed. I was, however, very surprised to then be denied a Negative Vetting clearance, a month or so later, on the grounds that I was supposedly a Communist myself and 'pro-terrorist' into the bargain. I would not have been surprised had the Defence Security Branch objected to my defence of Daniel Ellsberg; something to which I openly 'confessed' in the Negative Vetting interview. I was most surprised to learn later, however, that neither the interviewer nor her supervisor had made any mention of this matter in their reports, having not the first idea who Daniel Ellsberg was and never having so much as heard of the Pentagon Papers. Such was the condition of Defence Security Branch in the last days of the Cold War.

What should I have done at such a juncture? I felt rather like K in Franz Kafka's *The Trial*, with the difference that I was subject not simply to one nonsensical charge but to two antithetical charges of 'heresy' simultaneously. Staying in the academic world did not look promising and entering the world of government service not only appeared to be barred, but seemed also unattractive on account of the ignorance and blind prejudice I had encountered at the very outset. As it happened, the Defence recruitment people took up my cause, declaring that I was their 'prize recruit' for 1989 and threatening to appeal over the heads of Security Branch unless either I was given the clearance or they were provided with a compelling reason for it being withheld. I was given the clearance after a second interview. The problem was that rumour now preceded me and I ran into a world of mindless suspicion because I had had 'a problem getting a security clearance'. This led to unusual difficulties in getting a Positive Vetting clearance to work in the Joint Intelligence Organization and also to a ruling, so I was later informed by someone in a position to know, that I was never to be allowed to work on the United States as long as I was in government service.

This is not the place to recount the many absurdities and bafflements involved in that drawn out process. Suffice it to say, I quickly decided that DFAT would likely prove a more enlightened and hospitable environment than Defence and applied to move from Defence/JIO to the diplomatic service. I was rejected. The rejection slip arrived on almost the same day as the examiners' report on my PhD. The examiners had extolled my intellectual achievement. DFAT informed me that I had not made the cut and that 'while the interview committee acknowledged your achievements and abilities, they felt that you would be too impatient and too self-assertive'. This remark was not in the formal letter of rejection. It was a file note conveyed to me by a DFAT officer when I phoned to inquire as to why I had not been offered a position. Over the following few years, while gaining regular promotion in JIO, which had been renamed DIO (the Defence Intelligence Organization) in 1990, I twice more applied to the diplomatic service, but was rejected each time. I also applied for a position as a research historian in DFAT and was not only rejected but treated with remarkable rudeness in the interview.[17] I applied for a position in the Parliamentary Research Service and was rejected. I was later informed by one of its staff that the head of the PRS, Frank Frost, had told him he would not offer me a job because I was 'too independent minded'.

Despite all of this, I had gradually gained sufficient recognition and support within DIO that I was, by 1994, appointed head of China analysis. Not long beforehand, I had delivered a high level briefing on North Korea's nuclear weapons program. Paul Dibb, by then over at the ANU as head of the Strategic and Defence Studies Centre, phoned me afterwards and told me 'That briefing did you a lot of good!' He invited me to consider moving over to the University and working with him. Perhaps I should have done so, but I knew I was in the running for the China job and believed that it would be the better career move. Having been given the job, I tried everything I could think of to turn it into an effective launch pad for further career development, but nothing worked. Defence would not train me in Mandarin or arrange a posting for me. DFAT would not have me. I cultivated a relationship with the head of research for Bankers Trust in Hong Kong with a view to leaving Australia and finally getting into merchant banking. He was keen to recruit me, but headquarters in New York rejected me because I was not an economist. Ironically, after all my endeavours since 1981, I had run into a roadblock precisely because I had not been able to go to the Fletcher School as planned and pick up some law and economics.

The endgame began when Doug Kean, who had newly moved across from the Office of National Assessments as Deputy Director General of DIO, intervened to censor my writing of reviews and opinion pieces in the press. 'It's well known,' he told me, 'that you are a highly influential analyst. Suppose you were to write a piece in the press about China and then the government was to adopt a policy that your readers could tell was not consistent with your views?' I offered the suggestion that such readers might simply and with relief draw the conclusion that there were differences of opinion within government and that the proverbial 'gnomes of Russell Hill' were

---

17   The interview was conducted by the head of DFAT's history office at that time, a quite well-known academic historian by the name of Bill Hudson. I had never met him, but found him surly and insulting throughout the interview, for reasons that eluded me then and still do so. At one point, looking at my CV on the desk in front of him, he remarked, glaring at me in a patently hostile manner, 'There are those of us educated elsewhere who can't understand the way they throw around the word 'honours' at the University of Melbourne.' It soon became apparent that, for whatever reason, there was no way I would be offered the job for which I had applied. As I left, Hudson glowering at me in his baffling way, I extended my hand to him and remarked coolly: 'Well, thank you for your time. I'm sure you'll find someone to do your job for you, one way or another.' I never received so much as a rejection note or phone call from his office and did not bother to inquire about how I had gone, since it was all too evident.

not merely clones or drones who toed a policy line, but people with independent minds. This, he sharply reminded me, was not the role of a civil servant. 'You have to realize that you are a civil servant, not an intellectual; and you are not entitled to hold or express opinions that have not been cleared by the Public Affairs Office of the Department of Defence.' I unabashedly retorted, 'Sorry, but I beg to differ. I *am* an intellectual and I am here because I believe I have something to offer. Should I draw the conclusion that that is not what is wanted from me, I will not be staying.'[18] I offered to desist from writing about China, but he insisted that he would be censoring any writing I did on any topic. A few months later, I resigned and left a government which seemed to have no worthwhile place for me.

Looking back, I would say that perhaps I really wasn't suited to work in either Defence or DFAT; though I learned a great deal by being exposed to how they function. I had, by 1989, spent far too long charting my own intellectual course, studying history and international relations, to easily become a malleable and indoctrinated player in the national security or diplomatic teams. I would cheerfully have worked hard and learned new skills had there been a fast track of development open to me; but there was no apparent development track on offer and I was rather intractable in my preparedness to challenge any idea I saw as ill-informed or poorly argued. As one sympathetic senior diplomat confided to me in 1994, 'You need a place where you can spread your wings.' He was correct. I wanted to write and not be censored by any bureaucrat. I have done so now for twenty years. I cannot think of anything I might have done in government, had I remained in the Canberra bureaucracies at any level, that would have been nearly so free, creative or useful. My education, tenaciously acquired, has been put to good use. Here is the evidence.

Paul Monk
Melbourne
30 May 2015

---

18 My first academic monograph had been published in 1990 under the title *Truth and Power: Robert S. Hardie and Land Reform Debates in the Philippines 1950-1987*. Its cover featured a cartoon with the caption 'A Serious Offense' and a picture of a report—the Hardie Report of 1952—bound to a stake and about to be set on fire by a hunchback with a torch labelled 'bigotry'. 'What have I done?' asks the report plaintively. 'You spoke the truth!' retorts the hunchback with a malicious grin. This is the cartoon which sits at the beginning of the present book. Robert Hardie had been sent to the Philippines in 1950, by the Truman administration, to make a study of rural conditions and recommendations for land tenure reform. When he did so, however, recommending a neo-classical economic reform to spur growth and head off peasant rebellion, conservative landed interests in the Philippines denounced him as a Communist. When the Truman administration was replaced, in March 1953, by the Eisenhower administration, conservatives in Washington DC added their voices to the chorus and Hardie resigned from US government service in disgust. I corresponded extensively with him in 1988.

Part One
Late 20th Century Pieces

Section 1: 1990-91

The collapse of the Soviet bloc in Eastern Europe in 1989[19]

The image of the future, suggested George Orwell, in *Nineteen Eighty Four*, is that of a boot stamping on a human face forever. By 1984, it appeared that he just might be correct. Then, along came Mikhail Gorbachev. I was in Paris, in March 1985, when Gorbachev became what *Le Figaro* described as 'le nouvel tsar'. I remember thinking that he looked like Rod Steiger. Some four years later, *The Economist* itself was hailing this new tsar as 'Mikhail the Liberator'. The boot was off the face! In a moment of literary extravagance, Francis Fukuyama called it 'the End of History'; but to the contrary, it marked a great renewal of the vital forces of history and of hope for the future of the species. For it to begin immediately after 1984 was a curious coincidence. For it to have climaxed in 1989, the bicentennial year of the great French Revolution, was quite extraordinary.

In his slender but vigorous report on that 'year of wonders', '89', Timothy Garton Ash has given us an admirable political pamphlet, in the time-honoured sense of that term. 'The disadvantages of the witness, as against the historian,' he confesses, 'are those of partiality in space, time and judgement ... If things have gone badly in East-Central Europe by the time you read this, you will probably find what follows absurdly hopeful and terribly light-hearted. Carefully avoiding all quotations from Wordsworth, I would only say that this, too, belongs to the record. It felt like that at the time.'

In one luminous passage, Ash describes Czechs lining up in the freezing fog for copies of a newspaper called *The Free Word* and comments: 'The semantic occupation was as offensive to them as the military occupation; cleaning up the linguistic environment as vital as cleaning up the physical environment.' Noting that communism had done much to create the social and educational conditions for its own demise, Ash asks whether the culture of resistant memory and integrity in Eastern Europe will survive exposure to 'the perpetual noise of our media-driven and obsessively telecommunicative world.'

In most respects, Echikson's *Lighting the Night* is the least interesting of these four books. However, its conclusion is notable for the author's suggestion that the countries of

---

19 This reflection was originally published in *The Canberra Times*, on 8 December 1990. It was a review of four books: *We the People: The Revolution of '89*, by Timothy Garton Ash; *Lighting the Night: The Revolution in Eastern Europe*, by William Echikson; *Despatches from the Barricades*, by John Simpson; and *Chronicle of a Revolution: A Western-Soviet Inquiry into Perestroika*, by Abraham Brumberg, all written within a year of the collapse of Soviet rule in Eastern Europe in the second half of 1989 and a year before the collapse of the Soviet Union itself, in 1991. The book begins with this piece, because the downfall of Soviet power symbolically marked the end of the 20th century and ushered in a new era.

Eastern Europe will do well to look to Finland as a model for both their post-communist development and their post-Warsaw Pact relations with the USSR. Throughout the Cold War, 'Finlandisation' was a 'Bad Thing' in Western parlance, but it was a Good Thing for Finland and would have been much better for Eastern Europe than Stalinisation. Finland achieved peace without subjugation and prosperity without Marshall Plan aid. It had won the respect of Joseph Stalin because of its ferocious resistance to his invasion in 1939-40. Gorbachev's respect will not have to be bought with Eastern European blood, but with constitutional and territorial good sense.

John Simpson was fortunate in being present at the massacre in Tiananmen Square[20]; during crucial moments in the dissolution of communism in Poland and Hungary; the breaching of the Berlin Wall; the collapse of communist rule in Czechoslovakia; the violent overthrow of Nicolae and Elena Ceausescu in Romania, and the release of Nelson Mandela in South Africa. All of these experiences he relates, in *Despatches from the Barricades*, with a marvellous mixture of anecdote and historical reflection. The scope of his book far exceeds that of any of the other three. Moreover, his text is supplemented by numerous black and white photographs and several maps; making it, for a general readership, the most attractive and accessible of these four books. Simpson's account of the bloodshed in Beijing has the vividness of immediacy. His account of the overthrow of the Ceausescus features the testimonies of individuals who witnessed the last hours and execution of the tyrannical couple. The overall mood is exuberant. Like Ash and Echikson, Simpson is swept along in Wordsworthian wonder at being alive during such a time.

Brumberg's *Chronicle of a Revolution* is a book for students and specialists, where Simpson's is high-class news pictorial for a general readership. It is divided into essays by Western scholars and responses by Soviet specialists. There are pairs of essays on national and ethnic tensions, historical scholarship, the emergence of the rule of law, the new politics and poetry in the period of *glasnost*. Historian Roy Medvedev contributes a reflection on 'The Difficult and Painful Path to the Truth'. The essay I personally found most satisfying was Natalya Ivanova's 'Poetry in the Age of Perestroika and Glasnost'.

---

20 This took place on 3-4 June 1989 and great efforts have been expended by the Chinese Communist Party to airbrush it from history ever since. It very likely helped to precipitate the final revolt against Communist rule in Eastern Europe in the second half of the year. In the generation that has since elapsed, China has taken enormous strides economically and the Communist Party has retained its grip on power, presenting us with a unique example of such a combination. How things will transpire past this point remains uncertain, but there is a great deal of food for thought in what has happened, contrary to expectations, during that time.

Numerous long-banned authors are now appearing in print and their works, spanning decades, are playing 'an enormous role in the emancipation of public consciousness'. Ivanova welcomes the publication of such long suppressed poems as Anna Akhmatova's *Requiem*, the lament of Mother Russia for her children devoured by the GULAG; Alexander Tvardovsky's *By Right of Memory*, a long poem concerning the repression of the peasantry; Nikolai Klyuev's *The Holocaust* and Velimir Khlebnikov's ballad *Boss of the Cheka*, as well as the appearance of a full volume of Osip Mandelstam's lyrics. It is an extraordinary process. Like the mass graves near Minsk, the great memory hole of Stalinism has been dug open, but instead of rotted corpses, it has yielded up countless lyric verses, the effect of which on the moral sensibility of the public, declares Ivanova, 'cannot be overestimated.'

Hannah Arendt wrote, in *On Revolution* (1962), 'the French Revolution, which ended in disaster, has made world history; while the American Revolution, so triumphantly successful, has remained an event of little more than local importance.' The communist revolutions of the 20th century were all 'French', rather than 'American', revolutions. The revolutions of 1989 were overwhelmingly 'American'. Behind the many ironies in this turn of events there lies a massive weight of history, filled with enough tragic drama to underwrite a sustained revival of the ancient Festival of Dionysus. Yet, for many, what 1989 brought was 'simply' the triumph of common sense and the rights of man over dogmatism and oppression. Certainly, the spirit of Tom Paine animates *We the People*, *Lighting the Night* and *Despatches from the Barricades*. *Chronicles of a Revolution* registers more of the difficulties and complexities of the matter. Yet all four books bear witness to the resurgence of Enlightenment ideals out of the catastrophes of the 20th century. After the long years of the Cold War, this is, indeed, something to wonder at and celebrate.[21]

---

21 In late 1985, I wrote my first contribution to *Quadrant*, the venerable old magazine of anti-Communism in the Cold War. It was a letter to the editor, who was then Peter Coleman, taking issue with two senior scholars, my former lecturer Frank Knopfelmacher and the historian of ideas Eugene Kamenka, who had written for the magazine's August issue that the West was *losing* the Cold War. I reproduce it here, given how things worked out in the years that followed, during which I completed my PhD, handed it in for examination at the beginning of 1989 and then watched in wonderment as the Soviet bloc imploded:

> *Sir, the tone of downgoing in the reflections of Eugene Kamenka and Frank Knopfelmacher, in their articles 'A World We Do Not Like' and 'Against Forgetting', unrelieved as it is by any vision of overgoing, cannot, I think, do other than further the sorts of cultural disintegration and political nihilism they deplore. There is an unhealthy sort of Weimar Weltschmerz in their ruminations on the decline of the West which I distrust, much as I respect the fundamentally decent concerns of both men.*

> Much of what Dr Kamenka depicts as the metastasis of a sort of cancer of ressentiment *within the Western cultural body is arguably more ambiguous than he allows and by no means wholly cause for gloom. To take but one example, common to both his and Dr Knopfelmacher's* cahiers de doléances, *the rise of the 'new clerisy, produced by the enormous expansion in the upper levels of high school and the lower levels of the tertiary education' may be said to have swamped society in a great wave of half-educated* frondeurs, *'with little or no culture and knowledge'; but why should this be regarded as any more pernicious than the feasible alternatives? That our most prominent educators should be so dismayed by the outbreak of mass semi-literacy is a little paradoxical. Where is their sense of challenge? Of magnanimity? Of irony? At least we no longer have mass illiteracy. Regret that Thersites should have learned to read reflects badly on Odysseus's concept of his own authority, however much we may agree that it has complicated its exercise. So, what is to be done, you Olympians?*
>
> *If a somewhat ungracious and gloomy evaluation of the prospects for mass democracy informs Kamenka's and Knopfelmacher's view of the home front, they seem agreed, equally, that the prospect* extra muros *seems even darker. Both put 'the debacle of the Vietnam War' more or less at the centre of their misgivings about the Third World and Communism. Dr Knopfelmacher seems entirely convinced that 'the totalitarian apparatus covertly placed in our midst' is going to confine the lot of us to a global GULAG within a few decades. What better response could there be to such a dire prognosis than his own words: 'history is both impossible as a science and unpredictable'? Dr Kamenka, more restrained, simply claims that the Vietnam debacle 'created the false belief that the Cold War was not a justified response to Stalinist policies.'*
>
> *This is sticky ground to bat on. I would argue, however, that detestation of Stalinism 'justified' a range of policy responses, criticism of which was often well advised and not treasonous. In particular, the Communist victories in China and Vietnam were and are the source of multiple confusions in our Western policy debates, quite apart from the naïve or misbegotten contributions of any fifth columnists. For this not to be acknowledged is, to borrow Dr Kamenka's words, 'in many respects as appalling as the falsification and incomprehension of issues today.' The two are, of course, related.*
>
> *As a 'pre-malignant' product of the expansion of education that Drs Kamenka and Knopfelmacher seem to regret and as one without any roots in the privileged strata, I am disinclined to view the present state of things quite as unfavourably as they do. This is not, of course, to say that the present state of things is other than grim and tragic in the fullest sense. Nostalgia for some supposed liberal arcadia, however, impresses me not in the least. Where, precisely, is it to be located? In the 1950s? In the 1920s and 30s? In the last summer before the Great War? O Matthew Arnold! O Lord Palmerston! O for the world we have lost—the world of sweetness and light and gunboats that did the job! Are we not up to the challenges we face? Let us have a bolder, as well as a relentlessly honest, approach to them. That would be more impressive than this disconsolate liberal Spenglerism. It might even stir the enthusiasm of Thersites.*

My then friend and, much more recently my business partner, Tim van Gelder, wrote to me from behind the 'Iron Curtain', that he had been shown my letter by a professor of language studies in Bratislava; a fascinating piece of evidence that the anti-Communist magazine *Quadrant* was being read in Eastern Europe at least in the mid-1980s, or at least by one academic in Bratislava.

Less than three years later, as I completed my PhD dissertation, I wrote, in the spring of 1988:

> *Despite claims in anticipation, and in the aftermath, of the First World War, and again of the Great*

Depression, that the crisis was that of capitalism itself; that which has gone under, in both the short and the long run, has been every obstacle to the extension and maturation of capitalist system growth. The old dynastic empires went first, in the wake of the First World War; the threat of militaristic imperialism met with defeat in the Second World War; and recent developments suggest that the command economies of the anti-capitalist states could be next in line for capitulation in the face of the world-system and its unstable, all-consuming dynamism. It is within this context that we must situate the twentieth century revolutions and American response to them.

The very next year, the Soviet bloc fell apart. Unfortunately, I had not published my prediction beforehand.

Bread, circuses and classical scholarship[22]

The phrase 'bread and circuses' has for centuries been used to describe the alimentary and elementary demands of the masses which, if catered to by tyrants or oligarchs, enable them to rule. Among radical republicans, who believe in the political enfranchisement of the masses, it has long been a phrase indicating political decadence. Quite recently, a prominent member of the government of Singapore referred in this tone to the decline of Rome as having been caused by welfare state economics based on bread and circuses for the 'idle hogs' of the imperial city. From a book under the title *Bread and Circuses: Historical Sociology and Political Pluralism*, one is, therefore, entitled to expect a rich reflection on the roots in antiquity of modern democratic concerns. Certainly, that's why I wanted to read it. It is with considerable disappointment that I must inform other potential readers that they must look elsewhere for such reflection.

Paul Veyne's book is tantalizingly erudite, to the point of being esoteric. Those who have a taste for a sort of romantic meandering through Egyptian temples of arcane learning will surely find his philological ruminations and wealth of obscure footnotes delicious. I confess that I have that taste and that this is the reason why I finished reading the book, annotating it rather heavily. However, a serious book must make a clear and significant argument, as well as carry a weight of academic learning. While Veyne seems to have intended to present such an argument, I am not certain that he succeeded. By his own account, he wanted the book 'to be read by persons who are not specialists in ancient history'. His rather clotted and pedantic style and the unsystematic nature of his reference to modern political and sociological discourse defeat this aim, I think.

---

22   This review first appeared in *The Canberra Times* on 16 February 1991. It was, by then, the tenth year since I had completed my undergraduate degree in History, at the University of Melbourne. The central objective of my studies as an undergraduate was to gain a synoptic understanding of Western civilization, ancient, medieval and modern. The seminar in Roman Historiography, in 1981, run by Mr Ronald Thomas Ridley, was in some respects the culmination of that quest. In it, as noted in my Preface, I wrote three long papers (each of them around 8,000 words, which is very long for undergraduate papers and the more so given that I was, at the same time, writing an honours thesis that totalled some 20,000 words on the completely different subject of the general strike and student rebellion in France in 1968). That work had provided me with a solid foundation for thinking about the matter of political sociology and the matter of bread and circuses. Time permitting, I intend shortly to put together a book under the title *Reflections on an Education*, which will include annotated reproductions of all those papers and a number of other undergraduate research papers, on such things as feminism, Marxism and literature, the nature of the global economy and the philosophy of Ludwig Feuerbach.

Veyne set out to explain the phenomenon of donations by rich individuals to the community in the classical world and how it evolved into the proverbial extravagances of imperial Rome. His key classical world is 'euergetism', which means 'private liberality for public benefit'. Clearly much influenced by the work of Max Weber, he asks a characteristically Weberian sociological question: 'why do gifts to the community and acts of patronage towards the city bulk so large in the life of the ancient world ... between 300 BC and AD 300?' He seeks an explanation not in terms of classical or neoclassical economics, which he dismisses as irrelevant to an understanding of the classical mind, but in terms of 20th century anthropological theories of the gift, the potlatch and conspicuous expenditure. He then announces that euergetism 'is not redistribution, or ostentation or depoliticisation.' It is, he suggests, almost as an aside, the behaviour not of Machiavellian lions or foxes, but of social peacocks.

Never mind the fact that he has asserted earlier that it is not ostentation. Moreover, the Roman Annona, the institution through which grain was made available to large numbers of Roman citizens under the late Republic and the Empire, was, by his own account, a redistributive mechanism. As for depoliticisation, having expended much effort supposedly demonstrating that imperial largesse was not motivated by a desire to suppress or contain the liberty of the Romans, Veyne concludes his book with an odd *non sequitur*: 'Once more, we face the three issues of politics: Who commands? What does he command? In what tone does he command?' The overall effect of this convoluted argumentation, is a disconcerting sense that Veyne's erudition is considerable, but his political philosophy confused.

At several points, Veyne states that it is all but impossible for us to know now what life was like in the ancient world. That may be so, yet plainly the task of the historian is to render the available fragments of the past intelligible to his readers by relating them to a contemporary problem and illuminating, rather than merely insisting upon, the irreducible differences between past and present. Veyne might have done this by reference to such disparate phenomena as the evolution of modern sports and representative government. That would have been a truly Weberian undertaking and of great value. Instead, he has like so many classical scholars before him, wrapped himself in the mantle of philological obscurities and illuminated very little.

The genius of Ludwig Wittgenstein[23]

Ray Monk's *Ludwig Wittgenstein: The Duty of Genius* is, quite simply, the most marvellous, engrossing and thought-provoking book I have read in the first quarter of 1991.[24] It is the first full-length biography of one of the most complex and important figures in 20th century Western intellectual life, but it is also a rich and sympathetic biography, which vivifies Wittgenstein's abstruse philosophic concerns and his encounters with the likes of Bertrand Russell, Gottlob Frege, John Maynard Keynes, Piero Sraffa and Moritz Schlick.

Wittgenstein (1889-1951) was personally rather like a character out of an Ingmar Bergman film: brooding, intense, sexually and emotionally rather solipsistic; and often on the brink of suicide. He considered Mozart and Beethoven 'the true sons of God', but relaxed by watching American Westerns and musicals and was addicted to pulp fiction detective stories—as published in Street and Smith's *Detective Story Magazine* and mailed to him from the United States by his disciple Norman Malcolm.

He was a child of the overripe *fin de siecle* culture of pre-World War I Vienna and his great inner need was for clarity and simplicity. His philosophic work may seem less than clear and simple, but its motive was the clearing away of what he regarded as so much babble, nonsense and confusion. He remained pessimistic throughout his life that his work would be understood or that it would have any real effect in the world. This book tells his story and shows the emergence of his philosophic work superbly. It should interest any citizen of the contemporary West who is not quite brain dead.

---

23 This piece first appeared in *The Canberra Times* on 11 May 1991. Like many people, I had been rather fascinated by the figure of Wittgenstein for many years before that. Monk's biography was not the first I had read. It was, however, the best. It showed that Monk (who is no relation of mine, I have to confess) had delved into all the aspects of the philosopher's thought and life that those of us fascinated by him used to wonder about and had brought the story together wonderfully well. Years after I read this book, I read his two volume biography of Bertrand Russell, an essay on which appears in my book *The West in a Nutshell*. Most recently, I have been reading his biography of Robert Oppenheimer and marvelling, again, at his skills in research, analytical biography and human empathy.

24 My then friend of ten years and now business partner of fifteen years, Tim van Gelder, remarked at the time that this statement reads a little oddly, unless someone knows how many books I read in a quarter, since it would naturally be assumed that that number was small and therefore the compliment a hollow one. I trust that the remainder of the reflection adequately conveys my appreciation of the qualities of the book. Other than the book by Paul Veyne, my reflection on which appears immediately before this piece, I confess I cannot, after twenty three years any longer remember what other books I read in the first quarter of 1991.

Vienna before the First World War was described by one of its most notable citizens—the literary and social critic Karl Kraus—as the 'research laboratory for world destruction'.[25] It was this milieu that produced Sigmund Freud, Otto Weininger, Gustav Klimt, Oscar Kokoschka, Gustav Mahler, Arnold Schoenberg, Adolf Loos and Ludwig Wittgenstein, among others. If Schoenberg and his atonal music inspired Thomas Mann's *Doctor Faustus,* the Wittgenstein family might well have been (though it was not) the inspiration for his great novel *Buddenbrooks,* the tale of the disintegration of a high bourgeois family.

Karl Wittgenstein, the philosopher's father, was the Andrew Carnegie of the Austro-Hungarian Empire, immensely wealthy and determined that his sons would follow in his footsteps. His wife, Leopoldine, had a passion for music and musical evenings at the palatial Wittgenstein home on the Alleegasse, were attended by Johannes Brahms, Gustav Mahler and Bruno Walter, among others. Four of their five sons were musically or intellectually gifted, highly strung, sexually inverted and not at all inclined to follow their father into the steel industry. Hans was a precocious musical genius of Mozartian talent who fled from his father's demands and committed suicide in 1902.

Rudolf, also in rebellion against his father, committed suicide in a Berlin music hall in 1904. Kurt committed suicide in 1918, after Austrian troops under his command mutinied. Paul became a brilliant concert pianist, lost his right arm in the First World War, but resumed his career with one arm only. It was for him that Maurice Ravel, in 1931, composed his famous *Concerto for the Left Hand.* Ludwig himself hovered on the brink of suicide for years before World War I, gave away his inherited wealth; when still in his mid-twenties was hailed by Bertrand Russell as a philosophic genius, but remained a manic depressive throughout his life. His nervous temperament, peculiar life and remarkable work all alike germinated in the rarefied, opulent and neurotic *milieu* in which he was raised.

Wittgenstein did not believe in the 'gospel of progress.' He was deeply pessimistic about the destiny of scientific humanity, well before the horrors of World War II. And while, rather more than many great modern philosophers, he professed a certain belief in what he was prepared to call 'God', he was in no orthodox sense a Christian. Rather, he was a sort of post-Christian whose outlook on

---

25 Edward Timms has produced a remarkable two volume biography of Karl Kraus over the past thirty years and more. The first volume *Karl Kraus: Apocalyptic Satirist, Culture and Catastrophe in Vienna,* appeared in 1986. The second volume, *Karl Kraus: Apocalyptic Satirist, The Post-War Crisis and the Rise of the Swastika,* did not appear until 2005. Both volumes were published by Yale University Press. Kraus, like so many of the most interesting cultural and intellectual figures of the modern West, was Jewish, as of course was Wittgenstein. His ambivalences and his fastidious interest in the complexities of language and ethics are strongly redolent of Wittgenstein and his intellectual stance of satirical conservatism is one with which I have great empathy. Yet I am not, of course, a conservative in terms of my beliefs or my attitude to the significance of new knowledge. I am simply sensitive to the multitude of ways in which innovation and enthusiasm can go off the rails.

Christian belief was similar in important respects to Nietzsche's, though his outlook on Christian values was closer to that of Tolstoy or Dostoevsky. He once remarked of friends who had converted to Catholicism, 'I could not possibly bring myself to believe all the things that they believe.'

His abiding concern was with a unity of ethical integrity and intellectual clarity. Of many incidents from his life recounted by Monk, none perhaps captures this concern better than his famous outburst at Norman Malcolm in 1939—when Malcolm asserted that it was not in the British 'national character' to attempt to assassinate Hitler—'What is the use of studying philosophy if all that it does for you is enable you to talk with some plausibility about some abstruse questions of logic etc., if it does not improve your thinking about the important questions of everyday life; if it does not make you more conscientious than any journalist in the use of the dangerous phrases such people use for their own ends?'

Gnawed by this ethical concern, Wittgenstein abominated what he saw as the insincerity, pomposity and self-satisfaction at Cambridge University. He sought repeatedly to get away from academic life: by doing elementary school teaching in rural Austria; by living in cottages in Norway, Wales and Ireland; even by visiting the Soviet Union in September 1935, hoping to find work there as a simple manual labourer. Instead, he was offered a chair in philosophy at Kazan University, then a teaching post in philosophy at the University of Moscow. He returned to England. Yet he could never throw off the grip that philosophic questions had on him and kept writing and revising philosophic notebooks until the day before he died. Only after his death were the great bulk of his writings edited and published by his literary executors.

Why did Wittgenstein publish so little in his lifetime, when from his early twenties he was hailed as perhaps the greatest philosophic genius of his time? He was exceptionally fastidious about publication, as he was about most things. This infuriated Bertrand and others who were anxious to get Wittgenstein's ideas into circulation. Ironically, on the one occasion he anxiously sought publication—of his first major treatise, the *Tractatus Logico-Philosophicus*—he had great difficulty in finding a publisher. In that case, he drew the conclusion, 'What, in the final analysis, did it matter if his book remained unpublished?' By far the most important thing was to 'settle accounts with himself'.

He abandoned the manuscript of the *Tractatus* to the care of Russell and spent the summer of 1920 working as a gardener at the Klosterneuberg Monastery, just outside Vienna, in an effort to overcome the inner unhappiness that constantly threatened to destroy him. Thereafter, his attitude to publication might be said to have paralleled his attitude towards marriage and reproduction: the world being as it was, more books, like more children, would be *de trop*—superfluous. A man of rare intellectual acuity and cultural sensitivity, Ludwig Wittgenstein was a canary in the coalmine of the first half of the twentieth century in Europe.

His deep perplexity and pessimism regarding the opacity of language, the coarseness and mendacity of most human beings and the mushrooming of technological civilization found expression in reflections that are at once among the most hermetic and incisive in twentieth century writing. What informed them was ultimately a radically romantic longing for a purified, primal order of things: less hectic, less baffling, more aesthetic and spiritual. This romanticism was beautifully expressed, late in his life, to the American philosopher Oets Bouwsma, when Wittgenstein remarked on a moonlit night, 'If I had planned it, I should never have made the sun at all. See! How beautiful! The sun is too bright and too hot ... And if there were only the moon, there would be no reading and writing.' No reading and writing?! That is a radical romanticism indeed! To explore it, of course, one must read and re-read Wittgenstein's complex writings.

Not since reading Charles Hession's life of John Maynard Keynes have I come across a biography that so sensitively explores the intimate relationship between the sexuality and intellectual life of a great human being.[26] One of Ray Monk's purposes in writing this book was to examine the claims by William Warren Bartley III that Wittgenstein was promiscuously homosexual during certain periods of his life and that this was the root of his chronic inner unhappiness. Monk documents several homosexual infatuations that Wittgenstein had, but only one of actual homosexual intimacy (with Frances Skinner). He observes that Wittgenstein's feelings tended to be unspoken, unacknowledged and unreciprocated and suggested a 'certain indifference to the feelings of the other person.'

Monk comments on all this: 'The philosophical solipsism to which he had at one time been attracted and against which much of his later work is addressed ... has its parallel in the emotional solipsism in which his romantic attachments were conducted.' We are thereby offered a key not to Wittgenstein's psychological torment alone, but also to his obsessive concern with language, logic, meaning and communication. Since he was far more unusually bright and sensitive than he was unusually disturbed, his extraordinary life and personality offer much instruction to those who find being in the world disturbing. Ray Monk has done a superb piece of work in making that life and personality more accessible to others than it has been until now.

---

26 I read Hession's life of Keynes in the spring of 1985, on the train journey from Paris, via Lyons to Rome. I was particularly struck, as I recorded in my journal at the time, by the frank homosexuality of the Apostles at Cambridge and Keynes's own espousal before the First World War, of what he and others went so far as to call 'the higher sodomy'. In 1912, according to Hession, Keynes witnessed Rupert Brooke flirting with the beautiful Brynhild Olivier and wrote to Duncan Grant, 'Oh these womanisers. How on earth and what for can he do it?' Wittgenstein was, for some reason, unable to settle into that circle, despite his homosexual inclinations. That says quite a bit about his difficult and complex personality. Keynes, took an interest in Wittgenstein when the latter first arrived at Cambridge, but found him quite impossible to work out or to deal with.

The Western as a film genre[27]

Kim Newman's *Wild West Movies: How the West was Found, Won, Lost, Lied About, Filmed and Forgotten* is the best mail order catalogue I've ever come across. The consumer who is not already thoroughly familiar with the product line of this particular industry will find it a true Baedeker in the wild and diverse psychodramatic geography of the genre. And even those cinematic Lewises and Clarks who have covered a great deal of the territory will find Newman's arrangement of the tales about the West and his reflections on the birth of the Western out of the spirit of hero worship; its flowering, senescence and self-parody diverting and instructive.

I read this book in between viewings of Kevin Costner's linguistically and ecologically sensitive late Western, *Dances with Wolves*. I thoroughly enjoyed *Dances with Wolves* because it seemed to me to have qualities of tragic pathos, anthropological subtlety and reflectiveness about human violence which I did not associate with the Western. Reading Newman has compelled me to reconsider a number of these prejudices about the genre. For example, I considered *Dances with Wolves* an almost uniquely sensitive treatment of the fate of the Native Americans, but Newman argues cogently that, on the whole, the downgoing of the 'Indians' in the West is fairly sympathetically recounted in the genre.

Newman describes the 1970 Vietnam War era pro-Indian films *Little Big Man* and *Soldier Blue* as 'fairly thin', with *Soldier Blue* 'the sillier film', because 'lacking the ironic edge' of *Little Big Man*. John Ford's epic mea culpa, *Cheyenne Autumn* (1964) floundered, he writes, because 'the film was stuck with unbelievable Indians'. Yet he describes Charles Marquis Warren's *Arrowhead* (1952) as 'that rarity: a Western as enlightened about the Indians as the average 1943 war movie is about the Japanese'. He argues that Hollywood 'is ashamed of everything the white man has done to the red except patronising him'; but concludes that 'the Indian story is still too problematic and disturbing for mainstream American cinema to deal with'. For me, Newman's arguments have turned an otiose topic into a rather fascinating one.

Covering the whole century of cinema, Newman treats multiple versions of the same tale or historical episode. This provides special interest in the cases of those two most famous Western rebels without causes: Billy the Kid and Jesse James. He notes that Walter Woods's play *Bill the Kid* (1903) and Walter Noble Burns' *The Saga of Billy the Kid* (1926) changed the

---

27   This piece was first published in *The Canberra Times* on 18 May 1991. As the second paragraph records, Newman's book was read and reviewed in between viewings of the then newly released Kevin Costner film *Dances with Wolves*.

historic bandit into a semi-mythic hero. He first made the screen in *Billy the Bandit* (1916) and became a regular movie character after King Vidor's *Billy the Kid* (1930), featuring in such films as Howard Hughes's *The Outlaw* (1940), more or less wildly inaccurate versions of the tale in 1941, 1948, 1950, 1953, 1954 and 1955; encounters with the Three Stooges (1964) and Dracula (1965); Spanish, Mexican and French treatments; numerous cameo appearances in other Westerns; as well as better known dramatizations in Arthur Penn's *The Left-Handed Gun* (1957)—in which, had he not died young himself, James Dean would almost certainly have been aptly cast as Billy—Andrew McClaglen's *Chisum* (1970), starring John Wayne; and, of course, Sam Peckinpah's *Pat Garrett and Billy the Kid* (1973); starring James Coburn and Kris Kristofferson and featuring Bob Dylan. Peckinpah's last genuine Western, this film gives nuanced inflection to his gloomy, misanthropic perspective on the heroic days of the West and their decline into civilization.

In his brief Epilogue, Newman advances the elements of a theory of the death of the Western that, rather fascinatingly, parallels Nietzsche's well-known theory of the death of Greek tragedy and, to a lesser extent, George Steiner's argument in *The Death of Tragedy*. Around 1980, Newman writes, 'while Michael Cimino and United Artists were pouring millions of dollars into a toilet called *Heaven's Gate* and vigorously pulling the flush, the Western finally died with its boots more or less on.' Peckinpah is cast in the role of Euripides to John Ford's Sophocles and Howard Hawks's Aeschylus. *The Wild Bunch* (1969) is seen as heralding the end of the Western, as the machine gun, the automobile and the aeroplane intrude on the heroic stage. Newman quotes critic Howard Suber's Nietzschean view that: 'Self reflexivity is the death of any movement in the arts, because the moment you become totally conscious of what you're doing, you start tripping over your own ideas and you produce parodies or pomposity. What killed the Western was that it became self-reflexive.'

The result? Why, a sort of New Comedy, represented by *Butch Cassidy and the Sundance Kid* (1969) and *Silverado* (1985). The death of the genre might almost be said to coincide with that of its most famous thespian, John Wayne, in 1976. Thereafter, America's theatrical search for heroes and moral orientation moved increasingly to other frontiers. Significantly, in *Dances with Wolves*, Costner enacts a double nostalgia, declaring both with and within this film: 'I want to see the frontier, before it's gone.' Newman's book traverses that frontier in both its passings, historic and cinematic; taking flight, like Hegel's fabled Owl of Minerva, at dusk. It is not by any means Hegelian in its intellectual pretensions, but it does offer a genuinely reflective retrospective on a major era in modern theatre and is well enough written to be entertaining in its own right.

Charles De Gaulle as an epic hero[28]

Reading Jean Lacouture's monumental life of the man, I found myself persuaded as never before of the human and political greatness of Charles De Gaulle. I do not think I have read a political biography of comparable calibre since I immersed myself in Isaac Deutscher's exalted three volume biography of Leon Trotsky, when I was an undergraduate. Lacouture's work does not, perhaps, quite match Deutscher's as literature, but it surpasses it as historical scholarship. [29]

---

28   This piece was first published in *The Canberra Times* on 8 June 1991. It is a review of the first volume of Jean Lacouture's biography of Charles De Gaulle. My review of the second volume appears later in this book. I had first read a biography of De Gaulle in 1969: that by Alexander Werth (Penguin, 1967). I studied 20th century French History under Dr Charles O. Sowerwine at the University of Melbourne, in 1980. For some reason, I wrote inside the cover of my copy of Werth, in 1980, Dr Sowerwine's summary of the course of events which, in 1958, led to De Gaulle taking over as President and conservative strong man in a France dominated for the preceding decade by the Left.

The following year (1981), I wrote my History honours thesis on the general strike and student rebellion in France, in May 1968, against de Gaulle and Gaullism. That was an illuminating exercise, in which I found myself fascinated by the complex causes of the upheaval, but critical of the standard Left-wing theories about it and ultimately more sympathetic to De Gaulle than to the rebels whether of the Old Left (the Communist Party) or the New Left (the student rebels, with their fatuous enthusiasm for Fidel Castro and Mao Zedong). In the decade between that thesis and reviewing Lacouture's first volume, I completed my doctorate in international relations, saw much of the world and entered (with absurd difficulties not to be recounted here) the world of the Australian intelligence services. My appreciation for realism and maturity of judgment grew at every step.

29   It's curious looking back on this phrasing now. When I was still a twelve year old schoolboy, having read Deutscher's *Stalin*, I so much wanted to read his masterwork on Trotsky that I ordered it from the local bookshop (in those days a newsagency, which unlike any of which I am aware these days, actually stocked shelves of serious books) without first clearing the purchase with my parents. When it arrived, I surprised my mother with the announcement and was told I would have to go back to Mr Forbes at the newsagency and own up to what I had done, saying that I could not afford to buy the books and that my parents would not condone my behaviour by doing so on my behalf. That was a chastening experience. It was to be another decade before I obtained my own (paperback) copy and read it.

I was at that point very much impressed by Deutscher's portrayal of Trotsky as the tragic genius and Danton of the Russian Revolution. I have since learned a great deal more and have a rather different view of both his career and his unsuccessful struggle with Stalin. In particular, it became clear to me that Trotsky had failed as a political theorist before he failed as a political tactician and that Stalin defeated him because Stalin was not only the shrewder tactician, but was far more politically astute and capable than the presumptuous Trotsky ever gave him credit for. The trap which Trotsky laid for himself, having abandoned the Mensheviks (in 1917) for Lenin and the Bolsheviks, was agreeing to the famous 'ban on factions' at the Tenth Party Congress in 1921. Five years later, he tried to argue for the liberty to contest ideas, but prefaced his address to the Party apparatus with the self-defeating premise:

It is a more mature piece of work than Deutscher's masterpiece: more dispassionate, more ironic and more intimately humane. There is something a little too theatrically epic about Deutscher's Trotsky. Lacouture's De Gaulle seems to me a more authentic hero, though of no less epic proportions.

The great lover of France also seems to me a more appealing human being than the ill-fated proponent of permanent revolution. De Gaulle seems comparable to Caesar himself in his magnanimity, sense of destiny (like Caesar, he referred to himself in the third person in his memoirs) and force of character; but he resembled Brutus in his moral character and devotion to the republic. In the Anglo-Saxon world, De Gaulle was pilloried for his alleged arrogance, but Lacouture's portrait of him compels admiration. If some modern Plutarch were to compose a *Lives of the Noble Europeans and Americans*, I believe Charles De Gaulle would figure prominently among them.

Jean Lacouture is a biographer at the height of his powers and one deeply immersed in his subject matter. Foreign editor of *Le Monde* from 1957 until 1975 and concurrently director of the Paris publishing house Le Seuil from 1961 until 1981, he had written biographies of Ho Chi Minh, Andre Malraux, Leon Blum, Francois Mauriac and Pierre Mendes France before producing this massive study of De Gaulle. It is a towering biography of a towering figure and a fitting climax to Lacouture's life as a man of letters.

Lacouture opens his narrative with a stirring account of the adolescent De Gaulle's presentiment, in 1905, that he would one day lead the armies of France against the power of Imperial Germany. De Gaulle wrote in his memoirs, 'When I was an adolescent ... I did not doubt that France would have to go through enormous trials, that the whole point of life consisted of one day rendering her some conspicuous service and that I should have the opportunity of doing so.'

De Gaulle's sombre and equally brilliant, but ill-fated contemporary, Mikhail Tukhachevsky of Imperial Russia and then the Soviet Union had similar aspirations at the same time. Among the many fascinating encounters of De Gaulle's life, as recounted by Lacouture, were his encounters with Tukhachevsky. The first time was when Captain De Gaulle and Lieutenant Tukhachevsky were fellow POWs at the German prison for compulsive escapees: Ingolstadt IX, in 1916. The second was in late 1936, when Colonel De Gaulle and Marshall Tukhachevsky attended a dinner for 'the old boys of Fort IX' in Paris. De Gaulle was, by then, a rebel against the strategic orthodoxy of the French High Command, on account of his prescient advocacy of the use of armoured divisions as the spearheads of offensive and counter-offensive warfare.

'Comrades, I know that the Party cannot make a mistake, because it is the only vehicle given to us by History for discerning the truth. Nevertheless, comrades ... ' Stalin had him tied in knots; yet Trotsky, to the end of his days, insisted that Stalin was a 'grey blur' and a mediocrity. He never understood his deadly adversary and he paid the ultimate price for his blindness.

Tukhachevsky, by then Red Army Chief of Staff, sat next to De Gaulle at the dinner and congratulated him on his theories, as set out in his book *Vers l'Armée de metier*. Tukhachevsky presented De Gaulle with a copy of the Soviet edition of the book, the translation and printing of which he had himself seen to, being the foremost Soviet theorist of tank warfare. Six months later, Marshall Tukhachevsky was executed as the key figure in Stalin's ferocious purge of the Red Army officer corps.[30]

Far more significant in De Gaulle's career were his two encounters with Franklin Roosevelt of the United States and his dealings with Winston Churchill. These crucial political relationships form the background to the third and fourth sections of the book and Lacouture is at his best in recounting the subtleties and tensions involved in them. FDR's attitude to De Gaulle is especially intriguing and Lacouture's rendering of it leaves one in no doubt as to why France, under De Gaulle, later proved so recalcitrant a member of the Western alliance, insisting on the creation of its own *force de frappe* (nuclear deterrent) and independent military command. FDR refused to take De Gaulle seriously as the representative of Free France; treated sooner with Petain, Darlan, Laval and even Giraud as French leaders; and declared that France had become a non-nation (*res nullius*) as a consequence of its defeat in 1940, so that it would be, in 1944, not liberated so much as conquered and administered by a US military government. That De Gaulle was able to preserve his equanimity in the face of this attitude toward his beloved France and even to find a certain charm in the American president, testifies to his nobility of character.

In his dealings with both the British and the Americans, De Gaulle found the Anglo-Saxons, but especially the Americans, imperious and condescending. Lacouture dissects the relations between all three sides to this Western alliance triangle with superb sophistication and delicacy of judgement. His Chapter 27 'Charles Disowned: FDR and the Constable' is a gem. His nuanced

---

30   The failure of the French High Command to adopt De Gaulle's approach has at times been adduced as one of the reasons for the fall of France to the Nazis in 1940. But the situation was more complex and interesting than that. In a fascinating study of the fall of France, published in 2000, *Strange Victory: Hitler's Conquest of France*, Ernest May argued that Hitler lucked out and that only human error on the Allied side enabled the German forces to make their breakthrough in the Ardennes and outflank the Allied forces in both Flanders and along the Maginot Line. Every time computer simulations of the conflict were run, he points out, the Allies won.

Conversely, having purged the Red Army of almost all its leading strategic innovators and having failed to foresee the monumental folly of Hitler's invasion of the Soviet Union in 1941, Stalin quickly unleashed Tukhachevsky's protégés after the battle to save Moscow. The Red Army ended the war as a massively armoured force, hammering even the potent German armoured corps in major tank battles of unprecedented scale in 1943-44. History is full of ironies and beautiful complexities and of pitfalls for those who like to draw hasty conclusions or make sweeping judgements.

and appreciative view of FDR is crowned with the observation: 'What is so disconcerting about the anti-Gaullism of Roosevelt, a man of the greatest stature ... is that facts were only very minor elements in its composition.' De Gaulle was taught a sobering lesson in the psychology of great power politics which he never forgot. Roosevelt's idealism, he decided, 'clothed the will for power' and 'finally proved to me that, in relations between states, logic and feelings have little weight in comparison with the realities of power; what matters is what one seizes and what one can hold onto; and that, in order to recover its place, France should count only on itself.'

Yet De Gaulle admired both FDR and America. Lacouture notes, toward the end of his volume, how 'This man, so deeply concerned with the most traditional history, so ignorant of finance, economics and production, was immensely and instantly impressed by the sight of an America bursting with promise and industrial creativity ... this ... brought out everything that was modernist and even futurist in this medieval crusader.' As for his relations with Winston Churchill, these are one of the most engrossing and entertaining features of the book. It is worth reading for their sake alone, its other merits apart.

De Gaulle: The Rebel sets the stage magnificently for the subsequent treatment of the man's political career and the quality of judgement Lacouture has brought to this work suggests that his reflections on the affairs of the Fourth and Fifth Republics, the Indochina and Algerian wars, the Organisation Armée Secrete and its murderous vendetta against De Gaulle and the famous upheaval of May 1968 in France will make splendid reading. The only complaint to be made about the first volume is the surprising number of typographical errors and even what appear to be slips in translation. These are not such, however, as to significantly mar what is a magnificent piece of writing.

Israel's secret wars[31]

For those of us, the majority in the West, who have no links with the Arab world and little empathy with Islam, it takes a conscious effort to understand Israel as other than an impressive and heroic state. Our Biblical heritage, our awareness of the terrible genocide of the European Jews under Nazi rule and also, let it be said, a diffuse sense that somehow the Moslem Arabs threaten Western access to oil, all conspire to make us broadly biased towards Israel. Both the spectacular terrorist acts of various Palestinian rebels against Zionist domination and the spectacular coups of the Israeli secret service have, over many years, given pugnacious Israel a heroic image.

Ian Black and Benny Morris's *Israel's Secret Wars: The Untold History of Israeli Intelligence*; Dan Raviv and Yossi Melman's *Every Spy a Prince: The Complete History of Israel's Intelligence Community*; and Michael Palumbo's *Imperial Israel: The History of the Occupation of the West Bank and Gaza* help to put that image in perspective. One of them—Palumbo's book—does the image considerable damage.

Far and away the most famous branch of Israel's secret service is the Mossad. Mossad is an abbreviation for Ha Mossad le Modiin ule-Tafkidim Mayuhadim, which translate as The Institute for Intelligence and Special Tasks. In other words, Mossad means simply Institute. Alongside it, there are Shin Bet or Shabak, short for Sherat ha-Bitachon ha-Klali, meaning General Security Service[32] and Aman (Agaf ha-Modiin), the intelligence branch of the armed forces.

---

31 This piece was first published in *The Age* on 6 July 1991. It was, as far as I can establish, the first time I had written anywhere on Israel and the Middle East. It takes a line that, while fair-minded, is still one from which I have diverged in more recent years. It was written more than a decade before 9/11, prior to the two intifadas orchestrated by Yasser Arafat, the rejection by the Palestinian leaders of the olive branch offered to them under both the Oslo and Camp David accords, the rise of Hamas, the Israeli withdrawal from Gaza and the debacle of the so-called Arab Spring. The series of pieces in this book on Israel and the Arabs traces the evolution in my thinking over more than two decades.

32 In 2012, a very fine documentary about Shabak directed by Dror Moreh was released, under the title *The Gatekeepers*. It features extended interviews with six past directors general of the general security service, who speak with astonishing candour about the challenges of handling the Palestinian populations in Gaza and the West bank and ensuring the domestic security of Israel over the past thirty years or so. They do not pull their punches in terms of politics, errors, regrets or moral dilemmas. What is remarkable, of course, is that such a film was made at all and not censored or suppressed.

There is no state in the Muslim world, certainly not one in the Middle East, where any such candid film would be made. Indeed, there is nothing to match it in the Anglophone world either. It is right up there in terms of quality with Errol Morris's acclaimed 2003 documentary about Robert McNamara and 'the American century', *The Fog of War*. That, however, is an extended interview with one man, in his eighties, who had long since retired from the Pentagon. *The Gatekeepers* is the equivalent of six former heads of the FBI or perhaps the CIA, right up to the very recent past, talking candidly on camera about the Cold War and the war against Islamic terrorism. There is, thus far, no such documentary.

From 1957 to 1986 there was another agency, more secret than any of these: Lakam, short for Lishka le-Kishrei Mad'a, meaning Scientific Liaison Bureau. It was Lakam that ran the Israeli project for the acquisition of nuclear weapons. It was also Lakam that recruited Jonathan Pollard, an American Jew and passionate Zionist, who worked in the American Anti-Terrorism Alert Center as a spy for Israel in 1984-85. Pollard was recruited for Lakam at the instigation of its then director, Mossad and Shin Bet veteran Rafi Eitan, reportedly the model for Marty Kurtz in John le Carré's 1983 novel, *The Little Drummer Girl*. Kurtz was superbly played by Klaus Kinsky in the film of le Carré's novel, released in 1985.

The history of Israeli intelligence is more dramatic than most. Both *Israel's Secret Wars* and *Every Spy a Prince* provide excellent introductions to that history. The former has the more impressive apparatus of historical scholarship and is written, I think, in a stronger, better balanced fashion. The latter, however, supplies a useful table of the directors of Mossad, Aman, Shin Bet, Lakam and the Liaison Bureau for Jewish Immigration, as well as a list of the Prime Minister's advisers on counterterrorism. It also features a chart showing the structure of the Israeli intelligence community and has 25 photographs. The Black/Morris book has none of these features, although it does have a handy glossary of abbreviations that the Raviv/Melman book lacks.

Among the omissions from *Israel's Secret Wars* is an account of how Israeli prime minister David Ben Gurion obtained a nuclear reactor. On 21 September 1956, according to Raviv and Melman, French Defence Minister Maurice Bourges-Manoury, in order to ensure Israeli participation in the Suez operation, acceded to months of secret lobbying by Ben Gurion, conducted through his lieutenant, Shimon Peres, and offered Israel a nuclear reactor.

No safeguards or inspections were required. Ben Gurion and Peres then had a nuclear research station set up at Dimona, in the Negev desert, with the express intention of producing atomic weapons. This purpose was kept secret from all but a tiny circle of people in Israel and a special agency, Lakam, was created by Peres to keep the top secret project under wraps. The Americans discovered the site through U2 surveillance in 1960. Its full purpose only became public, however, in 1986, when the *Sunday Times* of London ran a long exclusive article entitled 'The Secrets of Israel's Nuclear Arsenal' based on information supplied by Mordechai Vanunu, who had worked as a technician at Dimona.[33]

Among the numerous virtues of *Israel's Secret Wars* is its lucid and extremely well researched account of the stunning failure of Israeli intelligence to anticipate the Egyptian/Syrian assault

---

33   Avner Cohen's *Israel and the Bomb* (Columbia University Press, 1998) superseded all these revelations in its systematic account of how Israel had developed atomic weapons. It centres on the debate over whether to declare the capability or seek strategic opacity by refusing to either confirm or deny the existence or size of the nuclear arsenal.

on 6 October (Yom Kippur) 1973.[34] A grand conception (*kontzeptziya*) had taken hold of virtually the entire Israeli military, intelligence and political establishment after the crushing defeat of the Arabs in the Six Day War of June 1967[35]: that the Arabs could not and would not dare to attack Israel in force for the foreseeable future. It is breathtaking, reading Black and Morris's deeply informed account of the matter, to learn how all manner of evidence that war was coming was dismissed, especially by Aman director Eli Zeira, on the basis of no more than the *kontzeptziya*.

Michael Palumbo's *Imperial Israel* is a book that should be read by any who believe that Palestinian violence against Israel is irrational.[36] Far more disturbingly than the other authors, Palumbo remorselessly exposes the darker side of Israel and Zionism: the brutalities of Israel in its oppression of the Palestinians and the Biblical bigotries of the Zionist Right, from Rabbis such as the late Meir Kahane and Moshe Levinger to ex-terrorists and recent prime ministers Menachem Begin and Yitzhak Shamir.

Yet the book provides, at the same time, clear evidence of the pluralism in Israeli society and the capacity for objectivity and fairness of much of the Israeli press. What it does above all, however, is compel recognition of the legitimate grievances of the Palestinians. For this reason, it should be widely read and discussed.

---

34   The origins of the Yom Kippur War and the major intelligence failure which preceded it have also been much better treated in more recent books, notably in Abraham Rabinovich's *The Yom Kippur War: The Epic Encounter That Transformed the Middle East* (Schocken Books, New York, 2004).

35   On the Six Day War see Michael B. Oren's *Six Days of War: June 1967 and the Making of the Modern Middle East* (Oxford University Press, 2002).

36   It is from Palumbo's verdicts and my own appraisal of his work that I have most diverged since 1991, not because I see no injustices in Israel's actions, but because I have found that I have less and less sympathy for the Palestinians who oppose not merely those injustices, real or imagined, but the very existence of Israel. Two pieces in particular, later in this book, will show the shift in my thinking: reviews of Efraim Karsh's *Palestine Betrayed* (Yale University Press, 2010) and Ahron Bregman's *Cursed Victory: A History of Israel and the Occupied Territories* (Allen Lane, 2014). In one sentence, I have come to believe that the Palestinian and Arab rejection of Israel and ever more vicious embrace of anti-Semitism, going back to the decades before Israel was even founded, have indeed been irrational and deeply counter-productive. I see no immediate prospect of these things being turned around and, therefore, I see no possibility of a negotiated peace settlement in the near future.

Indonesia's bloodletting of 1965-66 and the US ambassador[37]

When a diplomat of Marshall Green's calibre decides to write a memoir, there are many people who will be interested in reading it.[38] That interest arises, of course, from a desire to obtain clearer insights into some of the dramatic events to which the man has been a witness. There are certainly cases where such hopeful interest proves warranted. This is not one of them.

It is a book which takes us back to events that occurred in Indonesia, in 1965-66, just as the Vietnam War was escalating into a really large-scale American war. Those events involved the destruction of the Indonesian Communist Party (PKI) under circumstances that have never been adequately explained.

Green opens his story by observing that Sukarno had been leading his people towards Communism when, from October 1965, 'a miraculous transformation occurred'. Communist assassination of six top generals on the night of 30 September, he asserts, triggered 'the army's

---

37 This piece was published in both the *Canberra Times* (31 August 1991) and *The Age* (7 September 1991). It is the latter text, only very slightly different from the former, which I have reproduced here. It seems worth noting that I was, at the time, working in the Defence Intelligence Organization, where the whole subject of Indonesia and human rights was a very sensitive subject. Between late 1988 and mid-1990, I had been denied a Negative Vetting security clearance (enabling me to work for the Department of Defence at all) and then was given an unusually hard time getting a Positive Vetting clearance (enabling me to work in DIO and be given access to Top Secret material), writing this piece might be regarded as somewhat reckless.

Moreover, the spurious grounds on which clearances were withheld had to do with allegations that I was a Communist and had an unacceptable attitude towards the CIA. My attitude at the time, however, was that I regarded with considerable disdain the system which had treated me so incompetently and I had no intention of pulling my head in and conforming to mindless norms. As a great deal of material in the present book, including much dating from that time, surely makes clear, I was not remotely Communist or pro-Soviet and had a healthy respect for both serious intelligence analysis and hard headed realpolitik.

38 Marshall Green (1916–1998) was educated at Groton and Yale and then joined the US Foreign Service, becoming a specialist on Cold War politics in East and Southeast Asia. He was the senior American diplomat in South Korea at the time of the 1960 April Revolution, in which Park Chung-hee established a dictatorship which was to last, under him and his successors until the late 1980s and would catapult South Korea forward economically. He was also US ambassador to Indonesia when a coup took place there (the overthrow of the left-leaning Sukarno) followed by an enormous bloodletting in which hundreds of thousands of people were slaughtered as alleged Communists. Shortly afterwards, he became Assistant Secretary of State for East Asian and Pacific Affairs. He was a member of the party, led by President Richard Nixon that went to China to treat with Mao Zedong China in 1972. This review was of his 1991 memoir *Indonesia: Crisis and Transformation 1965-68*, published by Compass Press, Washington.

crushing of Indonesia's Communist Party, the eventual unseating of Sukarno and the emergence of a pragmatic new order led by General Suharto.'

Then he adds: 'The United States stood to gain much by these momentous changes. But it had no hand in bringing them about.' This last statement is sufficiently contentious that Green ought, surely, to have taken up the longstanding debate about the events of 30 September and after and possible American involvement in them, if only in order to try to demonstrate that the Communists did bring destruction on themselves and that the American government was a mere innocent bystander in the affair.

Instead, he takes refuge in the blithe disclaimer: 'This is the work of a diplomat, not a scholar'; as if that entitles him to ignore the claims of scholarship and trot out as his recollections long contested and even confuted statements about what actually happened in history.

The evidence and argument surrounding the upheaval of 1965-66 in Indonesia, in which some hundreds of thousands (estimates range up to one million) people, alleged to be communist or pro-communist, were slaughtered, are too complex to even begin to be presented here. From the work of Ben Anderson and Ruth McVey, as early as 1966, through the writings of Ralph McGehee and Peter Dale Scott, to the recent research by Kathy Kahane, however, the official Indonesian and American accounts of the matter have been shown to be inaccurate and even incoherent in ways which support a case that the real 'trigger' for the bloodbath was not, as the official account would have it, an attempted PKI coup, but a plan by Suharto and the Americans to topple Sukarno and 'clean out' the PKI.

McGehee, who worked for the CIA for 25 years, claimed in his own memoir, *Deadly Deceits*:

> *To conceal its role in the massacre ... the CIA in 1968 concocted a false account of what happened ... At the same time, it also composed a secret study of what really happened (one sentence deleted). The Agency was extremely proud of its successful (one word deleted) and recommended it as a model for future operations (one half-sentence deleted).*

Those deletions were made by the CIA censor, leaving the basic truth of the claim uncontested and indeed implicitly confirmed by the fact that the passage had been tampered with at all.

Perhaps the most succinct response to the sort of disingenuous account of the Indonesian bloodbath presented to us by Green is a letter to the editor of the *New York Review*, published on 1 June 1978, in which Ben Anderson responded to a similarly cavalier treatment of the matter by another senior American diplomat, Francis Galbraith. Anderson demonstrated that Galbraith's 'simple' account of the 1965 events was muddled even as regards what the published CIA study had concluded about the PKI's role in the affair. He added:

> *Like the Suharto regime, the CIA study fails to produce a plausible explanation of the motives of the purported coup-makers; indeed, its account unconsciously undermines the case it imagines it is making.*

Anderson's suggestion, derived from scholarship, not diplomacy, was that the six murdered generals were killed by soldiers under the command of Lieutenant Colonel Untung, whose oddly inept 'coup' attempt (with Brigadier General Supardjo and Colonel Latief, all three being former or current direct subordinates of Suharto) involved no attempt to neutralise the KOSTRAD (crack strategic army reserve) headquarters, from where Suharto promptly organised his devastating 'counter-coup'.

He asked rhetorically:

> *The CIA's interest in all of this? Perhaps merely scholarly historiographical concern. Or possibly the Agency had a closer connection to what its analyst concludes 'may well prove to be one of the most significant events of the post-World War Two period'.*

It would have been refreshing to see Marshall Green take up the claims made by Anderson and make a serious effort to buttress the 'official' story. Instead, he tries to pin blame for the whole brutal, bloody business on Sukarno and the 'hated' Communists.

It is often retorted, when one raises the notion of covert Western intelligence involvement in coups and such abroad, 'Oh, don't be such a conspiracy theorist! Indigenous forces were quite up to doing all that without the hand of the CIA being necessary.' Those inclined to such a sceptical reaction in this instance might do well to consider that, not only was the CIA itself involved, in 1958, in efforts to destabilise Sukarno, but as recently declassified materials reveal, the British and Australian secret services were also up to their elbows in the business.

Five years ago, *Pacific Affairs* published Peter Dale Scott's essay 'The United States and the Overthrow of Sukarno, 1965-1967', which goes far towards indicating the 'closer connection' of the CIA to the affair hinted at by Anderson. Then, last year, it was revealed that CIA officer Robert Martens had, at the time of the 'counter-coup', handed to the Indonesian Army a list of 5,000 names of PKI figures.[39]

The real question, at this hour of the day, is not whether the Agency was involved in bringing about the downfall of Sukarno and the decimation of the PKI, but what difference it makes that this occurred and continues to be denied. Isn't it the case that Indonesia is better

---

39 The implication is a little obscure here, but in the sources on which I was drawing the suggestion was that this list was less a set of names unknown to the Indonesian military than one the CIA thought would constitute an important hit-list of those whose elimination would most emasculate the PKI. To this day, I have not come across a clear and systematic account of the matter.

off under Suharto than it was under Sukarno, or would have been had the Communists come to power? Does it matter that a few hundred thousand Indonesians were killed, especially if they were Communists? Wasn't it a case, in Lenin's favoured phrase, of *kto kogo*—them or us?

Perhaps. One wonders, however, whether such a harsh attitude can ever be reconciled with a professed concern about human rights, in Indonesia or anywhere else. Is not the basic issue here the relation between our moral beliefs, including a fundamental commitment to truth, on the one hand; and political action, including the grim willingness to take responsibility for violence, on the other?

When it is possible that covert action has helped to precipitate the massacre of hundreds of thousands of people, the great majority of them innocent of any indictable offence, we should surely feel troubled enough to want to know the truth about the matter.[40] Where high political stakes are or were at issue, we might then wish to accept responsibility for such horrific things, with all that that acceptance implies. Marshall Green's memoir makes no attempt to lay out the truth and denies all responsibility. This makes it, both historiographically and morally, a weightless book—at best.

---

40 For a brief period in 2000, I was in Canberra doing some research in the National Archives on Australian relations with Indonesia. I took the opportunity to leaf through files on the events of 1965-67 and was struck by the extensive reporting on the killing and the general sentiment in the diplomatic cable traffic that it was to be hoped the Indonesian Army would 'finish the job'. In one cable, a senior Australian diplomat stated that he had visited Lombok and found that the prisons were overflowing and that there were mass executions every day, in which men, women and children were all being killed.

Another cable, dated January 1966, estimated that 600,000 people had been killed by then. Some years later, in a personal conversation, a retired former Australian ambassador to Indonesia informed me that he had joined the Foreign Service shortly after these events and would never forget 'the enormous feeling of relief in Canberra that this had happened'. It always struck me as incongruous that a decent human being (which he was) could see the massacre of many hundreds of thousands of human beings as something that could conceivably cause 'relief'; but of course he didn't mean the killing as such, he meant the destruction of the PKI as a political force.

James Jesus Angleton and CIA counter-intelligence[41]

Tom Mangold has given us a masterful contribution to Cold War scholarship, the history of the Central Intelligence Agency and the psychology of counter-intelligence. Anyone already fascinated by the gigantic struggle between the superpowers from 1945 to 1985 will find *Cold Warrior* a most rewarding and instructive study.[42]

Fans of John le Carré or Len Deighton are unlikely to find a better explication than this of the sort of realities those authors fictionalised. The book will be appreciated most of all, however, by those whose knowledge of these arcane matters already extends to an acquaintance

---

41 This was published in *The Age* on 24 August 1991. It was a review of Tom Mangold's *Cold Warrior: James Jesus Angleton, the CIA's Master Spy Hunter*, published by Simon and Schuster that year. This was, of course, the very year that the Soviet Union collapsed. In the years that followed a great deal was learned from formerly sealed archives in Moscow about the espionage activities of the Communist intelligence services (the KGB and the GRU) throughout the Cold War. It became clear that, contrary to the claims of many that the hunt for spies was a paranoid and unwarranted hunt for 'Reds under the bed', there had been far more Soviet spies at work than had ever been realized even by the 'paranoid' spy hunters, including hundreds of traitors and moles inside Western governments. To this day, the identities of many of them remain unknown, even where their codenames have been discovered.

42 It's curious that I dated the Cold War only to 1985 (when Mikhail Gorbachev became head of state in the Soviet Union), rather than 1988 or 1989, when everything changed so abruptly. A year later, I acquired Michael MccGwire's *Perestroika and Soviet National Security* (Brookings Institution, 1991) and discovered that there had been a major strategic reappraisal within the Soviet civilian and military leadership in 1983-84 with an explicit emphasis on avoiding a major war. This prepared the way for Gorbachev's strategic moves in 1987 and 1988 and for the peaceful Soviet withdrawal from Eastern Europe in the second half of 1989. It is a remarkable book and one I am often tempted to go back and re-read, in the light of subsequent events.

There has also long been a debate about when to date the beginning of the Cold War and what brought it about, with critics of Western strategy often alleging that it was avoidable in 1945-46 and was largely the fault of Washington and London. Robert Gellately's *Stalin's Curse: Battling for Communism in War and Cold War* (Alfred Knopf, New York, 2013) and S. M. Plokhy's *Yalta: The Price of Peace* (Viking, New York, 2010) are useful correctives to this view. One of the best expositions of it, conversely, is Melvyn P. Leffler *A Preponderance of Power: National Security, the Truman Administration and the Cold War* (Stanford University Press, 1992). For a fascinating study of how the end of the war in the Pacific and the American nuclear bombing of Japan set the scene for the Cold War, see Tsuyoshi Hasegawa's *Racing the Enemy: Stalin, Truman and the Surrender of Japan* (Belknap Press, Harvard University, 2005).

with something of the career of Angleton himself, along with awareness of the peculiar theories of Anatoly Golitsyn and the strange case of Yuri Nosenko.

James Jesus Angleton (1917-1987), the son of an all-American father and a beautiful Mexican mother, became an Anglophile as a schoolboy in England in the 1930s, but died intoning an Apache death-chant and told his wife he did not want Christian rites for the dying, as he had his own religion. His life was at once exotic and pathetic. He was a lover of poetry—notably that of Pound and Eliot—and of Italian opera; an accomplished fly-fisherman; a grower of orchids and a craftsman in jewellery and leather.

He was also a chain-smoker, an alcoholic, an insomniac and for the last 25 years of his life a dangerous paranoiac. From the time he was recruited into the Office of Strategic Services, in August 1943, until he was sacked from the CIA in December 1974, Angleton was also one of the most formidable figures in Western intelligence.

From the literary point of view, the Angleton that Mangold reveals to us invites comparisons with something out of a Gothic novel, or perhaps *Titus Groan*. Immured within the castle of secrecy and forbidden vaults, that it built for itself over twenty years as the CIA's unchallenged and unchecked master of counter-intelligence, Angleton's mind lost touch with sublunary reality. Mangold, in a memorable passage, describes the haunted man in his lair:

> *When a visitor entered Angleton's office, it was almost impossible to see the head of the head of CIA. His long, thin frame would be stooped behind a Berlin Wall of files. Since the blinds were firmly closed, the room was always dark, like a pool room at midday. The only lights came from the tip of Angleton's inevitable cigarette, glowing like a tiny star in the dark firmament of his private planet, and the dirty brown sun of his desk lamp, permanently wreathed in nicotine clouds.*

One can date Angleton's descent into the paranoia that haunted him in the 1960s and 1970s from the time that his esteemed British colleague and fellow *bon vivant*, H. A. R. 'Kim' Philby, fell under the suspicion of being a Soviet spy, in 1951.

Angleton had great difficulty in coming to terms with Philby's treachery. He denied it until, in 1963, Philby defected to Moscow; then he destroyed all the records his secretary had kept of his meetings with Philby, between 1949 and 1951, when Philby was MI6 liaison officer in Washington, even though (or rather because) the CIA was conducting a damage assessment and called on anyone who had dealt with Philby to put on record what had been discussed.

'I had them burnt,' Angleton later told Peter Wright. 'It was all very embarrassing.' His scandalous behaviour in this regard, however, was only the beginning of a decade of peculiar behaviour and caused grave damage to the CIA and its sister agencies in Britain, France, Norway and Canada. One of Philby's greatest triumphs, it has been remarked, was driving Angleton half mad. Ironically, it was a Soviet defector, named Anatoly Golitsyn, who completed the turning if Angleton's mind, after defecting in December 1961.

Golitsyn was either paranoid himself or a gifted charlatan and opportunist, who must have been amazed over the years at his ability to manipulate the great James Angleton and his counter-intelligence staff. What he cobbled together in the course of the early 1960s was a fantastic theory to the effect that the KGB had, since 1959, been working on a master plan to deceive the West by making it seem that the Communist monolith was fragmenting. In reality, Golitsyn solemnly informed a credulous Angleton, the Sino-Soviet split was a carefully created illusion. Likewise the Soviet-Yugoslav and Soviet-Albanian feuds, the apparent independence of Romania and, in 1968, the Prague Spring.

Moreover, Golitsyn added, there were highly placed Soviet moles everywhere: Harold Wilson, Lester Pearson, Henry Kissinger and Willy Brandt among them. Anyone who has read Golitsyn's book *New Lies For Old* (Bodley Head, London, 1984) and has any serious training in history, political theory or philosophy seems to me bound to conclude that it has about as much intellectual throw weight as the *Book of Mormon*. Yet Angleton and his staff and their allies throughout the Western counter-intelligence world swallowed this extraordinary confection many years before the book itself was published and they acted consequentially upon it.

Their saner colleagues within the CIA took to calling them 'the Flat Earth Committee'. Mangold calls them 'the Fundamentalists'. They were a bizarre little sect of Manicheans and James Jesus Angleton was their High Priest.[43] One of the better know victims of the Fundamentalists was the Soviet defector Yuri Nosenko. The Nosenko case is a famous one in the annals of counter-intelligence, because it was the pivot on which the great Angleton/Golitsyn *folie a deux* rested. Golitsyn had warned that the KGB would send false defectors after him to discredit him and mislead the CIA. Nosenko was, supposedly, the first and principal such false defector.

---

43   Long after I wrote this piece, I met one of Angleton's former colleagues from the counter-intelligence division of the CIA, on a visit to Brussels, in 2007, for a conference on the prospects for democracy in China. His name was Tennent 'Pete' Bagley and he had gone to live in Brussels many years before, after retiring from the CIA (before Angleton was sacked). He was a charming individual and we remained in communication until he died in 2014. At our first meeting, in Brussels, not far from his apartment, he told me about how, after the Cold War ended, he met his erstwhile enemies at a conference in Berlin: Markus Wolf who had headed the East German foreign intelligence service for many years; and a retired KGB general by the name of Sergey Kondrashev. They began by discussing the Cold War and ended up as friends. Finally, Kondrashev, who had been writing his memoirs, only to be told by the Putin government that he must not publish them, gave the materials to Bagley and asked him to write the book. He did so and it was published not long before he died. This is surely remarkable any way one looks at it. Either the former CIA counter-intelligence man wins the trust of the former KGB general and tells his story, or the KGB man takes his former opponent for one last walk up the garden path and feeds him disinformation.

Angleton spent years trying to prove that this was the case. In the process, not only was grave injustice done to Nosenko, but a whole range of people who vouched for his bona fides, including subsequent defectors who declared that the KGB had been distressed at his defection, became tainted in Angleton's eyes. Mangold, for the first time, tells the Nosenko story in full and relentlessly documents the harm done by Angleton's obsession.

One of the deepest ironies of the Angleton story is that, under the spell of Golitsyn, he became so convinced of the existence of a highly placed Soviet mole within the Soviet division of the CIA that he all but tore it apart looking for him; wrecking numerous careers in the process. Because the Soviets had discovered and executed two CIA agents within the GRU (Soviet military intelligence)—Peter Popov and Oleg Penkovsky—Angleton blamed the mole he couldn't find. Subsequently, he became convinced that a third CIA agent within the GRU, Dimitri Polyakov, was a triple agent. He leaked details about him through his friend, Edward Jay Epstein, which led to Polyakov's detection by the Soviets, followed by his arrest and execution.

Reading Mangold's carefully research and soberly written biography of Angleton, one begins to comprehend how it is that, under certain circumstances, real madness can become institutionalised. The harm that Angleton and the Fundamentalists did was considerable, although by comparison with the terrors perpetrated by other inquisitorial systems and secret police institutions, it remains almost trivial. While Angleton was given far too much latitude for too long, by Allen Dulles, John McCone and Richard Helms[44], William Colby was able to remove him very easily and many of his victims were offered apologies and compensation.

In the end, I think we may conclude that despite the circumstances of the Cold War, because they were hemmed in by America's powerful system of law and democratic institutions, even the Fundamentalists could not do the sort of massive harm that people of comparable psychological make-up have done in fascist, communist and theocratic states in this century. That is reassuring, I believe. Yet so often and so grievously has such terrible harm been done in our age that the appearance of paranoia in the heart of an institution created to guard democracy against the depredations of its more relentless enemies can only be deeply disturbing.

Angleton was not an evil man—not a Beria or a Kang Sheng—but he was unhinged.[45] His

---

44 Successive Directors of Central Intelligence between 1952 and 1972.

45 This is actually too severe a judgment, in retrospect. Angleton was a complex figure and by no means a wholly deluded one. He appears to have succeeded in protecting the CIA from Soviet penetration at a time when many other Western intelligence services were penetrated (including our own ASIO). When the KGB finally did penetrate the CIA, some years after Angleton had retired; one of the first things they sought was his manual on counter-intelligence. It was given to them by their mole, Aldrich Ames. Angleton's refusal to accept the good faith of the Soviet defector Yuri Nosenko and his obsessive hunt

successor, George Kalaris, drew the conclusion that the job itself was perilous and that no-one should hold it for very long—certainly not for twenty years. One is reminded of Nietzsche's aphorism, in *Beyond Good and Evil*: 'When you fight monsters, take care that you do not yourself become a monster; and when you gaze long into an abyss, the abyss also gazes into you.'

---

for a mole in the Soviet affairs division of the CIA are certainly controversial and his attitude has been labelled 'sick think' by those who reacted strongly against his suspicions and the destruction of quite a few careers. Yet the reverse of 'sick think' had been precisely what left Western intelligence services hopelessly vulnerable to penetration for many years before 1973, especially the British intelligence services, which were very seriously penetrated by multiple moles in the 1930s and right through until at least the 1960s. With so much still sealed in Russian archives, the definitive book has yet to be written on the full extent of Soviet operations in the West and in the US in particular on Angleton's watch. What we do know already is that they were far more extensive than anybody, including Angleton, guessed at the time.

Strategic bombing and the genocidal mentality[46]

Primo Levi, a survivor of the Nazi Holocaust, who took his own life a few years ago, once wrote regarding the constant threat of nuclear annihilation that loomed over the Cold War world:

> *Willingly or not, we come to terms with power, forgetting that we are all in the ghetto, that the ghetto is walled in, that outside the ghetto reign the lords of death and that, close by, the train is waiting ...*

Lifton and Markusen have written a book for those who would rise up in the ghetto against the lords of death and refuse with open eyes to board the waiting train.

Another Nazi Holocaust survivor, Samuel Pisar, has written:

> *It is as if an Auschwitz fever has taken hold of mankind ... an Auschwitz ideology ...*

Auschwitz, he observed, was exterminism 'on a pilot scale'. This is nothing but the simple truth. As early as 1948, the American war plan TROJAN called for the dropping of 133 atomic bombs on 70 Soviet cities in the event of a war against Stalin's evil empire that would have resulted in the annihilation of tens of millions of Soviet civilians within hours.

When Robert McNamara became US Secretary of Defence in 1961, he was briefed by the North American Air Defence Command (NORAD) and told that TROJAN had 'progressed' to the point where a nuclear assault against the Soviet Union, Eastern Europe and China would kill 350 million people in the first day or two of a major war.[47] The prospect appalled many analysts, even at the RAND Corporation, the self-styled bastion of unsentimental, 'hard'

---

46 This is a review of Robert Jay Lifton and Eric Markusen's *The Genocidal Mentality: Nazi Holocaust and Nuclear Threat* (Macmillan) and was originally published in *The Age* on 12 October 1991.

47 There is a first hand, graphic account of these estimates in Daniel Ellsberg *Secrets: A Memoir of Vietnam and the Pentagon Papers* (Viking, New York, 2002), pp. 58-60. He wrote that:

> *The total death toll from our own attacks, in the estimates supplied by the JCS, was in the neighbourhood of five to six hundred million. These would be almost entirely civilians. A hundred Holocausts. The greater part would be inflicted in a day or two, the rest over six months, about a third in allied or neutral countries. This was not a hypothetical calculation of what was needed to deter a Soviet nuclear attack on the United States (as such it would still have been obscenely absurd). It was the JCS's best estimate of the actual results, in terms of human fatalities, of our setting into motion the existing machinery for implementing the current operational plans of the JCS for general war ...*
>
> *I still remember holding that graph in my hand and looking at it in an office of the White House annex in the Executive Office building on a spring day in 1961. I was thinking: This piece of paper, what this piece of paper represents, should not exist. It should never in the course of human history have come into existence.*

The spring of 1961 being March, April, May, this recollection by Ellsberg is set eighteen months before the Cuban Missile Crisis, which almost triggered general war. Had it done so, the massive retaliation by the United States, involving the enormous death toll mentioned above, could well have been what resulted.

strategic analysis; and was denounced as 'a policy of genocide'.

Yet it remained in place, for all practical purposes and the means for causing unparalleled slaughter kept developing at a relentless pace throughout the 1960s, 70s and 80s.[48] *The Genocidal Mentality* is a sustained and superbly professional psychological inquiry into how this mentality became institutionalized and how we all, in varying degrees, accommodate ourselves to it, as if it were a 'normal' state of affairs. It should have a prominent place in unapologetic peace studies courses, alongside Jonathan Schell's *The Fate of the Earth*[49] and such films as *Doctor Strangelove* and *The Atomic Café*.

---

48   Since the end of the Cold War and the considerable scaling back of the American and Russian nuclear arsenals, a number of studies have examined the overall cost of the nuclear arms race even without the use of the weapons in war. See especially Derek Leebaert *The Fifty Year Wound: The True Price of America's Cold War Victory* (Little, Brown & Co, 2002) and David E. Hoffman *The Dead Hand: The Untold Story of the Cold War Arms Race and Its Dangerous Legacy* (Doubleday, 2009).

49   Jonathan Schell (1943-2014) was the author of a series books on nuclear disarmament, of which *The Fate of the Earth* (Picador, Jonathan Cape, 1982) was the first. When it was first published, the book was described by Kai Erikson in *The New York Times* as 'a work of enormous force' and 'an event of profound historical moment.... [I]n the end, it accomplishes what no other work has managed to do in the 37 years of the nuclear age. It compels us - and compel is the right word - to confront head on the nuclear peril in which we all find ourselves.' Writing in *Foreign Affairs* magazine, however, David Greenberg called *The Fate of the Earth* an 'overwrought doomsday polemic.' In Slate.com, Michael Kinsley characterized it as 'an overheated stew of the obvious and the idiotic.' Such are the passions that nuclear arms and strategic affairs arouse even in educated and articulate minds.

In 1998, Schell produced *The Gift of Time: The Case for Abolishing Nuclear Weapons Now* (Granta, 1998), in which a number of highly credentialed national security figures endorsed his 'overheated stew of the obvious and the idiotic' and agreed that nuclear weapons had no justifiable place in the US arsenal and should be abolished. These figures included General George Lee Butler, the last head of the Strategic Air Command and overall commander of strategic nuclear forces in the US in the early 1990s—the very years when I worked in the Defence Intelligence Organization, as it happens. A few years later again, Schell produced *The Unfinished Twentieth Century: The Crisis of Weapons of Mass Destruction* (Verso, 2001), published just after 9/11 and the increased urgency it had brought to counter-proliferation efforts.

'But proliferation to new countries,' he remarked, 'cannot be considered in isolation from possession of nuclear weapons by the old, Cold War powers, where the motherlode of nuclear danger still resides. In the policy debate now under way, I suggest, the inescapable, underlying question is whether the possessors of nuclear arms will insist on keeping them indefinitely or will be prepared to accept their abolition.' As of this writing and as of Schell's death from throat cancer in early 2014, there is no sign on the part of any of the 'old Cold War powers', which is to say the five permanent members of the UN National Security Council (America, China, Russia, Britain and France) of a willingness to give up their nuclear arsenals. Nor can they seem to agree on any effective or decisive action to pre-empt the development of nuclear weapons by recalcitrant states, whether non-signatories of the NPT (Israel, India, Pakistan) or signatories (North Korea and Iran).

Apart from anything else, it is unimpeachable in its reasoning and offers a sober history of the thinking that has taken us from strategic bombing to ruinous and insane expenditures on weapons systems which, whether or not they are ever used, are nothing but a terrible monument to the criminal delinquency or our species before God and Nature. In one of the blackest moments of that hilarious satire, *Doctor Strangelove*, General Buck Turgidson reads out to the assembled American National Security Council the words with which General Jack Ripper has committed his air wing to an attack on the Soviet Union:

> *Yes, gentlemen, they are on their way in and no one can bring them back. For the sake of our country and our way of life, I suggest you get the rest of SAC (the Strategic Air Command) in after them. Otherwise, we will be totally destroyed by Red retaliation. My boys will give you the best kind of start—fourteen hundred megatons worth—and you sure as hell won't stop them now. So, let's get going; there's no other choice. God willing, we will prevail, in peace and freedom from fear, in true health, through the purity and essence of our natural fluids. God bless you all.*

Is it any consolation that this specific scenario is only a caricature of the public positions of such figures as Edward Teller, Herman Kahn, Curtis LeMay, or Colin Gray? The point is, as Lifton and Markusen emphasize, in non-parodistic language, that detailed planning for nuclear war-fighting has been taking place for almost half a century—since the beginnings of the Manhattan Project—and that those of us who have not reckoned with this are like those incredulous Jews in the 1930s who did not flee the reaches of Nazi power, unable to believe rumours of genocidal intent.

Many will find the comparison with Nazi exterminism rebarbative. Let them read this book before voicing indignation. They have not perhaps allowed sufficiently for the extent to which even the Nazi doctors and SS killers were able to persuade themselves of the reasonableness of what they were doing—to say nothing of industrialists at Krupp or I.G. Farben, bureaucrats in the rear or ordinary German citizens.

The last thing we need is the sort of moral self-righteousness that would delude us into believing that Nazis or Stalinists prepare mass murder with satanic intent, while we in the West fight only just wars and deal out death only in just measure. We are far more in need of the sort of disturbing psychological insight provided by the famous Stanley Milgram experiments, which explored the willingness of ordinary people to inflict pain, even possibly lethal harm, under orders from acknowledged authority figures.

Lifton and Markusen have written with this sort of insight and the importance of their book is due in no small measure to the ways in which it throws light on the psychology of the 'national security state' and its professional cades. Hannah Arendt's description of Adolf Eichmann, as representing a shockingly 'banal' face of evil, is key here. Lifton and Markusen indicate how processes of dissociation, numbing and doubling enable human beings to engage in both normal personal lives and professional work that prepares and even perpetrates the most 'unthinkable' things.

Psychological parallels with the perpetrators of the Nazi Holocaust are a provocation to our reflections on the psychology of the nuclear war-planning state—of which we are all citizens, witting or unwitting—but even more disturbing is the direct root of this planning in the practice of strategic bombing of German and Japanese cities during World War II. The horrors inflicted on the cities of Hamburg, Dresden and Tokyo, before ever the atomic bombs were dropped over Hiroshima and Nagasaki, are easily forgotten; first in the relief and euphoria of victory and then with the passage of time. Yet the willingness to create firestorms that incinerated at least 40,000 people (Hamburg, July/August 1943), 100,000 (Dresden, 13 February 1945) and 130,000 people (Tokyo, 9-10 March 1945) indicate an escalating brutality parallel to the escalation in Nazi extermination of the Jews in the last years of the war and form the psychological and military pre-history of the nuclear age.

Lifton and Markusen perform an invaluable service in demonstrating both of these realities. This is a sombre book, but it is neither hysterical nor apocalyptic. It is written with an admirable blend of deep learning, moral engagement and cool reason. One would have to look very hard to find significant fault with it, I believe; and to do so would be to risk missing the point that it makes: that we all lead something of a double life, going about our ordinary lives as if the monstrous threat to everything we have ever touched or loved did not exist. This book is a call not to scientific or strategic awareness, but to moral awakening.[50]

---

50 The chief concern since 2001 has been that nuclear weapons will find their way into the hands of terrorists or terror states, especially chiliastic Muslims with a cult of death and martyrdom. For a thoughtful analysis of the slow, disturbing leakage of nuclear weapons technology to murderous places see William Langwiesche *The Atomic Bazaar: The Rise of the Nuclear Poor* (Allen Lane, Penguin 2007).

A dubious prophesy of US war with Japan[51]

A few months ago, there was something of a public flap in America when it was discovered that a small team of academics at the Rochester Institute of Technology had been commissioned by the CIA to produce a report on the threat to the United States presented by the rising power of Japan. Draft copies of this report, under the title *Japan 2000* were 'leaked' to a few interested parties and there was an uproar about CIA abuse of the integrity of academia and the 'Japan bashing' indulged in by the report's authors. Several well-known 'Japan bashers'—notably the San Diego based Chalmers Johnson—who had been consulted by the report's authors, moved quickly to dissociate themselves from the manuscript.

Having read the draft of *Japan 2000* myself, I think the Japan bashers were wise to distance themselves from the thing and would suggest that the CIA wasted its money on the project. Having read *The Coming War with Japan*, I think the 'Japan bashers' have been upstaged by Friedman and LeBard and that the CIA should consider funding these authors to pursue their work, writing off the Rochester Institute project as a false start. *The Coming War with Japan* is an incomparably more scholarly and interesting piece of work and probably should be required reading for all those who are anxious about the new dawn of the rising sun.

It is written in a clear and accessible style. It synthesises a substantial amount of historical and economic, political and strategic data. It presents an unambiguous, easily understood, sober and plausible argument about the shape of things to come. It is not an anti-Japanese polemic, but a sustained reflection on the fateful character of developments in train in the Pacific basin as the 20th century closes; which these authors contend, portend tragedy within a generation, in the form of a war between the United States and Japan.[52]

---

51   This piece was originally published in the *Sydney Morning Herald* on 26 October 1991, under the title 'Pacific's Bleak Prospect'. It is a review of *The Coming War with Japan* by George Friedman and Meredith LeBard (St Martin's Press).

52   We are now, in 2014, a generation removed from this prognosis and nothing seems less likely than a war between the United States and Japan, though there are growing warnings of a possible war between China and Japan, in which the United States would almost certainly enter on the side of Japan. Moreover, at no point in the intervening twenty three years has war between the United States and Japan become remotely likely. In this regard, not only were Friedman and LeBard in error in their prognosis, but I was in error in being insufficiently critical of their arguments. Interestingly, within a few months of writing this review I was appointed Japan and Koreas Desk Officer in the Defence Intelligence Organization. In that capacity, I had the opportunity to visit both Japan and South Korea and meet numerous government officials and military officers. I came away convinced that Japan presented no threat and, indeed, more impressed by it as a country than ever. I had first visited Japan as a graduate student in April 1985. The 1992 visit was far more substantial.

In his powerful history of the Roman republic, the great nineteenth century German historian, Theodor Mommsen, described the rise of the Carthaginian Empire in the western Mediterranean, in the 5th and 4th centuries BCE, as a matter of geopolitical fate. The Carthaginians, he wrote, became empire builders 'because they could not do otherwise.' Their stupendous clash with the rising power of Rome over control of the western Mediterranean was thus inevitable. The sense of fate and tragedy is quite Thucydidean. Friedman and LeBard approach their subject with a similar tragic sense of history and the effect is quite impressive, in both tone and substance, even if their style does not come close to that of Mommsen, let alone to what Peter Levi has called 'the dark thunder of Thucydides' prose.'

As Carthage rose from the ashes of the Second Punic War, in the first half of the second century BCE, the 'Carthage bashers' in Rome began to declare 'Carthago delenda est'—Carthage must be destroyed—despite the 'peace constitution' that Rome had imposed on its vanquished enemy, since it again threatened Roman commercial interests in Africa and the western Mediterranean and might yet rearm. Driven by these fears, of course, Rome went to war and annihilated Carthage.[53] Friedman and LeBard have written a provocative book, in which a similar-sounding scenario for another US-Japanese war is laid before us.

The Coming War with Japan is an oracular book. It is prophetic, not in the sense of foretelling an inevitable future, but in the sense of relating a possible future in a manner which might induce those who heed the oracle to chart a different course. The authors are quite explicit about this in their Preface. They describe themselves as being 'citizens engaged in a very old and respected tradition, that of pamphleteers.' They add: 'On what we hope is a more learned level than that of some other

---

Analysts, both military and civilian, whom I met in Seoul, on the other hand, assured me that the greatest threat to South Korea was not North Korea (as one would have thought), not China and certainly not Russia (with the Soviet Union having collapsed the previous year), but Japan. I asked them why they would see Japan as a threat and was intrigued by their response. Every time there is a major shift in the international balance of power, they declared, Japan becomes aggressively expansionist and we are the first in the firing line. I challenged them on this, pointing out that, while it was true that Japan had invaded the Korean peninsula in the sixteenth century (under Hideyoshi) and again in the early twentieth century, times had changed since those invasions and the Japanese now ran a $US10 billion annual trade surplus with South Korea, so why would they want to invade it? 'Because they are Japanese', was the reply, in all seriousness. Clearly, it was not only American 'Japan bashers' who were getting ahead of themselves with fear of Japan in the early 1990s.

53 See Adrian Goldsworthy *The Punic Wars* (Cassell & Co., 2000) pp. 331-356 and Serge Lancel *Carthage: A History* (Blackwell, 1995) pp. 409-427. The Third Punic War, in which Carthage was utterly destroyed, occurred between 149 and 146 BCE. Carthage was levelled to the ground and remained a ruin for decades, until it was refounded as a Roman colony on the same site. The Roman city of Carthage then endured until the downfall of the Empire five centuries later.

practitioners of the art, we wish to inform our compatriots of a coming danger and urge them to beware ... if there is any hope of avoiding a second US-Japanese war, it rests in our leaders becoming frightened.'[54]

Their hope, they tell us, is that 'finer minds than ours might be moved by what we say to discover what we have been unable to discover: the key to peace.' The chief merit of this book is that, while it is perfectly possible to take serious issue with its claims, doing so would require extended argument. This is not the case, for example, with *Japan 2000*, which can be dismissed as a crude polemic even on a cursory, commonsensical reading. The thrust of a critical review of Friedman and LeBard's work would be that the authors paint their scenario with too broad a brush and make insufficient allowance for the numerous international influences that stand between the United States and war with Japan as we approach the year 2000.

They too facilely draw direct comparisons between the circumstances of the 1920s or 1930s and those of the 1990s and after. Their sweeping historical view of things is underwritten by an ahistorical and rather tendentious interpretation of human affairs, made explicit in their concluding lines:

> *The struggle between Japan and the United States, punctuated by truces, friendships and brutality, will shape the Pacific for generations. It will be the endless game about which the philosophers have written, the game of nations—the war of all against all.*

Their sombre prognosis concentrates the mind and therefore should be widely read and debated. However, their description of the 'game of nations' is superficial. It excludes those numerous forms of discourse and exchange which are neither war nor substitutes for war and which have become dramatically deeper in the 20th century, as economic and communicational integration of the 'global village' has impacted on the atavistic tribalisms and violent proclivities of the species.

If there is hope for avoiding the sort of cataclysm they fear, it does not lie in policies based on the view of the 'game of nations' they espouse. Yet, if such policies fail their purpose, then the war predicted by Friedman and LeBard may erupt. It is, therefore, in a double sense possible to commend this book to the reader with the traditional warning *caveat emptor*—buyer beware.[55]

---

54 This now looks seriously misleading, since the danger was never as great as they suggested at that time and has now receded well beyond the point of being even plausible. Yet there is a case at present for being concerned about China. Will such concerns, a generation from now, look equally overblown and unwarranted? One can only hope so.

55 Looking back, I'm surprised that I did not bring into the reflection the fact that, at that juncture, US military power was so much greater than that of Japan that it was actually inconceivable that Japan would challenge the US in the Pacific. Nor was it remotely likely that the United States would do as Rome had done to Carthage: push it into an unnecessary war with the express purpose of destroying it. I no longer own a copy of the book, so it isn't possible to go back to it and highlight its errors of judgement, but it is possible to see my own in retrospect and that is a sobering—and useful—exercise.

Section 2: 1991-92

Noam Chomsky's critique of American democracy[56]

The front cover of this book—Noam Chomsky's bitter response to American euphoria over triumph in the Cold War—depicts a Lockheed Blackbird SR-71, the sinister looking, ultra-fast, high altitude, mostly titanium strategic reconnaissance super-plane that the US Air Force first put into service in 1966. What is the significance of this picture for the theme of the book? 'In the evolving world order', Chomsky observes in his introduction, 'the comparative advantage of the United States lies in military force, in which it is supreme.'

The Blackbird, it seems, is meant to represent this supreme military power. Perhaps the sinister appearance of the plane, rather than its function, is the point of the picture. Certainly, Chomsky's theme in this book, as in all his books over the past twenty years or more, since *At War With Asia* and *American Power and the New Mandarins*, remains the uses of American power. But the Blackbird in fact embodies less the uses of power than the informing of power[57] and, since much of Chomsky's concern is with the use and abuse of information by the powers that be, maybe the appearance of the Blackbird on the cover of *Deterring Democracy* is intended to update Orwell, as it were, and represent the reach of 'Big Brother' in the post-Cold War years?[58]

A clearly focused argument to this end and an explanation of the role of information or 'intelligence' in the workings of official and covert US policies abroad might have been very interesting. Are those policies bent on 'deterring democracy', as Chomsky alleges?[59] Alas, the book lacks a clear focus. Chomsky is prone to lump almost the entire 'establishment' together, as the object of his peppery critique, leaving us very little further enlightened as to the actual

---

56   This piece was first published in *The Age* on 4 December 1991. This was a decade before the 9/11 assault on America and twelve years before President George W. Bush's ill-fated invasion of Saddam Hussein's Iraq. It was seventeen years before the Global Financial Crisis and some two decades before the massive leaks of classified information by Bradley Manning, Julian Assange and Edward Snowden.

57   For an excellent history of American aerial reconnaissance programs throughout the Cold War see the work of William Burrows: *Deep Black: The Secrets of Space Espionage*, Bantam Press, 1988; and *By Any Means Necessary: America's Secret Air War*, (Hutchinson, London, 2001).

58   This has been the central allegation of alarmist critics of the increased role of the NSA and CIA since 9/11, under both Republican and Democrat presidencies. For a thoughtful and illuminating—at times wryly amusing—reflection on this see Shane Harris *The Watchers: The Rise of America's Surveillance State*, (Penguin Press, New York), 2010.

59   This has been a central point of contention in recent debates about the national security state, surveillance and the gigantic leakages of classified materials by Manning and Snowden.

institutional processes which produce the outcomes he deplores, much less what might be done to alter them.[60]

Deterring Democracy is Chomsky's most wide-ranging and ambitious book to date. An unrepentant Cold War dissident, Chomsky here continues his relentless assault on the American 'mandarins', arguing that the end of the Cold War leaves their power all but untrammelled, to the peril of democratic freedom the world over. The Cold War, in his view, was never a struggle between democracy and totalitarianism, but between two power elites, with democrats caught in the cross fire. The demise of the Soviet power elite, he suggests, leaves the power elite on 'our' side free to go on 'deterring democracy', where democracy means resistance to right-wing oppression around the world, wherever such democracy seems to threaten its interests.

The orthodox view, of course, since 1989, has been quite the reverse: Communism is dead, liberal democracy (and capitalism) are ascendant and the future looks brighter than it has for decades. Chomsky makes no concessions to this common outlook. His book would have had more enduring value had he attempted a monumental reassessment of the politics of containment in the light of the defeat of Soviet Communism. Instead, he has written a sweeping polemic, denouncing the whole spectrum of American 'establishment' politics as morally bankrupt.

Even if this were true, it would require better demonstration; and even were the demonstration impeccable, serious readers would want far more substantial suggestions as to what might be done about it than Chomsky provides. Too many readers, I think, especially those of a sound conservative disposition, will find his tone a bit shrill, his argument lacking in a sense of proportion and his political philosophy benign but simplistic. Perhaps I am being a little too 'mandarin' myself in criticising Chomsky's tone and sense of proportion. All things considered, there is ample cause in the areas of his concern for the sarcasm and indignation he vents. ('Jonathan Swift, where are you when we need you?' he ejaculates at one point, in the midst of a discussion of the US siege of Sandinista Nicaragua).

Yet, if I were to introduce this book to a university class, I would want to use it neither to inform them nor to guide their judgement, so much as to provoke them to rethink a whole range of problems in political philosophy and contemporary history. (The problem these days, of course, would be getting such a class to read the book at all, much less closely enough to be

---

60   A remarkable work directed at elucidating how the political institutions of the United States might best be adapted to deal with an epoch of terrorism and permeable borders is Philip Bobbitt's *Terror and Consent: The Wars for the Twenty-First Century*, (Alfred Knopf, New York, 2008). It has been criticised as too long, too dense and too elliptical, but it is a deeply learned reflection on the dilemmas of our time and vastly more substantial than Chomsky's polemics. Indeed, even to compare Bobbitt's work with that of Chomsky is an insult to Bobbitt.

provoked into rethinking problems in political philosophy that they had not so much as thought about to begin with).

The danger is that Chomsky's polemical style would encourage too many in such a class simply to adopt an unreflective posture of exasperation, based on scant knowledge, less experience and flimsy ideas. This was the problem with students reading Marx, Mao or Castro in the 1960s and 1970s. Now, after the Cold War, Chomsky ought be able to do better.[61] The defects of democracy in the United States and the abuses of power by its plutocratic elites and such ideological fanatics as Oliver North, which enrage Chomsky, are the subject of a considerable literature, most of them published in the United States itself. It is not a *samizdat* literature and its authors are, for the most part, not persecuted, even if some of them are reviled.

One is tempted to quip that, in a totalitarian state, books like Chomsky's are banned by the powers that be; while in a democratic state they are simply ignored, on the whole, by the powers that be. Even that, however, is not wholly true. Such books can have an effect. The problem with Chomsky's book is that it is based on too monochromatic a description of the American power elites he denounces, while the freedom he would substitute for their rule and propaganda remains maddeningly vague.

Even those highly sympathetic to Chomsky's howls of outrage at the lies and hypocrisies of those in the power game in Washington and its empire, must recoil somewhat from the simplicity of the political philosophy which seems to prompt these howls. Nowhere does he offer us anything more than a sort of evangelical demand for unvarnished truth and more 'popular participation' in political processes.[62] Nowhere does he offer a sustained analysis of the institutions whose deficiencies he, quite reasonably, blames for the malaise of democracy in America. In consequence, *Deterring Democracy* remains a provocative and disturbing book, but not a great one.

---

61   Two books that do much better, albeit written long after Chomsky's, are Jack Goldstone's *Power and Constraint: The Accountable Presidency After 9/11*, (Norton & Co., New York and London, 2010) and Benjamin Wittes' *Law and the Long War: The Future of Justice in the Age of Terror*, (Penguin Press, New York, 2008). Both books do precisely what Chomsky so signally failed to do and still fails to do. They examine in detail the institutional and legal processes underlying strategic policies and the very real dilemmas that the chief executive faces in handling national security challenges.

62   There is something of a plague of this kind of thinking abroad in the second decade of the 21st century, thanks in large measure to the much vaunted 'social media'. For an intriguing inquiry into one particularly notable example of anarchism on the web, see Gabriella Coleman *Hacker, Hoaxer, Whistleblower, Spy: The Many Faces of Anonymous*, (Verso, London and New York, 2014).

Israel, the bomb and a conspiracy of silence[63]

Considerable excitement was generated in the second week of November by the fact that, two days after the publication of *The Samson Option*, with its allegation that Robert Maxwell had worked for Israel's secret intelligence services, the media magnate was found floating naked and dead in the sea off the Canary islands. Seymour Hersh commented that his new book contained but a tithe of what he already knew about Maxwell's secret life. Then it emerged that, initial Spanish reports notwithstanding, Maxwell had not died of a heart attack and may have been murdered.

From the point of view of a book launching, the timing was impeccable. Doubtless, it will prompt a good few people to buy *The Samson Option*, just to read about Robert Maxwell. They will not learn very much about him. Indeed, Hersh now admits that he was misled about Maxwell's involvement in the kidnapping of Mordecai Vanunu. However, they will learn a great many far more interesting and dramatic things about the secret world of Israel and the politics of nuclear non-proliferation in the United States.

Seymour Hersh has written investigative exposes of the My Lai massacre, the work of Henry Kissinger in the White House and the shooting down of KAL-007. *The Samson Option* is, I think, his best book and his most significant investigation so far. What was the My Lai massacre

---

63 This piece first appeared in *The Age* on 23 November 1991. It was a review of Seymour Hersh's *The Samson Option: Israel, America and the Bomb*, published by Faber. It was, so far as I can recall, this article which prompted Colin Rubenstein of the Australia Israel Jewish Affairs Council to first get in touch with me and ask, over the phone, whether I really believed that Israel, as a democratic state surrounded by avowed enemies, should be treated in the same way, as regards the acquisition of nuclear weapons, as states such as Iraq, North Korea or Iran, all dictatorships with records of violence and recklessness very different to that of Israel.

At the time, I was sceptical about his stance, but as the years have passed I have become less so. Israel at least had the integrity to refuse to sign the NPT, while North Korea, Iraq and Iran all did so, only to then cheat under its provisions and seek to acquire nuclear weapons anyway. North Korea has now done so. Iraq was headed off by first the bombing of the Osirak reactor by Israel in 1981 and then UN intervention in the Gulf War of 1990-91. Iran is edging ever closer to nuclear capability and the United States seems unwilling to take decisive measures to prevent it from doing so.

That said, I remain deeply sceptical about secret government and the deliberate subversion of treaties by governments, especially that of the United States, which work to create them in the first place. It is well known that diplomacy and strategic affairs are fraught with deceit and deception. Yet the constraint of the abuse of power depends on the exposure of just such deceit and deception and the upholding of more transparent and accountable government and international agreements. The challenge of how to attain such a state of affairs when dealing with dictatorships and terrorists is difficult enough without our liberal democratic states directly undermining the agreements they themselves seek to put in place.

compared with the fact that for more than thirty years the influence of the pro-Israel lobby and the reach of Israeli intelligence in the US have led the White House deliberately to ignore or suppress evidence that Israel was building a nuclear research plant, then a reprocessing facility and finally a nuclear arsenal?

KAL-007 was blown out of proportion by the Reagan administration for propaganda purposes and ceased to serve this purpose once US forces shot down an Iranian airliner in the Persian Gulf, killing even more people than the Soviets had killed in shooting down KAL-007 in forbidden airspace over Sakhalin. Hersh's book on Kissinger, *The Price of Power*, is an inelegant, ill-proportioned piece of work, which verges at times on muck-raking and never puts its subject into serious historical perspective. *The Samson Option*, however, is a tightly written, incisive piece of investigative journalism that cuts to the heart of an issue of enormous importance and lays it open for sustained debate. It deserves to sell a million copies in half a dozen major languages.

According to Hersh, even as the Nuclear Non-Proliferation Treaty was prepared in 1968 and emphatically endorsed by President Lyndon Johnson, he told CIA Director Richard Helms to 'bury' a report that Israel was a nuclear power in the making. President Richard Nixon told the US Senate in February 1969: 'I will make it clear that I believe that ratification of the treaty by all governments, nuclear and non-nuclear, is in the interests of peace and in the interest of reducing the possibility of nuclear proliferation.'

Yet simultaneously, Hersh tells us, Nixon and his National Security Adviser, Henry Kissinger, circulated a memorandum within the US bureaucracies indicating that this public posture was to be disavowed in secret communications with France and West Germany. Morton Halperin is quoted as recalling that Kissinger, 'believed it was good to spread nuclear weapons around the world' and thought that Israel and Japan, for a start, should have nuclear weapons. If these details alone make you gasp or groan, get yourself a copy of Hersh's book and be prepared for a chronicle of such deceit and suppression of truth and intelligence which spans the years from Eisenhower to Bush.

The Old Man, as David Ben-Gurion was known in the 1950s, was determined that Israel should have nuclear weapons of its own, 'so that we shall never again be as lambs led to the slaughter.' Not everyone in Israel's leadership circles agreed with him that nuclear weapons were Israel's best means of defending itself against external threats, but the program went ahead and by the late 1960s the weapon of ultimate sanction belonged to Eretz Israel.

While the fierce determination of the Old Man and many others that there never again be a holocaust of Jews is entirely understandable, the choice of nuclear weapons threatened to wreak such a holocaust on the Arab people's should Israel's survival be threatened. For this reason, it was dubbed the Samson Option, after the ancient Hebrew hero who, blinded and bound, made sport of by the Philistine worshippers of Dagon, brought down the roof of their feasting house upon 3,000 of them with his last strength, declaring to his god: 'Let me die with the Philistines.' That, at least, is the phrasing according to the King James Bible. Hersh renders it, 'Let my soul die with the Philistines.' Perhaps it is the soul of Israel that Hersh believes to be at stake, rather than its physical survival.

If this book annoys those who prefer secret government programs to remain secret, or who believe that Israel has some special right to possess nuclear weapons and should be denied to other countries, such as Iraq, North Korea, Iran or Pakistan, I suggest that it is good to annoy them. Hersh has, by this criterion, written a splendidly annoying book. At a time when there is more talk than ever of disarmament, but at least as much danger of nuclear weapons proliferation and new conventional arms races, the long indulgence of Israel by the highest levels of the American government, under the influence of Jewish money and Jewish lobbying, simply has to be seriously debated.

At stake is the fundamental question of whether, after all, we human beings can create a set of universal moral and legal principles and abide by them, or are prepared to see such efforts mocked by a secret diplomacy which regards all such efforts as a convenient sham that the masters of the world will, at their whim, for reasons of state, subvert. At the close of the 20th century, which is it to be? Are we all such philistines that we can find security only in the Samson Option?

The Cambridge spies and the dark side of the force[64]

This book supersedes all previous accounts of how Kim Philby, Donald Maclean and Guy Burgess, among others, provided Stalin, at the height of his power, with many of the deepest secrets of the Western powers. Nigel West, Philip Knightley, Chapman Pincher, Peter Wright and the others can take a back seat now. Verne Newton's new study, based on far more detailed archival research and more extensive interviews with American, British and Soviet officials than any previous book on these matters, will be the standard history, until Soviet archives are fully opened.[65]

The Butcher's Embrace opens by describing how, in November 1938, General Walter Krivitsky, Stalin's erstwhile head of intelligence operations in Western Europe[66], fled to the United States to warn the West that Stalin was a man of the same kind as Adolf Hitler and that he had penetration agents at work in the West.[67] On 10 January 1939, Krivitsky was debriefed by the State Department's Loy Henderson and Edward Page on the meaning of the Great Terror.[68]

---

64 This is a review of Verne W. Newton's *The Butcher's Embrace* (MacDonald, 1991), first published in *The Age* on 7 December 1991.

65 This was a remarkable claim to make about such a book even in late 1991. As it happens, considerable Soviet archives did at least partially open in the 1990s and a great deal was learned about Cold War espionage. Newton's book does not appear to have enjoyed a very long shelf life and I have not seen it cited in any of the more recent literature on the subject.

66 More specifically, Krivitsky was a GRU operative. He was not the head of either KGB or Comintern intelligence operations in Western Europe. He went underground in Paris in 1937, when the Great Terror was in full swing in the Soviet Union and he came to fear that he would be executed on false charges of treason unless he defected. He was initially protected by the Trotskyist underground movement, before making his way to the United States.

67 Krivitsky was debriefed later in London by MI5 and divulged a good deal about how Soviet intelligence operated, including the separation between the KGB (OGPU) and GRU and the standard operating procedures of the latter, for which he had worked. The detailed report on his debriefing, which prepared by Jane Archer, was leaked to Moscow almost at once and since it was, at the time, in the custody of MI5's Roger Hollis, this is one of the earliest pieces of evidence that Hollis was himself, like the better know Cambridge spies, a Soviet mole—but for the GRU, not the KGB.

68 The Great Terror was the process by which Stalin purged the Bolshevik political apparatus, the Red Army high command, the security services and the various, already defeated oppositionist forces; while at the same time liquidating hundreds of thousands of 'potential fifth columnists' in a bloodbath that made Hitler's 1934 Night of the Long Knives look like child's play. For many years there were no exact figures regarding the numbers of people killed at this time (1936-38) and many inflated estimates were made. In the 1990s, when archival data finally became available, it was established that the number of official executions was around 750,000, with several million more being sentenced to long terms in the GULAG archipelago which many of them did not survive or which shortened both their lives and those of many close to them.

They were dumbfounded when he informed them that Stalin's motive was to annihilate the anti-fascist Bolshevik elite in order to forge a pact with Hitler, to whom he had been making overtures through a secret emissary since 1934. Krivitsky was almost completely disbelieved.

He further tried to warn both British and American authorities that Soviet agents had penetrated both the British Foreign Office and the US State Department. These warnings, too, went largely unheeded. Russians were listening, however. Lev Trotsky declared that Stalin wanted especially to kill two of his enemies: Trotsky in Mexico City and Krivitsky in Washington. Trotsky, of course, was assassinated on 20 August 1940. On 9 February 1941, at the Bellevue Hotel, in Washington DC, Krivitsky was shot dead by an agent of Stalin in what was made to look like a suicide.[69] The Krivitsky episode is crucial to Newton's story for two reasons. First, because Newton advances the argument that Philby, Maclean and Burgess were drawn to serve Stalin not out of idealism, but because they worshipped the dark gods of deceit, power and human sacrifice whose servants both Hitler and Stalin were. Second, because Krivitsky's warnings to both British and American security intelligence authorities of the existence of Soviet moles went almost entirely unheeded, so that the moles in question were not unearthed for more than another decade.[70] These

---

69 The timing here is worth keeping clearly in mind. Stalin finally made his pact with Hitler in late August 1939. As the Marxist historian Isaac Deutscher wrote many years ago, 'Stalin could not have had the slightest doubt that the pact at once relieved Hitler of the nightmare of a war on two fronts and to that extent it unleashed the Second World War.' (*Stalin*, Penguin 1968, p. 428). The two of them partitioned Poland at once. Hitler then turned against the Western powers and, in May 1940 invaded France, which fell within six weeks. Trotsky was assassinated two months after the fall of France. After spending months attempting to reduce Britain by air assault, Hitler fatefully began, in early 1941, to prepare a massive assault on the Soviet Union. It was as these preparations began, in early February 1941, that Krivitsky was assassinated. On 22 June 1941, to Stalin's utter disbelief, Hitler launched Operation Barbarossa and within six weeks had almost decapitated the Red Army, with the Nazi forces killing or capturing three million Soviet soldiers in that brief time. However, the Red Army withstood the battering, moved forces up to Moscow from the Far East and, from the winter of 1941-42 slowly and relentlessly began to turn the tide.

70 Maclean and Burgess were exposed in May 1951, when they fled Britain for Moscow. Philby was not definitively exposed until a decade later again, although he had fallen under suspicion and his career had been aborted from July 1951. Most of the Soviet moles in Britain and elsewhere were not, however, exposed in the 1950s and a good many have still not been exposed. Throughout the Cold War, partisans of the Left insisted that talk of moles was a paranoid conspiracy theory and that charges against such figures as Alger Hiss were symptoms of 'McCarthyism' and therefore should not be credited. The truth, it turned out, was that there were more Soviet spies in both North America and Western Europe than even the erratic McCarthy had alleged, though he made wild allegations against many individuals who demonstrably were not Soviet pawns or moles.

A full accounting of the extent of Soviet penetration of the West from the 1920s onwards, if it is ever achieved, may yet be some decades away. Crucial to it will be access to the GRU archives, since most

two points set the stage for Newton's drama of fateful intrigue and counter-intelligence.

The chief mole was Donald Maclean. Newton reveals that Maclean did far more direct damage to the West's diplomatic and intelligence work than did Philby. Above all, during his years in the British Embassy in Washington (1944-48), Maclean became the chief British liaison officer on nuclear matters. Newton's coverage of this side of the story is detailed and fascinating. Not the least fascinating aspect is his argument that Maclean kept Stalin better informed, during 1946 to 1948 on American military preparedness (more precisely lack of preparedness) than even the American Joint Chiefs of Staff and Strategic Air Command were—since neither of the latter 'were allowed to know anything about the size of America's nuclear arsenal'. In 1947, Newton tells us, that nuclear arsenal was practically non-existent. 'It is the thesis of this book,' he states, 'that because of Maclean, Stalin knew that he had nothing to fear from America.' Stalin's own blunders, however, enabled the West to pull together the Western alliance and keep the tide of totalitarianism in check.

The parts of Newton's book dealing with Maclean's espionage make absorbing reading. Almost as fascinating, however, are those dealing with the bureaucratic and international fears and jealousies that led both the British and American security, intelligence and diplomatic establishments to ignore, muddle and then cover up so much about the Soviet spies for so long. This phenomenon is of great intrinsic significance and Newton deserves high praise for the wry and detached manner in which he has presented the twisted tale.

Of many passages that bear on it, none perhaps more succinctly sums up the matter than that in which, writing of the reactions to the flight from Britain of Burgess and Maclean on 25 May 1951, Newton observes:

> By 7 June ... the pattern for the cover-up was established. The British were withholding information from the Americans. The CIA was withholding information from the FBI, which was withholding information from the State Department. The AEC (Atomic Energy Commission) would then join the fray and withhold information from all the others and Congress as well. Each organisation, in Washington and London, was determined to protect itself.[71]

---

of what has been exposed has come thus far from KGB archives. Even it has been astonishing. It turns out, for instance, than in addition to the Cambridge spy ring of five moles, there were similar spy rings recruited at the same time at both Oxford University and London University. A key case which remains to be solved is the identity of the GRU mole within MI5 in the early 1940s codenamed ELLI, whom the authorized historian of MI5, Christopher Andrew, in 2009, falsely claimed had been Leo Long. The available evidence overwhelmingly suggests that, in fact, ELLI was Roger Hollis, who went on to become first Deputy Director and then Director General of MI5 in a career that spanned 27 years (1938-65) and who was only forced out of MI5 in 1965 on the insistence of the US government.

71   It is notable here, looking back, that Newton mentions only American organisations specifically. Yet the greatest damage was being done and the most egregious cover-ups perpetrated in Britain. In the

Yet if the picture of Anglo-American intelligence than emerges from the book is a less than edifying one, the Soviet intelligence apparatus certainly does not emerge looking masterful. With a sense of irony more redolent of le Carré than of Pincher, Knightley or Wright, Newton argues that the Soviets squandered their prize assets. They did not do enough to assist the unstable Maclean; they made the amazing blunder of sending the dissolute Burgess to Washington and then allowing him to share lodgings with the valuable Philby; and then, when Maclean was blown, they allowed Burgess to flee with him in panic—instead of quietly liquidating him—and so threw away Philby's future as well.

Newton expresses wonder at the blunders of Stalin and the waste of Philby—just when he seemed poised to become the head of British foreign intelligence. The mythmakers on both sides of the Iron Curtain would spend the Cold War turning Philby into a super spy in the service of a fiendishly clever and ruthless apparatus. Newton puts things into perspective by quoiting the words Conor Cruise O'Brien used to describe the KGB as revealed by the memoirs of Arkady Shevchenko: 'a cumbersome, ill-informed, mutually suspicious, apprehensive and dimly improvising elite.' What else, one wonders, could Stalin's murderous paranoia and brutal tutelage have produced?[72] As le Carré's novels did much to suggest throughout the Cold War the world of 'intelligence' often seemed to be a struggle between elites on both sides who merited a wry description of this kind.

1940s, with MI6 penetrated by Philby, MI5 by ELLI (almost certainly Hollis) and Blunt (until 1945), the Foreign Office by Maclean and numerous other parts of the British government by other Soviet moles; and with the nuclear program penetrated by Soviet spies cleared by Hollis at MI5, Britain was as full of espionage holes as Swiss cheese, but the political as much as the intelligence establishment was deeply reluctant to either accept that this was possible or inform the Americans even when it had become incontrovertible.

72 In fact, at one point, there was a body of opinion within the KGB that Philby and the other Cambridge spies must be triple agents who were being cleverly used by MI6 to mislead Moscow. Why? Because the volume and quantity of secret material they were supplying was so vast as to be simply incredible. It was too good to be true. This fear does not seem to have prevailed, however. In any case, Moscow had a great many other highly productive spies, not least in the nuclear program from 1941 onwards and at high levels in both London and Washington.

Oliver Stone, *JFK* and conspiracy theory[73]

As a historian, I find the full-blown plot presented to us by Oliver Stone in *JFK* quite improbable. As a passionate lover of drama and cinema, I find his film, especially on a second viewing, to have the raw power, but also the lack of subtlety of his other films, such as *Wall Street*, *Salvador* and *The Doors*. As an analyst of world affairs, whose job it is to 'get it right', I might well join with those many critics who have assailed Stone's melodramatic blend of documented fact, contentious testimony and unbridled imagination. Yet, in all these capacities, I urge you to go and see *JFK*, as a provocative introduction to a great enigma of our time: the unsolved assassination of President John F. Kennedy on 22 November 1963.

I have lectured about the assassination of JFK in a tertiary course on political violence. I have had a serious interest in the case for years. I have followed the press reaction to Stone's cinematic treatment of the matter with fascination. My visceral reaction to the film, on a

---

[73] This piece was first published in *The Age* on 27 January 1992. It was a review of Oliver Stone's then newly released film *JFK*, starring Kevin Costner as Jim Garrison and dramatizing the farcical trial of Clay Shaw, in 1969, for alleged involvement in a US government plot that carried out and then covered up the assassination of President Kennedy in 1963. At the time it was written, I was still baffled by the case and inclined to believe that there could have been a conspiracy, perhaps along the lines of the well-known OAS conspiracy to assassinate President Charles De Gaulle of France in 1962-63, because he had given independence to Algeria. I was cautious as to who exactly may have been involved and how they could have arranged for it all to be covered up, but was prepared to consider rogue elements of the Western Hemisphere division of the CIA as having had a hand in it.

A decade later, with my colleague and friend Tim van Gelder, I mounted a three day workshop on the JFK case, in which the arguments were 'mapped' and systematically evaluated. We called this workshop the Advanced Reasoning and Analysis (ARA) workshop. Gradually, mapping and evaluating the arguments and discussing them with participants in multiple iterations of the workshop over about a decade, often for intelligence or financial professionals, I reached several conclusions: that there had not been a conspiracy; that Lee Harvey Oswald had acted alone; and that the Warren Commission had acted with integrity, but had left certain things vague or uncertain, which had been seized upon by conspiracy theorists and turned into decades of confusion and mischief-making. I came to see exactly where and why conspiracy theories had arisen and where they were in error.

By far the best book on the assassination is Vincent Bugliosi's *Reclaiming History: The Assassination of President John F. Kennedy* (W. W. Norton & Co., New York, 2007). It is encyclopaedic and meticulous in addressing every major conspiracy theory and every detail of the much controverted case. *Parkland*, written and directed by Peter Landesman (2013), is a vastly better account of the assassination than Stone's overblown and ultimately irresponsible film. It did not, of course, do nearly as well at the box office, because so many people want a conspiracy theory and far too many have become convinced, over the past half century, that there really was one in the case of the Kennedy assassination in 1963.

first viewing, was one of almost exuberant satisfaction that the subject had been presented on the big screen in a major feature film. At a second viewing, I became more dissatisfied with the movie's flaws. Nonetheless, I find that I have little patience with those critics who have attacked Stone for real or alleged misrepresentations of history. Let me explain why.

It needs to be emphasized that there are serious problems with the Warren Commission's findings—all of its findings, not just the central conclusion that Lee Harvey Oswald, acting alone, killed John F. Kennedy. Whatever its defects, Stone's film presents rather well the range of evidence that undermines the lone assassin case and the case against Oswald himself.[74] I find the reactions to *JFK* which contemptuously dismiss 'conspiracy theories' and affirm the bona fides of the Warren Commission fatuous.

For example, Gerard Henderson, in the *Sydney Morning Herald*, accused Stone of omitting from his film 'the documented fact that Kennedy was killed by a bullet fired from Oswald's rifle'. The plain fact is that the bullet which struck Kennedy in the head and killed him was never presented in evidence at all. Officially, it was never found. No bullet fragments of any identifiable significance were found in Kennedy's head, or indeed anywhere in his body, according to the official autopsy.

The only bullet presented in evidence to the Warren Commission was the notorious 'Magic Bullet', which was found on a stretcher at Parkland Hospital, Dallas, and which was subsequently credited with having inflicted a total of seven wounds on President Kennedy and Texas Governor John Connally (who was seated in front of Kennedy in the presidential limousine), without sustaining any discernible damage itself. The patent absurdity of this is especially well dramatized in Stone's film.[75] Now, once you discredit the lone assassin theory, you have a conspiracy of some kind, like it or not. You must then explain how the thing was pinned on Lee Harvey Oswald. Again, Stone does a good job of dramatizing the evidence, such as it is, which suggests that this was no accident and that Oswald was, as he claimed before he was silenced, a patsy.[76]

---

74   In fact, Stone seriously misrepresents that evidence and leaves those who watch his film and are otherwise poorly informed in a state of considerable confusion about what actually took place during the assassination, as well as before and after it.

75   In reality, the reconstruction in the film completely distorts the nature of the forensic evidence, the angles from which the bullets struck and the reasoning of the Warren Commission about the matter. It should be remarked, however, that clarifying what actually happened and getting participants in the ARA workshop to grasp the careful reasoning involved was always the most challenging part of the exercise.

76   I have come to understand, over years of careful parsing of the evidence and the arguments that have swirled around it that every one of these claims is false. A good many bullet fragments were, in fact,

Nor do I have much patience with the kind of critic who objects that Stone's putative conspiracy could not have occurred, because it is inconceivable that powerful figures in the United States of America would ever do that sort of thing. That is pious nonsense.[77] It all depends on which powerful figures you are talking about. Stone's problem is that he includes all sorts of powerful figures with a notable lack of discrimination. The point is that the assassination of President Kennedy is a crime that has not been solved and the unanswered questions concerning it do lead in quite alarming directions.

One is led, correctly enough, by Stone, into this labyrinth: Oswald's intelligence connections[78]; Ruby's lifelong links with the Mafia; and the CIA's links with the Mafia in

---

found in Kennedy's brain and traced to Oswald's rifle. Other fragments were found in the car. The so-called 'Magic Bullet' was not 'magic' at all and did not do anything absurd. Oswald was the shooter on the sixth floor of the Texas School Book Depository and there were no other shooters. Moreover, he acted for his own confused reasons and was not the pawn or accomplice of the CIA, the Mafia, Fidel Castro, the KGB, the Texas oil barons or any other cabal. In retrospect, I felt so concerned about my own errors in this 1992 piece that I considered omitting it from *Opinions and Reflections*. However, the book is not a book of proofs, but one of freedom of expression and learning. If anything, this old piece helps to show how even relatively well-informed and thoughtful people, intent on getting things right, are able to err egregiously in complex and contentious matters and even subscribe to conspiracy theories. Perhaps it is valuable for that reason alone, if for no other.

77 One way to think about this is Abraham Lincoln's assassination was achieved by a group of conspirators, although carried out by a lone gunman. More immediately relevant is the fact, as I pointed out to a university class as early as 1987, that the OAS conspiracy to assassinate the French President (De Gaulle) involved military officers, intelligence officers and political figures. It was triggered by a sense of grievance over the liberation of Algeria. The claim that a comparable group may have had a grievance against Kennedy because he failed to liberate Cuba has always seemed plausible. The problem is that the evidence available does not substantiate any claim that they actually arranged the assassination of the president. For an exploration of the Cuban connection, see Gus Russo and Stephen Molton *Brothers in Arms: The Kennedys, the Castros and the Politics of Murder* (Bloomsbury, New York, 2008). See also David Talbot *Brothers: The Hidden History of the Kennedy Years* (Free Press, New York, 2007) and James W. Hilty *Robert Kennedy: Brother Protector* (Temple University Press, Philadelphia, 1997).

78 The first book to draw attention to the background of Lee Harvey Oswald was Edward Jay Epstein's *Legend: The Secret World of Lee Harvey Oswald* (Arrow Books, London, 1978), but even before it came out there were speculations that he may have been a KGB operative or a CIA one. The film *Executive Action*, with a screenplay by Dalton Trumbo and starring Robert Ryan and Burt Lancaster, was released in 1973. It already depicted Oswald as someone with murky intelligence background who could be used for the purposes of the assassination plot and then eliminated. The film ran into a storm of controversy and was pulled out of theatres after only a fortnight. Two years later, with the Church Committee hearings into the CIA and the discovery that the CIA itself had been running a program called Executive Action in which it plotted the assassination of foreign political leaders, the idea that Oswald's alleged intelligence connections may have been significant came

Operation Mongoose (its attempts to destabilize Castro's Cuba and assassinate Castro himself).[79] He then almost certainly leads us astray by insisting that the answer to who carried out the conspiracy lies in Kennedy's alleged determination to withdraw from Vietnam in 1965, if elected to a second Presidential term in 1964.

Yet the essential materials of the enigma are there, as never dramatized before and I am inclined to think that it is better to have the viewing public wandering around in this labyrinth than to have them lost in Dealey Plaza with the Warren Commission's peculiar conclusions.[80] Other things need to be added, however; not least a demythologized knowledge of who John F. Kennedy really was, as compared with the enduring image of him as the King Arthur of an

---

back to the surface. Epstein's questions, however, centred on the possibility that Oswald had been a 'Manchurian candidate' for the KGB and that the Warren Commission had papered this over in order to avoid an international security confrontation with the Soviet Union.

John Newman's *Oswald and the CIA* (Carroll and Graf, New York, 1995) provides by far the most comprehensive account of the CIA's files on Oswald and the confusion caused by the Agency's refusal to acknowledge to the Warren Commission that it had such files. Newman's conclusion is that the intelligence services in general and the CIA in particular had had a much closer interest in Oswald than they have ever admitted and that, 'when Oswald turned up with a rifle on the president's motorcade route', the CIA may have 'found itself living in an unthinkable nightmare of its own making' (p. 430). Don DeLillo's novel *Libra* (Penguin, London, 1989) creates a brilliantly conceived fictional scenario in which the CIA is deeply implicated in the assassination, but in ways that even insiders find themselves unable to fathom. However, all these scenarios are covered off by Vincent Bugliosi, in his monumental *Reclaiming History: The Assassination of President John F. Kennedy* (W. W. Norton & Co., New York, 2007).

79 Fidel Castro himself and his long-time secret intelligence chief Fabian Escalante have waded into the JFK debate over the years, alleging that it was their old nemesis the CIA that carried out the assassination. Escalante has written a set of small books arguing this case, in particular the second of them *JFK: The Cuba Files—The Untold Story of the Plot to Kill Kennedy* (Ocean Press, New York, 2006). The book is fascinating to read, but it provides no new evidence and no compelling argument that what Escalante calls 'the US establishment' assassinated Kennedy.

80 This is the antithesis of what I now believe. It is like saying that one prefers to have the general public bamboozled by conspiracy theories about the Moon landing or 9/11 than well-informed and guided by serious thinking on such subjects. The Kennedy assassination, as it turned out, became the taproot of a growing tendency to unhinged conspiracy theory in the United States as the 1960s 'progressed'. There is now an interesting literature on this phenomenon itself. See Peter Knight *Conspiracy Culture: From Kennedy to the X Files* (Routledge, London and New York, 2000); David Aaronovitch *Voodoo Histories: The Role of Conspiracy Theory in Shaping Modern History* (Riverhead Books, New York, 2010); and Emma A. Jane and Chris Fleming *Modern Conspiracy: The Importance of Being Paranoid* (Bloomsbury, New York, 2014). A beautiful study in a reality around which much fanciful conspiracy theory has swirled for many years is Annie Jacobsen's *Area 51: An Uncensored History of America's Top Secret Military Base* (Orion, London, 2011).

evanescent Camelot in the White House.[81]

After all the anomalies concerning Dealey Plaza and the Warren Commission hearings have been tabled, one piece of the puzzle is legally and logically decisive and calls for special scrutiny: the autopsy procedure and the report that issued from it. This is something seldom appreciated and not addressed even by Stone, but he at least brings into the picture a little of the alarming evidence which has emerged that something was very odd indeed about the autopsy findings.

Quite simply, if the autopsy could be shown to have been above reproach, and if it could be shown that its findings were that Kennedy had been shot only from behind, then the Dealey Plaza anomalies would have to be imputed to confusion on the part of scores of eye witnesses to the events on the afternoon of 22 November 1963; including the doctors at Parkland Hospital in Dallas, who described the wounds to JFK in a manner irreconcilable with the description of his wounds in the autopsy report.

If, conversely, the autopsy findings were to be effectively impugned, then the Warren Commission's case would unravel in both directions—back into Dallas and up into the reaches of the US government—suggesting a conspiracy somewhere within the awesome spectrum thrown open by Oliver Stone. Why is that? Because, legally speaking, the autopsy findings amount to bedrock evidence or what in the law is called 'best evidence'. If the Warren Commission was misled by the autopsy report concerning the nature of Kennedy's wounds, its findings cannot be sustained. But if it was not misled, it becomes extremely difficult to sustain the case for a conspiracy—despite all the apparent ballistic evidence (or lack of it) and much cited eye and ear witness protestation.

That, perhaps, makes the matter sound simple. It is not. The abiding intellectual fascination of the case lies in the difficulties posed by the anomalies and unanswered questions about the events in Dealey Plaza, the identity of Oswald and the motives of Ruby, to say nothing of the highly disturbing medical evidence, or what has been presented as such evidence. The point is

---

81 Seymour Hersh's *The Dark Side of Camelot* (Little, Brown & Co., New York, 1997) is one of a number of books which highlights the seamier side of the Kennedy years and family background. Another is Ronald Kessler *The Sins of the Father: Joseph P. Kennedy and the Dynasty he Founded* (Warner Books, New York, 1996). A more scholarly and comprehensive account of the family background can be found in Doris Kearns Goodwin *The Fitzgeralds and the Kennedys: An American Saga* (Pan Books, London, 1988). Peter Dale Scott's *Deep Politics and the Death of JFK* (University of California Press, 1993) is an intriguing book that weaves together numerous elements of American underground politics and crime from the 1950s and early 1960s to suggest that JFK may well have been the victim of any one of a number of conspiracies. It fails, however, to make the case that he was in actual fact the victim of any of them. For a recent and scholarly account of Kennedy's inner circle, see Robert Dallek *Camelot's Court: Inside the Kennedy White House* (Harper Collins, New York, 2013).

that the autopsy has been impugned and no effective defence of it has been forthcoming.

Of the various pieces of evidence that Stone omits, to my surprise and to the significant dilution of his own 'hard-line' case, is the FBI report which indicated that, when the president's body was presented to the autopsy doctors, it was remarked that there was evidence of surgery to the president's head, namely in the top of the skull. Yet no mention of such surgery appeared in the final autopsy report, nor was mention of it made directly to the Warren Commission.

When James Humes, the chief autopsy doctor, was interviewed about this FBI report, he did not deny that such surgery had been evident. To the contrary, he stated that he believed that it ought to have come to the attention of the Warren Commission and that he would have liked to know where, when and by whom this surgery had been performed. Certainly, no surgery to the head was performed at Parkland Hospital in Dallas and none should have been performed by anyone, anywhere before the autopsy. Yet the FBI itself confirmed the validity of the agents' report.[82]

Like Stone's Jim Garrison, in the closing scenes of *JFK*,[83] I must leave it to the jury of readers to ponder what all this means and whether there is any justification whatsoever for documentation pertaining to this crime to remain classified for decades to come on national security grounds, as much of still is.

I regard Oliver Stone's film as a piece of theatre, not as a documentary; though documentaries, Leftist or conservative, have just as often misled their publics as any piece of imaginative theatre. I am, therefore, not appalled by its real or supposed excesses. I found it, in fact, less 'excessive' than critical reviews of it had led me to expect. I heartily recommend it to those who would have their political imaginations challenged. And I would urge those so challenged to go away, seek facts, read up and ask questions.

Among the numerous books on the subject, I would recommend that interested readers start with *The Kennedy Conspiracy*, by Anthony Summers and then try to obtain a copy of the most remarkable and chilling of all the books on the subject: David S. Lifton's *Best Evidence: Disguise and Deception in the Assassination of John F. Kennedy*. The first was published by Sphere Books in 1989 and reprinted in 1990. The second is published by Carroll and Graf and was reprinted for the eighth time in 1990.[84] Each has a very good bibliographic guide to sources and further reading.

---

82   On the autopsy, see Bugliosi's comprehensive treatment at pp. 382-449 of *Reclaiming History*. See also his withering critique of Lifton's work at pp. 1057-1070 of the same book.

83   Vincent Bugliosi provides a devastating critical analysis of both the Garrison trial and Oliver Stone's JFK in *Reclaiming History* pp. 1347-1436.

84   Here again my opinion has changed greatly in the 22 years since I wrote this piece in early 1992 or late 1991. I am now aware, as I was not then, of various flaws in the stories told by both Summers and Lifton. I remember well reading Lifton's book for the first time while on field work for my doctorate,

As for Stone's 'outrageous' artistic licence, my complaint is only that he could have made a finer drama of more enduring value with more care. Yet the reaction of too many of his critics, in my judgment, is as wrong-headed as Plato's critique of poetry and 'errant' opinion among the masses and the uninitiated in his *Republic* and *Laws*. Such critics would censor nightmare, anger and imagination in the name of an official version of history which is itself grounded in myth. Am I being sufficiently provocative? I think Oliver Stone is and, on the whole, I applaud him for it.[85]

---

in the Philippines, in 1987 and being flabbergasted by it. I immediately handed it to a highly intelligent friend and said to him: 'Do me a favour. Read this book and tell me where the author is wrong, because I cannot spot a flaw in his use of evidence or his reasoning, but I cannot accept his conclusion.' After going over the autopsy and medical evidence closely in many iterations of the ARA, I am convinced that he was not only in error but cannot have presented his evidence accurately in reaching a conclusion—that Kennedy's body had been hijacked by the US military and surgically altered to make it appear that he had only been shot from behind, in order to frame Lee Harvey Oswald—that was inherently preposterous. The fact that I found his book so spell-binding 27 years ago only goes to show that we are all susceptible to being seduced by a dramatic narrative and that it requires calm, careful and deliberate critical thinking to unpick such stories and free ourselves from their grip.

85   For all its many flaws, I still find the film valuable at two levels. It has been an excellent resource for running the ARA workshop over more than a decade; and it triggered the JFK Records Act by the US Congress, in 1993, which required the release of millions of pages of otherwise classified records. From all those millions of pages, no 'smoking gun' has emerged to support allegations of a conspiracy, but it is surely better to have them out in the open than to allow suspicion and paranoia to fester.

The strange persistence of anti-Semitism[86]

'The subterranean stream of Western history has finally come to the surface and usurped the dignity of our tradition,' wrote Hannah Arendt, in the summer of 1950.[87] She was referring, of course, to the murderous, atavistic and institutionalised irrationalism of Nazi totalitarianism. She was writing the Preface to her great work *The Origins of Totalitarianism*, the first part of which was entitled 'Anti-Semitism'.[88] Subterranean stream? Norman Cohn, writing some years later, entitled his study of the phenomenon *Europe's Inner Demons*.[89] Both were alluding to the ancient phobias and deep-rooted mythologies of the European peoples which, under the volcanic pressures of the 20th century, erupted in genocidal violence against the European Jews in the years of the Nazi ascendancy.

Robert Wistrich has, in this present book, provided a lucid and chilling survey of the

---

86   This piece was first published in *The Age* on 1 February 1992. It was a review of Robert S. Wistrich's *Anti-Semitism: The Longest Hatred* (Heinemann, 1992). That was more than twenty year ago. It is disturbing to see the rise of anti-Semitism in Europe in the last decade; to the point where substantial numbers of French Jews, for example, are leaving France and migrating to Israel.

87   Hannah Arendt *The Origins of Totalitarianism*, Andre Deutsch, London, 1986 p. ix. The fuller citation reads as follows, coming at the end to Arendt's Preface to the first edition, in 1950:

> We can no longer afford to take that which was good in the past and simply call it our heritage, to discard the bad and simply think of it as a dead load which by itself time will bury in oblivion. The subterranean stream of Western history has finally come to the surface and usurped the dignity of our tradition. This is the reality in which we live. And this is why all efforts to escape from the grimness of the present into nostalgia for a still intact past, or into the anticipated oblivion of a better future, are vain.

88   Hannah Arendt began her Preface to Part One: Anti-Semitism with a ringing rejection of the idea that anti-Semitism in the modern world was a direct outgrowth of religious anti-Judaism in Christendom:

> Anti-Semitism, a secular nineteenth century ideology—which in name if not in argument, was unknown before the 1870s—and religious Jew-hatred, inspired by the mutually hostile antagonism of two conflicting creeds, are obviously not the same; and even the extent to which the former derives its arguments and emotional appeal from the latter is open to question. The notion of an unbroken continuity of persecutions, expulsions and massacres from the end of the Roman Empire to the Middle Ages, the modern era and down to our own time, frequently embellished by the idea that modern anti-Semitism is no more than a secularized version of popular medieval superstitions, is no less fallacious (though of course less mischievous) than the corresponding anti-Semitic notion of a Jewish secret society that has ruled, or aspired to rule the world since antiquity.

David Nirenberg, however, has made a trenchant case that anti-Judaism does indeed go back into the ancient past and is, in fact, the seedbed of anti-Semitism. See his *Anti-Judaism: The History of a Way of Thinking*, (W. W. Norton & Co., New York, 2013).

89   Norman Cohn *Europe's Inner Demons*, (Granada Publishing, UK, 1975).

roots of this terrible phenomenon and of its afterglow, in both Europe and the Middle East, since the 1940s. It is not a book on the grand scale and is not a rich text that one might ponder and study. Its virtue is in its clarity and brevity, bringing a serious overview of the long history of hatred of the Jews within the reach of a wide readership of non-specialists and non-scholars. It has a useful bibliography, sufficient to guide any but the most demanding of readers and is enlarged by the inclusion of 49 black and white prints and photographs, often of a graphic and shocking nature.

If it has defects, they are, in my estimation, almost entirely the consequence of the author's attempt to cover the whole story from pre-Christian antiquity to Moscow and Warsaw in 1990. The result is, at times, a sparseness of narrative and reflection that significantly detracts from the book's quality and does less than ample justice to the gravity of its theme. Yet, for a general readership, this may make it digestible, instead of daunting or soporific. Perhaps one cannot have it both ways.

Wistrich opens his tale with some observations on the pagan antecedents of Western anti-Semitism. The Greeks and Romans, he notes, were repelled by the apparent misanthropy of the Jews, whose religion seemed to entail a bigoted rejection of the gods and customs of all mankind. Yet there was no racial anti-Semitism in the ancient world, he concedes. Indeed, the term 'anti-Semitism' is something of an anachronism as applied to anti-Jewish attitudes or activities before the late nineteenth century. It was a term invented by Wilhelm Marr, in the 1870s, to define a post-Christian, racial anti-Jewish prejudice, in which 'Semite' (Jew) stood opposed to 'Aryan' (northern European).

Nonetheless, the Jews, as both a religion and a race, were the object of many centuries of vilification and persecution by Christians—Catholic, Orthodox and Protestant - on account of their alleged 'Deicide' for killing Jesus of Nazareth, the so-called 'Son of God'. Pagan disdain for and exasperation with the Jews gave way to Christian slander and persecution of them, which became deeply ingrained in popular culture in much of Europe; forming that 'subterranean stream' that came to the surface in the 20th century, in the course of what Wistrich calls 'the great counter-revolutionary backlash'. That backlash was not specifically Christian, but it drew deeply on the longest hatred known to Christendom and found in the Jew the most vulnerable and time-honoured scapegoat on which to vent the paroxysms of its rage and paranoia.

One of the compelling and refreshing qualities of this book is its directness in laying the chief responsibility for the longest hatred at the door of Christianity. From the Gospel of St John down to the Vatican's edict *Nostra Aetate*, in 1965, 'absolving' the Jews of collective guilt for the killing of the Christ, some 1,930 years earlier; Christians had been taught to see the Jews as Christ-killers, as a God-denying remnant who would not accept their Saviour; as an evil brood of miscreants who practised child sacrifice. Pogroms a la Kristallnacht, expulsions, the racial badge, the ghetto, were not invented by the Nazis, but by medieval Christians in the age of Pope Innocent III, Thomas Aquinas and Dante. It was, Wistrich reminds us, the First Crusade, in 1096, which brought a decisive turn for the worse, as Christian warriors perpetrated massacres 'hitherto unprecedented in the history of Jewish-Christian relations'.

Wistrich might have lavished more attention on these roots of anti-Semitism, but he was most economical in his use of the materials available, if only because there was so much else to cram into his survey. The same is true of his account of the Nazi Holocaust itself, to which he devotes a mere 11 pages (Chapter 6). He avoids the contentious issues of Holocaust scholarship, providing only a simple summary of a grim but basically familiar story. The same then holds for most of the balance of the book, in which he briefly discusses the nature and virulence of anti-Semitism in the United States, Britain, France, post-war Germany and Austria, Eastern Europe and the Soviet Union; before turning to the rise and rise of anti-Semitism among the (Semitic) Arab peoples in the 20th century.

The most troubling aspect of the phenomenon of anti-Semitism for Wistrich, it seems, is not so much its dreadful past, but its tenacious persistence since the Second World War. His book appears, indeed, to have been prompted by this persistence and even recrudescence of anti-Semitism. This atavistic hatred of Jews, use of them as a scapegoat for anxieties about the erosion of traditional cultures, national identities, ideological orthodoxies and viable economies has the most disturbing implications concerning the workings of human mass consciousness.

And then there is the matter of the Middle East and Islam. Wistrich explains that, until the impact of Western imperialism and the creation of the state of Israel in its wake, Islam was, in general, more tolerant of the Jews than was Christianity. The real trouble began when Western power and Jewish revanchism collided with the ancient Islamic conceit of spiritual superiority and wrought what Wistrich dubs facetiously 'a truly wrenching dislocation of Allah's plans'.[90] The subsequent

---

90   The past thousand years, but especially the past three hundred years, have seen a relentless decay of the Muslim world and the contraction of any geopolitical evidence that Islam was or had any realistic chance of becoming universally supreme, as its devotees had believed from the 7th century. Its initial expansion from the Arabian Peninsula, between the hegira of Mohammed in 622 and the battles in France and Turkestan that brought it to the limits of its early extent by around 730 CE, was formidable. It overthrew and overran the Eastern Roman Empire and the Persian Empire, which had bled each other white over the preceding century, and fought its way to the outskirts of the nascent Frankish state in the West and the powerful T'ang Empire in the East. In many ways, as Edward Gibbon remarked in the late 18th century, the Muslims were fortunate in arising and striking when they did, since the two great empires of the Romans and Persians would almost certainly have been able to contain them had they not become mutually exhausted by the beginning of the 7th century.

Islamic adoption of Christian and post-Christian calumnies against the Jews and paranoid myths about Jewish conspiracies to dominate the world is nimbly and numbingly related by the author. His observation that the 'atavistic hatred between the sons of Isaac and the sons of Ishmael, between the followers of Moses and Mohammed, threatens to drown out the still small voice of reason', summarises quite beautifully the root of the matter and leaves one with no more hope than Elijah had on Mount Carmel. Wistrich, however, persists in offering us the still small voice of reason and shows us compelling grounds for why it should be preferred to the strident and dogmatic voices of anti-Semitic demagogues, religious believers and the crowds who are incited by them.

> That early success and the immense riches and heritage of learning that it delivered into Muslim Arab hands provided something of an illusion as to both the power and virtues of Islam. The Christian crusades from the 11th through to the early 13th century made very little impression on this vast domain. The Mongol invasions in the 13th and 14th centuries, by Hulagu and later Tamerlane, were another matter altogether. They devastated the heartland of Islam from Central Asia through to Syria and involved the sack of Baghdad and the destruction of its libraries. The Ottoman Empire arose on the ruins of the Abbasid Arab caliphate and for a considerable period looked formidable, especially with the capture of Constantinople in 1453. But the halcyon years of Arab Islam were over and have never returned. Now radical Islam is largely Arab in inspiration—with the exception of the Shi'ite regime in Iran—and it looks back with violent nostalgia to the Abbasid caliphate before the fall of Baghdad. The end of the Cold War and the sense that the Soviet Union and the United States were the modern counterparts to the Persian and Roman Empires has added to the vision of a revival of the caliphate, alas by only the most barbarous and fanatical means.

Alienating Russia at the end of the Cold War[91]

Is Russia part of Europe, or part of Asia? Whose problem is it now? The Soviet Union is dead and where it used to be there is growing economic chaos, which threatens to spiral out of control and generate dangerous political upheavals. There is also danger in the loss of central control over the vast stocks of armaments, especially nuclear arms, left behind by the Communist regime.[92]

---

91 This piece was first published in *The Canberra Times* on 26 March 1992. It was a response to remarks by then then head of the International Institute for Strategic Studies, in London, Francois Heisbourg, in a special seminar at the Australian National University a few days before. The seminar was supposed to have been conducted under 'Chatham House rules', which I violated by quoting Heisbourg directly. I do not apologize for this, even now, however, since what he said demanded a public response. I was told by a senior Russian diplomat a week or so after this piece appeared that the Russian Ambassador had shown him my piece and declared, 'This goes to the heart of the matter.' Given the stance adopted since the turn of the century by Vladimir Putin's Russia and the deep resentments among Russian nationalists at what they see as the humiliation of Russia by the West since 1991, I believe these reflections still stand up well.

For two useful accounts of Russia in the 1990s and the circumstances that led from the collapse of the USSR to the rise of Putin, see Daniel Yergin and Thane Gustafson *Russia in 2010 and What it Means for the World*, (Random House, New York, 1993) and Yegor Gaidar *Collapse of an Empire: Lessons for Modern Russia*, (Brookings Institution Press, Washington DC, 2007). Neither book anticipated the rise of Vladimir Putin and his regressive impact on Russian politics, economics and society. Even Gaidar's book, published in 2007, does not so much as mention Putin, though it does, in an Afterword, draw attention to worrying political trends after 2004. Yergin and Gustafson describe several alternative scenarios under which, by 2010, Russian capitalism might thrive or stagnate. Under the most favourable of them, with German and Japanese capital pouring in from west and east to fuel the renovation of Russian infrastructure and energy exploitation, Russia booms. But under most of them the legacy of Stalinism and command economics retards the country's development. This is what has transpired. For a critical account of Putin's authoritarian populism and its costs, see Robert Horvath *Putin's Preventive Counter-Revolution* (Routledge, London, 2013).

92 As it turned out, the greater danger was in stocks of biological and chemical weapons which vastly exceeded what the CIA had ever detected during the 1980s. In 1972, the United States and the Soviet Union signed the Biological Weapons Convention, pledging to abolish their existing stocks of biological weapons and not to develop any more. The United States did so. The Soviet Union utterly and completely violated its commitments. In the late 1970s and early 1980s, a few hardliners in the Pentagon argued that Moscow was cheating on the convention, but CIA analysts, including biological weapons specialists, insisted that this was paranoia and lacked evidential support.

Then, in 1989, Vladimir Pasechnik defected from the Soviet Union and revealed that there was a very large and super-secret biological weapons program in the Soviet Union. The CIA sceptics were won over after an extensive debriefing of the defector, who had worked as a scientist in the program. In 1991 the deputy head of the program, Ken Alibek, defected and revealed that the program was far larger than even Pasechnik had known. See his memoir *Biohazard*, (Arrow Books, Random House,

How, now, are we to think of Russia, the core of the fallen Communist empire? As a defeated enemy, like Germany and Japan in 1945, which now ought to be incorporated into the capitalist world system; perhaps as a part of the European community, or what Mikhail Gorbachev has called a 'common European home'?

Professor Francois Heisbourg, director of the prestigious International Institute for Strategic Studies, in London, was asked about each of these problems during a seminar he gave the Australian National University's Research School of Pacific Studies recently. His seminar presentation had covered a wide range of contemporary concerns, but the questions put to him zeroed in on the condition of Russia and the so-called Commonwealth of Independent States.

He was asked, on the one hand, whether his observations regarding the weapons stocks question had not been a little too optimistic and on the other hand what prospect he saw for a George Marshall of the European Community emerging to champion a Marshall Plan for the revitalisation of the CIS economies, most especially the Russian economy. No-one, I think, could draw much comfort from his answers.

In response to the questions regarding weapons, he replied good naturedly that he was relieved to be challenged for his 'optimism', as he had feared he would be accused of excessive pessimism. In sober fact, he averred, the situation was fraught with danger. It could be that CIS nuclear specialists would be bought up by foreign states eager to use their expertise. Nuclear weapons, especially of the older and less secure varieties, might indeed be stolen or sold to middle or lesser powers determined to have such weapons. Certainly, in its present condition of penury, there was now a raging fire sale of conventional arms by CIS states, in an effort to earn hard currency.

One of the chief purchasers, as he pointed out, was Iran. Within no more than a year or two, he asserted, Iran will emerge as a major military power in the Middle East once more, with unpredictable consequences. At the same time, the Republic of Kazakhstan, under President Nazarbayev, was something of a wild card in the CIS deck, both in its policy regarding nuclear weapons (its stock of which is greater than those of Britain, France and China combined) and its relations with other Islamic states.

Asked whether President Kravchuk's Republic of the Ukraine might not be more of a wild card—this by a man of Polish extraction—Professor Heisbourg demurred, declaring that

---

2000). The fear that nuclear weapons would find their way into terrorist hands nonetheless dominated Western security consciousness. For deeply informed accounts of this problem, see Jeffrey T. Richelson *Defusing Armageddon: Inside NEST, America's Secret Nuclear Bomb Squad* (W. W. Norton & Co., 2009) and Graham Allison *Nuclear Terrorism: The Ultimate Preventable Catastrophe*, (Henry Holt & Co., New York, 2004).

the Ukraine had behaved fairly reasonably, if only under the constraint imposed by its desire to become a part of the European Community.

Now, this last observation deserves emphasis; for Professor Heisbourg gave it to be understood that the Ukraine might indeed become a member of the European Community, provided that it met certain conditions and behaved properly. By contrast, in answering the question concerning Marshall Plan aid to Russia and its prospective incorporation into what Mr Gorbachev had referred to as a 'common European home', Professor Heisbourg dismissed out of hand the possibility of the Russian Federation becoming part of the EC 'at any time in the next century.'

Nor did he think that a Marshall Plan was feasible in the case of Russia, he said, since the original Marshall Plan had been like water poured on fertile, well-seeded soil; whereas, in Russia, the soil was rocky and did not contain much seed. The EC, he noted, had poured tens of billions of dollars into Russia 'and much of it has simply disappeared'—into Swiss bank accounts, the coffers of bodies sprung from the old Communist Party of the Soviet Union, or in reckless speculation and consumption.

In any case, Russia is an international problem, he opined, not a specifically European one. 'Why has the American contribution been so trifling?', he asked. And, as for the Japanese, their behaviour in this matter had been both 'clumsy and grossly irresponsible'. (One cannot, of course, but ask whether, if European money has gone to waste, the caution of the Japanese about pouring money into the CIS has been perhaps neither clumsy nor grossly irresponsible, but hard headed and prudent. No-one, however, found an opportunity to put this question).

Fundamentally, Professor Heisbourg sees no obvious solutions to Russia's difficulties and believes it will have to be left to cope with them outside the framework of the European Community, because 'Russia is not part of Europe, it is not wanted as part of Europe; it is simply not clubbable.' Nothing struck me as more thought-provoking, in what was a most interesting seminar, than this gloomy and exclusionist attitude on the part of a highly (French Marxist) educated and well-connected Anglo-French scholar towards Russia's fate after the end of the Cold War. Above all, I found it strange and alarming to hear such a man assert that Russia was not really part of Europe and could not readily become part of it.

The core of Mr Gorbachev's humane revolution was his appeal to what he called 'common and universal human values' and among the most hopeful of his aspirations was his desire to break down the 'Iron Curtain' precisely so that eastern Europe, including Russia, could re-enter the common European home. The reply from the director of the International Institute for Strategic Studies seems to be: 'Your collapse was inevitable; we shall try to see that you don't starve; but keep your distance, you are no brothers of ours.'

This attitude, which seemed to be grounded at least as much in anti-Russian prejudice as in economic rationalism, struck me as only marginally more generous or reasonable than the pathetic and disgraceful ethnic animosities among the Balkan and Caucasian 'tribes'. As I left the seminar, I raised this concern with a colleague, who happens to be of Italian extraction. I was disconcerted to find that his attitude was indistinguishable from that of Professor Heisbourg. Europeans, he said, see Russia as more a part of Asia than as part of Europe. 'As Napoleon once said, scratch a Russian and you'll find a Tartar,' he remarked.

Perhaps that had simply been sour grapes on Napoleon's part; or perhaps it was indicative of that very ignorance of Russia which had led him to invade it in the first place, believing he could conquer it with his Grand Army, only to come severely unstuck in the Russian winter, never to recover. Kiev Rus was, before the Tartar conquest, an integral part of medieval Europe. The princes of Muscovy expelled the Tartars and saw themselves as Europeans. Moscow styled itself the 'Third Rome' (after the Eternal City and Constantinople). Its rulers styled themselves Caesars (Tsars), not Khans. Christian Orthodoxy has been Russia's religion for more than a thousand years. Russian is an Indo-European, not an Asiatic tongue (are Hungary or Finland 'clubbable'?).

French was the preferred language of the imperial Russian court for decades before the overthrow of the Romanovs. Those same Romanovs were intermarried with the English and German royal families. The literature, music and ballet of Russia are incontestably regarded as classical elements of modern European culture. On the eve of the Russian revolution, German engineers and French capital were rapidly integrating Russia into the European and world economy. All this, one might think, should have led Professor Heisbourg to believe that there was some real substance to Mr Gorbachev's hope and vision. None of it appears to have registered with him. What are they to make of that in Moscow—or Kiev?

There is a real historical irony in the fact that, after the Bolshevik revolution, the British and French, Americans and Japanese intervened in Russia, trying to bring about the overthrow of the Leninist regime; whereas now, after it has finally brought about its own downfall, they seem reluctant to intervene in order to foster the new regime there. No-one should under-estimate the formidable difficulties involved in the enterprise, or the costs that may be involved. Yet one could not but feel sympathetic were contemporary Russians to react to this comparative indifference in the West and Japan in much the same way that Alexander Blok responded to Western intervention in his haunting 1918 poem 'The Scythians'.

Alluding to the long history of the Scythian and Slavic peoples standing between the Greco-Roman peoples and the Huns, Blok deplored the contemptuous indifference and even cold hostility of the Old World to the earthier folk of the great European plains. 'Bethink thyself, Old World,' the poet wrote, 'once more, before it is too late.' Would you have us recede into the marsh and forest of our backwardness and barbarism. To watch, in grim indifference, 'while the ferocious Hun rifles the pockets of the dead, burns churches, herds women and children like cattle? 'Once more we summon thee with the sounds of the Aeolian lyre, to the ancient, the civilized eternal feast and fire,' Blok wrote, as the anti-Bolshevik intervention and the Russian civil war began.[93]

'The Scythians' offers still a poignant insight into the Russian experience since 1917 and what the West looks like to Russian eyes. I would have thought that now, at last, Mr Gorbachev's vision offered a more hopeful prospect and a renewal of Blok's challenge to the West. That so civilized and prominent a citizen of the West as Professor Heisbourg should seem not only pessimistic but quite cold regarding such a prospect and such a challenge, I found rather disturbing. I suggest that all those who are concerned about our post-Cold War ordering of things might ponder seriously whether such pessimism and such coldness are our best counsel at this time.

---

[93] Isaac Deutscher made Blok's poem the centrepiece of his chapter on foreign policy and the Comintern between 1923 and 1933 in his biography of Stalin half a century ago. His reflections have a strange kind of resonance in the present decade, as Russian nationalist xenophobia and truculence under Vladimir Putin play out resentments going back to the perceived treatment of Russia in the 1990s. He spoke of the mood of the Russian people in the 1920s and 1930s as being captured by Blok's poem and of that poem providing 'a visionary anticipation of the attitude of Soviet Russia to the world.' Of course, in the 1930s, the 'ferocious Hun' was not coming across the steppes from the East, but was arising in the heartland of Europe, in the form of Nazi Germany and Stalin played out Blok's poem by standing aside, in his pact with Hitler, while the Nazis overran the whole of Europe. What Stalin did not count on, of course, was that once Hitler had conquered the rest of the continent, he would turn on the Soviet Union with a barbaric fury scarcely to be imagined from a Western power and that the West would come to his aid against the ferocious Hun with immense quantities of Lend Lease materiel.

Hector Bywater and the coming of the Pacific War[94]

There is definitely the material here for a TV drama series to rival *Reilly, Aces of Spies*. The famous Sidney Reilly, who was lured into Soviet Russia by the OGPU's brilliant Trust deception in 1926, never to be seen or heard from again, may not, in fact, have been so valuable an intelligence agent as Hector C. Bywater, whose end came in mid-August 1940, possibly at the hands of the Japanese secret service. Yet whereas Reilly's real or supposed exploits have become almost as legendary as those of James Bond, the achievements of Hector Bywater have, until now, remained rather obscure. This beautifully constructed, thoroughly researched and highly readable book makes the tale of his life accessible to a general readership for the first time. Along the way, it offers to such a readership an illuminating introduction to the history of naval armaments and geopolitics in the first half of the 20th century. Finally, at a time when Japan is acquiring a renewed prominence in world affairs and the Cold War has ended, this book makes Japan, instead of the Soviet Union, the subject of a great spy story.[95]

William Honan had been interested in the Pacific War for 26 years before, in 1967, in a small used book store in Greenwich village, he chanced upon a volume first published in 1925, entitled *The Great Pacific War: A History of the American-Japanese Campaign of 1931-33*, by one Hector C. Bywater. It was with astonishment that he discovered in this book, written sixteen years before the attack on Pearl Harbor, a remarkably accurate and detailed prediction of both the Japanese strategies of 1941-42 and the American counter-strategies in the Pacific War between 1942 and 1945. When he ventured into the Library of Congress in 1970 and looked up Bywater's name in the card catalogue, he discovered to his surprise that there were several entries in Japanese. Bywater's books, it transpired, had been translated into Japanese more than a decade before Pearl Harbor and one translation had been prepared specifically for the Japanese Imperial Navy General Staff for the use of top naval officers. This revelation triggered years of research by Honan into Bywater's background and the fate of his work; the fruit of which is the present book.

Like many a 'genius'—for, arguably, in his chosen field, he was just that—Hector Charles Bywater was born and raised into circumstances which directed his native wit to a particular

---

94 This piece was first published on 18 April 1992 in *The Canberra Times*. It is a review of William H. Honan *Visions of Infamy: The Untold Story of How Journalist Hector C. Bywater Devised the Plans that Led to Pearl Harbor* (St Martin's Press, London, 1991).

95 There is an even bigger and better spy story yet to be told in full about Japan and the Soviet Union: the life of Richard Sorge, a Soviet military intelligence master spy who, based in Shanghai and then Tokyo throughout the 1930s and into the early 1940s, achieved a great deal for Moscow, before being unmasked by the Japanese, arrested and executed.

subject and discipline, almost as if the interest and aptitude were congenital. He was born in London, in 1884, on the 79th anniversary of the battle of Trafalgar. His father, Peter Bywater, was a Welsh wanderer and man of many parts, who travelled much before his sons were born and took them, afterwards, to live, at intervals, in the United States, Canada, West Africa and Germany. Living in Brooklyn, in his late teens, young Hector spent much of his free time in the Brooklyn navy yard and, at the age of nineteen, got himself a job working for James Gordon Bennett, publisher of the *New York Herald* and a man obsessed with the sea. Bennet so liked the young Bywater's work that, in less than a year, he made him the *Herald*'s European naval correspondent.

While working in Europe, Bywater became a spy in Germany for the British secret service, following a personal interview with Sir Mansfield Cumming, 'C', as the head of SIS is known. Being a fluent German speaker who could pass as a native, Bywater spent nine years (1909-1918) on and off in Germany, as Honan phrases it, 'picnicking at naval anchorages, sightseeing at the Kiel canal and asking questions of naval arms manufacturers'. His careers as naval journalist and secret agent complemented one another well. His published articles soon won praise from naval specialists in Britain and the US while, from as early as 1911, Sir John Fisher was writing to Winston Churchill boasting of Bywater as 'our splendid spy in Germany'. As many spies do, Bywater found the strain of a secret life and low pay deeply disillusioning. In a book called *Strange Intelligence*, published in 1931, he declared that 'none of the survivors would ever dream of taking up intelligence work again under any circumstances whatsoever.' Yet the link was never entirely broken and, in the last decade of his life, it again became significant; as he relentlessly explored the Pacific naval arms balance and the threat of war.

Bywater's fascination with the Pacific had, in fact, developed as early as 1920. By that time, he had become an established member of the Fleet Street Press Gang, who used to gather informally and whose byword was 'the three most beautiful things in the world are a fighting ship, a nubile woman and a fast racehorse—in that order'. Honan provides a marvellous account of the personalities in this group, not least its doyen, Frederick Jane, who had a major influence on Bywater until his death in 1916. It was this man, of course, who founded the now world famous annual *Jane's Fighting Ships*—the beginning of what has become a virtual industry in weapons information. The Press Gang were his disciples.

The balance of Honan's book is concerned with Bywater's work on the coming of the war in the Pacific. Anyone concerned with military geography and geopolitics, the history of naval weapons and strategy, the origins of World War II, espionage in world affairs, the relationship between journalism, intelligence and high politics or even the study of human personalities could not but find chapter after chapter both instructive and entertaining. The book does not lumber. It skims through the water at a rate of knots. And it closes with a splendidly nuanced reflection both on Admiral Isoroku Yamamoto's use of Bywater's ideas in his Pacific campaign[96] and the question of whether Yamamoto or the Japanese secret service, the Kempeitai, had the journalist murdered in London at the height of the blitz, because he knew too much and was better placed than anyone else to blow the whistle on what they were planning. Honan's book rounds off a deeply interesting and almost completely satisfying book.

---

96   The role of Isoroku Yamamoto in all this is fascinating and is one of the richest parts of Honan's story. I'm surprised that I did not make more of it in my 1992 review. That deficit cannot be remedied now other than by writing a wholly new piece. However, two paragraphs from Honan's Preface do much to summarize the influence of Bywater's ideas on Yamamoto's strategic perceptions and actions between the mid-1920s and his own death over Bougainville in 1943:

> *Until now, historians have believed that Yamamoto's war plan was conceived independently, or at least that it origins 'remain obscure', as the American military writer Ronald H. Spector recently observed in his authoritative* Eagle Against the Sun. *But today, half a century after Yamamoto unleashed Japanese forces in the Pacific, it can be shown that, while serving as naval attaché in Washington in the late 1920s, he reported to Tokyo about Bywater's war plan and then lectured on the subject, adopting Bywater's ideas as his own. Years later—long after it had become encoded in his mind—Yamamoto followed Bywater's plan so assiduously in both overall strategy and specific tactics at Pearl Harbor, Guam, the Philippines and even the Battle of Midway that it is no exaggeration to call Hector Bywater the man who 'invented' the Pacific war.*
>
> *One may ask why, if Yamamoto was so deeply influenced by Bywater's analysis, he was not deterred from attacking Pearl Harbor by Bywater's unwavering conviction that Japan would lose a war against the United States. The answer is paradoxical. Yamamoto wholly accepted Bywater's belief that Japan could hold out against the United States for only about a year and a half, and for that reason vigorously opposed the resort to war. Once he became convinced that war was inevitable, however, Yamamoto came to believe that carrying out Bywater's strategy would place Japan in the strongest possible position to press for favourable terms in a negotiated settlement.*

Charles De Gaulle and the grandeur of France[97]

Among this century's countless petty politicians, corrupt power mongers and megalomaniac tyrants, Charles De Gaulle stands out for his nobility, his sobriety and his sense of proportion. In episode after episode, from the end of World War II through the decolonisation of the French Empire and the rise of the new Europe, he emerges, through Lacouture's measured and polysemic narrative, as a quite extraordinary human being. And all his impressive statecraft is cast into relief by the exquisite moderation and sombre intelligence with which, having finally withdrawn from political office in 1969, he set about writing his memoirs of hope (*Memoires d'Éspoir*), at his unpretentious home, La Boisserie, in Colombey-les-Deux-Eglises.

More than any other single figure, Charles De Gaulle enabled France to overcome the chronic crisis of political authority that had plagued it since the vicissitudes of its famous revolution of 1789. No monarch was ever more august than the general when he told the crowd of politicians of the Fourth Republic, in the first hours of 1946, that in the reconstruction of the republic they must take into account 'the lessons of our political history of the last 50 years' and above all 'the absolute need for authority, dignity and responsibility in government.' Or when he prepared to withdraw from the parliamentary arena, telling Jules Moch 'I don't want to be attacked, criticised, challenged every day by men who have no other distinction than the fact that they got themselves elected in some little place in France.' Yet he was not a monarch and disdained the idea of the *coup d'état* or arbitrary rule. He was neither a demagogue nor an ideologue, but an individual of lucid vision and incorruptible principle, with a rare genius for leadership. He was one of those human beings about whom, when they die, people justly murmur, 'We shall not see his like again.'

For all the importance of the times in which he lived, and his role in them, with which Lacouture deals in ample manner, it is the person, the presence of the man that leaves the most lasting impression when one at last closes the covers of this book. Charles De Gaulle revelled in the storms of nature even as rode the storms of human affairs. Lacouture depicts him, in the winter of 1947, living in his austere house at Colombey, which did not then have central heating, flinging open the doors in the middle of a gale, to the astonishment of a visitor, and exclaiming triumphantly, 'Ah! Ils parlent de la douce France! Voila la douce France! Elle est

---

[97] This piece was first published in *The Canberra Times* on 25 April 1992. It was a review of Jean Lacouture's *De Gaulle: The Ruler 1945-1970*, the second volume of his monumental biography of the French general and statesman.

terrible, la France!'[98] The biographer comments, 'In winter, treading the snow and braving the squalls, he would roam through the Foret des Dhuits like a wolf at the time of Charles the Bold.' Yet he was no wolf. He read a great deal, loved television (when it came to France, at the end of the 1950s), loved Westerns and the James Bond films, was a fine father and a most tender grandfather.

De Gaulle is, perhaps, best remembered in popular culture on account of Frederick Forsyth's novel, made into an excellent film directed by Fred Zinnemann, *The Day of the Jackal*. The theme of these two pieces of entertainment is, of course, the attempts by the OAS (Organisation Armée Secrete) to assassinate De Gaulle in 1962-63. They tried to kill him because they believed he had betrayed the army and French Algerians by his settlement of the colonial war in Algeria in 1962. Lacouture covers the Algerian question and De Gaulle's problem with the OAS in one hundred pages of Part IV of this volume, including a detailed account of the 22 August 1962 Petit-Clamart assassination attempt by a dozen hit men led by Colonel Jean-Marie Bastien-Thiry. Having survived a hail of automatic rifle fire, De Gaulle remarked only, 'It was touch and go this time!' A little later, he called Georges Pompidou from La Boisserie and told him, 'My dear fellow, those men shot like pigs!' He had earned such violent execration because, as Lacouture sums it up, he had 'with fearless lucidity ... freed France of her colonies', being both as strategist and as statesmen, a conservative of movement, not of fixed positions.

The high point of De Gaulle's relationship with America was his rapport with President John F. Kennedy. When JFK had just taken office, Jacques Chaban-Delmart, President of the National Assembly, went to Washington. De Gaulle instructed him to 'tell that young man ... not to get caught up in the Vietnam affair. The United States could lose not only its forces, but also its soul.' When the Kennedys visited Paris, in May 1961, De Gaulle was, of course, both dazzled and charmed by Jacqueline. Lacouture records the droll anecdote that, when asked by Jackie Kennedy which of the famous men he had encountered had had the greatest sense of humour, De Gaulle responded, 'Stalin, Madame.' When JFK was assassinated, the French statesman paid him a tribute which Lacouture tells us was 'without precedent and one that was never repeated.' He declared to his Council of Ministers, 'John Fitzgerald Kennedy has been assassinated. He was one of the very few leaders of whom it may be said that they are statesmen. He had courage and he loved his country.'

Nothing moved me more in this volume than the final two chapters: 'The Master of La Boisserie' and 'Without Music or Fanfare'. Shattered by the anarchic upheaval of May 1968, which had almost brought his Fifth Republic undone, De Gaulle retired, in July 1969, aged 79, to

---

98 'Ah! They speak of sweet France! Behold that sweet France! She is terrible, our France!'

live out his days in peace. Lacouture remarks, 'The suffering of the sovereign was the happiness of the writer. In eighteen months, a life was thus reinvented and turned back to its source: words. Now familiar with death, he abandoned himself meanwhile to the sweet demon of writing.' He did not live to complete his *Memoirs of Hope*, but the first volume was published before he died and was greeted with immediate and overwhelming acclaim. He was hard at work on his second volume, a series of imaginary dialogues on his foreign policy with great figures from France's past, from Clovis to Clemenceau. 'Time spurred him on,' Lacouture writes, 'Death lay hidden in the half darkness.' In the autumn of his eightieth year, the old man poured his memories into the mould of these dialogues, seated in the refuge of his study, looking out three windows across the valley of the Aube to the forests of Les Dhuits. And in the midst of this last labour of love and lucidity he died, on 9 November 1970.

This is an immense biography and how many people will have the stamina or the appetite to work their way through it all? The French original is longer: three volumes to the English translation's two abridged tomes totalling 1255 pages. Those many whose reading consists of ephemeral fiction or popular magazines will never attempt to read such a work as this. Yet even more serious people will find its scale and subject matter a bit daunting, I suspect. And how will university students be prevailed upon to read it, when few read in depth anymore and when recommended reading lists tend to be crowded with endless journal articles and books of the second or even third rank? It is, however, one of those monumental pieces of political biography which is something of an education in the nature of world affairs and public life. It is the kind of work which offers much to those more concerned with the enduring realities and challenges of human affairs than with the clutter and fuss of academicism. It is, in short, the sort of work that should be read, in all it bulk, but which for the most part, is likely to be used as little more than a reference work on details of the career of the half-forgotten French politician called Charles De Gaulle.

J. R. R. Tolkien's works at the centenary of his birth[99]

Once upon a time, when I was a young student, I asked the great scholar of English and Comparative Literature, George Steiner, in a letter about Virgil, Wittgenstein and reading, what he made of the phenomenon of J. R. R. Tolkien's *The Lord of the Rings*. The eminent man wrote back a generous letter, recommending readings from the dialogues of Plato, the letters of Van Gogh and the Sibylline writings of Martin Heidegger, but dismissing *The Lord of the Rings* as 'portentous fairy floss'. It had been the book of my childhood and youth—indeed, nothing in my primary schooling had made a deeper impression—and this contemptuous reaction by a man whose own writings on language, meaning and culture I had read avidly, jolted me. On mature reflection, I believe George Steiner had read too many serious and profound books to appreciate the uses of enchantment and the wonder that can be created in a more innocent mind by the imaginative vistas, the sense of language, of being and time that make *The Lord of the Rings* a unique work of fantastical fiction.

In many conversations over the years, asking and listening, I have sought to glean from different lovers of *The Lord of the Rings* what made the tale so satisfying. There are many appreciations of it and, of course, they vary greatly in thoughtfulness. Some are completely superficial, delighting only in the escapist fantasy of elves, goblins, heroes and magic rings. Others are absorbed by the romantic medievalism of Tolkien's world, what might be called the 'St George for England' colouration of the War of the Ring. The more sophisticated find echoes of Wagner and the Ring of the Nibelungs, or of Milton's *Paradise Lost*. Yet others are captivated by the suspense and drama of the Ring-bearer's quest. I call this the 'Thirty-Nine Steps' view of the tale. Readers of the tale who speak with appreciation of Tolkien's evocation of the deeps of time, the ancientness of kingdoms and languages; and the denseness of being in artefacts, dwellings,

---

99 This piece was first published in *The Age* on 25 April 1992. It was a review of Tolkien's achievement on the centenary of his birth and specifically of a pile of Tolkien books published that year by Harper Collins: a new edition of *The Lord of the Rings* illustrated by Alan Lee; *The War of the Ring: The History of Middle-earth Volume VIII*; *Sauron Defeated: The History of Middle-earth Volume IX*; *The Letters of J. R. R. Tolkien*; *The Complete Guide to Middle-earth: An A-Z Guide to the Names and Events in the Fantasy World of J. R. R. Tolkien from The Hobbit to The Silmarillion*; and *The Tolkien Family Album*. The second and third of these were two of the twelve volumes in Christopher Tolkien's remarkable account of how his father's masterpiece had evolved over several decades. They are a very rich study in literary composition and a priceless resource for anyone wanting to understand how *The Lord of the Rings* was written.

forests, rivers and mountains are the ones with whom I feel the greatest rapport.

I am a radical reader of *The Lord of the Rings*. At the risk of incurring snorts of scorn from those whose opinion of the book is closer to that of George Steiner than to my own, I would go so far as to say that, in this age of fractured disciplines, religious confusion and global ecological crisis, this book is one of the few that should be offered to children—indeed to all those *childlike* enough to immerse themselves in its deeply serious playfulness—as an indirect 'guide of the perplexed'.[100] It is my belief that Tolkien achieved, perhaps beyond his conscious intent, with this work of highly idiosyncratic fantasy, something close to the critique of modern 'realism' and return to the ground of Being that his close contemporary Martin Heidegger attempted, notably in his unfinished trilogy *Being and Time* (1927).

No other work of fantasy that I am aware of has this remarkable depth. And while I am modern 'realist' enough to prefer the professional study of international politics to being 'off with the fairies', there is no doubt in my mind that reading Tolkien (after initially having his tales read to me) when still young, prepared me as nothing else did, for an appreciation of language, time, poetry, phenomenology and my religious heritage in adult life. The young fifth grade teacher who introduced me to *The Lord of the Rings* in 1967 has my undying gratitude for these reasons.[101] The new, richly illustrated edition of *The Lord of the Rings* is surely the most aesthetically appealing presentation of the text since its creation in the early 1950s. Alan Lee's fifty illustrations capture engagingly many of the different moods and inventive movements in the tale.

The eighth and ninth volumes of Christopher Tolkien's account of the coming to life of his father's fabulous literary progeny will be engaging to a different set of minds and eyes, I imagine, than the addition to the master work of half a hundred coloured pictures. While I rather enjoy the latter, especially sharing them with the Tolkien lovers and little people in my

---

100 *The Guide of the Perplexed* was a three volume treatise on truth, meaning and ethics written in the 12th century, in Cairo, by the great Jewish sage Moses Maimonides. For a contemporary guide to Maimonides, see Moshe Halbertal *Maimonides: Life and Thought* (Princeton University Press, 2014).

101 Her name was Kathleen Gill, later Kathleen Rose. Five years after this review piece was published, she came to the funeral mass for my father, in the winter of 1997 and waited for me at the door of the parish church. I asked whether she had seen this piece in *The Age* and she exclaimed: 'Oh, I certainly did! I cut it out and ran around saying to my family and friends, 'Look at this! Look at this!'' That was a wonderful moment. I stayed in touch with her after that, beginning with a dinner invitation to my family's home, at which I served up a large plate of mushrooms. She at once recognized and laughed at the allusion to the passion for mushrooms shown by all hobbits. In 2009, I invited her to the launch of my book *The West in a Nutshell*, at the University of Melbourne, and repeated for the whole crowd gathered there what I had written in 1992. Kath bought an armful of copies of the book and, I trust, gave them to family and friends on the same basis that she had shared this review piece seventeen years before.

own family,[102] I personally find myself fascinated by Christopher Tolkien's exploration of his father's studio and the emergence of characters and plot lines in *The Lord of the Rings*, a tale which 'grew in the telling, until it became a history of the Great War of the Ring and included many glimpses of the yet more ancient history which preceded it', as the famous opening lines of J. R. R. Tolkien's Foreword to the tale relate.[103] Even more diverting are the *Letters of J. R. R. Tolkien*, collected and edited by Christopher Tolkien and Humphrey Carpenter. Uniquely, these letters allow us insights into how Tolkien regarded his own work and its place in his life.

Those who have an insatiable appetite for the *detail* of Tolkien's work, as against an appreciation of its *meaning*, may feel compelled to collect Robert Foster's *Complete Guide to Middle-earth*. I confess that I start to incline more towards the impatience of George Steiner at this point and feel that there are certainly numerous books and subjects which have a greater claim on our attention in detail than this sort of exhaustive taxonomy of fairy creatures. *The*

---

102   A few years after this piece was written, I had the privilege to read both *The Hobbit* and *The Lord of the Rings* to two young nephews, Damian and Christopher Barnett, just six and eight years of age when we started. They delighted in *The Hobbit*, but when they heard about 'the Necromancer' and I informed them that this was a very dark and powerful figure who played a much larger role in a far bigger story by Tolkien, they immediately wanted to know what that story was and whether I would also read it to them. Doing so was a wonderful experience, as both boys were highly intelligent and became passionately absorbed in the long story. It was quite a profound privilege to be able thus to share with a new generation something which had meant so much to me when I was young myself. When we reached the end of *The Lord of the Rings*, I remarked to them, 'Well, this is going to be a hard act to follow! What do we read next?' The older of the two boys, his eyes shining, declared unequivocally, 'We'll go straight back to the beginning and start again!' And so we did, completing a second reading perhaps a year later.

103   This interest grew deeper in the years that followed. I was intrigued by the way in which Tolkien had, as it were, discovered Middle-earth and its peoples, lands and histories as he went, rather than having plotted all these things out in detail before beginning his story. He had been making up stories of various kinds, as well as dabbling in 'legends of the Elder Days' and working on creating a genuine 'Elvish language' for many years before he began to write *The Lord of the Rings* and yet, when he did begin, in about 1938, he had no pre-vision of the novel becoming a grand creative synthesis of all these interests and lucubrations, or swelling into a large scale epic. It was to be sixteen years before the book was completed and then published. The year after its appearance in print, Tolkien wrote to the poet W. H. Auden, concerning the journey of discovery that writing the book had been:

> *I met a lot of things on the way that astonished me. Tom Bombadil I knew already; but I had never been to Bree. Strider sitting in a corner at the inn was a shock, and I had no more idea who he was than had Frodo. The Mines of Moria had been a mere name; and of Lothlorien no word had reached my mortal ears till I came there. Far away I knew there were the Horselords on the confines of an ancient Kingdom of Men, but Fangorn Forest was an unforeseen adventure. I had never heard of the House of Eorl nor of the Stewards of Gondor. Most disquieting of all, Saruman had never been revealed to me and I was as mystified as Frodo at Gandalf's failure to appear on September 22.*

Tolkien Family Album, conversely, is a slender and attractive companion to the volume of letters and worth adding to the Tolkien corner of the library in one's personal Bag End.

That I should incline towards the impatience of George Steiner with regard to Robert Foster's book is because I believe that the tonic effect of a childlike reading of *The Lord of the Rings* ought be a release of the adult mind to re-enter the real world with a refreshed and enlivened sense of all those dimensions of existence (*Dasein*)[104] that make being human peculiarly rich, terrifying and uncanny. Foster's sort of book takes one off in a quite different, basically frivolous and trivialising direction. As a writer, as a teacher, as an uncle, I would prefer to see *The Lord of the Rings* as a foundation on which a child or student might begin to build an appreciation of song and poetry; of the abysms of history underlying current startling, ill-understood realities; of the needs, within the realm of Being, for gathering and preservation, memory and the music of mnemonic forms; of the wonder of speech within the natural world; and of the melancholy and dignity inherent in mortality, ruin and moral consciousness.

Nor should Tolkien's paeans to simple, bucolic pleasures—the savouring of mushrooms, cold beer, hot baths, tobacco, long walks—be omitted from the list. 'Learn now the lore of living creatures', the ancient of days Treebeard sang to the hobbits, Merry and Pippin, who had strayed into his neck of the woods. Treebeard was an 'Ent', a name highly suggestive of the ancient Greek *onta*, Latin *enta* (beings) and thus with that concern with the Being of beings which Aristotle long ago identified as the deepest perplexity confronting the human mind. Treebeard's *Entness* embodies Tolkien's ontology and never more so than in his saying to the hobbits:

> *Elves began it, of course, waking trees up and teaching them to speak and learning their tree talk. They always wished to talk to everything, the old Elves did ...*

And, in a passage with powerful resonance now, even more than when it was penned, some forty years ago, Treebeard adds:

---

104 *Dasein* is Heidegger's term for conscious being. It translates literally as 'Being there', which curiously became the title of Peter Sellers' last film, *Being There*. Dasein is distinguished by moods, dispositions, and embeddedness in a world of things and artefacts which are all prior to any abstract thought on its part and condition its way of conceiving possibilities, taking actions or pondering the nature of its own existence. Any child is, in these respects, *Dasein*, in that it finds itself in a world full of states, objects and artefacts that it did not bring into being and with regard to which its own consciousness is shaped. The beauty of *The Lord of the Rings*, it has long seemed to me, is that in creating a whole other world, it provides the child an opportunity to experience what Heidegger might have called 'worldedness' abstracted from the immediate realities and demands of the 'actual' world and then to re-enter the latter with a fresh sense of what is possible, desirable, imaginable or ominous about being alive in a complex world at all.

> *Aye, aye, there was all one wood, once upon a time ... Those were the broad days! Time was when I could walk and sing all day and hear no more than the echo of my own voice in the hollow hills. The woods were like the woods of Lothlorien, only younger, thicker, stronger. And the smell of the air! I used to spend a week just breathing.*

Tell a child after this of the rainforests and the atmosphere.

Certainly there will be those (especially the politically and ideologically 'correct') who will scoff at or object to the 'reactionary', as well as 'merely' fanciful character of Tolkien's imaginative creation. Others (Steiner, I think, among them) find the 'eucatastrophic' (or happy ending) nature of *The Lord of the Rings* fatuous, in the world of stark tragedy and black absurdity that they take ours to be (not without reason). It is precisely the book's capacity to liberate young minds from the strictures of such various 'realisms' and open them to other hopes and possibilities that commends it to me. Learn those crafts and sciences necessary to a mastery (in fragmentary part) of the contemporary world (as human beings are making it), one might tell the young reader of Tolkien; but after reading the fable, perhaps you may see some point in integrating Homer and Thucydides, Dante and Chaucer, Milton and Shakespeare, Dickens and Melville—and Hegel, Husserl and Heidegger, if you are especially curious and mentally tough—into your life as *Homo faber*.[105]

---

[105] This piece, of course, was written a decade or so before Peter Jackson made his epic film trilogy of *The Lord of the Rings*, which evidently brought the story to the attention of millions of children and adolescents who had never actually read the book. The films, of course, grossly simplify and pare down the story, eliminating almost all its poetry and attempting to substitute for the language often beautifully conceived and executed cinematography. In many ways, they were a triumph of cinematic art, but they are no substitute for reading the original book on which they were based. The musical sound track, on the other hand, was an enhancement that had real beauty and value, not least the contributions by James Galway and Renee Fleming. Christopher Tolkien, who had lived inside his father's creation of the story from the beginning and had carefully edited his father's manuscripts in the 1970s and 1980s, was scathing in his judgment that the film-makers had 'gutted the book to make an action film for fifteen to twenty five year olds'. Yet it seems clear that those involved in making the film, including the actors right down to extras, did so not simply for Hollywood money, but because they loved *The Lord of the Rings*; and the elaborate design that went into the sets, the costumes and the re-enactment of many of the most famous scenes from the book surely show this love, whatever the other solecisms and even travesties.

International economic competition before China's rise[106]

It is sometimes alleged, by those who find economics impenetrable or frustrating, that economists hide behind algebraic hedges and cannot write about social problems and political challenges in plain English. Lester Thurow certainly makes nonsense of this allegation. His writing is crisp and clear, his arguments forceful and compelling. He provides keener insights into the inner logic of what is happening in the world around us than have a host of supply-siders, monetarists and their socialist critics over the past decade or more. He offers fair and rational proposals for tackling vexing problems of the present and outlines plausibly the shape of alternative tomorrows. If you read only one book on economic realities between now and Christmas—whether you are a student, a bureaucrat, a businessperson, a unionist, a white collar professional—this book has a strong claim for being that one book. Never mind that Australia rates only a passing mention. The problems with which Thurow is concerned concern all of us and the solutions he offers for America's problems speak also to ours.

If *Head to Head* has a single overriding theme, it is summed up in Thurow's declaration, towards the end of the book:

> In today's world economy, where American firms must match up against the business groups of Germany and Japan, American firms need to be able to form the same strategic alliances, the same self-help societies and the same joint strategies for conquering world markets. They must have an equal arsenal of weapons. To give them the necessary weapons, America's laws and regulations must be drastically overhauled.

Can they be? Certainly, he answers. Will they be? Not under the pernicious style of leadership that has become endemic in the United States, was epitomised by Ronald Reagan and is embodied in George H. W. Bush, he argues.

'Presidential elections have become contests,' he says, 'to see who can most successfully deny that America has any problems.' The problems, however, are real, deep and rooted in much that Americans have done and taken for granted for generations. 'History,' he warns rather ominously, 'is littered with the wrecks of countries whose mythologies were more important than reality.' Cutting across much of the rhetoric of the 1970s and 1980s, Thurow rejects the claims of the Thatcher and Reagan prescriptions—less government, lower taxes,

---

106 This piece was originally published in *The Age* on 13 June 1992 and is a review of Lester C. Thurow's *Head to Head: The Coming Economic Battle Among Japan, Europe and America* (William Morrow & Co., New York, 1992).

unfettered individual entrepreneurial capitalism—and points out that neither the Thatcher nor the Reagan experiment worked, whereas the German and Japanese economies, based on very different prescriptions, have been extraordinarily successful and would necessarily set the economic rules for the next generation or more.

As Thurow remarks, 'Japan and Germany, the countries that are outperforming America in international trade, do not have less government or more motivated individuals. They are countries noted for their careful organisation of teams—teams that involve workers and managers, teams that involve suppliers and customers, teams that involve business and government.' His discussion of all this, which is unusually lucid, will be of interest to all those Australians currently trying to discriminate between Fight Back and One Nation, between John Hewson and Paul Keating, as answers to this country's economic difficulties and social problems.

Much of Australia's current trade policy and foreign policy is guided by the thinking set out in the Garnaut report of 1989, *Australia and the Northeast Asian Ascendancy*, which has just been updated as *Australia and Northeast Asia in the 1990s: Accelerating Change*, produced by the East Asia Analytical Unit, in the Department of Foreign Affairs and Trade.[107] Reading Lester Thurow's *Head to Head* is a useful foil to reading these two basic guides to the Australian government's thinking on where this country is, and should be, heading. Thurow's view is, of course, an American one, but the fundamental point he makes is one Colin White made recently, with reference to Australia's casting in its economic lot with Asia.

The world is now tripolar, Thurow observes, with three huge economic hubs—the US, Japan and the European Community—dominating world production and trade. Moreover, he suggests, the 21st century is not likely to see this situation change markedly. Which of the big three, however, will most shape the rules of the international economic order in the coming century? Perhaps the US still, if it can undertake a major overhaul of its economic infrastructure and ideology; perhaps Japan, if it can overcome its serious cultural and political handicaps; but most likely the House of Europe, if it succeeds in bringing off the full integration of the EC, then draws central and Eastern Europe—including Russia—into what would become the world's largest, most affluent, most resource rich, best-educated market in the world.

---

107 When I wrote this piece, I had quite recently been appointed Japan and Koreas Desk Officer within the Defence Intelligence Organization. It was in that capacity, over the following twelve months or so, that I began to grapple as closely as I could with arguments that the Japanese model, emulated by South Korea, was superseding the American model as a path to economic growth. Like a good many of the pieces I wrote in the early 1990s, this one skated close to the terrain of my professional responsibilities.

The prospects for Asia and Latin America, by comparison, he regards as far less promising and Africa's prospects as dismal in every way. It by no means follows, of course, that Australia should orient itself to Europe, or that it could do so if it tried; but the global perspective sketched out by Thurow is one all of us would do well to ponder as we attempt to create a dynamic future for this country. Ross Perot, perhaps on the verge of challenging George H. W. Bush and Bill Clinton for the White House, has declared that the most fundamental answer to America's economic and social malaise is 'Education, education, education.' Thurow has a good many other suggestions beside this, but his views on American education are trenchant and cogent. Here again, we in Australia have much to learn from what is wrong with America and how it might be remedied.

Allan Bloom's *The Closing of the American Mind* focused on the universities and argued, rather turgidly and cantankerously, that they had been undermined in the 1960s and needed a stiff does of Plato to put them back on the right track. Thurow is more concerned about the elementary and secondary schools and their abject failure to produce literate and numerate citizens, whether for the college and university system or for the blue collar workforce. Here, the Germans and Japanese, he points out, do a far better job and through very deliberate government policies, whereas in America schooling and its standards are taken in hand by nobody if not by local school boards. A country which has any aspiration to remain among the wealthy in the 21st century, he reminds us, simply has no choice but to make its educational system rigorous and exacting, schooling its young citizens in the sciences and languages indispensable for competition (never mind mastery) in a world of vast trading blocs and relentless innovation in products, processes and marketing.

The role of government in making this happen is vital. Thurow's virtue is to make this clear in the context of an overall picture of what is happening in the world: something Allan Bloom signally fails to do in his much-vaunted polemic against intellectual and educational decadence. Last but not least among the virtues of this little book is that Thurow demonstrates more simply and accessibly than, say, Michael Porter, in his *The Competitive Advantage of Nations*, the relationship between various intellectual disciplines in the contemporary world. Interdisciplinary perspectives are indispensable now, if one is to avoid becoming baffled, not only about what the world is coming to, but even about the meaning and purpose of one's own profession or trade. Reading a book like *Head to Head* should enable people in many different walks of life to see quite clearly where skills in mathematics, languages, economics, history, the physical sciences and so on intersect and interact. Thurow does not, to be sure, offer much in regard to the place of the arts in all this, although there are passing allusions to Brueghel and Shakespeare; but the scope of his argument is dramatic in itself and an intelligent reader will appreciate where human drama and existential anxieties underlie the inexorable economic trends and fine processes of reasoning that he lays before us.[108]

---

[108] It is very striking that Thurow totally failed to foresee the rise of China, especially on the scale and at the rapidity with which it has occurred. Nor did he foresee the ballooning of Japan's national debt and the stagnation of its economy. Nor again did he anticipate the problems that the EU has run into with both economic integration and political coordination, or the ongoing alienation of Russia from the EU. It is only fair to confess, of course, that I did not at the time foresee these things either; but then Thurow had just spent some years writing a book on the subject, whereas I had spent only a few hours reading and reviewing his book.

That said, these failures point to an important issue in social science: the failure of expert economic and political prediction—and the failure of experts to acknowledge their failures even when the evidence is in and very clear. The reality is that prediction is a hazardous business, in which our cognitive limitations, unexamined assumptions and failure to explore competing hypotheses again and again betray us. Currently, there is a widespread view that China's rise will continue and that the United States is in irreversible decline. As I pointed out in *Thunder from the Silent Zone: Rethinking China* (Scribe, Melbourne, 2005) we would be very foolish to settle for linear projections in such complex matters and need to think in terms of various different future scenarios, while preparing ourselves to be able to ride out any given one of them.

Section 3: 1992-93

Australia and the wars in Southeast Asia[109]

'I write not to entertain a passing multitude, as other historians do,' wrote Thucydides in the preamble to his ancient and immortal work *The History of the Peloponnesian War*. 'I seek rather to write something which will last forever and which I hope will be of use to those who come after me. For it is my opinion that human nature being what it is, the things I describe here are likely to happen again in the future and in much the same way.' This might be an appropriate motto for official historians.

Certainly, one might argue that official histories are not intended to entertain a passing multitude and plainly they are meant to last and to instruct those who come afterwards. Thucydides, however, was not an official historian and it seems fair to observe that official histories fall under the suspicion of being the preferred interpretation of history from the point of view of the state or the establishment, being written under its auspices for the express purpose of 'correcting' interpretations of the affairs of state advanced by those denied the privileged access to secret documents that an official historian is often granted.

This issue was raised by Wilbur Edel, in a recent article in the *Political Science Quarterly*, called 'Diplomatic History—State Department Style', with regard to censorship in the 1980s of United States diplomatic records, specifically the deletion of documents indicating the CIA's involvement in overthrowing the governments of Iran and Guatemala in the 1950s. This is not the place to dwell on these episodes. Edel's point is that such deletions from the record result in history which greatly misrepresents the aims and actions of governments in crisis situations. The consequence is, first, an uninformed public and, second, when the truth begins to emerge, fundamental distrust of the government by the public.[110]

The Vietnam War has been, since the late 1960s and especially since the leaking of the famous *Pentagon Papers* to the *New York Times*, in 1971, the single greatest source of

---

109 This piece first appeared in *The Australian* on 27 June 1992. It is a review of Peter Edwards and Gregory Pemberton's *Crises and Commitments: The Politics and Diplomacy of Australia's Involvement in Southeast Asian Conflicts 1948-1965* (Allen and Unwin and the Australian War Memorial, 1992).

110 Given that, in early 1989 and again in late 1989 and early 1990, I had been refused security clearances (first a Negative Vetting one and then a Positive Vetting one) on the grounds that I was too critical of the CIA and was deemed to be 'pro-Soviet, pro-Communist and pro-terrorist', writing about the CIA and Iran and Guatemala as openly as this only a couple of years later was, perhaps, a bold and even reckless thing to do. My open expression of analytical and independent views may well have contributed to my reputation for an independence of mind and a self-assertiveness which led to my being shut out of career opportunities in Canberra.

confusion, anger and polemic in regard to this fundamental issue of state authority and credibility. Histories of the Vietnam War and its antecedents are, therefore, of great political sensitivity and importance.[111] While this is pre-eminently true in the United States itself, it is true, also, in Australia. Our involvement in the Vietnam War, in its modest way, raised many of the same conflicts in Australian society and politics as had occurred in the United States. In *Crises and Commitments*, Peter Edwards faced the unenviable task of grappling with all of this, as the official historian of Australia's commitments in Vietnam and elsewhere in Southeast Asia. His account will not satisfy partisans on either the Left or the Right. Yet it has this merit, that in a debate scarred by a great deal of polemic, his writing never becomes heated.

---

111 My doctoral dissertation, completed in 1988 and under examination in 1989, as I began a constrained year of training as a graduate recruit in the Department of Defence, following initial denial of a Negative Vetting clearance, was titled *Civilization and the Typhoon: Land Reform and 'Irrational Revolution' in the Philippines, Vietnam and El Salvador, 1950-1984*. It entailed a systematic grappling with the Vietnam War as well as a bold attempt to place it in comparative and geopolitical perspective. None of this seemed to cut any ice with those in Defence who had either recruited me or opposed my being given a clearance to work in the Department.

Even the head of the recruitment team who had both offered me a job and gone into battle with Defence Security to ensure that I was given a Negative Vetting clearance said to me that I needed to forget the PhD and just get my feet under a bureaucratic desk for a couple of years, proving that I could deliver what the Department wanted form me. That the central thrust of the dissertation had been the cognitive deficiencies of the Pentagon and the US security establishment more generally in dealing with the challenges of the Cold War was not only not *appreciated* by any of these people; it led to my being excluded from work on the United States, on the basis that I was apparently 'unsound' in that regard. Yet the longer I remained within the Canberra bureaucracy the clearer it became that the same cognitive deficiencies were powerfully at work there, quite as much as in Washington DC; just on a provincial scale.

My conclusion in the fifth chapter of the dissertation, 'Confusion's Masterpiece: Vietnam 1955-75', was unequivocal. It was that:

> *The Saigon regime known throughout its brief history as the Government of Vietnam (GVN) or Republic of Vietnam (RVN), fell before the conquering Communist armies of the Hanoi regime, known as the Democratic Republic of Vietnam (DRV), in April 1975, because of congenital weaknesses which a generation of American aid and intervention had failed to remedy ... The disintegration of the GVN in 1975 ... was not that of a well-built nation betrayed and overwhelmed. It was that of a colonially engendered rump government that had never demonstrated a capacity to command its own destiny.*

Slowly, in the years since, I have rethought some aspects of that judgment and I owe a considerable amount to those patient and tenacious historians who have combed through the voluminous and painful materials to re-examine the final stages of the war. See especially Lewis Sorley *A Better War: The Unexamined Victories and Final Tragedy of America's Last Years in Vietnam* (Harcourt, Brace and Co., New York, 1999).

He regards with a certain wry detachment the strident positions adopted throughout the 1950s and early 1960s by both the Communist *Tribune* and the Right-wing Catholic *News Weekly* and he records statements by public figures which, in some instances, are likely to embarrass them. It is rather hilarious, for example, to discover then Senator John Gorton declaring, in October 1953, that, should South Vietnam fall to the Communists, 'India, especially, would be isolated.' There is no indication as to what precisely he believed India would be isolated from. Nor did he appear to appreciate that the Indian authorities themselves did not view the French struggle to recolonize Indochina in this light.

The central argument advanced by Edwards is that the Australian government's decisions over what to do in regard to successive crises in Indonesia, Malaya and Vietnam, were fatefully entwined. The Labour Party, he argues, was right about Indonesia, but got Malaya wrong because it looked at it through the lens of the Indonesia case. The Liberal Country Party coalition was right, he goes on, about Malaya, but then got Vietnam wrong, because it looked at Vietnam through the lens of its Malaya experience. The argument is detailed, nuanced and immensely informative. The perspective is judicious and one which certainly should enlighten those seeking a clear account of Australian interventions in Southeast Asia in the post-Second World War era.

The historiography of the Vietnam War, however, is enormously complex, as well as contentious; and there are areas where critics might justly claim that Dr Edwards has shed insufficient light on crucial matters. In this brief space, I would nominate three such areas: the acutely sensitive matter of covert operations and intelligence agencies; the circumstances surrounding the Gulf of Tonkin incident—which provided the pretext for Washington's escalation of the war in 1964-65—and the controversial South Vietnamese 'request' for Australian troops, in April 1965. Should an official history candidly discuss the role of intelligence agencies in a government's foreign policy and overseas operations? There are those who have an unappeasable appetite for such revelations. Others insist that such matters should never be disclosed, since they are too delicate - especially in regard to 'sources and methods' - to suffer exposure without damage to the 'national interest.'

Still, it seems rather coy, even in an official history, to avoid so much as naming the Australian Secret Intelligence Service (ASIS), when its name has long since been used both in Parliament and in the press.[112] Treatment of the activities of such bodies in an official

---

112 This is plainly still the approach taken by the Australian government to certain categories of document regarding our relations with Indonesia and to evidence regarding Soviet intelligence operations in Australia during the Cold War, including penetration of ASIO (the Australian Security Intelligence Organization) by the KGB and perhaps the GRU (Soviet military

history ought to be such as to moderate suspicions and correct misapprehensions, where necessary by openly discussing questionable operations.

More serious is the treatment of the Gulf of Tonkin episode. Dr Edwards's language in this case obscures the fact that the incident consisted of a North Vietnamese response to South Vietnamese covert operations coordinated and supported by American military forces operating off the coast.[113] So crucial an episode, productive of such controversy ever since the late 1960s, warrants both scrupulous and exhaustive treatment, drawing upon all accessible Australian and US documents. The account in this official history draws upon no US sources; cites no informant interviews and makes reference to only two primary sources form the Australian archives. This is surely inadequate and unsatisfactory.

Finally, Dr Edwards softens and blurs somewhat the fact that the South Vietnamese government, in early 1965, did not request Australian troops, but acceded, rather, to Australian pressure to accept an offer of such troops. It was Canberra, not Saigon, that wanted to put Australian troops in the field. To evade this fundamental point does no service to candid and dispassionate debate on the causes and consequences of the Vietnam War for

---

intelligence). A report was prepared for the Prime Minister, Paul Keating, in the early 1990s (I was still in DIO at the time, but was entirely oblivious to this report being prepared or of the reason for it) on this sensitive subject, by Michael Cook. The Cook Report is said to have concluded that ASIO had, indeed, been penetrated by the Russians, at least in the 1970s and 1980s. The existence of the report was itself a closely guarded secret for many years, until I learned of it and wrote it up for *The Australian* in 2010, challenging the then newly appointed Minister for Defence, John Faulkner, to acknowledge its existence and release it.

I named and even quoted Paul Keating, his attorney general Michael Lavarch and Michael Cook in the piece. The silence in response to it was deafening. In subsequent conversations, however, I was able to confirm its existence and was unable to induce any senior figure to deny that it had concluded that ASIO had been penetrated by 'at least four Soviet moles' in the course of the Cold War. I gave a paper at the Attorney General's conference on intelligence and security the following year and, before a large audience of intelligence and security professionals, again argued for the release of the Cook Report, stating its reported findings. No-one debated the matter with me. The report has still not, as of this writing, however, been released. *The Australian's* veteran intelligence and security affairs reporter, Cameron Stewart, however, is pushing hard to get access to it.

113   The most detailed and trenchant account of the Gulf of Tonkin incident of which I am aware is that by Daniel Ellsberg in *Secrets: A Memoir of Vietnam and the Pentagon Papers* (Viking, New York and London, 2002). He was working in the Pentagon on 4 August 1964 when the incident occurred and had direct access to the classified cable traffic about it. He followed developments minutely and was dismayed when, by his account, President Lyndon Johnson and Secretary of Defence Robert S. McNamara lied about what had occurred first to the press and then to Congress, in order to shepherd through Congress a war powers resolution that would free Johnson to unleash greater American force on North Vietnam.

Australia. It is not that Edwards denies or misrepresent the truth, only that he does not address it directly and frankly. A truly strong and sound official history would have done better. Yet, these three criticisms aside, this is a meritorious and thought-provoking work of official historical scholarship. It is both an enlightened and enlightening contribution to our collective historical memory and to the long process of putting the Vietnam War is perspective.

The last Tsar and the fate of his family[114]

There are two tales here, that of the life of Nicholas Romanov, last of the Tsars of the Russian Empire, and that of the deaths (or rumoured survival) of members of the imperial family. Both will be found instructive by those who have seen the film *Nicholas and Alexandra*[115] and wondered what the real story was behind the drama on the screen. Yet the first of these, it seems to me, is too spare to really seize the imagination. The immense vortex of Russia before the 1917 revolutions, with its rich and fateful mixture of aristocratic decadence, intellectual ferment, cultural brilliance, rapid industrialisation and mass misery, is far better recreated within W. Bruce Lincoln's *In War's Dark Shadow*.

As for the conundrum of the ends that the imperial family met, the recent Koryakova forensic investigation purports to have demonstrated once and for all that all members of the family were, indeed, executed by the revolutionaries in the Ipatiev House, at Ekaterinburg, on the night of 16-17 July 1918, as 'orthodox' history has long maintained. Doesn't this mean that Professor Ferro's speculations are superfluous? Not quite. And the nature of the argument is actually rather fascinating. In this brief review I hope that I may be forgiven, therefore, if I dwell on it, rather than on the tale of the Tsar's life.

In one of the memorable moments in David Lean's classic film of *Doctor Zhivago*, Zhivago's father-in-law is handed a newspaper by his manservant and slumps when he discovers, as he announces to Yury and Tonya, that: 'They've shot the Tsar and all his family ... Oh, that's a savage deed! What's it for?' And Yury answers: 'It's to show there's no going back.' Ferro heads the final chapter of his book 'An Event—or an Item for News in Brief: An Enigmatic Death'

---

114 This piece first appeared in *The Age* on 11 July 1992 and was a review of Marc Ferro's *Nicholas II: The Last of the Tsars* (Viking, 1991). It was by no means the last word on the subject. In 2003, Greg King and Penny Wilson's *The Fate of the Romanovs* (John Wiley & Sons) went over the ground yet again. Peter Kurth, who had been preoccupied with the matter for twenty years or more by then, wrote a Foreword to it, in which he wrote that the whole subject is 'a quagmire and a minefield and ... has never been otherwise.' He concluded with the words, 'I am indeed a 'nut' on this story and am confident in predicting that many of you will be, too, when you discover what follows.' What the King and Wilson book shows is that debate over the fate of the Romanovs was far more intense and complex in 1992-93 than I had realized when writing this review. The matter was intensely politicised and powerful forces within Russia were determined to confirm the Sokolov verdict, regardless of the evidence. For this reason, the 2003 book is even more intriguing than the 1992 one.

115 The film, released in 1971, was directed by Franklin Schaffner and starred Michael Jayston as Nicholas, Janet Suzman as the Czarina Alexandra; as well as Jack Hawkins, Michael Redgrave, Laurence Olivier and Ian Holm. I remember watching it at a cinema when still very young and being horrified by the scene of the execution of the royal family. The film left no suggestion that any of them had survived.

and makes clear that, whatever may have been printed in the newspaper which these characters read in the film, the truth was very blurred and uncertain in 1918-20 (when *Doctor Zhivago* is set) and became more, not less so, in the 1970s and 1980s, when research into long secret German, Spanish and Vatican archives added further pieces to the puzzle.

The parameters of the dispute are roughly these: When anti-Bolshevik forces retook Ekaterinburg, in 1918, they discovered evidence that the imperial family may have been executed in the city before it fell. They appointed one N. Sokolov to investigate the matter. His findings were eventually published in Paris, in 1924, under the title *Judicial Inquest into the Assassination of the Russian Imperial Family*. The tale he told was essentially that told in Nicholas and Alexandra: the whole family being executed in the Ipatiev House cellar by a Bolshevik firing squad. However, in 1975, two BBC journalists, Anthony Summers and Tom Mangold, as Ferro remarks, 'managed to get hold of the complete file of the investigation' and showed that Sokolov 'had systematically eliminated (from the published record) those documents that might support the thesis that the Tsar's wife and daughters (not just the mysterious Anastasia, but Maria, Tatiana and Olga, also) had survived.'

Their book, *The File on the Tsar*, was published in 1976. Then, in 1987, Nikolai Ross published the file in what Ferro describes as 'a very carefully produced publication', fully ten times the volume of the book Sokolov had published in 1924. Cross-examining all these works and adding further archival research of his own, Ferro advances the elements of a fascinating, but as he describes it 'unavowable' hypothesis: that the Tsar was shot, along with his son and servants, but that the Czarina (who was, of course, German) and her four daughters (or perhaps only three of them—minus Anastasia, who had been 'lost' *en route*) were smuggled out of the former Russian Empire, in October 1918, in exchange for the release of Karl Liebknecht and Leo Jogiches, German Left-wing leaders then languishing in the Kaiser's prisons; following secret negotiations between the Bolsheviks and the German government. Thereafter, he argues, it suited all parties to the matter to insist that the whole family was dead. Instead of being *buried* in secrecy, in other words, they buried in *secrecy* and lived out their lives in secluded exile. Indeed, he argues, the remnants of the imperial family themselves denied the survival of the Empress and her daughters—specifically repudiating, inter alia, Anna Anderson's claims to being Anastasia—treating the late Tsar's family more cruelly than the Bolsheviks themselves had done.[116]

---

116 King and Wilson concluded that longstanding doubts concerning how many of the Romanovs were killed at Ekaterinburg and which ones had not been resolved by numerous, often extremely technical genetic inquiries throughout the 1990s and up to 2001. No-one could read their book, I think, without accepting that the investigations within Russia were seriously flawed, the motives of key parties to the case deeply warped by prejudices, passions and political agendas and the evidence itself exceptionally

Is this completely fantastic? Marc Ferro is a serious historian and he plainly believes that there may be here a remarkable diplomatic secret hidden beneath all this. Moreover, he argues, reconfirmation of the old version by post-Communist inquiries in Russia looks suspiciously like a political tactic itself. We are faced, he writes, with a case in which the most important witnesses disappeared, executed or assassinated; contradictions in the evidence have been omitted from published records; there remains serious doubt as to who the alleged executioners actually were; and many archival sources remain sealed. 'Only a full confrontation of the Soviet archives with the relevant foreign archives could enable us to be more positive about what happened at Ekaterinburg than about Pope Joan. We can be certain that the British and the Danes could help in this matter, since they must possess information with a bearing on it; and that is also true of the Soviets.'

And suppose Ferro's suspicions were to be confirmed from the archives he mentions? Of what consequence would this be now? Or, in other words, why do historians and investigative journalists inquire into such arcane matters? Leaving aside considerations as to Russian and Soviet history, where the ramifications are considerable, it seems to me that such a discovery would be intrinsically fascinating—indeed, quite breathtaking—for what it would say about the intricacies of international diplomacy and the keeping of secrets among the powers-that-be for decades. The imagination is tantalised at the thought of this dark and clandestine drama and rather appalled to contemplate the fate of the Tsar's four daughters—spirited away from certain murder, only to be denied their very identities and all 'actual' existence for the terms of their natural lives. Perhaps, however, Sokolov was basically right, after all, as Ms Koryakova has affirmed? In that case, unhappily as it may seem, our imaginations must be told to close their eyes and go back to sleep, assured that their nightmarish fantasies have no foundation in reality. And there is our answer, of course, to the question as to why historians and journalists pursue these things: they doubt the word of those 'parental' authorities who would lull them to sleep.

---

difficult to evaluate. Yet if any of the Romanovs survived Ekaterinburg, what became of them and why has no credible evidence of their lives after July 1918 ever surfaced? And if it was not them who were killed there, whose were the grim remains?

Anti-Americanism and political rationality[117]

There is a story, famous among students of the Vietnam War, about how the Pentagon's Victor Krulak and the US State Department's Joseph Mendenhall, returning from flying field trips to South Vietnam, gave President Kennedy such divergent assessments of the situation and prospects there that JFK asked incredulously, 'The two of you did visit the same country, didn't you?' If one reads Paul Hollander's *Anti-Americanism: Critiques at Home and Abroad 1965-1990*, in tandem with, say, Noam Chomsky's *Deterring Democracy* (Verso, 1991), or *Necessary Illusions: Thought Control in Democratic Societies* (Pluto Press, 1989), one is apt to ask of the two authors the same question Kennedy put to Krulak and Mendenhall in September 1963. Hollander and Chomsky present such incompatible accounts of the intellectual, ideological and political condition of the United States that it is scarcely possible to believe that they were both writing about the same country.

Readers of Noam Chomsky's work, whether hostile, bemused or persuaded, will be aware that he insists, marshalling all sorts of evidence, that the powers that be in the United States—the major political parties, the big business organizations, the Pentagon, the CIA, the FBI, the major media, the universities—govern the country according to the well-understood and informally coordinated dictates of a quasi-totalitarian capitalist and imperialist scheme for domination at home and intervention at will abroad. If Chomsky is to be believed, dissent and democratic freedoms barely manage to survive in the United States and are kept going, under duress, by small bands of activists, like him.[118]

Paul Hollander, on the other hand, advances the view, marshalling all sorts of evidence, that the United States is overrun by dissent and pseudo-democratic activism, which has penetrated and demoralised, if not taken over, many of the same institutions Chomsky assails

---

117 This piece was first published in *The Age* on 19 September 1992. It was a review of Paul Hollander's *Anti-Americanism: Critiques at Home and Abroad 1965-1990*.

118 Hannah Arendt's *Crises of the Republic* (Harcourt, Brace, Jovanovich, New York and London, 1972) is well worth reading on the era in which Noam Chomsky first rose to prominence as a Left-wing critic of the United States. For a brilliant critique of the decadence of Leftism in our own time, see Bernard-Henri Levy *Left in Dark Times: A Stand Against the New Barbarism* (Random House, New York, 2008), which is a bracing call for a new political and moral vision. He rounds in anger and dismay on the dangerous attitudes that have come to characterise the Left since the end of the Cold War, if not earlier: an unthinking loathing of Israel, an obsessive ant-Americanism; an idea of 'tolerance' that, in its justification of Islamic fanaticism, for example, could become what he calls 'the cemetery of democracies'; and an indifference, masked by relativism, to the greatest human tragedies facing the world today. This book, far more than Hollander's or any book by Chomsky, deserves to be widely read and taken to heart in the 2010s. In fact, Chomsky is a particular target of Levy's in his book and for good reason.

as quasi-totalitarian instruments of the establishment—most notably the major media (for example, the *New York Times*), the universities, the churches, mainstream politics and even the business world. What judgment should be rendered by a reasonably informed person, or by an educator, on this divergence of critiques of the Great Republic? Is one or other to be announced the winner and awarded a prize for his withering expose? Should both, instead, be offered to the uniformed as 'equally valid' views of the condition of America?

In the marketplace of ideas, as against some putative body of state censorship, certainly both should be available to the uniformed, as to the better informed. However, no educator should or I think could—simply offer them as 'equally valid' views of the United States; nor should either be awarded a prize. Both are strained and overdrawn polemics, which lack sociological depth and rigour of argument. Noam Chomsky has often been criticised on these grounds. Paul Hollander seems to me rather vulnerable to the same kind of critical response. His basic argument is that, since the 1960s, what he calls an 'adversary culture' has developed in the United States.[119] This adversary culture, as he describes it, consists of a widespread, irrationally intense hatred of, or predisposition to exaggerate the defects of the US, in particular, and in a more diffuse sense the West in general.

He finds all this both puzzling and disturbing, because he does not see the irrational element as a lunatic fringe, but as some sort of bacillus that has infected American society and institutions on a large scale. The trouble is that he lumps all sorts of manifestations of discontent, rebelliousness, social decay and moral and political criticism together into his 'adversary culture'; fails to provide anything resembling a systematic analysis of how these different elements of the phenomenon arose within American society; and, worst of all, offers no prescription whatsoever for treating what he clearly regards as a serious social malaise. His style of writing is rather cumbersome and the fact that the published text, even coming from Oxford University Press, is littered with elementary typographical errors detracts further from the overall impression his book makes.

---

119 For a largely sympathetic account of the student rebellions of the 1960s, see David Caute *Sixty-Eight: The Year of the Barricades* (Hamish Hamilton, London, 1988). Ingmar Bergman (1918-2007), the great Swedish film-maker and theatre director, was one of those who were most unsympathetic to the radicalism of the 1960s, especially as a 'cultural revolution'. Looking back, in his first autobiography, *The Magic Lantern*, published in 1987, he wrote that the damage done in 1968, in a short time, to cultural life and moral seriousness in the West 'was both astonishing and hard to repair' (p. 199). He always created serious and meaningful theatre, not trite or politically correct entertainment. He plainly felt that '1968', far from opening society up to honest critique and 'liberation', had actually undermined ancient standards of seriousness and meaning. It is not clear that he was in error.

Methodologically, Hollander's greatest vice, I think, is that he seems to believe that a compendium of examples of various sorts of error or expressions of opinion by those with whom he disagrees is an argument in itself; and that more substantial analysis or social history is quite superfluous. The effect is, at times, merely tedious, but at other points it becomes rather irritating. He has, of course, no great difficulty in assembling numerous examples of tendentious, ill-considered, fatuous or downright mendacious statements by various sub-luminaries of the radical Left or liberal milksop schools of thought. After a while, however, without a searching argument as to why we need read most of this material, it is hard to avoid muttering, 'Okay, but so what?'

There is certainly no end of comparably asinine or deplorable statements that one might string together from the writings and utterances of radical Rightists of various stripes, pompous conservatives, religious fundamentalists and so forth. These, too, abound in America. One has the impression that what Hollander has pasted together is intended for a readership of 'converted' Reagan-era conservatives, all alike convinced that the 1960s were a decade of decadence and disaster and that the 1980s would have seen the rebirth of America, were it not for all these adversarial enemies of the Great Republic and Economic Progress[120]. If Hollander had wanted to re-examine the roots of rebellion against 'the affluent society' or the Vietnam War, in the 1960s, he could have done far better than he has. Todd Gitlin's *The Sixties: Years of Hope, Days of Rage* is certainly a better reflection on that decade than Hollander's offering.[121]

But more generally, Hollander places himself in the sociological tradition of Tocqueville, Toennies, Weber and Durkheim without bringing anything like their breadth of learning or depth of conceptualisation to his work. Frank Knopfelmacher recently remarked that Tocqueville's *Democracy in America* is still the best introduction to understanding the foibles and virtues of

---

120 For an attempt at a systematic critical assessment of American economic policies since the 1930s, see David Stockman *The Great Deformation: The Corruption of Capitalism in America* (Public Affairs, New York, 2013). Stockman is scathing in his criticism of the development, over eighty years of what he describes as crony capitalism, misplaced fiscal stimulus and financial bailouts at public expense. He targets the Federal Reserve above all, but not from a Left-wing point of view. Lawrence Lessig, in *Republic, Lost: How Money Corrupts Congress and How to Stop It* (Twelve, New York and Boston, 2011), approaches the problem from a different angle, but emphasises the ways in which corporate lobbyists and special interest groups have hijacked the legislative and electoral processes in recent decades to the detriment of the republic. Meanwhile, Joseph Joffe, in *The Myth of America's Decline: Politics, Economics and a Half Century of False Prophecies* (Liveright, W. W. Norton & Co., New York and London, 2014) argues that criticisms from right and left alike are overblown and that America's virtues will continue to see it prosper and lead the world in the 21st century.

121 Alan Barcan *Radical Students: The Old Left at Sydney University* (Melbourne University Press, 2002) offers an illuminating guide to the antecedents, in Australia, of the student rebellions of the 1960s.

American society, even though it describes the United States of Andrew Jackson, in the 1830s, not that of George H. W. Bush.[122] It would be deeply satisfying to come across a book on this subject which might tempt one to disagree with Dr Knopfelmacher, even if it did not have quite the scope of *Democracy in America*. For all the praise that has been lavished on it by the likes of Jeanne Kirkpatrick, Edward O. Wilson and Peter Berger, I do not think that Hollander's *Anti-Americanism* would even make the short-list of candidates in this regard.

---

122 Alexis de Tocqueville's *Democracy in America*, in two volumes, (Alfred A. Knopf, 1945) was first published in 1834, but it was reissued in 1848, on the heels of the revolutions in Europe which occurred at that time. In his 1848 preface, he struck a note which remains of relevance to this day regarding the establishment of republics and was, when he wrote it, the soundest of rejoinders to the radical rhetoric of the communists, including Karl Marx and Friedrich Engels. He wrote:

> *It is not force alone, but good laws that give stability to a government. After the combatant comes the legislator; the one has pulled down, the other builds up; each has his office. Though it is no longer a question of whether we shall have a monarchy or a republic in France, we are yet to learn whether we shall have a convulsed or a tranquil republic, whether it shall be regular or irregular, pacific or warlike, liberal or oppressive, a republic that menaces the sacred rights of property and family, or one that honours and protects them both.*

When Marx and Engels first published *The Communist Manifesto*, at the beginning of 1848, they famously declared that they intended to do away with both private property and the family. Tocqueville knew well of what he spoke. The 20th century saw enormous attempts in many countries to impose the Communist system, with dismal consequences.

A fatuous potboiler on war in Asia[123]

Things are at a delicate and fascinating stage in Hong Kong as of the beginning of 1993. So are they in Beijing and on the Korean peninsula. It is, perhaps, a good time to be writing fiction about East Asia towards 2000. Simon Winchester, a Hong Kong based journalist, has had a crack at it. He has the whole region going up in flames before decade's end, sparked by the efforts of the Hong Kong triads, with the backing of Whitehall, to bring down the Communist regime in China. With remarkable ease and even more remarkable phlegm, these parties succeed in triggering civil war in China. This, in turn, prompts an outbreak of war in Korea, as Kim Jong-Il decides to try to overwhelm the South.

The Japanese, having abrogated their Mutual Security Treaty with the United States, in June 1994, are depicted as sending troops into China just five years later, with the explicit purpose of doing 'properly' what they had failed to do in the 1930s and early 1940s. And then President Benson of the United States saves the world from catastrophe (Winchester's phrase, not mine) by sending warplanes from Whiteman (sic) Air Force Base, Missouri, to drop a 50 kiloton atomic bomb over Tokyo Bay, thus pulling the Japanese back into line.[124]

Yet, looking back on all this, in March 2000, Winchester's narrator observes:

> *Those who take the long view will say that ... what is happening today is no more than the latest in an endless procession of irruptions of violence that tell us much about the nature of the Oriental mind.*

The Oriental mind, indeed? One might, far more realistically, describe *Pacific Nightmare* as no more than the latest in a long procession of British novels about the virtues of the Empire and the cruelty and stupidity of its enemies, who, of course, inevitably end up stumbling to sorry debacles.

Perhaps it is the fag end of this genre? There are occasional passages in the book in which Winchester seems almost to be echoing the John Buchan of a century ago. Is his book intended

---

123 This piece was first published in *The Canberra Times* on 23 January 1993. It was a review of Simon Winchester's *Pacific Nightmare: A Third World War in the Far East* (Sidgwick and Jackson, 1992). I was, at the time of writing Japan and Koreas Desk Officer in the Defence Intelligence Organization and my responsibilities included looking for any signs of possible conflict on the Korean peninsula, revival of Japanese military ambitions or strains in the American security alliances with both Japan and South Korea.

124 The very idea of Japan, in the 1990s, with its shrunken and constitutionally restricted army and non-existent amphibious lift capabilities and with major US forces still stationed on its soil would or could suddenly launch an invasion of China was preposterous. That Winchester would have a democratic Japanese government launch such a war with the battle cries of the imperialist Japanese forces of the 1930s and early 1940s demonstrates a lack of understanding of Japanese history, Japanese politics and contemporary geopolitics alike that is astounding for a journalist working in East Asia.

as a parody? No. I think Mr Winchester takes himself very seriously. Unfortunately, this does not save him from presenting us with what, in many respects, is an unintentional parody—of Orientalism, of strategic analysis, of British pretensions and racism and of serious writing.

The Buchanesque style is nowhere more in evidence than in chapter two 'Distant Thunder'. Setting: the British Embassy, Washington DC, Tuesday 11 June 1996. Scene: 'the most celebrated diplomatic event of 1996, the annual official birthday in honour of Queen Elizabeth II.' We discover, at this point, that in the closing months of George H. W. Bush's 'eight year presidency'[125] the friendship between the White House and Downing Street had never been stronger ... [and] British diplomatic parties were ... back to being recognised as the best on the circuit.'

Meanwhile, in the non-English speaking world, things are, as ever, dark and inscrutable. China, for example, 'was currently enduring yet another phase of inexplicable barbarism.'[126] And strolling around at this premier diplomatic party is a man called Wilkinson, who has the air of an Edwardian spy, a sort of latter-day Sidney Reilly, perhaps, who 'seemed ... to be making his life a progress through jungles and villages and into parts of foreign cities that it would be imprudent for a foreign diplomat to visit.'[127]

---

125   Which in fact ended after only four years, in November 1992, some few months after *Pacific Nightmare* had gone to press. It may have seemed probable that Bush would be re-elected in 1992, having won the Gulf War so resoundingly, but with an election looming and his book about to go to press, Winchester made a bold call and got it completely wrong.

126   This is another strange error of judgment on Winchester's part, since it was precisely in 1992, as he was writing his book, that Deng Xiaoping eased up on the repression in China that had begun in June 1989, after the massacre and mass arrests centring on Tiananmen Square and undertook his famous Southern Tour, declaring that China would pursue economic reform and opening again, as it had before 1989. Was Winchester paying no attention? Deng's journey and announcements were in January and February of 1992, well before Winchester finished his book, so the prediction of 'inexplicable barbarism' erupting very soon afterwards itself looks all but inexplicable. On Deng Xiaoping see Ezra F. Vogel *Deng Xiaoping and the Transformation of China* (Belknap Press, Harvard University, 2011). Vogel is weak on Deng's complicity in human rights abuses from the Anti-Rightist Campaign of 1957 to the crushing of the Democracy Movement in the late 1980s, but the biography is a rich resource on his overall political career and his statecraft after the death of Mao Zedong.

127   Britain has been served by such spies in the past and not only Sidney Reilly. Fredrick Marshman Bailey is one of my favourite case studies in that kind of espionage heroics. He was a British intelligence officer a century ago and one of the last protagonists of the Great Game - the legendary struggle for supremacy between the Russians and the British Empire in Central Asia and along the Himalayas. He is described by Wade Davis, in the latter's superb book *Into the Silence: The Great War, Mallory and the Conquest of Everest* (Bodley Head, London, 2011) as having been a master of disguises, travelling at different times as a Buddhist priest, an Austrian soldier and an Armenian prisoner of war. He became such a headache in places like Tashkent and Samarkand to the nascent Bolshevik regime in 1918-19 that he lived with a Soviet bounty on his head for the rest of his days—and he lived until 1967. He was also a talented naturalist and photographer, a writer and a collector of butterflies.

Asked, rather ingenuously, by Hugh Rackham Charlesworth III, Assistant Secretary of States for East Asian and Pacific Affairs, what he thought the Chinese (sic) might do to Hong Kong the next year[128], the worldly Mr Wilkinson replies, in his best London English: 'Odd that you should ask. Well—not odd that you should ask, but odd that I should meet someone here who was interested. Yes, I do have an idea or two.' How odd that it should seem odd to the Hong Kong-based Winchester's worldly Englishman, at the British Embassy in Washington DC, in June 1996, that someone there (and what a 'someone'—being the Assistant Secretary of States for East Asian and Pacific Affairs) was interested in the fate of Hong Kong. Yet the tone is the thing. It is surely from a different era. It is itself quite odd.

It seems to me improbable that serious or politically literate Englishmen or Americans are likely to give *Pacific Nightmare* any attention. One can only wonder, however, at the possible reception of this atavistic potboiler in China, Japan or Korea. The last British governor of Hong Kong, Sir John Courtenay, is made to exclaim in his first appearance in the novel, 'What bloody, bloody fools these Chinks can be!'[129] Yet he is party to an MI6 operation to arm the triads against the Communist Party and to trigger plots in Guangdong that start a civil war.[130] Who are the bloody, bloody fools: the 'Chinks' or the Poms?

Even more strangely, Winchester has the plot succeed with astonishing ease. The uprising against Communism ends up being led by Cantonese rebels who invoke the Christian God against Communism and, in no time at all, have all of southern China and half the PLA fighting for them against the aged veterans of the Long March, whom Winchester depicts as ensconced, in fear and inertia, in Beijing. The Japanese are then depicted as leaping into China without consulting anyone else and with rhetoric explicitly invoking their imperialist transgressions of half a century before. Not only that, but their troop transports fly right over the Republic of Korea with not so much as a Korean jet fighter being scrambled. Tell us another one, Mr Winchester.

---

128 That is to say in 1997, when China was set to resume (and did resume) sovereignty over Hong Kong, with the expiry of the 99 year lease the British Crown had had on it since the time of the Boxer Rebellion in 1898.

129 The actual last British governor of Hong Kong, of course, was Chris Patten. He tried to protect Hong Kong from the Communist Party to the best of his ability, but I know of no evidence of him holding the Chinese in contempt as a race in the manner Winchester attributes to his fictional John Courtenay.

130 That the triads would have connived with the British against the Communist Party at the very point of the handover of Hong Kong to China and given the long history of relations between the triads and the Party was a very dubious notion on Winchester's part. That they would then have been able to make headway in China, as an armed rabble, against the coordinated forces of the Party's military and internal security forces defies all common sense.

George F. Kennan as an American elder statesman[131]

It is always a pleasure reading a book by George Frost Kennan. The man is deeply civilised and neither his thought nor his prose has lost its crispness as he approaches the age of 90.[132] It is rather extraordinary, in a way, to consider that this diplomat and diplomatic historian has lived through the entire course of the Cold War and, indeed, went on his first posting to Moscow, as young Foreign Service Officer, in 1933. Throughout the intervening sixty years he has not ceased to reflect on the challenges facing American civilization and on the enigmas and terrors of totalitarianism.

From 1947 to 1959, he was Director of the US State Department's Policy Planning Staff, a unit set up by General George Marshall to ponder the rising challenges of the Cold War. He was one of the architects of the policy of 'containment' of Stalinism. In 1952, he was himself sent to Stalin's USSR as ambassador. Since 1951, he has written eleven volumes of diplomatic history and reflections on foreign policy and three volumes of memoirs. In this little book, we have a distillation of his personal values and outlook at the end of a long and richly reflective life. It is one of those small books which might be put into the hands of a bright young student by a good teacher, as a stimulus to a life of inquiry and public service.

Mr Kennan is a Yankee from the old eastern seaboard of the United States; a classic WASP

---

131 This piece was first published in *The Canberra Times* on 29 May 1993 and was a review of George F. Kennan A*round the Cragged Hill: A Personal and Political Philosophy* (W.W. Norton & Co., 1993).

132 George Frost Kennan (1904–2005) was an American diplomat and historian, known as 'the father of containment' from the very beginning of the Cold War. He wrote historical works on relations between Soviet Union and the Western powers and became at one time one of the foreign policy elders known as 'The Wise Men'. In his 'Long Telegram' from Moscow in 1946 and the subsequent anonymous 1947 article under the pen-name 'X' in *Foreign Affairs*, titled 'The Sources of Soviet Conduct', Kennan argued that the Soviet regime was inherently expansionist and that its influence had to be 'contained' in areas of vital strategic importance to the United States. These texts quickly emerged as foundation texts of the Cold War, expressing the Truman administration's new anti-Soviet Union policy. Kennan also played a leading role in the development of definitive Cold War programs and institutions, notably the Marshall Plan.

Soon after his concepts had become U.S. policy, however, Kennan began to criticize the foreign policies that he had done so much to articulate and encourage. As early as the end of 1948, he was confident that positive dialogue could commence with the Soviet Union. His proposals were discounted by the Truman administration and his influence marginalized, particularly once Dean Acheson became secretary of state, in 1949. The Korean War began in mid-1950 and American strategy became increasingly geared to preparations for war with the Soviet Union. Kennan left the Department of State and became a leading critic of U.S. foreign policy. He continued to be a leading thinker in international affairs as a faculty member of the Institute for Advanced Study at Princeton University for half a century, until dying at the great age of 101 in 2005.

(White Anglo-Saxon Protestant) as he himself confesses. The touchstones for his understanding of the America he identifies with and whose fate concerns him are still *The Federalist Papers*, *Democracy in America*, *The Education of Henry Adams* and *The Irony of American History*.[133] He professes a rarefied form of Protestant Christianity, which does not include adherence to any particular ecclesiastical authority and which, theologically, verges on Deism. He declares that man is not perfectible, but is rather 'a cracked vessel', yet he rejects the doctrine of 'original sin'.

He is a dualist, believing that the 'soul' has 'an existence wholly separate from that of the body'. As any good Weberian sociologist would expect, these beliefs underpin in him a strong commitment to ideas of vocation, integrity and individual responsibility in matters moral and political. While he pointedly does not seek to develop a systematic theory of morality and society based upon his personal beliefs, the relationships between the latter and his observations concerning a wide gamut of social and political problems of the late 20th century are implicit at numerous points and offer much food for thought to the attentive reader.

'Theory ... to me, as to Goethe, has always been grey,' Kennan writes, by way of defending his avoidance of systematic theoretical constructions, in contrast to the 'green quality' of what he called 'the golden tree of life'. Yet, at very many points, his dismay at much of what he sees around him at the end of his life, in the congestion, decay and demoralisation of urban America, cries out for just the sort of sustained conceptual analysis which he declares is not his dish. He recoils, for example, from the phenomenon of the post-Second World War, automobile dominated megalopolis, with its social infestations and alienations. He decries the insistence on unending economic growth as symptomatic of a 'diseased', 'cancerous' and 'unstable' form of society. He deplores what he describes as the gross and frightening over-population of the United States and the rapid depletion of its vast natural endowments.

He laments the impact of television and mass advertising on the standards of literacy and capacities for lucid thought of the present younger generation. He denounces the prevalence of pornography in popular culture and in much of what purports to be art. He sees both public

---

133 These four books range from the 1770s to the 1950s in vintage and constitute a kind of compact classical library of social and political thought about American democracy. *The Education of Henry Adams*, first published in 1918, after its author died, is a record of Adams's introspective meditation on the social, technological, political, and intellectual changes that occurred over his lifetime. He concluded that his traditional education failed to help him come to terms with these rapid changes. He repeatedly laments that his formal education, grounded in the classics, history, and literature, did not give him the scientific and mathematical knowledge needed to grasp the scientific breakthroughs of the 1890s and 1900s. The last of the four books mentioned, Reinhold Niebuhr's *The Irony of American History*, was published by Charles Scribner's Sons, New York, in 1952 and has, even in very recent years, been described by commentator on American strategic affairs Andrew Bacevich as 'the most important book ever written on U.S. foreign policy.'

administration and the making of foreign policy in America as having become hopelessly mired in bureaucratisation and the venality of electoral politics. He regards with serious misgivings what he sees as the erosion of constitutional government in the name of a sort of plebiscitary democracy. He chides his country for the immoderation of its pretensions and global commitments and he chastises its military establishment, as he has before, because of what he sees as its addiction to total war in strategic thinking, especially, until 1991 at least, with regard to nuclear weapons.

He does not, however, even at the broader conceptual level, pull these numerous and forbidding themes together into a deeper rumination on causes, consequences and cures for the maladies he sees afflicting America. Perhaps it is unfair to demand of such a book as this, or of a man of Mr Kennan's years, that he engage in the sort of massive cerebral exercise that would be required by the deeper rumination in question. Yet its absence is not merely due to oversight or incapacity on his part. Nor is it due simply to the fact that such rumination exceeds the modest scope of his book. Rather, it is, in part at least, a reflection of the author's avowed distaste for such systematic and theoretical reflection. This distaste is characteristic of Mr Kennan's particular conservative philosophical disposition. It is a dignified disposition. It is one not lightly swayed by fads, enthusiasms or ideological hubris.

However, dignified though it may be, it detracts at crucial points from both the originality and the cogency of a philosophy that it should consist of so many discontinuous observations and recoil from more rigorous reflection on both the premises and implications of those observations. The book takes its title from the famous lines of John Donne:

On a huge hill cragged and steep truth stands and he that will reach her, about must and about must go.

It is clear that, in the spirit of these lines, Mr Kennan would defend himself against the above criticism and declare, with characteristic modesty, that he does not claim to have reached the summit of the hill and he has offered us only what wisdom and insight he has been able to glean from where he stands.

That the summit can ever be reached by mortal man he plainly doubts. Yet he sees a great need for the infusion of deeper rumination and steadiness of reflection into American public life. To this end, he makes the book's most notable recommendation: that there be created a 'Council of State' in America, of carefully selected citizens, whose knowledge and wisdom would be devoted to pondering the major long term challenges facing the country and whose recommendations would be placed before the President and public as markers amid the hurly burly of telecommunications chaos, with which both struggle to cope. This recommendation, he confesses, is but a preliminary suggestion and, if it has any merit, those who implement the idea 'about must and about must go.' Quite so. But it is also worth going with Mr Kennan as far as he has; for he is a lucid companion, not garrulous, not pretentious, not arrogant—and of very long experience.

Pol Pot and the genocide in Cambodia 1975-78[134]

As I write this review, the long-awaited elections are proceeding in Cambodia, amid threats and violence by the Khmer Rouge. Whether these elections will bring anything like stable, effective and more or less humane government to that unhappy little country remains to be seen. Those who are interested in discovering how Cambodia has come to its present condition could do no better than to read these two short books.

Probably no more than a handful of people in Australia have studied Cambodia's history first hand. They will need no introduction to David Chandler's work. But the wider public is, in all likelihood, acquainted with the roots of Cambodia's present travail only through newspapers and television. How many, I wonder, have read Ben Kiernan's *How Pol Pot Came to Power* (Verso, 1985)[135], Someth May's *Cambodian Witness* (Faber, 1986) or Elizabeth Becker's *When the War was Over: Cambodia's Revolution and the Voices of Its People* (Touchstone, 1986)? One or more of these books would throw light on the subject for the puzzled, horrified and ignorant. But Chandler's two books trump them all. Not only is each unique, but between them they cover the whole story as economically and judiciously as the paucity of historical sources would seem to allow.

David Chandler has been a student of Cambodian history since he enrolled in Khmer language studies at the US Foreign Service Institute in Washington DC in 1959. Since then, he has, from close

---

134   This piece, a review of two books by David Chandler—*Brother Number One: A Political Biography of Pol Pot* and *A History of Cambodia* (2nd edition), both published that year by Allen and Unwin—was first published in *The Australian* on 12 June 1993.

135   I am surprised that I made no mention in this piece of Ben Kiernan's (and David Chandler's) early tendency (in the late 1970s) to defend the Khmer Rouge against accusations of genocide, as did Noam Chomsky, Edward Herman and others on the Left in America and elsewhere. Having been strenuous opponents of the American bombing of Cambodia from 1969 (in an effort to root out the North Vietnamese forces that had occupied eastern Cambodia and the Khmer Rouge, which were intent on overthrowing the regime in Phnom Penh), they found it impossible to believe that the Khmer Rouge would, on conquering Cambodia in 1975, engage in wholesale terror and the catastrophic de-urbanization of the whole society, which resulted in the deaths of well over a million of their countrymen.

Both Chandler and Kiernan came to terms with the grim evidence after 1979. Not so Noam Chomsky, whose writing on Cambodia was a disgrace and yet something of which he has never repented in well over thirty years. Chomsky and Herman insisted doggedly that accusations of genocide were nothing but American propaganda. The lengths to which they went in this campaign, the double standards they applied, the special pleading in which they engaged still beggar belief. It was this which, in the 1980s, turned me against Chomsky and made it scandalous to me that so many on the American and international Left continued to hold him up—as they do to this day—as some kind of moral paragon and beacon of enlightenment on international affairs.

quarters, including a diplomatic posting with the American Embassy in Phnom Penh, in the mid-1960s, observed more than three decades of upheaval and tragedy in Cambodian affairs and delved into 2000 years of the country's history. He has become familiar with many of the key protagonists in the modern political upheavals over those three decades, as well as with documentary sources in Khmer, Thai, French and English. From 1972, for almost twenty years, he taught Southeast Asian history at Monash University. So, these two books are the fruits of many years of painstaking research, which is reflected in the author's scrupulous use of evidence and temperate mode of argument.

I imagine that there are now a few key words which symbolize Cambodia for many a Western mind and the name of Pol Pot is surely among them; likewise the phrase 'the killing fields'. For those more familiar with the workings and geography of the Khmer Rouge regime of 1975-78, Tuol Sleng, location of the so-called S-21 interrogation, torture and execution centre of the Pol Pot clique epitomises its grisly rule of paranoia and terror. There are other, older key words, such as the names Sihanouk and Lon Nol, or the term 'sideshow', used by William Shawcross to describe the devastation of Cambodia by US forces, between 1969 and 1974; and, symbolising the ancient culture and exotic, ruined grandeur of Cambodia, Angkor Wat—even if, in the popular mind, Cambodia is perhaps no more than 'Angkor what?'

David Chandler's biography of Pol Pot, the only one of its kind, offers a way of turning that banal word-string of tags and stock names into an extended comprehension of the enigmatic figure whose assumed name (his real name is Saloth Sar) has become a byword for tyranny and mass murder. Along the way, the killing fields become more real and the full dimensions of the Cambodian tragedy become apparent. Behind both these things, something of the complex anterior history of Cambodia emerges, allowing us to anchor an understanding of the subject in more than political rhetoric or moral revulsion.

Two things stand out in Chandler's biography of Pol Pot. The first is the author's extraordinary restraint in the handling of his subject. This seems to have sprung not simply from his qualities as a scholar, but from his genuine surprise over years of patient research that Saloth Sar was not remembered by those who knew him in his childhood and youth, nor experienced by those who dealt with him in his mature years, as vicious, hateful, domineering or demented. Quite the contrary. A wide range of people testify to his apparent gentleness and charm, his 'school teacher' demeanour.[136]

---

136 'Cambodia', wrote Bernard-Henri Levy in 2008, 'is where everything unravels and the age finally realizes what's what, the Cambodian revolution of 1975—and the fatal blow it delivered not only to Marxism, or to the leaders of the Stalinist parties, or to the Communist dream, but to the very idea of Revolution ... '. As he points out, Pol Pot and his leading Khmer Rouge henchmen did not spring out of the Cambodian past or the jungles. They were educated in France itself, at the Sorbonne and the

This is both sobering and terrifying. Hannah Arendt's reflection upon the 'banality of evil' as exemplified by Adolf Eichmann in Jerusalem springs to mind. It is terrifying because it reminds us that massive evil is not necessarily the work of monstrous psychopaths, but of organized groups convinced of the righteousness or necessity of what they do. This brings me to the second thing that stands out in Chandler's biography: the way in which Pol Pot's regime had its roots not in some demonic foreign ideology, but in Cambodia's own inner demons. These, he argues, were stirred to a frenzy by the upheavals of the early 1970s and wracked the land like furies thereafter.

It is these inner demons whose ancient genesis and long past are revealed by Chandler's history of Cambodia. Bedevilled by the lack of detailed historical records, Chandler nevertheless creates a detailed and instructive narrative of the long drama of the Khmers, caught between the hill tribes and the civilisation of India, between Hinduism and Buddhism, between the Chinese Empire, the Kings of Siam and the lesser emperors of Vietnam. He shows how the hill and forest folk detested the Khmer, who enslaved and exploited them; while the Khmer themselves struggled to fend off the Vietnamese, who regarded them as barbarians; just as the Vietnamese, in their turn, fought to stave off Chinese domination.

And then along came the Europeans, most notably the French, with their assumed *mission civilisatrice*. Finally—or, rather, not finally, since that episode, too, has now begun to pass into history—along came the Americans, with their own illusions and excessive force. Out of all this, relating Pol Pot's style of rule to the Oriental despotism of earlier Khmer potentates, such as Jayavarman VII, in the late 12th century CE[137], as well as to the impact of centuries of imperial encroachment by the Vietnamese and then a century of colonial rule by the French, all climaxing in the fateful pressures of the Indochina wars of 1947-75, Chandler conjures the infernal spirits of the Khmer Rouge—and makes some sense of the tragedy that has been recent Cambodian history.

Ecole Normale Supérieure and imbibed the totalitarian utopianism of the latter day French Marxists, not least among them Louis Althusser. They accepted Sartre's judgment that past revolutions had failed because they had not gone far enough, or as Sartre phrased it had not killed enough people. They returned to Cambodia to unleash a 'super Great Leap Forward', to make an 'unprecedented attempt, important for the whole world, to change man in the deepest ways.' In this attempt, they in fact perpetrated 'one of the greatest insanities humanity has ever known'. *Left in Dark Times: A Stand Against the New Barbarism* (Random House, New York, 2008), pp. 59-63.

137   All this makes Chandler's history similar to histories of Russia which show Ivan the Terrible and Peter the Great as precursors of Stalin; or those of China, which show the worst excesses of earlier emperors of China as precedents for the abuses and misrule by Mao Zedong. These precedents do not, of course, excuse the modern tyrants for the extraordinary crimes and the sufferings they inflicted on their countries. Indeed, while the history does help to put these modern tyrants into historical perspective, such a perspective only throws into higher relief how vast their crimes were and how deeply barbarous and regressive were their policies.

The shape of things to come in the 21st century[138]

Here we have two ambitious attempts to peer through the still settling clouds of dust from the Cold War and discern the shape of things to come. Who has the keener sight: the academic historian Kennedy, or the erstwhile National Security Adviser to an American President, Brzezinski? The boffin or the man of practical politics? The author of *The Rise and Fall of the Great Powers*, or the author of *The Grand Failure*? While the keenness of their sight or insight might best be judged some years hence, after a good deal more dust has settled, there seems to me to be no doubt that Paul Kennedy's is incomparably the more impressive and interesting of these two books.

Whereas Brzezinski opens his book with a survey of 'the century of megadeath'— the immense bloodshed of the wars, political terrors and genocidal massacres of our age—Kennedy opens his with a reflection on the debate over the excess of births over deaths which has led to the plague-like multiplication of *Homo sapiens* on the face of the Earth in the 20th century: our numbers increasing by some five billion since World War I began, despite the violent deaths of, by Brzezinski's estimate, 187 million people in the intervening decades[139]. During the 1980s alone, as Kennedy points out, 842 million

---

138 This piece first appeared in *The Canberra Times* on 26 June 1993. It is a review of two books: Zbigniew Brzezinski's *Out of Control: Global Turmoil on the Eve of the 21st Century* (MacMillan, London, 1993) and Paul Kennedy's *Preparing for the 21st Century* (Harper Collins, 1993).

139 It isn't entirely clear how he arrived at this figure and, unfortunately, more than twenty years later, I no longer have his book at hand to check. It is commonly agreed that some 50 million people perished in the Second World War and perhaps half that number in the First World War. That still leaves well over 100 million to account for and Brzezinski, if my memory serves me well, attributes the lion's share of these to atrocities in the Communist world between 1917 and 1989.

However, both demographic and archival studies since 1991 have shown that the number of victims of Stalin's rule was considerably smaller than was often estimated in the Cold War; perhaps 10 million, but not the 20 to 40 million often alleged. Deaths under Mao Zedong in China were enormous and if we include the staggering toll from the famine caused by the so-called 'Great Leap Forward' in 1959-61 (35 million), may have totalled around 45 million. This would leave us to find some 55 million further deaths from war, terror and genocide in the 20th century, including wars in Africa and Asia (the Korean and Vietnam Wars not least), political terror in many countries (such as the bloodbaths in India between Hindus and Muslims in 1947 and in Indonesia in 1965-66, when the Communist Party was gutted and many ethnic Chinese were slaughtered along the way).

It isn't clear that that we would actually reach Brzezinski's grand total. But a more important point is that, while the figure, either way, is horrific in absolute terms; as a percentage of the world's human population at the time it was actually far smaller than the percentages killed in wars in earlier epochs. It

human beings were added to the world's population.

Whereas Brzezinski dwells on what he calls the 'megamyths' which dominated the 20th century, most notably that of Communism, Kennedy dwells rather on the staggering communications revolution which has, especially since World War II, thrown the megamyths of humanity, old and new, into confusion and onto the defensive. And whereas Brzezinski offers us a somewhat superficial comparison between the Communist 'coercive utopia' and the capitalist 'permissive cornucopia', Kennedy offers a far wider and more thought-provoking survey of the responses of different cultures, nations and regions to the tides of change sweeping the globe.

Brzezinski's central concern is that a morally and culturally decadent United States might prove unable to maintain order, or even offer a challenging universal vision to the world of the 21st century. 'American power,' he writes, 'is superimposed on a world that increasingly resembles a volcano of repressed aspirations and … an intensifying awareness of fundamental inequities.' Kennedy's analysis of what ails America and how its ailments relate to the broader currents of change in the world is both more profound and more lucid than Brzezinski's. He is less inclined to lapse into moral platitude than the Polish American and provides a cogent summary of much recent literature on the nature of technological and social change, demographic and ecological crisis, economic globalisation and political disarray, which is vastly more instructive than Brzezinski's somewhat taut and clichéd *tour d'horizon*.

Never before has the density of mankind on the face of the Earth been so great, the scale and pace of its impact on the biosphere so huge and unrelenting, the porousness of national

---

has been pointed out by historians of warfare that, had the same proportion of the 20th century global population been killed in wars and other forms of violence as were killed in traditional tribal societies in the Americas, Africa and the Pacific, for example, before European colonisation, the dead would have numbered not one or two hundred million, but two billion.

This wider question of the prevalence and costs of violence in human affairs is both a fascinating and important one. Lawrence H. Keeley's *War Before Civilization: The Myth of the Peaceful Savage* (Oxford University Press, 1996) is a very thought-provoking exploration of the problem. Even more interesting, however, because of the counter questions it raises is Raymond C. Kelly's *Warless Societies and the Origins of War* (University of Michigan Press, Ann Arbor, 2000). Steven Pinker attempted a grand synthesis of the subject very recently, in *The Better Angels of our Nature: The Decline of Violence in History and its Causes* (Allen Lane Penguin, 2011). The paradox, then, would have to be that war did not commence until relatively recently—perhaps ten thousand years ago—and then it escalated relentlessly for millennia, only to decline in recent centuries for reasons Pinker attempts to discern. Contrary to very widespread perceptions, he points out at the very beginning of his book, 'today we may be living in the most peaceable era in our species' existence.' This takes some believing when we think of the nuclear arsenals in the world (though they have not been used, it is worth remembering), the wars in the Middle East and the insurgent nature of radical Islam with the mayhem and terror it perpetrates. Yet that is what a careful analysis of available data leads Pinker to conclude.

borders and cultural barriers to flows of information and capital so complete, the gulfs between wealth and poverty, backwardness and technological sophistication so immense, the intensity of human inventiveness so incandescent. It is all this which, with the respite we have just gained from the looming threat of nuclear apocalypse, these two authors assay to comprehend on our behalf. It is Paul Kennedy, however, who has comprehended more and presented it to us better. If you read only one of these two books, therefore, make it his.

In a number of reviews of *Preparing for the 21ˢᵗ Century*, which have been published since the book was released, it has been asserted that Kennedy is less impressive as a futurologist than as an historian of the sinews of power. One recent reviewer even opened his piece by rather caustically remarking that 'be prepared' is a boy scout's motto and beneath the dignity, surely, of a 'grown up historian'. Now, it has to be said that the weightiness of *The Rise and Fall of the Great Powers* does make *Preparing for the 21ˢᵗ Century* seem a little on the once over lightly side. Yet the tone of the criticisms Kennedy's new book has attracted has more to do, I think, with sensitivities about the issues he raises than with any real deficiencies in his scholarship.

For Kennedy adopts quite trenchant positions on the population question, problems of ecological change, of culture, education, economic philosophy and political responsibility. His critics carp at him from positions of what might be called sheltered scepticism: sniping at his alleged Neo-Malthusianism, for example, without offering any sustained argument of their own with regard to the grave challenge of population pressure as we approach the next century.[140] I cannot empathise with this sort of criticism.

---

140 The population and resources question is clearly a vital one, but is far too often addressed in terms of either Malthusian or anti-Malthusian rhetoric. The dynamics are extremely complex. It is demonstrable that humanity has, collectively, not only increased its numbers exponentially, but increased per capita consumption enormously, decreased levels of infant mortality, general morbidity and poverty across the world and used raw materials with ever more remarkable efficiency in the course of the last hundred or two hundred years, i.e. since the industrial revolution began. Yet the strain on the ecological fabric of the Earth does seem palpable, whether in terms of soil erosion, depletion of the oceans, falling water tables, extinction of exotic species or grave questions about the atmosphere and climate.

Perhaps as good an index of all this as any is the debate over the reserves, use and impact of fossil fuels as part of the human impact on the biosphere. Over the past decade we have seen claims that we had reached 'peak oil' and would soon run out of the single most important fuel of the 20ᵗʰ century industrial and technological boom; and that coal was the worst source of greenhouse gas emissions and should be phased out as rapidly as possible less the biosphere be irreparably damaged. Yet coal remains overwhelmingly the cheapest and most abundant fuel for industrial and economic development, while oil prices have plummeted in recent months and the shale or fracking revolution has revealed hitherto untapped and even unguessed reserves of fossil fuels which have put the 'peak oil' claim to rest.

See Kenneth S, Deffeyes *When Oil Peaked* (Hill & Wang, New York, 2010), Peter Tertzakian *A Thousand*

My own chief criticism of the book would be, rather, that having laid before us so many of the critical issues that must be addressed in the next generation or two, Kennedy does not offer very much at all by way of reflection on how these problems are to be adequately addressed in the fractured, crowded, 'borderless' world we now inhabit. With that caveat, however, I would suggest that, directed as it is at a general readership, Kennedy's book is one of the most responsible and judicious of its kind available. It should help to bring many a bewildered mind into tolerable focus.

Barrels a Second: The Coming Oil Break Point and the Challenges Facing an Energy Dependent World (McGraw Hill, New York, 2006), Peter W. Huber and Mark P. Mills *The Bottomless Well: The Twilight of Fuel, the Virtue of Waste and Why We Will Never Run Out of Energy* (Basic Books, New York, 2005); Charles C. Mann 'Coal: It's Dangerous, It's Dirty and It's the Future of Clean Energy' (*Wired* April 2014 pp. 72-81, 114, 116) and *Foreign Affairs*, May-June 2014 'Big Fracking Deal: Shale and the Future of Energy'. The price of oil has fallen from $US110 a barrel in September 2013 to $US53 a barrel in January 2015, with major economic and geopolitical implications around the globe. The United States has gone from massive and troubling oil import dependence to looming energy independence within a few short years. All of which means that the energy and ecological questions remain as complex and uncertain as ever, but that our capacity to innovate in order to rise to challenges seems undiminished and, indeed, on the increase.

Werner Heisenberg and the atomic bomb[141]

'Germany's failure to build an atomic bomb was not inevitable,' Thomas Powers[142]

---

[141] This piece first appeared in *The Canberra Times* on 7 August 1993. It is a review of Thomas Powers *Heisenberg's War: The Secret History of the German Bomb* (Alfred A. Knopf, New York, 1993).

[142] Powers, many years earlier, wrote what is still widely regarded as one of the best books ever written about the CIA: *The Man Who Kept the Secrets: Richard Helms and the CIA* (Alfred A. Knopf, New York, 1979). He graduated from Yale University in 1964 with a degree in English and, from 1970, at the age of 30, has made a living as a freelance writer. His book on Helms and the CIA was one of those that enabled me to develop a balanced perspective on the subject in the 1980s, as I undertook my PhD on counter-insurgency in the Cold War. Yet Powers was far from writing a history of the CIA that was reassuring or bowdlerized. On the contrary, what has always impressed me about his writing on the subject is his ability to ask the most probing questions, dig out the most troubling facts and draw the most disturbing inferences without ever lapsing into the kind of Leftist polemic that has marred Noam Chomsky's work and that of many others for decades.

He was writing, of course, only a few years after the hearings into the CIA in 1975 had broken open the secrecy which had covered its covert operations for almost thirty years—revealing a great many activities which stunned large numbers of Americans. His remarks toward the end of his book are almost a prelude to his book on Heisenberg:

> *The history of the CIA is the secret history of the Cold War. CIA people are cynical in most ways, but their belief in secrets is almost metaphysical. In their bones they believe they know the answer to that ancient paradox of epistemology which asks: If a tree falls in the forest without witness, is there any sound? The CIA would say no. It would agree with historian David Hackett Fisher that history is not what happened, but what the surviving evidence says happened. If you can hide the evidence and keep the secrets, then you can write the history. If no-one knows we tried to kill Castro, then we didn't do it. If ITT's role in Chile is never revealed, then commercial motives had nothing to do with the Allende affair.*

> *If the CIA's role in overthrowing Mossadegh remains hidden, then the Iranians did it all by themselves ... So it wasn't just himself and the CIA which Helms was protecting when he kept the secrets. It was the stability of a quarter century of political arrangements, the notion of a Free World, a 'history' of American response to 'aggression', a stark contrast of American 'morality' with Communist 'expedience', an illusion of American rectitude unclouded by reality. The true history is not the antithesis of the child's history; it is not all crime, greed and imperial reaching. But the true history is a long way from what we tell ourselves on the Fourth of July.* (pp. 297-98)

Of course, as I discovered in 1989 and 1990, even so honest an approach as this to the history of the CIA was not one the Defence security people—or the security officers at the ONA or what was then the Joint Intelligence Organization, shortly to be renamed the Defence Intelligence Organization - themselves held or welcomed in anyone they were vetting. One was supposed not only to keep the secrets within the secret world, but not even to acknowledge that they were realities. I had studied this problem as a scholar in the 1980s and was not prepared to tolerate it as an intelligence analyst in the 1990s. Discretion is one thing; denial altogether another and institutional amnesia a serious cognitive malady.

observes, towards the end of this splendid study. 'If a serious effort to develop a bomb had commenced in mid-1940, one might have been tested in 1943 ... But no serious effort to build a German bomb ever began ... Heisenberg did not simply withhold himself, stand aside, let the project die. He killed it.' This conclusion is electrifying and the historiography behind it profoundly sobering. For it was, in 1941-42, the conviction in the West that the brilliant physicist Werner Heisenberg was building an atomic bomb for Adolf Hitler that led ant-Nazi physicists to persuade President Franklin Roosevelt to launch the Manhattan Project. It produced the bombs that were dropped on Japan in early August 1945 and which triggered the nuclear arms race of the Cold War.

Heisenberg is best known for his brilliant 1927 paper on the uncertainty principle, which led him to exclaim: 'I think I have refuted the law of causality!' Thomas Powers is best known for his examination of American Cold War secret intelligence operations in his biography of Richard Helms. In this present book, after twelve years of meticulous research and writing, he has presented us with a magnificent study in the uncertainty principle at work in strategic judgment and its implications for the causes of geopolitical conflict. *Heisenberg's War* is a wonderfully lucid inquiry into science and politics, science and ethics, the roots and consequences of government secrecy and the psychology of genius. It is eminently worth reading on all these levels. But it provides, also, a gripping tale, filled with drama and intrigue, piercing insights into the everyday life of the scientific elite in Hitler's Third Reich and a marvellous portrait gallery of that generation of brilliant mathematicians, physicists and chemists of the 1920s and 1930s who gave the world nuclear weapons. The portraits of Niels Bohr, Robert Oppenheimer and Heisenberg himself are perhaps the richest and most intimately drawn. They are real gems. So is Powers' portrait of Albert Speer.

The book opens with an account of Heisenberg's visit to the United States in the summer of 1939, when many physicists and other intellectuals, especially if they were Jewish, had already fled Hitler's Germany and taken refuge in the West. Heisenberg was offered such refuge, but declined it, saying that his place was in Germany, to take responsibility for German science. This is where the misgivings about him began. How could a genius such as Heisenberg not both understand the evil of Nazism and flee from it? It is Powers who does justice to Heisenberg's sense of both uncertainty and principle. Heisenberg, he points out, felt he had either to stay in Germany and face pressure to build a bomb for an evil master, or leave Germany and face pressure to build one that would be used against the Germany he loved. Under these circumstances, he opted to stay in Germany, try to prevent a German atomic bomb from being built and hope that Western scientists would similarly try to restrain politicians and generals in Britain and America.

The irony, of course, is that his peers in the West believed he was working for Hitler and therefore proceeded to do for Roosevelt and Churchill what Heisenberg would *not* do for Hitler.

At a time when so many issues springing from scientific innovation and the impact of technology confront humanity, the early history of the invention of nuclear weapons holds lessons that are well worth pondering. The incandescent genius of the generation of Einstein, Bohr, Born, Fermi, Szilard, Oppenheimer, Teller and Heisenberg is legendary. Some of Powers' most finely crafted prose is lavished on the portraits of these men. But the ethical and political dilemmas they faced are the central object of his concern. It was Otto Hahn, one of Heisenberg's colleagues, who remarked, in 1939: 'If my work should lead to a nuclear weapon, I would kill myself.' Well, of course, his work did not. And, after the Nazi era, in 1957, Heisenberg was one of eighteen prominent scientists who flatly refused 'to participate in any way whatever in the manufacture, testing or use of atomic weapons.'

Yet the scientists in America and Britain, faced by the perceived threat of a Nazi—and later a Soviet—atomic bomb, did build nuclear weapons. And when Robert Oppenheimer - who had done everything he could to ensure that the atomic bomb would be terrible enough to end the Second World War and regretted that it had not been developed early enough for use against Germany—expressed qualms about the development of the hydrogen bomb in the early 1950s, the US Atomic Energy Commission stripped him of his security clearances, terminated his official career and shattered his personal life with accusations of treason.[143] When Niels Bohr, as early as 1944, began a campaign against the secrecy of nuclear research programs, in the hope that a more open world might help prevent a post-World War II East/West arms race, Winston Churchill suggested that Bohr be imprisoned, or at the very least 'made to see that he is very near the edge of mortal crimes.'

Now, Niels Bohr was, in some respects the presiding genius of that fateful generation of gifted nuclear scientists. His Institute for Theoretical Physics in Copenhagen was the 'Mecca' of these pioneers, who, after all, in the 1920s, numbered only a few score scientists with their circles of students. He was, by all accounts, a rather extraordinary man, with an immense, relentless passion for thinking, for clarity about things and for political and ethical decency. He was, in the 1920s, the mentor of Werner Heisenberg. In 1927, they stood together at the Solvay Conference and argued against Albert Einstein that 'God' does, indeed, 'play dice'. And it was to Bohr that Heisenberg turned, in 1941, in the vague and quixotic hope that a scientists' strike or secret pact could be arranged, which would prevent the development of atomic bombs. Bohr,

---

143   For a luminous exploration of the character and career of Oppenheimer, see Ray Monk *Inside the Centre: The Life of J. Robert Oppenheimer* (Jonathan Cape, London, 2012).

however, misunderstood Heisenberg's message and became convinced that his former protégé was working for the Nazis.[144]

The rest, as they say, is history. Only that, until Powers' book was published, that history was confused. Contrary to the fears of his old teacher and friend Bohr, Heisenberg succeeded in preventing a German bomb from being built, even as others energetically built one for the Allied powers. 'What happened matters,' Powers argues, 'because truth matters ... Whether the Soviet/American arms race was both inevitable and necessary is too large a question to address here, but the truth about the German bomb program—that it was fatally crippled by lack of scientific zeal—might have contributed a note of caution about the Russian danger at the outset of the Cold War ... when Americans again feared there was nothing and no-one on the other side they could trust.' Too bad that such insight is rare and tends to be the product of sustained historical and ethical inquiry rather than that of practical political debate or strategic intelligence analysis. The Cold War is over, but the lessons Powers draws remain of pressing relevance, both in the geopolitical arena and in wider areas of debate concerning science and the future of the species. Read his book and be edified.

---

[144] About five years after this review was written, Michael Frayn wrote a play called *Copenhagen* dramatizing the meeting between Bohr and Heisenberg and exploring what was said and what it meant. It was published in 2003 in a Methuen Drama edition. The artful thing about the play is that it is written as if the characters were revisiting the past to discuss what had actually happened and the consequences of misunderstandings or interpretations. The play is a very nice complement to Thomas Powers' book. Twice in recent years, I have arranged readings of it at my apartment, followed by discussion of its meaning and importance. Frayn, by his own account, made a number of changes to the play between its first writing, its London stage run, its New York stage run and its publication in 2003. In a Postscript and then a Post-Postscript to the published version, he went to great pains to address the controversies and complexities associated with the case.

The Postscript was intended, as he wrote, to make as clear as possible 'how much of it is fiction and how much of it is history'. The Post-Postscript addresses criticism that he had whitewashed Heisenberg, who was on the record as having stated that he believed Germany's conquests in Eastern Europe were justified and that if it could subdue Soviet Russia, this should be welcomed. The question remains, however, given that Heisenberg was a German nationalist who approved of these devastating and ruthless conquests, why would he not have attempted to develop an atomic bomb for the regime which carried them out? The answer of Allied intelligence after the war was that, as far as they could ascertain, he had tried and failed. This is the version of history that Thomas Powers believed he had undermined. There were many nationalists in Germany in the 1930s and well into the Second World War who wanted to see a strong Germany, but many of them were not Nazis and slowly came to realize that Hitler was bringing ruin down on the country by his reckless war-making. We need to ponder the question of Heisenberg and the atomic bomb in this complex context.

Premonitions of the end of Hong Kong[145]

It is just over 150 years since British warships and soldiers compelled Imperial China to submit to opium importation on a staggering scale and made the harbour of Hong Kong the headquarters of both drug trafficking and free trade in East Asia. Under the Treaty of Nanjing (29 August 1842) and the Convention of Beijing (24 October 1860), Britain extracted from China the cession, in perpetuity, of Hong Kong island and the Kowloon peninsula, respectively. On 9 June 1898, the premier diplomat of late Imperial China, Li Hungchang, signed the Second Convention of Beijing, under which Britain obtained a lease on the New Territories for 99 years, giving the crown colony of Hong Kong a much extended hinterland.

China was then weak and was much bullied by the vigorous and self-righteous Europeans, the 'foreign devils' as they were called in the Middle Kingdom. It did not become strong for many years afterwards and, in the interim, it became an axiom of the British Colonial Office that it would be unthinkable ever to return either Hong Kong and Kowloon or the New Territories to China.[146] It was only in the mid-1980s, after Deng Xiaoping had begun to open up China to foreign trade for the first time since 1949 that the unthinkable was thought through. When it was, the realisation dawned on the Foreign and Commonwealth Office that Hong Kong could not be held and that a resumption of Chinese sovereignty had to be anticipated, as of 1997, when the lease on the New Territories expired.

In this small book, Robert Cottrell, who lived and worked as a journalist in Hong Kong for most of the 1980s, offers an account of this realisation and of the negotiations with China that followed,

---

145 This piece first appeared in *The Canberra Times* on 16 October 1993 and was a review of Robert Cottrell's *The End of Hong Kong: The Secret Diplomacy of Imperial Retreat* (John Murray, London, 1993). I was, at that time, head of arms trade and defence industry analysis for East and South Asia in the Defence Intelligence Organization. I had not yet visited China itself. As I retype it, in January 2015, the authorities in Hong Kong have just suppressed the Occupy Central democracy movement, led by students like the eighteen year old Joshua Wong, who were not even born when the piece was first written. They were demanding full enfranchisement for the people of Hong Kong, consistent with the Basic Law agreed upon by the British and Chinese governments before the crown colony was handed over the People's Republic in 1997. It was clear throughout the protest movement that the Hong Kong government was receiving direct orders from Beijing about what it could or could not concede and how to handle the students. Since 1989, the Communist Party has firmly set its face against any kind of political liberalisation or modification of its dictatorial powers in China. With this control of events in Hong Kong, in 2014, it showed that the Basic Law, which was to usher in full democratization in Hong Kong over a period of fifty years, is a dead letter and that the special autonomy of the city is purely nominal.

146 For a history of Hong Kong under the British see Frank Welsh *A History of Hong Kong* (Harper Collins, London, 1993).

conducted on such different terms from those of the 19th century. Those negotiations have turned the unthinkable into a controversial blueprint for the Chinese future of Hong Kong, starting within four years. Since 1984 and even more since 4 June 1989, it has been asked again and again whether 1997 will bring the 'sack' of Hong Kong, or at least its demise as the great trading entrepôt it has long been? Will it lose its special characteristics and revert to the status of just another Chinese coastal port. Will there be a large-scale Communist intervention and a purge of civil society in the 'special autonomous region', as in that of Tibet? Or will it become even more vigorous than before, as the gateway to a burgeoning Chinese capitalist marketplace; even the catalyst for a non-catastrophic political transformation of the People's Republic?

Perhaps the most salient and poignant point made by Cottrell is that the people of Hong Kong have been little consulted about all this in the negotiations over their future between London and Beijing. They have been treated as subjects, not as citizens. Almost, one might say, they have been treated as children and their obedience has been expected. The running of a household is not, after all, something to be decided *devant les enfants*. Why was it not possible for these six million people to be asked whether they wanted to remain a colony of Britain—without democracy, but with capitalism—or be incorporated into the People's Republic of China ending up, perhaps, with neither capitalism nor democracy? Or if they would prefer to become an independent Republic of Hong Kong, both capitalist and democratic, with cultural, economic and political links to both China and Britain, but subordinate to neither?

Why? Because the burden of history and the logic of *raison d'état* dictated that the matter would be settled as it has been. Britain has never been accustomed to consult the people of Hong Kong regarding their political preferences and the memorious rulers of China see the recovery of Hong Kong as the correction of a deep wrong and humiliation inflicted on the Middle Kingdom long ago by the British Empire. Both have a stake in the preservation of Hong Kong as a thriving *entrepôt* and therein lies its best hope; but its political fate is another matter. Cottrell makes all this quite plain in a concise manner and the general reader will find his account of it illuminating.

Hong Kong, as China is likely to recover it, bears, of course, not the slightest resemblance to Hong Kong as it was when China was compelled to cede it in perpetuity in 1842. Cottrell waxes lyrical, in the opening pages of his book, in describing the electric and tropical beauties of the city seen from Victoria Peak at night, the unceasing dynamism of the great harbour and the atmosphere of 'fugitive, even romantic excitement' which uncertainty about its future now imparts to the city. His paean to its virtues deserves to be quoted:

> *The beauty of Hong Kong lies in its plasticity, its fertility, its capacity to invent and reinvent itself a dozen times in a single generation. Tomorrow, there might be anything here or nothing.*

That has, clearly, been the judgment of many of Hong Kong's best and brightest since 1984 and especially since 1989. Several hundred thousand of them have emigrated—most often to other, more secure parts of the former British Empire. In a move symbolic of the tidal change in Hong Kong's affairs, the oldest and greatest of the 'hongs', the old trading houses that founded the city and made it what it is, Jardine Matheson, the original 'noble house', withdrew its legal domicile from Hong Kong on 28 March 1984—transferring it to Bermuda.

Ironically, though its insistence on reclaiming Hong Kong is rooted in resentment of the deeds of William Jardine, drug trafficker, in the 1840s, Beijing was furious when his great-great-great-great nephew, Simon Keswick, announced the retreat of the old trading house. The rules if the game in Hong Kong are changing and the capitalists will hedge their bets accordingly. But, as Cottrell reminds us, whatever the rulers of China may decide to do with or in or to Hong Kong, the majority of its inhabitants do not have the sort of option that was exercised by Jardine Matheson. They have no real choice but to stay, even though many of them are there because they fled Communist rule in China many years ago.

Cottrell did much of the work on this book in Hong Kong in 1991-92. By then, the panic which followed the severe repression in China in the second half of 1989 had subsided to some extent. The book reflects this calmer mood. It is not apocalyptic. It is a reflective account of the negotiations of the Sino-British Joint Declaration of 19 December 1984. It provides just enough of the earlier history of Hong Kong and of Sino-British relations for the reader to be able to make sense of the course of the negotiations. It includes the full text of the Joint Declaration, with its various annexes, which will be very useful to the student of these matters for many years to come.

It is non-committal on the future of Hong Kong, but perhaps leans toward a certain guarded optimism. Its keynote, however, is the observation, at once romantic and realistic, that Hong Kong is 'a small and fragile place' whose virtues and wonders will not survive rough handling. That is the common wisdom. Yet Hong Kong has bred tough entrepreneurs under undemocratic conditions. Just possibly, they will prove ideally suited to the China that is now emerging and Hong Kong will become, even more than it has been in the 1980s, the fountainhead of Chinese progress. Just possibly.[147]

---

147 This turned out to be the case both before and after 1997, with Hong Kong providing banking, accounting and management skills for the rapidly emerging new industrial centres that mushroomed in China, starting in Guangdong, just up the Pearl River from Hong Kong, after Deng Xiaoping's Southern Tour of 1992. In the 21st century, beyond anyone's expectations, China boomed and numerous new centres of innovation sprang up, chiefly along the coast at first, but then spreading inland. The staggering growth that ensued catapulted China from an economic backwater to the chief creditor and statistically the largest economy in the world by 2015. That is a true 'revolution', the like of which Mao Zedong can never have imagined.

Allan Bloom on love and friendship[148]

I flew into Melbourne two days before Christmas and was met at Tullamarine by a homosexual friend whom I have known for nineteen years, but had not met for two years. We drove into the heart of town and spent six hours in a good Brunswick Street café immersed in wide-ranging conversation about his life in Palo Alto and mine in Canberra; about consciousness, metaphysics and the world's disorders; and about love and friendship. I had Allan Bloom's *Love and Friendship* with me, planning to read it over my Christmas break and shared it eagerly with my friend.

In the course of our conversation, I discovered to my astonishment that he not only had not read Michel Foucault's *History of Sexuality*, but did not know who Foucault was. To my dismay, I learned also, for the first time in our long acquaintance, that he had never read Plato's *Symposium*. Here, in other words, was a homosexual male of mature years, trying to articulate his feelings about eroticism, love and friendship, but who had no acquaintance with Plato or Foucault.[149] What a deprivation! This, precisely, is the argument of Allan Bloom's marvellously civilized and beautifully composed book, which was written in the very shadow of the author's approaching death.

Those who have read Bloom's famous polemic of 1987, *The Closing of the American Mind: How Higher Education Has Failed Democracy and Impoverished the Souls of Today's Students*, may or may not share this reviewer's opinion of it as a provocative, but uneven and incomplete piece

---

148 This piece was first published in *The Canberra Times* on 15 January 1994. That is now over twenty years ago and until I came to assemble this book, I had more or less forgotten having written it. It is a review of Allan Bloom *Love and Friendship* (Simon & Schuster, 1993). As of this writing, however, I am fortunate in being able to say that I have more and better friends, male and female, than ever before in my life and that I have come to appreciate love and friendship more with each passing year. I have revised the wording of the piece more extensively than any other piece in this collection, however, because when I re-read it, I found it unusually prolix and unattractive in style.

149 I have long since ceased to be an admirer of Michael Foucault (1926-1984), not least because of his nihilism and his life-long friendship with and defence of Louis Althusser, an equally destructive French intellectual. Even as an undergraduate, I had difficulty comprehending the widespread citation of these and other then fashionable Left-wing French intellectuals, whose thought was often all but impenetrable and whose influence on serious thinking and lucid writing was deeply pernicious. Foucault was homosexual, but when he contracted AIDS he refused to exercise any responsibility and was notorious for remaining promiscuous and engaging in unprotected sex with people unaware of his illness. Plato is a far more complex matter. His works and life I continue to find fascinating and certainly important. The greatest abuse of which he can be charged, in my opinion, is his desire to burn all the books of Democritus, the great pioneer of atomism and materialism. But that is a subject for another space and time.

of argument about the purposes and contemporary dilemmas of higher education. Most will, however, find in his last book, or so I believe, a more rounded and less cantankerous meditation on the deepest things, on the sublime and on the spiritual pitfalls of scientific modernity, to say nothing of so-called post-modernity.

Beginning with a reflection on the fall of Eros, Bloom proceeds to meditate on Rousseau and the idea of romantic love in the novels of Stendhal, Austen, Flaubert and Tolstoy. He then sets against that meditation a comparative reflection on love and friendship in Shakespeare's *Romeo and Juliet, Antony and Cleopatra, Measure for Measure, Troilus and Cressida* and *The Winter's Tale*. But as if that was not enough to give wings to the flaccid and reductionist cynicism of the shrunken spirits of our age whose impoverishment after the loss of Eros is his great concern; he follows up with a wonderful essay on friendship. It is called 'Interlude on Two Strange Couples—Hal and Falstaff, Montaigne and La Boétie.'

He then crowns his masterpiece with a 118 page discussion of Plato's *Symposium* and the erotic underpinnings of philosophy. All things considered, *Love and Friendship* is a very academic book and surely will seem altogether indigestible to the illiterate or semi-literate denizens of modern society who were Bloom's chief concern. That is not a damning objection to the book, but it does run the risk that the only people who will read it will be those who least need what it has to say. If read more widely, it might well run the risk of being scorned or even denounced for undermining the 'pieties' of our permissive, demotic, consumer society. Yet that, in a sense, is just what it is intended to do.

Like many scholars, Bloom faced an abiding dilemma; one which, I think, he never really came to terms with: how to communicate the value of classical literary works to a public increasingly unfamiliar with them. This was his problem in *The Closing of the American Mind*, in which he argued that the failure to teach young people Plato and Aristotle, among other classics, was stunting their intellectual and moral development. His last book is a pleasure to read if you already have some familiarity with, say, *Emile, The Red and the Black, Madame Bovary*, the plays of Shakespeare, the essays of Montaigne and the dialogues of Plato. Yet if you do, there is a good chance that Bloom does not need to weave his Socratic spell on you. If you don't, on the other hand; if your world is 'illuminated' chiefly by *Playboy*, the tabloid press and pulp fiction, the book is unlikely to seem intelligible to you.

Love and Friendship is a deeply serious and humane book and, if you have ever experienced deep love or enduring friendship, you ought to find it nourishing and 'anchoring'. If you found Martin Scorsese's *The Age of Innocence* more engaging than his *Taxi Driver*, then *Love and Friendship* is a book for you. If *Casablanca* and *Doctor Zhivago* are films which helped to shape your sense of the integrity of the heart, then *Love and Friendship* is a book for you. If you have recently enjoyed Kenneth Branagh and Emma Thompson in *Much Ado About Nothing*, then *Love and Friendship* is a book for you. These are mostly films, of course, because I would not lightly assume than many people have recently re-read—or read at all, in many cases—the novels of Stendhal, or even those of Tolstoy; the dialogues of Plato (even the delightful and luminous *Symposium*) or even much of Shakespeare. But all these roads lead to Rome: Bloom's central argument that love and friendship lie at the very root of our all-too-human spirituality and are actually the keys to self-knowledge.

Section 4: 1994-97

The evolution of 'total war'[150]

John Keegan is a distinguished historian of warfare who has, for 30 years, brought to this grim subject a passionate commitment to clear-sighted reckoning with the nature of human conflict and a deeply humane revulsion from the horrors that men inflict during those paroxysms of organized and sanctioned violence that we call war.[151]

A history of warfare is his tenth book and its design suggests that, if it is not his *magnum opus*, it is at least a sort of testamentary essay. I suspect that many readers will feel a magnetic attraction to this book with even a first glance at the titles Keegan gave his chapters: from 'War in Human History' to 'interludes' on stone and the limitations on war-making; fortification and the vulnerability of human flesh; armies and iron; fire and the work of logistics and supply.

The starkness of his use of the elemental words stone, flesh, iron and fire has about it the flavour of pre-Socratic or even more specifically Heraclitean cosmology. We are being offered by Keegan the keys to one of the abiding enigmas of human existence. His project is to plumb the depths of the human propensity to violence and its extraordinary escalation in that cosmic blinking of an eye-lid we call 'world history'—the past ten thousand years.[152]

Certainly, this is a project more ambitious in scope than anything Keegan has previously attempted. Sixty four photographs (alas, all black and white prints) and twelve maps provide

---

150 This piece was first published in *The Canberra Times* on 5 March 1994. It was a review of John Keegan's *A History of Warfare* (Hutchinson, London) and Alvin and Heidi Toffler's *War and Anti-War: Survival at the Dawn of the 21st Century* (Little, Brown & Co). The following month I was appointed head of China analysis at the Defence Intelligence Organization, a job I was to hold until November 1995, when I resigned from DIO and departed from government service in Canberra.

151 Keegan (1934–2012), as the Wikipedia biographical entry on him records, was a British military historian, lecturer, writer and journalist. He was the author of many published works on the nature of combat between the 14th and 21st centuries concerning land, air, maritime, and intelligence warfare, as well as the psychology of battle. When asked about the Vietnam War, Keegan replied: 'I will never oppose the Vietnam War. Americans were right to do it. I think they fought it in the wrong way. I don't think it's a war like fighting Hitler, but I think it was a right war, a correct war.' He similarly defended the invasion of Iraq in 2003.

152 However, see n107 above regarding Steven Pinker's argument that violence has actually decreased in historical time, with the paradox that the means for perpetrating it have escalated relentlessly and the absolute numbers of fatalities in war likewise. The subtle statistical calculations involved seem to elude almost all scholars, to say nothing of non-specialists. Yet the reasoning involved is immensely important and right up there with reasoning about epidemiological data and the 'battle' between the human species and diseases. On that subject, Daniel E. Lieberman's *The Story of the Human Body: Evolution, Health and Disease* (Pantheon Books, New York, 2013) is enormously instructive, though it does not deal explicitly with epidemiological statistics and how to understand them.

a graphic focus and enticement for the mind's eye, but the text itself commands sustained examination and should provoke much reflection.

The pivotal section of *A History of Warfare* is the first 'Interlude': 'Limitations on Warmaking'. For it is Keegan's purpose in this book to take issue with what he sees as a Clauswitzian orthodoxy in the analysis and practice of warfare in the 20th century. His opening sentence—'War is not the continuation of policy by other means'—sets the stage for a sustained inquiry into the origins and meaning of the terrible 'total' wars of the 20th century. Clausewitz, he declares, was 'the ideological father of the First World War … The ideology of 'true war' was the ideology of the First World War's armies and the appalling fate that those armies brought upon themselves by their dedication to it may be Clausewitz's most enduring legacy.'

The author's stated belief is that the 'ideology of true war', pronounced at the dawn of the industrial era by Carl von Clausewitz, in his classic *On War*, in a sense generated that addiction to *la guerre a outrance* (war to the limit or total war) which, from 1945, with the advent of atomic weapons, has threatened the very survival of the species. He discerns, as a direct consequence of the excesses of modern warfare, 'the beginnings of a profound change in civilization's attitude to war.'

His first Interlude 'Limitations on Warmaking' is the foundation on which he builds his case for rational limitation of warmaking as we approach the 21st century of the Common Era—roughly the 71st century of recorded history.[153] Keegan's account of the warlike history of human culture, rendered as it is in a spare and lucid prose, is a wonderful introduction to the subject. His outline of the limitations which both taboo and technology have placed on killing in the wars of mankind over millennia is beautifully narrated and quite coherent.

Keegan guides his reader through the invention of the instruments for killing, from the primitive bow to iron weapons, the chariot and the man on horseback, siege engines and gunpowder, the arts of fortification and those of shock and manoeuvre; and, finally, the panoply of logistical and lethal means which, underwritten by the doctrines of Clausewitz—themselves rooted in the French Revolution's *levee en masse* and the campaigns of Napoleon Bonaparte—made conceivable the First and Second World Wars.

---

153 Dating 'recorded history' back 70 centuries is somewhat arbitrary. That would date it from 5,000 BCE, which is intermediate between the beginnings of Neolithic agriculture, after the end of the most recent ice age; and the invention of writing in Sumer in the fourth or fifth millennium BCE. In any case, that period of 7,000 years remains a very brief one in the longer context of human evolution, since the Palaeolithic remains of our own species date back at least ten to twenty times that period and our last common ancestor with the chimpanzee was 1,000 times as far back—or 7 million years ago. Yet it is only in the Neolithic that we find evidence for what can rightly be called 'warfare', as distinct from other forms of violence, such as homicide, capital punishment or intermittent raiding and feuding.

His reconstruction of the wars between the nomads of the Eurasian steppe and the agrarian civilizations of the Fertile Crescent and Western Europe is especially well crafted. Indeed, his survey of the intensification of human violence from the end of the last Ice Age through to the bureaucratically organized and magnificently engineered brutality of the Roman legions is superb. Likewise his summary of the human capacities for warmaking from the downfall of Rome and the invention of gunpowder. At every point in the argument, he draws our attention to the interplay between the shocking increases in the human capacities for slaughter made possible by technological innovations—which always spread fairly rapidly—and the lingering human reluctance to engage in relentless killing.

However, just where one hoped to see the scholar sheet home his argument, at least as an intellectual *tour de force*, Keegan falters: towards the end, where the phenomenon of 'true war' or 'total war' comes into historical view and living memory. His quarrel with Clausewitz is a nice way to pinpoint what he is driving at; but it seems to necessitate a more thorough grappling with Clausewitz's own writings and their ramifications in the wars of our century than Keegan delivers in the last part of his book. After an impressive laying down of the groundwork and placement of his pieces, Keegan's argument, like a miscarried ambush, allows his prey to slip away at the last moment. What he needed was a relentless and dense last section, embodied in a long and powerful conclusion, which would have pounded away at the Clausewitzian doctrine in the 20th century context and, crucially, laid out the grounds on which a post-Clausewitzian doctrine might be developed for the world in the wake of the nuclear Cold War.

Keegan's actual conclusion does neither of these things and, as a result, the force of his argument dissipates just when it ought to have been decisively concentrated. He concludes the penultimate section of the book, 'Fire', with what is something of a compact cliché: 'Unless we unlearn the habits we have taught ourselves, we shall not survive.' By 'we', he plainly means the human species, but the point is not proven, for the means now available to modify rather than unlearn the habits of historic time are more diverse and the habituation itself more profound than he allows.

His plea, in the final sentence of his book, for a rediscovery of 'the principles of intellectual restraint and even of symbolic ritual' which, he argues, constrained primitive warfare is noble in its inspiration, but not adequately undergirded by the historical evidence the book provides. This evidence largely suggests that those espousing the restraints and ritual habits in question invariably perished at the hands of the masters of the evolving technological and 'decisive' approaches to warmaking—many centuries before Clausewitz enunciated the idea of war as 'an act of violence pushed to its utmost bounds'.

Might advanced technologies make it possible for post-industrial states in the coming century to defeat the 'total war' barbarism of new Saddam Husseins without causing massive bloodshed? Keegan does not so much as pose the question. Yet if, as he so clearly shows, the bow and the horse long ago made man a predator against his own kind, how will the restraint and ritual he invokes reprogram such proclivities in the age of semtex, smart bombs and stealth platforms? Here was Keegan's true quarry, but he did not close in for the kill, settling instead for ritual pieties and platitudes.

It is just where Keegan falls away that the Tofflers take off. *War and Anti-War*, as one would expect from a book authored by Alvin Toffler, is a book which moves at a relentless pace, has its eyes fixed resolutely on the day after tomorrow and pivots on the dizzying dynamic of the information revolution as the key to what is transforming our world. In short, *War and Anti-War* is an altogether different sort of text from *A History of Warfare*. It is far less discursive, far more breathless and almost totally devoid of what I would call 'phenomenological humanism'—reflections on the actual human experience of warfare and violence. Alvin Toffler is a man on the run, trying to overtake a future which is unfolding at a staggering speed.

Those familiar with Toffler's previous books, most notably *Future Shock*, *The Third Wave* and *Powershift*, will be familiar with the style in which he writes. His conceptual reach is impressive and his creative neologisms are suggestive, but he appears to compose his texts with a striking lack of concern for the resonance of his futurism against the poetics of what he dubs First (Agrarian) and Second (Industrial) Wave human experience. His Third (Information) Wave civilization comes across as a vast blur of technological innovation, with a kaleidoscope of consequences across the planet, which he anticipates in reportorial language somewhere between *Penthouse* hip and *Omni* forecasting.

Despite its breathless style, the content of this book, like that of Toffler's earlier books on the beginning of post-industrial, Third Wave civilization, is immensely suggestive and stimulating. That is markedly so with regard to the insights this book offers concerning the nature of politics, the challenges to intelligence in the age of the Internet and the probable future of war. Indeed, had Keegan's book included a more thorough critique of Clausewitz, a denser reflection on the world of nuclear arms and a reckoning with the prospects for innovation that the Tofflers lay out before us, his would have been a work of surpassing power.

It is the distressing implication of the Tofflers' sweeping argument that all modes of being human which do not surge along the crest of the Third Wave are destined for the notorious 'dustbin of history'. Yet their survey of the nascent means for warmaking in the era of the Third Wave, which reads like a blend of Arthur C. Clarke and *Jane's Defence Weekly*, powerfully communicates the sense that war has a future beyond the stormiest contradiction, in a crowded world seething with ethno-linguistic divisions and impulses to violence springing from a bewildering variety of historical sources.

The Tofflers talked to a fascinating range of people in preparing this book and the panoramic vision they impart of a world of Prigoninian instabilities[154] amid global hyper-connectivity and a 'trisection' of technological orders of civilization is full of vitality and has a refreshing boldness of conception. Above all, it is a book calculated to provoke iconoclastic thinking about almost any comfortable assumption clung to by those still grounded in First and Second Wave material and intellectual cultures.

Finally, though not very coherently, the Tofflers, having sketched out all sorts of possibilities for the fragmentation of the current order of things and for numerous new modes of warfare[155], suggest ways in which information technologies might, in the decades to come, supply novel means for the dilution and control of conflict. Read them. Doing so will pretty certainly get your neurons firing.

---

154 Ilya Romanovich Prigogine (1917-2003) was born of a Jewish family in St Petersburg shortly before the Russian Revolution in February 1917. His family fled the Bolsheviks in 1921 and he grew up in Belgium, where he became a chemical engineer and physicist. In his book *The End of Certainty: time, chaos, and the new laws of nature* (1997), Prigogine contended that determinism was no longer a viable scientific belief. 'The more we know about our universe, the more difficult it becomes to believe in determinism,' he wrote. This was a major departure from the approach of Newton, Einstein and Schrödinger, all of whom expressed their theories in terms of deterministic equations. According to Prigogine, determinism loses its explanatory power in the face of irreversibility and instability. He notes numerous examples of irreversibility, including diffusion, radioactive decay, solar radiation, weather and the emergence and evolution of life. Like weather systems, organisms are unstable systems existing far from thermodynamic equilibrium. Instability resists standard deterministic explanation. Instead, due to sensitivity to initial conditions, unstable systems can only be explained statistically, that is, in terms of probability.

155 For two among many more recent books on technological innovation and warfare in the 21st century, see Max Boot *War Made New: Technology, Warfare and the Course of History 1500 to Today* (2006) and P. W. Singer *Wired for War: The Robotics Revolution and Conflict in the 21st Century* (2009). For a reflection on the adaptation of American military strategy to the new technologies, see Frederick W. Kagan *Finding the Target: The Transformation of American Military Policy* (Encounter Books, New York, 2006).

China as the next economic superpower[156]

In the dedication to his prophetic and controversial book *The Emerging Japanese Superstate: Challenge and Response*, in 1970, Herman Kahn wrote:

> To the Japanese superstate and its successful and peaceful integration into the international system.

William Overholt might well have written a dedication to this book simply substituting the word 'Chinese' for 'Japanese'. He went only half way, however. He concluded his author's prefatory note with the observation:

> I hope that some readers will weigh the unpopular ideas expressed here with some of the same open mind that I had when Herman Kahn told me that he was going to rub my nose in the reality of South Korea.

Nevertheless, *China: The Next Economic Superpower* clearly and self-consciously echoes Kahn's book of a generation ago.

The difference between the two is due chiefly to the fact that, in the generation since Kahn wrote *The Emerging Japanese Superstate*, much of what he predicted has come to pass, while South Korea, Taiwan, Hong Kong and Singapore have also emerged as exceptionally dynamic economies in Asia. All this lends weight, by example, to Overholt's central argument concerning China's incipient emergence as a super economy. There is a further reason, however, why *China: The Next Economic Superpower* is an even more portentous book than *The Emerging Japanese Superstate*: it deals with China; and, if Overholt's prognosis is at all on the mark, China will indeed become, in the 21st century, as Lee Kuan Yew has put it: 'The biggest player in the history of man.'

---

156 This piece first appeared in *The Canberra Times* on 26 March 1994. It is a review of William H. Overholt *China: The Next Economic Superpower* (Weidenfeld & Nicolson, 1993). I had stumbled upon Overholt's book in a bookshop, read its Preface and decided that I liked the way his mind worked. I bought and reviewed the book and then sent him a copy of the review. He was based in Hong Kong in those days, as Head of Asia Research for Bankers Trust. As it happens, I had arranged to fly to Hong Kong for a RAND conference on the Chinese armed forces shortly before sending him the review. We met the morning after I arrived and became acquainted over a long breakfast at the Marriott Hotel, on the Island.

I was appointed head of China analysis at the Defence Intelligence Organization shortly after writing this piece and it was in that capacity that I spoke with Overholt. We candidly discussed the possibility of my making the move from Canberra to Hong Kong to work with him at Bankers Trust. Many years later, Chicago-based China specialist David Hale said to me privately, 'If you'd been able to make the move to Hong Kong, it would have transformed your life'. I feel quite certain he was correct. Yet had I made that move, nothing of what I have done since the turn of the century would have happened and it is now impossible to imagine my life without those things: workshops for Austhink Consulting, relationships and writings.

William Overholt is a man with an interesting past. He studied Chinese history and politics at Harvard University in the early 1960s. He went to the Philippines as an undergraduate to research the failure of the Communist Huk rebellion. He participated in the civil rights struggle back in the United States in the mid-1960s; took a conservative view of the Vietnam War (which is to say, he approved of the attempt to suppress the Communist revolution in South Vietnam); worked as a researcher on the Cultural Revolution at the Pentagon in 1968; did his graduate studies at Yale University; then went to work for Herman Kahn at the Hudson Institute.

The formidable Doctor Kahn became notorious in the early 1960s, with his exercise in 'thinking about the unthinkable', *On Thermonuclear War*; some of the language of which was reflected in Stanley Kubrick's classic black comedy *Doctor Strangelove*, in 1964. The Hudson Institute was one of the first futurological think tanks and Kahn's book on Japan was one of its hallmark products. Kahn used to introduce the young Overholt to distinguished visitors by saying: 'This is Bill Overholt. He spent seven years at Harvard and Yale and it nearly ruined him, but we're trying to rehabilitate him.'

The rehabilitation worked. In 1976, Overholt and Zbigniew Brzezinski founded a journal called Global Political Assessment and both joined the staff of Jimmy Carter. Overholt found himself consistently at odds with the prevalent view among Carter's advisers that South Korea under President Park Chung Hee was nothing more than a corrupt and vicious dictatorship which did not merit US support. He also drafted, at that time, a paper entitled 'The Coming Crisis of Soviet Communism', which, when presented to the full National Security Council staff, in May 1977, was rejected as crazy by the NSC's resident Sovietologists.

In 1980, Overholt left government to work for Bankers Trust, heading up a global political risk analysis unit. Since 1985, he has been based in Hong Kong, still with Bankers Trust, concentrating on the reforms in and future of China under Deng Xiaoping. Shortly after the massacre in Tiananmen Square, on 4 June 1989, he wrote a piece which no major newspaper or magazine in the world would publish, arguing that 'although this looked very bad for China, in the end Deng Xiaoping would come out a hero and Gorbachev, then at the height of his popularity would be seen as a fool and lose his job.' He got both those predictions right. The man has balls as well as brains and *China: The Next Economic Superpower* deserves a close reading on its author's track record alone.

The book stands up extremely well on its own, though. Overholt provides us with seven lucid and cogent chapters: The Rise of China's Economy; The Politics of Economic Take-off; The Emergence of Chinese Financial Markets; The Golden Age of Hong Kong and Guangdong; The Diplomacy of Hong Kong's Transition: The Transformation of International Relations; and The United States and China. The argument which knits them together is one which should be reflected on by all those concerned with economic development, foreign policy and the political economy of human rights. It boils down to a number of core propositions, each of which is supported by evidence and reasoning of a kind which make the book digestible for any intelligent reader.

The core propositions are these: under Deng Xiaoping, China 'bought the whole Pacific Asian policy package'. The consequent policy reorientation has catapulted it into a prominent and burgeoning position among the world's great trading nations. Within a generation, this will make China the great arbiter in Asia and a power the United States will have to treat with a great deal more respect. The most fundamental of these propositions is the first. The second is statistically irrefutable. The third is well-argued and thought-provoking, but remains a speculation; since various things could yet happen to confound it. [157]

The first, however, itself entails a radical reassessment of widely prevalent theories of both economic development and the nature of Chinese Communism. The 'Pacific Asian policy package' in question is summarized by Overholt as consisting of the following elements:

- A reduced military budget
- Subordination of politics to economic growth
- Strategic reliance on the United States
- Subordination of ideology to economic pragmatism
- Acceptance of foreign corporations and technology
- An increasingly market-oriented economy
- Encouragement of domestic economic competition; and
- An increasingly outward looking economic and social posture

---

157 It has to be said that we have now arrived at the very threshold of this overall transformation anticipated by Overholt more than twenty years ago. China has assumed a vastly greater place in world trade and finance than it had in 1993-94, it has begun to vastly upgrade its military capabilities and it openly aspires to become the 'great arbiter in Asia' which will not brook interference by the United States. This has provoked considerable debate in Australia about our strategic choices in the decade or two to come. The United States, meanwhile, under President Obama, seems unable to decide exactly what to do with regard to the rise and rise of China.

The next five to ten years have now become crucial, both in terms of American rebalancing and in terms of China's capacity to sustain its rise, strategically, politically and even economically. As I prepare this piece for reprinting, a fine opinion piece has appeared in *The Australian*, by John Lee of Sydney University and the Brookings Institution, in which he challenges the widespread premise that China is inevitably set to keep rising. He writes: 'China's economic problems are more than simply cyclical. The US seems to be roaring back, regaining manufacturing prominence and reinventing itself as a net energy exporter, while remaining, by a considerable margin, the world leader in innovation and technology.' Let us not, therefore, he argues, capitulate or kowtow pre-emptively to China on the assumption that it will in fact become the great arbiter in Asia. It may not escape the 'middle income trap' and its political system may yet come apart at the seams. I explored all these things in greater detail a decade ago in *Thunder from the Silent Zone: Rethinking China* (Scribe, 2005).

Overholt's trenchant remarks on the superiority of the East Asian (and even Southeast Asian) policy package to the nostrums of free marketeers and democratisers foisted so recently on the Soviet Union and Eastern Europe are especially worthy of attention.

Nowhere is Overholt's argument more incisive and iconoclastic than in his reflections on the diplomacy of Hong Kong's transition. Hong Kong, as he writes, 'is where the tectonic plates of Chinese and Western civilizations engage most firmly'. He points out that, since 1979, Hong Kong's 'GDP' has quadrupled; its total exports have sextupled (from $US15.3 billion in 1979 to $US98.6 billion in 1991); and its re-exports have increased *seventeen*-fold, catapulting Hong Kong from 20th to 10th among trading states and creating a 'Greater Hong Kong' in southern and seaboard China which dwarfs the old 'Little Hong Kong'—the British crown colony.

It is the latter, however, especially under Governor Chris Patten, has clung to, mistrusting and seeking to undercut China and, in the process both misrepresenting and undermining what is actually happening to the real Hong Kong. This fifth chapter of Overholt's book is a *tour de force* of unblinkered and unflinching political analysis and should become compulsory reading for all 'China watchers', to say nothing of those who intend not only to watch China but to act with some effectiveness in regard to it.

There are a few minor solecisms in the book, which should be imputed to the proof-readers, rather than to the author, but which I cannot help noting. At footnote 6 on page 68, the author refers us to 'Jonathan Spence *The Rise of Modern China* (New York, W. W. Norton & Co., 1990)'. Jonathan Spence's great book of 1990, of course, was *The Search for Modern China*. *The Rise of Modern China* is an equally massive tome by the Taiwanese scholar Immanuel C. Y. Hsu. On page 84, there is a sentence which reads, 'President Kennedy tried futilely to force South Korea to rescind Park Chung Hee's military coup in 1961 and protested Park's authoritarian Yushin Constitution in 1972.' Perhaps this last phrase was meant to read 'and President Nixon protested Park's authoritarian Yushin Constitution of 1972'? But this is nit-picking. The book is vigorous, rigorous, spiced with anecdotes, crammed with useful statistics; and it addresses with boldness and vision one of the greatest issues of the coming generation. Every serious person in Canberra should read it and mull over its argument.

Henry Kissinger and power politics[158]

Henry Kissinger achieved virtual pop-star fame in the early 1970s, as the shuttle diplomacy trapeze artist and architect of American détente with the then Soviet Union and with Mao's China. Those over thirty will remember the *Time* magazine covers. He was to American diplomacy in those days what Bob Hawke was to Australia industrial relations. The glossy-mag fame and popular notoriety of the man found expression, in the late 1970s, in a rag-time Monty Python ditty which went:

> *Oh, Henry Kissinger*
> *How I'm missing yer*
> *You're the Doctor of my dreams*
> *With your curly hair*
> *And your glassy stare*
> *And your Machiavellian schemes ...*

With his heavy-duty spectacles and gravelly German Jewish accent, his very European approach to American foreign policy and the dramatic events on which he stamped his name, Dr Kissinger surely endures as a figure in the popular imagination, though somewhere towards the back of the cupboard, in most cases, to be sure.

This book, more than any of Henry Kissinger's earlier ones, lends itself to cementing a place for his ideas in the popular mind. It has the makings, as Harvard University's leading specialist on crisis diplomacy and intelligence matters, Ernest R. May somewhat grudgingly admitted, in reviewing it of 'the mind-provoking qualities of great teaching'. Kissinger's name and the subject matter are surely guaranteed to make it a big, if not a best seller. It could, however, have done with a sub-title. *Diplomacy* is both too laconic for the reflections of so colourful a figure and too suggestive of a monumental academic treatise—something which the book is not.

A suitable sub-title might have been *A Realist's Epigrammatic Survey of Modern Times*. For it is a survey of modern times, from Richelieu and the Thirty Years War to Reagan and the end of the Cold War. It has the kind of sweep and conceptual gravity which make it a superb text to require undergraduates, or trainee officers and diplomats to read from cover to cover. But it is the epigrams and asides which make it Henry Kissinger's *piece de resistance*. Declaring that undergraduates and trainees should read the book may seem like a kind of put down, but the

---

158 This piece was first published in *The Canberra Times* on 2 July 1994 and is a review of Henry Kissinger's *Diplomacy* (Simon & Schuster, 1994), a massive tome at over 900 pages, but not a well-balanced one.

remark was not intended in such an impertinent spirit at all. Many people more learned and with greater responsibilities than undergraduates would certainly benefit from reading the book and enjoy the experience a great deal, as I did.

Diplomacy is, in fact, addressed primarily to practitioners of American foreign policy. It's central argument is that the liberal internationalism which Kissinger sees as having been the most distinguishing characteristic of American foreign policy since the presidency of Woodrow Wilson (1912-1920), while well-intentioned, has always needed and now needs more than ever to be tempered by an appreciation of the logic of interest and power in international affairs. It is not a complicated argument, but he uses the whole of modern history to try to impress it upon his readers.

The argument never becomes very complicated because Dr Kissinger is not much enamoured of international relations theory, except in an intelligent practitioner's sense. And even his most relentless critics will concede that he was a highly intelligent practitioner of the art of diplomacy. Art, not science; hence the hesitancy to delve very far into theory. To be sure, if one wants rigorously to understand and explicate much of the history and many of the practical judgments Kissinger presents in this book, then theory necessarily enters the picture. Refined theory. Graduate seminar and even school of advanced studies rumination. But Kissinger's concern is not with theoretical niceties. He somewhat ungraciously refers to such concerns, at one point in the book, as 'hair-splitting academic exegesis'. He is more concerned with what might be called—though he does not call it this—a sort of Weberian ethic of responsibility for statesmen. He dwells, again and again, on both the pitfalls of unbridled power politics and unrestrained moral or ideological fixations. Much of the dry wit and a good deal of the worldly wisdom that *Diplomacy* offers spring from this central concern.

Given the vast scope of *Diplomacy*, one might choose any one of a number of topics on which to pause and reflect about the accuracy of the author's history or the cogency of his argument. Let me choose two only: Kissinger's portrait of Stalin and his observations about the Vietnam War. While deploring Marxism in all its manifestations and celebrating the demise of the Soviet Union and its dominion in Eastern Europe, Kissinger depicts Stalin as a kind of dark genius for whom he cannot suppress a certain professional admiration. 'Stalin was indeed a monster,' he observes, 'but in the conduct of international relations he was the supreme realist—patient, shrewd and implacable—the Richelieu of his period.'

Certainly, this is a far more accurate appraisal of the greatest tyrant in world history than, for example, the appraisal of Stalin that President Franklin D. Roosevelt offered to his cabinet, in the wake of Yalta, to the effect that Stalin's early education in a seminary had imparted to his nature 'something of the way a Christian gentleman should behave.' And Kissinger's reflections on Stalin's interaction with both Hitler and the leaders of the Western democracies, between 1933 and 1953, buttress his appraisal. Yet he attributes to this diabolical practitioner of power politics the conviction that he was 'servant of historical truth'. He would have done better to have drawn the parallel with Cardinal Richelieu more closely and have highlighted the gulf that separated the professed metaphysical or ideological beliefs of the two men from their ruthless political and geopolitical behaviour.

Many of the portraits of statesmen in *Diplomacy* are deft and insightful, but this assertion that Stalin was motivated by a sense of service to 'historical truth' turns the depths of the man's psychotic cruelty and perilously cool vindictiveness into a mere ideological abstraction. If you want to understand the psyche of Stalin, then you need to cast Marx aside and pick up Machiavelli, Sade, Dostoevsky and Nietzsche. It is worth contemplating how it could be that Henry Kissinger, like a great many other people—to their cost—could find Stalin somehow admirable and fascinating. To be fascinated by the living Stalin was to be a mouse fascinated by the mesmerising snake coiled up and looming above it.[159]

Vietnam takes up more pages of *Diplomacy* than any other single topic: three whole chapters filling more than eighty pages. Kissinger's argument is neither new, nor particularly controversial, unless you remain a partisan of the Left-wing view that he and President Nixon were, in Terry Lane's recent phrase, 'the butchers of Southeast Asia', responsible for the Khmer Rouge genocide in Cambodia and the 'unconscionable' bombing of North Vietnam. If one

---

159 The literature on Stalin has continued to grow as more archival sources open up and further, probing historical inquiries are conducted. Ten years after this piece was written Donald Rayfield's *Stalin and His Hangmen* was published by Viking in 2004. In 2012, Anne Applebaum's *The Iron Curtain: The Crushing of Eastern Europe 1944-1956* threw new light on the purges and repression by which Stalin imposed Communism on the countries occupied by the Red Army as it drove the occupying Nazi forces back into Germany in 1944-45. Robert Gellately's *Stalin's Curse: Battling for Communism in War and Cold War* (Alfred A. Knopf, New York, 2013) advanced a systematic argument that Stalin was an enemy with whom peaceful co-existence was never going to be a possibility and that it was Soviet, not Anglo-American actions which made the Cold War inevitable in the 1940s.

Stephen Kotkin has set out to write an authoritative biography of Stalin. The first volume, *Stalin: Paradoxes of Power 1878-1928*, was published by Penguin, New York, in 2014. In a long coda to this first volume, Kotkin ponders the question of what alternatives there were to Stalin's leadership in the USSR by 1928. He concludes that, given the straitjacket of Bolshevik ideology, there really wasn't one. 'Rykov and others in the politburo had come to see not only a prickly, self-centred, often morose, vindictive person in Stalin, but also an indomitable communist and leader of inner strength, utterly dedicated to Lenin's ideas, able to carry the entire apparatus, the country and the cause of the world revolution on his back' (p. 731). They all paid with their lives for this judgment.

wanted to conduct a graduate seminar on the Vietnam War, one could certainly do worse than have the class read these eighty pages and then prepare critical and historical papers on points of detail in Kissinger's presentation of the matter.

No presentation of it, after all, least of all one of a mere eighty pages, will ever exhaust the tragedy and moral complexity of the Vietnam War. Kissinger's account, however, has the merit of being coherent, concise, dignified and written from the point of view of a man who had to take responsibility for the extrication of a superpower from a quagmire, with all that that extrication entailed on the global scene. We were deeply involved in that quagmire, in our own modest way. Yet Kissinger's map of the Cold War world, with its spheres of influence and conflict, marking out US allies and associates, does not include Australia in the latter category for some reason. Thailand and South Korea, Egypt and Guatemala feature as American allies and associates, as of course do the NATO states; but Australia draws a blank.[160]

The concluding chapter of *Diplomacy* offers a reflection on the 'new world order'. It is not a stirring or original piece of writing. It merely applies the uncomplicated realism laid out in Kissinger's long survey of modern history to the prospective multi-polar world of the 21st century. Much of it dwells on Russia, NATO and the Atlantic Alliance. As an Australian, I found myself impatient to learn what he thought about Asia and the Pacific. When Kissinger does turn to Asia, however, he has nothing whatever to say about Australia's role in it. He mentions APEC, but not Australia's role in its creation. His focus is overwhelmingly—and perhaps understandably—on China and Japan. And his message is simple: these two nations are, more than ever, great powers which the United States will have to treat on more equal terms than it has done throughout the 20the century. America's Wilsonian goals will, therefore, have to be sought patiently, in a journey that has no end, he concludes. He does not suggest any clear path towards their attainment, leaving us instead with a Spanish proverb: 'Traveller, there are no roads. Roads are made by walking.'

---

160 There is a scene in Seymour Hersh's book on Kissinger and Nixon in which the Chilean leader Eduardo Frei is in Washington and tells them that Chile is being neglected and even damaged by their policies. Kissinger says to Frei that Chile does not matter, because 'history runs on an axis that begins in Moscow and runs through Berlin and London to Washington.' This preoccupation with the northern hemisphere may explain why Australia did not register with him when he was writing his book.

The looming danger to Hong Kong's liberties[161]

Books about Hong Kong these days are rather like books about *Homo sapiens* and the ecosphere. There are doomsayers, relentless optimists and just about every shade of disposition in between. Mark Roberti, a journalist who worked in Hong Kong for almost a decade, up until last year, as a correspondent for *Asiaweek*, falls somewhere in the doomsaying part of the spectrum. His sub-title contains the basic message: Hong Kong as a 'free city' is about to fall into the hands of 'barbarians'.

Most of this book consists of a narrative account of the Sino-British negotiations over the future of Hong Kong from 1982 to 1990. Mr Robert's claim to originality is that he, in his own words, 'worked full time for more than two years, interviewing 142 people in Hong Kong, London and Beijing, including almost all of the major players and filed over a hundred Freedom of Information requests with the United States government, thereby reconstructing a more or less definitive record of the negotiations.'

His argument is uncomplicated: 'Britain is stripping the people of Hong Kong of the protection of British democracy and forcing them to live under a Communist dictatorship.' Or, as he puts it a little less baldly, towards the end of his book: 'Having failed to provide the Hong Kong people with either a truly representative government to protect them after 1997 or a place of refuge, Britain has left her colonial subjects to the mercy and whims of China's leaders. The Basic Law gives Beijing the means to control every facet of Hong Kong's administration through its hand-picked governor.' Even more damning: 'The gap between what the Hong Kong people needed in order to keep living in freedom and what China was willing to give could not be bridged, so the Foreign Office and Thatcher's government simply covered it up.'

---

161 This piece first appeared in *The Canberra Times* on 29 October 1994, a decade before the Occupy Central democracy protests erupted in Hong Kong. It is a review of Mark Roberti's *The Fall of Hong Kong: China's Triumph and Britain's Betrayal* (John Wiley & Sons, 1994). As I prepare it for reprinting, a short piece in *The Australian* (08 January 2015, p. 7) reports that the Hong Kong legislative council has 'announced new proposals for how Hong Kong should choose its next leader, but made clear that candidates would still be screened—the key issue behind more than two months of mass protests. More than 20 legislative councillors carrying yellow umbrellas—the symbol of the pro-democracy movement—walked out of the chamber as the consultation document was about to be presented by government No 2 Carrie Lam. They shouted 'I want universal suffrage', as they left, forcing a brief adjournment ... China has pledged that voters in Hong Kong can elect the city's next chief executive in 2017—the first time there has ever been a public vote. But it insists that only two or three candidates can stand and that they will be vetted by a loyalist committee.' Meanwhile, Beijing has denounced Martin Lee, the democracy leader, as a 'running dog' of the colonialists, in a tired re-run of old Maoist rhetoric from the Cold War years.

Mr Roberti's account of the Sino-British negotiations may prove to be the most complete we will get this side of the repeal of the Official Secrets Act in London. Certainly, it is quite detailed enough for anyone who desires a working record of the process. Perhaps it might have been made more useful, though, by inclusion of the text of the Basic Law, or at least its most significant clauses, much as Robert Cottrell includes the text of the Sino-British Joint Declaration of 19 December 1984 as an annex to his 1993 book *The End of Hong Kong*.

However, Mr Roberti's book conspicuously lacks two things which are vital to the sort of case its author tried to build. First, an opening chapter setting out a historically reflective and conceptually sophisticated account of what has made Hong Kong such a vibrant and prosperous city state in the colonial era. Second, a much more substantial conclusion, setting out with dispassionate rigour the grounds for the author's opinion that 'Hong Kong, as we know and love it' is about to pass into history and that its people may suffer serious oppression in the process. The absence of both these elements makes *The Fall of Hong Kong* a thinner book, in both senses of the term, than its subject warrants.

What seems to elude Mr Roberti, in his concern over the possible end of freedom in Hong Kong, is the tremendous historical irony involved in what is about to happen to that great enclave of colonialism and capitalism. If we stand back just a little from the recent drama over democratic reform and fears of Tiananmen style Communist repression in Victoria Park or Nathan Road, what stands out in the grand sweep of Hong Kong's history from the Opium Wars to 1997?

Let's remember that the barren island of Hong Kong and its mainland toehold were extracted from Imperial China as part of a British campaign to prise the Middle Kingdom open to foreign trade. The Emperor Qianlong, after all, had written to King George III, in 1793: 'We have never valued ingenious articles, nor do we have the slightest need of your country's manufactures.' His Britannic Majesty's envoy to the Celestial Kingdom, George Macartney, noted on that occasion that the Chinese Empire, awesome though it appeared at first glance, suffered from grave internal weaknesses that could lead to its disintegration.

We are still hearing variations on Macartney's prediction after two centuries, during which the Empire did indeed disintegrate due to its grave internal weaknesses, was dragged back together kicking and screaming, by Communist terror and totalitarian governance and now teeters once more on the brink of disintegration owing to the brittleness of Communist rule and the Party's ruthless suppression of all other stabilizing civil or political bodies. Yet the attitude of Beijing to foreign trade and manufactures has changed *in toto caelo*.

Taking Hong Kong as an enclave worked for Britain sooner and better than it did for China, but now it has become both the model for China and the most immediate source for the expertise and finance required to spur its voluntary opening to world trade and investment. China now insists on reversing the outcome of the Opium Wars, but only because it has finally decided to embrace exactly what those wars were about: the reform and opening of a decrepit and reactionary China to the forces of liberal capitalism and the tide of innovation it brings with it.

What is at stake, therefore, is no longer the old issue of whether China will be open for business and the importation of 'ingenious articles', but whether its repressive and xenophobic governing power—the Communist Party—can be changed further; whether China can, at last, be converted into a less arbitrary and repressive polity—one in which the rule of law and not of men (which is to say a totalitarian party) prevails. The Communist Party fears that 'perfidious Albion' is trying, none too subtly, to use Hong Kong for this end. Hong Kong cannot, of course, be held for this purpose, but if it could be reformed before being returned, it might prove to be a veritable Trojan Horse of democratization.

Mr Roberti sees things the other way around and is concerned about immediate possibilities for political repression and human tragedy. His moral concern does him credit, but perhaps it vitiates his political and economic judgment. He asserts that Britain should have introduced full democracy in Hong Kong years ago and so presented China with a *fait accompli* before the imminence of retrocession made the issue as sensitive as it has now become. Perhaps this is so; but by his own account there has long been and is still a powerful constituency in Hong Kong which opposes democratization for its own reasons and not because of any fealty to the Communist Party.

Mr Roberti nowhere spells out how or when the massive changes he calls for might plausibly have been introduced against such opposition and in view of the colony's historical character—being run by a governor appointed in London. Tacitly conceding this point, he declares that Britain should have allowed any or all of Hong Kong's citizens to emigrate. He argues that this would have proved an economic boon to Britain. This, also, may be true; but it might well have destroyed Hong Kong, which would surely not have been to anyone's benefit. He wavers on the matter of Hong Kong's economic future, for better or for worse, before entering the judgment that it will cease to be an Asia/Pacific financial centre within twenty years from 1997. This is a highly contestable claim, given both current trends and China's economic prospects.

Mr Roberti concedes that China's burgeoning middle class (estimated in 1993 at 200 million) and booming economy are drawing record amounts of foreign investment and that vast quantities of this are being channelled through Hong Kong. He does not explore the ways in which Hong Kong is itself financially colonizing China. But he concludes that international companies are 'unlikely to expose their regional operations to the risks of a legal system that cannot protect their assets, to a government that could blacklist them ... to political uncertainty and perhaps to social turmoil.'

If this is so, why is foreign investment pouring into Shanghai, the Bohai Rim and ever deeper reaches of the Chinese hinterland? Mr Roberti makes insufficient allowance for the complex interaction of China's forbidding ways with the powerful pull of international engagement and all the incentives this now provides to the Communist Party to begin to play by different rules. In all this, in part because he does not look back over its history with any great detachment, he shows his lack of appreciation of the triumph that Hong Kong now represents in a long view of the history of modern China.

Keeping the rise of China in perspective in 1995 [162]

One generation ago, China was still viewed by conservative strategic analysts as a threat to Australia's security because of a fear that it was bent on spreading Communism throughout the region. The full implications of the then decade old Sino-Soviet split were still not taken altogether seriously by many such analysts. The ancient Sino-Vietnamese antagonism was practically ignored. The poverty and backwardness of Maoist China were regarded as the taproot of its threat to Western values and its appeal to the poor of Asia. Its self-destructive radical ideology was seen as a threat to the capitalist West, in part because of its appeal to the lunatic fringe of the student Left in Western societies.

Some few brave and pragmatic souls looked for ways in which China might be drawn away from its isolation, radicalism, revolutionary politics and backwardness, if only to become at last the vast China market of old Western dreams. Beyond almost anyone's realistic expectations, this has happened since 1979. Yet now China seems increasingly to be regarded as a threat to the region, to Southeast Asia, to Australia, even to the West at large or the global balance of power, because of its conservative nationalist ideology, its increasing economic prosperity and its sound relationship with a post-Communist Russia.

There is a rising chorus of voices expressing alarm at the real or imagined military implications of China's rapid economic growth; at the alleged massive increase in its defence budget in this

---

162 This piece was first published in *The Australian* on 16 May 1995. It may well have been one of the pieces which prompted Doug Kean, as Deputy Director General of DIO in 1995, to want to rein in my contributions to public debate on the grounds that I was 'well known' to be a 'highly influential analyst' and if I wrote something and then the government could be seen to be taking a different path, people might start asking awkward questions. In the twenty years that have since elapsed, China has relentlessly increased its military expenditures and is—in the present decade—now rapidly becoming a first class military power for the first time in modern history. A decade ago, in *Thunder from the Silent Zone: Rethinking China* (Scribe, 2005, pp. 59-62), I warned that one possible scenario for China's development in the years ahead was 'militarization'.

This danger has become far more acute in the decade since I wrote that than it was at the time. Yet there were, in 1995, quite other possibilities and, to a considerable extent, there still are. There were four scenarios that I sketched out in 2005: Mutation, Maturation, Militarization and Metastasis. As of 2015, there has been relentless resistance by the Party to Mutation, which is to say, political liberalization as envisaged in the 1980s, in a context where the Democracy Wall (1978-79) and student movements (1986-89) challenged the Party's monopoly of and arbitrary exercise of power. It was always the most attractive of the four. All three others have seen signs of development and the next decade will be crucial in determining what kind of China we will have to deal with by the 2020s.

decade; at its allegedly ominous military 'build-up'; at the 'objectionable' nature of its political regime; and also at the possibility of political or even geopolitical instability should that regime actually disintegrate. Sober-minded Chinese might be forgiven for thinking that their long-suffering country can do nothing right in the eyes of its neighbours and the world. If China is poor and radical, it is a threat. If it is prosperous and pragmatic, it is also apparently a threat. If it supports revolution in Southeast Asia, it is a threat; but if it gives up any such aim and seeks to become a normal great power consistent with its size and historic dignity, then it is also a threat.

If it drastically reduces the defence budget as a share of national revenue and seeks to gradually convert its armed forces into a modern and professional fighting force, this is more threatening than reassuring, it seems. So, at least, things might appear to many a Chinese patriot in Beijing or Shanghai as of 1995. But is China, from the point of view of a rational Australian patriot, actually a looming threat, now that it is becoming economically, politically and militarily 'normal'? Should we fear what China is doing, or might conceivably do in 10, 20 or 30 years? What kinds of threats could China pose in the medium to long term, if its power should continue to grow and become truly formidable? What does Australia have to fear from such hypothetical threats?

The chief reason that apprehension has been increasing is China's sheer size, weight and mass. If the economy that is growing so rapidly was merely that of Hong Kong or Singapore, there would be no occasion for projecting a sense of possible danger onto the screen of the future. China, however, is a behemoth and, when it stirs, it causes a shiver of apprehension among the smaller beasts in the ocean deeps of international politics and even among the larger creatures cognizant of its presence. There is talk of China's economy becoming larger than that of the United States within a couple of decades.[163] It has been plausibly described as set to become the world's next economic superpower. What if this emerging economic superpower should decide to invest heavily in military power and then use its new military muscle to impose its will in Asia?

Some analysts believe that it is already doing both of these things. They point to five consecutive years of double-digit increases in China's defence budget.[164] They point to its stance

---

163 In purchasing power parity terms, there have been claims that that point was actually reached in 2014. That is an astounding development, given where things stood in 1984 and even 1994. Yet China's economy remains structurally cumbersome and backward in very many ways and it is far from clear that its upward ascent can be sustained much beyond this point, especially under the heavy hand of the Communist dictatorship. Moreover, with a population four times that of the United States, it's per capita income remains far smaller than that of the leading OECD countries. Its environmental problems are severe and its financial system, dominated by the Party run state banks, is not in good order and condition; though this is camouflaged by the state's control of information flows.

164 Those annual double digit increases in the defence budget have now been sustained for twenty four

in the South China Sea; the ongoing modernization of its nuclear arsenal; its acquisition of advanced combat aircraft and new conventional submarines from Russia. Don't these things mean that, as international affairs commentator Malcolm Booker recently asserted, the rising potential enemy and threat to the security of the Asian Pacific?

The single biggest threat to Asian Pacific security in the years of China's emergence from Maoism onto the world stage as a normal great power is not, in fact, China's size, nor its prosperity, nor its current level of military expenditure, nor the modernization of its nuclear arsenal, nor its territorial claims in the South China Sea. It is the risk of miscalculation of the relative power and strategic intentions of China resulting in either ill-advised appeasement of the behemoth or unwarranted confrontation with it. In many ways, China's size—geographically, demographically and economically—is a liability to it. It faces enormous institutional and resource challenges to sustain its impressive rate of economic growth. To meet these challenges, it will almost certainly have to open up even more and become better integrated with the external world of trading states.

If it does so, it is likely to develop an ever-increasing stake in regional and global peace and stability. If it does not do so, it is likely to find its resource base for military modernization shrinking and its intractable problems pulling it in on itself, rather than driving it to external aggression. In any case, its military spending would have to increase enormously in real terms if it was to develop truly formidable power projection capabilities much beyond its own periphery. All we have seen in the early 1990s is annual double digit increases in nominal terms, which have yet to return China's military spending in real terms to the levels it stood at in 1979, before its steep decline in the 1980s, when Deng Xiaoping froze it in order to give priority to economic development.

China's acquisitions of advanced weapons systems from Russia have been extremely modest and the modernization of its nuclear forces will still leave it, in 2010, the least formidable of the five major nuclear powers. Nor is it clear that the nuclear arsenal it would possess by then would have any practical utility in any of the hypothetical regional conflicts which might occur in the 2010s. China is growing in power, both relatively and absolutely, though not yet as decisively or rapidly as the more alarmist analyses would have us believe. We need to take

---

years and the consequence has been to rocket China to No 2 on the table of international military expenditures, behind only the United States. Whereas, however, the US has global bases and provides security for numerous and substantial allies from Japan and South Korea to Germany and France, as well as shelling out generous veterans' benefits and pensions, China protects no-one but itself and has a vastly smaller proportion of its defence budget allocated to overhead costs and entitlements. In real terms, therefore, especially when both budgets are adjusted in purchasing power parity terms, China spends almost as much as the United States now and it is still increasing its outlays, while those of the US have been shrinking.

careful stock of how this maturing of the Chinese revolution necessarily alters the balance of power in the Asian Pacific region and to adjust our strategic outlook accordingly. We do not, at this point, need to become seriously alarmed.

Plainly, our interest and that of our regional neighbours has long been in China becoming a normal and benign great power, instead of revolutionary state. Neither aggravated Chinese nationalism, nor hubristic great power pretensions on China's part, nor the failure of China's economic surge and a consequent lapse into political anarchy is to be desired. We should see gradual military modernization—and that, for now, is all we are seeing—as merely one aspect of its overall post-Maoist course of normalization and not as the beginning of a bid to dominate Asia. We should neither expect nor wish that China would continue to settle for a level of military backwardness that we, even as a small to middling power, would regard as intolerable.

It is in this context that China's most recent nuclear test should be seen. We should continue with patient and persistent efforts to draw China into multilateral security dialogue and greater strategic transparency, but understand that it is beginning to stretch limbs that have been cramped for a considerable time and that it will seek to stand fully upright. Let us seek to balance its increasing vigour as need may dictate, but not leap to the conclusion that China is an enemy. The fact that it is large and vigorous is enough (or ought to be) to prompt sober and responsible measures to maintain an acceptable regional security balance. The ringing of too many alarm bells too hastily will only cause confusion and miscalculation, perhaps generating an action/reaction syndrome which will bring about the very arms race and confrontation with China feared by the ringers of the bells to begin with. We are a long way from such an arms race and confrontation yet and, for the time being, we should keep our imaginations as well as our powder good and dry.

Hidden aspects of Nazi eugenics[165]

Reading William L. Shirer's *The Rise and Fall of the Third Reich* when I was thirteen years old was a deeply formative and disturbing experience. Far more than any religious talk at school about 'original sin' and the 'fall of man' from the grace of the Garden of Eden, Shirer's pioneering documentation of the horrors of the Third Reich and the Final Solution convinced me that I lived in a world of violence and evil otherwise inconceivable in the environment within which I was growing up.[166]

I have wondered ever since how people who lived through those times could have been able to psychologically digest their experiences and go on living 'normal' lives.[167] This book is about a category of individuals whose lives were shaped by that era in a particularly intimate and inescapable fashion: children born or kidnapped and raised as genetic specimens in a Nazi racial program overseen by Schutzstaffel (SS) chief Heinrich Himmler. This was the so-called Lebensborn Experiment.

Lebensborn means 'fount of life'. The word is, of course, cognate with one more commonly associated with the Nazi catastrophe - *Lebensraum*, 'living space'. The Nazi ambition, rooted in a misconceived and mongrel mix of pseudo-science and bastardized history, was to dominate the European continent, eliminate or enslave the mass of 'non-Aryan' peoples and repopulate the east, in particular, with a Germanic 'master race'.[168] The extermination and enslavement parts of this barbarous project have made a lasting impression even on the popular imagination, since the fall of the Third Reich; though, as we have seen in the past few years in Bosnia, such barbarism has not been done away with even in Europe.[169]

---

165   This piece first appeared in *The Canberra Times* on 28 October 1995. It is a review of Catrine Clay and Michael Leapman *Master Race: The Lebensborn Experiment in Nazi Germany* (Hodder & Stoughton, 1995).

166   Notoriously, there have been attempts to deny that the Holocaust occurred. One of the worst or at least best known offenders was the pro-Nazi British historian David Irving. For a systematic refutation of his views see Richard J. Evans *Lying About Hitler: History, Holocaust and the David Irving Trial* (Basic Books, New York, 2001). On the actual roots of the Holocaust, see Christopher R. Browning *The Origin of the Final Solution: The Evolution of Nazi Jewish Policy September 1939—March 1942* (Yad Vashem, Jerusalem, 2004). Bettina Stangneth has provided a most revealing account of the unrepentant genocidal racism of Adolf Eichmann in *Eichmann Before Jerusalem: The Unexamined Life of a Mass Murderer* (Alfred A. Knopf, New York, 2014).

167   See Christopher R. Browning *Remembering Survival: Inside a Nazi Slave Labour Camp* (W. W. Norton & Co., New York and London, 2010).

168   Rolf-Dieter Muller *Enemy in the East: Hitler's Secret Plans to Invade the Soviet Union* (I. B. Tauris, London, 2015) provides a deeply informed account of the roots of the Nazi onslaught on the Slavic world.

169   For an overall perspective on the upheavals that marred Europe in the 20th century, see Mark Mazower *Dark Continent: Europe's Twentieth Century* (Penguin, London, 1998).

What is less well known is the far smaller and less spectacular breeding program by which the same SS which performed extermination duties in the East were encouraged to perform what can only be described as 'stud' duties with carefully selected 'Aryan' or Nordic women. They were also assigned the task of identifying and kidnapping children in the occupied territories who were deemed to be of 'Aryan' genetic stock. Such children, after minute testing and examination, were then adopted out to good, solid German families to be raised as Germans, with new identities. They were then to be given a comprehensive Nazi re-education.

Master Race does not make the same deeply shocking or even overwhelming impact on one's moral consciousness as do serious accounts of the genocidal mania and devastating war-making of the Nazis.[170] It is, after all, concerned with something which, apart from being on a far smaller scale than the genocide or the war, about the generation of life, rather than its mass extinction. Yet the practices whereby the Lebensborn Experiment was carried out and the equanimity with which its chief administrators defended their actions, during Case No 8 in Nuremburg, before the American Military Tribunal No 1, in 1947-48, merit close attention, precisely because they represent the 'positive' side of the Nazi racial program. This is the central thrust of *Master Race*.

Chapter 2 'The Racial Utopia' introduces the reader briefly not only to the racial doctrines set out in *Mein Kampf*, but to their roots or parallels in the writings of Arthur de Gobineau (*Essay on the Inequality of the Human Races*, 1855) and Houston Stewart Chamberlain (*The Foundations of the Twentieth Century*, 1899). These racist writers are well known as progenitors of Nazi racial myth-making. What is less well appreciated, Clay and Leapman argue, is that much

---

170 The Nazi conquests of 1939 to 1944 have been dubbed 'internal colonialism', with the implication that they saw practices pioneered by European imperialists in the late nineteenth and early twentieth centuries imported into the European heartland with devastating consequences. There is only limited truth to this claim. Nothing that was done in the British Empire justifies such a comparison. The Spanish impact in the Americas is a different matter and the Belgian impact on the Congo (Zaire) under King Leopold II, in the first decade and a half of the 20th century, was certainly genocidal and reckless in its violence. It is ironical, in the circumstances, that it was the fate of 'little Belgium' that triggered British entry into the First World War.

An even greater irony was that the practice of class warfare and social revolution in the USSR matched the worst imperialist practices in its expropriation of property, flagrant injustice and massive violence. On the destructive impact of the Spanish conquests in the Americas, see Charles C. Mann *1491: New Revelations of the Americas Before Columbus* (Alfred A. Knopf, New York, 2005 pp. 31-133). On looting under the Bolsheviks, see Sean McMeekin *History's Greatest Heist: The Looting of Russia by the Bolsheviks* (Yale University Press, New Haven and London, 2009). The problem of genocide, of course, is far from being one begun by or uniquely practised by Europeans of any kind. For a reflection on the plague of killing in the late 20th century, see Samantha Power *A Problem from Hell: America in the Age of Genocide* (Harper Collins Perennial, New York, 2003).

better remembered figures, among them H. G. Wells, Francis Galton, T.S. Eliot, Virginia Woolf, George Bernard Shaw and Marie Stopes all, at various points, embraced, or at least flirted with, rather radical theories of racial purification through selective breeding.

Clay and Leapman also point out that Hitler admired the British Empire and the way it had subordinated and ruled what Rudyard Kipling called 'the lesser breeds without the law' in wide parts of the world. The final chapter in their book, 'Born-Again Eugenics', draws conceptual parallels between the Lebensborn Experiment and the work of various population scientists, human geneticists, psychiatrists and sociobiologists in the West up to the present, including the well-known 1994 book *The Bell Curve*, by Richard Herrnstein and Charles Murray.

The core of Master Race, chapters 3 to 9, is concerned with 'Himmler's Children', 'Poles Like Us' and 'Maids of Norway'. A number of the personal stories reconstructed by the authors are deeply moving testimonies to the moral foundations of human intimacy and the need of individuals for a sense of identity and personal integrity. It is the historical and moral anchoring of the book, however, which gives it its real bite. Tracing the origins of the Nazi Party back to such pre-World War I racist and nationalist bodies as the Racial Hygiene Society and the Thule Society, Clay and Leapman point to such non-German bodies, still in existence in Britain and the United States, as the Galton Institute, the Pioneer Fund and the Cold Spring Harbor Laboratory as seedbeds for ideas genetically similar, as it were, to those which inspired the Nazis.

As we approach a 21st century which will, inevitably, be an era of congestion and immense challenges to the social and moral imaginations of civilized human beings around the globe; it will be well to bear in mind that the roots of racial and genetic theories have a great deal to do with notions of 'cleansing' and 'order' and 'living space' and that all these things have been called for in the name of 'higher civilization' long before the rise of the Nazis. While the core tale of *Master Race* and the individual stories of the Lebensborn Experiment it tells are moving, it would be facile to read the matter simply as the bizarre story of a Nazi eccentricity. What we need to absorb and reflect upon is more hauntingly represented, I suggest, by a passage from H. G. Wells, still a widely read and admired science fiction author.

The passage is something that Wells published in 1901, at the height of European imperialism, but long before the rise of Nazism in Germany. It reads as follows:

> *The ethical system which will dominate the world state will be shaped primarily to favour the procreation of what is fine and efficient and beautiful in humanity ... and to check the procreation of base and servile types ... The method that must in some cases still be called in to the help of man is death ... For a multitude of contemptible and silly creatures, fear-driven and helpless and useless ... feeble, ugly, inefficient ... and increasing and multiplying through sheer incontinence and stupidity, the men of the new Republic will have little pity and less benevolence.*

What kind of new Republic, then, would that give us? But equally, what are we to do with the pullulating multitudes to which Wells referred, when the world's population was only a fraction of what it has since become? There is a question for the coming century.

The rise and fall of totalitarianism[171]

Totalitarianism is a word which, like the word revolution, has a host of connotations. Explore those and you will find yourself worming your way into the heart of darkness of 20th century political sociology. Almost on a global basis now, the word totalitarianism carries with it, by association of ideas, the names Hitler and Stalin and, especially since about 1978, that of Pol Pot.[172]

If you were lying on the psychoanalyst's couch and were asked what were the first things that came into your head when the word totalitarianism was mentioned, those names would very likely be among the first words to bubble to the surface and tumble off your tongue. Likewise such shibboleth terms as doublethink, Big Brother (or Brother Number One), Gulag, Auschwitz, Final Solution, Gestapo, KGB, Great Terror, purge, killing fields and so on.

Totalitarianism has its own unique and sombre literature, among which, perhaps, Arthur Koestler's *Darkness at Noon*, George Orwell's *Nineteen Eighty-Four* (and his *Animal Farm*) and Alexander Solzhenitsyn's *The Gulag Archipelago* are the most proverbial. For a time in mid-century and even for a few years in the early to mid-1980s, there were those in the West

---

171 This piece was first published in *The Canberra Times* on 25 November 1995. It is a review of Abbott Gleason *Totalitarianism: The Inner History of the Cold War* (Oxford University Press, 1995) and Roger Eatwell's *Fascism: A History* (Chatto & Windus, 1995). I had left the Defence Intelligence Organization by the time this piece was written and was beginning to explore ways to create a new way of life, free of the apparatus of supervision in a secrecy obsessed government bureaucracy.

172 I do not know why I failed to include in this short list the name of Mao Zedong, who was as bad as any of the others and, in absolute terms, responsible for more deaths among his own people than any of them. The Left like to claim that Stalin and Mao cannot be equated with Hitler because class warfare is somehow legitimate, unlike racial extermination. As one China scholar remarked to me many years ago, with a gentle smile, when I raised the matter of the deaths by starvation under Mao of at least 35 million people, 'But Mao didn't *mean* to kill those people, so you can't compare him with Hitler.' It has always staggered me that he could so readily pass over the deaths of tens of millions of people and exonerate Mao of blame for them, despite the indisputable fact that they died for no reason other than Mao's insistence on both a mad economic policy and totalitarian control of information.

But in any case, Mao was responsible for the deaths of other millions whose deaths he clearly did intend—from the terrors of the late 1940s and early 1950s to the anti-Rightist campaign and the incarceration of millions in the Laogai to the Cultural Revolution. On the roots of the Great Leap Forward, see Frederick C. Teiwes and Warren Sun *China's Road to Disaster* (M. E. Sharpe, New York, 1999). On its consequences, see the particularly fine study by Dali L. Yang *Calamity and Reform in China* (Stanford University Press, 1996). The most exhaustive documentation of the famine can be found in Yang Jisheng *Tombstone: The Great Chinese Famine 1958-1962* (Farrar, Straus and Giroux, New York, 2008). The most recent systematic analysis of the matter can be found in Frank Dikotter *Mao's Great Famine* (Bloomsbury, London, 2010).

who feared that totalitarianism was the future—that the Communists would win the Cold War. The future prophesied in Orwell's *Nineteen Eighty-Four*, of 'a boot stamping on a human face forever', still seemed alarmingly possible.

I remember an edition of *Quadrant*, in August 1985, in which the late Eugene Kamenka and the late Frank Knopfelmacher bemoaned the susceptibility of Western societies and statesmen to the propaganda (as they saw it) of the Marxists and (in the case of Dr Knopfelmacher) predicted that we would all end up in a global Gulag within a generation, bound in the darkness by 'the totalitarian apparatus covertly placed in our midst.'[173] That was the very year that Mikhail Gorbachev became General Secretary of the Communist Party of the Soviet Union. Six years later, the Soviet Union itself disintegrated. And shortly thereafter, Francis Fukuyama published *The End of History and the Last Man*, heralding the end of Communism and the triumph of the West. What had become of totalitarianism?

These two books by Abbott Gleason and Roger Eatwell, *Totalitarianism* and *Fascism* go far towards providing an answer to that question and access to a wider literature on the subject in a lucid and readily digestible form. Gleason, a distinguished scholar of Russian and Soviet affairs has given us what must surely be the best review of the literature on totalitarianism available. While it lacks the originality and brilliance of Hannah Arendt's *The Origins of Totalitarianism* (1951), it has the advantage of looking back on the phenomenon and the historical epoch, rather than, as it were, 'down the barrel' at it. At a time of resurgence of interest in Arendt's work, Gleason also draws upon the reflections of those who have pointed out the oversights and excesses in Arendt's seminal analysis—from Stephen Whitfield's *Into the Dark: Hannah Arendt and Totalitarianism* (1980) to Margaret Canovan's *Hannah Arendt: A Reinterpretation of Her Political Thought* (1992).

Gleason's chapter headings will give some idea of the breadth of his survey of this haunting subject. He begins with 'Fascist Origins' and 'A New Kind of State: Italy, Germany and the Soviet Union in the 1930s'. Here he takes up the vexed and controversial topic of the similarities and dissimilarities between the regimes headed by Benito Mussolini, Joseph Stalin and Adolf Hitler and how the description 'totalitarian' came to be used in reference to them. In chapters 3 and 4, he turns to 'Wartime in the English-speaking World' and 'The Cold War', in which he makes clear how the term 'totalitarianism' became shorthand for the nightmare of the democratic West about Communism, but also a pejorative term used with considerable lack of discrimination by conservatives in the Cold War to taint or discredit a wide spectrum of political and economic opinions.

---

173   This is, of course, the subject of the first piece in the present book, published in 1990.

In chapter 5 'Brainwashing: Communist China as a Totalitarian State', Gleason extends his analysis beyond the Eurocentric locale of most of the discourse on totalitarianism to explore the rise and nature of Maoism. The second half of his book is devoted to an illuminating and admirably sober exploration of the debate over totalitarianism in the West and in the Soviet bloc itself. Chapter 6, 'Searching for the Origins of Totalitarianism', pivots on the pioneering works by Hannah Arendt and Jacob Talmon in the early 1950s. Chapter 7, 'Totalitarianism among the Sovietologists', provides an excellent introduction to the world of Cold War Sovietology, especially in the United States, showing how the revisionism of Stephen F. Cohen, Jerry Hough and Sheila Fitzpatrick emerged and how it clashed with the ideological stances of the old Right and the neo-conservatives.

Chapter 8, 'The Cold War in Post-War Europe: France, Italy and Germany', and chapter 9, 'The Cold War in Eastern Europe', are beautifully complementary. The sketches of Raymond Aron, Jean-Paul Sartre and Albert Camus are, to my mind, a highlight and a keynote as regards Gleason's own outlook. Anyone who has read Simone de Beauvoir's memoirs *Prime of Life* and *Force of Circumstance* (or for that matter her novel *The Mandarins*) will appreciate the acuteness and economy with which Gleason portrays the French intellectual milieu in the years immediately after the Second World War.[174]

---

174 Simone de Beauvoir was, for various reasons, a controversial figure, but her memoirs were superbly written and are a great document for the era. Beginning with *Memoirs of a Dutiful Daughter* (1958), they proceeded through her life with *The Prime of Life* (1960), *Force of Circumstance* (1963) and, almost a decade later, *All Said and Done* (1972). All these volumes were preceded by a great deal of other writing, including *The Second Sex* (1949) and *The Mandarins* (1954). I read all these books as an undergraduate and found their author a fascinating figure. My heavily underscored and annotated copies still hold pride of place in my library. Within a short time, I came to hold a higher regard for the integrity and political opinions of both Aron and Camus than those of Sartre and de Beauvoir, but there is a scene in *Prime of Life* that has always stayed with me. It dates from their youth, when, by de Beauvoir's account, they were all 'anarchists', sceptical of the Communist Party and even more of Communist splinter groups, despite having 'the very highest opinion of Trotsky'.

She recalled how Aron had been studying Husserl's phenomenology at the French Institute in Berlin in the very early 1930s and, during an evening at the Bec de Gaz on the Rue Montparnasse spoke to Sartre and de Beauvoir about what he had been learning:

> *We ordered the speciality of the house, apricot cocktails; Aron said, pointing to his glass, 'You see, my dear fellow, if you are a phenomenologist, you talk about this cocktail and make philosophy out of it.' Sartre turned pale with emotion at this. Here was just the thing he had been longing to achieve for years—to describe objects just as he saw and touched them and extract philosophy from the process. Aron convinced him that phenomenology exactly fitted in with his special preoccupations: by-passing the antithesis of idealism and realism, affirming simultaneously both the supremacy of reason and the reality of the visible world as it appears to our senses. On the Boulevard San Michel, Sartre purchased*

Gleason's book concludes with chapter 10 'The Evil Empire' and an Epilogue entitled, with a touch of irony, 'The Russians Call Themselves Totalitarian', which brings the debates between Western analysts to a rounding. I especially enjoyed this closure. The issues it circles around were personalized for me, in 1992, when I entertained Russian Orientalist Professor Lev Deliusin at my Braddon home, talked for hours with him about Stalinism, Communism in China, Brezhnev's Soviet Union and the legacy of Mikhail Gorbachev—and made a gift to him of Hannah Arendt's classic set of essays *Crises of the Republic*.

Roger Eatwell's *Fascism: A History*, covers less ground than Gleason's book on totalitarianism. It is not concerned with Communism, or what was once dubbed 'red fascism'. It is, nonetheless, a highly valuable survey of the subject in three parts: 'In the Beginning', 'Inter-War Fascism' and 'Fascism since 1945'. Eatwell is especially concerned with the social preconditions for the rise of what he regards as a pathological phenomenon and why Britain—or Anglo-Saxon democracies in general—seem especially immune to the phenomenon.

He argues that Fascism's different forms, ranging from the reactionary conservatism of Franco in Spain to the theatrical pretensions of Benito Mussolini, to the monstrous, Wagnerian epic of Adolf Hitler, conceal a core, coherent ideological foundation: a compound of Romantic anti-modernism, anti-rationalist nihilism and atavistic anti-cosmopolitanism, which remain part of the 'biochemistry' of the contemporary world, lurking in its bloodstream as sado-masochism lurks in the psyches of an unknown number of human beings. Whether it breaks out again, like Albert Camus's plague at Oran, will depend on both the overall stability of social systems and the attention paid by the citizens of the democracies to—how can I put this delicately?—the purity of their blood.

> *Levinas's book on Husserl, and was so eager to inform himself on the subject that he leafed through the volume as he walked along, without even having cut the pages. His heart missed a beat when he found references to contingency: had someone cut the ground from under his feet, then? As he read on, he reassured himself that this was not so. Contingency seemed not to play any very important part in Husserl's system—of which, in any case, Levinas gave only a formal and decidedly vague outline. Sartre decided to make a serious study of him, and took the necessary steps to succeed Aron at the French Institute in Berlin for the coming year—this on Aron's own instigation.* (pp. 135-36)

When I read this, in 1980, I had already abandoned the formal study of philosophy for that of history and I did not follow up Sartre's interest in Husserl. It was only many years later that finally turned my attention to or discovered an interest in Husserl's thought. That interest centred on his last work, *The Crisis of the European Sciences and Transcendental Phenomenology*; an unfinished study written in Prague as Nazism rose ominously in Germany and threatened to overrun the continent. For a good introduction to Husserl, see Barry Smith and David Woodruff Smith *The Cambridge Companion to Husserl* (Cambridge University Press, 1995) and David Woodruff Smith *Husserl* (Routledge, New York and London, 2013).

The August 1945 communist revolution in Vietnam[175]

This important book is the kind which justifies the existence of elite universities and requires the tenure and facilities they have traditionally provided. Ten years in preparation, it is the culmination of three decades of commitment by its author to understanding the tangled roots of the devastating upheavals that occurred in Indochina between 1945 and 1975.

Preceded by two volumes on Vietnamese anti-colonialism covering the periods from 1885 to 1920 and 1920 to 1945, *Vietnam 1945: The Quest for Power* provides what is surely the most lucid account in any language of the international circumstances and conditions within Indochina which made it possible, in August and September 1945, for Ho Chi Minh and his Communist lieutenants to lead the Viet Minh establishment of an independent and anti-colonial Vietnamese republic.

It shows us the confluence of French, Japanese, American, British and Chinese geopolitical interests in Vietnam in 1945 and how these shaped events. It also draws on an extraordinary

---

175 This piece first appeared in *The Canberra Times* on 13 January 1996. It is a review of David Marr *Vietnam 1945: The Quest for Power* (University of California Press, 1995). I had known David Marr, by then, for well over a decade and knew the personal story of how he had shifted from being a US Marine intelligence officer in Vietnam, in 1961-62, to becoming an historian of the Vietnamese revolution and a critic of the American war against it. Since this piece appeared, he has taken his history at least one step further, in *Vietnam: State, War and Revolution (1945-1946)* (University of California, 2013). Pierre Brocheux's authoritative, if brief, *Ho Chi Minh: A Biography* (Cambridge University Press, 2007) has also been added to my collection on the roots of the Vietnam War. My reading of all these books, as even the 1996 review makes clear, has been strongly influenced by the story Daniel Ellsberg relates in *Papers on the War* (Harper and Row, 1972) about his conversation with General Andre Beaufre at IISS, London, in 1968.

Beaufre told Ellsberg that it had been too late for the French to win in Indochina by 1946, or 1947 at the latest, because by then all the Vietnamese with whom the French might have allied themselves in an effort to defeat the Communists were already dead. The French had killed some of them in the 1930s, the Japanese more of them in the early 1940s, but the Communists had liquidated thousands of them in 1945-46—an aspect of the history of Vietnam that has received altogether too little attention on the part of those who too readily depicted the Communists as the 'good guys' and the authentic Vietnamese nationalists fighting against the French and then the Americans, as if there had never been any authentic Vietnamese nationalists who were not Communists. Lewis Sorley's *A Better War: The Unexamined Victories and Final Tragedy of America's Last Years in Vietnam* (Harcourt, Brace & Co., 1999) goes far toward arguing that, despite the toll taken by the Communists in the 1940s and the many errors and tragedies of the war to check the Communists, they could still have been kept in check in the 1970s, but that the American people had lost the will to persevere in the fight. Certainly, he underscores the very high cost to the Vietnamese people of the Communist victory, which left the country oppressed and impoverished for a generation.

range of Vietnamese sources to render a remarkable account of the fissiparous tendencies within Vietnam itself, even within the Viet Minh, at that time; as they, too, shaped events.

In both respects, it performs an enormous documentary service. Above all, however, it is of importance for the classical sobriety of its tone and its dispassionate representation of a subject so long ruined and overgrown by the jungle plants of propaganda and political passion. David Marr's long and intimate acquaintance with his subject makes his Preface especially interesting from an historiographic point of view.

'The idea for this book goes back to 1961,' he recalls, 'when I listened to my Vietnamese language teachers at Monterrey describe their experiences in the August Revolution ... Six years later, I had the opportunity to interview some prominent Vietnamese and Japanese participants; unfortunately I lacked sufficient knowledge of events in 1945 to ask many of the right questions. At any rate, this specific line of inquiry was shelved for years, while I studied earlier decades.'

Of particular historiographic interest, I think, are his remarks about the need to avoid the 'teleological trap' of 'considering events entirely from the point of view of what occurred subsequently, forgetting the standpoint of history as 'becoming'. When this happens, it is but a short step to crude deterministic expostulation, rather than history as a study of the possible.' At numerous points, this philosophic concern is evident in the pages of the book, as Marr brings to our attention the experiences and aspirations, dilemmas and perplexities of the countless people caught up in the tides of history in 1945: among them, Gaullist and Vichy Frenchmen; regional and central Nationalist Chinese; Japanese occupation forces; American OSS officers in Vietnam, in Kunming and in Washington; Vietnamese royalists, religious nationalists, Trotskyists, provincial Viet Minh cadres, leading Communists figures and political prisoners on Con Son, the French prison island.

The structure of the book, between its introduction and its epilogue, is indicative of the vast task the historian faced. The chapter headings are: 'The French and the Japanese', 'The Vietnamese Deal with Two Masters'; 'The Indochinese Communist Party and the Viet Minh'; 'The Allies: China and the United States'; 'The Allies; Great Britain and Free France'; 'The Opportune Moment'; 'Beyond Hanoi' and 'A State is Born'. The final chapter provides a compelling picture of the indelible impression made by Ho Chi Minh across Vietnam when, on the afternoon of 2 September 1945, before crowd estimated at 400,000 Vietnamese, in Ba Dinh Square, Hanoi, he read a declaration of independence, pausing after a few sentences to ask his audience: 'Countrymen, can you hear me clearly?' He received a roar back from that vast crowd, 'Clearly!'

Several hundred thousand people had also gathered in Saigon, in Norodom Square, to hear the declaration by radio, but the transmission failed. Sabotage was suspected. A march down Paris Commune Street was fired upon and an anti-French riot ensued, which began to set the scene for a polarisation of sentiment that would lead to the First Indochina War by late 1946. We cannot too carefully go over that period if we wish to understand the roots of the colonial war and the entrenchment of the Communist regime, first in the north of the country and then in the countryside in the south in the 1950s.

A poignant vignette in the in the book is a facsimile of the letter written, in August 1945, by Ho Chi Minh to Lieutenant Charles Fenn, his former American contact in Kunming, in which the Communist leader wrote, concerning Japan's surrender: 'The war is won, but we small and subject countries have no share, or very small share in the victory of freedom and democracy. Probably, if we want to get a sufficient share, we still have to fight. I believe that your sympathy and the sympathy of the great American people will always be with us … '[176]

The bitterness of internecine political strife among the Vietnamese themselves at this time is a significant sub-plot in the historical narrative. Marr reveals that, in the period of August and September 1945 alone, nationwide 'several thousand alleged enemies of the revolution' were assassinated by the Viet Minh and 'tens of thousands' imprisoned. These are staggering figures for the first weeks of any revolution, or indeed any dictatorship. In fact, it is very difficult to conceive of how the infant regime could have acted with such effective ruthlessness so quickly.

These statistics, carefully documented by a historian who is meticulous in such matters, belong for me in the context of General Andre Beaufre's remark, to Daniel Ellsberg in London in 1968, looking back on the French defeat in Indochina, that the war was unwinnable for France by no later than 1947, 'because by then most of the Vietnamese we might have allied ourselves

---

[176] Ho Chi Minh had seen all this before. He had attended the Versailles Conference, in 1919, as a young Vietnamese nationalist, hoping that US President Woodrow Wilson would support self-determination for colonized peoples and had been seriously disappointed. He then read Lenin's *Theses on the National and Colonial Questions* and decided that the Bolshevik leader was serious about independence for colonial peoples. He therefore joined the French Communist Party, was sent to Moscow, trained as a revolutionary and sent to China to help organize a Communist movement in the Far East. By 1945, he was a hardened revolutionary and it is difficult to believe that he would have done other than what he did—assassinating political opponents, launching a political terror in the countryside and collectivizing agriculture, even had Truman's State Department chosen to talk with him and support Vietnamese independence. Those OSS officers who had actually dealt with him had formed a favourable impression of him, however, and urged that he be accepted as a 'Southeast Asian Tito'. That was a path never seriously contemplated in Washington, where the Atlanticists held sway and wanted France in NATO and chose, therefore, to support its determined effort to take back its colonies in Indochina after the Japanese surrender. In any case, Tito was also a mass killer.

with to defeat the Communists were dead.' It cannot be said that the French helped their own cause in that regard, but David Marr's work appears to make clear that the people around Ho Chi Minh knew exactly who their political rivals were and systematically killed them, leaving nothing to chance.

Whether such ruthlessness was necessary in order to ensure Vietnamese independence or was, instead, very much a product of implacable Stalinist paranoia is something an authoritative history of the Vietnamese revolution must ponder. It is bound to become more accessible to such reflection when the Communist Party can finally be compelled to relinquish its monopoly on power in Hanoi and its secret archives are opened up to scrutiny. That, however, may still be many years away. In the interim, students of the Communist seizure of power have, in David Marr's excellent book, an unrivalled account of the international and indigenous context for that coup by the fabled Ho Chi Minh and his well-disciplined Communist cadres.

Contemplating the end of the world[177]

This is a book that sits well alongside Jonathan Schell's *The Fate of the Earth* and Bill McKibben's *The End of Nature*, as an ethical cry from the heart. John Leslie, professor of philosophy at the University of Guelph, Canada, advances a threefold argument in it. First, that the human race faces a range of threats to its long-term survival. Second, that we have an ethical obligation to demonstrate a greater concern about the future of the ecosphere than we have been showing. Third, that as a matter of probability theory, the chance that our species faces extinction sooner rather than later is disturbingly high and ought to lead us to redouble our efforts to ensure against our demise.

Leslie's book is mentally taxing and is not for the impatient or the faint of heart. His primary contention, that the human race faces extinction, may seem a truism to some, but it is dismissed by many as a doomsday fantasy. As Leslie points out, not only are there those who argue that extinction is improbable; there are also those who, allowing the possibility, regard it either with remarkable philosophic detachment or even applaud the prospect. In many respects, his book is a polemic against such outlooks. The first three chapters are devoted to a consideration of the many risks now facing humanity.[178] The last three chapters are devoted to a meticulous explication of his probability argument. In between, he answers the seemingly unnecessary question: Why prolong human history?

Is human extinction in fact probable? In the long run, of course, unless we presuppose the spread of the species throughout the galaxy, to other habitable worlds, it would appear inevitable. After all, the Sun itself will eventually expand into a red giant, destroy the

---

177 This piece was first published in *The Australian* on 20 July 1996. It is a review of John Leslie *The End of the World: The Science and Ethics of Human Extinction* (Routledge, London, 1996).

178 Warnings of impending apocalypse have religious roots in the West and the Middle East, dating back millennia. The modern warnings have all been largely Malthusian and have sprung from concerns about the human impact on the biosphere as our numbers exploded in the 20th century. The literature on the subject is now voluminous and has been greatly increased by the debate about greenhouse gas emissions and the fear that we may be irreversibly harming the atmosphere and endangering the biosphere through our prodigal use of fossil fuels. Derrick Jensen and Aric McBay's *What We Leave Behind* (Seven Stories Press, New York, 2009) is representative of a widespread mood. William H. Calvin's *A Brain for all Seasons: Human Evolution and Abrupt Climate Change* (University of Chicago Press, 2002) offers a highly unusual and thought-provoking angle on the subject. Richard Leakey *The Sixth Extinction: Biodiversity and its Survival* (Weidenfeld & Nicolson, London, 1996) and Elizabeth Kolbert *The Sixth Extinction: An Unnatural History* (Bloomsbury, London, 2014) provide deeply informed overviews of our impact on the rest of life on Earth and its implications.

Goldilocks Zone in which we happily reside, and burn our Earth to a cinder—a couple of billion years from now; but what about the short run—the next few centuries or millennia? Consider that, since life began on Earth, about 3.8 billion years ago, some thirty billion species of plant and animal are estimated to have existed at one time or another. Only thirty million species now exist. This means that 99.9 percent of all species of plant and animal that have ever existed are already extinct; or, as one wit expressed it, to a first approximation, *all* species are already extinct.

Species are, in other words, as evanescent as individuals in the larger scheme of things; they are mortal and pass away. Perhaps more significantly, over the past two decades some remarkable work in evolutionary biology has demonstrated that catastrophe and chance have played a far larger role in shaping the nature of the biosphere than had been believed since Charles Lyell and Charles Darwin[179] dismissed 'catastrophism' a century and a half ago. Biologist Stephen Jay Gould[180] has observed that life has been 'more a grand scale

---

179 Edward O. Wilson has produced a beautiful edition of the collected works of Charles Darwin called *From So Simple a Beginning* (W. W. Norton & Co., New York, 2006). It is over 1,700 pages long, but it is a book that every citizen of the 21st century world should read and reflect upon, because more than any book before it and certainly more than any religious scripture, it opened the doors for us to understanding what we actually are and how we came to be what we are in the natural world.

180 Stephen Jay Gould (1941-2002) was an American palaeontologist, evolutionary biologist and historian of science. He spent most of his career teaching at Harvard University and working at the American Museum of Natural History in New York. In the later years of his life, he also taught biology and evolution at New York University.

His most significant contribution to evolutionary biology was the theory of *punctuated equilibrium*, which he developed with Niles Eldredge in 1972. The theory proposes that most evolution is marked by long periods of evolutionary stability, punctuated by rare instances of radical innovation. This contrasts with the 'phyletic gradualism', espoused by Charles Darwin, according to which evolution follows a pattern of smooth and continuous change over geological time.

Gould was a great popularizer of evolutionary biology, with books such as *Ever Since Darwin: Reflections on Natural History* (Penguin, 1986, but first published in 1978). While he campaigned against religious creationism, he attempted to hose down conflicts between religion and science by declaring that they are 'separate magisteria' (Gould, S.J. (1997). 'Nonoverlapping magisteria', *Natural History* 106 (March): 16–22), a view with which I do not agree. The two have clearly overlapped at many points and still do so, with various religions making claims which are unwarranted by science and have no other epistemological foundation. Gould also stated that he had been very much influenced by the political writings of Noam Chomsky, which I find quite as troubling as his unnecessary concession to religious beliefs.

However, he wrote an excellent short reflection on his experience of being diagnosed, in July 1982, with peritoneal mesothelioma, a deadly form of cancer. I read this piece some years ago, after being diagnosed with melanoma. Published in *Discover* magazine, it was called 'The Median

lottery than a race with victory to the swift and powerful'. Or, as Richard Leakey has put it, the world as we have found it is: 'just one of many possible biological worlds' that could have emerged, even on Earth, but for various unpredictable occurrences. It therefore cannot be taken for granted, whether in terms of composition or in regard to its 'destiny'. Leslie's world is populated by lucky survivors in a game of chance; in which, to contradict Albert Einstein, 'God' *does* play dice and *is* mean.

The really original part of Leslie's argument is based on the probability theorizing which he, Cambridge mathematician Brandon Carter and Princeton University astrophysicist J. Richard Gott, have done since 1980, which indicates that we ought to consider the danger of 'doom soon' rather than 'doom deferred' to be disconcertingly high. Why is that? Well, they reason, as a matter of probability 'we could hardly expect to be among the very earliest—among the first 0.01 percent, for instance—of all humans who would ever have been born. On the other hand, it would be none too startling to be among something like the very last 10 percent, which is where we would be were the human race to end shortly.'

If that reasoning puzzles you, try looking at it this way: if you are in a lottery and you don't know whether there are 10 or, say, 1,000 balls in the draw, but find that your ball is drawn among the first three, you ought to infer that it is far more probable that there are 10 rather than 1,000 balls in the draw. This is such an unusual way of looking at things—because human beings are, in general, very poor at estimating probabilities—that, as Leslie observes, the implications are widely and even scornfully dismissed. But the case turns out not to be vulnerable to any simple counter arguments, each of which is considered in the final three chapters of Leslie's book.

Let me assure those who might be prone to dismiss a book with such a title as *The End of the World* with a snort of presumptuous derision that John Leslie is no crank. The book has been described by the philosopher J. J. C. Smart, for example, as 'possibly the most important book of the year'. The distinguished physicist, Paul Davies, describes the doomsday argument by Leslie as 'a philosophical poser that is startling, yet informative; seemingly outrageous, yet intriguing; and ultimately both disturbing and illuminating.'

Isn't the Message'. It explains his thinking after being informed that mesothelioma patients had a median survival period of only eight months from diagnosis. He reasoned that the median being the halfway point, 50% of patients die within eight months, but the other half live longer, potentially much longer. His personal characteristics placed him, he realized, on the long right hand side of the curve. Gould actually lived another 20 years, dying finally from a form of lung cancer unrelated to the mesothelioma.

Though *The End of the World* is not recommended bed-time reading, it is the sort of book one should read when taking time out to collect one's thoughts and adjust one's sense of perspective—as one of a brilliant and rampant species, whose days could be numbered.[181]

---

181 The great extinctions of the past, of which there are generally considered to have been five, were catastrophic events that seem, in each case, to have been due to causes that caught vast numbers of the species then extant, in each case, totally by surprise, allowing no time for adaptation. Michael J. Benton's *When Life Nearly Died: The Greatest Mass Extinction of All Time* (Thames and Hudson, 2003) is a study of the great Permian mass extinction, which wiped out the vast majority of species of both land and sea creatures on the planet. That was some 250 million years ago. In a remarkable article in *New Scientist* (9 February 2008), Peter Ward, a professor of biology at the University of Washington in Seattle, argued that the chief cause of mass extinctions may well have been attempts by the original inhabitants of the Earth—microbial bacteria and archaea—to wrest back control of the biosphere from the larger life forms that had emerged during the so-called Cambrian Explosion, some 543 million years ago. Microbes have inflicted far more deaths on human beings throughout history than have our weapons and it has only been over the past one hundred and fifty years that we have begun to push back against them with effective drugs and public sanitation. However, the battle is ongoing and the 21st century could well see dramatic developments. See Nathan Wolfe *The Viral Storm: The Dawn of a New Pandemic Age* (Allen Lane, London, 2011) and, more generally, John L. Ingraham *March of the Microbes: Sighting the Unseen* (Belknap Press, Harvard University, 2010).

Tales of Holocaust survival[182]

I am one of those who believe that David Irving, the historian who denies the reality or scale of the Holocaust, should not have been denied permission to visit Australia. Instead, he should have been granted such permission, on condition that he agreed to a nationally televised, prime-time debate, in which he would have been subjected to a systematic and relentless cross-examination by a panel of experts.[183] The matter of the Holocaust is central to the 20th century and our knowledge of it and reactions to that knowledge are a litmus test of our humanity.

This is not because other genocides have not occurred, both before and since. They have and they continue to occur. Rather, it is because none has been more continent-wide, more utterly ruthless, or more massive. Moreover, the Holocaust took place not in 'darkest Africa' or 'remote' Cambodia, or even in the Balkans, as have our most recent horrors, but in the very heartland of what we have been accustomed to call 'civilization' or even 'Christendom'. Its genesis, its horrific nature and its implications should be part not simply of Israeli or ethnic Jewish mourning and commemoration, but of the core curriculum of historical, political and moral education for all citizens of the West.[184]

---

182 This piece was first published in *The Canberra Times* on 8 February 1997. It was the last piece I wrote for *The Canberra Times*. I had by then retreated from Canberra to Melbourne and things had not gone well for me. My father was dying and I withdrew into myself for much of the following three years. I did, however, begin writing longer essays, chiefly for *Quadrant*, at the invitation, initially, of Robert Manne, when he was still the editor. An era in my life had ended and a new one had yet to begin. When it did begin, at the turn of the century, it involved the writing of a large number of longer essays, many of them in the *Australian Financial Review's* Friday Review supplement.

183 I am retyping this in the immediate wake of the *Charlie Hebdo* massacre in Paris, which has generated a considerable debate about the nature and limits of freedom of expression in Australia and elsewhere around the world. The single most troubling issue, I now believe, is the intractable difficulty in demonstrating that many passionately held or merely mendacious opinions are in fact in error. A television debate is, in fact, poorly suited to achieving this and that leaves us with dilemmas about how to limit the contagion of fanatical or otherwise wrong-headed ideas. In the case of David Irving, it was only after I wrote this piece that Irving was taken to court by Penguin Books and Deborah Lipstadt and systematically hammered over his denial of the Holocaust. See *The Irving Judgment* (Penguin, 2000). Unfortunately, it is seldom possible to achieve such clarification and debates remain very messy and unresolved.

184 I am now tempted to add 'and of the Muslim world', since there the double plague of anti-Semitism and Holocaust denial seems every bit as virulent as it has ever been in Europe and has the deeply pernicious effect of encouraging genocidal attitudes towards the Jews, not in Israel alone, but globally. Just as with Christianity, so with Islam, the roots of anti-Semitism can be traced back to ineradicable and explicit statements in the 'sacred scriptures', but the truly vicious anti-Semitism of the modern world is political and ideological and is now sedulously propagated by Islamists of both the Sunni and Shia factions.

Martin Gilbert has laboured to make available the materials for such education. *The Boys: Triumph Over Adversity* is his fifteenth book on the history of the Jews. It is the story of hundreds of Jewish adolescents who, by extraordinary turns of fortune, survived the Holocaust, while their whole families, neighbourhoods, urban cultures were annihilated. It makes remarkable and deeply moving reading, primarily because it makes so personal and immediate the staggering barbarism that was inflicted on the Jews by the Nazis and their European henchmen during World War Two.[185] The other highly remarkable characteristic of the story is the evidence of the breathtaking resilience of the survivors: their capacity to restart their lives and to raise healthy and successful families, despite the overwhelming traumatic shocks of 1938-45.

The book opens with an evocation of the world of Polish Jews in the 1930s, when the subjects of the collective memoir were children, living in an anti-Semitic but peaceful Poland. Roman Halter, who was to become the artist for the gateway to Yad Vashem, the Holocaust Memorial in Jerusalem, was born in a Polish village called Chodecz, or in Yiddish 'Hotz', on 7 July 1927. Eight hundred Jews lived in Hotz in 1939. By 1945, only four were left alive. Half a century after the war, Roman Halter met one of the other three survivors.

'We reminisced', he told Gilbert, 'about the walks through the hills covered in pine trees and about the places where in June we picked wild strawberries and in August and September collected baskets full of mushrooms. Hotz was a lovely place for us. It was our world, as we didn't know any other.' Most of his family were deported from Hotz to the death camp at Chelmno and murdered there. The rest were sent to the ghetto at Lodz and there all of them, except him, died by the spring of 1942. He survived to be deported from Lodz to Auschwitz, in late 1944.

---

185 Two indispensable books for getting one's mind around the Holocaust are Mark Roseman *The Villa, the Lake, the Meeting: Wannsee and the Final Solution* (Penguin, 2002) and Leni Yahil *The Holocaust: The Fate of European Jewry* (Oxford University Press, 1990). I did not acquire a copy of the latter until 2010. By then Professor Yahil (1912-2007) had died. She was born in Düsseldorf and raised in Potsdam, a classic product of the assimilated Jewish culture in Germany, as she was to become a classic victim of its disintegration. She was a sixth-generation descendent of the great 18th century German Jewish intellectual Moses Mendelssohn, who did so much to advance the cause of Jewish emancipation in the Germany of Goethe and Schiller. Her father, Ernst Westphal, was a judge. She studied history at the universities of Munich and Berlin, before being accepted into the College of Judaic Studies in Berlin, in 1932. Her education was interrupted by the Nazi rise to power in Germany in 1933. She emigrated to Palestine in 1934, and resumed her studies at the Hebrew University, where she majored in general history, with a dual minor in Jewish history and Hebrew literature. She received her master's degree in 1940, with her thesis being about 'The Concept of Democracy in Tocqueville.' She married in 1942 and had two sons, one of whom was killed in Jerusalem in 1967 fighting in the Six Day War. *The Holocaust: The Fate of European Jewry* was her masterpiece and the culmination of her life's work.

'About three quarters of all those on that train (which was full of the last survivors of the Jewish population of Lodz) were immediately sent to the gas chambers when the trains arrived at Auschwitz.' He survived until the end of the war as a slave labourer.

The personal aspect of this book is underscored by the poignant remark of one of the survivors, Moniek Goldberg, that: 'as I grew older I came to realize that I could not expect people to understand; or to comprehend the incomprehensible ... The tragedy that befell our people was so great, so complete, that one cannot imagine it ... '. Daniel Goldhagen's *Hitler's Willing Executioners* caused a stir because of its vigorous assertion that ordinary Germans participated enthusiastically in the mass murder of the Jews and that the genocide was not something which can simply be passed off as a secret horror perpetrated by sadistic fanatics in the SS.[186]

The recollections of the survivors brought together by Martin Gilbert overwhelmingly reinforce this argument. Moreover, it was not only ordinary Germans who brutalized and killed without compunction, but Poles, Hungarians, Ukrainians, Balts. As survivor Jack Rubenfeld wrote to Gilbert: 'I am fully aware of the enthusiastic participation of the majority of Germans, Poles and Ukrainians in the hatred and gross mistreatment of the Jews. As a group, I have not forgiven them. For me, the main responsibility lies within Catholic, Eastern Orthodox and Protestant clergy and churches that planted and nourished the seeds of this hatred.' Those who returned to Poland after the defeat of the Nazis found an undiminished and violent anti-Semitism among the Poles. Nor is Nazism dead even now, as Yaron Svoray found when, only a couple of years ago, he infiltrated the Nazi underground in Germany and found it to be flourishing.

The story of the rehabilitation of 'the boys' (there were very few girls who survived at all) fills the second half of this book. It is a story of healing and recovery, physical, psychological and social, which does much to reinforce the stark contrast, established in the opening chapters, between the civilized life of a settled community and the catastrophe of barbarism that was Nazi power. That is salutary. The survivors did not take a single path, whether political or religious, as Jews after the Holocaust. They developed an enduring bond with one another, however; as well as an evident faith in the values and virtues of civilized life, family life and freedom of speech under the law. They did not themselves become vengeful, hate-filled racists, like their ruthless persecutors. Perhaps this was their greatest victory over the Nazis.

---

186 Gita Sereny's *Albert Speer: His Battle With Truth* (Alfred A. Knopf, New York, 1995) is a superb study in the moral psychology of those Germans who were both enthusiastic supporters of Hitler and his conquests and yet wanted to claim that they did not know about or participate in the genocide of the Jews or other mass atrocities.

Intermezzo: Seven turn of the century essays (1998-2001)

Kim Jong-Il's Paranoia[187]

Speaking in Seoul on 22nd January, US Defense Secretary William Cohen urged that South Korea not allow its present financial crisis and consequent defence budget cuts to 'send the wrong signal' to North Korea. Proposed cuts to the defence budget were reported to have put in doubt South Korean plans to purchase C-17 air transports, AWACS radar surveillance aircraft and Apache attack helicopters.

Such warnings, of their nature, invoke perennial fears that North Korea is poised to take advantage of an opportunity to unleash its huge army against the South and try to reunify the peninsula by force. Indeed this is precisely what senior North Korean defector Hwang Jang-yop warned last year was the North's overriding strategic objective. Stressing the "total domination" within North Korea of Kim Jong-il, Hwang Jang-yop declared that the regime in Pyongyang was obsessed with military preparations, possessed nuclear weapons, had no intention of reforming and was bent on military action to reunify the peninsula. This is the "rogue" North Korea which has been the object of fear and loathing since 1950. But there have to be serious doubts as to how realistic a picture this is of North Korea's capabilities or intentions.

---

187 This essay first appeared in *Quadrant*, in March 1998. It had been written while Robert Manne was still editor, but he resigned before it could be published. I was wholly unacquainted with the internal politics at *Quadrant* and was caught entirely by surprise when he resigned. He had clashed with both Les Murray and the late Ray Evans and offered an ultimatum to Leonie Kramer that either they had to go or he would. He was shocked and aggrieved when she accepted his resignation. He was succeeded by the late Paddy McGuinness, who rang me and asked in a polite manner whether I would consider writing for the magazine under his editorship. I saw no reason not to do so, as the change of editor had nothing to do with me and as he had said nothing at all about adhering to any editorial line. I offered him this piece on North Korea and he ran it.

That was the beginning of a flourishing relationship, in which I always found McGuinness to be candid and impartial. When I wrote a piece about East Timor a couple of years later, he said to me by phone: 'I disagree with you about East Timor, but this is a very good essay, so I'm going to publish it.' That, to me, summed up the way we related as writer and editor throughout his tenure at *Quadrant*. Robert Manne, unfortunately, was another matter altogether. When I went to talk with him in his La Trobe University office in 1999, he was very cool. He accused me of having 'joined the other side' and stated that he was too busy to spend time talking with me. I remarked that *Quadrant* was a national institution and I saw nothing personal in continuing to write for it under a new editor, any more than I would have done had it been a matter of writing for, say, *The Age* and seeing a change of editors. Of the various possible reactions he might have had, his seemed to me the least dignified. I saw no reason why we could not have continued to become better acquainted and to discuss the very issues that so exercised him. That was not his preference, however, and we have never had a conversation in the sixteen years since.

Abundant reports, over nearly a decade now, indicate that North Korea's economy is under enormous stress and that it lacks the capacity, unaided, to feed its people, fuel its factories and transport systems, or generate sufficient foreign exchange to cover its basic needs. Last May, South Korea's ambassador-at-large, Dr Kim Ki-Hwan, gave it as his opinion that the near-famine conditions in North Korea made it 'highly probable' that the regime in Pyongyang would "collapse". While a desperate North Korean attack on the South was conceivable, he said, it was most improbable, because North Korea's strategic isolation and poverty would make such an attack suicidal. The challenge for the South was to ensure that the North did not collapse, since this would entail costs of an order which could seriously destabilize the economy of the South, as well as unsettling the strategic balance in the region.

The balance of probabilities is on the side of the Kim Ki-Hwan assessment, rather than that of Hwang Jang-yop, but sound policy under present circumstances cannot balance on the knife-edge presented by two such antithetical assessments. A more cogent analysis is required and with it a more assured policy in regard to the future of the Korean peninsula.

The debate over North Korea's propensity to initiate a second war has made little conceptual progress in many years. The underpinnings of the belief that it is likely to launch a war given half a chance are of very long standing, and they are what I call "analytically primitive", by which I mean that they consist of a number of tenacious, but largely unexamined and poorly integrated, perceptions and suppositions. The first is: they did it in 1950, which gave us a shock, and they have never signed a peace treaty, so they could do it again. The second is: they have a pronounced forward posture militarily, which can only mean that they have offensive intentions.

The third is: they have total control over their population, so dissent is not possible and a decision by a fanatical leadership to go to war could not be checked by countervailing forces. And, finally, there is the overriding judgment that the leadership in North Korea does not think 'logically' but ideologically, being communist or, as one sometimes hears, 'Confucian', so that there is no telling *what* they might do. Statements such as those of Hwang Jang-yop, of course, tend very much to reinforce these analytically primitive beliefs. This, however, has the effect of inducing something close to policy paralysis. Such policy paralysis in regard to North Korea is conspicuous in Canberra and has to some extent afflicted even Seoul, Tokyo and Washington. It is time to put our analytical house in order.

The first postulate, that North Korea is likely to recommence the war it started in 1950, if only because it has never signed a peace treaty, begs the question. We need to ask why and under what circumstances did Kim *père* invade the South in 1950 and, given the fate of that initiative, what might have induced him to restart the war subsequently (which he never did), or might induce Kim *fils* to restart it under current circumstances. In 1950, the revolution in the North was newly accomplished and appeared to be possible, also, in the South. Certainly, Kim Il-sung believed that is was possible, but that it would require military intervention from the North, because the left had been ruthlessly crushed in the South under the Rhee regime.

In 1950, both Seoul and Pyongyang itched for a war of reunification. Washington held Seoul on a leash, but Moscow unleashed Pyongyang. In 1950, there was widespread credence given to the notion that communism might, indeed, be the economic and political wave of the future. Stalin was still in power and Mao had just proclaimed the People's Republic of China. Communism had been imposed on Eastern Europe and was insurgent in Indochina. The United States was ambivalent about defending South Korea, as Dean Acheson had publicly indicated, and was even contemplating either abandoning Taiwan to Mao, or conniving in a coup to remove Chiang Kai-shek from power before the communist attack came.

There was, in short, every reason for Kim Il-sung to believe that the whole of Korea was ripe for the taking. Certainly reunification would have rendered the economic foundations of Korean communism and its strategic position very much stronger. There was, therefore, nothing at all irrational about Kim's decision to go to war in 1950, or about the way he then fought that war. None of the above conditions now obtain and, therefore, a North Korean decision to go to war in the late 1990s would be *radically inconsistent with* and not a revisiting of the decision to go to war in 1950.

Yet North Korea has maintained a forward military posture for many years. Doesn't that indicate an offensive intent? Besides, its propaganda has again and again spoken of and threatened a war of reunification. There are various ways to tackle this shibboleth of the fear and loathing party. One is to draw a heuristic parallel with the Soviet forward posture in East Germany throughout the Cold War. So long seen as threatening a massive invasion of the West at any time, it was in fact a posture intended to ensure that, should the Third World War become unavoidable, as much as possible of it would be fought in Western Europe. During the 1980s, as its grand strategy was strenuously re-examined, the Soviet Union looked for cost-efficient ways to pull back from these deployments and eventually did so. There is no *prima facie* case for construing North Korea's posture in any other terms.

While much is made of its massive artillery emplacements along the war zone behind the DMZ, which, we are told, could wreak terrific damage on Seoul and its hinterland within hours, it seems to escape the exponents of this notion that the artillery in question could not be used to support a deep thrust into South Korea, since it is dug into mountain defences. Or, again, much is made of the numbers of North Korean armoured vehicles and tanks, but without regard to the fact that the terrain across which they would have to move and the weapons systems they would face render a massed armoured attack against the South an extremely dicey strategic position. Finally, the infrastructure behind North Korea's lines is so poor and its air power so obsolescent, fuel-deprived and under-exercised that the North's capacity to launch and sustain a *blitzkrieg* campaign must be viewed with great skepticism, irrespective of whether its leadership is or is not of sound mind.

A key part of Hwang Jang-yop's warning about the North is that Kim Jong-Il is totally in control. Various recent reports appear to support the claim that Kim Jong-Il has, indeed, consolidated his succession to the power his father wielded, at least, for the present. The question is whether this, in itself, has any particular bearing on the regime's propensity to go to war. There are at least two components to this question. First, is it the case that absolute control by a ruler correlates with a propensity to start wars? Second, does Kim Jong-Il's personality or do the conditions under which he holds power indicate that he, in particular, is likely to go to war?

As to the first question, the most pertinent analogies would seem to be with other communist dictators, the nature of whose rule and ideological outlook might reasonably be seen as similar to that of Kim Jong-Il. Yet, in this regard, the evidence is surely weighted *against* the fear and loathing party. Stalin and Mao, every bit as strongly entrenched as with Kim Il-sung or Kim Jong-Il, showed themselves to be strategically very canny and cautious. They exhibited a sound grasp of the balance of power and the psychology of deterrence. Kim Il-sung must be said to have been at least as realistic in this respect.

Had he not been, one might have expected him to have restarted the war in 1975 or 1979, when the United States was on the back foot, but he did not chance his arm. Why should we expect Kim Jong-Il to do so now? I have never yet seen a plausible answer to this question. It all seems to come down to the fourth supposition: that Kim Jong-Il and his colleagues are in some sense irrational, delusional or obsessive. This is a thin reed on which to lean one's strategic assessment, but let us dispose of it, since the way will then be clear for a more cogent analysis of North Korea's prospects.

Kim Jong-Il is a princeling, born to the purple and raised under extremely privileged circumstances. He has a reputation for extravagant tastes and is said to possess a large collection of pornographic films. According to South Korean secret intelligence reports and the testimony of defectors, he is also given to bouts of drunkenness and depression, as well as cruel and even capricious punishment of those he suspects of disloyalty. He is said to live in fear for his life and to move around, much as Saddam Hussein does, from one secure residence to another to avoid possible assassination. Reports of this kind, widely rumoured or circulated, lay behind

Jim Hoagland's headline for the *International Herald Tribune*, after Kim Il-Sung's death in 1994: "Scenario for North Korea: Exit Stalin, Enter Caligula".

Yet what was there in even these rumoured patterns of behaviour to suggest that Kim Jong-Il was, in any clinical sense, insane or unbalanced? It was not exactly a 'balanced environment' in which he grew up or acceded to power. The extravagant tastes are indistinguishable from those of many a wealthy individual elsewhere in the world and indicate nothing whatsoever about Kim Jong-Il's capacities as a statesman. The alcoholism and cruelty sound disconcerting, but even if the rumours are accurate they may as well indicate reactions of an intelligent man under intolerable circumstances as symptoms of uncontrollable madness. Indeed, I would argue that they are clinically speaking more likely to indicate the former than the latter. As for capriciousness and paranoia, not only do these not demonstrate a likely propensity to start a war, they may well indicate, to the contrary, that the heir of Kim Il-sung has a well-developed fear of the forces which close him in on all sides and could easily destroy him.

And there is another consideration. If it is true that he is in constant fear of assassination, then the claim that he is in 'total control' must be qualified by the observation that he does not believe this himself and sees himself as having many real or potential enemies. It is also a reminder that he lives within an elaborate structure which has supported his succession to power and which has interests that are certain to be ill-served by irrational or self-destructive behaviour on the part of the princeling. For all these reasons, the supposition that irrationality or madness on the part of Kim Jong-Il is likely to lead to war in Korea must, at the very least, be regarded with the greatest caution.

There are, in fact, reports that Kim Jong-Il is, despite the characteristics mentioned above, an intelligent and capable administrator, troubled by the condition of his principality and anxious to find ways of preventing its collapse. This is consistent with the tenacious manner in which North Korea has stuck to its guns in negotiations with its neighbours and the United States and the cautious, but discernibly practical, measures it has experimented with to hold things together. This is not to say that he is a man of great gifts and insights who will turn his state's economy around; there is little evidence of that. Rather, there is evidence of circumspection and a grim rearguard action against the many forces which threaten his state and power with disintegration.

The regime's propaganda, meant chiefly for domestic consumption, about tough times for socialism and the challenge of holding up the red banner in a period of capitalist resurgence, can be read superficially as indicating an inability to face reality, but on the whole it indicates just the opposite: that the regime is well aware of the formidable challenges it faces. That being so and given its careful, defensive negotiations with the United States and South Korea over its nuclear installations, energy requirements and food supplies, it would be completely at odds with its pattern of behaviour for North Korea to suddenly throw everything to the high winds and lash out with war. Having gradually risen to power over many years and slowly assumed the succession over three and a half years, Kim Jong-il must be considered the leader of a coalition of survivors, not a band of berserkers.

It is, in the light of all these considerations, not paranoia on the part of Kim Jong-Il or his lieutenants which is the real problem on the Korean peninsula now, but paranoia on the part of the rest of us. Kim Jong-Il's paranoia is perfectly understandable and is most unlikely to prompt him to start a war against overwhelming odds. There is, of course, the residual supposition that the mind-set of his whole regime is one of ideological fixation and that as communists they will never see reason. But this is an insupportable assertion. Nothing in the now widely opened history of the communist regimes lends credibility to any such proposition.

Several years ago, I had to deal with the wild assertion of a defence attaché in Seoul that the North Koreans would start a war by Christmas 1993, when the ground hardened. They would do so, he asserted, because being 'Confucian' they did not assess the odds according to 'Western logic'. This curious proposition was disturbingly congruent with the widespread paranoia of the party of fear and loathing, even in very high circles in Canberra. The notion that the North Koreans would start a war with reckless disregard for the probable consequences under the influence of 'Confucian' ideas ought to have struck all concerned as risible. That it did not, meant that it needed to be confuted.

What reason had the defence attaché, I asked, to believe that Pyongyang based its strategic reasoning on the precepts of Confucius? Surely, if classical Chinese wisdom was going to guide their actions, it would be Sun Tzu's *The Art of War* to which they would turn. And if they were guided by Sun Tzu, then they would certainly not start a war in their present circumstances. It was Sun Tzu's maxim that every battle is won before it is started. Would his guidance, then, counsel that one start a war which would be *lost* before it was started?

It is Kim Ki-Hwan's fears, rather than Hwang Jang-yop's, which should be at the centre of our thinking about North Korea in the near future. The authentic danger is not that North Korea will lash out with fire and the bayonet against the South and the United States, but that it will finally collapse as a state under the accumulated burden of its economic and political deficiencies, as the Soviet Union and its East European client regimes did between 1989 and 1991. To get this into serious perspective, it is necessary to focus on the dynamics which have shaped North Korea since the 1953 armistice brought a halt to the destructive war Kim Il-sung had started in June 1950. Information on North Korea is notoriously sparse, since the regime is possibly the most secretive in the world, but there is enough for the crucial indicators to be registered with sufficient clarity to render the policy implications plainer than they appear to be in policy-making circles.

For the decade after 1953, North Korea concentrated on reconstructing its devastated economy and Kim Il-sung on eliminated his political rivals. By 1964, the reconstruction had been vigorous enough for Joan Robinson to declare that an 'economic miracle' had been achieved. Indeed, she made the extraordinary pronouncement that 'All the economic miracles of the post-war world are put in the shade by these achievements'. Leaving aside, for the moment, the question of how warranted such an encomium was, the most significant facts were that there was a typically Stalinist emphasis on heavy industry, which had led to dissent within the party itself in the late 1950s; and that military expenditure in this period was kept within quite modest bounds. A turning point came in 1965, coincident with American escalation in Vietnam, after which North Korea's military expenditure grew rapidly, reinforcing the over-commitment to heavy industry. This imbalance in resource allocation and output, exacerbated by the inherent inefficiencies of a command economy, led the North into economic difficulties as early as the mid-1970s.

While various complex accounting measures have led some observers to suggest that North Korea's GDP continued to grow rapidly as late as the mid-1980s, a more realistic analysis is that it stagnated both structurally and dynamically in the late 1970s, at the very time that South Korea began to grow explosively. At the same time, the North became institutionally locked into its military expenditures, as much due to the sheer size of the interest groups created by the military build-up as to ideological zeal or strategic planning. By 1985, the gulf between South Korea's economic performance and that of the North was so wide that the North's leaders were faced with a fact which threatened the very foundations of their rule: their present economic system could not compete with that of the South, which meant that the South would soon be able easily to outstrip the North's military expenditure in absolute terms. This is when the North's crisis originated. It is also the point at which they appear to have redoubled their efforts to develop a small nuclear arsenal.

Since that time, but far more since the dramatic events in 1989, the North Korean nuclear weapons program has attracted a great deal of attention. There are sound enough reasons, in the context of non-proliferation anxieties, for this attention. But the underlying realities received insufficient attention until much more recently. The nuclear program was driven by the combination of the North's perfectly realistic fear of growing military vulnerability *vis-à-vis* the South and the rent-seeking of the huge military bureaucracy that had grown over previous decades. The vulnerability, however, was at bottom a consequence of poor economic performance, and the same economic decrepitude, drastically worsened by the collapse of the

Soviet Union in 1991, made the rent-seeking orientation of the bloated military-industrial establishment more precarious than ever. From as early as 1991, therefore, the leaders of North Korea were very much caught 'between the ROK and a hard place' as the common joke had it. Their weapons sales have been, in this context, more like a *Gorky Park* drama than part of a bid for a strategic breakout. The real focus of our analytic attention and policy-planning should be the economic pincers in which they are caught.

No informed observer of North Korea questions the fact that it is in very serious economic difficulties. The problem is getting any precision into estimates of the depth and structural dynamics of those difficulties. In a chapter devoted to 'North Korean Statistics' for a forthcoming monograph from the Brookings Institution, Heather Smith begins by confessing that:

> *Relatively little can be stated with certainty about North Korean statistics. In attempting to quantify North Korea's economic performance, one must not only cope with the theoretical issues that have dogged such estimates for the USSR and communist Europe, but also with the fact that these countries made available vastly more information about their economies than has North Korea.*

Yet such impediments to systematic analysis notwithstanding, she concludes, the available evidence and what data North Korea has released indicate both that its economic performance has faltered badly over the past decade and that it faces multiple, mutually reinforcing problems which it cannot overcome with the means currently at its disposal. It is being sustained against industrial collapse and famine by substantial foreign aid, especially from China, and has begun halting steps towards economic reforms of a kind which might offer a way forward. The solution to the long-standing gridlock on the Korean peninsula is to be found in the closer analysis of these matters, if it is to be found at all.

One may gather from both official North Korean statistics, as submitted to the United Nations from the North Korean Central Office of Census in 1997, and data compiled by the Bank of Korea, the gravity of North Korea's economic contraction over the past decade, even if the lack of substantial data bases renders both sets of figures no better than indicative. North Korea's own statistics indicate a staggering contraction, from a GNP of $US17.7 billion in 1989 to one of $5.2 billion in 1995, or from $US868 per capita to $239. These figures are significant in two important ways, even if they cannot be regarded as accurate. First, they indicate a dramatic admission on the part of a regime notoriously given to inflating its achievements that it is in dire straits. Second, they indicate that even before the massive contraction began, the economy was simply not comparable in size or dynamism with that of South Korea. The Bank of Korea's figures, interestingly, do not suggest as severe a contraction as North Korea's own figures but this serves only to underscore both the fact that there is a serious crisis in the North and that the regime is starkly aware of that fact.

That the regime has not fallen is, on the whole, quite remarkable. The reason is that it pivots on a vast military-industrial establishment which has everything to lose by doing anything to precipitate things in dangerous directions. This harsh reality throws their self-interest, their options and their doubts into relief, if we can once put aside our fear and loathing and look upon their predicament with strength and confidence. The precise details may be elusive, but the fundamentals of the analysis are rock hard: North Korea cannot fight a war and it cannot, unaided or unreformed, sustain itself much longer. Since neither South Korea nor any other state wishes to see war inflicted on North Korea, the debate now hinges on whether collapse of the regime is something to be precipitated, postponed or prevented, given the huge costs that such a collapse could entail.

These are the realities which South Korea's new President, Kim Dae-Jung, has inherited. By a striking turn of events, the leading proponent of democratic reform and peaceful reunification of Korea has come to power in the South at just that juncture when the North, always contemptuous and spiteful towards the military regime in the South as a government of reactionaries, fascists and traitors, has become incapable of pursuing further its armed revolution and has begun groping towards some sort of economic reform, simply in a bid to survive.

South Korea's own financial crisis ought to chasten it and put it in a frame of mind to understand the difficulties and painful costs entailed in fundamental reform of economic institutions. As a clement victor who has declared that he will pardon the abuses for which his two predecessors were jailed, Kim Dae-Jung has the temperament, the mandate and the historic opportunity to reach out to North Korea. Such an initiative will have to be realistic in assessing both the vulnerability and the pride of the North and in framing proposals for change and for reconciliation consistent with these realities. And such proposals must, surely, pivot on two basic institutional realities: that the North cannot move towards reform unless the huge military-industrial, rent-seeking, rusting establishment can be attracted to market economics and pragmatic, integrationist nationalism; and that, in any such process, the South Korean *chaebols* (giant conglomerates such as Samsung and Hyundai) will necessarily play a leading role.

They have worked for decades with a military industrializing regime in the South. The challenge during the presidency of Kim Dae-Jung will be for them to find ways to work with the regime in Pyongyang on a gradual course of economic resuscitation and integration. Once the first couple of hurdles are overcome, the huge forces that are still arrayed on either side of the DMZ will come to be as anachronistic as those which were, until a few years ago, deployed on either side of the Iron Curtain in Europe. Our own outlook in this matter should be informed along these lines and our policies constructed accordingly, rather than being governed by a confused misunderstanding of North Korea's posture and prospects.

Looking back at the 1960s[188]

The sixties were *not* for me a decade of civil disobedience, antiwar activism, experimentation with drugs, sexual revolution or oedipal rebellion. They were the years of a sheltered, gentle, conservative Catholic childhood in suburban Melbourne, touched only at the outermost margins by a dim awareness of the world outside, in which all these things were going on. I have no idea what I was doing, as a seven-year-old boy, on the day JFK was assassinated. I dimly recall black-and-white television coverage of the funeral of Bobby Kennedy, in June 1968. And I remember hearing over the public address system, in a sixth-grade classroom, in August 1968, a radio news report of Soviet tanks entering Prague. My father was an NCC man, a Santamaria man, and each Sunday the television would be tuned in to Mr. Santamaria's program *Point of View*. That was the ambience; that and singing 'Hail, Redeemer, King Divine' at school. Oh and being read *The Lord of the Rings* in 1967, utterly innocent of any awareness of Che Guevara's death struggle in Bolivia.

In consequence, I cannot look back to the sixties with that heat or exasperation which characterize the debates of aging New Leftists and revanchist conservatives. Their 1960s are something I have reconstructed for myself, by many stages, over some twenty years of university studies, tertiary teaching on politics and violence, work as an intelligence officer in the federal government and citizenship in a changing world. I write 'reconstructed' quite deliberately, for my wider immersion in the sixties, retrospectively, was not something which happened merely in snatches of second-hand mythology picked up along the way. It was something which I found myself engaged in as a recursive process of coming to terms with the world in which I had grown to adolescence and adulthood; a world which others had shaped ahead of me; or, more precisely, behind me. For, by the time I reached late high school, in the mid-1970s, I had the disturbing sense that things which had happened in the sixties, and of which I was only vaguely aware, had undermined the very foundations of that small, sheltered world in which I had spent my childhood. Such, in a rather more traumatic form, must have been the experience of many a middle- or upper-class child whose life was overtaken by revolution in other times and places. Harry Wu in late 1940s Shanghai, or Vladimir Nabokov in the Russia of 1917, are examples which spring to mind, but I found consolation in their far grimmer experiences many years after I had been driven to reflect on my own.

---

188 This piece first appeared in *Quadrant* in May 1998. It led to an interview with Philip Adams on *Late Night Live*, alongside two of the Leftist luminaries of the era, Tariq Ali, then in London, and Daniel Singer, in Paris. I was, as Philip cheerfully announced to his listeners, in 'a beach house somewhere south of Melbourne'.

For all that my childhood was sheltered; it was not one of stifling or narrow conservatism. I was a precocious reader and was encouraged in this by my parents. In late 1968, stirred by what seemed to be the seriousness of its contents, I asked my parents to give me, as a present on my twelfth birthday, a copy of Isaac Deutscher's *Stalin*. They did so, writing inside the cover, 'Happy birthday to dear Paul, love from Mummy and Daddy'. The warmth, openness and striking incongruity of those words in such a context I have long found so fetching that I have treasured that battered old book to this day. I read it, with half-comprehending fascination, that summer at the seaside, altogether unaware of the debates between Old Left and New Left or fissiparous leftist groupuscules which had raged through the decade and a half since Khrushchev's secret speech to the Twentieth Party Congress and the Soviet invasion of Hungary in 1956. It was long afterward, as a student at Melbourne University in 1981, writing an honours thesis on the May 1968 upheaval in France, that I learned, for example, how, on 8th May 1968, as Louis Aragon, the old communist writer, had addressed a street meeting outside the Odeon in Paris, the student rebels around Daniel Cohn-Bendit had heckled him, shouting derisively, 'Long live OGPU! Long live Stalin, the father of all the people!'

Back in the sixties, since Tolkien's Dark Lord was a more vivid idea to me than any historical figure, I readily associated Stalin with Sauron, the KGB with the Black Riders and the Kremlin with the Dark Tower. By the time Ronald Reagan, as President of the United States, had started to describe the USSR as the 'Evil Empire', I was older and world history—my chief object of study in the intervening years—had become a more substantial thing. But in 1968 evil meant oppressive power and Mordor was as 'real' as the Soviet Union or the Roman Empire. The good which stood opposed to it was a dreamy amalgam of the romantic *longue durée* of Tolkien's High Elves and the simple world of family picnics, football, television and Sunday mass. The closest to social protest my world of ideas came in those years was, so far as I can now recall, the warm, ethical resonance of Peter, Paul and Mary singing songs like 'Where Have All the Flowers Gone?', 'If I Had a Hammer' and 'Le Déserteur'; save that I knew no French and had little idea what the latter song actually meant.

If by 'the Sixties' one means the breakout into cultural and personal revolt, then my 'sixties' began in 1975, my first year out of secondary school. It was the year that the Communist armies took Saigon and Phnom Penh, bringing to a head the bitter debates which had riven the West for a decade and more by then. I had subscribed to *Time* magazine during my secondary school years and had read about the antiwar movement, the *Pentagon Papers*, My Lai, Watergate and the demoralization alike of the US armed forces in Indo-China and their New Left critics. This was the denouement, but what to make of it? At the same time, a decade after the closing of the Second

Vatican Council, the Catholicism of my childhood was fraying. The shock of stepping outside the conservative milieu of my sixties childhood into a university world in which Catholicism was openly derided as antediluvian was more than even my precocious reading had prepared me for.

In 1975, as the Whitlam government unraveled, I discovered Leonard Cohen, the Rolling Stones and Friedrich Nietzsche. The years that followed were not ones of marijuana (much less LSD) and rage maintained (I voted Liberal in the historic election at the end of 1975), but of almost ascetic immersion in trying to recover the history of my world, from pre-Classical antiquity to the 20th century revolutions. Gradually the sixties started to come into focus as I looked backwards. But the angle of vision was personal, strenuously though I sought to grasp what had really happened. Every inquiry, every reading was provisional and perspectival and there were questions I kept coming back to over the years. There were some I was not even equipped to ask when still an undergraduate. That, in itself, is a clue, perhaps, to much of the confusion of the New Left before me, when *they* were undergraduates.

Never having discovered the supposed allure of the world of Timothy Leary and Allen Ginsberg; never having thought of Communism as other than a catastrophic storm blowing through the 20th century, in 1980, I met Albert Langer, the fading icon of sixties student radicalism in Australia. The brief encounter with Mr. Langer occurred after a public meeting on poverty and unemployment at Melbourne University's Public Lecture Theatre. After a number of other speakers, such as Tom Uren and Don Chipp, had spoken about social and economic challenges facing Australia, Mr. Langer rose to address the meeting of some hundreds of people. I knew only vaguely of his glory days as a Maoist activist at Monash University and had no particular predisposition as to what he might say on an occasion such as this. 'You've heard all these bourgeois proposals about what this country needs,' he declared to the gathering. 'I put it to you that what this country needs is a revolution. If you want to do something useful, go out and learn how to use a rifle.'

I was less shocked than bemused. Can he be serious? I thought. Or is this a sort of theatrical provocation? After the meeting concluded, I approached him and invited him to join me for a coffee in the Student Union. On the way across to the Union café, I asked him, 'Albert, suppose for the sake of argument that it was possible to actually organize an armed revolution in this country and that you succeeded in seizing state power. Just suppose. What would you *do*? What would your revolution consist of?' To my enduring fascination, he responded, 'That's a good question.' A good question, no doubt. The problem was that he offered no substantive answer.

'Alright,' I returned, 'let's suppose, further, that you actually had an agenda for revolution, that you seized state power and began to implement your agenda, but then found yourself running into all sorts of problems with implementation, including all the old problems of degeneration into bureaucratic despotism and economic chaos. What would you do then?' His answer all but took my breath away: 'Well, we'd have to have another revolution, wouldn't we? And why not? If things *did* work out, it'd get boring. Revolutions are fun!'

I had not, at that time, ever heard of Abbie Hoffmann and *Revolution for the Hell of It,* but I had read Dostoyevsky's *Notes from Underground* and *The Possessed.* From that point on I was unable to take Mr. Langer seriously and have always regarded his vacuity and irresponsibility, expressed in his own words that evening, as the epitome of why the young rebels of his generation aroused so much contempt among their elders and betters from the late 1960s onward. When we sat down in the Union café and he solemnly announced, 'I'm a Marxist-Leninist-Stalinist-Maoist', he struck me as a caricature of a literary figure, devoid of ethical or political substance. Was this the sixties? Not mine. Not at all. Frank Knopfelmacher reportedly took Albert Langer seriously. Seriously enough to have remarked that, in the event of significant threats to social order, he believed Mr. Langer should be thrown into prison as a menace to our commonwealth. That is, he did not regard Mr. Langer as a clown.

I couldn't take Albert Langer seriously, but I took Frank Knopfelmacher seriously. It was his lectures on Marx, Weber, Durkheim, Toennies, Lukacs and Gramsci, in 1979, which gave me some sort of conceptual foundation on which to look back at the sixties from more than a personal standpoint, in 1981. Even more significant were his earthiness and wry world-weariness, as one who had fled Czechoslovakia to escape the Nazis, in the late 1930s, lived and labored as a young Marxist in Palestine, discovered Orwell in wartime England, fought gun in hand at D-Day and returned to Czechoslovakia after the war, only to flee it a second time, to escape Communist tyranny, in 1948. Here was a teacher with things to say and above all with the message, 'Be wary of utopian daydreams. Develop an ethic of responsibility.' Yes. Knopfels, as we called him, one could take seriously. But the sixties drew me backwards and Paris had an allure as the locale in which to study this question of utopian daydreams, an ethic of responsibility and the legacy of the sixties.

Perhaps no slogan more enduringly encapsulates the mood of the sixties, at least as a decade of New Left rebellion in the West, than the phrase scrawled on a wall in the Sorbonne, 'L'Imagination au pouvoir!' (All power to the imagination). In 1981, I still found that slogan arresting, along with other memorable ones, such as the denunciation of boredom, 'Metro boulot, metro dodo' (Train work, train sleep) and 'Je prends mes desirs pour la réalité, parce que je crois en la réalité de mes desirs' (I take my desires for reality, because I believe in the reality of my desires). But it was with a Nietzschean cast of mind tempered by a Catholic cultural orientation, not a Marxist one, to say nothing of a beat Ginsbergian, Situationist or lysergic acid diethylamide disorientation, that I viewed the idea of 'imagination'.

The summer before beginning work on my honours thesis, while working the 'graveyard' shift on the Victorian Railways, at Flinders Street Station, I read Marx's *Capital*, but I also read Augustine's *The City of God*, Dante's *Divine Comedy* and Spinoza's *Tractatus Theologico-Politicus*. It was, therefore, with something other than a New Left mindset that I plunged into reading about *les évènements de Mai soixante-huit* (the events of May 68); and the idea that a proletarian revolution, the nationalization of the means of production, or a mass of anarchist councils might constitute an imaginative solution to the travails of industrial society was not one with much plausibility to my way of thinking. What I was interested in was the psychology of rebellion and the rhetoric of 'cultural revolution'.

Books with titles like *Les Travailleurs Vaincront*, *Prelude to Revolution* and *Writing on the Wall* were the standard fare on the subject, with their variations on the theme that the upheaval marked the beginning of the end for capitalism. Yet it seemed clear, looking back over more than a decade, that the events had signified nothing of the kind. None other than Regis Debray, erstwhile comrade in arms of Che Guevara, wrote in 1979, in the *New Left Review*, that the rebels in Paris, who so defiantly invoked Mao, Fidel and Che, thought they were landing in China or Cuba, but were in fact landing in California. Yet this struck me as too glib and even as supercilious. It was the writings of Simone Weil on oppression and liberty that I found most useful in trying to think through the social significance of a revolt in which a whole society had come to a halt in a sort of political saturnalia. She, of course, had been writing not about 1968, but about the general strike of 1936. What stood out in both instances was the way in which a latent disgruntlement with being frog-marched into a questionable future had overflowed all available theorizations and authorized boundaries to put in question the structures of everyday routine.

What is now commonly believed, but was by no means obvious in the immediate aftermath of the events of 1968—in America and Australia quite as much as in France—is that this saturnalia did not simply subside, but flowed through our universities and other institutions, attacking 'bourgeois' society and authority at virtually every level. In 1981, this was still not obvious to me. Rather, I was interested in the then brewing civil rebellion against communism in Poland and dedicated the thesis to Lech Walesa. To be sure, he represented workers against the state and was championed by the Catholic Church; but it was his movement's demand for the right to question and contest things at all which moved me. Nor was the comparison indirect. The events in Paris in 1968 had coincided with the reform movement and its suppression in Prague. Raymond Aron and Annie Kriegel, in Paris, appalled at the saturnalia, denied any similarity between events there and those in Prague. But, as Klaus Mehnert pointed out, in his book *Moscow and the New Left*, it looked different from Moscow, whose conservative authoritarians saw disturbing parallels and wanted none of them.

Not only was Solidarity rising in Poland in 1981, but civil war was raging in El Salvador, and ideological passions which had their roots in decades of Cold War, going back through the Vietnam War to the Cuban revolution and even the Spanish Civil War, were all being roused again. It was in this context that I found myself enrolling in 1983 to undertake a PhD on the roots of rural insurgency and US counterinsurgency. And it was against this background, as a researcher in the United States, El Salvador and the Philippines and *on* Vietnam, through the mid-1980s, that I rediscovered the American sixties, as a great deal of modern history bit by bit was ploughed up and sown with questions so that I could harvest understanding. In this quest, Abbie Hoffmann and Jerry Rubin had no more place than Charles Manson, or for that matter Jim Morrison or Jimi Hendrix. But Carl Oglesby, Tom Hayden, Dave Dellinger, Mario Savio and others assumed a presence and a meaning I'd not accorded them before: just as David Halberstam, John Paul Vann, Daniel Ellsberg and many others became real to me for the first time. This was the sixties as history, but as near-contemporary history, and in the immediate context of events which still resonated against those of the sixties, if one was able to place an ear to the ground and listen.

Again it was 1968 that stood out, because of the Tet offensive, encapsulated for so many television viewers by the notorious footage of Nguyen Ngoc Loan shooting a Viet Cong captive through the head at point blank range during the defence of Saigon. My undergraduate studies had enabled me to avoid becoming either a Manichaean or a millenarian, so it was not with an ideological axe to grind that I approached the great controversies over the Vietnam War, but with a relentless desire to understand what I already, by 1982-83, tended to think of, with reference to Thucydides' history of the Peloponnesian War, as America's Sicilian Expedition. That was how I put it to Robert O'Neill, then head of the Strategic and Defence Studies Centre at ANU, when I first spoke with him about doing a PhD on the subject. Being, at that point, still ignorant of American military and intelligence links with the Sicilian mafia, going back to the 1940s, and only vaguely aware of how these links had contributed to the demoralization of the US counterinsurgency war in Laos and Vietnam and the evil flowering of heroin addiction in the US armed forces in the late 1960s, I did not describe the Vietnam War as the Sicilian Expedition with any intended irony. I simply considered myself, as it were, a citizen of Athens concerned about the disasters of his city's war against Sparta. Professor O'Neill did not demur at the analogy I offered, only commenting that he hoped the Cold War as a whole would not end the way the Peloponnesian War had—with the defeat of Athens.

Tet was a metastasis. Going back over the bitter debates it had generated concerning counterinsurgency war, the media and the numbers games played by General Westmoreland and

Robert McNamara, it always seemed to me that these debates were largely beside the point. The problem went deeper than how the war was reported or how many Communist foot soldiers lost their lives when General Giap imprudently gambled on a general uprising in January 1968 and sent his infantry into the open against the overwhelming fire power of the United States army. The question was what the United States really thought it was trying to *accomplish* in Indo-China, or more precisely how lucidly its decision-makers were conducting a strategy and policy of trying to check the spread of Communism. In the 1960s, activists could not, for the most part, do what I did in the 1980s and search patiently for answers to this question in the US National Archives. Dissent in the early 1960s ran out of patience after the escalation of US involvement in 1965 and a mood of growing anger and even apocalyptic frustration grew as the decade advanced and the bloodshed increased without any tenable answer being supplied to the insistent question.

The stock responses invoked the so-called Domino Theory and the need for the US to stay the course for the sake of its credibility. But it was precisely its credibility that the nature and conduct of the war were putting in question. As for the Domino Theory, none other than Robert Komer, who had been LBJ's pacification czar in 1966-67, told me, at the Washington DC office of the RAND Corporation, in early 1985, that he had never subscribed to it. Yet in the early 1980s it was again being invoked by the Reagan administration in regard to Central America. Watching the 1967 CBS documentary *The New Left*, in the US National Archives in early 1985; hearing Tom Hayden saying, 'We have found that when push comes to shove this society is very resistant to change, much more so than we thought seven or eight years ago'; watching film footage of Hubert Humphrey embracing racist Georgia Governor Lester Maddox; hearing the voices of pre-electric, pre-acid folk singers intoning, 'Call it peace or call it treason, call it love or call it reason, but I ain't a marchin' to war any more', I developed more affinity with the ethos and anger of the New Left than I had ever had as an undergraduate. Yet the Left was not for me. I kept delving in the archives.

There was a growing feeling among the public at large, remarked US Assistant Secretary of Defense John McNaughton in 1967, that the establishment was 'out of its mind', that it was 'carrying things to absurd lengths'. This was central to my concern in the 1980s and it was pivotal to my whole way of reconstructing what had happened in the 1960s. Was 'the establishment out of its mind'? Was this only in regard to Vietnam, or did it go deeper? And if it was, why had the New Left also gone out of its mind? Indeed, why did many of its luminaries seem devoted to blowing their minds and to mindless ranting about the evils of bourgeois civilization, the state, industrialism and rationality? That was, of course, many inquiries, and I had a PhD to do. One figure on whom many of these questions came to focus for me, however, was a former assistant to John McNaughton; an individual who in many ways epitomized both the virtues of the establishment and American bourgeois society in the 1960s and the crisis it underwent in the second half of that decade, especially on account of the Vietnam War. That individual was Daniel Ellsberg.

I was in what we now call Year Nine at school, in 1971, when Daniel Ellsberg briefly became famous for leaking 7,000 pages of a secret Pentagon study to the *New York Times*, exposing to public scrutiny much of the classified history of US decision-making which had led to the imbroglio in Vietnam. I still remember *Time* magazine running coverage of the sensational story. Yet Ellsberg remained only a fleeting and abstract figure to me until I found myself, in 1985, acquiring my own copy of *The Pentagon Papers* and reading all four volumes of the documents cover to cover, as well as Ellsberg's book of reflections, published in 1972, *Papers on the War*. Here was that sort of primary source material which could provide an answer of sorts to the questions of a troubled Athenian about that business in Sicily.

If John McNaughton had pointed in the right direction, by asking whether the establishment had gone out of its mind, Ellsberg's *coup de main* had revealed the actual thinking process of that mind. As a close student of its thinking over more than a decade at RAND, the Pentagon, the National Security Council and the State Department, he had been committed to ensuring the cogency of that mind. From 1966, however, he became increasingly convinced that that thinking was going seriously awry. By 1971, he had despaired of being able to help correct things from inside the US government's mind. There was nothing *Leftist* here. This was *cognitive* rebellion. I found myself riveted by its implications, which put the whole question of sixties dissent in a different light and had plain relevance, at a non-ideological level, to the questions I was grappling with in the 1980s.

It was crucial to my appreciation of Ellsberg's 1960s that he was neither of the beatnik nor of the neo-Marxist persuasion and that he had no interest in revolution for the hell of it. As a PhD student at Harvard before the Cuban missile crisis, he had been concerned with decision-making under conditions of uncertainty, issues of statistics, cybernetics and economic philosophy, which he had been studying since the early 1950s. Before and after receiving his doctorate, he worked at high levels within the US government on problems of crisis management and strategic decision-making. He believed in rationality and in the possibility of the executive branch of the United States government handling the excruciating challenges of the Cold War intelligently.

In the mid-sixties he began to discover that the Vietnam War had put all of this very seriously at issue. He found that the whole information analysis and decision-making system was suffering from pathologies which defied either simple explanation or identifiable solution; and that these pathologies were what had made the war so prolonged, fruitless and murderous in Indo-China and socially destructive in the United States. 'The process of reaching these conclusions was', he wrote in 1972, 'quite simply, the most frustrating, disappointing, disillusioning period of my life. I had come to Vietnam [in 1965] to learn, but also to help us succeed; and the learning was as bitter as the failure.'

The significance of such words for me went well beyond the vexed question of the Vietnam War itself. For one thing, I was, by then, immersed in a learning process which was showing me that the very pathologies identified by Ellsberg in the case of Vietnam War intelligence systems and decision-making were identifiable, also, in the history of United States involvement in the Philippines from the 1950s and in Central America over decades leading up to the civil wars of the 1980s. Nor was I under any illusion that such pathologies had much to do with 'bourgeois' society, American 'imperialism' or capitalism. I knew too much, by then, about the Russian and Chinese revolutions and the staggering pathologies of totalitarian government to see Marxist class analysis in any of its forms as very useful in the task of understanding why systems of authority became Cyclopean. I saw Ellsberg as Odysseus, not as a Leftist fellow traveler.

No passage in Ellsberg's reflections made a more lasting impression on me than this observation, concerning the conclusions he had arrived at by early 1967:

> *The urgent need to circumvent the lying and the self-deception was, for me, one of the 'lessons of Vietnam': a broader one was that there were situations—Vietnam was an example—in which the US government, starting ignorant, did not, would not, learn. There was a whole set of what amounted to institutional 'anti-learning' mechanisms working to preserve and guarantee unadaptive and unsuccessful behaviour: the fast turnover in personnel; the lack of institutional memory at any level; the failure to study history, to analyze or even record operational experience or mistakes; the effective pressures for optimistically false reporting at every level, for describing 'progress' rather than problems or failure, thus concealing the very need for change in approach or for learning. Well, helping the US government learn—in this case learn how to learn—was something, perhaps, I could do; that had been my business ...*

This touched not one but a whole set of responsive chords in me. It made not only the Vietnam War, but the whole psychodrama of the sixties conceptually intelligible, from the point of view of a crisis of learning in industrial civilization. It resonated against my very personal effort to use the disciplines of university study to learn about the deep past which had shaped the very 'beach' on which I had found myself thrown in adolescence.

What was it that the founding manifesto of Students for a Democratic Society (SDS) had declared, at Port Huron, in 1962? 'We are people of this generation, bred in at least modest comfort, housed now in universities, looking uncomfortably to the world we inherit ... But we are a minority—the vast majority of our people regard the temporary equilibriums of our society and world as eternally-functional parts'. As Todd Gitlin phrased it, looking back in 1988, the founders of SDS 'were not only willing to be marginal, they felt there was a kind of nobility in being devoted to public good in an unconventional way. In a nation devoted to private pursuits, they believed in public action.'

Well, of course, the conceit of being devoted to 'the public good' as a luminary minority had led many a group astray before the SDS and it certainly led the SDS in over its head in the sixties. What caught my attention increasingly, as I recovered the history of the SDS two decades after its heyday, was the *aspiration* it had embodied to rethink the modern world in critical and renovative ways. None of their denunciations of 'imperialism' or capitalism or 'bourgeois society' impressed me in the way Ellsberg's analysis of the cognitive pathologies of power structures did, but I, too, was uncomfortable looking at the world I'd inherited and all the more so because the residues of the SDS's aspirations of the sixties looked so sickly in the 1970s and 1980s.

Maurice Isserman wrote in 1987, in *If I Had a Hammer: The Death of the Old Left and the Birth of the New Left,* that the Port Huron statement 'placed the university at the centre [of the SDS's] design for remaking America, the potential home for a student left 'with real intellectual skills', a 'community controversy', a base for the assault upon the loci of power ... ' Ah! Assault? There was the old Leftist impulse to violent struggle. Wasn't it possible to use the universities as a base for truly understanding the challenges of the modern world and reforming things intelligently? Daniel Ellsberg, of course, had entered government service with this sort of faith in intelligence working within established structures and he did not surrender that faith easily, but he did end up apostatizing.

By the time I was at university it seemed to me that the legacy of the SDS was one of anti-intellectual and morally irresponsible assault-mongering, both on and off campuses. Yet who could gainsay the need to think, rethink and intelligently come to terms with the intractable challenges of the contemporary world? It's just that ever more convoluted post-Marxian jargon and variations on late-sixties yippy and hippy cynicism, accompanied by ever more cacophonous and offensive rock culture, seemed to me to be a spiral downward into *Sympathy for the Devil.* No hope there at all. Better to join the conservatives than to spin out with Jim Morrison and invoke *The End.*

But of course it wasn't that simple. Having completed my PhD I sought to take the old Ellsberg path: sober, rational, enlightened work in government service. I wanted to use my intelligence in intelligence work, the better to understand the world and, understanding it, to help change it in constructive ways, as far as I was able. That was at the beginning of 1989: the year of Tiananmen; the year the Soviet bloc in Eastern Europe underwent an 'American' revolution and Communism went into headlong retreat; the year the Berlin Wall came down. To enter government service, of course, I had to undergo security vetting procedures hammered out in the course of the Cold War—in London and Washington mostly—and here I collided, to my lasting astonishment, with that other side of the sixties: the same Neanderthal conservatism and mandarin mindlessness, the same anti-learning mechanisms and bureaucratic pathologies that had driven the SDS and Daniel Ellsberg to rebellion a generation before.

I found myself denied a security clearance on the astonishing grounds that I was 'pro-Soviet, pro-Communist, pro-terrorist', with a 'library full of books on Russia, Communism and terrorism' and an 'attitude towards the Central Intelligence Agency' which rendered me unsuitable for work in policy or intelligence areas, where I would have access to 'sensitive information'. The situation was truly Kafkaesque. In the process of fighting for the clearance and then, having gained it, spending six years in the intelligence system, I came to realize more than ever that the history which had taken place in the sixties, when I was cocooned from it, was the very stuff of which the world I lived and moved in was formed. I came to see myself as, in a double sense, a *child* of the sixties: skeptical of both the Old and the New Left, uncomfortable with the world as I inherited it, impatient with arbitrary authority, insistent on freedom of speech. Yet weren't these liberal values, quite extricable from the psychobabble, hallucinogenics, bombast, antinomianism, anti-scientific green-hornedness and sheer moral profligacy of the hippies, yippies and yahoos? I would certainly like to think so.

It was from my teacher Frank Knopfelmacher that I learned the term 'reconstructive conservative' and it is a style I have always felt to be saner and more responsible than that of the radical who presumes to turn the world upside down in the name of Eden or History. Not to start history anew at the Year Zero, but, to the contrary, to consider our circumstances and our actions in terms suggested by the remembrance of things past is, I believe, the way of wisdom. In a world which increasingly appears to be without moorings, this seems to me to be the single most salient lesson that the sixties have to teach us, in the perspective of thirty years since 1968: the Year of the Barricades.

Habemus Papam: an appreciation of Pope John Paul II[189]

At the beginning of Canto III of *The Inferno*, Dante tells us that the lintel over the Gates of Hell has an inscription on it which concludes with the words, 'Abandon all hope, ye who enter here'. Such has been the reaction against Papal power, the tradition of the Inquisition and Roman Catholicism itself, since the sixteenth century, that one might almost suggest that the Gates of Modernity have inscribed on their lintel, in a parody of Dante, the words, 'Abandon the Pope, all ye who enter here.' Modern secularists have long anticipated the demise of the Papacy, of Roman Catholicism and even of religion as such. Yet all three endure. Are they, indeed, mere slowly eroding anachronisms? Or is it possible that they contain deep sources of spiritual vitality, which will sustain them and challenge the world even in the 21st century?

Those who believe the first of these propositions might pause to consider how decisive the authentic charisma of the present Pope proved to be in the downfall of Soviet communism. 'How many divisions has the Pope?' Stalin once famously asked. 'And how much moral authority has the Kremlin?' came the reply from the Pope in the 1980s. The outcome of that contest, as much as any trial of the strength of the Catholic Church in its history, warrants reflection on the famous passage in the Gospel of St Matthew (16:18-19) in which Jesus is said to have declared to St Peter, 'Upon this rock I will build my Church, and the Gates of Hell shall not prevail against it.' As if challenging the very Gates of Hell depicted by Dante, Pope John Paul II wrote a book, after the downfall of Soviet communism, called *Crossing the Threshold of Hope* (1994). Its title is no empty rhetorical flourish. It taps into a universe of symbolism, of meaning more deeply rooted in the millennia of Western and Mediterranean civilization than any symbolism Modernity has generated.[190]

---

189 This essay first appeared in *Quadrant* in July 1998. John Paul II had been Pope by then for almost twenty years and in the eyes of many on the broad Left the shine had long since gone off him, if they had ever truly admired him. His conservatism regarding the key moral issues, starting with contraception, and his insistence on the authority of the Vatican over Liberation Theology activists in Nicaragua and elsewhere led to much criticism. Rarely have I met anyone who, while not sharing his beliefs or acknowledging his authority, confessed to admiring his charisma, his integrity and his statesmanship.

190 Dante's *Divine Comedy* remains a core text of Western civilization regardless of one's theological beliefs or lack of them. For a recent and acclaimed commentary on its significance, see Prue Shaw *Reading Dante: From Here to Eternity* (Liveright Publishing, W. W. Norton & Co., New York and London, 2014). She comments pointedly in her Introduction:

No Pope since time out of mind has shown a keener, more authentic grasp of that universe of symbolism and where it stands in relation to Modernity than has Pope John Paul II. He has steadfastly believed and has demonstrated to the secularists, who had considered his religion moribund that, in the much quoted words of Hamlet to Horatio, 'There are more things in Heaven and Earth than are dreamt of in your philosophy.' His pontificate has left many of his constituents, both Tridentine and Latitudinarian, dissatisfied; but those disposed to a less fractious and self-absorbed view of the Church and the world will, I think, allow that he has been one of the towering figures of the twentieth century. I will venture to go further and assert that Pope John Paul II stands among the handful of popes who have truly been both masterful ecclesiastical statesmen and authentic spiritual figures.[191]

> *Two writers I know, liberal humanists both, on being asked if they had read Dante, answered almost in unison: why would I bother? A nineteenth century Italian poet, writing when evolutionary ideas had begun to permeate popular consciousness and challenge traditional religious thinking, put the point with epigrammatic neatness in the final line of his sonnet on Dante. Even if God is dead, great art survives:*
>
> > Muor Giove, e l'inno del poeta resta
> > *(God dies, and the poet's song remains)*
>
> *It is interesting that the poet in question (the author of the sonnet) wrote that Jove dies, which might be interpreted to mean the ancient pagan sky god, rather than the God of Christianity. Yet he was writing of Dante's 'song'. The inference we must surely draw is that he was likening the durability of Dante's poetry, after the death of God, to that of the poetry of Homer and Virgil, after the death of Jove, long ago.*

191 George Weigel, a conservative Catholic theologian and advocate, has written an impressive biography of Karol Wojtyla: *Witness to Hope: The Biography of Pope John Paul II* (Cliff Street Books, Harper Collins, New York, 1999). At nearly 1,000 pages, it is a formidable book, but well worth reading. David Yallop has written a very different appraisal of the papacy under John Paul II: *The Power and the Glory: Inside the Dark Heart of John Paul II's Vatican* (Carroll & Graf, New York, 2007). His emphasis was on the secrecy and defensiveness of the Vatican as an institution and the way it has, even in the recent past, dismissed or persecuted those from within or those on its periphery deemed to have compromised those secrets. I need hardly say that in such matters I am aligned with Yallop and not with the Vatican.

For an overview of the history of the Papacy, bringing the story right up to the present, see Eamon Duffy *Saints and Sinners: A History of the Popes* (4th edition, Yale University Press, New Haven and London, 2014). The book includes an appendix with a complete chronological list of Popes and anti-Popes. It concludes with a clear-headed reflection on the prospects for reform of the Vatican under Pope Francis I. It was not clear, Duffy wrote in 2014, whether the Argentinian Jesuit and septuagenarian with one lung:

> *... would be able to carry through the deep structural changes he seemed to favour in the Vatican's entrenched and byzantine bureaucracies. Many suspected that the pope's age and lack of Vatican experience might in the end frustrate even the best intentions. Behind the scenes, some feared, the temple police need only regroup and wait for the flood tide of reform to ebb away. Those familiar with his record as Jesuit Provincial and as Archbishop of Buenos Aires insisted, however, that Bergoglio's canniness and determination would be a match even for the grey eminences of the Vatican, and that a process had begun whose momentum might well survive its initiator. Only time will tell.*

His achievements in the 1980s put him at least on the level of Pope Leo the Great (440-461), who turned back Attila the Hun at Mantua, and Pope Gregory VII (1073-1085), who humbled the Emperor Henry IV at Canossa, as a tamer of secular potentates. His social encyclicals, notably *Solicitudo Rei Socialis* (1987) and *Centesimus Annus* (1991), truly lay a foundation for a modern Catholicism. They simultaneously and seamlessly transcend the notorious narrowness of Pope Pius IX's *Syllabus of Errors,* reach beyond Pope Leo XIII's *Rerum Novarum* or Pope Paul VI's *Populorum Progressio* and issue a clear moral challenge to liberal capitalism: all in the name of a human solidarity grounded in transcendental principles.

Pope John Paul II's devotion to the Blessed Virgin and his admiration for Padre Pio jar against many a Protestant, Latitudinarian and secularist sensibility, but is that a decisive objection to the integrity of his Catholic piety? His strong endorsement of Opus Dei, similarly, is widely regarded with distrust. Yet it might be allowed that he sees this movement as playing a comparable role in the late 20th century to the Cluniac movement in the tenth century or the Society of Jesus in the sixteenth. It is, of course, just such an analogy as that with the Jesuits which tends to excite suspicion of the Popery which has been so vehemently repudiated in the modern Western world. I make the comparison, however, only by way of underscoring the tenacity of a faith and an institution which so many have, for so long, expected to see wither away.

One of the *loci classici* of the view that the Papacy was a doomed anachronism is that passage in *Thus Spake Zarathustra,* Part IV, 'Retired from Service', in which Nietzsche's prophet of the death of God, Zarathustra, meets 'the last Pope', who has served God up until the old Deity's final hours and has watched Him die.[192] Published in 1885, this passage makes curious reading now. It is one of the passages in Nietzsche likely to prompt the response of the graffiti artist "God is dead'—Nietzsche. 'Nietzsche is dead'—God."). It is a sublime passage and it goes to the heart of Nietzsche's actually very complex attitude toward Christianity. But to what Pope who has actually sat in the chair of St Peter since 1885 might Zarathustra have spoken on such spiritually intimate terms? Gioacchino Pecci (Pope Leo XIII)? Eugenio Pacelli (Pope Pius XII)? Perhaps Angelo Roncalli, the widely praised Pope John XXIII? Giovanni Battista Montini (Pope Paul VI)? Perhaps none of them so much as Karol Wojtyla, the spiritual witness to and survivor of Nazism and Communism, whom Vaclav Havel welcomed to Prague in

---

The secularized West will not return to the Papal fold in any foreseeable future, least of all under the aegis of an unreformed and secretive Vatican. If, however, the Catholic Church wishes to exert significant moral influence in the 21st century, it will have to put its house in order and demonstrate an integrity that others find convincing. Neither secrecy nor dogma will avail it in this matter.

192 All citations from *Thus Spake Zarathustra* are from the Penguin translation by R. J. Hollingdale, first published in 1961. 'Retired from service' is at pp. 271-75 of that version.

April 1991 as 'The Messenger of Love ... the Living Symbol of Civilization ... the Apostle of Spirituality'.

Zarathustra encounters the last Pope as a figure sitting by the side of the road and is greeted by him. The last Pope had climbed into the mountains after the death of God, seeking out an old hermit who had not yet heard that God was dead, in order to celebrate with him 'a festival of pious memories and divine services'. He had served the old God until his last hour and now wanders in the mountains in a world that is 'strange and remote', where he hears the 'howling of wild animals' and where 'he who could have afforded me protection is himself no more'. But he finds that the hermit is dead, also. Therefore, in a moment of inspiration, he had decided to seek out Zarathustra, 'the most pious of all those who do not believe in God'. That, in itself, is a point worth noting. In any case, Zarathustra, when he comes upon him 'sitting beside the path', takes his hand with veneration and asks him, thoughtfully, after a profound silence, 'Do you know *how* God died? Is it true what they say, that pity choked him?'

They then discourse on the life and times of God, as faithful servant and pious sceptic. But at last Zarathustra urges the Pope to let go of the dead God whose memory he cherishes, since that God was, after all, a God full of secrecy, contradictions and wrath, who followed 'strange paths' before finally growing old and tired. 'He had too many failures, that potter who had not learned his craft! But that he took vengeance on his pots and creations, because they had turned out badly—that was a sin against *good taste*.'[193] To which the Pope-in-mourning responds: 'O Zarathustra, you are more pious than you believe, with such an unbelief! Some god in your has converted you to your godlessness ... In your neighbourhood ... I scent a stealthy odour of holiness and well-being that comes from long benedictions: it fills me with joy and sorrow.' He asks Zarathustra might he be his guest, there in the mountains, for a night. 'Amen!' responds Zarathustra 'in great astonishment' and points the way to his eremite's cave.

Both his youthful experience as a thespian and his deeply reflective 20th century life, as well as his love of walking in the mountains, might place Karol Wojtyla in this dialogue, alone among the modern Popes. Yet he plainly does not believe that God is dead. Nor does it seem probable that he

---

193   This looks very much like an allusion to the famous verses of the Persian poet Omar Khayyam, very freely translated into English by Edward FitzGerald (1809-1883) in his celebrated long poem *The Rubaiyat of Omar Khayyam*, first published in English in 1859, then in new editions in 1868, 1872 and 1879. Stanzas 78 to 89, in particular, evoke the idea that God might be seen as a potter; but then ask what potter would 'toss to Hell the luckless pots he marred in making?' On Omar Khayyam, see Mehdi Aminrazavi *The Wine of Wisdom: The Life, Poetry and Philosophy of Omar Khayyam* (Oneworld Publications, Oxford, 2005). The book includes (as Appendix B) the complete text of FitzGerald's translation of the Rubaiyat. The book itself is dedicated 'to the democratic movement of the people of Iran. May Khayyam's spirit of free-thinking prevail in our native land'.

will be the last Pope.[194] Why, therefore, imagine this historic Pope in a dialogue with the fictional Zarathustra? Why, indeed, tell any story which does not stick strictly to 'the facts'? Surely because, as Frank Kermode remarks, in his wonderful reflection on the Gospel of St Mark and James Joyce's *Ulysses - The Genesis of Secrecy: On the Interpretation of Narrative* - the telling of stories is a *midrash* on 'the facts', a probing beneath their surface appearance to get at their various significances. The idea of the death of God throws into high relief what the persistence of religion is ultimately about.

Roberto Calasso observes, in *The Ruin of Kasch,* that 'the civilized West', since the 18th century has 'seemed (and still seems to be) separated by a lead wall from everything that might turn one's gaze toward the *atman-brahman*'—the appreciation of life in conscious awareness of its strangeness and brevity. The civilized West, including vast numbers of Latitudinarians who more or less still call themselves Catholics, does not share the Pope's faith or hope. A lead wall stands between his way of experiencing reality and that of the worldly and libertarian societies he would like to re-evangelize. The forms and ceremonies, devotions and prayers which have informed his spiritual life are substantially as inaccessible, as devoid of living meaning, to the citizens of those societies as the Latin in which the Catholic liturgy was celebrated until a generation ago. This is not to say that his beliefs are true; only that they embody a ritualized way of being in the world that has become foreign even to most of those who still call themselves Catholics.

God has, indeed, receded from Western societies. In seeking to re-evangelize them, the Pope has more in common than might seem plausible on the surface of things, with Zarathustra. He is uncannily akin to that madman whom Nietzsche describes in aphorism 125 of *The Gay Science.* The madman runs into the marketplace in the morning hours, with a lantern, crying incessantly that he is looking for God. The famous aphorism continues:

> *As many of those who did not believe in God were standing around just then, he provoked much laughter. Has he got lost? Asked one. Did he lose his way like a child? Asked another. Or is he hiding? Is he afraid of us? Has he gone on a voyage? Emigrated?—Thus they yelled and laughed.*

Thereupon, the said madman leaps into the middle of the crowd and cries out,

> *'Whither is God?... I will tell you. We have killed him—you and I. All of us are his murderers. But how did we do this? How could we drink up the sea? Who gave us the sponge to wipe away the entire horizon? ... What was holiest and mightiest of all that the world has yet owned has bled to death under our knives: who will wipe this blood off us? What water is there with which we might cleanse ourselves? What festivals of atonement, what sacred games shall we invent?'*

---

194 Since this essay was written, in 1998, John Paul II has died (2 April 2005) and been succeeded first by Pope Benedict XVI and then, in March 2013, by Pope Francis I. There is no immediate sign of the Papacy crumbling. The Vatican, however, is still widely seen as a corrupt and self-serving cabal of clerics, whose motives and dogmas are widely distrusted and repudiated. Pope Benedict XVI sought to re-evangelize the secular West, but the prospects for that happening do not look promising, even under his apparently good-hearted and reforming successor.

His listeners look at him in dumb astonishment, no more alive to the madman's concerns than is the marketplace to those of the Pope. The madman therefore walks away, saying to himself that the death of God is something that has not even come to their attention yet. It is more distant from them than the most distant star; and yet they have killed God themselves. That and not a mere cynical or arid atheism, sums up Nietzsche's attitude to Christianity over a century ago.

Like Zarathustra, or Nietzsche himself, the madman is a pious soul. Upon leaving the crowd behind in the marketplace, he makes his way into various churches and sings a requiem for the deceased God. 'Led out and called to account', Nietzsche's aphorism concludes, 'he is said always to have replied nothing but, 'What, after all, are these churches now, if they are not the tombs and sepulchers of God?'' He might, surely, have been talking about the great monasteries and cathedrals of the West in the last decades of the 20th century. My point is that there is more in common between the madman's bearing in such places and that of Karol Wojtyla as Pope than there is between the Pope and the insubstantial after-religion, vacuous pop-liturgy, and ontological tourism of so much that passes itself off as modern religion in the contemporary West. The unbelievers in the marketplace, of course, have a hard time understanding why that matters.

It matters a great deal. If the barbarisms of the 20th century and the terrible emptiness of so much 'post-modern' urban life have taught us anything, it is surely that there has always been more to religion than enthusiasm and superstition. The challenge lies in getting at the ontological kernel beneath the forms of religious belief and ceremony, without killing it in the process of stripping down the altars. In 1884, the year before *Thus Spake Zarathustra* was published, Leo Tolstoy wrote an essay called 'My Religion' (or 'What I Believe'), in which he made a damning attack on organized Christianity in the name of the Gospel. He wrote:

> *I was driven from the [Russian Orthodox] Church, by the strangeness of its dogmas, and the approval and the support which it gave to persecutions, to the death penalty, to wars, and by the intolerance common to all sects; but my faith was chiefly shattered by the indifference of the Church to what seemed to me to be essential in the teachings of Jesus, and by its avidity for what seemed to me not essential.*

Conversely, as regards the accumulating evidence that modern science and scholarship were advancing against long-established Christian beliefs, he commented:

> *They are attacking the last of the outworks, and if they carry it and demonstrate that Christ was never born, it will be all the more evident that the fortress of religion is impregnable. Take away the Church, the traditions, the Bible and even Christ himself: the ultimate fact of man's knowledge of goodness, that is, of God, directly, through reason and conscience, will be as clear and certain as ever, and it will be seen that we are dealing with truths that can never perish—truths that humanity can never afford to part with.*

Yet Tolstoy, excommunicated by the Russian Orthodox Church for his radical theological views, found himself unable to live out his 'truths that can never perish' and ended up fleeing from his wife and family at the age of eighty-two, in search of a lonely place where he could draw closer to God. Instead, he died of pneumonia at Astapovo. Did he mutter to himself as he died, 'My God, my God, why have you abandoned me?' Within a decade, the *kerygma* not of Tolstoy but of Lenin swept across Russia. Where were the 'truths that can never perish'? They were more exposed than ever by the tyranny of Communism.

It was the evocation of 'truths that can never perish' which, in the end, brought down Soviet Communism. To those truths there had been many witnesses and many martyrs, but it was their evocation by the Pope in the 1980s that was decisive. Whereas Tolstoy spoke out with little effect against the repressions of the last Tsar, the Pope spoke out with world-historical effect against the lies and repressions of Soviet Communism and brought about its demise. Pope Benedict XV had tried in vain to bring about an end to the First World War, Pope Pius XII is still accused of doing too little to denounce or seek to hinder the Nazi genocide of the Jews and, indeed, of assisting Nazis to escape Europe at the end of the Second World War. Pope John Paul II brought down Soviet Communism. And he did so not by suspect or Machiavellian Popery, but by inspirational mass moral and political dissent.

The Pope was not, or course, alone in this, nor can it be said that circumstances and other pressures did not contribute to the collapse of the Soviet Union and its East European empire, but it was Mikhail Gorbachev himself who wrote, in 1992:

> *Everything that happened in Eastern Europe these past few years would have been impossible without the Pope, without the political role he was able to play.*

In terms of the old maxim, attributed to Archimedes, 'Give me a lever that is long enough and a place to stand and I will move the world', the lever was the Catholic faith and the place to stand was the office of the Roman Pontiff. Karol Wojtyla was the man who, at the appointed hour, was, as all those steeped in that ancient tradition would put it, chosen by God to wield that lever and stand in that place—and move the world.

It is important that this argument not be misconstrued. It is, after all, more commonly perceived that the White House and President Reagan, not the Vatican and Pope John Paul II, precipitated the downfall of Soviet communism; or that it fell of its own weight, due to the cumulative effects of economic mismanagement and political sclerosis. Doesn't it verge on the mystical or unscientific to attribute the fall of the Soviet empire to the influence of the Pope and religion? It might, in the manner of claims that God worked a miracle at the Battle of Lepanto to save Christendom from the infidel Turks, if it was misconstrued. The argument is, however, completely hard-headed and based on the evidence.

As Mark Kramer, Director of the Harvard Project on Cold War Studies told Jonathan Kwitny, author of *Man of the Century: The Life and Times of Pope John Paul II*, the declassified records of the Soviet government from the 1980s make it clear that:

> *books that credit US policy for the collapse are just plain wrong. The Reagan military policies were a background thing. Poland was of vastly greater importance.*

Poland was the pivot on which Karol Wojtyla placed his lever, with his feet planted in Rome. And the lever was not fanaticism, it was not hatred, it was not 'divisions', it was not a covert alliance with the White House and the CIA. It was that very ontological kernel of 'truths that can never perish' which Tolstoy sought beneath the trappings of organized religion; which Zarathustra and the last Pope found they had in common; which the madman revered in singing his requiem to the deceased God; which Karol Wojtyla saw in some measure even beneath all the lies and barbarisms of Soviet Communism; and which he has striven to draw out from within the depths of Roman Catholicism, in order to render it, as the Second Vatican Council hoped, a light among the nations.

This was at all times the Pope's own reading of the nature of the struggle in Poland, in Eastern Europe as a whole and in the world at large. In the immediate aftermath of the overthrow of Communism in Poland, in 1989 he wrote: 'I think that, if any role was decisive, it was that of Christianity ... of its content, its religious and moral message, its fundamental defence of the human person and his rights. I have done nothing other than call to mind, repeat and insist that this principle be observed.' Two years later, as the Soviet Union itself fell apart, he wrote, in *Centesimus Annus*:

> *The fall of this empire ... was accomplished almost everywhere by means of peaceful protest, using only the weapons of truth and justice. While Marxism held that only by exacerbating social conflicts was it possible to resolve them, through violent confrontation, the protests that led to the collapse of Marxism tenaciously insisted on trying every avenue of negotiation, dialogue and witness to the truth, appealing to the conscience of the adversary and seeking to reawaken in him a shared sense of human dignity ... This disarmed the adversary, since violence always needs to justify itself through deceit and to appear, however falsely, to be ... responding to a threat posed by others.*

The astonishing thing is that all this should have emerged, contrary to every expectation of the prophets and praetorians of modernity, precisely from the Papacy. From *that* institution? Indeed. And what other institution could have done it? Or what other Pope this century? The answer in both cases, surely, is 'No other'. That should lead us to ponder more carefully than we commonly do, in our libertarian, consumerist, postmodern post-culture, the uses of long levers, firm pivots and sound places to stand.

Karol Wojtyla's life has been absorbed, very plainly, in just such pondering and with a degree of commitment, of engagement, which must surely put any Sartrean existentialist to shame.

Yet his pontificate has been marked by a great deal of dissent from within the Catholic church about his use of Papal authority, his firm defence of doctrinal and moral tradition and his real or alleged sins of omission as regards the advancement of human rights within the Church and in the world as large. At a time when the Catholic Church was clearly in a state of institutional crisis and confusion, following the remarkable renewal attempted at the Second Vatican Council (1962-65), it elected the first non-Italian pope in centuries and he became the most redoubtable of modern Popes. Yet his critics within the church, especially in the West, and his critics outside the church have been unrelenting in their complaints against him as a leader.

I do not wish to suggest that there are no grounds for criticism or complaint. I do think, however, that much of the criticism directed at the Pope, especially from within the Church, is ill-considered and even incoherent. If, of course, one simply wishes to do away with the Papacy, with Roman Catholicism, perhaps with Christianity itself, in the manner of the Utilitarians or the League of Militant Atheists, then any barb fired at them might be considered a useful contribution to what has been a very long siege. If, on the other hand, one is more concerned with civilization than with domination, then the matter becomes more complex and interesting. Above all, however, if one is putting a case for what Catholicism or Christianity really is or ought to become, then it will not do at all to simply fire at will. Certainly, it will not do to demand of the Pope, of all leaders, that he become a thoroughly flexible Latitudinarian and libertarian immoralist—however liberal one may personally be.

What precisely it *is* reasonable to demand of the Pope, in the name of Catholicism or Christianity, must be consistent with the foundations and traditions of that religion. This imposes limits and a development logic, as John Henry Newman argued in the mid-nineteenth century. Outside of those limits and that logic the critic is part of the besieging army, either *extra muros* or disgorged by the Trojan horse within the walls. The present Pope is a defender of the faith. A Catholic Hector, he has slain the Patroclus of Communism. He or his successors may yet by slain, in turn, by the Achilles of liberal capitalism, but who among the Greeks would even respect him if he threw open the gates and said, 'We are all Greeks here!'? That he has not done—and Troy still stands, under his leadership.

John Henry Newman, the celibate Anglican who found himself driven by his studies of the primitive tradition of Christianity to embrace Roman Catholicism, despite its extremely reactionary condition in his time, wrote in 1833, more than a decade before his conversion:

> *Oh that Rome were not Rome; but I seem to see as clear as day that a union with her is impossible. She is the cruel Church—asking of us impossibilities, excommunicating us for disobedience, and now watching and exulting over our approaching overthrow.*

Twelve years later, on the eve of his conversion, he wrote, in *The Development of Christian Doctrine*:

> *There is a religious communion claiming a divine commission and holding all other religious bodies around it heretical or infidel; it is a well-organized, well-disciplined body ... It is a natural enemy to governments external to itself ... and tends to a new modeling of society ... it is despised by the intellect of the day; it is frightful to the imagination of the many. And there is but one communion such.*

As a Roman Catholic, Newman was a strong critic of Ultramontanism (the belief that the authority of the Pope should be absolute) and opposed the definition of Papal infallibility at the First Vatican Council. For this and other reasons, he has widely been dubbed the eponymous hero of the long struggle within the Catholic Church throughout the twentieth century over how to overcome the defensiveness of the Roman Curia and engage the modern world as *Mater et Magistra* (Pope John XXIII's encyclical of 1961). The Second Vatican Council, convened in 1962, is sometimes referred to as 'Newman's Council'. [195] Yet there have been few sterner or more consistent critics of Latitudinarianism than Newman and, though this might be contested, I would be astonished if he, revisiting the world in the past twenty years, were to be other than an enormous admirer of Pope John Paul II.

Writing at the very beginning of Pope John Paul II's reign, James Hitchcock spoke for many conservative Catholics (and discerning non-Catholic observers) when he remarked, in *Catholicism and Modernity: Confrontation or Capitulation?*:

> *One of the great human mysteries of modern times is the amazingly swift process by which the Roman Catholic Church, apparently one of the most solid, self-confident and enduring institutions in the history of the world, was plunged into an identity crisis of cosmic proportions. The crisis still goes on, with no satisfactory outcome yet in sight.*

The crisis was very real and Pope John Paul II has been beset by it throughout his twenty-year reign. The mystery is not, however, so unfathomable as James Hitchcock believed in 1979. For what Pope John XXIII did in summoning the Second Vatican Council was akin to what Louis XVI did in summoning the Estates General, or what Mikhail Gorbachev did in declaring an era of *glasnost*.

---

195   Ian Ker, a fine Catholic scholar and biographer of John Henry Newman, has recently produced a compact book, *Newman on Vatican II* (Oxford University Press, 2014), which advances a closely reasoned and conservative account of both Newman's theological opinions and the documents of the Second Vatican Council. It concludes, however, with a chapter called 'Secularization and the New Evangelization' which urges that a belief in the 'real presence' of the 'body and blood' of Jesus be made the focus of an attempt to re-evangelize the secular West in the early 21st century. It is difficult to believe that an intelligent man could seriously entertain such an idea at this point. That he should do so goes to underscore the gulf that still separates religious literalists from well-informed anthropologists of religion. The latter point of view is set out with notable lucidity in Roy A. Rappaport *Ritual and Religion in the Making of Humanity* (Cambridge University Press, 1999).

As Alexis de Tocqueville long ago observed, despots who begin to reform are like armies who begin to retreat: they expose themselves to the furious onrush of their enemies and the demoralization of their janissaries. Although, as Robert Aubert wrote in 1978, the Second Vatican Council was intended to serve as 'the vital bridge' for the church between the Counter-Reformation and an imagined new era of modern renewal and enlightened evangelism, that bridge was stoutly held by modernists against the church's soldiers of Christ. If the Emperor Constantine was supposed to have seen a vision of the cross at the battle of the Milvian Bridge (in 312) and the words *in hoc signo vince* (in this sign conquer), the ecclesiastical heirs of Pope Sylvester I (Constantine's contemporary) may be said to have seen a vision of a condom and the words *in hoc signo cede* (in this sign surrender). It was Karol Wojtyla who rallied the *milites Christi*, just when a real rout threatened.[196]

The idea of a vision of a condom and the accompanying words may sound flippant and even blasphemous. Yet few things in Catholic teaching since the 1960s have so offended the modern secular sensibility, or what many people within the church would simply call common sense, as the Papal ban on contraception. Mockery follows. On no single issue has the internal division of the Catholic Church and its confrontation with the modern world been more exposed since the Second Vatican Council than on this one. It is, on the other hand, now merely part of the broad-ranging agenda among Latitudinarians for the wholesale revision of the Church's moral and magisterial character, with demands for the abolition of clerical celibacy, the ordination of women, the acceptance of divorce and remarriage, the renunciation of ancient strictures against masturbation and homosexuality and, in general, a sort of thoroughgoing reconstruction of Catholicism along Frankfurt School or even New Age lines. This Pope John Paul II has resisted.

The ban on contraception may well go the way of the Index of Prohibited Books, or the long prejudice against the Jews as the killers of Christ, in due course. After all, as recently as 1929, the Cardinal Secretary of the Holy Office, Rafael Merry del Val, could still write, in his preface to the latest edition of the *Index Librorum Prohibitorum*, that the Vatican continued to fight a stern struggle against that 'terrible instrument of Hell, the wicked printing press'. The Index remained on the books, as it were, until 1966 and even the 1945 edition contained 4,000

---

196 Looking back seventeen years, I am surprised and a little dismayed at the extent of my defence of Pope John Paul II, especially on the matter of contraception. I have revised the wording of several passages in the essay, including this one, to make it read better; but I have not altered the original argument or sense of any of the essay. This is what I argued at the time and, as the following paragraphs show, I was 'bending over backwards' to understand the conservative position, while still being far more in Zarathustra's camp as far as actual beliefs were concerned. That remains more than ever the case after all the intervening years.

titles, including works by Boyle, Bruno, Hobbes, Hume, Voltaire, Descartes, Kant, Locke, Mill, Gibbon, Montaigne, Stendhal and Flaubert. That, clearly, was the sort of Catholicism which Newman deplored. If the Church is truly to act as a morally redemptive influence in the world as it now is, it can ultimately no more condemn the contraceptive regulation of fertility than it can reasonably prohibit the regulation of seminal works of Western thought.

Understanding why it would ever have taken this stance at all, however, is vital to any attempt to do justice to it as an institution and to the integrity with which Pope John Paul II has led it. The premium placed on sexual chastity and even sexual renunciation goes so far back in the history of Catholicism that it may justly be said to constitute the taproot of its spirituality. In his 1971 essay on the redefinition of Western culture, *In Bluebeard's Castle*, George Steiner ventured the suggestion that the twentieth century has seen a rebellion against 'the singularity, the brain-hammering strangeness of the monotheistic idea'. Whatever the merits of either that suggestion or the putative rebellion, the debate over contraception and sexuality generally, at least as regards the teachings of the Catholic Church, can only rise above confusion and mutual exasperation if those who take issue with the Vatican on this matter can recapture a just sense of the singularity, the 'brain-hammering strangeness' of the ancient Catholic veneration of sexual renunciation and chastity.

I know of no better or more illuminating exploration of this subject than Peter Brown's extraordinary 1988 book, *The Body and Society: Men, Women and Sexual Renunciation in Early Christianity*. What he wrote in his preface to this book might with equal justice be said of those who have embraced celibacy and asceticism over the many centuries since the practices were first hammered out in late antiquity:

> *It would be deeply inhumane to deny that, in these centuries, real men and women faced desperate choices, endured privation and physical pain, courted breakdown and bitter disillusionment, and frequently experienced themselves and addressed others, with a searing violence of language.*

Yet this marvellous scholar is able to do justice to the fierce striving for spiritual and personal redemption that this ferocious renunciation and harsh regimen entailed in the world of the Roman Empire. His tribute to 'the towering genius of Origen' (the remarkable 3rd century Alexandrian theologian) and his 'peculiarly majestic ideal of virginity' encapsulates this capacity to do justice to 'the disturbing strangeness' and the 'sharp and dangerous flavour of many Christian notions of sexual renunciation'.

The Christian Platonism of Origen envisioned the body as:

> *Poised on the edge of a transformation so enormous as to make all present notions of identity tied to sexual differences, and all social roles based upon marriage, procreation and childbirth, seem as fragile as dust dancing in a sunbeam ... Identified in this intimate manner with the pristine soul, the*

> *intact flesh of a virgin of either sex stood out ... as a fragile oasis of human freedom. Refusal to marry (in a society in which this was an early and relentless duty) mirrored the right of a human being, the possessor of a pre-existent, utterly free soul, not to surrender its liberty to the pressures placed upon the person by society.*

This point of view is, of course, so antithetical to the Marcusean ethos of desublimation, with which two generations in the West have grown up since the 1960s, that when Karol Wojtyla invokes such ancient ideals, which he has done consistently throughout his life as a priest, he is simply not understood. In a tradition going back via Diderot and Voltaire to Boccaccio and Chaucer, we are apt to mock such ideals in the breach, but we are increasingly out of touch with their contribution to the psychological and cultural deepening of Western civilization. It was none other than Nietzsche who remarked, concerning this uncanny and disturbing matter, 'Who is sufficiently rich in gratitude not to be impoverished in the face of all that the 'spiritual men' of Christianity ... have hitherto done for Europe?' Karol Wojtyla is of that company. One may well choose not to walk in the mountains with him; but to lightly ask that he resile from such traditions, as the foundation of Catholic moral and spiritual teaching, is to fundamentally misconceive the nature of the issue.

The former Jesuit Malachi Martin described Pope John Paul II as having been 'left with a shattered institution waiting at the crossroads of history with only the gravest of doubts and the deepest of problems as his constant companions'. Local Latitudinarian Father Paul Collins declares that the Catholic Church does not want any more Popes like John Paul II. The Russian Orthodox patriarchs denounce his desire to extend Catholicism eastwards. Muslim zealots denounce his desire to proselytize in Africa and the Middle East. Above all, millions who, as Nietzsche dryly remarked, 'have forgotten what religions are supposed to be for and as it were merely register their existence in the world with a kind of dumb amazement', regard with puzzlement and even exasperation the insistence of this man that *his* religion is rooted in deep commitments and which views the transactions of everyday life *sub specie aeternitatis*. Yet isn't that what Popes are supposed to be for? In Karol Wojtyla, whose life and pontificate are drawing to a close, the world and the Catholic Church—which he clearly does not regard as a shattered institution—truly have a Pope of this kind. Will he be the last such? Or will the next Pope, perhaps from Africa or Latin America[197], be an even more astonishing figure, who will take the challenge of arcane beliefs and austere morality right up to the last men in the marketplace?

---

197   There has not yet been an African Pope, but we got a German Pope after the Polish one and now have a Latin American one, in the Argentinian Pope Francis I. These three elections have shown, at least to some extent, the broadening out of the Catholic Church's central governing body and its willingness to break the long Italian monopoly on the Papal office.

Christianity and the cathedral of the mind[198]

Christmas is an ancient feast in the calendar of Western civilization. Indeed, its roots are pagan and antedate Christianity itself. Wryly commenting on its growing tendency to be a merely commercial Saturnalia in the 20th century, Tom Lehrer quipped, a generation ago, that it:

> *gives us a chance to reflect on what we all most deeply and sincerely believe in. I refer, of course, to money.*

Perhaps it might be better used to reflect on the sheer antiquity of Christianity and ask, against that background, what it actually is that we all most sincerely and deeply believe. For it makes at least figurative claims on what we believe about ourselves as human beings; claims which the extensive reconfiguring, in recent decades, of our knowledge of the past must surely put in serious question.

Taking up the challenge of that question is not a simple matter. It involves trying to disentangle several quite closely interwoven strands of ourselves and our cultural patrimony, without having the whole fabric unravel on us. Maybe I can convey something of what I mean by this if I state that my impulse to seek an answer to this question is prompted by, among other things, unease at the absurdity of the Gospel story as depicted in Franco Zeffirelli's *Jesus of Nazareth*, compared with the powerful exaltation still induced by listening to Handel's glorious musical rendering of the salvation drama in *The Messiah*. I believe the question can only be answered at all satisfactorily by a deep reckoning with the archaeology of our religious tradition.

I am talking here of far more than the quest for the historical Jesus. Recent decades have seen a revolution in our scientific understanding of how we human beings became what we are. The profound and ancient symbolism of Christian faith must be seen in the context of that scientific

---

198 This essay was first published in *Quadrant* in December 1998. It was probably my first more or less systematic attempt to play out my stance as regards religion in the modern world: an ongoing inquiry and not one in which I feel much affinity with the polemical and reductionist approach of Richard Dawkins or the unreconstructed Trotskyist polemics of the late Christopher Hitchens (1949-2011). Religion has been a human universal and has to be understood not in historical materialist terms or in reductionist sociobiological ones, but in terms of the human propensity to symbol, ritual and transcendent vision. One of the best rationalist critiques of religious belief is Daniel C. Dennett *Breaking the Spell: Religion as a Natural Phenomenon* (Viking, New York, 2006). J. G. A. Pocock has written a magisterial multi-volume study of the collision between Western religion and Enlightenment rationalism and materialism in *Barbarism and Religion* (Cambridge University Press, beginning with two volumes in 1999). For a far broader survey of the problem, however, see Robert N. Bellah *Religion in Human Evolution: From the Palaeolithic to the Axial Age* (Belknap Press, Harvard, 2011). The weakest part of Bellah's book is his conclusion. He recoils from the judgement that what is needed in the 21st century is a 're-axialization' of our religions in the light of our cosmology, biology and cognitive science.

understanding, if the question about what we truly believe is to find an authentic answer. In a special, fiftieth anniversary edition of the journal *Archaeology* this year, Brian Fagan contributed a short essay headed 'Fifty Years of Discovery: How Archaeology Has Reconfigured the Human Past'. He wrote that 'computers and an awesome array of new scientific methods have allowed us to make discoveries unimaginable at mid-century.' He lists such innovations as pollen analysis, the calibration of carbon dates with tree rings, zoo-archaeology, remote sensing, mitochondrial DNA research and carbon isotope analysis.

He draws attention to the fact that such technological advances have extended our reach back into the human past in manifold ways. Mary Leakey's astonishing discovery of the 3.6 million year old hominid foot prints at Laetoli, Tanzania, in 1978; climatological studies, reconstructing the world of the late Ice Age, between 50,000 and 30,000 years ago; brilliant work on the origins of agriculture, 10,000 years ago, with a sudden onset of global warming have all been part of the archaeological work of the past half century; formidable in both its scope and achievements. Yet the implications of all this for our common understanding of what it means to be human have barely begun to penetrate our general culture or habits of thought.

Archaeology, in fact, appears widely to be regarded as a matter of idle curiosity; a kind of retroactive tourism into the realms from which popular entertainments like *Raiders of the Lost Ark* emerge. In this respect, it is perched on the other end of a see-saw from astrophysics. Although the latter every now and again produces discoveries that briefly seize the popular imagination, there is a certain distrust of the expense involved in exploring space, when we have so much to clean up down on Earth. In the case of archaeology, the very effort to look more closely at the Earth and the human presence on it is viewed with distrust, because it is antiquarian, even though, now and again, it turns up some spectacular object or forgotten city which briefly captures the popular imagination. Astrophysics is acknowledged to be looking out to the stars and, therefore, it is inferred, to the future. That our instruments actually detect things as they were long ago, given the immense distances involved in light years, seems to elude many people. The two disciplines blur or blend, it might be said, in such potboilers as *Chariots of the Gods*.

It is not popular culture with which I am principally concerned, however, when I remark that the implications of half a century of archaeology do not seem to have deeply penetrated our general culture. I am more concerned with the dissonance between what the brilliant research of our archaeologists now tells us and the strongly institutionalized and culturally ingrained habits of mind which govern our conversation about what it means to be human; about what it is that, in fact, we are. This is true at many levels of our Western civilization and is even more true in the case of non-Western cultures. It is pre-eminently true in regard to our shared sense of the nature of human civilization as such—as a process in the biosphere. The question of the authenticity of Christianity is simply a point of entry into this far larger field of inquiry; but it is both a deeply fascinating issue in itself and an aappropriate one on which to reflect as we approach Christmas in 1998 of the Common Era, until recently known as the years Anno Domini—in the Year of the Lord and Master.

For this reason, I am concerned not simply with our understanding of the material record of the past and what it can tell us about our changing technologies and cumulative impact on the biosphere; but more fundamentally with what the cognitive implications are of discoveries that have revealed things long hidden from us, out of the obscurity of which we projected our religious myths and spiritual speculations. I believe that such recent works as John North's *Stone Henge: Neolithic Man and the Cosmos* (1996), Paul Jordan's *Riddles of the Sphinx* (1998) and Robert Drews's *The End of the Bronze Age: Changes in Warfare and the Catastrophe Circa 1200 BCE* (1993)— to name them in the chronological order of the archaeological periods with which they deal—are enormously fascinating studies, with tremendous utility in reclaiming ground from both genuine uncertainty and confabulated poppycock. Yet none of this seems to be nearly as important as the remarkable work which has been done in recent years on reconstructing the evolution of the human mind itself.

Ever since Charles Darwin first published his work on biological evolution, the most intractable resistance to the idea that human beings were creatures who had evolved from earlier life forms has been grounded in the insistence that the human mind or soul is of so remarkable a character that it is laughable to liken it to that of apes and monkeys. Biological science was widely declared to be drastically reductionist in its account of how human beings are able to think, dream, create and engage in reverie. The great religions of the world, all rooted in philosophic or pre-philosophic ideas dating back to the so-called Iron Age, between 3,000 (Hinduism and Judaism) and just under 1,500 years ago (Islam) mingled with ritual and symbolic practices that dated back much further, have all proclaimed the transcendent nature of the human 'soul' and its need for some form of salvation from a world of suffering, illusion, evil and death. How could they abandon their dreams, their efforts to dignify and discipline the species, in the face of a science which declared that we are not fallen angels, but risen apes? Conversely, how could the biologists even begin to explain the phenomena of religion and ritual in human culture?

Though my own field of study was strongly directed towards the geopolitical and sociological challenges of the 20th century world, I was riveted by this problem throughout my years at university. It always seemed to me to be the most fundamental of all problems, but I abandoned philosophy for modern history and then international relations; because the problem seemed unanswerable within philosophy and so abstruse that I didn't think I could justify dwelling on it full time, when there were so many more urgent problems to try to grapple with. Still, I pondered it; and no book made a more profound impression on me in relation to the human mind or 'soul' than George Steiner's *After Babel* (1975). Steiner's insistence that we are the *language animal* and that the prodigal multiplicity of languages on Earth offers a vital clue as to the protean nature of language itself stuck with me. It kept drawing me back to the fundamental underlying problem; not as a primary researcher into it, but as one alert for what others who were doing such primary research might be able to tell me.

Colin Renfrew's *Archaeology and Language: The Puzzle of Indo-European Origins* (1987) was a wonderful discovery, because it took the matter out of the realm of linguistics, philosophy and literary criticism and connected it with the prehistoric world of human migration and the the scientific study of the diffusion and confusion of tongues—to which the Biblical fable about the Tower of Babel was an ancient mythological response. Yet, still the problem was not resolved; for the human mind, already equipped with language 5,000 to 10,000 years ago, was the very phenomenon that constituted the root of the problem.

Derek Bickerton's *Language and Species* (1990) was another compelling step forward. As Bickerton expressed things:

> *The concept of something known as 'mind' and regarded as somehow problematic goes back to the dawn of recorded thought ... Over the centuries, almost every possible answer ... has been espoused by someone. No solution seems to have worked, least of all the solution of claiming that there was no problem. In this, the mind-body problem rather resembles language origins. In both cases, we have been told that the issues were insoluble, or illusory, or not worth thinking about ... Curiously enough, few seem to have suspected that the mind-body problem and the problem of language origins might turn out to be related ...*

Now, here was someone talking my language!

The challenge, beyond this point, was to develop a cognitive archaeology—an archaeology of the evolution of primate and hominid cognitive capacities and the neurological foundations of language itself. Not surprisingly, passionate scholars were hard at work on just this aspect of the matter—closing in relentlessly on the fundamental, underlying problem as Derek Bickerton had described it. In 1991, Harvard University Press published Merlin Donald's path-breaking study *Origins of the Modern Mind: Three Stages in the Evolution of Cognition and Culture*. His brilliant, lucid and exciting cognitive archaeology offered something breathtakingly close to a solution and one which truly appeared to 'square the circle' when it came to reconciling biological science with human cultural realities.

As Donald wrote, in an exuberant flourish at the conclusion of his book:

> *One thing is certain: if we compare the complex representational architecture of the modern mind with that of the ape, we must conclude that the Darwinian universe is too small to contain humanity. We are a different order ... Nineteenth century biology was absurdly, grotesquely wrong in its classification scheme, because it had no adequate vocabulary for assessing the cognitive dimension of human evolution ... Our genes may be largely identical to those of a chimp or a gorilla, but our cognitive architecture is not ... we are symbol-using, networked creatures, unlike any that went before us. Regardless of whether our current chronological framework is verified or radically changed by future research, this much is not speculation: humans are utterly different. Our minds function on several phylogenetically new representational planes, none of which are available to animals. We act in cognitive collectivities, in symbiosis with external memory systems ...*

What an analysis this was! Yet still there was much that remained to be hammered out. How did language actually work in the brain? And what were the cognitive characteristics of this symbol-using, networked creature which had got us into so much strife over the millennia since our records began—characteristics which, in the Christian tradition in which I was raised, had since ancient times been dubbed 'original sin'?

Steven Mithen's *The Prehistory of the Mind: A Search for the Origins of Art, Religion and Science* (1996) went far towards providing a basis for answering that last, huge question. Terrence Deacon's astonishing piece of work *The Symbolic Species: The Co-Evolution of Language and the Brain* (1997) took a huge step in the direction of answering the other one. Mithen described himself as filling in certain archaeological lacunae in Merlin Donald's work. And Donald himself remarked of Deacon's book: 'This is essential reading for anyone interested in what makes us human.' Edward Manier, Professor of Philosophy and of the History and Philosophy of Science at Notre Dame University, went so far as to declare:

> *The Symbolic Species should transform the foundations of the human sciences ... it is not another grandiose lyric about the global properties of the brain. When this author finds 'nascent heart and mind' where most fear clockwork, he doesn't persuade his readers to believe; he shows them where to look.*

It is impossible to do justice in so brief a space as this essay to the wonderful qualities of Terrence Deacon's book, but the touchstone of it, as far as cognitive archaeology is concerned, is surely his observation that:

> *We live in a world that is both entirely physical and virtual at the same time. Remarkably, this virtual facet of the world came into existence relatively recently, as evolutionary time is measured; and it has provided human selves with an unprecedented sort of autonomy or freedom to wander from the constraints of concrete reference and a unique power of self-determination that derives from this increasingly indirect linkage between symbolic mental representation and its grounds in reference.*

Here was the 'spirit', the transcendent self, the 'soul', restored through neuroscience to the seat from which biology had apparently tumbled it! But where did this leave religion, with all its arcane trappings? Deacon fastidiously left that topic alone. Steven Mithen did not.

The Prehistory of the Mind takes up from where Merlin Donald leaves off and deepens the archaeological reach of the argument, while grappling insistently and penetratingly with the most interesting 20th century debates in the philosophy of mind: most notably, the modular theory of the mind and the multiple intelligences theory of the mind advanced by Jerry Fodor and Howard Gardner, respectively, both in 1983. The findings of the book are acutely interesting. The following passage struck me as so resonant that I transcribed it into the front of my copy of Karl Rahner's *Foundations of Christian Faith*:

> *The human mind is a product of evolution, not supernatural creation. I have laid bare the evidence. I have specified the 'whats', the 'whens' and the 'whys' for the evolution of the mind. I have explained how the potential arose in the mind to undertake science, create art and believe in religious ideologies, even though there were no selection pressures for such abstract abilities at any point during our past. I have demonstrated that we can only understand the nature of language and consciousness by understanding the prehistory of the mind—by getting to grips with the details of the fossil and archaeological records. And I have found the use of metaphor and analogy in various guises to be the most significant feature of the human mind. I have myself only been able to think and write about prehistory and the mind by using two metaphors: our past as a play and the mind as a cathedral.*

The mind as a cathedral?! What an arresting metaphor for one trying to reconcile the ancient doctrines and hopes of Christianity with the modern sciences of the mind.

In one sense, Mithen's metaphor is disconcerting: Merlin Donald had used the metaphor of the Internet to create his brilliantly insightful picture of the gradual development by the genus *Homo* of external or prosthetic devices for cognitive leverage, culminating (so far) in our staggering technologies for global communications, information processing, graphic display and data storage in the late 20th century. Mithen seems to be taking us back into a Gothic world of far more structured and hieratic communication systems, compared with the dynamic and demotic systems so graphically comprehended by Merlin Donald. Yet the metaphor is not arbitrary and it is not obfuscatory. Perhaps it occurred to him because he was a graduate from the School of Fine Art, Sheffield, before going on to specialize in archaeology at Cambridge?

At any rate, he uses the metaphor to get us to picture the evolution of the mind as consisting of the 'construction', through processes of natural selection, of a 'nave' of general intelligence and, around it, a series of 'chapels' of specialized intelligences, which he calls technical, natural history, social and linguistic intelligence. The key to the puzzle of human intelligence, he argues, is that these chapels were initially constructed without mutual inter-connection and at different rates. Linguistic intelligence—the capacity to encode the world in grammatical terms and communicate about it semantically by vocalization—developed primarily in relation to social intelligence and still shows the traces of this affinity.

We can see the evidence of the segmented and limited cognitive capacities of early humans in the physical remains of artefacts they have left behind and which our science has—in Fagan's half-century—enabled us to recover and decode with increasing sensitivity. Only with *Homo sapiens* did all the chapels become connected with one another as well as with the nave. The direct consequence was the cultural explosion of the Upper Palaeolithic from about 60,000 years ago; manifested in the sudden proliferation of specialized tools and weapons and the astonishing murals of the Chauvet Cave and Lascaux (as well as the Kimberley Gorges in Australia). Sudden, that is, compared with the two million years of agonizingly and puzzlingly slow progress since early humans had first exhibited the technical intelligence, in Oldowan flaked stone tools, which set them decisively apart from chimpanzees and marked them as our ancestors.

This interconnection of the chapels and the nave Mithen calls cognitive fluidity and he argues that it is precisely the earlier specialized and segmented development of the chapels of intelligence which gave the modern mind its extraordinary creative power, once the chambers of the mind were interconnected by what he sees as linguistic penetration of the interior walls of the cathedral. It is the semi-compartmented structure of the mind which makes possible the brilliant creative leaps of metaphor, technical creativity, humane sympathy and artistic vision which have exalted us; but also the dark lapses into dissociation and destructiveness which have plagued and puzzled us for millennia.

This process seems to have occurred over tens of thousands of years before the Upper Palaeolithic and to have had a cascade of consequences once the interior walls were breached. Was it, one ventures to speculate, some dim apprehension of this primal epiphany which undergirded the aetiological myth, three millennia or so ago, of the Garden of Eden and the Fall of Man? *Homo sapiens*, after all, emerged from Africa, it seems, some 100,000 years ago and has been present in the Fertile Crescent ever since. Incidentally, having come out of the Garden of Eden, we encountered our less cognitively gifted hominid brethren and drove them to extinction before the end of the Upper Palaeolithic 30,000 years ago, as we fanned out across Eurasia and Australasia. Remember the fable of Cain and Abel?

Summarizing his findings, Mithen wrote:

> *The critical step in the evolution of the modern mind was to switch from a mind designed like a Swiss army knife to one with cognitive fluidity, from a specialized to a generalized type of mentality. This enabled people to design complex tools, to create art and believe in religious ideologies ... The switch from a specialized to a generalized type of mentality between 100,000 and 30,000 years ago, was a remarkable about turn for evolution to have taken. The previous six million years of evolution had seen an ever increasing specialization of the mind. Natural history, technical and then linguistic*

> intelligence had been added to the social intelligence that was already present in the mind of the common ancestor to living apes and humans. But what is even more remarkable is that this recent switch from specialized to generalized ways of thinking was not the only about turn that occurred during the evolution of the modern mind. If we chart the evolution of the mind not just over the mere six million years of this prehistory, but over the 65 million years of primate evolution, we can see that there has been an oscillation between specialized and generalized ways of thinking.

This arresting realization goes to the heart of the quest to understand the nature of human cognition and metacognition: the capacity to concentrate on a task, compared with the capacity to grasp the context and purpose of a task and reconceive the scope for possibilities in the task environment. What Mithen has done for us is condense millions of years of unself-conscious cognitive evolution into a startling and illuminating metacognitive narrative. His synthesis enables us to see a great deal of human activity and the labours of countless other thinkers in a new light and to conceive new possibilities for ourselves as the being he describes.

Against this deep scientific background, we must now re-read the whole three or four millennia of Eurasian religious reflections; the Bible not least. More than a century ago, Friedrich Nietzsche wrote, in *Human All-Too-Human* #113, of Christianity as antiquity, as something 'gruesomely wafted to us, as if out of the grave of a primeval past':

> *In the context of our age, the Christian religion is certainly a piece of antiquity intruding out of distant ages past ... A god who begets children on a mortal woman; a sage who calls upon us no longer to work, no longer to sit in judgment, but to heed the signs of the imminent end of the world; a justice which accepts an innocent man as a substitute sacrifice; someone who bids his disciples drink his blood; prayers for miraculous interventions; sins perpetrated against a god atoned for by a god; fear of a Beyond to which death is the gateway; the figure of the cross in an age which no longer knows the meaning and shame of the cross—can one believe that things of this sort are still believed?*

Our century has seen various efforts to grapple with this radical question, from materialist doctrines denouncing the whole thing as a gross superstition, to the efforts of scholars like Albert Schweitzer, Rudolf Bultmann, Karl Rahner and Jürgen Moltmann to reach behind the enigma of arcane doctrines in search of the spiritual and ethical foundations of Christianity.

It was as if they were cross-checking the grave of the primeval past, to see whether the Roman and Pharisee stone sealing it was immovably in place, or might have been rolled away in the long, dark night of the modern soul. To phrase things in this manner is, of course, to engage in precisely the capacity for metaphor and analogy the roots of which Steven Mithen has so profoundly elucidated. Therein lies the key to understanding what is at issue for us as human beings in the quest to recomprehend ourselves, where we have come from and how our minds work. What is vital at this point is to keep the rigour of scientific integrity, as we find it in the work of Mithen, Donald and Deacon, without lapsing into an impatient and errant scientific positivism, which would consign our religious patrimony to the grave of the primeval past.

In the Prelude to his mighty novel of 1948, *Joseph and His Brothers*, Thomas Mann wrote:

> *Very deep is the well of the past. Should we not call it bottomless?...Thus, there may exist provisional origins, which practically and in fact from the first beginnings of the particular tradition held by a given community, folk or communion of faith; and memory, though sufficiently instructed that the depths have not actually been plumbed, yet nationally may find reassurance in some primitive point of time and, personally and historically speaking, come to rest there.*

If, with Mann, we shift from the grave to the well as a way of thinking about the past and its depths and what it contains, we do well. For, as we now know, it is indeed deep—far deeper than even he guessed in 1948—and we have plumbed its depths now in ways he could barely have imagined, writing in the very year that *Archaeology* was first published.

It was also in 1948 that Robert Graves published his brilliant anti-Christian polemic *The White Goddess*, an attempt to break back into the depths of the past buried beneath the Roman and Rabbinical canon of the Judaeo-Christian religions, to a time before religious patriarchy, when the young Yahweh still walked with his consort Asherah and Isis was the Queen of Heaven and the Star of the Sea—and further back again, into the days before history in which our symbolisms and totemisms germinated. It is a marvellous book, even if, as Graves himself confessed, 'a very difficult book, as well as a very queer one, to be avoided by anyone with a distracted, tired or rigidly scientific mind.' His ingenious and romantic iconoclasm is, like Harold Bloom's marvellous polemical poem *The Book of J*, a mouthful of water from the depths of the well just below the deepest reaches of Christian and Rabbinical orthodoxy (to say nothing of Islam, which is even nearer to the surface). Yet both Graves and Bloom, being Romantic aesthetes, failed to see their poetic intuitions and iconoclastic leaps of imagination in a sufficiently ascetic/scientific light, with the consequence that their work lacks the rigorous clarity and intellectual power of the cognitive archaeologists—Donald, Mithen and Deacon.

Almost the opposite might be said of those who have, in recent years, renewed the Schweitzerian quest for the historical Jesus. To read, for example, Robert Funk's *Honest to Jesus: Jesus for a New Millennium* (1996), or John Dominic Crossan's *The Birth of Christianity: Discovering What Happened in the Years Immediately After the Execution of Jesus* (1998), is to discover a disconcertingly earnest faith that, if we strip away the soteriological metaphors with which two millennia invested Jesus of Nazareth as the Christ/Messiah, we shall discover the true *kerygma* that Jesus intended to teach all along. There is much admirable scholarship in these books and considerable ascetic virtue, but the guiding assumption seems to me quite naïve. Crossan's attempt, for example, to raise a 'sarcophilic' (flesh-loving) prophet of justice out of the grave of 'sarcophobic' (flesh-fearing) Pauline Christianity and to discover in the pre-canonical germ of Christianity revelatory, divinely commissioned communism, seems to me to be a quite quixotic venture. If Jesus was, in fact, just one more itinerant preacher in the Roman province of Judaea, executed because he got on the wrong side of the occupying power, why should his obscure teachings particularly concern us in the 21st century?[199]

We would do better, I believe, to recomprehend the stunning poetics of the Biblical religions, including those very aspects of Christianity which Nietzsche thought wafted 'gruesomely' to us out of the grave of a primeval past, in terms of the astonishing capacity for metaphor which has made us *Homo sapiens* for some 100,000 years and especially over the past 30,000 or so. To paraphrase John Henry Newman, we might thereby formulate a 'grammar of ascent'—except that, as Terrence Deacon has so brilliantly shown, it is not grammar but reference which is the key to how language works in the brain. It is metaphor which holds the keys to the 'Kingdom of God' that is within us. It is metaphor that is the key to the Logos—the spirit of thought within us which is our spark of divine fire and has, for millennia, given us intimations of transcendence.

These considerations light up, also, I believe, a reading of that singularly fascinating breakthrough in Biblical archaeology of the decades since 1948, the *Dead Sea Scrolls*. It was on 15 May 1948, the very day that Israel declared its existence and independence, that William Foxwell Albright, the leading Biblical archaeologist and Semitic epigrapher of his time, informed the American School of Oriental Research in Jerusalem that what he had seen of the *Dead Sea Scrolls* left him in no doubt that they were 'the greatest manuscript discovery of modern times'. As Herschel Shanks remarks, in *The Mystery and Meaning of the Dead Sea Scrolls* (1998):

---

199   Books purporting to unveil the historical Jesus continue to appear. A notable recent example is Reza Aslan's *Zealot: The Life and Times of Jesus of Nazareth* (Allen & Unwin, 2013). Aslan is Iranian and his family fled Iran after the mullahs seized power and imposed a coercive theocratic regime there in 1979-80. Once in the United States, they abandoned Islam and he became a Christian. As he grew to maturity, however, he began to ask more and more probing, secular questions about how Jesus of Nazareth had come to be understood as the Messiah—the Christ. His book offers an account systematically at variance with the Christian depiction of Jesus as a 'turn the other cheek' pacifist and argues that he was a rebel against Roman authority who was executed, like many others, for this sedition. Like others before him, he then argues that Christianity as we know it was largely a fabrication by St Paul.

All this might be debated at various points, whether by Christian scholars or those of a more secular, but analytical bent. The most disturbing—but unstated—deduction of the book, however, which may or may not have been intended by Aslan, is that Jesus was another of the Jewish prophets and that he was justified in his ill-fated rebellion against Rome. Since Aslan has reverted to Islam in recent years, this leaves open the possibility that he see the use of the sword by Mohammed against infidels as 'justified' and current radical Islam as standing in a tradition going back to Jewish zealots between the times of the patriarchs and the crushing of the Bar Kokhba rebellion by the Emperor Hadrian in 135 CE. It would have been reassuring had he clarified this point—in the negative.

> *From them, we get a direct glimpse into the world out of which Christianity grew. This was the soil. Here are the roots. For those who want to understand the history of Christianity, the scrolls are exciting and enriching.*

Absolutely so, but this is itself only a metaphor for what the great codex of cognitive archaeology now makes possible: a direct glimpse into the world out of which grew not only Christianity, but the very possibility of a religious imagination and a mind able to see itself as incomplete and in need of 'salvation'. Qumranology is a refreshing new avenue down which to approach the complex roots and early growth of those eschatological metaphors which form the central seed-stock of Christian faith. Yet it is still too tempting to become caught up in the metaphors themselves—as Graves and Bloom were caught up in their romances of strong misreading—and so miss the far more profound reality which lies behind and beneath all of them, as the awesome phenomenon of language as such lies behind and beneath all particular languages and poetries.

In the mid-20th century, Dietrich Bonhoeffer attempted to formulate a 'Christianity without religion', convinced that the dogmatic doctrines and hierarchical magisterium of centuries had actually caused a sort of evangelical artero-sclerosis to develop within the Church. As his biographer and friend Eberhard Bethge put it in 1977, Bonhoeffer 'encourages us to sail quickly out of harbours that have silted up.' This was itself in the spirit of Qumran and of Jesus, in their ascetic relation to the Second Temple. Bonhoeffer's *The Cost of Discipleship* surely belongs with the *Dead Sea Scrolls* and the Gospels, as a strenuous effort to wrest the life and reach of soteriological metaphor out of the hands of the high priests.

Qumran, of course, was destroyed by the Romans even before they destroyed the Second Temple, having no defences; but even before those catastrophes befell classical Judaism, Jesus had set alight a fire in the hearts of his disciples that triumphed over his ignominious execution at the hands of the Romans and the high priests and was, in time, to become the Roman religion itself. What I want to suggest is that this whole process can be seen in a clearer light than ever now—the light of cognitive archaeology—and by that light reincorporated into our humanity in ways which shows us why the Sabbath was made for man and not man for the Sabbath. Yet in no easy or literal sense can we discover the historical Jesus and declare that, therewith, we have lit upon the 'true Messiah'. No; our task of reinterpretation is far more radical than that.

Unfashionable as he now is among those who would like to resurrect Christianity as more 'sarcophilic' and less patristic, Augustine of Hippo remains a remarkable and luminous figure in the long history of Christianity and one with a more than usually acute understanding of the profundity of soteriological metaphor in the New Testament and the Old. His *Confessions* are an astonishing journey into the cathedral of the mind, as their author sought to fathom his humanity, with its many enigmatic flaws and secret doors. In his stunningly beautiful study *Augustine the Reader: Meditation, Self-Knowledge and the Ethics of Interpretation* (1996), Brian Stock explores how Augustine made his inward journey into the many mysteries of language, consciousness and the life of the mind.

Now, Augustine was doing quite the opposite of what Funk and Crossan, for example, are doing in trying to strip away metaphor and symbolism to get back to the 'real', the 'irreducible' historical Jesus. He was seeking to explore the phenomenology of the incarnation of the word—something which the work of Donald, Mithen and Deacon now makes it possible for us to do anew and with utter scientific integrity. In trying to fathom how we can make sense of Christianity and Christmas in a non-trivial way, without mooring our spiritual boats in silted up harbours, we must, I think, journey more with Augustine than with Crossan or Funk. For the quest for the historical Jesus anchors us to what Thomas Mann would have called a merely provisional, folkloric point in the past; whereas Augustine is a figure of immense significance in our long effort to raise ourselves with the support of our own metaphors and then to comprehend what we have done and where it has landed us. That is a truly transcendental exercise and, far from requiring the sacrifice of the intellect, as Blaise Pascal thought, engages the intellect at its most extraordinary and reaches back to its very foundations.

For my money, the ancient feast of Christmas and the doctrine of the incarnation are bound up with the profound mystery of our being the language animal, for whom the Word become flesh as Everyman, the Teller of parables which confound arid doctrine and the Sage who taught that the powers and vanities of any given time are transient and re-imaginable, might indeed be conceived as the Saviour of souls from darkness and spiritual oppression. This seems to me, at least, a way to find more human truth in Christmas than the mere faded, jaded Roman Saturnalia, which in so many ways our relentlessly commercialized and consumerist 'Christmas' has become. It frees us to draw upon the stories of departure and liberation that constitute the central axis of the Bible—from the Garden of Eden to Ur, from Egypt of the Pharaohs to Babylon, from the rule of the Seleucids to the rule of the Romans and to see in all the metaphors heaped around the cradle of Jesus the longing for simplicity and transcendence that lie at the root of religious evangelism. It also enables us to do all this without recourse to dogma or the authority of the high priests.

Atlantis and the science of archaeology[200]

Although I defected from philosophy and classical studies to history and political science, as an undergraduate I loved reading the dialogues of Plato. Indeed, it was the year after I defected, and was immersed in studying early modern history, that I bought myself the wonderful Bollingen *Collected Dialogues of Plato*, including the letters, beautifully printed on fine paper, and read it with the passion and awe of the young initiate. I was fascinated by A.N. Whitehead's remark, made earlier this century, that 'the whole of Western philosophy consists of footnotes to Plato' and wanted to know why someone would make so astonishing a remark. I loved Socrates' *Apology* and *The Symposium*, in particular, but it was *The Republic* I studied most closely, being an apprentice political scientist and historian.

One thing I paid only scant attention to, though, was the tale about the downfall of the archipelagic civilization of Atlantis twelve thousand years ago, which Plato tells in the *Timaeus* and *Critias*. I assumed that it was, in the words of Francis Bacon, 'poetical and fabulous', and nothing inclined me to believe that it had any foundation in historical reality. Even its relationship to Plato's utopian political philosophy seemed uncertain. So I let it be. The publication last year of Rodney Castleden's *Atlantis Destroyed* gave me the opportunity to revisit my judgment and it was with considerable pleasure that I learned from it about the ways in which twentieth-century archaeology has gradually been able to unearth the roots of Plato's tale—the archaeology, as it were, of utopia.

Before I read Castleden, I could not make sense of Plato's story about Atlantis and I was bemused by the regular reports from various theosophical geographers and wide-eyed parahistorians that they believed Plato's Atlantis to lie on the Atlantic sea-bed, somewhere between the Azores and Hispaniola. I have two clippings tucked inside my Bollingen Plato; kept there out of just such bemusement. One is from *The Age*, 5th April 1981; the other is from *The Australian*,

---

200 This essay first appeared in *Quadrant* in May 1999. I was at that time resident tutor in Politics at Trinity College, at the University of Melbourne. At the end of that year I received a number of letters from students thanking me in the warmest terms for having been an inspirational tutor and intellectual role model. However, the Warden, Don Markwell, refused to renew my appointment, because I had written a poem for one of the female students, which he declared was 'a stick of dynamite'. She had liked the poem and was indignant at Markwell's intervention, but no effort on my part to conciliate the authoritarian and insecure Markwell made any difference and I had to depart Trinity College on unpleasant terms. In our final interview, he refused even to acknowledge that the poem had been the reason why he would not renew my residency for 2000. Yet again, I had fallen foul of an institution and its inflexible determination to subordinate my freedom of expression to its authority. I vowed, in 2000, that I would never again accept a tutoring position at such an institution under any circumstances.

29th December 1997. The first records the claim by Soviet oceanographers to have 'discovered the lost land of Atlantis—the sunken land referred to by the ancient Greek philosopher Plato—hundreds of kilometres west of Portugal'.

The second records the efforts of a twenty-member team of Russian scientists, led by Viatcheslav Koudriavtsev—'an internationally respected classical scholar' and director of the Moscow Institute of Metahistory—to succeed where their Soviet colleagues had presumably met with disappointment sixteen years before. It states that the British Foreign Office was about to give the Russian scientists a six week licence to explore Little Sole Bank, about 128 kilometres off Land's End, England, where Koudriavtsev said he believed the capital of Atlantis to lie. I gave no credence to these claims. I put them in the same category as the search by emissaries of the Edgar Cayce Foundation for the Atlantean Hall of Records under the Giza plateau. Why? After all, Cayce was the weird chap who claimed, in the 1930s, to have been a survivor of Atlantis and to have actually built the Sphinx and the Great Pyramid in 10,500BC, whereas Koudriavtsev and his countrymen are apparently quite serious scientists.

I have lumped virtually all searches for Atlantis into the same broad category because the whole Atlantis tale has consistently held that the civilization in question existed 12,000 years ago and was therefore completely out of sync with everything we have so painstakingly pieced together in the past one hundred years or so about the origins and development of human civilization. Even Koudriavtsev describes Plato's tale as something 'handed down from the end of the last Ice Age'. This simply could not be woven into my web of belief. And when that strange little fringe publication *The X Factor* came out, a year or so ago, with the truly astonishing notion that Atlantis lies under the Antarctic ice cap, I was prompted to laugh heartily and pop the story in my hanging file labelled 'Lunatic Fringe'. Here's a delightful *reductio ad absurdum*, I thought: Why can't Atlantis be found in the Atlantic? Because it's hidden under the Antarctic ice cap! Given that I had always thought that intellectual seriousness required that Atlantis be 'put on ice', it seemed to me a superb sort of absurdist revelation to discover that the ice has been put on Atlantis. This really was a joke worthy of Luis Bunuel. But it's only a wonderful joke, of course, for those of us who are confident that the Antarctic Atlantis notion really is absurd. Why are we confident? And what makes us see the joke here? After all, odd as it seems, there clearly are many people who credit such things.

Rodney Castleden's book is, therefore, a first-class opportunity to try to clarify the difference between sound history and archaeology on the one hand and peculiar imaginings such as those of Cayce and the Antarctic Atlantis theorists on the other. Reading *Atlantis Destroyed*, I found myself asking: Why exactly is it that I find Castleden's argument credible and interesting, when everything else I have read about Atlantis, from Plato to the Antarctic, has seemed so patently lacking in credibility? There are several possible answers to this question, but I think that the heart of the matter has to do with the fact that Castleden marshals his evidence and lays out his inferences with a view to showing precisely where he could be mistaken, whereas the general run of claims about Atlantis make huge demands on our credence and fail to deliver any hard evidence at all. And Plato's 'original' account is one of these. He has Critias assert that the tale, strange though it sounds, really is true and that Egyptian records show that Atlantis existed, describe its geography and culture and record its downfall. Unfortunately, no such records have come down to us.

The really intriguing thing about Castleden, though, is that it is precisely his evidence which leads him to conclude that Plato was not fantasizing when he wrote about Atlantis in the 350s BC—he was just drawing on inadequate evidence and making some basic but explicable errors of geography and chronology. The excavations of the past three decades have, he argues, gradually made it possible for us to piece together enough of the broken and damaged jigsaw of really ancient Mediterranean history—that is, that going back in to the second millennium BC and earlier—as to be able to see that Plato was almost certainly telling the truth when he wrote of having heard the tale of the glories and downfall of Atlantis from his grandfather, whose own grandfather had heard it from Solon, who had learned it in Egypt, in the early sixth century BC, from scribes in the now vanished city of Sais, who would appear to have had in their temple archives a quite detailed record of the passing away of Minoan Aegean civilization between 1520 and 1380 BCE.[201]

---

201 Long after I wrote this essay, while on a visit to Harvard, I discovered a book by Eric H. Cline, classical scholar and anthropologist at George Washington University, called *1177 BC: The Year Civilization Collapsed* (Princeton University Press, 2014). It makes no mention of Atlantis, Thera (except for a single reference to it as Santorini, its modern name) or Akrotiri and so does not add to the matter under discussion in the essay. His one mention of Santorini states that the great eruption there 'has now been pushed back to at least 1550 and more likely 1628 BCE, based on radiocarbon and ice-core dates' (p. 93), which sharply separates it from the collapse of Bronze Age civilization half a millennium later.

Cline does, however, add substantially to our understanding of the downfall of Bronze Age urban civilization when it did occur and has a wonderful and very extensive bibliography. In a diffuse sense, his account of the late Bronze Age makes it all seem like an extended version of the Atlantis of legend. As he writes: 'The period of the Late Bronze Age has rightly been hailed as one of the golden ages in the history of the world and as a period during which an early global economy successfully flourished.' His book provides an excellent background reading in the nature of the civilization within which the little trading entrepôt of Thera was situated and therefore gives the mind purchase on the archaeological and historical realities so lamentably lacking in the ongoing searches for the 'lost continent of Atlantis'.

The idea that Plato's Atlantis tale was based on the fascinating and long-vanished Minoan civilization is not by any means wholly new, nor does it yet have unquestioned assent within the archaeological profession. Castleden's argument, however, appears to have put together more of the pieces of the jigsaw puzzle than anyone before him, and the picture that emerges is not only incomparably more plausible than the fanciful Atlantis notions which tease the popular imagination and embarrass or amuse the scholar; it is also deeply interesting in itself, as an historiographic exercise for the mind. It certainly led me to go back and re-read Plato's *Timaeus* and *Critias* with renewed interest and to find that this re-reading, in turn, prompted me to reconsider some of Karl Popper's remarks, in *The Open Society and Its Enemies*, about Plato and his utopian political philosophy.

Castleden's argument is qualified and his evidence carefully marshalled. As regards the central claim that Minoan civilization lies at the root of the Atlantis legend, he states:

> *The hypothesis, revived in the twentieth century—that Minoan Crete was Atlantis—has proved inadequate to the case and has rightly been rejected. The parallel hypothesis, based on more recent archaeological evidence, that Cycladic Thera was Atlantis is also in itself inadequate. Because these hypotheses can be rejected separately, many have rejected the idea that Atlantis might have existed in the south Aegean, understandably overlooking the possibility that if the two hypotheses are combined they do meet the needs of Plato's description.*

Come again, you may be asking: Did not Plato state that Atlantis lay out in the wild Atlantic Ocean opposite the 'Pillars of Hercules'? So, how could Castleden's south Aegean 'Atlantis' answer Plato's description, even if it could itself be validated? Well, that is just where the careful work of the archaeologist becomes truly interesting.

Reconstructing the remote past is a more than usually challenging task. Indeed, those who take the historical record for granted, or who ingenuously believe that imaginary pasts are just as credible as carefully and critically reconstructed ones, fail to grasp the care and ingenuity that are involved in our figuring out the actual course of events in ancient times at all. As Paul Jordan remarked last year, in the introduction to his beautifully crafted and meticulous study *The Riddle of the Sphinx*:

> *The history of the ancient world is not easy to reconstruct and it has taken an immense amount of patient reasoning on the basis of rigorously sifted evidence, together with the necessary exercise of ingenuity of mind on the part of many scholars, to put together a coherent picture of the likely course of events in remote times and different parts of the world.*

It is all too easy to forget or overlook this when reading Plato himself, or for that matter the great historian Thucydides, a generation earlier than Plato. Reading these powerful and hugely influential writers from our present vantage point, from within a vast library of historical and philosophical works, one is struck by the enormous vagueness of their sense of the past, once it extended back beyond quite recent and readily available records.

It was because he was groping about in the fog and darkness of a past only, scantily recorded and set amid a narrow and uncertain geography, full of legend and anthropomorphic deities, that Plato lit upon the tale of Atlantis in the way that he did. His use of the tale is marked by uncertainty and ambiguity. But it was not until more than two thousand years after his death that the techniques for unravelling the puzzle he set us started to become available. And it is only in the past one hundred years that we have, incontestably, pieced together an understanding of the course of pre-classical Aegean history which not only leaves Plato's knowledge and understanding of the matter completely in the shade, but has finally, it seems, enabled us to decipher the very story he had to hand and which he plainly did not quite understand himself.

Ever since Plato's death, in 351 BCE, the Atlantis legend has exercised an enduring fascination on his countless readers. His disciple Crantor went to Egypt to seek to verify the story, but whatever he found has not come down to us in documentary form. Eight centuries later, the great Neo-Platonist Proclus, in his *Commentaries on Plato's Timaeus*, written as the Roman Empire went into eclipse, declared that the Atlantis story was historical and true. Handed down as part of the Platonic canon, the story gained renewed interest in the sixteenth century, with the growth of trans-Atlantic navigation and the Western European discovery of the Americas. Thomas More's *Utopia* (1517) alluded to the possibility that America was Atlantis. A century later again, in his *New Atlantis* (1627), Francis Bacon entertained the same idea, though it is not clear that he was serious.

Rather curiously, Bacon ventured to 'correct' Plato, by having his sources declare that Atlantis had, indeed, flourished in the Americas until some three thousand years ago. This would, of course, date the downfall of Atlantis (in the Americas) to around the fifteenth or sixteenth century BC—exactly the time at which Minoan civilization flourished in the Aegean. This seems astonishingly proleptic on Bacon's part; for although the classical world had never forgotten that there had been a civilization in the ancient Aegean (in the first century CE Pliny the Elder remarked, for instance, on the ruins of Knossos), there was no clear sense of its history and no claim anywhere that it had had anything to do with the Atlantis of Plato. Besides, Bacon made no mention at all of the Aegean in his *New Atlantis*.

What might be called the Aegean Hypothesis concerning the legend of Atlantis seems to have first been made, or suggested, in 1872, by French vulcanologist Ferdinand Fouqué, after he did some tentative archaeological work on the tiny island of Thera, in the Aegean Cyclades—an island generally known today as Santorini, which had been partly obliterated by a huge volcanic eruption long ago. It is from Fouqué's bold but tentative hypothesis that Castleden's present account of the matter has ultimately sprung.

What happened after Fouqué's first tinkerings in the volcanic ashes of Thera is best illuminated by comparison with the rather better-known story of the recovery of Troy, Mycenae and the ruins of the world of Homeric legend, beginning with the famous excavations by Heinrich Schliemann. The great mathematician and mystic Blaise Pascal had written, in the seventeenth century:

> *Homer wrote a romance; for nobody can believe that Troy and Agamemnon had any more existence than the golden apples of the Hesperides. He had no intention to write a history, but only to amuse us.*

Yet, some 250 years later, after his excavations on the very site Homer had described Troy as having occupied three thousand years before, Schliemann wrote:

> *I have proved that in a remote antiquity there was in the plain of Troy a large city, destroyed of old by a fearful catastrophe, which has on the hill of Hissarlik only its acropolis, with its temples and a few other large edifices, whilst its lower city extended in an easterly, southerly and westerly direction ... and that this city answers perfectly to the Homeric description of the site of sacred Ilios.*

The truly astonishing thing is that such reconstruction has been possible at all—from legend to history, reversing the destructive effects of time. Yet Troy was only the start, even for Schliemann. As Robert Drews argues, in *The End of the Bronze Age: Changes in Warfare and the Catastrophe Circa 1200 BCE* (1993), we have gradually put together a picture of what happened three thousand years ago which is vastly more detailed and accurate than anything known to Homer, for all the gaps and uncertainties which still remain. Castleden's re-examination of the Atlantis legend belongs in this context.

Plato's sources related that 9000 years before Solon visited Egypt (in about 590 BCE) there had been a great island far to the west (of Egypt), with a marvellous, temple-centred capital city and a far-flung archipelagic maritime empire, whose outliers extended as far as Libya and which had prospered exceedingly, threatening to subdue the whole Grecian world, before catastrophe, in the form of volcanic eruptions, earthquakes and floods destroyed it utterly. The great island, he says, lay off from the 'Pillars of Hercules' and was 'larger than Libya and Asia (Turkey) combined'. From his description of its geography, its religion, its arts, its commerce and its engineering, in his *Critias*, one is able to form a tolerably detailed picture of Plato's Atlantis. The chronology, the location in the Atlantic, the dimensions of the great island, however, have all confused the picture for millennia.

Castleden advances the intriguing suggestion that these problems can all be resolved and that the solutions converge remarkably on the Aegean Hypothesis. He then attempts to show how the structure and extent of the Minoan trading empire meets the corrected description of Plato's Atlantis. Finally, he gives us a breathtaking scientific reconstruction of the great volcanic eruption which destroyed Minoan Thera and battered the northern coasts of Crete and much of the Minoan Aegean with tsunamis and falls of volcanic debris in 1520 BCE.[202] This last is one

---

202   None of what follows would appear to be seriously affected by the fact that the Santorini catastrophe has now, in Cline's words, been pushed back by somewhere between thirty and a hundred years. Clearly, however, the further back it is pushed the less connection it has with the series of catastrophes that destroyed Late Bronze Age civilization in the 13th and 12th centuries BCE. It was a stand-alone disaster, but perhaps all the more memorable for that reason.

of the truly awesome aspects of the book and of what contemporary archaeology is capable of doing. It recreates the sixteenth-century-BCE trading town of Therassos (Akrotiri), on Thera (Santorini), on the eve of its destruction; brings its folk to life and then tells graphically how they and their town perished in a catastrophe which was far more dramatic than the one which buried Herculaneum and Pompeii nearly 1600 years later.

The script used by Minoan civilization in the sixteenth century BC was what we know as Linear B. Castleden tells us that the symbols for 1000 and 100 in Linear B are notably similar and that a simple explanation for the implausible antiquity assigned by Plato to Atlantis could be that the Sais records had actually been in Linear B originally and, in translation, the 900 years between the Thera eruption and Solon's sojourn in Egypt was rendered as 9000 years. This hypothesis is supported by the odd fact that the dimensions for the great island of Atlantis supplied by Plato happen to be exactly ten times those of Crete.

A further corruption in translation, but this time from Linear B or even Egyptian script, simply in the Greek rendering of the tale, appears to have occurred, he says, where Atlantis is described as being larger than Libya and Asia (Turkey) combined. As it happens, he reasons, the Greek for 'in between' is strikingly similar to that for 'larger than' and if a Greek scribe—even Solon himself—had an account which described Atlantis as being ten times the size of Crete, then it could be that the corruption occurred in order to make sense of the earlier error in translation. If all three of these putative errors are corrected, we get an island precisely the size of Crete in between Libya and Turkey, which was the chief island of a civilization which met with catastrophe some 900 years before Solon visited Egypt. Now, isn't that interesting?

The Egyptian account had described Atlantis as lying 'far to the west' and 'outside the Pillars of Hercules', though. How can Castleden's 'corrections' of Plato accommodate these awkward facts? Well, it is true that Crete is far to the west of the Nile delta, especially if you are an ancient Egyptian contemplating the vast and mysterious 'Great Green', as they called the Mediterranean Sea. If you were a classical Greek, of course, your orientation and your sense of space and geography would have been somewhat different from this. Far to the west would certainly not be to the south-east of the Peloponnese. And the Pillars of Hercules appeared to settle the matter, since to the classical world they were what we call the Strait of Gibraltar. It turns out, however, that in pre-classical times, the two southernmost promontories of the Peloponnese—Capes Mallea and Tainaron—were commonly known as the Pillars of Hercules, so that a great island of the precise dimensions of Crete lying off the Pillars of Hercules, far to the west of the Nile delta and subjected to an ill-defined catastrophe which ended its great civilization 900 years before Solon's visit to Egypt, would again give us Crete as the main island of Atlantis.

If all this can be so readily resolved, however, what has the scientific disagreement and hesitation been about since Minos Kalakairinos and Arthur Evans began the excavation of Knossos (the famous Cretan capital with the Labyrinth of King Minos) and unearthed its famous labyrinth temple-palace a century ago; or at least since Michael Ventris deciphered Linear B in 1950-52? Well, there are a number of considerations, as it happens. For one thing, to their great credit, the archaeologists in question were fastidious about detail and disinclined to leap to fanciful or self-indulgent conclusions. That discipline has not come easy to human beings and still requires considerable effort.

The simplest way to summarise these considerations, as Castleden himself hints, is that Crete and later Thera were considered separately as possible sources of the Atlantis tale and, much as the above 'corrections' of Plato point to Crete, taken on its own it was not deemed sufficiently close to Plato's Atlantis to convince the scholarly fraternity of the Aegean Hypothesis. And Thera, on its own, seemed an even less plausible candidate. For one thing, Minoan civilization had not perished when Thera did. It lasted at least another century or more[203], before Achaean warriors overwhelmed it, in the early fourteenth century BC. Crete did not seem to match the vulcanology and Thera was too small. Besides, it was only in the 1970s and after that the excavations of Thera of the archaic town of Therassos (Akrotiri)[204] threw new light on Thera's connection with Knossos. It was, Castleden points out, a sort of Hong Kong of the Minoan empire, an entrepôt for Minoan trade throughout the Grecian and northern Aegean world. Its catastrophic downfall was, he surmises, the beginning of the end for Knossos itself, even though the older and larger chief city of the Minoan world endured after the catastrophe for some time.[205]

One of the most fascinating details Castleden provides is that the northern and eastern region of Crete was known, in Linear B, as Atlunus. It was this region that was especially hard hit by the tsunamis generated by the Thera eruption of 1520 BCE. Since the people of Thera seem to have perished in their entirety, the account of the downfall of Atlantis which Solon found preserved 900 years later in Sais—a city which itself was founded just before the final downfall

---

203 Several centuries, in fact, if the eruption at Santorini occurred in 1628 BCE

204 It was only in 2014 that I was finally able to visit Santorini, while on a field trip for a novel I am writing. The archaeological site at Akrotiri is beautifully maintained and very impressive. The museum is quite exquisite and well laid out. The caldera left by prehistoric eruptions and widened by the ancient eruption which destroyed Santorini is awesome in its size and its hint of what occurred there long ago.

205   The destruction of Santorini would certainly have sent shockwaves throughout the Minoan world, both literally and figuratively, but Knossos dominated the whole of the Cyclades, of which Santorini was and is only a small component part. Given the redating of the eruption, therefore, it seems reasonable to assume that the loss of Santorini did not seriously degrade the capacity of Knossos and Minoan Crete to flourish, as it did, for several centuries more.

of Knossos—may well have been based on Linear B records brought to Egypt by those fleeing Mycenaean depredations in Atlunus. And that may be where the name 'Atlantis' entered into the tale. In the manner of so much history when clear and cross-referenced records are not available—and therefore of almost all ancient history as it was first recorded and handed down in legend—the destruction of Thera, the Atlunus tsunamis and the invasions by Mycenaean warriors may well have become conflated very early. Later corruptions of the record, as we have seen, literally translated Atlantis in time and space and made it the object of huge and mysterious legends, which are only now being cleared away by the patient work of our historical scientists.

Castleden's reconstruction of the life and fate of archaic Thera is haunting and has entirely altered my sense of Plato's far vaguer evocation of the life and fate of Atlantis. As the archaeologist remarks, when Thera's harbour-town, Therassos (now commonly referred to as Akrotiri) was overwhelmed by the great eruption, it was already a very ancient human settlement—to be precise, about 3000 years old. It had flourished during the golden age of Minoan civilization for hundreds of years and its citizens, going by the astonishing evidence unearthed from the pumice and ash under which it had lain buried for 3500 years, were the imaginative and expansive citizens of a Bronze Age trading city of perhaps 12,000 inhabitants. The nature of Thera's fate meant that much was preserved which elsewhere in the Minoan world later perished through exposure to the ravages of man and time. Castleden comments:

> *Akrotiri's sudden burial under a blanket of ash means that an unusually detailed record of the Aegean culture has been preserved, far more complete than anything found on any of the other islands, including Crete. Akrotiri offers us a window onto Atlantis.*

The pottery, the breathtaking frescoes, the stone masonry, the sanitary engineering—redolent of that in Knossos, which was the basis for the legend of the Cretan engineer Daedalus, after whom the American Academy of Arts and Sciences has named its journal—all came to light in the excavations begun in 1967 and slowly pursued since.

Castleden relates how, among these antique remains of early human civilization at is noontide, an exquisite round table was recovered:

> *The legs were not only fretted into intricate silhouettes—surprising enough - but relief-carved as well, in a design centring on a large crocus-blossom (dedicated to the goddess). This single object hints at what may have been lost in the way of carpentry and wood-carving in Thera.*

Such details give us a portrait of Atlantis which is arresting and deeply realistic. Then, in the ninth chapter of his book, Castleden reconstructs for us the awful events which brought about its sudden and terrible end. According to Plato, as Castleden phrases it, 'Atlantis was destroyed by a major geological convulsion, a series of earthquakes accompanied by a massive subsidence that took the land area below sea level.' There was, we have been able to establish, an earlier earthquake in 1580 BCE, after which the town was repaired.[206] Then, in 1525 BCE there was a series of premonitory earthquakes, which did substantial damage, but Theran engineers began to rebuild the town once more.

They had not completed their work, however, when in 1520 BCE, what Plato later described as a series of 'portentous earthquakes' signalled the beginning of the end. There was a massive emission of steam and white pumice from the volcano at the heart of the island, covering the whole island to a depth of ten centimetres. A huge cloud soared some thirty-five kilometres into the atmosphere above the island. Then the volcano really blew and huge chunks of the island around the ancient caldera which had been blasted out by prehistoric eruptions collapsed four hundred metres and more into the ocean, filling the surrounding sea with mud and ash and rock. Plato was later to write of how the catastrophe had made the waters near Atlantis unnavigable, because of mud and rock in the sea. Castleden's account, which I summarise only very briefly here, is apocalyptic:

> The collapse of the volcano must have been accompanied by colossal shallow-seated earthquakes measuring as high as 10 on the Richter Scale. Ear-splitting explosions were heard as deafening roars all around the Aegean, and would have been audible 4800 kilometres away... an eruption of a violence and intensity probably not since equalled... The area of the Santorini caldera is about twice that of the Krakatoa caldera, and we can be sure that more energy was released in the Bronze Age Thera eruption, that it was more violent, that like Krakatoa it did produce tsunamis. The Krakatoa tsunamis drowned 36,000 people.[207]

It was this awesome event, Castleden persuasively argues, which later formed the foundation of the legend of the destruction of Atlantis, but never before now, unless I am mistaken, have we been offered anything like so carefully assembled, accurate and moving a description of Atlantis being destroyed. What this description now does for us is to destroy the legend of Atlantis and relocate it in real historical time. Indeed, since the Linear B name for Thera was Quhera, we might say that, after all these thousands of years we finally have a *Quherant* account of the downfall of Atlantis. That is a breathtaking cognitive achievement, by any measure.

What are the implications of this for critical reflection on Plato's utopian political philosophy? At the very beginning of this book, Castleden remarks:

---

206 This is a curious detail, if the major eruption was in 1628 BCE, as Cline states. Plainly, this is a matter of archaeological detail which needs sorting out. See S. W. Manning *A Test of Time: The Volcano of Thera and the Chronology and History of the Aegean and East Mediterranean in the mid-Second Millennium BC* (Oxford, Oxbow Books, 1999) and Manning's 2010 article 'Eruption of Thera/Santorini' in The Oxford Handbook of the Bronze Age, edited by Eric Cline himself.

207 This is almost certainly an overstatement, since the huge caldera was not caused only by the historic eruption under consideration, but by prehistoric ones which created the great harbour long before human beings settled on the island.

> *Plato's story of Atlantis has the unenviable reputation of being the absurdist lie in all literature. One major problem has been the long eclipse which Plato's reputation as a philosopher and a political thinker suffered during the twentieth century. Some scholars have written about Plato in such vitriolic terms as to test the boundaries of the term 'scholarship'.*

One such scholar, of course, was Karl Popper. In the first volume of his great polemic work of 1945, *The Open Society and Its Enemies*, Popper asserted that Plato's political philosophy was rooted in nostalgia for a 'closed society' of aristocratic, landowning conservatives and that he was an enemy of the commercial, democratic culture, the 'open society' of fifth-century Athens. Popper contended that Plato was reacting against 'the breakdown of the closed society' and that his utopia was grounded not in future possibilities but in the past.

He wrote:

> *Perhaps the most powerful cause of the breakdown of the closed society was the development of sea communication and commerce ... These two, seafaring and commerce, became the main characteristics of Athenian imperialism, as it developed in the fifth century BCE. And indeed they were recognized as the most dangerous developments by the oligarchs.*

Now there is no doubt that when Plato described the utopia of his *Laws*, 'Magnesia', at the end of his life, he conceived it as a 'closed society' (situated, oddly enough, in Crete) and I do not propose to defend Plato's idea of the ideal republic against Popper's anti-totalitarian spirit of the 1940s. What is curious, though, is that Popper thought seafaring and commerce to have been what got the 'open society' going and brought about the 'breakdown of the closed society', but somehow imagined that all this occurred only with the rise of Athenian maritime imperialism, after the defeat of the Persians in the fifth century BCE.

We now know better. What is striking is that Plato himself described Atlantis precisely as a seafaring, commercial civilization and cast no opprobrium on these characteristics of it all. Somehow this seems not to have made any impression on Popper. After reading Castleden, however, one is led to the peculiar sense that Popper's 'open society' may very well have been ideally instantiated primordially in just that lost civilization which Plato looked back to with admiration and whose downfall he reflected on so evocatively that we have pondered the roots of the tale for millennia. Isn't that ironical? Isn't archaeology fascinating? Isn't truth so much more interesting than fiction?

Secret intelligence and escape clauses[208]

Preamble

Since the creation of Indonesia half a century ago, the dialogue between Washington, London and Canberra about Indonesia's future has been at the heart of their strategic concerns with Southeast Asia and even Asia as a whole. The most obvious reason for this is that Indonesia

---

[208] This essay was first published in *Critical Asian Studies* Volume 33, No. 2, June 2001, under the title 'Secret Intelligence and Escape Clauses: Australia and the Indonesian Annexation of East Timor 1963-76'. In the summer of 2000, I was invited up to the Australian National University as a visiting scholar to read and reflect upon the newly published 885 page volume of declassified diplomatic papers titled *Australia and the Indonesian Incorporation of Portuguese Timor, 1974-1976*. I had previously written, for the conservative magazine *Quadrant*, about the controversies surrounding the annexation of East Timor by Indonesia and the Australian government's handling of the matter, including the killing by Indonesian Special Forces, at Balibo and in Dili, of six Australian-based journalists. Those who invited me to come up to Canberra were aware of my earlier writing.

I seized the opportunity not only to read the thick volume closely, but to conduct further research in the Australian National Archives on the deeper background to Australian relations with Indonesia, going back to the 1940s. When I presented my seminar paper on the subject, at the end of a fortnight's research and writing, I began by remarking that I had arrived in Canberra armed with a hypothesis as to what had happened in 1975 and why and, within a few days of reading into the declassified record, I had had to reject that hypothesis and come up with a new one, because of what I learned. This paper sets out what I learned and shows that Gough Whitlam's wilfulness and lack of diplomatic sophistication were the chief cause of Australia getting itself into an embarrassing situation when Suharto's Indonesia decided to use force to take over East Timor.

There is plainly still a great deal that we do not know about Australian deliberations and actions at that time, because much has remained classified. The Australian government, in September 2000, released some 68,000 pages of documents, only a tiny fraction of which were published in the book under review. About 2,600 pages of diplomatic documents were withheld, along with Cabinet papers, intelligence materials and Defence Department records. Moreover, the documents that were released cover only the period from early 1974 to mid-1976. They do not document the Indonesian war in East Timor between 1976 and 1998, and its human costs. What they do document is the process whereby Australia acquiesced in Indonesian annexation of East Timor.

Above all, they show that secret briefings by the Indonesians kept the Australian government closely informed of Indonesian intentions and operations at every step. In the light of these secret briefings and related documents, it is clear that Prime Minister Gough Whitlam's claim that he wanted to see a 'genuine act of self-determination' by the East Timorese is and always was hollow. This was a fig leaf covering his desire to see East Timor incorporated into Indonesia, as West Papua had been in the 1960s. The patina of moral responsibility and legal respectability were his alibi, or as Richard Woolcott put it in late 1974, 'escape clause', if and when Indonesian actions led to accusations of Australian complicity with Jakarta. Mr Whitlam was complicit. The record is clear.

has always been the geographically and demographically largest state in Southeast Asia. It is also a resource rich archipelago sitting astride the Malacca, Sunda, Lombok and Ombar-Wetai Straits. These straits are indispensable to the passage of enormous volumes of commercial shipping from the Indian Ocean to the South China Sea and the Pacific Ocean. They are also crucial to the passage of military shipping, especially for the United States with its global naval power. Australia's abiding interests have been that Indonesia develop into a stable, prosperous and friendly neighbour. Under President Sukarno (1947-66) that prospect seemed at times to be at risk on all counts. Under President Suharto (1967-98) it seemed for a time that it could be achieved on all counts. The prospect now looks quite uncertain again.[209]

Since the downfall of President Suharto, in 1998, the possibility of the political disintegration of an economically stricken Indonesia has arisen for the first time since the late 1950s. As *The Economist* pointed out, in December 2000[210], the vote for independence in East Timor has led to revitalized demands for independence in Aceh and Irian Jaya and even in Riau, East Kalimantan, North Sulawesi, Makassar (South Sulawesi) and the Moluccas. These stirrings have very serious implications for Anglo-American strategic interests in the future of Indonesia. At the same time, the incoming Bush administration has indicated that it wants Australia to deepen its alliance with the United States and, in the words of Secretary of State Colin Powell, lead alliance policy on Indonesia.[211] Under these circumstances, it is vital that all concerned critically and carefully examine the way that Australia thinks about Indonesia and the way in which its foreign and defence policies concerning Indonesia are made. The publication, in September 2000, of an important book of Australian government documents, *Australia and the Indonesian Incorporation of East Timor: 1974-1976*, provides an unparalleled opportunity for such critical and careful examination.[212] The book shows in detail how the Australian policy system worked at a critical juncture in the history of Indonesia—the decision by President Suharto, in 1975, to take over East Timor from Portugal in the face of clear and armed opposition from its inhabitants.

---

209 This is an interesting judgment to look back upon after fourteen years. During those years, Indonesia has emerged as a quite stable democratic state and its economic growth has been quite respectable. Moreover, its relations with Australia have been very sound and largely relieved of the tensions which, for different reasons, existed in our relations with Indonesia under both Sukarno and Suharto.

210 *The Economist*, 9-12 December 2000, 'The Fire Next Time: Indonesia—Disintegration Dreaded'.

211 *The Australian Financial Review*, 19 January 2001, p. 1 'U.S.: Key Role for Australia'.

212 *Australia and the Indonesian Incorporation of Portuguese Timor: 1974-1976*, (Melbourne University Press, Carlton, 2000). All citations from this book from this point will cite it as 'AIIPT' with reference to documents from it according to their numbered sequence in the book.

Ever since the Indonesian invasion of East Timor, on 7 December 1975, there has been international controversy over whether Australia and, indeed, the United States, gave President Suharto a 'green light' to send military forces into the former Portuguese colony. The scale of violence inflicted on the East Timorese by the Indonesian armed forces, in their ultimately unsuccessful effort to crush all resistance, horrified a great many people. Yet, in 1979, Australia gave *de jure* recognition to Indonesia's annexation of East Timor and both the United States and Britain supplied military equipment for the brutal Indonesian campaign against East Timorese resistance. Australian political leaders and senior diplomats asserted for many years that they had not given President Suharto any sort of 'green light'. American leaders, especially Henry Kissinger, who was President Gerald Ford's Secretary of State at the time and who visited Jakarta with Ford on the eve of the invasion, have likewise professed their innocence of any complicity in the matter.

Before the release of thousands of classified documents, in September 2000, the debate in Australia over the matter of East Timor had centred on two questions: Did Australian Prime Minister Gough Whitlam give President Suharto a 'green light' to use force in East Timor; and, if not, could Australia have done anything more than it did to dissuade Indonesia from using force to incorporate East Timor, in 1975? Whitlam has adamantly maintained, ever since 1975, that he did not give Suharto any reason to believe that the use of force would be condoned by the Australian government.[213] Defenders of Australia's policy have also argued, right up to the present, that nothing else Australia could realistically have done would have made any difference at all in the way things worked out.

The declassified documents show that neither of these statements is true. They show that Whitlam, as Prime Minister, gambled that an Indonesian covert operation would bring about incorporation of East Timor into Indonesia without significant bloodshed and that it would come to be accepted for the same reasons as Indian annexation of Goa in 1961-62. They show further that he told Suharto he would place greater importance on good relations with Indonesia than on self-determination for East Timor if things got tough. They show that Australia's handling of the matter was flawed, because the policy adopted was both insincere and incoherent. The documents make it possible to pinpoint the flaws in policy-making and the errors in thinking behind those flaws. This is invaluable. It means that we can, with a weather eye on future contingencies, , learn crucial lessons about Australia's national security, intelligence and policy-making processes in a

---

213   Gough Whitlam died in 2014, at the great age of 98. To the best of my knowledge, he neither publicly nor privately expressed any contriteness or regret over the way he had conducted his dealings with President Suharto in 1974-75. Whether he had any reason to is one of the issues at the heart of the present paper.

sober, incisive and systematic manner. We can do so, in the famous phrase of the Roman historian Tacitus, *sine ira et studio* (without anger and bias), thus doing justice to the participants in the process while learning useful lessons for the future.

The 1963 Jockel Report: Elements of a more cautious policy

Portuguese Timor, until 1974, was a remote and sleepy corner of one of the last European colonial empires. It was the sort of little place that is easily overlooked by national security policy-makers, whether in Washington or Canberra—until something startling happens that calls for 'crisis management'. A left-wing coup in Lisbon, in April 1974, led to startling developments in Timor, over the next year and a half. However, the question of the future of Portuguese Timor first came under close consideration over a decade before the 1974 coup in Portugal—due to another startling event: India's annexation of the Portuguese enclave of Goa, in late 1961.

In the wake of the Indian seizure of Goa and other tiny Portuguese colonial enclaves in India,[214] in December 1961, and the incorporation (under a UN mandate) of Dutch New Guinea (West Irian or Irian Jaya), in 1962-63, the US State Department urged Australia to take the initiative, with some sort of preventive diplomacy, to head off a possible military seizure of Portuguese Timor by Indonesia. The idea was raised of assisting Portugal to develop the territory economically. Canberra was sceptical. The Australian Minister for External (Foreign) Affairs, Garfield Barwick, cabled Howard Beale, the Australian ambassador in Washington: 'I completely fail to see how pouring money into Timor to raise the standard of living is going to solve this problem. Does the State Department imagine that there is any future for an independent East Timor?'[215]

In a 'Submission to Cabinet', in February 1963, Barwick stated that: 'it is difficult to see a practicable alternative to the Timorese people joining Indonesia,' but 'we must be at pains to

---

214 These enclaves, it is worth remarking, had been in existence for about 400 years and had been annexed not from a nation state of India, but from the margins of a vaguely defined Mughal empire in the sub-continent, at the very beginning of what is now sometimes dubbed 'the Vasco da Gama era', the era of European maritime and military supremacy which led to European powers dominating the entire world for several hundred years.

215 National Archives of Australia (hereafter NAA), CRS (Correspondence Files of the Department of External Affairs) A1838, File No. 3038/10/1 (Portuguese Timor: Relations with and policy towards), Outward Cablegram to Australian Embassy Washington, 5 February 1963, SECRET PRIORITY for Beale from Barwick. All further citations from the NAA, when they have not been published elsewhere, for example in AIIPT, will be cited as 'NAA *n, n/n/n', reflecting the series and file numbers of the document cited. Cabinet papers have only the series number Cn, not the fuller file numbers of External (or Foreign) Affairs documents.

impress on Indonesia our disapproval of a military attack on Timor.'[216] The question was how to handle this matter, given that Washington's 'quiet approaches' had not prevented India's military attack on Goa and Indonesia had been supported by Washington and London (to the discomfort of Canberra) in pressuring the Dutch out of their colony in West New Guinea and then taking it for themselves.[217] Both the Minister for External Affairs, Barwick, and Prime Minister Robert Menzies were keenly aware of the dilemma confronting Australia, even though they did not expect imminent military moves by Indonesia.

In early January 1963, the Department of External Affairs had cabled the Australian Embassy in Washington:

> *Please emphasize our wish to keep in close touch with the US on this matter. Because of our geographical situation, we naturally have a close interest in the problem. However, our studies are at an early stage and we would not expect to be in a position to let the State Department have any considered views for some time. We would be glad to have any ideas on tactics.*[218]

Both Menzies and Barwick, each of whom was among the most formidable individuals to have held their respective offices in Australia's history; clearly wanted the matter given very careful thought. Against this background, on 25 February 1963, Secretary for External

---

216 NAA C3739 Barwick to Cabinet, 7 February 1963, SECRET.

217 Two illuminating PhD dissertations, completed in 1999 and 2000 respectively, between them, lay out the processes whereby all this came about. The first is Stuart Robert Doran *Western Friends and Eastern Neighbours: West New Guinea and Australian Self-Perception in Relation to the United States, Britain and Southeast Asia, 1950-1962* (Australian National University, Research School of Social Sciences, 1999). The second is John Francis Saltford *UNTEA and UNRWI: United Nations Involvement in West New Guinea During the 1960s* (University of Hull, 2000). Doran's eleventh chapter 'Sukarno's Move and the Anglo-American Decision to Force a Dutch-Australian Capitulation, December 1961-January 1962' is masterful. Especially striking is his analysis of a letter from Harold MacMillan, the British Prime Minister, to Sir Robert Menzies, then Australia's Prime Minister, dated 27 December 1961.

> He wrote that he had meet with President Kennedy in Bermuda some few days earlier and that they had agreed that the situation regarding Dutch New Guinea confronted them with 'a choice of evils', in which the handing over of West New Guinea to Sukarno seemed the lesser evil. In any event, he wrote, neither Washington nor London would support Australia should it seek by force of arms to prevent such an outcome. Menzies was quite deeply disturbed by this development, but the view of Cabinet was that it left Australia with no practical alternative than to accede and thus accept a land border (in what was still at that time the Australian UN mandate colony of Papua New Guinea) with an aggressive and expansionist Indonesia under President Sukarno. The bottom line was, as Doran phrased it, that 'Washington and London had simply ignored Australian views.' (p. 225). He went on to remark: 'The shock ... of finding that the British and Americans were capable of placing their peripheral interests above what they recognized as a central concern of Australian defence thinking was tremendous—particularly at a time when Australia could do nothing for itself.' (p. 226).

218 NAA A1838 3006/4/3, Outward Cablegram, 9 January 1963, SECRET.

Affairs Arthur Tange instructed a small working group within his department to prepare a report on the future of Portuguese Timor.[219] The working group was headed by Gordon Jockel, a senior officer in the department, who was later to become Australia's ambassador to Indonesia (1969-71), and then the second director of Australia's Joint Intelligence Organization (1971-78), replacing the founding director, Robert Furlonger, who, in turn, took over from him as ambassador in Jakarta. I shall refer to the report that the group produced as the Jockel Report.

The report, which was submitted to Tange on 5 April 1963, recommended that action be taken to 'steal the Indonesian wind' and open up the possibility of the territory being decolonized without any use of force by Indonesia. Excerpts from the report were published in 2000, in *Australia and the Indonesian Incorporation of Portuguese Timor: 1974-1976*, but the full version repays a close reading and belongs in any documentary history of the subject from now on. In his instructions to Jockel, Tange had written:

> *The United States and the United Kingdom are looking to Australia to take some initiative to avoid the Western world finding itself in a situation where a nationalist revolutionary power, backed by Russian arms, can achieve its ends by force of arms. This power is at Australia's doorstep.*[220]

What leaps to the eye here is that Tange's perspective in 1963 was, geopolitically speaking, the reverse of the conservative concern by 1975: a Leftist regime in East Timor potentially being used by the Communist powers against Indonesia, in a situation where Indochina had just fallen to Communist revolutions and the United States had suffered a humiliating set-back on the global scene.

Tange's instruction to Jockel is of interest, all the same, because he wanted a report that would 'explore all possible measures and analyse developments which, if they can be initiated or encouraged, would produce the least embarrassment to Australia's foreign policy and national interests.'[221] The key phrases are 'initiated or encouraged' and 'least embarrassment'. The Whitlam government a decade later neither initiated nor encouraged measures that might have directly inhibited Indonesia from taking the unilateral action it did to incorporate

---

219 For a fine biography of Tange which throws a good deal of light on the development of Australian foreign and defence policy between the 1930s and the 1980s, see Peter Edwards *Arthur Tange: Last of the Mandarins* (Allen & Unwin, Sydney, 2006). The chapter most immediately relevant to the present paper is chapter 7 'The policy adviser triumphant: serving Menzies and Barwick 1960-64', pp. 114-142. In this account, the capacities of Tange as a thinker and his standing as an independent and thoughtful adviser to the Prime Minister and Cabinet emerge very clearly.

220 NAA A1838 3038/10/1, Part II.

221 Ibid.

Portuguese Timor. The result was a considerable embarrassment to Australia over the course of a generation—to say nothing of the high costs to Indonesia and the huge suffering inflicted on East Timor. Yet apologists for the Whitlam policy have argued that Australia had nothing to be embarrassed about and that, in any case, Indonesian annexation of East Timor was in Australia's national interest in all the circumstances. The 1963 Jockel Report is useful, above all, because it allows us to put such claims in deeper perspective.

In the summary of the report, Jockel remarked that early discussion of the future of the colony in the United Nations could help to head off the unwelcome possibility of unilateral, violent action by Indonesia. He added:

> *What we have to fear, in particular, is an uprising and bloody suppression leading to Indonesian intervention. If the matter is already actively before the United Nations, Indonesia may itself allow the main action to be determined in the United Nations. In any event, there would be better chances of a realistic engagement of the United Nations in such a situation and better chances for Australia avoiding a head-on clash with Indonesia.*[222]

There were, he observed, 'some pointers which suggest that Indonesia may act in a more cautious and more acceptable fashion.' Indonesia would not wish to appear expansionist, he believed, and if the matter were handled pro-actively by Australia, Jakarta 'may be somewhat flexible on the international status of Timor after the Portuguese have gone.' For all these reasons, he concluded, 'the sooner the question is brought before the United Nations, the better.'

The crucial paragraph in the Jockel Report, in the light of subsequent developments, is paragraph 35:

> *While letting Indonesia understand that Australia would not oppose the territory eventually becoming a part of Indonesia through satisfactory processes of self-determination, we might also urge that there are other worthwhile possibilities for consideration. For example, the territory might acquire a measure of autonomy under the protection externally of Indonesia ... In talking to the Indonesians, we should avoid being over eager to suggest that inevitably the territory of Portuguese Timor should pass to them and that we don't have any scruples about that eventuality except the use of force. We should make continued reference to the argument for self-determination. Otherwise, we place ourselves in the position of being an accomplice of Indonesia in an exercise in realpolitik which we believe would earn the reverse of their healthy respect.*[223]

What the Jockel Report recommended tactically was that Australia take steps to slow or inhibit Indonesian moves toward unilateral and violent action in regard to Portuguese Timor. The idea was to give Australia's policy some traction in the event that Portugal proved obdurate in Timor, as it had in Goa, and a need arose to restrain Indonesian impatience.

---

222   Ibid. Hereafter referred to as 'Jockel Report'. Summary, paragraph 6.
223   Jockel Report, paragraph 35.

To this end, the Jockel Report made six key tactical recommendations:

1. *Call for the progressive development and self-determination of Portuguese Timor in the United Nations.*
2. *Take the initiative in this matter to 'steal the Indonesian wind' and pre-empt any move toward unilateral action aimed at annexation.*
3. *Make clear, in early talks with the Indonesians, that there are other possible futures for Portuguese Timor than incorporation into Indonesia.*
4. *Avoid giving the Indonesians any reason to believe that we regard incorporation as inevitable.*
5. *Make clear that satisfactory processes of self-determination have priority over any particular outcome of those processes.*
6. *Do not become an accomplice in any Indonesian exercise in realpolitik.*[224]

The course that Gough Whitlam unilaterally embarked upon, at his own initiative, in 1974, disregarded every one of these tactical recommendations. If we wish, therefore, to reach a considered judgment as to whether the accusation against Whitlam is justified—that he gave a 'green light' to Suharto to take unilateral action in East Timor in 1974-75—then these recommendations are the place to start.

In fact, there is some reason to believe that the desire to see Portuguese Timor incorporated into Indonesia—in a manner that would not involve Australia in any military obligations and would cause it the least possible embarrassment—was the shadow side of Australia's policy even as Jockel and his colleagues prepared their recommendations. In a short, hand-written memorandum, Keith Waller, a senior officer in the Department of External Affairs, made the following observations to Gordon Jockel on 13 March 1963:

The Secretary said this morning that the Working Group should look for the circumstances which would make it easiest for any Australian government not to become involved with military obligations while acquiescing in the passage of Timor to Indonesia.

At that point, the Working Group still had several weeks before it was to submit its findings to the Secretary. It is quite clear, however, that Jockel had not and did not interpret his brief as Waller suggested; since Waller's proposal is by no means what Jockel and his colleagues submitted for Tange's consideration. It is clear from Barwick's cable to Beale, on the other hand, that the Minister had little patience with the idea that Portuguese Timor might ever become independent. Waller's remark to Jockel seems, therefore, to have reflected not only the views of the Secretary, but those of the Minister. Little wonder, then, that the report's recommendations were stillborn. Yet they were committed to print. They show, therefore, a possible course of action for the Australian government. In 1974-75, however, Whitlam was to take the Barwick line and doing so was to have all the consequences foreseen by Jockel in 1963.

224 Jockel Report, paragraphs 32-35.

Arguably, the single most crucial determinant of Australian policy in this matter after 1965 was the fact that, in 1965-66, Colonel Suharto and the Indonesian army destroyed the Indonesian Communist Party (PKI) and pulled the rug from under the left-leaning regime of Sukarno. This transformed the security outlook regarding Indonesia from Canberra's point of view and that of Washington. It was also, in those very years, that the American war in Indochina escalated and Australia committed military forces to it. In these circumstances, Australian relations with Indonesia grew steadily more cordial between 1966 and 1974. The matter of Portuguese Timor lost its apparent urgency—until the failure of America's war in Indochina and a left wing coup in Lisbon that catapulted Marxists to power in East Timor transformed the situation for the worse and gave a wholly new accent to the old Barwick and Tange line on the future of the Portuguese enclave.

The coup in Lisbon directly prompted suggestions from within the Australian Embassy in Jakarta that an Indonesian takeover of Portuguese Timor might be a good thing. A month after the coup, the Minister in the Embassy, John McCredie, wrote to Graham Feakes, First Assistant Secretary for Southeast Asia and Papua New Guinea in what was now called the Department of Foreign Affairs, in Canberra:

> *Indonesian absorption of Timor makes geopolitical sense. Any other long term solution would be potentially disruptive of both Indonesia and the region. It [absorption] would help confirm our seabed agreement with Indonesia. It should induce a greater readiness on Indonesia's part to discuss Indonesia's ocean strategy. We might be able to provide some assistance to a smooth transition [to absorption of East Timor by Indonesia].*

This, of course, comes very close to embodying what critics long accused the Whitlam government and subsequent Australian governments of conniving in, from 1975 until 1999. Certainly, it represented a totally different approach to that recommended in the Jockel Report, as can readily be seen. The fact that Indonesia was now seen as under a more tractable and pro-Western regime must be regarded as accounting for some part of the shift, but what McCredie called 'geopolitical sense' was unambiguously part of it as well, due both to the Cold War calculus and to the seabed interest.

Had it been possible to arrange what McCredie called 'a smooth transition', there would, arguably, have been little problem with his reasoning—at least from the point of view of Australia's national interest. But smoothness was always going to be a problem, as Jockel and his colleagues had understood all too well. There was a need, consequently, for an Australian policy with some traction, lest 'smoothness' become an unconstrained slide into Indonesian military action. By 'traction' I simply mean the capacity, which one relies upon with good tyres on a motor vehicle, to grip the surface if it is necessary to slow down or even brake sharply. As we shall see, the policy

Australia adopted under Whitlam conspicuously lacked such traction. The consequence was that all hope for a smooth transition was made dependent on factors beyond Australia's control. The policy failed and, instead of a smooth transition, there was a dangerous slide into disaster for East Timor, brutal aggression by Indonesia and prolonged embarrassment for Australia.

Responding to McCredie from Canberra on 6 June 1974, Feakes wrote:

> *My own feeling, which I think would be widely shared in the Department, is that there will have to be an internationally acceptable act of self-determination ... In our view, the best result of that act of self-determination would be for the Timorese to choose union or some form of association with Indonesia. The diplomatic problem for us is how to bring that result about. We have to face up to the possibility that the Timorese may choose independence ... Timorese resistance to absorption by Indonesia may come as a shock to the Indonesians; and we may have a role in suggesting to the Indonesians that they take into account the possibility of such resistance and start to think seriously about how Indonesia might live with an independent Portuguese Timor. We should not assume that it would be beyond the Indonesians' capacity to do so and fairly quickly to gain a dominant influence there.*

From this, note three things. First, the aim of policy, even among the cautious, has moved from inhibiting unilateral Indonesian action, through pro-active and constructive measures, to facilitating, if possible, the absorption of Portuguese Timor into Indonesia. Second, Feakes allowed that the Timorese might choose not to accept absorption, but he offered no suggestions as to how their freedom to choose might be guaranteed. Jockel had been more cautious, eleven years before. Third, the fact that Feakes was speculating about whether Australia might have a role to play in suggesting to Indonesia that futures other than absorption be considered indicates, in itself, that no such initiative had been undertaken in all the year since the Jockel Report had recommended just such an approach to Jakarta. Indeed, given the attitude of Barwick and Tange in the early 1960s, it seems probable that any such idea had been quashed as a matter of deliberate policy.

Enter Harry Tjan

As it happened, the clock was ticking. Just at this point, the Australian Embassy in Jakarta began to receive a remarkable series of back-channel briefings from the Jakarta-based Centre for Strategic and International Studies (CSIS) and from OPSUS (the special operations outfit which had done much to facilitate the incorporation of West Irian in the 1960s).[225] These briefings

---

225   The official document set that was published gives no indication that this contact between Harry Tjan and Jan Arriens was anything but a new development. In correspondence with Arriens, however, I learned otherwise. I sent him a copy of this paper and he responded warmly and at great length. He remarked that he thought the paper itself 'quite outstanding', knowing especially 'how difficult it is to synthesize what happened and to come up with a coherent interpretation. Yours is remarkably coherent and fair.' He went to point out, however, that the briefings by Harry Tjan 'did not start in 1974, but in 1973.'

were delivered in person by Harry Tjan, director of CSIS, and Lim Bian Kie, personal secretary to Ali Murtopo, Suharto's key intelligence adviser and special operations czar. Tjan himself had been a close confidante of Murtopo's since 1967 and in contact with the Australian Embassy even earlier, as an anti-Sukarno student activist during the upheaval of 1965-66. Both Tjan and Lim (Jusuf Wanandi) were protégés of the Dutch Jesuit, Father van Beek, a strong supporter of the Suharto regime, who developed a major intelligence organization in the 1960s, as a bulwark against both Communism and Islam.

On 3 July 1974, Ambassador Robert Furlonger sent a top secret cable to Canberra, reporting that Harry Tjan had had an extraordinary conversation with Jan Arriens, First Secretary in the Embassy. Tjan's earlier intelligence links with the Australian Embassy, during the upheaval of the mid-1960s, had to do with the destruction of the PKI. This conversation, however, was the beginning of a long series of briefings in regard to Portuguese Timor. In the published documents alone there were another forty five, in an uninterrupted sequence up to June 1976. There content is the kind that secret intelligence officers dream about. If we use the Jockel Report as our benchmark for policy formulation, the first document is the greatest importance, as Furlonger's own wording makes plain.

He wrote to Canberra:

> *Harry Tjan told Jan Arriens on 2 July that he intends to submit a paper to the president this week recommending that Indonesia mount a clandestine operation in Portuguese Timor to ensure that the territory would opt for incorporation into Indonesia ... Ali Murtopo ... would appear to have directed Tjan to draft a paper setting out the operation. Tjan's extreme frankness indicates that the Indonesians are confident that we would favour an independent Portuguese Timor as little as they do.*[226]

His account of this is of considerable interest, though too long to reproduce here. The gist of it is that he had arrived on posting in May 1973 and had met Harry Tjan for the first time then. He (Arriens) already had an interest in Portuguese Timor and visited it shortly after his arrival. On his return, he met Tjan and discussed with him the idea that Portuguese Timor 'was bound, sooner or later to become a significant issue for Indonesia and Indonesian/Australian relations.' He then added: 'Harry remarked that he had had a similar conversation a few weeks before with Peter Wilenski.'

The crucial consideration, wholly missing from the published record, is the following: 'When I went to see Harry the next week, the first thing he said was that apropos of what I had said and his earlier conversation with Wilenski, he had put a position paper up to the President. This was, quite literally, page 1 of Indonesian thinking on Portuguese Timor in the Suharto era.' In other words, Furlonger's cable gives a misleading impression that the whole conversation began in July 1974. It appears that Peter Wilenski, presumably at Whitlam's instigation, had made contact as early as April 1973 and had already raised the idea. As we shall see, when the whole thing had blown up, Harry Tjan would say to Allan Taylor that it was the Australians who had first put the idea into Indonesian heads. We need, it seems, an account of what Peter Wilenski said to Harry Tjan and what understanding he had with the Prime Minister at that early point on the subject of Timor.

226 AIIPT #10.

They may, however, have been doing more than assuming. Whereas there had been considerable mutual suspicion between Indonesia and Australia before 1965, this had changed as Suharto's grip on power strengthened in 1966-67. In 1971, Indonesia's intelligence agency BAKIN (*Badan Ko-ordinasi Intelijen Negara*, or State Intelligence Coordination Agency) had established a regular liaison relationship with Australia's Joint Intelligence Organization (JIO), the roots and nature of which remain classified. CSIS had been set up under the guiding hand of Ali Murtopo, deputy director of BAKIN, in the same year. The briefings initiated by Harry Tjan in July 1974 were plainly intended to cement a geopolitical and intelligence relationship. Tjan's 'confidence', in mid-1974, seems to have been grounded in prior, still classified intelligence exchanges between BAKIN and JIO. He had also, however, had a conversation with Peter Wilenski, principal private secretary to Whitlam, in Jogjakarta, the week before his conversation with Arriens.[227]

> Reporting the Tjan/Arriens exchange, Furlonger went on to say:
>
> *It is interesting to note the Indonesian preoccupation with Portuguese Timor which is now coming through to us—from Ali Murtopo at the discussions (half a line deleted)*[228] *last week and now with Tjan. It is true that all these discussions were initiated on our side, but the Indonesians clearly decided to take the opportunity offered by the talks to take us along on a Realpolitik approach to the problem; and they are speaking surprisingly frankly. We are, in effect, being consulted. They clearly expect a response from our side. A failure to do so will be taken by them, I fear, as tacit agreement. Although I recognize that there are sometimes evolving situations where policy is best left grey and obscure, I doubt that that is desirable in this case.*[229]

This makes fascinating reading against the deeper background of Gordon Jockel's tactical recommendations of 1963. It suggests that Canberra had not worked out a policy position on Portuguese Timor between 1963 and 1974, but had raised the matter with the Indonesians in order to draw them out, only to be asked to cooperate in arranging for the incorporation of Portuguese Timor into Indonesia. Furlonger's remarks show that he was aware of the problem adverted to by the Jockel Report (that Indonesia might be tempted to embark on a Realpolitik approach unless Australia handled the matter very deftly), but he did not himself recommend any pre-emptive action 'to steal the Indonesian wind'. He sought guidance from Canberra.

---

227 AIIPT #10. In retrospect, I would amend this judgment slightly. Gordon Jockel was director of JIO by 1971 and it seems improbable that he would have allowed the message to go to Murtopo that Australia wanted to see incorporation. Wilenski is another matter. It seems possible that he passed on the already set opinion of Whitlam that the Barwick line would be adhered to on his watch. Certainly, this is the way Whitlam played the matter from the time he met Suharto in Jogjakarta a few months later.

228 It seems probable that the deleted half line referred to the latest round of talks between JIO and BAKIN.

229 AIIPT #16.

The response from Canberra came, once again, from Feakes. He wrote, on 26 July:

> The information conveyed to Jan Arriens by Harry Tjan was most valuable, but ... we should not encourage the Indonesians in any way to talk to us along those lines. Australia could not afford to be associated with an Indonesian covert operation because of the risk of exposure. Any hint of Australian involvement or even acquiescence, would be damaging to the government's reputation overseas, to its domestic credibility and to the confidence in us of small countries, especially PNG. In terms of domestic opinion, there are enough problems in maintaining our present policy towards Indonesia without the complication of association with a doubtful operation in Timor, which would scarcely be consistent with the government's support for self-determination in Portuguese colonial territories.[230]

Wilenski, as it happens, informed Secretary for Foreign Affairs Alan Renouf, on 23 July, that Tjan had 'pleaded' for Australian cooperation in working toward early incorporation of Portuguese Timor into Indonesia.

Renouf responded that an earlier report to him had indicated that the East Timorese 'favoured either independence or remaining with Portugal' and that clearly the matter would need careful thought.[231] Yet it was not given sufficiently careful thought for Feakes' misgivings to lead to the development of what I have called 'traction' in Australia's policy on the matter. As the record shows in exhaustive detail, the Indonesians were in no way discouraged from talking to the Australian Embassy 'along those lines' between July 1974 and the Indonesian invasion of East Timor in December 1975. This did, indeed, carry the risk of exposure, but for that reason great efforts were made to conceal the fact that Australia knew of Indonesian machinations and to deny or ignore the fact that the covert operation was going on, once it got under way.

That, however, was still some months away when Feakes was writing to Furlonger, in late July 1974. Feakes added a judicious comment which shows that he had an inkling that traction might be needed. His suspicions, however, did not take him far enough and so they remained interesting but idle reflections. If he and his colleagues had gone back to the reasoning of the Jockel Report, Feakes' suspicions at this juncture might conceivably have led to some rigorous thinking about pre-emptive steps and policy initiative:

> I wonder whether the Indonesians may not underestimate the difficulties of a covert operation in Portuguese Timor and the risk of exposure ... One can guess at the thinking underlying Harry Tjan's idea. It might go like this: Indonesia can have the best of both worlds by employing covert tactics for expansion in Timor; OPSUS (Ali Murtopo's special operations outfit) has the necessary skills and has demonstrated them in West Irian; the agency and political interest that secured Portuguese Timor for Indonesia would gain great kudos domestically. It seems to us that the danger that this approach illustrates is that self-interest may distort rational thinking and the assessment of risks.[232]

---

230 AIIPT #16 n4, 72.
231 AIIPT #16.
232 AIIPT #24

Despite making these astute observations, which would turn out to be grimly prescient, Feakes did not urge that Tjan be challenged on the advisability of such an operation. While he saw possible problems for Indonesia, he does not seem to have fully appreciated that Australia could not simply look the other way and keep its innocence. Once such an operation started, it would have direct implications for Australia.

Urgent and vigorous action at this juncture might have pre-empted the operation in question. Clearly, Renouf understood that there was a potential problem and his apprehension was shared by both the ambassador, Furlonger, and the official chiefly responsible for Indonesia policy analysis, Feakes. Yet no rigorous thinking or policy planning took place. Feakes was circumspect, rather than decisive. When it was arranged that Whitlam would visit Indonesia for meetings with Suharto, at the beginning of September 1974, Feakes coordinated the preparation of the briefing paper for the prime minister. His paper was much weaker in structure, however, than the Jockel Report. The meeting of the two leaders was an unprecedented opportunity for Australia to create an understanding with Indonesia about how to handle the matter. Had Whitlam used Jockel's formula, or even Feakes' less robust advice (which, in the event, he cavalierly disregarded), things might have worked out differently.

In his briefing paper, Feakes informed Whitlam of Tjan's covert operation plan and suggested that 'we should aim ... at maintaining a dialogue about the problem that Portuguese Timor represents to divert them from a forward policy in Timor that would place our other interests at risk.' He suggested that Australia adopt the position that 'any future disposition of Portuguese Timor which was contrary to the wishes of its people would be likely ... to have a destabilizing influence in the region.'[233] What he did not do was to make any reference for the need for something other than a diffuse dialogue to give traction to Australia's policy, in the event that Indonesia inclined further toward Tjan's covert intervention. Feakes advised the prime minister to tell Suharto that self-determination for the Timorese was firm Australian government policy and that this 'should not exclude any of the three future options for Portuguese Timor', namely, sustained links with Portugal, independence, or association in some form with Indonesia.

Whitlam, however, had his own views on the subject and he disregarded Feakes' advice without further consultation with his foreign policy officers. With the high-handed self-confidence that was his political style, even in areas in which he conspicuously lacked expertise, Whitlam advised Suharto at Jogjakarta, on 6 September 1974, that his personal views tended to become Australian government policy. His views on the subject of Portuguese Timor were

---

233 AIIPT #26 95: Record of meeting between Whitlam and Suharto, State Guest House, Jogjakarta, 6 September 1974, 10.00 AM.

double-sided, as it happens: East Timor 'should become part of Indonesia' and 'this should happen in accordance with the properly expressed wishes of the people of East Timor.' Whitlam told the Indonesian president that while a belief that Portuguese Timor should become part of Indonesia was 'not yet government policy ... it was likely to become so.'

We need not conclude too categorically that Whitlam intended at this point to give Suharto a 'green light' to go ahead with the plan proposed by Harry Tjan. His words do appear, however, to have been so understood by Suharto. Given that Whitlam knew of the Tjan plan, he surely had a clear responsibility to warn against it, if he believed that it could interfere with the genuineness of East Timorese self-determination. Not to so much as mention the covert action plan was to give what Furlonger had earlier described as tacit support for the idea and this is what Suharto took away from the meeting.

Commenting on Feakes' briefing notes after the completion of Whitlam's talks with Suharto, Furlonger wrote, on the cover sheet of his copy:

This was all very cautious and rather different from the line the PM actually took.

The briefing paper had been sent to Furlonger from Canberra by Dick Woolcott, who, in a handwritten postscript to his formal note of transmission, asked Furlonger: 'Are you satisfied with the way the PT issue is working out?' [234] Furlonger's own comment suggests that he was not completely satisfied, but he seems to have thought that the matter could be handled satisfactorily, as Feakes had written, by keeping some sort of dialogue going.

Why did the prime minister disregard the advice given to him in such a sensitive matter? There are a number of possible explanations. Two of them seem to be the most plausible. First, he had been assured by Furlonger that Suharto saw Australia as 'unique among countries of Western origin in the degree of understanding that it showed towards the problems of Indonesia and the region' and that 'he and those around him admire your reshaping of Australian foreign policy.' So, Whitlam perhaps allowed the heady sense of working with Indonesia's strongman in reshaping the region to cloud his judgment. He allowed himself to believe that the two of them could work it out and never mind the details for the time being. Second, he had no patience with 'micro-states', whether in the Southwest Pacific or the Baltic, and he was highly susceptible to the argument that Portuguese Timor could never be a viable independent state. Its absorption into Indonesia was, therefore, inevitable and should be helped along, not retarded, by Australian policy.

Whitlam's approach was contrary not only to the 'very cautious' brief given to him by the Department of Foreign Affairs, but, whether he knew it or not, even more to the strategically

---

234 NAA A10463, 801/13/11/1, Part III. Marginalium scribbled on covering minute by Woolcott, 8 October 1974.

thoughtful assessment by Tange's working group in the Menzies years. It was, however, consistent in spirit with the views expressed by Barwick and Waller, especially given the rise of Suharto in the intervening years. Whitlam's position was a characteristically extravagant gesture by a man who was well-known for an overweening sense of his own vision and importance. From this point, in consequence, Australia's policy was caught or ground between the millstones of Whitlam's two professed desiderata (incorporation and self-determination) and these were only ever likely to be reconciled by the means Harry Tjan had proposed—with all the dangers that Feakes and Furlonger had foreseen. To the extent that the Timorese exhibited an unwillingness to be absorbed into Indonesia, Australia would be faced with an invidious choice between these two desiderata. Suharto, however, having been told what he had by Whitlam, would expect Australia to quietly support its covert—but as the months went by increasingly blatant—efforts to 'ensure that the territory would opt for incorporation', as Tjan had phrased it. The results would be embarrassment for Australia, frustration for Indonesia and massive loss of life in East Timor.

Feakes concerns about encouraging the Indonesians to talk to Canberra, as Tjan had begun doing, went by the wayside now. Tjan told the Embassy that talks with the Indonesian foreign minister, Adam Malik, and with the Indonesian Department of Foreign Affairs, were likely to prove unproductive because Malik was 'not being kept fully informed of developments' regarding covert plans for Portuguese Timor. The best channel for such information, he said, was CSIS, especially through Lim Bian Kie.[235] The secret briefings by Lim and Tjan that followed were priceless intelligence and are invaluable historical documents. One can only wish always to have this level of access to the inmost counsels of foreign governments, but the Australian Embassy in Jakarta was engaged in a conversation about covert action. Furthermore, it had created no traction of the kind that Jockel had recommended in 1963 to inhibit Indonesian use of force. Whitlam had, in short, sent Australia down the very path Furlonger had apprehended in July 1974: being drawn into complicity in Jakarta's Realpolitik gambit.

If this had not been so, one would expect to find more evidence of divisions and uncertainties in Indonesia being 'exploited' by Canberra to try to open up a path to self-determination for Portuguese Timor—one that would have precluded the covert operation. Feakes had suggested a dialogue at least along these lines. The prime minister, however, had left the matter wide open to the Realpolitik approach at the Jakarta end, but without, it seems, realizing where this was likely to lead. He may well have believed that East Timor would be swallowed up by Indonesia as easily as Goa had been by India. His confidence was excessive, in any case, and his mind, presumably, on many things other than the fate of the people of the tiny Portuguese colony. One has the

---

235 AIIPT #36

impression that, from this point, Furlonger believed he had the guidance he had sought: to play along with the Suharto/Murtopo/Tjan line, while assuming that good will and dialogue and 'discretion' would prevent everything from ending in disaster and exposure. That it did end with both these things was clearly the direct outcome of the policies adopted by the two leaders, Suharto and Whitlam.

Was Whitlam, having been briefed on the covert operation, tacitly giving Suharto a nod and a wink in September 1974? He has strenuously maintained ever since the policy unravelled that he did not do this, but the record, closely read, suggests that he did. In a cablegram to Foreign Minister Don Willesee, then in New York, in his capacity as acting foreign minister, he stated on 24 September:

> *I think it is important that the Indonesians and Portuguese should understand that, while one major element in our policy towards Portuguese Timor is that we favour incorporation into Indonesia, the other main element in our attitude is that the Timorese should have the opportunity for a genuine act of self-determination to decide their political future. We also think that the Timorese should be allowed to proceed deliberately towards the decision about their future.*

On the other hand, Whitlam added, 'We have no intention of raising the question of Portuguese Timor in the United Nations.' This, as we have seen, had been one of the key initiatives suggested by Jockel to head off an Indonesian Realpolitik approach.

Rather tellingly, Whitlam went on to remark that:

> *The best informed person about Portuguese Timor among the Indonesians in New York will be Ali Murtopo's private secretary Lim Bian Kie. A later telegram from Jakarta makes it clear, however, that Malik has been fully informed of Indonesian policy and is now in sympathy with it. You may, therefore, consider it more appropriate for contacts with Lim Bian Kie to be pursued at the official level.*

Now Gough Whitlam was a highly intelligent man and it seems to me that we would be doing him an injustice to assume that he failed to understand 'Indonesian policy' at this point. He understood and he sought to manoeuvre Australian policy in accordance with Indonesia's Realpolitik gambit—while avoiding any military obligations for Australia and, so he thought, minimizing any embarrassment to it.

If there was any doubt at the highest levels in Canberra regarding Indonesian policy, it ought to have been dispelled by the next secret report on Harry Tjan's briefings to Jan Arriens in Jakarta. It came on 30 September. They key passage is crystal clear:

> *I (Arriens) saw Harry Tjan this morning ... He said that he had now developed a 'grand design' on the future of Portuguese Timor, which had been submitted to the president ... The first stage of securing legal access by Indonesia to Portuguese Timor through economic cooperation. Australia will be invited by Indonesia and Portugal to join in this cooperation. The second stage will be to invite the UN to send a team to inspect conditions in Portuguese Timor. At the earliest stage, this would take place in 1975, but probably not until 1976. The third stage would be a referendum, the*

> *result of which would be ensured by the territory's exposure to Indonesian influence. Tjan said that the president had endorsed the plan as the 'basic guidelines' for Indonesian policy. It still remained, however, for the plan to be converted into operational terms by Ali Murtopo.*

How did Tjan and his master, Murtopo, expect Indonesian influence to take effect so quickly, after 450 years of Portuguese rule? And what if the Timorese proved resistant to that influence? From an Australian point of view, given the declaratory policy, laid down by Whitlam, to say nothing of other considerations, these should have been fundamental concerns. I can find no evidence in the archives, however, that Whitlam had any strategy for inhibiting the Indonesian policy from sliding in the direction of the use of force. This is not simply the wisdom of hindsight, of course, because we know that just such considerations had exercised Jockel in 1963 and had also occurred to Furlonger and Feakes as soon as Tjan had raised the very idea of a covert operation, in July 1974.

Whitlam's stated commitment to self-determination for the Timorese and their being allowed to proceed deliberately toward their decision about their future was well and fine in principle. He may have been perfectly sincere, but this desideratum was not supported by any active or practical diplomacy designed to ensure that self-determination would take place. One is left with the impression that either the prime minister was being strategically naïve, which I feel certain he would not want to accept, or that he was being Machiavellian in a twofold sense. He knew what the Indonesians were thinking and he believed that their covert plan would provide the appearance of self-determination, while ensuring his other desideratum: incorporation of the colony into Indonesia. That was the first sense. The second was that he believed that if things did somehow go wrong, he had provided himself with an alibi: he could say that he had never endorsed any covert operation or blatant Indonesian intervention. Indeed, we know that he did make and continues to make this claim. It was a subtle game to play, but it did not work in Portuguese Timor, in Australian relations with Indonesia, or in domestic political terms. The former prime minister has no alibi. He gambled and lost.

The real danger, to some extent hidden by Tjan's language and Suharto's real intentions, in September 1974, was that covert intervention would either become exposed and backfire, or escalate into military intervention. Freudians talk of the 'return of the repressed'. It could be said that this is what happened in the case of Australian policy on Portuguese Timor in 1974-75. The longstanding fear of Indonesian military intervention in the colony were repressed, due to the overriding desire for good relations with Jakarta and the strong rapport developed between the two 'great leaders', Whitlam and Suharto. Therefore, no roadblocks were created in its way—since creating them would stir the fear and unsettle the good relations with Jakarta.

It should be emphasized that there was every indication that Suharto did not intend to use military force—unless it was absolutely necessary. He told Murtopo and Tjan in September that he wanted the matter handled 'in a discreet and honourable manner' and in such a fashion that he would 'not be embarrassed or implicated.' The problem is that covert operations have a dangerous tendency to roll downhill in the direction of dishonourable and embarrassing action. From the time of the 6 September 1974 meeting between Suharto and Whitlam onwards, the whole relationship between Canberra and Jakarta was made hostage to the dubious assumption that Harry Tjan's covert operation would succeed without running out of control.

If Whitlam had any doubts that this was, indeed, the latent danger in the Realpolitik gambit being designed by Tjan for Murtopo, they should have been dispelled by the two alarming briefings that Lim Bian Kie and Tjan gave to Furlonger and Arriens in October 1974. On 16 October, Furlonger sent a Secret Austeo (Australian Eyes Only) letter to Feakes summarizing the conversation with Lim, on his return from New York. He wrote:

> *Lim is rather concerned about the impact that Ramos Horta is likely to make on the Committee (of Twenty Four, the UN's consultative body on decolonization) and that there will be nobody in Apodeti (the small pro-integration East Timorese party) capable of matching him ... Lim feels that if the Indonesians cannot influence matters in the direction they want within eighteen months, they will be unable to do so at all. Lim said that by 1976 it should be possible for Indonesia to gauge fairly accurately what the likely outcome of a plebiscite would be. If it was clear that the territory would not vote for incorporation into Indonesia, Lim said that the use of force could not be ruled out. Harry Tjan agreed. He spoke of the possibility of fomenting disorder in Portuguese Timor and of Indonesian forces stepping in to salvage the situation at the request of certain sections of the population.*[236]

Needless to say, this is exactly what was to occur. Indeed, it is a little haunting to consider that this Secret Austeo letter from Furlonger was sent on 16 October 1974, a year to the day before the Indonesian covert military intervention began and five Australian network journalists in East Timor to investigate reports of possible Indonesian intervention were killed by Indonesian special forces or their East Timorese allies at Balibo.

If Australia's tacit policy—and certainly Whitlam's—was to accept a West Irian solution (that is, an Indonesian controlled and manipulated process of incorporation) while avoiding Indonesian use of force, this letter of Furlonger's ought to have caused very serious alarm in Canberra. All the more so, because Lim went on to tell Furlonger and Arriens that 'the operation would be considerably more difficult than that in West Irian'. Moreover, Furlonger wrote that he had asked Lim whether Indonesia was not exaggerating the difficulties it would have with an independent Portuguese Timor and whether it might not be better to exert a preponderant influence over such a little state than use force to incorporate it. 'Lim indicated that the latter was

---

AIIPT #49.

not a real alternative for the Indonesians.'[237] In short, Lim, whom Whitlam had already identified as the best informed Indonesian on Timor policy, was telling the Australian government, through its Embassy, that incorporation was Indonesia's goal and never mind about self-determination.

Shouldn't this have set off alarm bells? Didn't this mean that Indonesia had no intention of allowing a genuine act of self-determination in Portuguese Timor? That it had no intention of a gradual and careful preparation of the territory for self-determination, but was set on a course of precipitate action? Surely this indicated that Whitlam's policy was not viable, that he could not have both of his desiderata, much as he might have wanted to—unless, of course, the gamble worked and Indonesian influence won the hearts and minds of the Timorese inside eighteen months.

On 26 October, Arriens again spoke with Tjan and was told that Ali Murtopo had been replaced by Lieutenant General Leonardus Benjamin Murdani, a rapidly rising figure in Indonesian military intelligence, as real operational chief of the covert action plan; that the grand design had hardened into policy; and that Indonesian 'determination to take over Portuguese Timor had now developed an almost irresistible momentum.'[238] The telling thing about this briefing from Tjan is that it came six months before the second round of Whitlam/Suharto talks in Townsville, on 4 April 1975, giving Whitlam ample time to have reconsidered his policy.

It was also a full year before Suharto gave Murdani permission to start a covert military invasion of the territory controlled by Fretilin (the Revolutionary Front for an Independent East Timor, a leader in the independence struggle since 1974). In other words, there had been ample time in which to adjust Australian policy, if the desire had been to 'steal the Indonesian wind' and head off unilateral Indonesian use of force. Yet the record shows that Whitlam did not adjust his policy. He continued to gamble that one or another form of Indonesian covert operation would yield incorporation of East Timor into Indonesia—without Australia having to take any responsibility for the means used to achieve this end.

The momentum was far less irresistible at this point than it would become after August 1975 and, if Australia did not wish to slip down the slope of the Realpolitik approach now so frankly spelled out by Lim Bian Kie, surely this was the time to put on the brakes. The problem was that the Whitlam policy did not have any braking capacity built into it. Jockel was the brakes man. Whitlam, as he more than once remarked in domestic politics, was a 'crash through or crash' man. Not only was his policy without any traction, but he did not seem particularly aware of this or concerned about it. If the danger of Indonesian military intervention in East Timor was to be

---

237   AIIPT #54.
238   AIIPT #56.

headed off, Whitlam's policy had, at this point, either to be jettisoned or radically re-engineered to give it such traction. Instead, the 'dialogue' Graham Feakes had recommended continued into 1975—and then all the way down the slope to near genocidal bloodshed and Australia's *de jure* recognition of the Indonesian conquest of East Timor, in 1979.

October 1974, not October 1975, was the end of the line for the Whitlam policy. Having been told what it had by Lim Bian Kie and Harry Tjan, the Australian government had either to find the means to oppose Indonesia—i.e. to harden and clarify its own policy by giving self-determination unambiguous priority over incorporation or to acknowledge its acquiescence in their Realpolitik project. This was the time for a more pro-active policy to be undertaken. Granted, there would be awkwardness in doing so, but for the pretense to continue that Whitlam's declaratory policy had any substance or integrity amounted to either delusion or mendacity.

It is also clear that, contrary to widespread perceptions, it was not the fall of Indochina to Communism, in April 1975, that led Suharto or Murdani to shift from eschewing expansionism, honouring self-determination, consulting Australia and taking things slowly, to plans for precipitate and uncompromising action. This shift must be attributed to endogenous, not exogenous influences on Jakarta. Finally, it is also clear from the October 1974 documents that Woolcott's line, in mid-1975, about Jakarta having made up its mind and expecting Australia to go along with it, was not something confected by him after his arrival on post in Jakarta, in March 1975. It was something which had become clear many months before that.

Sotto Voce Dissent, December 1974

In a secret cable from Jakarta dated 1 November 1974, Ambassador Furlonger wrote to Gordon Jockel, director of the Joint Intelligence Organization, concerning the 'series of conversations with Tjan, Lim Bian Kie and Yoga (Sugama, the head of BAKIN) regarding the possible resort by Indonesia' to military action of some sort to advance its policies in Portuguese Timor.' He told Jockel that 'the Indonesians can be in no doubt that we regard talk of military action as misplaced in current and foreseeable circumstances.' He then added: 'I assume, in any event, that you will be using the resources available to you to keep a close watch on military activity and deployment, just in case our judgment of likely Indonesian behaviour on this whole question should be excessively optimistic.'[239]

---

239 AIIPT #157. In July 1975, when Foreign Affairs challenged the Embassy on whether Tjan's briefings should be taken completely seriously—let me repeat, this was in July 1975, after a full year of such briefings, backed up by talks with Lim Bian Kie and Yoga Sugama—Malcolm Dan, the political counsellor in the Australian Embassy in Jakarta, responded at length, forthrightly setting out the many reasons for taking Tjan completely seriously. He then added an intriguing comment, which has found

Two things stand out about this. The first is that Furlonger had shifted from questioning the advisability of a covert operation to qualified optimism that Indonesia would not finally resort to force. He had slipped down the slope some distance, but gives no sign in this cable of unease at having done so. Of course, he was in good company back in Canberra. Yet among the 'currently foreseeable circumstances' was there not already the possibility that Portugal would not agree to a rapid transition, or that it would simply hand over autonomy to the Timorese, or that if there were a plebiscite the Timorese would not vote for incorporation? And had not Lim Bian Kie plainly told Furlonger that, in such circumstances, the use of force could not be ruled out? Had not Tjan hinted that Murdani was in the wings waiting to endorse such a use of force?

The second striking thing about Furlonger's cable is that he writes of Jockel using 'the resources available to you' to keep 'a close watch on military activity' in Indonesian territory with a view to possible action directed at Portuguese Timor. Exactly what these resources were remains classified, but in general terms such resources would include surveillance by signals intelligence monitoring and photo-reconnaissance, as well as defence intelligence liaison with other foreign intelligence services, especially the Americans and the British. This surveillance of Indonesia had long been one of Australia's primary tasks within the UKUSA signals intelligence treaty arrangements and has become increasingly important since the mid-1970s. The question of surveillance resources is worth noting, simply because intelligence records of the period under discussion have not been released, but there have been unconfirmed claims for nearly twenty years that a report based wholly on them, covering the entire Indonesian covert operation and invasion of Portuguese Timor, was compiled at Jockel's direction, within JIO, in 1976 and no later than 1977.[240]

---

its way into the published documents, despite the censoring of intelligence material in general:

> *With regard to Portuguese Timor, we have enough evidence from other [words expunged] sources to know that what Tjan is telling us is accurate. The [words expunged] sources are fascinating. I have suggested that someone in Australia might compile a report exclusively from these sources.*

It seems to me conceivable that Malcolm Dan's suggestion that such a report be compiled may have been the first germ of the idea for the creation of a highly classified document which insiders have long referred to as *The Blue Book*: a set of Australian signals intelligence materials on Indonesia and the whole matter of East Timor. In the early 1980s, not long after all this had taken place and while the fighting in East Timor remained severe and brutal, this file was described to Desmond Ball, Australia's leading academic specialist on intelligence matters, based at the Australian National University, by a senior JIO officer who had worked closely with Jockel in 1974-75, as 'the best study of Australian operational intelligence he had ever seen'. However, as far as I am aware, it was not until more than a year after Dan's suggestion that Jockel took up the idea and arranged for the creation of such a report.

240 This is *The Blue Book*. To the best of my knowledge, it was not put together until late 1975 and after, at

The slide of Australian policy down the slope to inextricable entanglement in Jakarta's Realpolitik gambit began at Jogjakarta, on 6 September 1974. It was given ominous momentum by the cable traffic through October and into November 1974. On 11 December 1974, senior foreign affairs and intelligence officers met to discuss the situation and Gordon Jockel, as Director of JIO, raised the question of military calculation. His analysis has been strongly vindicated by what happened after October 1975, so it is all the more significant that it was put on the record as early as it was. The record of the meeting tells us that:

> *Mr Jockel said that what concerned him was the appreciation of the situation on the ground; there was a risk that Portuguese Timor could turn out to be a 'running sore' for Indonesia. The situation was very different from West Irian; many of the inhabitants had military training (1,000 in the army, 15,000 formerly in the army and therefore with some military experience and 3,000 in the reserves who received regular training); given the nature of the terrain, it would be easy to mount and sustain a liberation movement with outside support. If a liberation movement did in fact develop, it would gradually attract international attention and Portuguese Timor would become more of an international issue.*[241]

Now what this fairly plainly indicates is that thinking—even in Jockel's canny and thoughtful mind—had shifted from heading off an Indonesian intervention, to hoping that a covert political intervention would work, to reflecting on whether a military intervention could succeed. Once this was where the issue stood, it all became a matter of competing intelligence estimates. The available evidence suggests that JIO's projections were more sceptical than BAKIN's, but Ambassador Woolcott—in late 1975, when the die was cast in any case—would reject JIO's arguments, in a Secret Austeo Priority cable from Jakarta.[242] He would accept Murdani's assurances that Indonesia would do whatever it took and would clean up Fretilin by the end of the year.

Given that Jockel had been the author of the 1963 report on the future of Portuguese Timor, his views of December 1974 are more than usually interesting. Having offered his estimate of the 'situation on the ground', the record declares that he went on to say that:

the instigation of Jockel. It reportedly consisted of two blue-coloured loose-leaf folders, one of them a 200 page dossier of raw intelligence on Indonesian covert operations against East Timor; the other a much slimmer volume of careful analysis of the use of that intelligence. I discussed this matter in an essay in *Quadrant* in November 2000 called 'Balibo: Murdani and the Memory Hole', which caused quite a stir. Paul Dibb, who had been Des Ball's informant, denied emphatically to me that he had ever heard of any such thing while in JIO. Yet when my sometime mentor in Defence Frank Lewincamp became Director General of DIO (formerly JIO), in the early 2000s, he personally confirmed its existence to me. It has long been my assumption that the considerable number of documents, including Defence and intelligence materials, that are still classified include sensitive materials to do with the Indonesian invasion of East Timor and Australia's internal deliberations about how to respond.

241 AIIPT #262
242 AIIPT #257

> *He had sympathy for the Indonesians in the present situation, in wanting to take control of Portuguese Timor now in order to prevent the realization of their worst fears. The real danger, however, was that the Indonesians would alienate those not in favour of integration and so push them to some form of extreme action. There were signs of a strong stiffening of Portuguese resistance to recent Indonesian activity; the situation was therefore becoming more difficult.*[243]

At this point, Michael Cook, then First Assistant Secretary of the North and West Asia Division, Foreign Affairs, who was to become Director of the Office of National Assessments (ONA) and in the 1980s and later be appointed Ambassador to Washington, commented that:

> *He agreed with Mr Jockel ... There seemed to have been a basic assumption that Portuguese Timor would be like West Irian: the people would accept integration,*[244] *and from this assumption followed our commitment to an international acceptable act of self-determination. However, what was now clear was that the people of Portuguese Timor were not malleable; integration was not a winnable goal ... so that in the long run independence may be better than integration.*

This was a very telling implicit admission. Cook was saying that agreement to an internationally acceptable act of self-determination was predicated on the assumption that the Timorese would accept integration (never having been consulted on the subject). But isn't the very idea of self-determination grounded in uncertainty as to its outcome? And should not Australia's policy toward Indonesia have been predicated on precisely this uncertainty? Wasn't that what Jockel himself had urged in 1963 and Feakes as recently as September 1974? And had not Harry Tjan's and Lim Bian Kie's briefings made it clear that the Indonesians themselves were not confident that the Timorese were 'malleable'?

What, then, to do about the Whitlam policy? That is the question these senior officials mooted, on 11 December 1974. It is sobering to discover that even Jockel, who had so lucidly set out the options in 1963, had no policy suggestions to offer at this critical juncture. All he

---

243 AIIPT #66

244 That the people of West Irian accepted integration is a highly questionable statement. They were not offered any choice. Under Indonesian occupation, in a rigged ballot, it was declared that West Irian was part of Indonesia. Anyone who had been opposing integration openly had been suppressed and such suppression has continued since. The whole matter is covered in great detail by John Francis Saltford in his PhD dissertation of 2000. The people of Irian Jaya sought genuine self-determination, while Sukarno insisted that any negotiations with them or the Dutch would have to be based on the pre-condition that the territory would pass to their control. A state called West Papua was created in December 1961, but suppressed by the Indonesians with UN and Australian acquiescence and even connivance. For Cook to have described what happened as acceptance of integration was a serious misrepresentation of what had actually occurred. It has not proven convenient for Australia to resist Indonesia's colonization of West Papua and so the realities on the ground have been consistently papered over and no comfort or support has been offered to the resistance movements that have existed there since the start. That is a matter of *raison d'état*, for better or worse. That such resistance has existed and has been ruthlessly suppressed is a matter of record.

was able to say was that 'incorporation into Indonesia should not be regarded as a foregone conclusion.' Truly? But had not the Indonesians stated plainly that they intended to 'ensure' this outcome? What now stood between their determination and an escalation of their covert machinations into military intervention; an intervention that Jockel apprehended could turn into a 'running sore for Indonesia'? The only such thing was Suharto's word to Whitlam that he did not intend things to end up that way; an assurance which Suharto seems to have meant sincerely enough.

Suharto did not want to be embarrassed by a violent intervention in East Timor. He miscalculated quite as badly as Whitlam did. What Whitlam did not make sufficient allowance for, on the other hand, was that Suharto and those around him had a track record of the ruthless use of force when it was expedient. The problem at the Canberra end was that the Whitlam policy was now based on a tenuous assumption that, if the Timorese failed to prove 'malleable', Suharto would pull back from the covert plan and refrain from military intervention. But Lim Bian Kie and Harry Tjan had expressly indicated that he probably would not. What this meant was that Suharto did not wish to use force unless it was absolutely necessary, but he had advisers around him who would urge him to use it.

By 11 December 1974, Jockel and Cook seemed to appreciate that it was what the Bible people call 'come to Jesus time'. Feakes appreciated that, as he put it to Foreign Minister Don Willesee on 13 December, 'there are grounds for regarding the outlook in Portuguese Timor as ominous.'[245] Woolcott, who was also, at the 11 December meeting, as Ambassador designate to Indonesia, did not agree. He certainly did not believe that the Whitlam policy needed to be modified in the circumstances. He told the 11 December meeting that he was 'not sure that the situation was a s bad as some seemed to think; the Prime Minister thought it would be better if Portuguese Timor was incorporated into Indonesia; but he had escape clauses if necessary.'[246]

Escape clauses? What a remarkable admission by the Ambassador designate to Jakarta. Escape clauses? Surely this is confirmation of the reasoning that what Whitlam had sought to create for himself was an alibi, in the event that Indonesian military intervention proved to be the only way to ensure the incorporation of Portuguese Timor? It would have been quite a different matter had Woolcott stated that the Prime Minister had a clear understanding with President Suharto that military intervention would be both unacceptable to Australia and destabilizing in the region. That's not what he said, however. He said the Prime Minister had 'escape clauses'.

---

245 AIIPT #66
246 AIIPT #67

In a lengthy submission to Foreign Minister Willesee, following the 11 December talks, Graham Feakes suggested that Australia might make a number of points to the Indonesians to the effect that, if an act of self-determination led to an independent Portuguese Timor, that would not necessarily damage the interests of either Indonesia or Australia. In other words, Australia should continue the dialogue with Indonesia about the subject; but any more robust action, he thought, would only impede Australian freedom of manoeuvre. He told the Foreign Minister: 'the less we become involved ... and the less we are called upon publicly to explain our views about self-determination, the freer we are in our choice of policies and tactics ... and the more options we can keep open the better.'[247]

Just what options he believed would be open, if OPSUS proceeded to implement the Murtopo/Tjan plan, the United Nations was not involved and the Timorese insisted ion independence, he did not even attempt to spell out. What was going through his mind? He conceded the situation was ominous, but thought that Australia's freedom of manoeuvre would be best enhanced or at least maintained by continuing nothing other than continuing a dialogue that had already implicated Canberra in Indonesia's covert efforts to have its way. This was not freedom of manoeuvre, I suggest; it was free fall. The fascinating thing is to observe how the diplomatic establishment kept imagining for months after this that it was being very clever, when all it was doing was falling short of cementing the relationship with Jakarta that Whitlam professed to want and that Tjan was actively seeking; deluding itself about what was likely to happen; lying to the outside world about its commitment to genuine self-determination for the Timorese; and laying up trouble for itself domestically. Yet, when all of this broke over its head in late 1975, it would insist that it had done everything possible to ensure a different outcome. It plainly had done nothing of the kind.

Policy Coherence and Realpolitik

On 22 January 1975, the two largest political groupings in Portuguese Timor, UDT (the Timorese Democratic Union) and Fretilin, declared that they had merged and that jointly they sought 'total independence' for the colony, to be arranged under UN auspices, without either Indonesia or Australia (which they saw as under Indonesian influence) being involved. This was the point of no return for Australian policy. Foreign Minister Willesee had already written to Whitlam on 14 January, stating that the 11 December meeting had indicated that the two desiderata of the established policy were incompatible—'self-determination is likely to yield a result other than the association of Portuguese Timor with Indonesia.'[248]

---

247 AIIPT #71
248 AIIPT #75

On 30 January, Harry Tjan briefed Allan Taylor, the new First Secretary in the Embassy, who had replaced Jan Arriens the previous month, to the effect that the UDT/Fretilin joint communique had strengthened the influence of Indonesian hardliners, led by Murdani, on the special committee that made policy on Portuguese Timor. He said that Suharto and members of the special committee 'had difficulty in understanding why Australia placed so much emphasis on the need for an act of self-determination.' If, at this point, the desideratum of incorporation, with its corollary of good relations with Indonesia, was to be allowed to stand (which it was), then it logically entailed giving up both the desideratum of self-determination for the Timorese and fastidiousness about Indonesia's means in denying it to them. This had been the approach taken with West Irian only a decade before, under Menzies. But under Whitlam things remained unresolved.

On 28 February 1975, the Australian Prime Minister signed a letter to President Suharto, which was delivered by Richard Woolcott on 8 March, when he presented his credentials as Ambassador in Jakarta. In the letter, Whitlam did raise with the Indonesian leader the possibility of a new understanding about the situation in the Portuguese colony. The letter would repay close analysis, but I shall not linger over it here, since no such new understanding in fact emerged. On 10 March 1975, Tjan told Taylor that, in all the circumstances, Suharto 'placed great store on what Mr Whitlam had told him about Australian policy. He believed that he could trust Mr Whitlam to fulfil his word.' What 'word' was that? We have to assume it was—at least in Suharto's mind—that Australian policy would remain in favour of incorporation and that Australia would give priority to its relationship with Indonesia over its concerns about self-determination for the East Timorese.

Whitlam had his chance to personally clarify any possible misunderstanding on this matter when he met with Suharto on Australian soil, in Townsville, on 4 April 1975. Although both leaders stated that they did not want the matter to come down to the use of force, the record indicates that Whitlam reiterated to Suharto that ultimately desideratum number 1 (incorporation) had priority over desideratum number 2 (self-determination). I believe the record also shows that Suharto made a serious effort between April and October 1975, in good faith with Whitlam, to avoid the use of force. He explored all other avenues for ensuring rapid incorporation of the colony into Indonesia, but none of them worked. He held back Murdani and the military interventionists in August 1975, when the opportunity to intervene with some semblance of legitimacy was most open because of the civil strife that erupted between UDT and Fretilin over the internal governance of the territory.

Nothing worked for him, but instead of pulling back and cutting his losses, he finally, in October 1975, permitted Murdani to proceed with covert military intervention. Murdani had assured him that this would turn the trick, but it simply became an embarrassment, first because of the Balibo incident on the first day and then because the whole operation, having run into serious resistance, became bogged down. Even then, Suharto would not pull back. In early December 1975, he allowed Murdani to unleash the dogs of war with an open and large scale invasion. Australia slipped with him all the way down the slope, hoping each new effort would work. None of them did, but both Whitlam and his diplomats insisted that their own hands were clean. In sober truth, their hands were clean only in the sense that they had long since washed their hands of any responsibility for the fate of the people of East Timor. When, under the Fraser government, Canberra endorsed Indonesian annexation, the Australian government became an accomplice after the fact to the means as well as the end that had been involved.

On the eve of the 4 April 1975 Townsville talks, the new Ambassador to Indonesia, Richard Woolcott, wrote to Whitlam:

> *My own belief is that we should seek to disengage ourselves as much as possible from the Timor situation, which could well become pretty messy. Indonesia is very unlikely to mount a military invasion of Timor unless it regards the situation there as hopeless and as a real threat to its security. But the Indonesian government has not abandoned its ultimate objective of integrating Timor and it will pursue both covert and overt activity to influence Portuguese Timor to decide in favour of integration at the eventual act of self-determination.*[249]

This was carefully worded, of course, since there had been no agreement on any act of self-determination and Canberra had long since been informed that the senior Indonesians could not really see why Australia was so concerned that there should be one. Was Woolcott as ignorant of the West Irian precedent as Michael Cook, or as willing to stick with the threadbare cover story that had been created for the so-called 'Act of Free Choice' there in 1969? It would certainly seem so.

That said, in the months that followed, from the Embassy in Jakarta, Woolcott was to become the clearest-minded advocate within the government for a policy that was at least *coherent*, given that the two desiderata of the Whitlam policy had manifestly come asunder by late 1974. And it is his testimony, in a cable to Canberra dated 15 October 1975, - the eve of the covert military invasion of East Timor by Murdani's special forces—that Whitlam had made plain to Suharto at Townsville that if it came down to a choice between the two desiderata, then he (Whitlam) would side with Suharto rather than insist on self-determination for the East Timorese.

I quote Woolcott's cable at length, because this was, it seems to me, where the final slide began, even though Canberra dragged its heels and persisted in its muddled and self-serving double-talk all the way to its *de jure* recognition of Indonesian annexation of East Timor, in 1979:

> *On the basis of the Townsville talks, President Suharto will assume that the Australian government will make every effort to give Indonesia what support and understanding it can. The Prime Minister's statement in the House of Representatives on 26 August confirmed this assumption. An example of Indonesia's confidence that the Australian government understands and is sympathetic with its objective*

---

249 AIIPT #262

of integration is the extent to which it keeps us informed of its secret plans. The Indonesian government is aware of the different views in Australia on relations with Indonesia and on the Portuguese Timor issue. It expects criticism in Australia. It expects the government to react critically against the future of Portuguese Timor being decided without the wishes of the people of the territory being ascertained. But there is no doubt in my mind that the Indonesian government's fundamental assessment of our position is predicated on the talks between Whitlam and President Suharto in Townsville.

Particularly important to the Indonesians was the Prime Minister's view expressed in the Record as follows: 'He wished to reaffirm, however, that we strongly desired closer and more cordial relations with Indonesia and would ensure that our actions in regard to Portuguese Timor would always be guided by the principle that good relations with Indonesia were of paramount importance to Australia.' While the way in which the situation has evolved—the collapse of Portugal's decolonization policy and UDT and Fretilin's resort to force—was not foreseen in Townsville, the President would, I believe, make the assumption that, if the two main strands of Australian policy, namely understanding of Indonesia's position and support for integration, on the one hand; and support for self-determination, on the other, were to become irreconcilable, - as they appear to have become—then the Australian government would attach more weight to the former consideration than the latter.[250]

Some would judge this passage damning of both Whitlam and Woolcott. I do not. I think Woolcott's reasoning was pellucid. This was, indeed, the position in which Whitlam had long since placed Australia's policy; and had that policy been guided by Garfield Barwick or Keith Waller there is every reason to believe they would have acted just as Whitlam had done—with the same results. No-one in the Department of Foreign Affairs to whom Woolcott was writing in October 1975 had suggested any robust steps toward amending the policy or reversing its priorities in all the months between Tjan's first briefings to Arriens and a briefing which took place on 13 October 1975, at which Malcolm Dan and Allan Taylor were informed that Indonesia was about to undertake, at last, a covert military invasion of East Timor.

If one disagreed with Woolcott's reasoning at that late stage—and many did, from William Pritchett in Defence Planning to Alan Renouf, the actual Secretary of Foreign Affairs—then one needed to be able to propose an alternative policy with some traction. Such traction, as I have shown, never had been built into the Whitlam policy. Nor had an alternative policy with traction been developed or submitted for Whitlam's consideration after the September 1974 talks had left the gate dangerously ajar. Feakes had, of course, quietly suggested points for dialogue and a small number of people spoke up within internal meetings about the possibility that the Timorese might prove less than 'malleable'; but the governing desideratum of policy was that incorporation take place and that Australian relations with Indonesia not be adversely affected by any stand Australia might choose to take. There was no coherent fall-back position. To the extent that self-determination ever received serious consideration, no plan was so much as proposed as to how it might actually be engineered. Nor were there any practical plans about how to inhibit Indonesia use of force except through 'dialogue'. When Bill Pritchett in Defence suggested a 'major effort of statesmanship' to this end, on 9 October 1975, it was very late in the day and he still failed to spell out of what such an effort should actual consist.

This is not to argue that Woolcott's line of reasoning was correct, only that it was rational and at least had the merit of being coherent. It is conceivable that, even in October 1975, it would have been possible for Whitlam to break his word to Suharto and take a firm stand against any kind of Indonesian military intervention in East Timor. Logically, or abstractly, that was possible. In reality, it was both vanishingly unlikely and would have entailed considerable risks. Clearly, Whitlam believed that incorporation had to happen. He did not believe that an independent East Timor was either a viable or desirable idea. He firmly believed—and in this he was in good bipartisan company—that Australia's relationship with Indonesia was much too important for it to be made hostage to the fate of tiny East Timor. He almost certainly did not believe that military intervention would be other than a quick, decisive affair resulting in Indonesian control of the enclave. The Indonesians clearly thought the same. They were, as Jockel and Cook foresaw, badly in error. The grim reality was that, by October 1975, Whitlam had left himself no options other to avert his eyes while Suharto acted. Woolcott understood that and advised that this be Australia's formal policy.

Having listened to the briefings from Harry Tjan and Lim Bian Kie for so many months, Australia's policy and intelligence officers knew perfectly well that they were being complicit in a covert plan to subvert genuine self-determination in Portuguese Timor. They had also learned, step by step, that the plan was not working. Yet they adopted a policy of 'studied detachment'—a policy of the clever alibi. They had a dialogue with the Indonesians about purely notional alternatives all the way down the slippery slope and then, to Woolcott's frustration, in December 1975 and for some months thereafter, Canberra let Jakarta down by protesting against the use of force, rendering Australian policy doubly incoherent, since the only rationale for not taking self-determination seriously had been better relations with Jakarta. The now declassified documents show in detail just how uncomfortable many of the diplomats and intelligence officers were at the course of events from October 1975 onwards. Yet there was no turning back and the 'bargain' with Jakarta was finally sealed by *de jure* recognition of its annexation in 1979.

Should we single Whitlam out in all this for some special blame? Blame for a policy gone awry; for the catastrophe that the Indonesian invasion inflicted on hundreds of thousands of East Timorese? Ultimately, as the Prime Minister and the self-styled architect of Australia's policy on the matter, as well as the immediate interlocutor with Suharto, he has to take responsibility for what happened, even though the worst of it happened after he left office in December

1975, rejected overwhelmingly by the Australian people. The crucial policy lessons make a good subject for reflection. They seem to me to be threefold: no-one was able to constrain the Prime Minister's headstrong lack of caution and presumption that he knew best; there was no shared sense that practical measures would be required if Australia was to have any influence on Indonesia's actions; and there was no apparent mechanism for ensuring that the problems raised by the lack of options would be systematically addressed. The consequence was that everything Jockel had foreseen and warned against in 1963 happened in 1974-79.

The greatest irony of Whitlam's approach to the problem is that even the Indonesians felt betrayed when Canberra voted in favour of a censure motion against Indonesia in December 1975 at the United Nations. To be sure, Whitlam had never said that Australia would condone the use of force; but he had clearly encouraged Suharto down a path which was only ever going to end in the use of force and he cannot have been so naïve as to have failed to see what was happening in 1975. As Woolcott argued, Australia had given what the Indonesians took to be assurances of tacit partnership in what they embarked upon. Furlonger had warned in July 1974 that this would be the case unless Australia made very clear that it did not support the whole covert action plan and was committed to genuine self-determination for East Timor. Had Whitlam sincerely supported Suharto, he had the option of backing him in August 1975 to intervene in the East Timorese civil strife under a UN mandate to 'restore order'. He did not have the courage of his convictions and lost this opportunity to accept the unworkability of his confused policy and throw in his lot with Suharto on a realistic basis.

In June 1976, with the invasion in East Timor turning into a bloody mess and a running sore for Indonesia, Harry Tjan came to see Allan Taylor once again; the briefings never having ceased since July 1974.[251] Taylor summarized the meeting in a cable to Canberra as follows:

> We had a long discussion about the history of the Timor issue. Tjan's main point was that Australia, with good intentions, had planted the idea that that East Timor should be part of Indonesia and events had moved so quickly that it had not been possible to work out a solution with the Portuguese. I said that I did not accept that Australia had determined the general direction of Indonesian policy to the extent that he claimed. He said that what he was really claiming was that Australian interest had focused Indonesian attention on East Timor.[252]

This is an extraordinary exchange and quite fascinating in its implications. Tjan was implying that Australia had in fact *exercised* a degree of influence that its diplomats never *sought* to exercise[253];

---

251 But see note 192 on p. 155. As Jan Arriens wrote, the briefings had not started in July 1974, but in May 1973.

252 AIIPT #457

253 This almost certainly remains true, despite what Jan Arriens revealed to me; since it appears highly improbable that Wilenski, speaking for Whitlam, would have sought to influence Tjan and through

such was their uncertainty about what to do. Taylor evaded the central problem clearly present to Jockel in 1963 and Furlonger in 1974: that *unless* Australia actively sought to influence Indonesia in constructive directions and to corral its possible proclivities to use force, things could get out of hand - as they plainly had. And *both* avoided the significance of Whitlam's statement to Suharto in September 1974, in express disregard of the advice from Foreign Affairs; that he believed Portuguese Timor *should* be part of Indonesia and that his view would very likely soon become Australian policy.

This preference had been the shadow side of Australia's policy all along, as we have seen, with reference to the views of Garfield Barwick in 1963. The fact that Whitlam, in his defence of his prime ministership, *Abiding Interests* (1997), cites the views of Barwick from 1963 as evidence of the soundness of his own policy reinforces this surmise. The circumstances which would have made it 'easiest for any Australian government not to become involved with military obligations while acquiescing in the passage of Timor to Indonesia', in Waller's words to Jockel of 1963, would surely have been those suggested by Whitlam to Suharto at Jogjakarta in September 1974: an internationally acceptable act of self-determination by the Timorese resulting in incorporation into Indonesia. This was, indeed, what Barwick hoped, in 1963, could eventually be engineered—along the lines of the arrangements in West Irian at that very time. Had there been, in 1974-75, any serious prospect of such an act and such an outcome being genuine, no-one is likely to have objected. When it became clear that a genuine act would not yield 'passage to Indonesia', Australia had to choose where its interests truly lay.

The Whitlam government, did not want any military obligations in 1975, any more than the Menzies government had in 1963; and official Canberra liked the Indonesia of Suharto a great deal more than it had that of Sukarno a decade earlier. That made the choice difficult, but it was a false choice, or would have been, had Jockel's pro-active diplomacy informed policy before 1974. Australia would have served the Timorese and the Indonesians, as well as itself, better by having in place a policy that would have supported Suharto in not intervening covertly and then militarily in the affairs of the Portuguese colony. Ironically, the unravelling of the Indonesian annexation of East Timor, in 1998-99, landed Australia with all but ineluctable military obligations in the passage of the territory *from* Indonesia, while causing some considerable difficulties for Canberra's relationship with Indonesia.

Little states are often morally and strategically inconvenient in the geopolitical affairs of the

---

him Suharto in the direction of taking over Portuguese Timor. But it does seem as though first Wilenski and then Arriens, by his own account, raised the matter of Timor with Tjan in the first instance; not the other way around.

world. Portuguese Timor was an awkward geopolitical anachronism in the 1960s and early 1970s. Indonesia's concerns about it were comprehensible. It is now, as a newly independent state, less an anachronism in the archipelago to Australia's north than a geopolitical aneurism, as it were. There seems no good reason to believe that the problems caused by its internal realities have now been dealt with. There are good reasons to believe that it is now only one of an increasing number of Melanesian and Islamic would-be micro-states in Australia's immediate region whose uncertain status and restiveness will require vigilant attention for many years to come. The largest of these is West Papua itself—West Irian or Irian Jaya. In a marvellous historical irony, that whereas the 1962-63 passage of West Papua to Indonesia prompted the governments of Australia and Indonesia to turn their attention to the future of Portuguese Timor; the 1999 passage of East Timor from Indonesia to independence has led both governments to turn their attention to unrest in West Papua.

The wheel has turned, if not full circle, then 180 degrees. Under these circumstances, all those concerned with stability and security in island Southeast Asia would be foolish not to reflect on how the Whitlam's government's efforts to avoid responsibility produced compromised and flawed diplomacy. Australia cannot ultimately avoid responsibility for the stability and security of its region by seeking the path of least resistance. Nor can it sustain the confidence of regional governments, beginning with that of its largest near neighbour, Indonesia, by adopting incoherent policies. This was demonstrated in slow motion, over twenty five years, in the case of East Timor. It should be recognized and acted upon in the years ahead in regard to West Papua and the many little states or would-be states of the Southwest Pacific. Australia must be imaginatively and responsibly pro-active, rather than disengaged or inclined to settle for 'dialogue'. And in such cases, it needs to develop policies with some resilience that have traction in a dangerous world and are not founded on wishful thinking or on slippery exercises in Realpolitik.[254]

---

254 In a long letter to me in 2001, as I was preparing this paper for publication, Jan Arriens wrote:

> *I was in the Policy Planning Group in 1972 and 1973 (under Roger Holdich). I think we produced some very thoughtful, well-researched papers ... Portuguese Timor is precisely the sort of thing the Group should have looked at, but never did. The subject needed a lengthy paper covering previous official consideration of the topic, in the way that comes out now in the documents that have been published. As it was, I feel that our collective memory was very short or even non-existent. Certainly in Jakarta we regarded the history of Australian/Indonesian relations over Timor as starting in 1973/74. We were dealing with a clean slate ... .Hardly anyone was standing back and looking at the broader historical, political and strategic sweep. We did not have any collective memory to draw upon in Jakarta. On top of that, Whitlam smashed through the cautious pirouetting of his policy briefs.*

He also confessed:

> ... some years after I resigned, in the 1980s, as the scale of the killing and cruelty in Timor became clear, I felt a terrible sense of complicity, combined with guilt and shame that we had not foreseen how dreadful it all would be ... Most of all, I was appalled that Australia was tacitly acquiescing in what was going on and seemed too craven to condemn the Indonesian atrocities. The picture of Gareth Evans in the aeroplane at the time of signing the Timor Gap Treaty must surely be one of the most shameful images in our entire foreign policy.

Yet, he adds, at the time he was in the diplomatic service: 'I was totally infused with the spirit of Realpolitik. Had I stayed on [in the Embassy in Jakarta into 1975], I think I would have served very comfortably under Dick Woolcott.'

The allure of Mary McCarthy[255]

Who, under the age of thirty, now remembers Mary McCarthy? She was the George Orwell of women's liberation—the genuine article—but she has not achieved the iconic status of the author of *Animal Farm* and *Nineteen Eighty-Four*. Her writings seem to be fading into comparative obscurity only twelve years after her death. This is a pity, because the way she lived her life and the spirit in which she wrote deserve to be a role model for young women for a long time to come.

Pauline Kael, the noted American film critic, said of McCarthy that she 'really was *the* cultural heroine of my generation ... before feminist writing got bogged down in victimization.' Decades before Germaine Greer and Gloria Steinem, McCarthy lived a full, free, bold and iconoclastic life, with no quarter asked and none given. She wrote more than twenty books, went through four marriages and many love affairs, mixed it with the most formidable intellectuals of her time without fear or favour, had a son, travelled widely and never lost a passion for truth and beauty. As her friend, Niccolo Tucci, expressed it, 'She loved to drink, she loved to cook, she loved to make love, she loved to have friends, she loved to fight. You don't often find that.'

This was a woman to remember and to esteem. Frances Kiernan's biography *Seeing Mary Plain: A Life of Mary McCarthy* shows why. It highlights the opinions of many of McCarthy's contemporaries concerning her and a lot of other things. It recalls the Warren Beatty film about John Reed and Louise Bryant, *Reds*, in which the action is interrupted at regular intervals by interviews with ageing contemporaries of the couple. It is a fascinating supplement to earlier biographies by Carol Gelderman and Carol Brightman.

McCarthy was a *rara avis*, a rare bird: a truly sexy intellectual, who was nonetheless more interested in truth than in merely being fashionable or exhibitionist. There is a beautiful passage in Elizabeth Hardwick's foreword to McCarthy's posthumously published *Intellectual Memoirs: New York 1936-38*, in which her friend of four decades wrote: 'Intellectual responses are known as opinions and Mary had them and had them. She was so little of an ideologue as to be sometimes

---

[255] This essay was originally published in *The Australian Financial Review's* Friday Review, under the title 'A truly sexy intellectual', on 3 August 2001. I have always been attracted to intelligent women and have never understood men who were afraid of them. Mary McCarthy struck me as the epitome of the attractively intelligent woman, but it was Hannah Arendt, as she had been in the 1920s and 1930s, with whom I 'fell in love' as a graduate student. There was a photograph of the young Hannah Arendt on the back cover of Elizabeth Young-Bruehl's biography *Hannah Arendt: For Love of the World*; a book which I read while in the United States on fieldwork for my PhD, in 1984-85. I was besotted by the dark intensity of Hannah's eyes and her evident intelligence. And, of course, the story of her life and writings was utterly absorbing.

unsettling in her refusal of tribal reaction—Left or Right, male or female, that sort of thing. She was doggedly personal and often this meant being so aslant that there was, in this determined rationalist, an endearing crankiness; very American and homespun somehow.' There, in a nutshell, is the role model for a new generation of women—and men.

Kiernan pays her own tribute to McCarthy: 'She was a great heroine to many young women of my age for her independence and her courage in speaking out in defence of lost causes and for her ability to combine great personal glamour with a ferocious intelligence.' Both the great personal glamour and the ferocious intelligence are amply testified to by the numerous contemporaries of McCarthy whom Kiernan quotes. Arthur Schlesinger Jr, for example, declared: 'I absolutely adored Mary. I was transfixed by her. She was so beautiful, so witty, so much fun to talk to.' Carmen Angleton declared: 'She was very beautiful ... both witty and sparkling ... like something out of Shakespeare, something out of *A Midsummer Night's Dream*.'

Others remarked that 'She looked primeval, like the Venus de Milo'; 'She was like a goddess in our midst' and 'She was like a black-haired Grace Kelly.' Oddly, the photographs published in Kiernan's book, like those in Gelderman's, do not show an especially beautiful woman. The exception is a stylized picture used on the cover of McCarthy's book of short stories, *The Company She Keeps*, in 1943. In that photograph, she does, indeed, look as beautiful as Grace Kelly. Otherwise, she looks much plainer. Perhaps, like Cleopatra, her greatest charm was her intelligence in conversation? The ferocious intellect was described by a wounded Alfred Kazin as 'a wholly destructive critical mind'; but praised by Isaiah Berlin for its 'masculine quality ... strong, direct, cutting ... tough ... and utterly honest.' Norman Mailer called McCarthy 'our First Lady of letters.'

The combination of glamour and ferocity was inimitably described by William Barrett. He observed that she was one writer whom the notoriously spiteful and egomaniacal intellectual circle 'could not intimidate in any way'. 'I see her,' he commented, 'in the image of a Valkyrie maiden, riding her steed into the circle, amid thunder and lightning, and out again, bearing the body of some dead hero across her saddle.'

In 1933, fresh out of Vassar College, the 21 year old McCarthy plunged into the intellectual world of New York. It was the height of the Great Depression and there were so many Communists among the New York intelligentsia that Norman Mailer later dubbed the Big Apple of that time 'the most interesting part of the Soviet Union.' As Jason Epstein remarked, in 1994, the Stalinists 'were a very powerful gang in those days, like the political correctness lot now.' While coping with an ill-considered first marriage and struggling to make her mark as a young freelance writer, McCarthy found her feet in this milieu—and stayed on them.

The New York Left, with whom McCarthy was intimate, was broken apart by the Moscow Trials of 1936-37 and the 1939 pact between Hitler and Stalin. McCarthy avoided ever becoming either a Stalinist or a Trotskyist, while nonetheless writing for the leading Left-wing journal of the time, *Partisan Review*. She acquired a reputation for being both literate and pugnacious— and sexually quite voracious. After breaking free of her first, unsuccessful marriage, McCarthy went through a period of rather remarkable sexual promiscuity. Her candour on the subject, in her *Intellectual Memoirs*, is so astonishing as to be almost uproariously funny. 'Of all the men I slept with on my studio bed on Gay St (and there were a lot; I stopped counting),' she wrote of her sexual binge in the winter of 1936-37, 'I liked Bill Mangold the best—until I began to see Philip Rahv.' Rahv (1908-73) was one of the editors of *Partisan Review*; a charismatic and fiercely independent Marxist Lothario.

'It was getting rather alarming,' she reflected in her 70s. 'I realized one day that in 24 hours I had slept with three different men. And one morning, I was in bed with somebody while over his head I talked on the telephone with somebody else ... I did not feel promiscuous. Maybe no-one does. And maybe more girls sleep with more men than you would ever think to look at them.' What was she looking for? She herself was quite unsure, which was reflected in her impulsive decision to marry the literary critic Edmund Wilson in 1938. Yet, on the whole, she seems simply to have seen it all as a time of exploration and free experiment.

'I was able to compare the sexual equipment of the various men I made love with,' McCarthy wrote, 'and there were amazing differences in both length and massiveness. One handsome married man who used to arrive with two Danishes from a very good bakery, had a penis about the size and shape of a lead pencil. He shall remain nameless. In my experience, there was usually a relation to height, as Philip Rahv and Bill Mangold, both tall men, bore out. There may be dwarfish men with monstrously large organs, but I have never known one. It was not until later, after my second divorce, that I met an impotent man or a pervert (two of the latter) ... None of my partners, the reader will be relieved to hear, had a venereal disease.' Her tongue was surely in her cheek in writing these wry lines.

Diana Trilling told Kiernan that she found McCarthy's account of her promiscuity 'chilling', but this is someone who also found McCarthy's irrepressibly iconoclastic approach to politics 'irresponsible' and 'stupid'. Susan Sontag's remarks are both more perceptive and more humane. She commented not simply of McCarthy's promiscuous binge but of her sexuality more generally that McCarthy seemed never to have enjoyed sex. 'There's no sensuality in her writing,' Sontag commented.

There is a fascinating passage in McCarthy's most famous short story, 'The Man in the Brooks Brothers Shirt', published in 1943, which perhaps goes to the heart of her sexual persona, though Sontag does not appear to have seen this and Trilling not at all. McCarthy's heroine, Meg Sargent, is reflecting on how, ever since her adolescence, her boldness and willingness to swap 'dirty jokes with the college boys' had provoked men into tackling her 'like a football dummy'. She reflects, 'and of course she had invited it, just as she was inviting it now; but what she was really asking all along was not that the male should assault her, but that he should believe her a woman. This freedom of speech of hers was a kind of masquerade of sexuality ... But the men, she thought, did not look into it so deeply; they could only respond by leaping at her—which, after all, she supposed was their readiest method of showing her that her impersonation had been convincing.' Impersonation? Of what, precisely?

Coming suddenly out of her reverie, she tells the man in the Brooks Brothers shirt, 'You know what my favourite quotation is?...It's from Chaucer ... Criseyde says it: 'I am myne owene woman, wel at ese.' That, at least, is what McCarthy wanted to be. In many ways, she was. That's what makes her so admirable a role model for women even now. If she did not seem always to enjoy sex, it was surely because becoming her own woman well at ease required a lot of work, given her Catholic upbringing, her lack of independent means and the tendency of men to lunge at her without too much regard to her enjoyment. It rather astonishes me that neither Trilling nor Sontag could see how remarkable her adventurous achievement was against this background.

Memories of a Catholic Girlhood, published in 1957, is perhaps McCarthy's most memorable book. It is beautifully written and, as much as anything she wrote, it invites favourable comparison with Germaine Greer's *The Female Eunuch*. Nothing that happened to her ever turned McCarthy into a female eunuch: neither the loss of her parents, when she was still a child; nor bewilderment at Catholic dogma; nor loneliness in adolescence; nor poverty as a young writer; nor abuse by the alcoholic Edmund Wilson; nor the scorn of critics. There is a passage in the book which seems to me to convey much of the humanity of McCarthy and to show how she developed an anti-dogmatic and resolutely humanistic credo as she matured.

As with much else in the book, it comes in a reflection on her grandmother:

> *Combativeness was, I suppose, the dominant trait in my grandmother's nature. An aggressive church goer, she was quite without Christian feeling; the mercy of the Lord Jesus had never entered her heart. Her piety was an act of war against the Protestant ascendancy ... articles attacking birth control, divorce, mixed marriages, Darwin and secular education were her favourite reading. The teachings of the Church did not interest her, except as they were a rebuke to others ... The extermination of Protestantism, rather than spiritual perfection, was the boon she prayed for.'*

Later, it would be the extermination of Communism, rather than civic virtue and the good society—not for her grandmother, but for all too many of her American contemporaries.

McCarthy's capacity for irony and aversion from dogma carried her right through the hurly burly of American Leftism, from the 1930s to the 1980s, without her ever becoming either a party hack or a born again conservative. It is striking that, in the critical study of the Congress for Cultural Freedom and its links with the CIA, published in 1999, Frances Stonor Saunders referred to remarks by McCarthy again and again, as almost a touchstone for what a truly independent democratic intellectual should have been like in the 1950s and 1960s. One of the things that infuriated Mary McCarthy was the reluctance of the anti-Stalinist Left in America in the 1950s to attack 'McCarthyism' – the red-baiting and anti-intellectual populist rhetoric of Senator Joseph McCarthy.

Saunders quotes the outspoken Senator William Fulbright as remarking of the Joseph McCarthy phenomenon:

Our leaders became liberated from the normal rules of evidence and inference when it came to dealing with Communism. After all, who ever heard of giving the Devil a fair shake? Since we know what he has in mind, it is pedantry to split hairs over what he is actually doing ... '.

Mary McCarthy, however, avoided this trap; not because she wanted to give the Stalinist Devil a fair shake, but simply because of her passion for truthfulness. Unfortunately, her passion was not matched by a capacity to make a major impression as a political intellectual. Her true calling was surely literature and perhaps memoir.

When she tried, in the 1960s especially, to take on the world of international relations and the Vietnam War, her writings fell flat. Even those of her greatest friend, Hannah Arendt, provoked controversy and mixed reactions, but they were on an altogether different level from her own efforts. Indeed, after her early promise as a story writer, even her literary creativity never quite fulfilled its promise. Norman Mailer, like John Updike, felt that she began at the top of her form ('Like Hemingway', Updike said), only to fall away afterwards, Mailer told Kiernan that 'he was in awe of Mary McCarthy' as a young man. 'I read *The Company She Keeps* my sophomore year at Harvard. It was a consummate piece of work. It seemed so finished ... I hoped for more from her in later work. I kept thinking she'd write a great novel. In those days, I had no idea how difficult it is to write a great novel.'

Her best seller *The Group* (1963), which has sold more than five million copies worldwide, was not a great novel. It was, rather, a quasi-memoir which exhibited an invincible preoccupation with her undergraduate days at Vassar College. The most instructive contrast is, I think, with Simone De Beauvoir's *The Mandarins*. McCarthy detested De Beauvoir as 'an odious, athletic nun', but her novel is a far more accomplished and interesting piece of work than *The Group*. Too much of McCarthy's writing was, in Kiernan's phrase, 'nakedly confessional', so that, for all her wit and honesty, she never quite became an artist of the first rank. Why, however, should this be held against her? The real beauty of her life and work is that she was an explorer who never compromised her freedom or integrity. Her writing was symptomatic of this. It never quite became an end in itself, but remained, throughout her life, a means for articulating herself as 'her own woman'. In that, she succeeded marvellously and it is the way in which she did it for which she deserves lasting respect and emulation.

Part II: Early 21st century pieces

Section 1: 2007-08

Integrity, secrecy and the public interest[256]

The best film in town is *The Lives of Others*, a German drama about the Stasi, the secret police, in East Germany. If you have not seen it, you must. It is a deeply moving and theatrically accomplished film that goes to the heart of the great questions of accountability in government and moral integrity in citizens. It's a great stimulus right now to clear thinking about issues we face in our own society—issues to do with leaks, ethics and the public interest.

Written and directed by Florian Henckel von Donnersmarck, *The Lives of Others* explores the way in which a senior government minister, Bruno Hempf, uses the Stasi to blackmail a woman he desires (the actress Christa Marta Sieland) and to keep under surveillance and try to destroy her lover (the playwright Georg Dreyman). It is set in the mid-1980s, but concludes with the breaking down of the Berlin Wall and the downfall of the sinister regime it protected for a generation. At centre frame, however, is Stasi officer Gerd Wiesler, an ascetic, a committed communist, an accomplished Stasi interrogator—and, as it turns out, a man of integrity; a good man.

Wiesler is assigned to put Dreyman and Sieland under surveillance. Their apartment is thoroughly bugged and he listens in on their lives for a whole shift every day, whence the title of the film. He suspects Dreyman is a subversive; an arrogant and self-indulgent artist who secretly opposes socialism. He learns that he is mistaken. He also learns that the minister is coercing Sieland into providing him with sexual favours and that his own boss, Anton Grubitz, is playing along with all this for his own venal motives. Out of a sense of duty, he does his job; but gradually, overhearing the lives of Dreyman and Sieland drives him to subvert the agenda of Hempf and Grubitz, at the cost of his own career.

The turning point, the plot point in cinematic terms, of the film comes when the blacklisted theatre director, Albert Jerska, who had given Dreyman, as a 40th birthday present, the piano score of a piece of music called *Sonata for a Good Man*, commits suicide in despair. Dreyman plays the piece in shock at the news and says to Sieland, "How could any man who listens to

---

[256] This opinion piece dates from 2007. There is a six year interval between it and the Mary McCarthy essay, chiefly because during that time I wrote dozens of other essays and almost no short pieces. I had thriving relationships with Hugh Lamberton at the *Australian Financial Review* and Paddy McGuinness at *Quadrant*. When Lamberton left the AFR in 2007 and was replaced as editor of the Friday Review by Robert Bolton, this era came to an end. Since my consulting business had become relatively busy by then, I decided it was time to move on. One fruit of this was the decision, in 2008, to bring together thirty of the AFR essays in a book called *The West in a Nutshell: Foundations, Fragilities, Futures* (Barrallier Books, 2009).

this music—I mean really listens to it!—not be a good man?" Wiesler is listening and the whole situation affects him so directly that a single tear rolls down his cheek.

Now Dreyman decides that enough is enough. Still oblivious to the fact that he is under surveillance, he decides to write an article about suicides and the death of hope in East Germany and to smuggle it out to the West, for publication in *Der Spiegel*. Wiesler overhears everything, but covers for Dreyman and foils Hempf and Grubitz. In the process, however, the meat-grinder of the Stasi destroys Sieland. Grubitz calls her in, submits her to coercive interrogation and, under pressure, she weakens and betrays her beloved. Even then, Wiesler secretly intervenes to save Dreyman. But he cannot save Sieland from her own despair. She throws herself under a truck and is killed—the very theme Dreyman has written about.

Years later, after the end of the regime, Dreyman learns that the Stasi had had him under comprehensive surveillance. He discovers, in the Stasi's massive secret file on him, how Wiesler, code named HGW XX/7, had protected him and tried in vain to protect Sieland. Deeply moved, he does something he had not done since Sieland's tragic death: he writes again. He writes a novel called *Sonata for a Good Man* and dedicates it to HGW XX/7. Wiesler discovers the book and buys it in the newly commercialized Karl Marx Bookshop in liberated East Berlin.

There is an ethical beauty about all this that gripped me by the throat every time I saw the film—three times in a week. And here is where I see its relevance to issues in our country right now. Former Customs officer Allan Robert Kessing faces imprisonment for leaking to the press a classified report that revealed serious flaws in airport security and the influence of organized crime within airport terminals. There has been no suggestion that he did this with anything in mind except the public interest. Yet the trial judge instructed the jury not to take into account the public interest argument.

This is shocking. Whether, in the considered judgment of the citizens of this country, a leak has been in the public interest or conducted for unethical and improper ends should, surely, be the determining criterion of whether it is justified or not. We do not live in the East Germany of the Stasi, but that is so chiefly because of the mechanisms we have in place to hold government to account and to keep in check the human propensities to corruption and abuse of power. Principled leaks decidedly serve these ends. For my money, Mr. Kessing is a good man and he should be recognized and treated as such.

Silencing even the hint of dissent

On 4 July the Chinese Communist Party shut down the Beijing-based China Development Brief. This small body had produced a newsletter, published over the past twelve years, which reported on the emergence of civil society in China. The irony of its being shut down is that its founder and editor, Nick Young, had a reputation for being friendly to the Communist Party. He regularly informed the world at large that China was not as repressive as its critics alleged. He was shut down, however, for conducting 'unauthorized surveys'.

This is just one more incident indicating not only that the Communist Party is repressive, but that it cannot abide anything resembling open inquiry into how things are and what people think. Hu Jintao declares that he seeks to build a "harmonious society", but the only harmony he will tolerate is everyone singing to the Party's tune. Now it seems that even this is insufficient. "Unauthorized surveys"? Consider what a stark contrast this represents with what we take for granted in this country. It's like John Howard shutting down Sol Lebowitz for reporting that Kevin Rudd has become the preferred prime minister.

The name Nick Young is easy to remember, because it is English. The problem with Chinese democracy activists, human rights lawyers, journalists and writers who languish in the Party's prisons is that their names are Chinese and most Westerners find that they all blur into one another. These prisoners of conscience suffer, also, from the strange mystique of China, which leads far too many of us to subscribe to the myth that "Western" notions of human rights and democracy do not apply to China. We need reminding that basic human rights are not "Western" and that the Chinese Communist Party has no right to suppress them.

Yet suppress them it does—and also reporting of its suppression of them. Do you know the name Qin Yongmin? He is serving a twelve year sentence for the "crime" of applying to register a provincial preparatory committee for the Chinese Democracy Party, in 1998. Dozens of others are in prison on similar charges. Dozens of journalists are in prison—more than in any other country in the world. Have you heard of Shi Tao? He is a writer, poet and journalist, arrested in late 2004 and sentenced to 10 years in prison, for having sent to the Asia Democracy Foundation, via his Yahoo email account, news of the Party's call for the media not to run pro-democracy stories on the anniversary of the Tiananmen massacre of 1989. This alert was, supposedly, a "state secret."

Have you heard of Guo Guoding? He is the human rights lawyer who represented Shi Tao, pointing out that the confiscation of his property and his detention were illegal. That did not save Shi from prison. All it did was lead to Guo being stripped of his license to practice law. He was harassed so fiercely that his wife divorced him to get away from the stress. He himself finally fled into exile in Canada. I met him recently and was astonished by his gentleness and openness. A society of Guo Guodings would be a harmonious one. The society dominated by the Party of Hu Jintao cannot possibly be one.

Have you heard of Lu Jianhua or Chen Hui or Ching Cheong? Lu is a renowned Chinese sociologist; Chen an official of the Chinese Academy of Social Sciences; Ching a distinguished journalist who worked from Hong Kong for the Singapore *Straits Times*. All three were arrested in 2005 for allegedly leaking or seeking to obtain "state secrets". The "secrets" in question? A manuscript of the last reflections of the aged former Chinese premier and reformer Zhao Ziyang before he died, in January that year. This is the equivalent of the memoirs of, say, Malcolm Fraser being suppressed and treated as "state secrets" by the Howard government. It is, truly, a different political world in China; but for all the wrong reasons.

Just a week after Nick Young's newsletter was abruptly shut down by the Communist Party's Public Security Bureau, I had the privilege of having to dinner Wang Juntao, one of the veterans of the democratic cause in China. In the early 1980s, Wang founded the first public opinion polling organization in China since the Communist seizure of power, as well as a newspaper called *The Economic Weekly*. Both were shut down by the Party. He was one of the leaders of the Tiananmen demonstrations in 1989 and was arrested and sentenced to 13 years in prison. Released on medical parole in 1994, he has lived in exile since.

Wang's quiet and determined character, not the harsh and neurotic repression of dissent by the Communist Party, represents the genuine traditional wisdom of China, if not its traditionally repressive political culture. He lives for the easing of repression and the deepening of governmental accountability in his country; but he is a sage in the best Chinese manner, not a firebrand or a swaggering rebel in the Maoist mould. He works to bring democracy activists together and to spread abroad the understanding that there is nothing at all "unChinese" about accountable government and basic human rights.

Never mind Nick Young. He should have known better than to befriend the gigantic Mafia that runs China. Remember Qin Yongmin, Shi Tao, Guo Guoding, Lu Jianhua, Chen Hui, Ching Cheong. Remember Wang Juntao when you conduct your own unauthorized survey of the Chinese scene and the possible meanings of the rapid growth in China's wealth and power. For these are the names of a China we could all live with and should want to see. May their cause prevail.

Iraq and Vietnam: three analogies

The Vietnam War has been invoked as an analogy by critics of the invasion of Iraq from the outset. Last week President Bush invoked it to defend his determination to persevere with the occupation of Iraq. These analogies are of some use in understanding the situation, but they need to be handled with care.

The analogy that critics of the Iraq invasion make is the 'quagmire'. The more severe among them depict both wars as immoral, imperialist and even genocidal. The more temperate see both wars as well-intentioned but massively costly undertakings, marred by very serious errors and inefficiencies—in short, as tragedies.

Bush points to the genocide and mass repression which occurred in Indochina after the American withdrawal and declares that the same is likely to happen if America withdraws from Iraq before a stable government is in place. On this reading, both wars were honorable interventions against totalitarian regimes, for which a high price was paid and we should seek a different outcome in Iraq to that which occurred in the case of Vietnam.

There are regrettably many grounds for criticizing Bush's handling of the Iraq war from the outset. This does not mean that he is altogether wrong in this case. One of the most respected critics of the American war in Vietnam, William Shawcross, wrote, in 1993, that 'those of us who were opposed to the American effort in Indochina should be humbled by the scale of suffering inflicted by the Communist victors—especially in Cambodia, but in Vietnam and Laos as well.'

In Cambodia, 1.7 million people perished by torture, execution, starvation and disease, due to the terrifying brutality of the Khmer Rouge. Vietnam was not so appalling, but the Vietnamese Communists did establish a totalitarian regime, which kept the country poor and grimly repressed for a generation and drove hundreds of thousands of its oppressed citizens to flee by sea, large numbers losing their lives in the process.

Should we see this as a useful analogy in the case of Iraq? Three grim prospects could follow a hasty American withdrawal from Iraq. First, a rapid descent of Iraq into full scale civil war, with violence an order of magnitude worse than anything so far. Second, open intervention by other states in the region, such as Iran, or Turkey. Third, the redoubling by Islamists of their *jihad*, based on a belief that would they had won a great victory over the United States and were on a roll.

Despite similar misgivings, however, the United States did withdraw from Vietnam. Only some of the misgivings turned out to be warranted. South East Asia did not suffer wider destabilization and, although for a few years, the American position in the world at large appeared to have been weakened, the tide actually turned against Communism within about a decade. We should not, therefore, simply assume that withdrawal from Iraq would lead to dire consequences and feel 'trapped' into staying there.

At the same time, we should think carefully about how and when to withdraw, rather than assume that the war is 'lost' and should be abandoned. A third analogy with Vietnam may be instructive here. The Vietnam War was lost politically and not on the battlefield. As Lewis Sorley argued, in *A Better War* (1999), the American forces in Vietnam made marked progress with pacification in South Vietnam after crushing the 1968 Communist Tet offensive and then the 1972 North Vietnamese Easter offensive. The American political system was not prepared, however, to support the war beyond 1973 and certainly not in 1974-75, when the North Vietnamese launched their final offensive against the South.

Some progress is being reported from Iraq under David Petraeus and we might usefully explore the parallel. A senior Australian officer in Iraq wrote to me recently: 'My view is that the counter-insurgency here is nearly done. American sacrifice and military skill (which have both been prodigious) have been necessary but not sufficient to get us to where we are. Of more importance is that starting early this year the people of Iraq began to turn their back on both Sunni and Shi'a insurgents ... I explain this to people all the time and, outside of Iraq, I get blank looks or open incredulity. People here on the ground are notably more optimistic than those on the outside because we can see what is happening.'

The extent to which this is true should concern us all; for by early next year, a drawdown of American forces seems unavoidable. The endgame is on, for better or worse, and if the Iraqi government collapses, the consequences could be both very ugly and very difficult to contain. But we must, surely, seek to contain them. I suggest that, in these circumstances, it is this third analogy, rather than the other two, more common ones that is most useful.

Wake up and ban the bomb

There is talk of bombing Iran to force a halt to its nuclear weapons program. Certainly, if at all possible, Iran should be stopped from getting nuclear weapons. However, Iran's program is only a symptom of the real problem: the existence of nuclear weapons in the arsenals of eight other nations. Fear of Iran's aspirations should serve not merely as an occasion for reactive measures, but as a wakeup call to the larger menace. What we truly need to do is to abolish nuclear weapons altogether.

That can't be done, 'realists' will say. They are in error. It can be done. The question is only whether the nuclear powers, starting with the United States, can exhibit enough vision and moral leadership to do it. Many deeply informed realists have argued recently that nuclear abolition is both necessary and possible. Among them are General George Lee Butler, nuclear deterrence theoretician and former commander of the US nuclear forces; General Charles Horner, commander of the allied air forces in the 1991 Gulf War; and Robert S. McNamara, former US Secretary of Defence.[257]

One of the most compelling figures to argue for abolition was the late Paul H. Nitze. A consummate Cold War realist, Nitze argued, after the Cold War, that he could think of *no* circumstances in which it would be wise for the United States to use nuclear weapons. He recommended that it dismantle its nuclear arsenal *unilaterally*. This is all the more notable, because Nitze was a nuclear deterrence champion during the Cold War and no-one could accuse him of being a 'peacenik'.

Nitze argued, after the Cold War, that America's huge lead in high precision conventional weaponry meant that it had nothing to fear if it took the bold move to unilateral nuclear disarmament. What the present confrontation with Iran suggests is that it would, in fact, have a great deal to *gain* by doing this. Such a claim is strategically counter-intuitive, but a moment's reflection will compel the thought that morally and politically, it would garner enormous credibility if it set a decisive example of nuclear disarmament.

After all, the United States began the nuclear age by developing atomic weapons during the Second World War; it is the only nation to have *used* nuclear weapons in war and it is the self-appointed guardian of international security and 'stability'. Having begun the Nuclear Age, it needs to lead in ending it. It started down this path in the 1990s, under the Strategic Arms

---

257 All these figures spoke of their concerns and their vision with Jonathan Schell, the great campaigner for abolition of nuclear weapons. He died of cancer early in 2014 and must have felt, as he did so, that his campaign had ground to a halt. Abolition is nowhere in sight as of 2015.

Reduction Treaty with Russia. But under first Bill Clinton and then George W. Bush, nuclear disarmament ground to a halt.

The dilemma with which we are confronted now is bound up with that fact. The fanatical and brutal nature of the Iranian regime, its wild threats to wipe Israel off the map, its inflammatory rhetoric about spreading Islam around the world, its open defiance of the UN Security Council and the fact that it is in flagrant violation of its obligations under the Nuclear Non-Proliferation Treaty (NPT) are all, to be sure, reasons for the rest of us to seek to check the progress of its nuclear weapons program. But even if we do, the underlying problem of great power hypocrisy will remain.

That hypocrisy has two components. First, the five permanent members of the UN Security Council (the United States, Russia, China, Britain and France) are *themselves* in violation of the NPT, because they committed themselves to work toward the abolition of nuclear weapons, but are not doing so. There is, therefore a certain hollowness to their insistence that others not develop nuclear weapons. This is why, in the 1990s, India denounced them for what it dubbed 'nuclear apartheid' and, never having joined the NPT, openly went nuclear in 1998.

Second, as long as the five great powers retain their nuclear weapons they lend credence and legitimacy to the idea that such weapons *serve a genuine military purpose*. But if this is so, why should not lesser powers, with more to fear, avail themselves of such weapons? Conversely, if Butler and Nitze are correct and nuclear weapons actually do *not* have any justifiable military use, what excuse is there for the great powers to cling to them? There is none. There is only psychological inertia and the special pleading of the interest groups which make their living out of nuclear weapons.

Iran is unlikely to be able to complete a nuclear weapon in less than three years and it may take considerably longer, according to the best informed estimates. There is a window of opportunity, therefore, to retrieve the situation. It will be made vastly easier if the United States can find the magnanimity to initiate a breakthrough in nuclear disarmament. That would give it the moral high ground and far greater global support than it now has—even if, in the end, it requires the use of force to bring Iran to heel.[258]

---

258 As of this writing, in January 2015, the Obama administration claims that it has got very close to a satisfactory deal with Iran that will head off Iran's acquisition of nuclear weapons. The Republican Congress is deeply sceptical, as are the Israelis. The question remains, what options exist for ensuring that Iran comes to heel? There appear to be no good ones. Just possibly, the collapse in oil prices, if it was exploited, might make it possible to put extra pressure on Iran. But North Korea pushed through to testing nuclear weapons under far more dire economic circumstances than those currently facing Iran. It isn't clear, therefore, that pressure will have the desired effect.

The children of democratic principles foil Hugo Chavez

A week after we enjoyed a rejuvenating democratic election[259], the people of faraway Venezuela were asked to vote away their democratic institutions. In a referendum last Sunday, the flamboyant, Bush-defying Hugo Chavez sought the power to control the central bank, expropriate private property, suppress dissent and remain president for life. In his hubris, he thought he would win. But a broad coalition, inspired by university students, opposed him and he lost. He conceded only that he had lost 'for now', but neither he nor any ruler anywhere should ever have the dictatorial powers that he sought in this referendum.

Chavez has been lionized, in John Pilger's latest film, *The War on Democracy*, as a brave and visionary rebel against American imperialism and neo-liberalism. Pilger blames repression, corruption and poverty across Latin America on the United States and depicts Chavez as a genial Robin Hood in a red shirt, who seeks to right the wrongs actually or supposedly inflicted on his country by the Yankees. But Chavez is more a symptom of the illiberal malaise that has long marred both Latin America and much of the global Left than an authentic liberator of his country from wrongs real or imagined.

That is not to say that the policies of the United States in Latin America have been especially enlightened over the past century. They have often left a great deal to be desired. Pilger's film includes some telling interviews, in this respect, including a remarkable one with the former CIA covert operations chief for Latin America, Duane 'Dewey' Clarridge. On camera, Clarridge denies outright that thousands of people were killed in Pinochet's Chile in the 1970s and tens of thousands in Guatemala and El Salvador in the 1980s, on his watch. He

---

259 I was clearly referring to the Federal election of 2007, which brought Kevin Rudd and Julia Gillard to power as Australia's prime minister and deputy prime minister respectively. Like many Australians at the time, I believed that these two would form a good team and that their youth, energy, intelligence and stated commitment to sound fiscal management would be good for the country. How wrong one can be! I clearly knew too little about Kevin Rudd's character defects, too little about the hidden animosities within the ALP and too little about the factional and labour affiliations of Julia Gillard. Instead of a new era of reform and steady governance in Australia, their prime ministerships and feuds marked the end of an era of sound government in Australia. As of this writing, similar tensions are evident within the Liberal Party and as senior and level-headed a political analyst as Paul Kelly is declaring that our political system is actually 'broken' and that, in place of adult government we are being given 'adolescent chaos'. Australia remains, nonetheless, light years ahead of Venezuela in terms of government. We simply need to steady the ship a bit in the next few years.

dismisses all this is 'propaganda'. It isn't. It happened.²⁶⁰

To indict Clarridge, however, is one thing; to pretend that Chavez is a white knight of democracy is altogether another. To be sure, Chavez won a series of popular elections, starting in 1998, and appeared to be committed to addressing the needs of the country's poor majority. However, as Jorge Castaneda, the noted Mexican political scientist, has written, there are two kinds of Left in Latin America now, the intelligent and the irresponsible. Chavez is of the second kind. He has been running the Venezuelan economy into the ground, creating a climate of rampant crime and corruption, driving the middle class into exile or poverty, establishing a one party state, inflicting Marxist indoctrination on even the independent schools and denouncing all his critics as 'fascists' and 'traitors'.

The increase in violent crime under Chavez is appalling. Homicides have *doubled* since he came to power. There are now as many murders in Venezuela every *week* as there are in Australia in a year. In Australia, in 2006, there were 281 murders; in Venezuela, with a similar population, more than 12,200.²⁶¹ Even as basic social order has deteriorated, Chavez has plundered his country's soaring oil revenues to build up a system of patronage, power and surveillance. Last month, his long-time ally and former Defence Minister, Raul Baduel, denounced the referendum proposals as "a constitutional fraud and a *coup d'état*". Baduel saved Chavez from a conservative *coup d'état* in 2002. Just possibly, his defection marked the high tide of Chavez's bid for dictatorial power.

One of Chavez's most articulate critics has long been Moises Naim, a distinguished Venezuelan economist, now resident in Washington D.C., where he edits *Foreign Policy*. In a seminal essay in 2001, Naim deplored Chavez's pretensions and extravagance, as well as his poorer countrymen's delusion that theirs is a 'rich country' because of its huge reserves of oil. This, he pointed out, is the "oil curse" that afflicts much of the Arab world, stifling economic initiative and tempting incompetent governments to buy off their people's discontents.

Naim was an architect of unsuccessful attempts at liberal reform in Venezuela in the 1990s and laments the lapse into crackpot socialism under Chavez. Sustainable reforms of the kind

---

260 One of the most intense parts of my PhD inquiries was into death squads in Central America. I never found evidence that the death toll was propaganda cooked up by the Left. After the resignation of Pinochet, the commission of inquiry in Chile concluded that the number of people executed under his rule was around 3,000, which is a fraction of the figure 15,000 that I had gleaned from other sources. In the cases of Guatemala and El Salvador, there were better kept statistics and the toll was high. In the case of El Salvador, it peaked in 1980-81 and then slowly declined.

261 By 2014, things had become far worse. In the United States that year, with a population of over 300 million, there were 14,000 homicides. In Venezuela, with just 30 million people, there were 22,000. This made Venezuela one of the most violent countries on Earth.

Naim would like to see are taking place elsewhere in Latin America, notably in Mexico and Brazil, as Michael Reid explains, in *Forgotten Continent: The Battle for Latin America's Soul* (Yale, 2007). In Venezuela, however, oil money has been used to try to create a state modeled on the Cuba of Fidel Castro—even as Chavez bails out the impoverished Cuba of the dying Castro with heavily subsidized oil.

As with Castro, so with Chavez: the problem is less one of declared social justice *goals*, than of political and economic *methods*. Chavez is an incompetent spendthrift and a loud-mouthed demagogue, not a principled democratic reformer. Tens of thousands of students campaigned against his referendum; not in the name of the old order, but on behalf of basic principles of democratic politics and accountable government. *Los hijos de los ricos*, Chavez called them, the children of the rich; but they are, rather, *los hijos de los principios democráticos*—the children of democratic principles—and this victory, which owes a lot to them, is immensely heartening.

The death of Suharto and our judgment

President Suharto was a blackguard, a mass murderer and a kleptocrat, with whom we should have been seriously at odds, if not at war, according to his critics. To the contrary, urged several prominent figures; he was a white knight, a charming fellow who did a lot for his country, as well as for the region; and a great friend to Australia.

There is actually a good deal of truth in both sets of claims. The man was a 'prince', in Machiavelli's sense, and assessing our relationship with him is a test of our capacity for dispassionate judgment about international politics, "princes" in general, our security interests and our moral commitments.

Suharto is dead, but our need to be able to make dispassionate judgments in these domains, with regard to Indonesia and many other countries, will be enduring. That's why thinking a bit harder about Suharto at this juncture is worthwhile. We need to go beyond a few one-sided evaluations about his deeds, whether the facts adduced in either case be true or false'.

More fundamentally, we need to come to terms with the fact that, in external affairs, we often face intractable dilemmas and must make a choice between evils. This very idea makes many people feel uncomfortable, but it is an inescapable aspect of statecraft. Few things illustrate this more starkly than the history of Australia's relationship with Indonesia, before, during and since Suharto's long rule.

In the late 1940s, Australia's leaders had to choose between supporting the Dutch in their attempt to hold onto their colonies in the 'East Indies', or the Indonesian nationalists under Sukarno. They chose the latter, but Sukarno proved a very difficult neighbour to deal with.

In the mid to late 1950s, there was serious debate at the highest levels in Australia regarding whether our interests would best be served by a fragmented or a unified Indonesia. It was decided that, all things considered, the latter would be our best bet, but that Sukarno was a problem and the Indonesian Communist Party (PKI) was looming as an even greater one.

Sukarno was determined, in the late 1950s, to acquire Dutch New Guinea, though it was Melanesian and not, therefore, self-evidently part of a nation centered on Java. A top secret intelligence study in 1957 advised that our interests would best be served by seeking the cooperation of the Dutch in developing the whole island of New Guinea and giving it independence as a unified Melanesian state. Robert Menzies made this his policy.

But Menzies had a problem. The Dutch would not cooperate. And Sukarno kept pressing his claim. At the psychological moment, in late December 1961, Menzies received an eyes only letter from British prime minister Harold Macmillan saying, more or less in these words, 'Dear Bob, I've had a chat with Jack (Kennedy) in Bermuda and we think you should roll over on this Dutch New

Guinea thing ... We'll throw this bone to Sukarno, separate the Indonesian nationalists from the communists and then find some other way to deal with the PKI.'

This was the origin of the so-called 'act of free choice', by means of which West Papua was handed over to Indonesia between 1962 and 1968. Menzies's hand was forced by the attitude of Washington and London. If he defied them and resisted Sukarno, he risked a war with Indonesia on most uncertain terms. The alternative was to sacrifice West Papua and that choice was made, as the lesser of two evils.

As for finding another way to deal with the PKI, Western analysts were in agreement, in the early 1960s, that Sukarno could not contain the increasing power of the Communists and that only the Indonesian Army had the strength to do so. Led by the young Colonel Suharto, in 1965-66, the Army neutralized Sukarno and destroyed the fabric of the PKI. In the process, it slaughtered an estimated 500,000 people, including the families of PKI cadres and sympathizers, who were executed wholesale without trials or rights of appeal.

These events, the setting for Christopher Koch's fine novel and Peter Weir's excellent film, *The Year of Living Dangerously*, were unambiguously welcomed by Australia's leaders and the hope was expressed, in late 1965, that the Army would 'finish the job'. The late Alan Taylor told me a few years ago that he had joined the Department of Foreign Affairs just after these events and would never forget the 'enormous feeling of relief in the place' at what had happened.

Even before Suharto overthrew Sukarno, thoughtful people within Foreign Affairs were thinking ahead about Portuguese Timor. Gordon Jockel wrote a particularly fine analysis of the problem for Arthur Tange in 1962. But in 1973, good friends of Australia in Indonesian national security circles approached our Embassy and indicated that they were proposing to Suharto that Portuguese Timor be absorbed into Indonesia.

The debate that then took place in Canberra was vigorous and intelligent, but it led, ultimately, to Gough Whitlam's choice, subsequently endorsed by Malcolm Fraser, to do nothing to oppose Indonesian annexation of East Timor and to publicly play down the brutalities entailed in that annexation, between 1975 and 1983. Was this a good choice? There have always been those who have asserted that it was the wrong choice. What has never been clear is what better alternative was open to the Australian governments of those times.

All these events are the background to a reasoned assessment of Suharto as 'prince' or a mature approach to Australia's diplomatic relations with Indonesia. There are, alas, no neat, morally ideal solutions to problems of this nature. Nor was Suharto a neat or morally ideal solution to Indonesia's difficulties in the 1960s and 1970s. But he *was* a prince of very considerable abilities and our only effective option for decades was to work with him as best we could.

Beware China's emerging naval ambitions

According to naval intelligence sources in London and Washington and a recent MI6 briefing to *Jane's Intelligence Weekly,* China is building a massive, highly secure naval base at Sanya on Hainan Island. This has been independently confirmed, using commercially available satellite imagery, by the Federation of American Scientists. It turns out that the EP-3 incident, in April 2001, when a US reconnaissance plane was harassed and forced to land in Hainan, was all about Sanya. It had been the EP-3's surveillance target. That's why the Chinese were so concerned about the matter. The question is, should we be concerned about Sanya? Yes.

The naval base centres on a huge underground complex that even the most sophisticated spy satellites cannot penetrate. It is being prepared with berths for up to 20 of the most advanced Chinese submarines, the C94 Jin-class boat, which will be capable of firing both anti-satellite and nuclear tipped missiles. It is also being fitted out to house several aircraft carriers—something China does not even have yet. In short, Sanya is a very clear signal of the scale of China's emerging blue water naval ambitions.

We are very used to Anglo-American naval dominance and to China not even having a significant blue water navy. Moreover, American naval dominance remains overwhelming. Sanya, however, raises the twofold question: will that dominance endure and what would be the consequences if it did not? We need to put Sanya in geopolitical and historical perspective and we need to remind ourselves that the future could take any one of several paths from here, whatever the intentions of China's current leaders might be.

Several episodes from modern history show us, by analogy, what Sanya could signify: the development of German naval power in the 1910s, to rival British dominance; the rise of Japanese naval power in the 1920s to rival Western naval dominance in the Pacific; and the attempt by the Soviet Union, in the 1970s and early 1980s, to build a blue water navy that could challenge American dominance of the world's oceans. None of those attempts succeeded, but they were part of what became the First World War, the Second World War and the last anxious phase of the Cold War.

Consider the case of Germany one hundred years ago. The intention of the Germans, when they began their naval buildup, was not to fight Britain, but to develop enough naval muscle to apply pressure to Britain in a possible future crisis that would induce Britain to come to terms and make concessions. The Kaiser's Navy Laws of 1898 and 1900 gave Navy Secretary Alfred von Tirpitz a mandate to develop a fleet of short range battleships that could challenge the Royal Navy in the North Sea. It was also hoped that the naval buildup would rally both conservative interests and the new middle classes around the flag and buttress the legitimacy of the monarchy.

Sanya, on the South China Sea, is about China being able to put enough pressure on the United States in a possible crisis to extract concessions from it. The aim may also be to rally Chinese citizens around the Communist Party, whose dubious legitimacy depends more and more on nationalism rather than communism. In the 1910s there were many people in Britain itself who did not see the rise of German naval power as necessarily a cause for alarm. There are plenty today who will be inclined to say, Why shouldn't China have a blue water navy? Doesn't it have legitimate interests in sea lines of communication and maritime claims it has a right to defend? Wouldn't a rising great power naturally build such a capability?

Yes it does and yes it probably would. But consider where all this could lead and do not rest on your laurels or your cynicism. Admiral Liu Huaqing designed a long term naval strategy for China from 1985. He was appointed by Deng Xiaoping as military mentor to Jiang Zemin in the 1990s. He fell out with Jiang Zemin a decade ago, but the strategy is slowly maturing. It has a clear objective: to dominate the waters around the first island chain (the great chain of islands that runs from the Kuriles through Japan and Taiwan to the Philippines) and then to challenge US dominance in the Pacific by 2050.

As Alan Wachman has shown in his monograph *Why Taiwan*[262], *this* is why China seeks to assert sovereignty over Taiwan; not because of any historical sentimentality about old imperial territories or 'unequal' treaties. It no longer seeks sovereignty over the vastly larger territories of Mongolia or the Russian Far East that also belonged to the old Manchu empire, but it does seek Taiwan—because of its pivotal place in the first island chain, its strategic position straddling the trade pipeline that is the Taiwan Strait and its first class harbors with their direct access to the wide waters of the Western Pacific. The Sanya naval base is a key move in the grand plan and we should all sit up and take note.

---

262   Alan M. Wachman *Why Taiwan: Geostrategic Rationales for China's Territorial Integrity* (Stanford University Press, 2007). This is a particularly fine monograph, which I suspect has not been read nearly widely enough.

Open the book on cold war spies

The nomination of John Faulkner as Minister of Defence, in place of Joel Fitzgibbon, is a statement of intent on the part of the Prime Minister. He wants to sort Defence out. In his new job, Senator Faulkner will find his stated commitment to freedom of information and transparent government tested, especially with regard to security and intelligence. He could make a bold and long overdue contribution to openness in the public interest by—jointly with the Prime Minister and the Attorney General—releasing crucial materials on Soviet penetration of our intelligence system during the Cold War.

He should start with the Mitrokhin archive. Voluminous KGB files were smuggled west in 1992 and published in two hefty volumes, totaling 1,700 pages, by Allen Lane Penguin in 1999 and 2005. They deal with KGB operations in the Americas, Europe, Asia and Africa and also behind the iron curtain. But there is a notable omission in these books: material dealing with KGB operations in Australia. Such material exists. It was sent by the British intelligence authorities to Canberra in September 1992, but has been suppressed.

That should never have happened and should now be remedied. What reason can there be for suppressing the entire file on Australia, when so much was published about the rest of the world? Were the materials on Australia so bland and uninformative that they were deemed of no interest and consigned to the waste paper bin? That would have been an absurd reason for suppressing them; but it plainly was not the case. Something quite substantial and unsettling is in the Australia file. That something must now see the light of day.

The Mitrokhin materials so alarmed Canberra that two inquiries were set on foot. The AFP was asked to conduct a check on ASIO. This inquiry was called Operation LIVER. It was halted, in 1995, by then Attorney General Michael Lavarch, on the disturbing grounds that there was no knowing where it would all end. Indeed. Separately, the Prime Minister, Paul Keating, asked senior diplomat Michael Cook to conduct an inquiry into Soviet penetration of ASIO. He did so in 1993-94 and is reported to have found such a counter-intelligence mess that the whole organization was compromised. But his report was classified and remains very tightly guarded. We need to know, at long last, what he found.

What Cook found in 1994 had long been suspected. The 1977 Hope Royal Commission on Intelligence and Security made damning judgments about ASIO's counter-intelligence ineptitude. 'Many of the more thoughtful and responsible ASIO officers who gave evidence before me sought the opportunity to voice their fears of a penetration,' wrote Justice Hope. Cook is reported to have concluded that there had been *four* Soviet moles inside ASIO right through to the end of the Cold War. All four were quietly retired on full pension. George Sadil was arrested and charged, but he was at best small fry whose prosecution was bungled.

In short, while Aldrich Ames and Robert Hanssen were being prosecuted and jailed in the United States, their Australian counterparts were being retired on full pensions. Why? Because the AFP and Cook suspected, but could not actually deduce who the guilty parties were? What confidence does that inspire in our capacity to ensure the integrity of our counter-intelligence and security services? Or was it all too embarrassing, especially to the Labour Party, so many of whose members and supporters had spent the Cold War denouncing the 'reds under the bed' mentality and the 'witch hunts' of McCarthyism? What a parlous defence that would be for suppressing the truth.

This is of more than merely historical significance. Russian and Chinese espionage have been resurgent in Australia in recent years. ASIO set up a new Counter-Espionage and Interference Division a few years ago to deal with it. But how can we have confidence in such a Division as long as the truth about what happened in the Cold War years remains suppressed? And the Mitrokhin archive itself only deals with KGB operations. Those of the GRU (Soviet military intelligence) remain a disturbingly closed book. Yet we know the GRU was active in Australia and have reason to believe it successfully recruited agents here.

KGB and GRU moles in Australia may have been recruited as early as the 1960s, but we still do not even know their codenames, because the Mitrokhin archive on Australia has been withheld under what used to be called a D Notice. The KGB recruited British spy rings in the 1930s not only at Cambridge, but also at Oxford and London universities. The head of the Oxford ring was codenamed SCOTT, we learned in 1992; but for many years no-one could find out who SCOTT had been.

It turns out he was Arthur Wynn, who served his KGB masters for decades while a prominent British civil servant. His recruiters reported to Moscow Centre that they considered him a second SOHNCHEN (Kim Philby's codename) with 'even greater possibilities than the first.' Did the Mitrokhin archives point to an Australian SOHNCHEN and SCOTT? It is high time we learned, Senator Faulkner.

Iran, the bomb and the war of ideas

There has been much anxious speculation for some years now about whether Israel or the United States would take military action to try to pre-empt Iran's acquisition of nuclear weapons. Emanuele Ottolenghi, Executive Director of the Transatlantic Institute in Brussels, who is in Australia at the moment, believes that Europe would be more endangered by an Iranian nuclear capability than would the United States and that it is time the European Union took action on the matter.

Further negotiation is fruitless, he believes, because the regime in Iran has strung out talks for six years while continuing to develop the wherewithal for manufacturing nuclear weapons. Military action is beyond Europe's capabilities, even if it seemed advisable. What he urges is a regime of targeted sanctions that, he believes can inflict such stress on the regime that it might be toppled. And Europe is uniquely well-placed to impose such sanctions, without the need to wait on the US or face frustration at the UN.

Ottolenghi is the author of *Under a Mushroom Cloud: Europe, Iran and the Bomb*. In it, he argues lucidly that the UN will not act on Iran, for the usual reason—that Russia and China will block any Security Council resolution—and that the United States is still feeling its way. The EU, however, has unique economic leverage over Iran and the credibility that comes from having patiently and imaginatively negotiated for years, only to have the Iranian regime treat it with scorn. Now, he urges, it must demonstrate that it is serious.

One possible response might be that it is not only the hardline mullahs in Teheran who seek nuclear weapons; but a broad cross-section of Iranian nationalists. Pressure on the country would cause such nationalists to rally round the flag. Iran might suffer, but it would dig in its heels and even accelerate its 'Manhattan Project'. Though conceived as an alternative to military action, serious sanctions might cause the situation to actually deteriorate to the point where only military action could put an end to the Iranian nuclear program.

In any case, Europe would quickly find itself under terrorist threat if it imposed serious sanctions on Iran. The Islamist movement worldwide and its Left-wing allies would without doubt start a clamorous campaign against 'Western imperialism', which Tehran would play up to the hilt. The regime and its fellow travelers would remind all and sundry of Anglo-American intervention in Iran in the 1950s and 1960s to buttress the Shah. The EU's policy cohesion would quite probably fall apart under such pressure; assuming that its present lack of cohesion or will could be remedied to begin with.

The cautious and timid in Europe are likely to urge that President Obama should be followed on this, not led. He has made it clear he wishes to invite Iran to the negotiating table, though he has indicated that its nuclear ambitions will have to be traded for otherwise generous treatment. Why take hasty and condign steps at such a juncture? In any case, if push comes to shove, Iran will get its nuclear arsenal and will have to be deterred—and it will be the primary responsibility of the United States, not the EU, to orchestrate and underwrite such deterrence.

Ottolenghi's case is a morally and politically serious one. Yet, unless the EU undergoes a dramatic acceleration in the shift to geopolitical earnestness that Angela Merkel and Nicholas Sarkozy have tried to engineer, it is very difficult to see the proposed sanctions being agreed, enforced and sustained against a backlash from the Iranian regime and its various allies. It may be, therefore, that President Obama will soon face a dread choice between military action against Iran and putting in place a whole new regime of deterrence and arms control in the Middle East.

There is a crucial ingredient missing here, though: the need to drive a wedge between the theocratic regime and the broad currents of Iranian nationalism. This would actually require making clear that it is *not* the bomb that is the outside world's most pressing concern. The real worry is the belligerent and ideologically possessed regime that would then possess it. Change the regime and a more even handed dialogue about regional power could become vastly easier.

After all, the Shah sought nuclear weapons. Yet neither the United States, nor Israel, nor the Europeans would have imposed condign sanctions on him, to say nothing of going to war. There would still be an effort to dissuade a changed regime from completing a nuclear weapons capability; but there would not be the acute anxiety that currently has American, European, Israeli and Sunni Arab security analysts and statesmen up at nights.

The Iranian elections have shown again that there is widespread frustration with the economically incompetent and recklessly belligerent regime. We need now, in real earnest, to talk directly to that frustration and court it. The time has passed for seeking to cajole or appease the theocrats. If we do not want to settle for confrontation with Iran, or see a nuclear arms race in the Middle East, as Sunni Arab regimes rush to reassure themselves against the aspiring hegemon, we must address Iran as a nation and bring its better parts to the fore. We must defeat the theocrats in the war of ideas.

Stalin, Trotsky and the Soviet archives

Why do we need more books about the history of Soviet communism when there are many more pressing things to read about? Isn't the basic story well known? Isn't it time to move on? Perhaps such books are merely, as the old saying has it, 'the propaganda of the victors'? These three new books demonstrate that there are still things to be learned and that good history is not propaganda at all.

Moreover, we can move on only if we learn how to prevent the recurrence of what happened in the Soviet Union. *Master of the House* and *Stalin's Police* are aids to such learning. *Stalin's Nemesis* is less so, but is a useful accompaniment to reflecting on the killing of dissidents such as Alexander Litvinenko and Anna Politkovskaya by the heirs of the Soviet KGB in recent years.

Vladimir Putin and others have declared that the collapse of the Soviet Union was 'the greatest geopolitical catastrophe of the 20th century'. These books are a timely reminder of why such an assertion is not only wrong-headed but morally abhorrent. Surely one of the great moral scandals of the 20th century was that, despite early and abundant evidence of its totalitarian and lawlessly repressive nature, the Bolshevik regime and Stalin's rule in particular was somehow seen as a bold experiment in progressive government. It was, supposedly, the vanguard for a world revolution that, as Jean-Paul Sartre notoriously phrased it, would 'come through the Soviet Union or not at all'.

Throughout much of the 20th century, there was a widespread belief that the world could do with some kind of radical revolution. Alas, this enabled first the Bolsheviks, then Stalin, then other communist leaders, not least Mao Zedong in China, to get away with murder, repression and misrule on a staggering scale for decades. The challenge has long been to get the history of these matters right, with Stalin in centre frame, in order to be done with this moral scandal.

When the works of Alexander Solzhenitsyn began appearing in the 1960s and 70s, they caused a stir in this regard, but his estimate that 60 million people had perished in the Gulag and in Stalin's terror fuelled controversy, because this seemed highly implausible. Some, perversely, asserted that Solzhenitsyn's revelations about the Gulag archipelago should be disregarded even if true, for the sake of the 'greater good' of world revolution against American-style capitalism. Certainly, there have always been many who wanted to assert that Stalin's supposed 'class struggle' could not be morally equated with Hitler's racial genocide.

The collapse of the Soviet bloc 20 years ago had the great benefit that significant communist archives started to be opened to researchers for the first time. Finally, longstanding debates based on anecdote, defector testimony, allegation, rumour and ideological rancour could be tested against a documentary record compiled by the accused themselves: the communist authorities and their security apparatus.

Oleg Khlevniuk, senior researcher at the State Archive of the Russian Federation, has been one of the leading figures in this work. In 2004, Khlevniuk published *The History of the Gulag: From Collectivisation to the Great Terror*, including numerous key documents on how the system of forced labour camps was set up and administered. This followed Anne Applebaum's path-breaking *Gulag: A History of the Soviet Camps* (2003).

Both books are models of objective scholarship: careful weighing of evidence, caution in inference, allowance for uncertainty and for the importance of asking the right questions in order to get sound answers. They are vital contributions to research work correcting estimates such as Solzhenitsyn's and putting the case against Stalin on a much better-documented historical footing. They conclude that approximately six million people died of starvation due to the famines caused by Stalin's forced collectivisation in the early 1930s; and that approximately 1.2 million were executed on political grounds (about three quarters of a million of these in the Great Terror of 1937-38), while at least 2.7 million died in the Gulag and other centres of deportation between 1921 and 1953, most of them after 1929.

That yields a total of about ten million deaths attributable to Stalin's policies of coercion and repression. This figure - conservative and carefully documented - is one half to one sixth of estimates made during the Cold War, but is far more solidly based. And, of course, it is only the most evident and quantifiable measure of the suffering inflicted by the Soviet regime, not least among the families of those who starved or were executed and among those who spent years in the Gulag, even if they did not die there.

Try imagining deaths due to government coercion on a comparable scale in Australia: 140,000 people shot and buried in secret mass graves, often after being tortured, 100,000 of them in an 18-month period, orchestrated out of the prime minister's office in Canberra; 750,000 people dying of starvation as a result of a government policy of confiscating all rural property; three million people deported to concentration and forced labour camps in places like the Kimberley and far north Queensland, with 300,000 dying of malnutrition, disease and abuse. It is, fortunately, inconceivable that such things would occur in Australia, but they have occurred in many countries during the past 100 years. We need to better understand them if we are to restrict the incidence of such practices in this century.

Khlevniuk's *Master of the House* is a meticulous study of how Stalin acquired and abused his dictatorial power. His central conclusion explodes the apologist and relativist historiography that has often deflected damning verdicts on Stalin personally and on the ideological shambles that made his misrule possible. He writes:

> *Theories about the elemental, spontaneous nature of the terror, about a loss of central control over the course of mass repression, and about the role of regional leaders in initiating the terror simply are not supported by the historical record.*

He goes on:

> *Now that we have access to essentially all of the key documents associated with the mass repression of 1937 and 1938, we have every reason to see the Great Terror as a series of centralised, planned mass operations that were conducted on the basis of Politburo decisions (that is, Stalin's decisions) aimed at the liquidation of a 'fifth column' ... The special role played by Stalin in orchestrating this eruption of terror is beyond doubt and is fully supported by documentary evidence. His role can be put even more starkly ... without Stalin's orders, the Great Terror simply would not have taken place.*

These trenchant findings make *Master of the House* a bracing study in the fundamental principles of historiography and historical argument. It is more than that, though. It is a great moral accomplishment after decades of polemic, propaganda and statistical confusion.

Stalin needed servants, however, to perpetrate his appalling rule. Paul Hagenloh, a fine young historian at Syracuse University in New York, provides a scholarly analysis of how those servants were formed, under the Bolshevik regime, into an instrument for mass repression and mass killing. *Stalin's Police* makes somewhat dry reading, but is a very serious contribution to the field. Its single most telling finding is that the primary target of the Great Terror was not the communist elites but whole cohorts of disaffected and uprooted people, as well as Poles, Germans, Koreans and other ethnic minorities living in the USSR.

Stalin had all these people rounded up as the usual suspects and killed *en masse* lest they constitute a fifth column in a future war. According to Hagenloh, some 440,000 'kulaks, criminals and other anti-Soviet elements' and 250,000 members of national minorities were shot in the mass operations of 1937-38. It is as if Franklin Roosevelt had rounded up all Japanese and German Americans in 1937-38 and had them shot out of hand as potential traitors.

Research by various scholars now suggests that the number of Communist Party members shot during the Great Terror was 'only' about 40,000 (not the half million alleged by Roy Medvedev and long accepted as conventional wisdom). The number of Soviet military officers executed was about 6000 (not the 30,000 or more long believed) and the number of security personnel executed perhaps another 6000.

In other words, the Great Terror was primarily directed not at the 'true revolutionaries' - the old Bolsheviks - but at huge numbers of ordinary people. This was, Hagenloh observes,

> *not an abrupt change in policy on Stalin's part but rather the culmination of years of regime policies toward population groups deemed 'dangerous' to the security of the state.*

This was censored from the historical record after Stalin's death, Hagenloh points out, as the Communist Party attempted 'to create a usable Leninist past while ignoring widespread repressions that called into question the legitimacy of the entire Soviet experience'.

Leon Trotsky argued in *The Revolution Betrayed* (1936) that Stalin had hijacked the Bolshevik revolution, but he nonetheless endorsed the basic program of dictatorship and forced industrialisation that Stalin had undertaken. He depicted the Great Terror as a "counter-revolution" against the Bolsheviks and called for a new Bolshevik revolution to oust Stalin.

But Stalin was too shrewd and ruthless for his Bolshevik rival. His propaganda machine depicted *Trotsky* as the personification of counter-revolution. He purged the communist elite under the banner of crushing vast Trotskyist conspiracies. But he also physically liquidated anyone who might lead or join a *real* counter-revolution. And this, Hagenloh argues, was possible because of the approach to policing and law that the Bolshevik regime, including Trotsky, had created and espoused from the outset.

Stalin's Police shows that:

> *The mass repression of 1937 and 1938 was no mere expansion of ongoing purges within the Communist Party and the Soviet state; it was an explosion of police repression with roots in the histories of Soviet policing, social engineering and state violence stretching back to the very beginnings of the Bolshevik regime.*

This is a remarkable and important finding. Police and judicial power are crucial aspects of a modern polity. Marxists have always misunderstood them.

Embedded in Bolshevik ideology was the idea that such things were of their nature instruments of class dictatorship and should be used ruthlessly to enforce the revolution. Lenin seized power from the elected representatives of the Russian people, dispersing the Constituent Assembly in January 1918, and imposed a one-party dictatorship, which was then upheld by terror and violence. Lenin, Trotsky and the Bolshevik mainstream scorned 'bourgeois' legal and constitutional principles. They were, at best, blind to where this would lead. It led tens of thousands of them to execution in Stalin's dungeons in the Great Terror, but they were the least among his victims.

Trotsky, however, never repented of his Bolshevism. That is the subtext to Bertrand Patenaude's *Stalin's Nemesis*. Trotsky believed in the use of arbitrary police and judicial terror against real or perceived enemies of the revolution. He defended the use of terror when in power and engaged in it with revolutionary fervour. Just as with his absurd belief that the party was 'the only vehicle given to us by history for discerning the truth' and therefore could not err; this commitment to arbitrary police power and ruthless social engineering left him no place to stand against Stalin.

Having firm hold of the arbitrary police power the Bolsheviks created, Stalin hunted Trotsky to death across the globe. As Pavel Sudoplatov, wrote in his 1994 memoir, *Special Tasks*: 'Beria suggested I should be put in charge of all anti-Trotskyite operations ... to mobilise all available NKVD resources to eliminate Trotsky, the worst enemy of the people.'

Patenaude, a lecturer at Stanford University, updates from Soviet archives the story of how "the worst enemy of the people" was hounded and eliminated. It is a dramatic tale, most of it long known or surmised. It made Trotsky the model for George Orwell's Snowball to Stalin's Napoleon in *Animal Farm*. It forms the denouement to Isaac Deutscher's classic three-volume biography of Trotsky: *The Prophet Armed, The Prophet Unarmed, The Prophet Outcast*.

Trotsky, however, was a false prophet. Patenaude calls him Stalin's nemesis, but this rings hollow. Stalin was Trotsky's nemesis. Stalin won, hands down. And Trotsky's prophecy that a new revolution would bring down Stalin in the name of communism was never fulfilled. Communism itself was brought down, and not in the name of Trotsky. It was its own nemesis: baleful, murderous, mendacious, incompetent and detested by those it claimed to have liberated.

Section 2: 2008-09

Freedom is the name of the game

The Chinese Communist Party's attempts to impose censorship on the Melbourne Film Festival and the National Press Club regarding Rebiya Kadeer; the recent remark by Abu Bakar Bashir that even those thinking critical thoughts about Islam deserve violent retribution; and the various doubts about the future of the West prompted by things like the GFC and fears of ecological crisis all call for reflection on what the West is about; what we stand for. The common denominator is freedom—and the rights and responsibilities that go with it.

The idea of freedom is our most fundamental Western heritage. It has universal relevance, but it is the creation of Western civilization. It is the underpinning of our civil rights, our political institutions, our classical and modern theatre, our literary and poetic traditions, our legal codes, our expectations with regard to the press, our philosophical schools and our remarkable breakthroughs in natural science, first in the ancient world and again since the Renaissance. It finds expression, also, in our music and fine arts.

Other civilizations have produced engineering and architectural wonders, schools of philosophy, innovations in mathematics, major religions, cultural beauties, wealth, empire and bureaucratic order of various kinds; but *no* other has autonomously generated and sustained this tradition of freedom, the idea of the open society and the rights of the individual. It may be unfashionable to say this, but it is true, nonetheless, and its implications are crucial in our time, as we wrestle with the dilemmas of globalization and what Samuel Huntington dubbed 'the clash of civilizations'.

To state this is not, of course, to assert that good government or virtue have always been the monopoly of the West. On the contrary, the discovery and practice of freedom were in the beginning and have remained perennially, difficult and exacting matters. Hypocrisy and corruption, the failure of republics, the suppression of religious and philosophical freedom, censorship, torture, slavery, genocide all mar the history of the West. Yet the voice of freedom has, again and again, been the rallying cry of Western culture for 2,500 years. It remains so now and must remain so on the world stage.

Freedom, political and intellectual, was *invented* by the ancient Greeks. It was pioneered, in the 6th and 5th centuries BCE, in conscious rejection of the monarchical pretensions of the Great King of Persia and in prolonged argument with the proponents of tyranny or oligarchy in Greece itself. Freedom of inquiry sprouted in the trading cities around the Aegean coastlands, not least in the cities of Ionia (the sea coast of modern Turkey), before the Persians conquered them. Here the pre-Socratics initiated uninhibited inquiry into the truth about the natural order of things, the nature of the gods, or even whether they existed. Elsewhere in Greece the ideas of speaking out fully and frankly in debates about public policy, as well as holding public officials accountable and being able to elect and expel them from office, also started at this time.

Defiance of the Persian Empire by (a minority of) the Greek city states and their remarkable defeat of the Great King's forces were a defining moment in the development of Western civilization. The Great King demanded submission from the Greeks. They rejected that demand. He could not believe that these little states would defy him. He set out to teach them a crushing lesson. They taught him one; humiliating his fleet at Salamis and then his massive army at Plataea. Greek freedoms were already under way before then, but after that they flourished.

Didn't the Athenians build an empire themselves, subordinating many other Greek cities; practise slavery; put Socrates to death for 'corrupting the youth'? Yes. Such things look objectionable, however, only if your assumption is that individuals have a right to be free and to speak out and reflect critically on traditions and prejudices without fear or favour. That assumption originated in ancient Greece. Often honoured in the breach or even suppressed by religious and political powers, it has revived again and again, in church, state and civil society. We are electrified by it in Sophocles and Demosthenes, in Cicero and Tacitus, in Erasmus and Galileo, Montaigne and Shakespeare, Voltaire, John Stuart Mill and George Orwell. It is the basis for the hope Barack Obama kindled in so many hearts and minds.

In the midst of present challenges, it is important to recapture a bracing sense of all this. This is especially so as China's wealth and power increase and Islamists seek a new caliphate by martial or propagandist means, while the decadent Left decries capitalism, champions 'militants' of almost any stripe and repeatedly calls for 'political correctness' in both public policy and public debate; while the unregenerate Right embraces conservative religion and 'business-as-usual' in economic and ecological affairs. There is a great need for clear minds and clear voices.

We need to revitalize both our education and our public discourse as things rooted in liberty, rational inquiry and freedom of dissent. They, not religious dogmatism or dictatorial politics, are what have given the world modern law, economics, science and democratic politics. Above all, they have thrown open the horizons of modern humanity and enlarged its possibilities as no religion or authoritarian polity has ever done. They have enabled us to see back to the foundations of the Earth billions of years ago, to grasp the evolution of life itself, to wonder at the immensity of the cosmos beyond the wildest imaginings of myth makers. They have begun to make the world one.

Despite all the challenges we face, therefore, this is not a time for capitulation, despair or cynicism. It is the time for a vast renewal of civilization around the world. That's not something which will be achieved overnight, nor is it something that can be directed by any central authority. It is something that requires freedom—of inquiry, of speech, of assembly and association; the freedom to hold and to change opinions, the freedom to criticize religious dogmas and to hold government officials accountable. It is something that will demand tremendous patience and imagination and innovation. It is something that will make very great demands on our own integrity. It is, precisely for these reasons, the bedrock of our debates with one another about the West, our shock at the attitude of Islamic fanatics like Abu Bakar Bashir and our refusal to buckle before the demands of the Chinese Communist Party.

Balibo: theatre and history

Robert Connolly's *Balibo*, in cinemas this week, graphically reconstructs the murder by Indonesian special forces, on 16 October 1975, of Greg Shackleton, Gary Cunningham, Tony Stewart, Malcolm Rennie and Brian Peters, because they had tried to capture on film Indonesia's covert invasion of East Timor. It does this through the story of Roger East, another Australian journalist who, having gone to find out what had happened to the Balibo five, was himself summarily shot by Indonesian soldiers on the docks in Dili on 7 December 1975, in the first hours of Indonesia's conventional invasion of East Timor.

Neither the Indonesian nor the Australian government has been keen to see this story publicly aired. It is refreshing to see that, nonetheless, it has been unsparingly dramatized. But *Balibo* provides too little historical background to what occurred. If it prompts viewers to inquire further that will be good. They should not settle for the over simple version it offers. The Balibo case has so long been a touchstone for public perceptions of the so-called Jakarta Lobby in Canberra. It is very important, for that reason, that the history be better understood.

There has been a long and complex debate within Australian government circles, ever since the 1940s, about how to come to terms with Indonesian nationalism and the ambition of the Javanese to control the entire archipelago that had made up the Dutch East Indies. Canberra opted to support Indonesian nationalists against the Dutch, in 1948, but for two decades after that struggled to come to terms with Sukarno, his loose alliance with the powerful Indonesian Communist Party (PKI) and his tendency to resort to force over territorial disputes. When Suharto rose to power in 1965-66, destroying the PKI and overthrowing Sukarno, there was enormous relief in Canberra. Thereafter, there was a strong disposition to work with Suharto—a feeling that was reciprocated in Jakarta.

Crucial to Canberra's perceptions of what scope it had for containing Indonesian territorial ambitions was the case of Dutch New Guinea (West Papua or Irian Jaya). A Top Secret study by Army Intelligence in 1957 advised that Australia's national interest would be best served by inducing the Dutch to cooperate in developing New Guinea and giving the whole of it independence eventually, as a unified and economically viable Melanesian state. Menzies agreed. The Dutch, however, were ambivalent. Sukarno was truculent and both Washington and London, in 1961, urged Canberra to accede to Sukarno's determination to annex West Papua. Menzies and his advisers were vexed, but felt that they had no effective choice left.

This set the stage for thinking about Portuguese Timor. It was far less well-endowed than Dutch New Guinea and governed even more negligently. It seemed highly likely that Sukarno would seek to annex it in due course. Significantly, just as the Dutch New Guinea issue came to a head, in December 1961, the Indians invaded Goa, the 451 year old Portuguese enclave in India. The fighting was all over within 36 hours, with 14 Indian and 31 Portuguese fatalities. The precedent seemed clear. Canberra had to think through what its position would be as regards Portuguese Timor.

In early 1962, Arthur Tange, Secretary of External (Foreign) Affairs, asked Gordon Jockel to write a study paper on the question. Jockel recommended that Australia openly press for the development and self-determination of Portuguese Timor; that it raise this matter in the UN, to head off Indonesian ambitions; that it make clear to Jakarta that incorporation was not inevitable and that Australia would not be an accomplice to any Indonesian exercise of *Realpolitik* in the matter. None of this was done, in part because both Tange and his Minister, Garfield Barwick, were looking for ways in which Australia might *acquiesce* in the passage of Portuguese Timor to Indonesia—as it was about to do in the case of Dutch New Guinea.

Gough Whitlam inherited this tacit policy history and took the Barwick line. This was all the more so because, from 1966, Canberra had decided to throw in its lot with Suharto as it's least bad option in regard to the future of Indonesia. Whitlam's thinking was further affected by several things which precipitated the case in 1974-75. A left-wing coup in Portugal brought Marxists to power in 1974 and they urged leftist forces in the country's colonies to take them over. Indonesian intelligence officers approached the Australian embassy, in early July 1974, requesting support for an Indonesian takeover of Portuguese Timor. And, in late 1974 and early 1975, the wars in Indochina reached their denouement, with the Communists seizing South Vietnam, Laos and Cambodia.

The debate in Canberra in these circumstances was both nuanced and fascinating. Tange was now Secretary of Defence and Jockel Director of the Joint Intelligence Organization. Against the explicit advice of Foreign Affairs and the strongly expressed views of senior Defence officials, Whitlam took the Barwick line. But he did not wish to publicly espouse it and seems to have expected that a Goa outcome would occur—as did Indonesia's military planners. Both Whitlam and the Indonesians were seriously in error on this score. At a meeting of senior officials with Secretary of Foreign Affairs Alan Renouf, in December 1974, Michael Cook and Gordon Jockel, in particular, made clear that there would be protracted and bloody fighting if Indonesia sought to annex the territory and that Canberra urgently needed to rethink its policy.

The Barwick/Whitlam approach would lead to 'a running sore for Indonesia', so integration was 'not a winnable goal', as Cook phrased it; and independence would have to be looked at in the long run. But the prime minister wanted to see incorporation, Richard Woolcott responded, and he had 'escape clauses if necessary.' Those 'escape clauses' were his refusal to openly support the use of force by Indonesia. He did, however, privately tell Suharto, in April 1975, that if push came to shove he would give priority to the relationship with Jakarta over the right of the Timorese to self-determination.

Jakarta then prepared a covert invasion, in the mistaken belief that it could quickly overrun Fretilin, raise a false flag in Dili, and then occupy the territory under that cover. Australian intelligence kept a close and anxious watch on the situation and, at Woolcott's urging, sought to deflect Australian public opinion from interest in or concern about the matter. But such interest and concern went all the way back to the Second World War and was not to be deflected. It was into this vortex that the five journalists stepped, in mid-October 1975. The rest, as they say, is history—but only a small, all-too-human part of that history is captured in *Balibo*.

Perfidious Albion and the merits of Zionism

The Balfour Declaration, in 1917, was the foundation stone on which, with British support, the Zionist movement was able to set about creating what would become the state of Israel in 1948. It consisted of two simple, but pregnant sentences:

1. His Majesty's government accepts the principle that Palestine should be reconstituted as the National Home of the Jewish people.
2. His Majesty's government will use its best endeavours to secure the achievement of this object and will discuss the necessary methods and means with the Zionist Organization.

Jonathan Schneer, in his path-breaking new study of how this declaration came to be made, comments:

> Note that the first sentence implies an unbroken link between Jews and Palestine despite the nearly two thousand year separation. Note that the second sentence posits the Zionist Organization as official representative of Jewish interests.

He is correct in both cases. Yet if there was, in fact, to be a national home for the Jews, where else would it naturally have been, if not in Palestine? And since the Zionist movement had been the advocates of just such a reconstitution of Jewish nationalism for decades before 1917, were they not the logical partners for such an endeavour on the part of the British government in 1917?

The more important questions, surely, are why did the British government see fit to make such a declaration and why were the Arabs so opposed to it then and ever after? The first of these questions is the chief object of Schneer's inquiry. The second question he only ever addresses obliquely and not, in my judgment, satisfactorily. This may be because his professional specialty is modern British history, not Middle Eastern history. It may also be because, as a founding editor of *Radical History Review*, he tends to accept without too much critical reflection the idea that the Arab rejection of Israel is rooted in justified grievances, exacerbated since 1948 by the power and toughness of Israel as a state. Certainly, he nowhere digs down into the roots of Muslim or Arab anti-Semitism, confining his explanation of Arab grievances to the double and, indeed, triple dealing in which Britain engaged during the First World War. This, I think, is a weakness in an otherwise fascinating and very well written work of history.

The great strengths of the book are Schneer's mastery of his British sources and his wonderful portrait gallery of the key British, Jewish, Arab, Turkish and other figures involved in the intrigues which led up to the declaration. Nowhere is this more in evidence than in his fine grained depiction of the many personalities in the Jewish community in Britain and their sometimes nuanced, but often vehement disagreements about the merits of Zionism. He is notably even handed and deeply humane in his descriptions of both the characters and their opinions. His book is not an anti-Zionist polemic. Rather, it underscores, in rich and fascinating detail the many considerations that played in the minds of Jews in the West's most liberal and tolerant society regarding the fate of Jews elsewhere, the feasibility of creating a Jewish homeland in Palestine, its acceptability in the light of Judaic religion and its likely impact on anti-Semitic feeling across Europe rather more than among the Arabs or other Muslims.

Above all, what Schneer shows in sometimes exquisite and occasionally excessive detail, is that the British decision to support Zionism was due much less to the lobbying of the Zionists than to the opportunism of British statesmen in the increasingly desperate struggle against the Central Powers and their illusions regarding the true global power and influence of the Jews. He remarks that:

> *the Balfour Declaration sprang from fundamental miscalculations about the power of Germany and about the power and unity of the Jews.*

Given that some of the most wealthy and powerful British Jews were not Zionists and that Britain's design in finally backing Zionism was an opportunistic gambit in a terrible war, Schneer argues that the idea would almost certainly never have gotten up had it not been for the British establishment forming the erroneous opinion that the Jews carried enormous influence in world finance and the secret counsels of governments and that this should be brought to bear against the Central Powers before the Central Powers themselves exploited it. Schneer doesn't say so, but the terrible irony of the history he shows us is that the pernicious libels against Zionism and the anti-Semitic myths that have so long gone with them are shown to be *false* by the historical archives but actually seemed to be *confirmed* by historical events.

Schneer begins his book with a few lines from Apollodorus about Cadmus, Athena and the sowing of dragon's teeth which then rose up from the ground in the form of armed men. He concludes with the lines:

> *During World War I, then, Britain and her allies slew the Ottoman dragon in the Middle East. By their policies they sowed dragons' teeth. Armed men rose up from the ground. They are still rising.*

His account of Allied ambitions and intrigues aimed at dismembering the Ottoman Empire and the manipulative promises made to the Arabs in an effort to enlist them against the Turks—rather like David Fromkin's *A Peace to End all Peace*—make clear enough how the dragon's teeth were sown. But Schneer leaves almost untouched the question of why it was always going to be so difficult for the Jews to find a homeland again in Palestine. True, there had not been a Jewish state there for almost two millennia. But there had never been a Palestinian Arab state. The prospect in 1917 was a Middle East made up of many new nations. There were many hundreds of thousands of Jews in the Islamic world. Why should they not have been a welcome and constructive part of the Semitic world? That question takes us into the dark heart of Islam. There Schneer does not venture.

Overthrowing Rudd: the system worked

The events of the last few weeks, culminating in the toppling of Kevin Rudd a week ago today, were a wonderful live tutorial in the workings of Australian democratic politics. Whatever one's interests or ideological leanings, they merit close study as demonstrating beautifully how the system works - and why it is so much better than the brutal and opaque system of authoritarian government practiced in China and being touted at present as the likely benchmark for 21st century politics around the world.

All the parts of the democratic system played their assigned roles with admirable efficiency. The free press hammered away at policy flaws and the increasingly problematic political style of the prime minister. Public opinion polls, conducted by independent organizations, gave voice to shifting popular sentiment. The political opposition, long on the back foot, but having regrouped under Tony Abbott, saw its opportunity and went on the offensive. The caucus of the governing party took note of the dramatic shift in popular sentiment and, fearing for their electoral future, cast around for a way to head off catastrophe. The factional leaders within the governing party quietly canvassed opinion, marshalled the numbers, approached their candidate and offered her their support, if she would agree to move decisively against the incumbent leader. The mining companies assailed by a poorly thought through government taxation initiative took their concerns to the public. And public intellectuals of various stripes vigorously debated the merits of the candidates for leadership of the Labour Party.

There are those who are calling the overthrow of Mr Rudd from within caucus an 'execution', but of course it was nothing of the kind. It was a consensual and peaceful process done by the numbers and gracefully accepted by Mr Rudd when he saw that his number was up. We don't do executions in the liberal democracies. That's the whole point of our system of government. And we have, in the place of Mr Rudd, a lively, intelligent and emotionally balanced prime minister, who also happens to be the country's first woman to hold that office.[263] Those with any misgivings about the manner of her elevation know that she must and will go to the polls before the year is out to seek an electoral mandate in competition with a resurgent opposition that has committed to prudent and constructive governance.

---

263   These lines stand as witness that I was not an anti-Labour or anti-Gillard partisan as of 2010. I was simply unprepared for the degree of fecklessness, recklessness and internal factional bitterness that ruined the Rudd/Gillard government under both prime ministers. I welcomed their rise, somewhat naively. I cannot say that I lament their falls. Unfortunately, the Coalition government that has replaced them is now exhibiting signs of similar dysfunction, while the ALP under Bill Shorten does not show any signs of having learned or changed its ways, since the defeat in 2013.

Yet despite all of this, there have been some commentators, on both side of politics, making wild claims that the removal of Kevin Rudd from the driver's seat was like the assassination of Julius Caesar. Not only was it not an assassination at all, but those making this claim would appear to have forgotten that the assassins of the real Julius Caesar acted because they believed he was seeking to establish a monarchy that would bring an end to the cherished, if troubled republican institutions they sought to revive. They failed. Our democratic system has not. We should all be celebrating its virtues right now.[264]

---

264 Not many months after the removal of Rudd as prime minister, I was in Sydney as a speaker at a small workshop on the Uighur minority in China and its treatment by the Chinese Communist Party and Han majority. I was asked to introduce Paul Howes and quipped that he would be interesting to listen to because he had had 'personal experience in overthrowing a Mandarin speaking tyrant'. He looked a little sheepish at that remark, but Michael Danby, the ALP member for Melbourne Ports and an old acquaintance, confided in me during a walk through the Botanical Gardens that the caucus had removed Rudd not because they feared he would lose them the next election, but because they feared he would win the next election 'and then we'd be stuck with the bastard'. On the basis of pure and surely misguided expediency he and others voted Rudd back in again, however, when it looked Like Julia Gillard would lose them their seats in 2013.

The climate debate: more heat than light

An argument can become intellectually interesting for various reasons, but three of the most important are its complexity; its dependence on subtle pieces of evidence or inference; and the perception that there are significant stakes in the matter. The climate debate has all three of these characteristics; so, it is a very interesting debate indeed. Unfortunately, the things that make arguments interesting also tend to trigger the cognitive biases and illusions to which human beings are generically prone. As a consequence arguments all too often generate more heat than light.

Over a period of years, this problem has gotten rather out of hand in the case of the climate debate. We have those committed to the view that anthropogenic global warming (AGW) is real and dangerous dismissing those who disagree with them as 'denialists' or 'climate skeptics' and even suggesting that they are moral miscreants, like Holocaust deniers. On the other hand, quite a number of the skeptics are prone to dismiss or attack the proponents of the AGW hypothesis as 'green fascists' or as believers in a new 'religion' and the like. Such epithets are symptoms of frustration and bewilderment; but they do nothing to resolve the substantive matters in dispute.

Fierce sectarian battles of this nature have marred human history for millennia. It was with a view to getting past them and discriminating better between truth and opinion, reality and illusion that both critical rationality and scientific method were developed. Neither of these things is hard-wired into the human brain; most human beings never master either of them; and even highly educated human beings all too readily fall away from the exacting mental disciplines they require when arguments in which they find themselves involved are complex, subtle, or seem to involve significant stakes.

Before exploring some of the ways in which this has played out in the debate over AGW, it is worth thinking about the credulousness of the ordinary human mind and just what it takes to carefully sift truth from error and illusion. We need to remember that the human brain is a "sense-making" organ that looks for patterns. It will find them - whether they are there or not. Belief in what are actually *illusory* patterns, which we dub superstitions, is very common, even in what we like to think of as a 'scientific society'. Misinterpretation of the significance of dramatic events is common, because the brain readily leaps to conclusions and, once this happens, they can be very difficult to dislodge, because we are generically prone to confirmation bias—seeking evidence to confirm our hunches or beliefs, while overlooking or devaluing what is at odds with them.

A charming anecdote about the philosopher Ludwig Wittgenstein nicely captures the problem of 'common sense' illusion as compared with scientifically deduced reality. It is a handy mental model for thinking about illusions, superstitions and over hasty conclusions. It goes like this: a student says to Wittgenstein, 'You know, it's really not surprising that people believed for so long that the Sun revolves around the Earth, because it looks like that is what happens.' To which the philosopher responds, 'Really? So, what *would* it look like if, actually, the Earth revolved around the Sun, while turning on its axis?' The answer, of course, is that it would look exactly the same. In other words, the truth of the matter does not spring to the eye and the human being unequipped with the intellectual tools and data to test the apparently obvious will never guess, much less be able to demonstrate, what the truth actually is.

To overcome this problem, which applies to an enormous range of things, we have had to develop highly specialized and very exacting methods for discriminating between truth and falsehood in natural science. Those methods have themselves been the subject of intense debate, first in the Hellenistic world, long ago, and then in the modern world. Among the most thoughtful philosophers of science and the scientific method was the 20th century philosopher Karl Popper. In *Conjectures and Refutations* and *Objective Knowledge: An Evolutionary Approach*, he argued that the gold standard for seeking truth was to formulate testable hypotheses and then try to *refute* them, *not* confirm them. If you cannot refute them, despite your best analytical and experimental efforts to do so, then you can have some confidence that you are in the ball park. And the most fruitful experiments are those which enable you to refute various competing hypotheses, leaving either one or none still standing. The whole idea of science, Popper once quipped, is to make the mistakes as quickly as possible.

This Popperian approach has been strenuously debated for decades and it is safe to say that it is not the way that 'normal science', as Thomas Kuhn put it, is actually done. However, it might be seen as ideally enacted at the 1927 and 1930 Solvay conferences, in Brussels, at which Albert Einstein, along with Hendrik Lorentz and Max Planck, confronted the proponents of the new theory of quantum mechanics and the famous 'uncertainty principle'. Einstein, Lorentz and Planck were the three grand masters of early 20th century physics. At Solvay, in 1927, Niels Bohr and his 'Young Turks', not least among them Werner Heisenberg and Paul Dirac, both only 25 years old, challenged the grand masters by presenting a hypothesis at odds with their basic view of how the physical world worked. Einstein was especially resistant to the new hypothesis. 'God', he famously remarked, 'does not play dice.' Again and again, over days, he came up with thought experiments designed to show Bohr and his protégés that they must be in error.

Again and again, after hours of debate, they would demonstrate that his efforts to refute their hypothesis did not work. He would accept the exacting logic of their counter-arguments each time—only to come up with a new thought experiment, which forced them to keep thinking. He failed to refute their case, but he returned with more arguments in 1930. As Heisenberg later wrote, this was a great test for them and left them much better off, because such a man had tried again and again to show them that they were wrong and had been unable to do so. Even if much science is not or cannot be done quite this way, this is surely a very nice example of scientific debate at its best. If we conduct debates in that manner, they are more likely to yield genuine insight: light, as we say, rather than simply heat. They are also likely to be more efficient than a drawn out process in which scientists doggedly seek to confirm their opinions without directly engaging in something like these debates.

Against that background, let's now turn to the AGW debate. We have been told many times in the past few years that "the science is settled" and "the debate is over". What does this mean? What science exactly? What does 'settled' mean in this context? And what precisely was the "debate" that is now ended? Well, the simplest possible answer to these questions would run as follows: there has been a kind of protracted Solvay conference about the hypothesis that dangerous anthropogenic global warming is occurring; the conference has concluded and those present have tried very hard to *refute* the hypothesis and have failed. Consequently, we have to report that AGW seems to be occurring, that it seems to be driven by greenhouse gases, most notably carbon dioxide (CO2) and we recommend that governments around the world take note of this and develop public policies to address the problem. Because CO2 appears to be the fundamental problem, we urge that serious steps be taken to decrease and even eliminate CO2 emissions.

At this point, several questions naturally arise. First, what precisely was the nature of the 'Solvay conference' in question? Second, what is the primary evidence that global warming is occurring at all, that it is anthropogenic, that it is dangerous and that the fundamental problem is CO2 emissions? Third, what was the nature of the effort to refute this compound hypothesis and why did that effort fail? Fourth, *how* dangerous, exactly, is this problem? And, fifth, what does it make most sense to *do* about it, in all the circumstances? But consider that, had the debate been about any number of fields of scientific or scholarly enquiry, we would not—as a general public—bother to ask such questions. In *The Humans Who Went Extinct* (2009), Clive Finlayson advances a novel hypothesis about human evolution. In *Fire: The Spark That Ignited Human Evolution* (2009), Frances Burton has advanced a bold new hypothesis on the role of fire in human cognitive evolution. In *The Horse, the Wheel and Language* (2009) David Anthony has set out a challenging new theory on the origins of the Indo-European languages. Some of us will read these books, but it is extremely unlikely they will become matters of public debate and name-calling. Other examples are legion. Why in *this* case, then, is there such public debate? Quite simply, because we are being told that the very future of civilization and even of life on Earth, is at stake and we need to drastically change our economies, our energy infrastructure and our consumption habits.

Given such stakes, isn't there a case to be made for guillotining debate and saying, 'We have to act quickly to cut CO_2 emissions?' Shouldn't Joe Public and the politicians accept the word of the scientific specialists that 'the science is settled' and fall in line behind urgent public policy measures—the Stimulus Package and then some, to use another mental model—and not put civilization at risk by refusing to accept the clear implications of so portentous a scientific finding? Indeed, if the science is truly 'settled' and civilization at imminent risk in the face of potentially catastrophic climate change, isn't it actually reprehensible, even downright immoral, to stand in the way or remain in denial? Well, that's what we are hearing from some quarters. And, if we were clear about both the science and the danger, there might be reasonable grounds for judgments of these kinds.

But if things were so clear, shouldn't there be transparent and testable answers to all five of the questions listed above? All the more so precisely because of the alleged gravity of the situation? The problem with 'denial' at this juncture is that it comes from multiple sources. One might well expect many people to be in denial of so shocking a reality, however good the evidence, simply because it would upend so many assumptions and expectations with which they have long been comfortable; or because it will directly affect their perceived material or institutional interests. But the complexity of the debate and the difficulty in the way of understanding the science behind the AGW hypothesis compound the problem. Perhaps the biggest problem has arisen, however, because the 'Solvay conference' in this case has been mediated by the Inter-Governmental Panel on Climate Change and the impression has been growing slowly for years that the IPCC has not conducted its work in the Solvay manner at all. It has *not* been a clearing house for attempts to *refute* the AGW hypothesis, but rather a political body committed from the outset to finding evidence that AGW is a reality.

Given all these considerations, surely there is a requirement that those holding positions of responsibility in such an inquiry adhere to the highest possible standards of scientific debate—standards that should ideally be applied, also, to debate over public policy. Those standards might consist in setting out the AGW hypothesis as clearly as possible; actively soliciting efforts to test and possibly refute it; and allowing that the way to test a hypothesis is not to seek evidence consistent with it, but to seek diagnostic evidence—evidence *inconsistent* with it, which would force us to either revise or abandon the hypothesis; likewise with public policy proposals, such as the ETS. In the wake of the recent disclosures about hasty acceptance of findings by the IPCC consistent with the AGW hypothesis, Chief Scientists John Beddington in the UK and Penny Sackett in Canberra have called for the IPCC to be more careful in checking the truth of claims. But considerably more than that is incumbent upon the IPCC: it must, in the nature of the case, seek as transparently as possible for evidence that its hypothesis is *false*. That might not be the normal standard, but it would be a standard of unimpeachable integrity.

Needless to say, what applies to the IPCC applies also to independent scientists investigating the matter; to journalists writing about it or to others venturing to think about it. One has only to read the literature to see that, for the most part, this is not what is happening. Consider just a few of the recent books on the subject. Al Gore's *Our Choice: A Plan to Solve the Climate Crisis* (Bloomsbury, 2009), James Hansen's *Storms of my Grandchildren* (Bloomsbury, 2009), Clive Hamilton's *Requiem for a Species: Why we resist the truth about climate change* (Allen & Unwin, 2009), Christopher Booker's *The Real Global Warming Disaster* (Continuum, 2009), and Ian Plimer's *Heaven and Earth: Global warming: the missing science* (Connor Court, 2009) are all recent contributions to the literature outside specialist journals and websites. Only two of the authors, Hansen and Plimer, have any claim to scientific expertise, but all of them take strong positions. None of them observes the Popperian standards.

The conclusion to Ian Plimer's book is a particularly notable case in point. He heads it 'What if I'm wrong?', then loads the dice by posing the question in the form 'What if all the solar physics, astronomy, history, archaeology and geology presented in this book is wrong?' This is very different from setting out a hypothesis and indicating how it might be tested. But he then proceeds to quote Lord Monckton on eighteen reasons why the *AGW* line of thinking is wrong. This is a rather odd way to address his initial question. He then closes with a quote from, of all people, Pope Benedict XVI and the final remark, 'Human stupidity is only exceeded by God's mercy, which is infinite.' Against that last remark, I scribbled in the margin, 'Meaning what? Do you have any evidence for this at all?' None of which is to say that Plimer has all his facts wrong, or that the AGW hypothesis is correct. Many a hypothesis has been refuted based on getting just a subtle point of evidence or inference wrong, while having almost all its facts right. Alas, those whom he dismisses as stupid exhibit many of the same tendencies as he does; which does not advance the debate, but bogs it down in rhetoric and vituperation.

Al Gore has been an energetic proponent of the AGW hypothesis for decades. His film, *An Inconvenient Truth*, seems to have had a considerable influence around the world in persuading vast numbers of people that the hypothesis is correct and that only the venal and the stupid are still in denial. After its release, the film was heavily criticized for its misleading claims and scientific errors. One would not guess this from reading *Our Choice*. Mr. Gore is a crusader, whose profound conviction seems to be that the natural world is a wonderful, balanced place that human beings are wantonly polluting and that the science of dangerous AGW is so well demonstrated that those who so much as challenge it are the intellectual equivalent of Flat Earthers. So fixed is his view in this regard that he continues, for example, to cite Hurricane Katrina as evidence that AGW is causing an increased frequency and intensity of hurricanes and tropical storms. Yet the scientific evidence on this is now apparently quite clear: there has *not* been any such increase. Mr. Gore is determined to offer sweeping proposals for the solution of a problem the existence of which he sees not as an alarming hypothesis, but as established fact. Yet he chooses to overlook inconvenient evidence at odds with that belief.

James Hansen, unlike Gore, at least has some claim to being a serious climate scientist. He has a long history of activism on the matter of AGW. Early in his book, he makes the disarming statements that he is not a very good communicator and has had to work hard, at the age of sixty, to write a book clearly setting out his analysis of AGW; and that he is a scientist who seeks to be a witness, not a preacher. He speaks of his beautiful grandchildren and his concern about the future, which is touching. And he makes a genuine effort to set out clearly the scientific considerations behind his belief in the most alarming version of the AGW hypothesis: that if we use fossil fuels through to the end of the 21st century, including tar sands and tar shale, then a runaway greenhouse effect that 'will destroy all life on the planet, perhaps permanently'—something he calls the Venus syndrome—'is a dead certainty.' Along the way, while naming almost none of them, he manages to assert repeatedly that the only people opposing this analysis are 'special interests' and a few scientists who have a record of serving those interests. He names MIT's Richard Lindzen, for instance, as having helped Big Tobacco defend itself against claims that cigarettes cause cancer.

Now, ask yourself, even if you have the impression that AGW is a reality and a genuine problem for humanity, had it occurred to you that this Venus syndrome was what was coming? If you accept AGW on the basis that 'the science is settled', what do you make of Hansen's remarkable claim? Is *that* settled? He claims that it is 'a dead certainty'. Let's allow, for the sake of argument, that he might be right. How would we know? Surely we would want at this juncture to go back to our five questions about the provenance and reliability of his 'dead certainty'. But if it is warranted in *this* case, where would we draw the line as we work our way back to less extravagant versions of the AGW hypothesis?

If, for example we read *Fixing Climate: The Story of Climate Science and How to Stop Global Warming* (Green Profile, 2008), by Robert Kunzig and Wallace Broecker, we get a very much more temperate and moderately optimistic account of what the problem is and how we might address it. But even there, the central underpinnings of the AGW hypothesis are not really made explicit for testing. Kunzig and Broecker set out quite clearly the very *basic* and settled science that CO_2 is a greenhouse gas (as Svante Arrhenius demonstrated a century or so ago), that industrial civilization has been putting considerable quantities of CO_2 into the atmosphere for well over a century (as Charles David Keeling first demonstrated many years ago) and that, in the late 20th century, global temperatures edged up by a fraction of a degree (though they have failed to further rise somewhat in the past decade). It is past this point, however, that the debate about climate *sensitivity* to CO_2 begins with regard to climate models, projections and assumptions 'forcing'.

Christopher Booker, in *The Real Global Warming Catastrophe*, is on the case of all those who profess certainty about AGW. He is a debater, skilled at repartee and he mocks those 'warmists' who have been meeting in conditions of extreme cold and even record snowfalls in the past couple of years, kept warm by coal-fired electricity for the most part, to discuss how to prevent global warming. But Booker, like his opposite numbers, is not trying to make the best case against his own preferred belief or hypothesis; only to score clever points in debunking a hypothesis which he believes to be dangerous nonsense. If you are uncertain what to believe in this matter, or if you are inclined to believe that truth and virtue are all on the side of the AGW people, you should read Booker and take his various punches, sometimes quite telling in points of detail, on the chin. Think, don't dismiss, is the rule here.

Clive Hamilton's *Requiem for a Species* leans somewhat in the Hansen direction as regards his view of the science, but having declared that he sees 'the science' as settled, he proceeds to do several somewhat tendentious things. He says anyone who disagrees must demonstrate that there is something wrong with the science, which is quite correct; but then dismisses anyone who goes down that path as 'right-wing' and therefore, it seems, self-evidently wrong or having ulterior motives. Likewise with the public policy debate, in which he is dismissive of highly credentialed critics of the Stern report such as William Nordhaus and Richard Tol. He laments the mess we are putatively making of the planet and asserts this has come about because of the West's 'Cartesian' science; capitalism's encouragement of greed and over-consumption; and male psychology or testosterone, on which he appears to want to pin blame for science and capitalism arising to dominance in the first place. Oddly enough, he then declares that technological innovation in renewable energies will set things to rights, if only we set science and the market free to deliver it. His is, by a fair margin, the least illuminating or disciplined of the books under discussion.

Collectively we need to do better than this. Not only is that so because the stakes in climatic and economic terms, as everyone agrees, are about as high as they can get, whether the AGW hypothesis is correct or not; but because, more generally, we need to cultivate better habits of debating matters of moment, as regards both what is so and what is to be done. And it is for precisely this reason that the recent disclosures about the IPCC's sloppy handling of evidence and the scandalously anti-scientific behaviour of the AGW proponents at the East Anglia Climate Research Centre and elsewhere are so disturbing. These people have been—supposedly—conducting the AGW 'Solvay conference' for about twenty years. What we are beginning to see is that they have not been following the Solvay rules at all. In fact, they have been seeking for some considerable time, to prevent or discredit any attempt to refute their hypothesis and have manipulated evidence in an effort not merely to confirm it, as bona fide evidence might be taken to do, but to *appear* to confirm it, when they knew that there were all kinds of uncertainties in the data. This is, quite simply, inadmissible.

Georges Monbiot has lamented recently, in the wake of the Copenhagen conference, that 'climate skepticism' is 'spreading like an infectious disease'. He may or may not be right, but his attitude is dead wrong. The AGW hypothesis is, in the nature of the case contestable, a claim based on highly complex data. Where inferences from the data or the reliability of the data itself seem unclear or tendentious, skepticism is completely natural. But more importantly, skepticism is the life blood of both science and democracy. Those who sincerely believe AGW is threatening civilization should themselves be as actively and rigorously skeptical as possible. They should be *soliciting* challenges to their data and inferences. That's what the scientific method *is* and it doesn't end because someone, scientist or otherwise, feels certain of their ground. It goes on and we need it to do so. It is the same with the proposal for an ETS as public policy. Let's have an end of denunciation, vituperation and exasperation. For the sake of science, civilization and democratic governance, we need clarity in this matter. And clarity comes through making one's arguments explicit and then trying to find where one could be in error. That's the gold standard—for all parties to all serious debates.

Michael Scammell on Solzhenitsyn and Koestler

'Oh! Is GULAG an acronym? I always thought the Gulag Archipelago was the name of a group of islands where there just happened to be prisons,' exclaimed a friend recently. I explained that it stood for Glavnoe Upravlenie ispravitel'no-trudovykh LAGerei—main administration of corrective labour camps—a vast system of prisons extending the length and breadth of the Soviet Union. My friend's remark shows how vague the world is in general to the ordinary citizen. But it was ever thus—even in the Soviet Union under Stalin. That's why it requires special witnesses and extraordinary writing to bring such realities alive for people.

Solzhenitsyn's opening to *The Gulag Archipelago* captures beautifully the vagueness which prevailed then, as it does still, regarding the sinister realities of the concentration camp world:

> How do people get to this clandestine Archipelago? Hour by hour planes fly there, ships steer their course there, and trains thunder off to it—but all with nary a mark on them to tell of their destination. And at ticket windows or travel bureaus for Soviet or foreign tourists the employees would be astounded if you were to ask for a ticket to go there. They know nothing and they've never heard of the Archipelago as a whole or of any one of its innumerable islands.

He went on to describe how almost everyone contrived to overlook the reality of the system until it struck them down like a bolt of lightning, at the moment of their arrest, which for him came in 1945, when he was serving with the Red Army in East Prussia:

> If you are arrested, can anything else remain unshattered by this cataclysm? But the darkened mind... drawing on all life's experience, can gasp out only, 'Me? What for?'... We have been happily borne—or perhaps have unhappily dragged our weary way—down the long and crooked streets of our lives, past all kinds of walls and fences made of rotting wood, rammed earth, brick, concrete, iron railings. We have never given a thought to what lies behind them. We have never tried to penetrate them with our vision or our understanding. But there is where the Gulag country begins, right next to us, two yards away from us. In addition, we have failed to notice an enormous number of closely fitted, well-disguised doors and gates in these fences. All those gates were prepared for us, every last one! And, all of a sudden the fateful gate swings quickly open, and four white male hands, unaccustomed to physical labour, but nonetheless strong and tenacious, grab us by the leg, arm, collar, cap, ear, and drag us in like a sack, and the gate behind us, the gate to our past life, is slammed shut once and for all.

So it was for millions in the Stalin years. But a moment's reflection on the above passage will reveal that Solzhenitsyn's words act not only as a description of the shock of being arrested and flung into Stalin's prison system, but as a description of the vagueness with which almost all of us live in general—until the shock of reality hits us out of the blue, whether it be a terrorist assault on New York, a global financial crisis or the discovery that we have a terminal illness.

It is only relatively rare individuals who make it their business to think about and look into such things pro-actively. And, of those, the ones who are able to describe what they discover in powerful language are even rarer. During the darkest years of the 20th century, Arthur Koestler and Alexander Solzhenitsyn were among them. Michael Scammell has written biographies of each of them. Doing so has been a major part of his own awakened life, as a translator of Russian novelists (Tolstoy, Dostoevsky, Nabokov) and Soviet-era dissidents (Marchenko, Bukovsky, Solzhenitsyn) and a teacher of non-fiction writing and translation at Columbia University. Published a generation apart, both biographies are monumental studies in what it means to be a rare witness and an extraordinary writer.

The sub-title of *Koestler* in the British edition is 'The Indispensable Intellectual'; in the American edition it is 'The Literary and Political Odyssey of a Twentieth-Century Sceptic'. The second is better. Koestler was not 'indispensable' and most of his intellectual work, while notable for its iconoclasm, was not of the first rank. He was a good journalist and a tenacious explorer, but of his published work, probably only *Darkness at Noon*, his 1940 novel about the moral and human catastrophe of Stalinism, can rightly be called a classic. Its strength was and is rooted in the author's personal experience of being in a fascist prison and his intimate acquaintance with prominent communist figures, on whom his literary characters are based.

Koestler's literary and political odyssey through the twentieth century was remarkable. A Hungarian Jew, he flirted with Zionism, embraced Communism, worked as a left-wing journalist and anti-fascist crusader, saw the evil in Stalinism and became an anti-Communist, helping to found the Congress for Cultural Freedom in the 1950s. Journalist and novelist, iconoclast and explorer, he mingled and sparred with the leading Zionist, communist, existentialist, liberal and conservative intellectuals of the mid-20th century. A restless free spirit, he travelled to the North Pole on the *Graf Zeppelin*, lived on a primitive *kibbutz* in British Palestine, journeyed through Stalin's Soviet Union, lived dangerously in war-torn Spain, lived in half a dozen great cities (Budapest, Berlin, Moscow, Paris, Jerusalem, London), experimented with hallucinogens and ended his life at a time of his own choosing, when he realized that he was terminally ill.

Having read Scammell's *Koestler*, I found myself compelled finally to read his monumental *Solzhenitsyn*, which had been sitting on my library shelves for 23 years. Reading the two biographies so close together and in reverse order was a rewarding experience. Not only was each a study in a writer's development; but the two books, taken together, were a study in the development of the biographer. The books afforded an opportunity to compare the lives of two witnesses to the nature of Stalin's prisons. I had found the Koestler biography astonishing. I found the Solzhenitsyn biography utterly absorbing. The latter was necessarily an "unfinished life", since it was published in 1984, while Solzhenitsyn lived until 2008. But by 1984, he had done his greatest work; and Scammell's exploration of the life world out of which that work grew was remarkable, especially given the serious restrictions on his freedom to do research inside the Soviet Union.

Scammell was born in 1935 in Britain. His immersion in the Russian world dates back to the early 1950s, when, at the age of eighteen, drafted for national service and assigned to the intelligence corps, he was directed into two years of Russian language study. By his own account, he 'emerged with a passion for classical Russian literature', which lasted through three years of undergraduate studies at Nottingham University and four at graduate school in New York. Upon his return to Britain, he says, 'I was drawn to reading and translating Soviet dissident literature, and it was this experience that led me to found the magazine, *Index on Censorship*. Although the latter's field of view was global, it was inevitable that the countries of the Soviet bloc would figure prominently in its pages.'

It was then that he discovered Solzhenitsyn, 'that quintessential dissident ... whose profile perfectly matched my two principal obsessions: good writing and freedom of expression.' Wonderful obsessions - nourished for thirty years, before he completed *Solzhenitsyn*, by a passion for classical Russian literature. And this is evident in the manner of his writing about the great Soviet dissident. Chapter after chapter exudes a profound appreciation of the world of Russian landscapes and letters. He paints richly sympathetic portraits of Solzhenitsyn's forbears in the Tolstoyan world of the North Caucasus before the Bolshevik revolution shattered it. His cast of characters, not least Solzhenitsyn's ill-fated mother Taissia Shcherbak, his first wife Natalia Reshetovskaya and the great poet, literary critic and editor of *Novy Mir* (*New World*), Alexander Tvardovsky, are worthy of the great Russian novelists themselves. He follows Solzhenitsyn through more than sixty years, as always wanting to emulate Tolstoy, but compelled by the times to become a new Dostoevsky.

To see Solzhenitsyn in perspective, however, it is necessary not only to appreciate the great Russian writers who preceded him, but the many great Russian writers who were destroyed by the Soviet regime. It was already possible to do something of this in the early 1980s, when Scammell was writing his biography. But the collapse of the Soviet Union made it possible to render a fuller account of the destruction wrought on Russian life and letters by the communists. Vitaly Shentalinsky's *Arrested Voices: Resurrecting the Disappeared Writers of the Soviet Regime* sketches something of this story. Later this year, there will appear in English for the first time the full text of a novel by Andrei Platonov, who died in poverty and obscurity in Stalin's Russia in 1951, his works banned. It is called *The Foundation Pit* and is one of the chief reasons why Platonov, almost sixty years after his death, is coming to be seen as the greatest prose stylist in 20th century Russian literature—greater than Solzhenitsyn or Pasternak.

Some 1,500 writers perished under the Soviet regime. It was taken for granted in the Stalin years, moreover, that the wives and children of executed writers should also be shot or imprisoned. The regime suppressed their writing, tortured them, shot them and invented false dates for their deaths, because they had not been sentenced to death, but to '10 years without the right of correspondence'. Pavel Florensky was shot in Solovki in 1937, but officially died in exile on 15 December 1943. Isaac Babel was shot in Moscow on 27 January 1940. Officially, he died in a prison camp on 17 March 1941. Robert Conquest remarks, in his introduction to Shentalinsky's book, that the average age of death of creative Russians who fled into exile when the Bolsheviks seized power was 72; that for those who remained was 45.

The sheer brutality of the world of the Gulag is poignantly captured by Rachel Polonsky, in her beautiful, newly published book *Molotov's Magic Lantern* with a passing reference to the tragedy of the lovely Bolshoi Opera contralto, Olga Mikhailova. The child of a working class family, she studied singing in Moscow in the 1920s and then became a professional opera singer. She 'was arrested in August 1937 for attending receptions at foreign embassies.' The fact that she was the (second) wife of Marshall Budyonny, one of Stalin's military henchmen, did not save her. 'After nineteen years in prison and the Gulag, she returned to Moscow, her physical and mental health broken, with stories that no-one wanted to hear of her repeated gang rapes in the camps.' She was one of countless people destroyed by the Stalinist system even though they were not executed outright. This is the world to which Solzhenitsyn bore witness, having survived it—and outlived Stalin.

'Solzhenitsyn led me to Koestler', Scammell says, 'for having written Solzhenitsyn's biography, I was approached by Koestler's literary executor to write about him, too. In my own mind, *Solzhenitsyn* is the more romantic and passionate book, the one in which I let loose (and went on for too long), *Koestler* is calmer, more controlled, more cannily composed - and covers a lot more ground, of course - so you could say yes, I felt more masterful while writing it.' As a finished piece of work, which brings its subject's life to a close, it does have the qualities Scammell claims. Reading the two books in reverse order, however, I did not find myself thinking that the 'more romantic and passionate book' went on too long. Greatly though I enjoyed the biography of Koestler, I found that of Solzhenitsyn more compelling; perhaps because its author was more passionate and less controlled; but also because Solzhenitsyn was the greater figure. *Darkness at Noon* stands up well in comparison with such good recent novels about the Great Terror, such as Alan Furst's *Dark Star* or Robert Littell's *The Stalin Epigram*. But *The Gulag Archipelago, In the First Circle, Cancer Ward* and *One Day in the Life of Ivan Denisovich* invite comparison with the great novels of Dostoevsky.

Koestler was far more of an adventurer and *bon vivant* than Solzhenitsyn and would have been better company. Solzhenitsyn's vocation was writing and he subordinated everything else to it—comfort, love, friendship, safety. His work habits were relentless and, even when cohabiting with a wife—he married twice, each time to a woman named Natalia—he insisted that his writing was not only his own priority but must be hers. Koestler loved to party, drank like a fish and was a quite remarkable Casanova. Yet he, also, had astonishingly disciplined work habits. According to Scammell, for most of his adult life, regardless of how much he had drunk or how late he went to sleep the night before, he rose with the sun, had a cold shower, ate a light breakfast and sat down to his writing desk.

If Scammell himself believes he went on too long in *Solzhenitsyn*, it might be said that both of his subjects wrote too much, always wanting to write more and thinking they could write better. Neither entirely realized his ambitions. Koestler was prolific, but after *Darkness at Noon* he struggled to write things of enduring literary value. He was at his best as a polemicist in the Cold War. He wandered off, later, into increasingly eccentric preoccupations with parapsychology and idiosyncratic reflections on the history and philosophy of science. Solzhenitsyn persisted in trying to write a gigantic Tolstoyan epic about the Russian revolution, *The Red Wheel*, thinking it was his chief work. His chief work, in fact, was his Dostoevskyan writing about the Soviet world of the 1940s and 1950s. Each did his best writing when he had something of profound seriousness to write about and when freedom of expression was a life and death matter. Scammell's deeply researched and judicious biographies help us to see all this in the perspective of his subjects' lives.

One of the most generous and judicious aspects of Scammell's life of Koestler is his account of the writer's relationships with the key women in his life: his mother and his wives and lovers - Eva Striker, Dorothee Ascher, Daphne Hardy (who translated *Darkness at Noon* into English as it was written in Paris), Mamaine Paget, Eva Auer and Cynthia Jefferies. His compulsive promiscuity outside these relationships is astonishing. In 1943, Daphne Hardy found a notebook he'd kept with the names of about two hundred women he had bedded. Like Solzhenitsyn, he seems to have wanted in his wives less a mother substitute than a house servant and amanuensis. He did not partner, strictly speaking. He was a solitary. In this respect, he was not unlike Solzhenitsyn, but incomparably more hedonistic. Controversially, he took his last wife, Cynthia, many years his junior, with him in suicide at the end. The final chapter of *Koestler*, before the Epilogue, is about this choice of his—and hers. It is called 'An Easy Way of Dying'.

It was characteristic of Koestler that, confronted by degenerative disease at 78, he chose to end his life pharmacologically, rather than fatalistically accept his growing helplessness. He just as characteristically wrote a lucid suicide note, more than six months in advance, making it clear, as Scammell records, 'that the decision to kill himself was his own, that he had legally collected and stored the necessary drugs over a period of time, and that he would take the drugs 'without the knowledge or aid of any other person', a phrase intended to spare Cynthia any unpleasant legal consequences.' At the point when he wrote this, he plainly expected her to survive him. The hardest part about making the decision to end his own life, he wrote, was knowing the pain it would inflict on those close to him, 'above all my wife Cynthia.' Transcending the Lothario instincts of a lifetime, he added, 'It is to her that I owe the relative peace and happiness that I enjoyed in the last period of my life—and never before.'

Cynthia made her own free decision to go with him. Scammell remarks that, had she lived, she might have prevented what was a precipitate decline in his literary reputation 'by acting as keeper of the flame and tending to Koestler's literary heritage, much as Sonia had done after Orwell died ... That she decided otherwise is a mystery the bystander cannot penetrate, but it became clear soon afterward that she knew what she was doing.' Having read Scammell's account of the matter, I do not believe that Cynthia's decision is the mystery he claims. She had loved not Koestler's fame, or money, but him. She yearned not to be the keeper of a flame, but to remain with him, in death as in life. Koestler was not to blame for her death. He wished to leave a final witness to the virtues of voluntary euthanasia. Cynthia's decision to join him rather than survive him was one he neither prompted nor, it seems, was able to veto. Both of them, individually, made free decisions about when and why they would bid life goodbye.

Choosing one's death remains morally and legally controversial, but it is, surely, the antithesis of that state of astonishment and helplessness at one's arrest to which Solzhenitsyn so memorably testified in *The Gulag Archipelago*. Doing so was a fitting end to Koestler's robustly free life. Both Koestler and Solzhenitsyn were passionate and uncompromising witnesses to the violence of tyranny and the horrors of imprisonment. Each explored the psychology of human bondage and moral freedom. Neither was vague or asleep. Each was a prodigy of wakeful energy: observing, thinking, intent on the craft of writing and committed to freedom of expression. That's why their stories are compelling—both the stories they wrote and the stories of their lives. We owe to them the stories they wrote themselves. The stories of their lives we owe, in an important sense, to Michael Scammell. Both are eminently worth absorbing into our own lives.

Latin America and the Washington consensus

Paul Keating warned, in 1986, that unless Australia embraced economic reform it would 'end up being a third-rate economy ... a banana republic'. Under the Hawke, Keating and Howard governments, Australia did reform. The result was an economic revitalisation. We rode out the Asian financial crisis with notable resilience and we have done the same in the recent global financial crisis. Australia is not a banana republic or a third-rate economy, because of all those reforms.

Many countries have done less well and the crises of the past decade have engendered widespread misgivings about liberal economic principles. Misgivings arose in Asia from the 1997 financial crisis. They arose in Latin America in the wake of the 2001-02 Argentine debacle. They went global with the GFC. In Australia, Kevin Rudd sought to carve out a political leadership role by declaring, in *The Monthly*, that we were seeing the demise of neo-liberalism and that social democracy was the solution. Now, both sides of politics in Australia appear to have lost the nerve for liberal economic reform.

Meanwhile, China's achievements have suggested that the so-called Washington Consensus is not all it was cracked up to be; that in fact it has cracked up; and that a 'Beijing Consensus' - an illiberal political order and a state-directed economy - offers an alternative. In *The Beijing Consensus: How China's Authoritarian Model Will Dominate the Twenty-First Century*, Stefan Halper argues that this is the challenge China is setting before the US. In *The Forgotten Continent: The Battle for Latin America's Soul*, Michael Reid has analysed the emergence of comparable tendencies in Latin America, most notably in Venezuela under Hugo Chavez and Argentina under Nestor and Cristina Kirchner.

We in Australia need to engage in economic debate in a manner that is nuanced, analytical and historically informed, rather than ideologically impassioned or platitudinous. Paul Kelly's *The March of Patriots* is an excellent aide to such debate. But we would do well to look closely at the debates playing out elsewhere, because they throw into sharp relief many of the issues with which we are concerned. This is especially true of Latin America, the continent of "banana republics" and third-rate economies, though it tends to be neglected by Australians.

Reid's book is invaluable. But Sebastian Edwards, a professor of international business economics at the University of California, Los Angeles, has just published a shorter, crisper, updated analysis of the issues involved, under the title *Left Behind: Latin America and the False Promise of Populism*. Both books reflect on the debate over the Washington Consensus and each is concerned to clarify why successful reform and sustained increases in reasonably equitable economic growth have been so difficult in Latin America.

What exactly is the Washington Consensus? The term was coined by economist John Williamson in 1990, in his monograph *Latin American Adjustment: How Much Has Happened?* He listed 10 criteria as a benchmark against which to assess the vigour and flexibility of Latin American economies:

Achieve fiscal balance as a means of reducing inflationary pressures and stabilising prices.

Target public expenditures on the poorer groups in the population. Give priority to government expenditures aimed at improving social conditions and reducing poverty; avoid generalised subsidies that benefit mostly the middle class.

Implement deep tax reforms in order to reduce evasion, increase government income and eliminate perverse incentives as regards both production and investment.

Free interest rates and modernise the financial sector, since a well-functioning capital market tends to allocate scarce capital to the most productive uses and market-determined interest rates discourage capital flight.

Avoid having an artificially strong currency, since this discourages exports and tends to trigger a potentially devastating currency crisis.

Reduce the extent of protectionism and rationalise trade policy.

Encourage foreign direct investment, since foreign capital will provide both the funds for new economic initiatives and the technology and management methods that are needed to raise productivity.

Privatise inefficient state-owned enterprises. Sell them to private investors, domestic or foreign.

Deregulate business transactions, including investment decisions. Cut red tape that raises barriers to entry in key industries.

Improve legal protection of property rights in order to secure greater investment by both foreigners and nationals.

Edwards comments that all this was 'not defined by the Washington bureaucracies at the International Monetary Fund, the World Bank or the US Treasury' and could quite easily have consisted of a dozen or 20 broad policy principles. It was limited to 10 for simplicity's sake. He adds various other considerations and pays particular attention to the subtleties and complexities of reform in four countries: Chile, Mexico, Argentina and Venezuela.

His net assessment is crucial: there was a Latin America-wide willingness to embrace liberal economic reform in the 1980s, and by 1992 every country in the region except Cuba and Haiti had done so. Yet the reforms that were implemented:

only barely scratched the surface of Latin America's policy environment. In fact, most Latin American economies are still among the most regulated, distorted and protectionist in the world. In many of them, it is difficult to start a business, regulations are stifling and taxes are very high. With very few exceptions, institutions continue to be extremely weak: property rights are not protected sufficiently, the judiciary is inefficient, contracts are difficult to enforce, corruption is pervasive and the rule of law is wanting. Moreover, throughout the region governments continue to be very large and highly inefficient and fail to provide basic services, including quality education, infrastructure and support for research and development.

Chile, Edwards observes, is the standard-bearer of sustained and successful liberal economic reform in Latin America. This has long been contested, because the reforms were carried out under Augusto Pinochet, who seized power in a brutal *coup d'état* in September 1973. Moreover, the reforms were identified with the disciples of Milton Friedman, known as the Chicago Boys. Those resistant to his economic philosophy looked to find fault with how it was applied in Chile. Edwards's account shows that Chicago-style liberalism was far from being the military's preference. However, the liberal economists won key policy debates and, crucially, the government persevered with reform through a currency crisis in the early 80s, with such striking results that the post-Pinochet democratic governments endorsed and supported the new economic order.

'By 1990 there was little doubt that Chile's new approach to economic policy had produced an export boom, an acceleration in productivity gains, rapid overall growth and a reduction in poverty'. Indeed, in the period between 1975 and 2006, Chile's income per capita increased from 25 per cent of the US level to 40 per cent, while across Latin America as a whole it decreased from 24 per cent to 19 per cent. This should inform reflections on whether neo-liberalism has failed in Latin America. But the cases of Mexico, Argentina and Venezuela are widely seen as showing that it did; which makes Edwards's analysis of these cases even more important than his account of Chile's success.

Mexico's liberal reforms led to the signing of the North American Free Trade Agreement and the financial markets' infatuation with Mexico's prospects. But its performance was far less impressive than that of Chile. It grew at an annual average rate of 2.8 per cent compared with Chile's 7.1 per cent; productivity growth was almost flat, export expansion was unimpressive, real wages did not increase, private savings declined, while the incidence of poverty and inequality continued to be very high. Also, the Mexican currency, the peso, was pegged to the US dollar rather than allowed to float, with the result that it became seriously overvalued as foreign money poured in, much of it speculative. The warnings of a few perceptive observers such as Rudi Dornbusch and Paul Krugman about the danger this presented went unheeded. The consequence was a currency collapse in 1994 that devastated the Mexican economy and set back the cause of reform for years.

The nature of the Mexican crisis anticipated in many ways what occurred in Asia a few years later. Yet the same error was spectacularly and tragically repeated in Argentina. It had also been at the heart of Chile's 1982 crisis and Chilean policy-makers had learned their lesson, but Argentina didn't heed Chile's experience or that of Mexico. Edwards calls his chapter on Argentina 'The Mother of all Crises', because in late December 2001 Argentina defaulted on its foreign debt and entered one of the most traumatic currency crises of modern history. The Argentine peso lost two-thirds of its value in two months, the country went through five presidents in a matter of weeks and the number of households in Buenos Aires living in poverty leaped from 12 per cent to more than 40 per cent.

The Argentine meltdown led to widespread attacks on neo-liberalism. Joseph Stiglitz blamed the Washington Consensus and the IMF for the catastrophe, and went on to champion China's approach to economic reform and development as an alternative. Edwards argues that Stiglitz is wrong. The Washington Consensus called for avoiding fiscal deficits in times of economic growth, avoiding an overly strong currency and seeking to increase both flexibility in the labour market and a business environment receptive to foreign investment and supportive of export industries. Argentina violated every one of these prescriptions.

Crucial to Stiglitz's case is his claim that Argentina's misfortunes were caused by external shocks, which 'were compounded by the strong dollar; since the Argentine peso was tied to the dollar, it was increasingly overvalued'. But as Edwards points out, 'The problem was not the shocks themselves; the problem was that Argentina was ill-prepared to survive them.' Australia, of course, rode out these same shocks remarkably well precisely because it was *well* prepared to survive them, having adopted exactly the kind of reforms that are integral to the Washington Consensus.

Not least among Australia's 'neo-liberal' reforms was the decision to float the dollar. The Howard government further buttressed the economy by getting the federal budget into surplus as the economy grew and paying off national debt. The attempt to take reform further, by increasing the flexibility of the labour market, ran into a political brick wall in 2007. It has been represented as part and parcel of a neo-liberal 'brutopia'. The real brutopia, however, happened in Argentina in 2002.

Venezuela's story is even sorrier than that of Argentina. Chavez describes his Bolivarian economic policies as a corrective to the excesses and failures of neo-liberalism. But they are actually the culmination of a populist trend of long standing that cries out for reversal through serious and patient liberalisation of the economy. Such attempts as there were at liberal reform in Venezuela were only ever half-hearted and came to an end in 1993, when Rafael Caldera won the presidency on a populist platform and undid even the rudimentary liberal reforms of his predecessor, Carlos Andres Perez. As of 1998, when Chavez took power, Venezuela had implemented the fewest reforms in Latin America.

Venezuela suffers from the notorious 'oil curse'. Big increases in oil prices in the 70s enabled successive Venezuelan governments to spend irresponsibly. Chavez has taken this behaviour to unprecedented heights. Superficially, oil made Venezuela a wonderful place to be back then. But it fuelled corruption on a grand scale, protectionism, thoughtless social expenditure and political complacency. The consequences were destructive. Between 1980 and 1995, Venezuela's per capita income declined by 18 per cent, compared with an increase of 45 per cent in Chile.

When Andres Perez took office in 1989, Venezuela's economy was on the brink of collapse. 'The external debt was enormous, the fiscal deficit was out of control, there were food shortages and credit had all but disappeared.' A shock program was designed to halt the slide, but the social and political reaction to it stopped the reforms in their tracks. Chavez rode to power on the back of that reaction and, failing utterly to understand the underlying problems, proceeded to attempt what he has described as a socialist economic transformation.

All this is surely instructive from an Australian point of view. It is also a sobering context in which to reflect on the huge economic problems dragging the US down and the apparently relentless rise of China. That is what makes Halper's book timely and thought-provoking. The two concurrent, and connected, developments are, he argues, shrinking the West and enabling China to tout in Africa, the Middle East, Central Asia and Latin America an alternative model of economic development combined with authoritarian politics.

Australia, economically and geo-strategically, is caught between a rising China and an America widely seen as being in serious if not precipitous decline. We must think very hard about these things as we seek to chart a course ahead. Chinese general Liu Yazhou recently declared that China's rise will not be sustainable unless it democratises on broadly American lines. That remains uncertain. What is certain is that our freedom and prosperity will not be sustained if we cease thinking, reforming and innovating to stay flexible and competitive.

Conspiracy theory vs learning: Assange and Ellsberg

The single most important reference point in the debate over the WikiLeaks case is the leaking of the *Pentagon Papers* to the *New York Times*, in 1971, by Daniel Ellsberg. Those who see Ellsberg as a hero tend to see Julian Assange as one. Those critical of Assange tend to denounce what he has done for the same reasons and in the same language that Henry Kissinger used in 1971, when he described his old Harvard University colleague Ellsberg as 'the most dangerous man in America.' Ellsberg himself has come out in support of Assange. But the *differences* between the Ellsberg and Assange cases are more important than the similarities.

Ellsberg was a Harvard educated economist who did his PhD on decision-making under uncertainty and worked at the highest levels of classification for the Rand Corporation and the Pentagon in the 1960s. He worked with a sense of patriotism and vocation. His job, as he saw it, was to help the US government think well and learn efficiently at the highest levels on vital matters of strategy and security. Like many senior US officials, including the Secretary of Defence, Robert McNamara, he slowly came to the conclusion that the Vietnam War was a seriously misconceived, inefficient and ultimately immoral exercise in futility.

In 1967, he was a member of a team of thirty analysts assigned by McNamara to review the whole history of decision-making that had led to the mess in Vietnam. The *Pentagon Papers* were the papers assembled and written by this team. Ellsberg leaked them four years later because he believed that the lessons they laid out had not been learned and that the only way to help the Republic overcome the problem was to take them to the most reputable newspaper in the country and inject them into public debate.

In *Papers on the War*, in 1972, Ellsberg wrote:

> The urgent need to circumvent the lying and the self-deception was, for me, one of the 'lessons of Vietnam'; a broader one was that there were situations—Vietnam was an example—in which the US government, starting ignorant, did not, would not, learn. There was a whole set of what amounted to institutional 'anti-learning' mechanisms working to preserve and guarantee unadaptive and unsuccessful behaviour: the fast turnover in personnel; the lack of institutional memory at any level; the failure to study history, to analyse or even record operational experience or mistakes; the effective pressures for optimistically false reporting at every level, for describing 'progress' rather than problems or failure, thus concealing the very need for change or for learning. Well, helping the US government learn—in this case, learn how to learn—was something, perhaps, I could do; that had been my business.

Compare this with Assange's outlook, in essays written in 2006 under the titles 'State and Terrorist Conspiracies' and 'Conspiracy as Governance.' Describing the US government as an authoritarian conspiracy, he declared that his strategy was to disrupt its ability to share information and thus disable the functioning of the 'conspiracy'. He wrote, as if this constituted a profound insight into the workings of government: 'We can marginalize a conspiracy's ability to act by decreasing total conspiratorial power until it is no longer able to understand, and hence respond effectively to its environment.... An authoritarian conspiracy that cannot think efficiently cannot act to preserve itself.' In other words, Assange set out not to help the US government learn, but to *prevent* it from learning, from 'thinking' effectively at all. He wants to cripple it.

The difference between these two points of view or objectives could hardly be greater. But ironically, the leaks show that the US government is *not* an 'authoritarian conspiracy' at all. They show, notably in the case of relations with the Arab states of the Middle East, an American government served by generally candid diplomats, trying to keep its balance and think its ways through a devilishly challenging set of problems, chief among them how to dissuade the theocratic and dangerously anti-Semitic regime in Iran from developing nuclear weapons. They show nuance and scruple, not authoritarian conspiracy. They show honest assessments of world leaders like the corrupt and domineering former KGB thug Putin, or the corrupt and irresponsible Italian leader Berlusconi. Moreover, as Robert Gates, heir to Robert McNamara, has pointed out, the leaks were possible precisely because the US government had been trying to circulate more information to more of its civil servants in order to facilitate learning. That was Ellsberg's agenda. Assange wants to *prevent* just such learning.

A good deal in the cables has been interesting, but that would surely be a frivolous criterion for assessing whether they were justified. In making such an assessment, we should weigh up several overriding considerations. First, has there been a clear matter of public interest of an urgent nature that the leaks address, which might outweigh the possible harm they could cause? Second, do the leaks provide us with finished analysis laying out the judgments of senior officials, thus allowing us to assign responsibility for some misdeed or major error?

Third, was the intention of those who leaked the material morally responsible, in the sense of a careful and discriminating judgment about the good intended? The answers to each of these questions would appear to be 'No'. One imagines it was for these reasons that Larry Sanger, founder of Wikipedia, which is designed to help people learn and to do good, wrote to Julian Assange and his colleagues, saying, 'Speaking as Wikipedia's co-founder, I consider you enemies of the U.S.—not just the government, but the people'. The problem, in short, is not leaks, but responsibility. Efforts to hold government to account and to understand the business of diplomacy need to bear this in mind and to design strategies that enhance responsibility in government, rather than simply trying to sabotage standard operating procedures.

On challenging the scientific consensus

Few things have more bedevilled the debate about global warming than the question of scientific consensus: what the scientific consensus on the subject is and about what degree of deference should be paid to scientific consensus as such. Both debates have been seriously aggravated by two other factors. Global warming seems to have colossal economic implications, which has activated the concerns of many interested parties; and the ecological nature of global warming has stirred up heated ideological passions that go well beyond the science. It's all very well to *feel* either passionate or sceptical about these matters, but how are we to *think* clearly about them?

David Weintraub's *How Old is the Universe?* offers five useful clues. The author has nothing to say about climate science and all parties to the climate debate can, therefore, chill out and think dispassionately here. His general argument is about how we can *know* the age of the universe. He asks:

> How have 400 years of science brought us to this point at which astronomers, cosmologists and physicists can claim that the universe came into existence at a specific moment 13.7 billion years ago? And how much confidence should you have in this statement?

These are similar in kind to the big questions that need to be asked (and answered) regarding the anthropogenic global warming hypothesis. Just one of his chapters provides the five useful clues to which I referred.

That chapter is about the discovery that the Milky Way is not the whole universe, but actually a very tiny part of it. The early breakthroughs in modern cosmology had been the shift from a geocentric to a heliocentric view of the solar system and then to a realization, as telescopes became more sophisticated and the understanding of the light spectrum more refined, that there were vastly more stars than anyone had imagined and that they were much further away than ever previously guessed. Among them there were strange phenomena called spiral nebulae, wispy cloud-like formations that called for explanation. In 1755, the great philosopher Immanuel Kant, in his *Universal Natural History and Theory of the Heavens*, speculated that spiral nebulae might be what he called 'island universes' outside the Milky Way. A debate about this went on for many decades, but there was no scientific consensus one way or the other.

However, in the first decades of the twentieth century, a strong scientific consensus developed that the Milky Way was, in fact, the entire universe. A range of detailed studies in the 1910s, by leading astronomers Vesto Slipher, Harlow Shapley and Adrian van Maanen, seemed to confirm this. Shapley's work was especially brilliant. He upended the consensus that had reigned since Copernicus that the Sun was the centre of the universe; showing that we should see it as being 40,000 light years away in the heart of the Milky Way. The debate now appeared to be over: Kant had been wrong. But it turns out he wasn't. In Weintraub's words:

> *The steady accumulation of evidence from a decade of work by Slipher, Shapley and van Maanen appeared to have driven the astronomical community toward broad consensus. Spiral nebulae are part of the Milky Way. They are not island universes. The Milky Way encompasses the entire universe. A few years later, new observations proved this consensus completely wrong.*

In 1923-24, the brilliant young astronomer Edwin Hubble, having collected a great deal of data using the newly commissioned 100 inch telescope at Mount Wilson Observatory, wrote to Shapley to say that it looked as though Andromeda and M33 were well outside the Milky Way. 'The straws are all pointing in one direction,' he commented, 'and it will do no harm to consider the various possibilities involved.' Shapley responded with disarming humility, 'I do not know whether I am sorry or glad ... perhaps both.' Quite suddenly, it had been shown that the universe was vastly larger than the scientific consensus had allowed.

Weintraub asks, 'How had the astronomy community, including Slipher, van Maanen and Shapley, been led so far astray?' Slipher, he points out, had made some good measurements but had misinterpreted them and also made statements that were "rash and not supported by sufficient evidence". Van Maanen's measurements had been simply incorrect. 'Eager to discover what he believed must be true, he misled himself, finding the answers he thought should be in his data rather than the answers truly revealed by his photographs.' Shapley had actually made 'excellent measurements, but he did not make enough of them.' Incredibly, he concludes, despite all these errors in trying to bring closure to the island universe debate, the research of Slipher and Shapley was to actually help provide the basis for the next momentous step in Hubble's research—the discovery that the universe was not only enormously larger than the Milky Way, but was expanding.

How does all this help in regard to the climate science debate? First, it shows that we are justified in being wary of foreclosing major debates based on scientific consensus, since it can be in error. Second, it shows that the way to challenge and correct scientific consensus is not through polemic or denial, but through specifying crucial variables and deductions and testing them scrupulously, in the manner of Hubble. Third, it shows that there is, nonetheless, such a thing as scientific consensus and that when handled in the manner just described it tends to prove self-correcting. Fourth, it shows that ideally such correction will occur, as it did between Hubble and Shapley, on the basis of lucid examination of "the various possibilities". Finally, it shows that overwhelmingly human beings have always lived oblivious to the truth about the natural world and that only exacting and brilliant science has been able to discover what that truth is. In the climate science debate, we would all benefit from taking note of these five lessons as we seek to develop a rational consensus on the subject.[265]

---

265 For a very recent study in the philosophy of science with a comparative perspective on the climate change debate, see James Lawrence Powell *Four Revolutions in the Earth Sciences: From Heresy to Truth* (Columbia University Press, New York, 2015). The four revolutions he looks at are Deep Time (the discovery that the Earth is 4.5 billion years old), Tectonic Plates (the discovery of continental drift), Meteorite Impact (the realization that meteor impacts have been regular occurrences and have at times had catastrophic consequences in the biosphere) and anthropogenic global warming. Powell states (p. 289):

> *Why did scientists reject the four theories discussed in this book for so long, only to have later generations come to regard them as virtually self-evident? The answer is now plain: scientists accepted the theories when the data demanded that they do so. To call themselves scientists, they had no choice.*

Galileo, science and religious authority

In 1600, Giordano Bruno was burned alive by the Inquisition, in the Campo dei Fiori, Rome, for having advanced a heliocentric cosmology at variance with Catholic orthodoxy. It was a grim beginning to the century that would bring the scientific revolution to Western Europe. In 1616, Galileo Galilei was expressly forbidden to hold, teach or defend the heliocentric theory of the solar system, as set out in Nicolaus Copernicus's controversial treatise of 1543, *De revolutionibus*.

In 1633, following publication of his book *Dialogue Concerning the Two World Systems* (the Aristotelian or Ptolemaic and the Copernican), in which he had effectively done just that, Galileo was forced on pain of severe punishment to renounce before the Inquisition any belief in the heliocentrism of Copernicus. He was confined thenceforth under permanent house arrest. His *Dialogue* was placed on the Vatican's *Index of Prohibited Books* and remained there for the next two hundred years. The scientific revolution, however, had begun. Galileo has ever since stood out as its most famous hero.

But all this has been known for a long time. One could learn as much on Wikipedia. Why, as John Heilbron wrote last year, in the Preface to his magisterial *Galileo*, burden the world with a new, 500 page biography of the man? 'Is there anything fresh to say?' he asked rhetorically; and answered:

> Yes. Galileo's biographers tend to rush their gladiator prematurely into an imaginary arena filled with pig-headed philosophers and fire-spitting priests. He did spend time arguing with and suffering such people. But Galileo the gladiator and martyr of science began as Galileo the patrician humanist. I hope to have introduced something fresh by locating Galileo more firmly among Florentine cultural institutions than others have done. That makes space for character development.

He delivered on that hope. But Mark Peterson's even newer, albeit much shorter book on Galileo inadvertently shows that Heilbron performed another, more important service. He laid out in scrupulous detail and with delightfully mordant wit the very real conflict between the Catholic Church and early modern science which Peterson perversely dismisses as merely 'imagined'.

Mark Peterson is Professor of Physics and Mathematics on the Alumnae Foundation, Mount Holyoke College, a leading liberal arts college in western Massachusetts. Like Heilbron, who is Professor of History Emeritus at the University of California, Berkeley and Honorary Fellow of Worcester College, Oxford; Peterson believes that there is a fresh and important story to tell about Galileo's roots in Renaissance humanism.

He tells that story well and makes the fascinating argument that Galileo's interest in applied geometry arose not from the study of orthodox philosophy and mathematics, but from his interest in the application of geometry to poetry, painting and architecture. He makes this case well and it complements Heilbron's, because it is not simply a story of the development of a man's character, but of the counter-intuitive emergence of the physical sciences out of the liberal arts. One can quite see how this would be a fine case to make at a liberal arts college.

However, after devoting most of his 336 pages to this quite beautifully worked argument, Peterson then advances a second argument, almost at unawares, at the very end of his book. He writes that Galileo, according to 'the standard myth' is less an historical person than

> *a symbol, the personification of an imagined conflict between science and religion, truth and authority, or almost to put it baldly, right and wrong. Such a caricature is a misrepresentation of him, not just mistaken, but pernicious in its widespread acceptance.*

Imagined? Caricature? Mistaken? Pernicious? To make claims of this nature, given the historical record, is nothing short of remarkable. Between the prosecution and imprisonment of Galileo by Pope Urban VIII (1633) and the 'exoneration' of Galileo by Pope John Paul II (1979), the record of the Catholic Church was one of strenuous attempts to prevent the teaching of a cosmology apparently at variance with the 'authority' of both Aristotle and the Bible, followed by a long drawn out apologetics about how the science had no bearing on the 'mysteries' of religious revelation.

What is pernicious is to paper this long controversy over and pretend that all is basically well with Biblical religion. It simply isn't. The Renaissance was triggered by the recovery of Aristotle's long lost work in the Latin West from the twelfth and thirteenth centuries. What is less widely understood is that the scientific revolution, in the sixteenth and seventeenth centuries, was triggered by the recovery of the great treatises on geometry, mechanics and optics of Euclid, Archimedes and their lesser known Hellenistic colleagues. Insights inspired by these sources overturned both Aristotle's physics and the medieval notion that the Bible should be seen as a source of information about the nature of the cosmos.

Galileo was dubbed the 'Tuscan Archimedes' and with very good reason. He revered Euclid and Archimedes and his revitalization of their approach to science, taken further by Descartes, Newton and others, *was* the scientific revolution. As Lucio Russo showed, in his classic *The Forgotten Revolution: How Science was Born in 300 BC and Why it had to be Reborn* (first published in Italian in 1996), we simply cannot understand modernity unless we understand this transition. Heilbron illuminates this. Peterson, deplorably, muddies it.

Section 3: 2009-10

Why democratization would be good for China

Prime Minister Julia Gillard's visit to China this week coincides with a nervous and reactionary campaign by the Chinese Communist Party to suppress any possibility of a "jasmine revolution"—given what has been sweeping the Arab world recently. Scores of leading intellectuals, human rights lawyers and activists, journalists and scholars have been arrested to silence and intimidate them. The case of the artist Ai Wei Wei has made headlines, but many others have been swept up by the Party's forbidding security organs.

This suppression should concentrate our minds on how we think about the rising power of China. Human rights abuses are generally considered ugly and a regime that treats its own citizens in this manner does not look like a trustworthy or pleasant neighbour; to say nothing of a prospectively benign regional superpower. The real lesson from the current repression in China, however, is not the strength or unpleasantness of the regime, but its insecurity. A regime which imprisons a man like Liu Xiaobo and denounces the award of a Nobel Peace Prize to him as 'an obscenity' is deeply insecure and politically immature.

For three decades, the Communist Party has declared it wishes to move from the rule of an arbitrary dictator (Mao Zedong) to the 'rule of law'. But it violates its own laws with astonishing frequency. It still rules arbitrarily and its legal system is farcically subordinate to political dictation. The Party insists it is building a 'harmonious society', but it takes condign measures to suppress any voice which displeases it. Its propaganda organs accuse Western critics of wanting to contain and weaken China, using democracy as a fig leaf. In reality, democracy has been called for by the most principled and independent Chinese intellectuals since before the Communist Party even existed.

Understanding this is critical to our future dealings with China. Political reform has always been excruciatingly difficult in China, but calls for it are not a Western plot and they are not designed to weaken China. They are intended to strengthen it and provide for better, more resilient, more responsive governance. They are intended to make it possible for China to become a more fully accepted and welcome member of the international society of states. As Wang Jisi, Dean of the School of International Studies at Peking University, put it in a recent essay, 'China's Search for a Grand Strategy', China won't be able to exert positive influence globally unless it can enhance its reputation for 'good governance and transparency'.

How can it do that? Wang is unequivocal: China's continued resurgence depends on "greater transparency and accountability, as well as on a firmer commitment to the rule of law, democracy and human rights, all values that are widely shared throughout the world today." Let's drum this into the heads of everyone who says we should not 'lecture China' about democracy and human rights: the whole idea is (1) being articulated best by eminent Chinese thinkers; (2) vital to the flourishing of China, not part of any plot to weaken it; and (3) a complex but indispensable element in China actually becoming influential and universally respected on the world stage.

Wang's essay was about the need for China to devise a coherent grand strategy— something he argues it currently lacks. Just as he points out the need for China to undertake responsible political democratization, he argues that it badly needs to reassure the world that its rapid military build-up won't lead it to bully its neighbours. Most of its neighbours are becoming apprehensive that it will. The irony of Chinese testiness is that the United States seeks *not* a weak China, but a cooperative and confident China—a partner in orchestrating and maintaining global security and coping with global challenges. This is lucidly set out by a very fine American China specialist and State Department official Thomas Christensen in his recent essay 'The Advantages of an Assertive China'.

Last year, in a conversation with Hillary Clinton, which emerged from WikiLeaks, then Prime Minister Kevin Rudd described himself as 'a brutal realist on China'. With refreshing candour, Mr Rudd described the Chinese leaders as 'sub-rational and deeply emotional' about Taiwan. He told the US Secretary of State that our intelligence agencies are closely watching China's military expansion. The planned build-up of Australia's navy, he told Mrs Clinton, was 'a response to China's growing ability to project force'.

Much was made of Mr Rudd's candour and there was speculation that the disclosure might adversely affect our relations with China. But the context of his remark was crucial. He stated that, of course, our common goal must be to integrate China into the international community, 'while also preparing to deploy force if everything goes wrong'. That is to say, we should seek to *ensure* that China's rise will be peaceful, not *assume* or merely *hope* that it will be. As things stand, that will be a particularly challenging—but unavoidable - project for Australia, given our vast economic stake in China's resurgence.

Here, then, is the watchword for our relationship with China in the years ahead: we want a secure and mature China, not a tetchy, insecure and bullying one. What would work for us—for the international system as a whole—would also, as it happens, serve China's interests best. It might not, however, suit the perceived interests of the Communist Party. There's the problem.

Six true heroes of modern China

The announcement on Monday that Osama bin Laden had been run to ground in Pakistan and killed in a fire fight with US special operations personnel swamped post mortems on Julia Gillard's visit to China. But it is worth juxtaposing the two. The struggle against al Qaeda and the struggle for political liberalization in China are akin. Each is a long, often twilight struggle for liberal norms in global society. The popular revolts in the Arab world this year have highlighted what is at stake and what is possible. The arrests in China have highlighted the Communist Party's nervous and repressive attitude to such possibilities.

In the immediate wake of the prime minister's visit to China, US human rights official Michael Posner, who had been holding talks with Chinese officials, declared that the recent crackdown in China constituted 'serious backsliding'. He added that disagreements between Washington and Beijing on the subject are serious and profound. Julia Gillard, on the other hand, was low key about the matter. She declared that had sought and received reassurances from premier Wen Jiabao that China was *not* backsliding on human rights.

Naturally, the Chinese government preferred her tone to that of Posner. His attitude, declared Chinese Foreign Ministry spokesperson Hong Lei, constituted "interference in China's internal affairs." Given Australia's booming trade with China, it's easy to see why the prime minister chose to keep her remarks on the subject of human rights bland. But let's not allow the interference charge to deflect us from supporting human rights in China. For more than a hundred years, tyranny in China has been judged by China's own leading intellectuals and denounced in the name of political liberalization and human rights.

Given that the Communist Party still apologizes for Mao Zedong, who was responsible for the deaths of tens of millions of his fellow citizens, and has again and again crushed dissent during the reform era, Wen's assurances count for very little. The problem is, popular and political memory in the outside world tends to be very short. We need to remember that the true heroes of modern China are those denounced, imprisoned and exiled by the Party. Here are six you should see as representative of what the Party continues to stifle any way it can.

Qin Benli (1917-1991). Denounced as a 'Rightist' in 1957 and banished from journalism for twenty years, he was rehabilitated in 1978. He then created a newspaper in Shanghai called *The World Economic Herald*. It was a beacon of free thought and liberal ideas. In late April 1989, it was shut down for refusing to heed instructions from the propaganda organs of the Party to refrain from publishing a round table discussion by liberal intellectuals of the legacy of Hu Yaobang.

Liu Binyan (1925-2005) joined the Party in 1944 as an idealistic youngster. In 1956, he wrote scathing critiques of corruption and abuse of power under Communist rule. He was labelled a 'Rightist' and expelled from the Party in 1957. He spent the next 21 years in and out of labour camps. In 1978, like Qin Benli, he was rehabilitated. He then resumed his gadfly function and became popularly known as 'the conscience of China'. In 1985, when the Chinese Writers' Association was, for the first and last time, allowed to elect its leadership, he won the second most votes, behind the veteran dissident Ba Jin. He was expelled from the Party again in 1987, left for the US in 1988 and was never allowed back into China.

Hu Jiwei (1916-2012) was editor in chief of the Party's main newspaper, *People's Daily*, between 1977 and 1983. He championed political reform and the protection of individual rights. In March 1989 he openly criticised the State Council for blocking political reform. He called for freedom of the press and declared that democratic norms, not autocratic authority, would give political stability to China. He was sacked from the Congress for opposing the declaration of martial law. In January 2005, he circulated a letter calling on the Party to give the deceased reforming premier Zhao Ziyang a grand memorial. It did nothing of the kind.[266]

---

266 Hu Jiwei died in September 2012. *The South China Morning Post* ran a story about him which read, in part, as follows:

> *Hu Jiwei, a former* People's Daily *chief editor and one of the most vocal advocates for political reform, made vindication of the Tiananmen protest movement his dying wish. He died on Sunday, one day after his 96th birthday. A close family member who declined to be named said the liberal party elder died of heart failure in a Beijing hospital. He had been suffering from heart problems for years and was readmitted to the hospital earlier this month, having spent most of the summer there.*
>
> *He was already in intensive care and in a frail state when his closest friends Li Rui and Du Daozheng visited him four days before he died. Speaking sparingly, Hu nonetheless told them the truth about the Tiananmen pro-democracy movement must be told, his close relative said. Li, a former secretary to Mao Zedong, and Du, a former propaganda chief, are also reform-minded party elders. 'He didn't have much energy to speak', his relative said. 'But he put up his hand and said to them: 'Seek vindication for June 4'. That was the most fervent wish in his heart.'*
>
> *Born in Sichuan in 1916, Hu joined the underground Communist Party at 21 while at university - a dangerous move during Kuomintang rule. In 1939, he went to the revolutionary base, Yenan, where, for the next decade, he edited regional pro-communist newspapers. He transferred to the* People's Daily *in 1952 and worked there until 1983, when he became a member of the Standing Committee of the National People's Congress. During his leadership at the party newspaper, he was often criticised by the conservatives for his liberal positions.*
>
> *Hu was charged by liberal leader Hu Yaobang with drafting a media law to protect press freedom, but the initiative - like other reformist measures - was scrapped after the Tiananmen crackdown in 1989. The law's failure became a lasting regret for Hu. Owing to his support for the Tiananmen*

Fang Lizhi (1936-2012) An astrophysicist and vice president of China's University of Science and Technology, Fang was a major proponent of liberal ideas who inspired students to challenge the Party's dictatorship in 1986-87 and 1989. When the bloody crackdown came, in June 1989, he found asylum in the US Embassy. A year later he was flown into exile in the US, where he remained until his death in 2012, working at the University of Arizona.

Ruan Ming (1931-) was one of the leading lieutenants of the reformer Hu Yaobang in the mid-1980s. He sided with the democracy movement and fled China after its brutal suppression in 1989. He has since lived in Taiwan and has become a vocal proponent of democracy and independence there. In the years after he left China, he wrote a number of books: *Essays on the Character of the Chinese Communist Party*; *Hu Yaobang and the Turning Point of History* and *Deng Xiaoping: Chronicle of an Empire*.

Yan Jiaqi (1942-), a prominent member of the reform movement in the 1980s, was director of the Institute of Political Research in the Chinese Academy of Social Sciences between 1985 and 1989 and a political adviser to Zhao Ziyang. A leading light in the 1989 protests, he fled abroad in June 1989 and helped to organize the Federation for a Democratic China, becoming its first president. He was expelled from the Party. He now lives in New York and is a member of the Chinese Constitutional Reform Association and a proponent of a Federal Republic of China.

Remember these names and invoke them whenever someone tells you that democracy is not for China. Remember these names and invoke them when the Chinese Communist Party denounces calls for human rights and democracy as interference in its internal affairs. And remember that their fate has been benign compared to that of many others, not least in Tibet and East Turkestan (Xinjiang).

---

movement and his condemnation of the June 4 crackdown, he was sacked from official duties in 1990 and kept under investigation for several years. In his later years, shielded by his status as a party elder, Hu used his influence to push liberal causes, such as urging the release of human rights activist Liu Xiaobo, who was jailed in 2009 on subversion charges.

Hu was among 23 party elders who issued a strongly worded petition to the top legislature in late 2010, calling for an end to media censorship. In 2010, Hu told the South China Morning Post: *'China nowadays looks strong on the outside, but it's actually very weak and afraid ... the regime is rotten from within'. He said he had not given up hope because people were no longer ignorant in the age of the internet.*

Politics, reason and gay marriage

The reaction by conservative religious leaders and political commentators to the decision by the ALP on gay marriage has been that this tilt will imperil the party at the next Federal election. It may well do. But the reasons supplied are shocking arguments against a call for legitimising gay marriage. I am not a member of the Left-wing intelligentsia, I am not gay and I am not standing for political office. I am, however, a believer in clear reasoning; and what has been written on the subject cries out—if not to Heaven, then to the intellect—for a response.

The case for gay marriage has been advanced by various parties and it is not my business to defend either their specific arguments or their political ideologies. However, surely one might make the following argument for such a move, without regard—for the moment—to the moral prejudices of religious conservatives or the psephological calculus of the pundits (some of whom I number among my friends).

1. There are a significant number of our fellow citizens who are gay.
2. Their sexual orientation is not a matter of 'sin', but of biochemistry.
3. They are, in this sense, a minority which has long been persecuted and vilified in conservative religious societies.
4. This has too often forced much of their love underground and rendered its practice furtive, undignified and opportunistic.
5. Making marriage possible would be a step in the direction not only of dignifying homoerotic relations, but of making them *more* moral.

It is surely important here to get a few elementary distinctions clear. First, there is a sanctimonious claim by conservative Christians and Muslims and perhaps Jews that their 'holy scriptures' confine marriage to heterosexual relations. But the idea that any of us should still have our moral reasoning overshadowed by these arcane and morally dubious books is highly challengeable.

Surely a liberal, secular society will assess the merits of moral arguments on a more rational basis than this? Such a basis might be that there is simply nothing inherently objectionable about homosexual relations and that making it legally and morally possible for homosexual lovers to form a lasting bond would be a constructive step in our society. Let those who insist that they derive their morals from 'holy scripture' live their moral code without hypocrisy. But there is no sound basis for permitting them to dictate standards of morality in a liberal and tolerant society.

Second, it is argued that the ALP has been self-destructive in espousing a right to gay marriage, since this may cost it heavily in the polls. Cardinal George Pell has been quoted, from far away Rome, as declaring that 'any Australia wide party' which supports gay marriage 'does not want to govern'.

Perhaps. But whether or not the ALP will suffer at the polls on account of its support for a right to gay marriage has no bearing on whether such support is morally sound or rationally defensible. One could not, for a century, have hoped to win electoral office in many southern states of the USA if one stood for desegregation and civil rights. Did that make those causes morally wrong or intrinsically indefensible? One would not have thought so.

There are many issues, both moral and practical, on which is very difficult to win the consent of a majority of our fellow citizens, for a wide range of reasons. That may make it politic to avoid espousing them on the hustings. Yet many of us decry the lack of courage and imagination shown by the political class. They are too driven by opinion polls and concerns in marginal electorates and the single issue lobbying of special interests, it is again and again lamented. Well, we have a case study right here.

Let it be conceded that the ALP may have miscalculated electorally in this matter. That does not mean that those who support gay marriage are in *moral* error. It may simply mean that too many of our fellow citizens are narrow-minded, fearful, bigoted and led astray by clerics of one kind or another. If those who have called for gay marriage are in error, let the case be argued on rational and empirical grounds and not on the grounds that such a moral and legal reform would be inconsistent with Deuteronomy or the Koran.

Those who do not have gay friends or do not know gay couples are not well placed to have a sensible opinion on this subject; for it is the freedom of such lovers and couples to live open and dignified lives that is at stake here. Is there anything about actual heterosexual marriages that makes them the gold standard of morality and decency and fidelity? Surely not. The idea of love and fidelity in marriage is again and again honoured in the breach.

Yet if those who see themselves as the moral guardians of our society—an office to which none of us elected them, incidentally—wish to see higher standards of love and fidelity in homosexual relations, might not marriage be a way of signifying precisely that? And if they recoil from such an appeal, perhaps they need to be reminded that many of us—even if we might still be a minority—have long since repudiated their religious beliefs and claims to moral authority.

What we look for is an enlightened and open society, not a theocratic and reactionary one. We do not see the Bible or the Koran as having any weight in serious matters, moral, historical or scientific. Consequently, we applaud those who raise challenging issues and are prepared to stand up for reforms in the face of conservative reaction and popular prejudice.

Meaning and secular nihilism: the Dreyfus case

Hubert Dreyfus is a fascinating American philosopher, long ensconced at the University of California, Berkeley. He is best known for his polemical books *What Computers Can't Do* (1972/79) and *What Computers Still Can't Do* (1992) and for his illuminating exposition of the core philosophical ideas of Martin Heidegger in *Being-in-the-World: A Commentary on Heidegger's "Being and Time," Division 1* (1990). Sean Dorrance Kelly is much younger, but is Professor and Chair of the Department of Philosophy at Harvard University. They have teamed up to produce a beguiling little book under the title *All Things Shining: Reading the Western Classics to Find Meaning in a Secular Age*.

The reason they see any point in writing such a book is that they subscribe to an opinion which is fairly widely diffused: that the secular world has been stripped of much of the "meaning" which earlier generations of human beings found in an 'enchanted' world. The genealogy of this perception is well enough known. The ancients experienced the immanent presence of the gods in the world and saw "soul" in many things and intentionality and design in the cosmos. This was heightened, but rigorized by monotheism, which made the divine loftier and more abstract. It was stripped away by Cartesian rationality and modern science, which denied that there was anything other than indifferent mechanism in the cosmos.

This 'disenchantment of the world', in Max Weber's famous phrase, left modern human beings, or at least those most subject to the forces of rationalization and scientific culture, increasingly bereft of meaning, purpose, ethical guidance and consolation. Hence the desolate plays of Beckett and the emphasis on 'nothingness' and anomie in modern philosophers from Nietzsche to Sartre and Foucault. Hence, also, Dreyfus and Kelly argue, the despairing confrontation with meaninglessness and boredom in the novels of David Foster Wallace, *Infinite Jest* and the posthumous *The Pale King*. Their argument is that it is possible to find a way out of this apparent *cul-de-sac* and to recapture what they describe as the world of wonder and meaning experienced by pre-scientific peoples.

Their first two chapters, 'Our Contemporary Nihilism' and 'David Foster Wallace's Nihilism' are devoted to describing what they see as a modern (Western) culture driven to distraction by meaninglessness and addicted precisely to distraction, which is to say entertainment, drugs, pornography and trivial or arbitrary pursuits. Most of the book, chapters three, four, five and six of seven, are devoted to retracing what they see as the development of the malaise of disenchantment. Chapter three, 'Homer's Polytheism' centres on the idea that "the Greeks ... held the world in constant wonder." This was the world before disenchantment and it is a version of this that the authors want to argue we can recapture. Not through metaphysical belief, but through the phenomenology of experience.

The keynote to this line of reasoning, which might be called phenomenological re-enchantment of the world, is perhaps their claim, at p. 77:

> *Homer describes an array of situations in which something outside our control evokes, or ought properly to evoke, a kind of amazement and gratitude from us.*

They add (p. 79):

> *The modern view that we are entirely responsible for our existence, stands in radical contrast with the Homeric idea that we are at our best when we open ourselves to the world.*

They spend the following three chapters, 'From Aeschylus to Augustine: Monotheism on the Rise', 'From Dante to Kant: The Attractions and Dangers of Autonomy' and 'Fanaticism, Polytheism and Melville's 'Evil Art'', setting out their case that a growing Western obsession with responsibility, autonomy and truth disenchanted the world to our cost.

Those at all familiar with the writings of Nietzsche and Heidegger will recognize this general line of thinking. They do not, however, offer the dubious prescriptions recklessly propagated by Nietzsche in the 1880s and they are suitably wary of the gnomic work of Heidegger which too easily enabled the philosopher to embrace Nazism as a way out of this modern condition. Instead, they suggest an approach which they derive from the Homeric world, to which they give the Greek name *poiesis*: the crafting of meaning into both objects and experiences. This is not, they emphasize, a mere throw back to Homer. Rather, it is a reframing of the experiences we have in terms of the phenomenology of perception, instead of the stark, depersonalized objectivity of natural science.

There is a good deal to be said for this approach and Dreyfus and Kelly are far less reckless than Nietzsche, far less gnomic than Heidegger and far less nihilistic than Sartre. Their approach is, they suggest, clued into "a whole new understanding of who we are" and what meaning actually is. 'Living well in our secular, nihilistic age', they conclude, requires a kind of *meta-poiesis*: an understanding of when to be immersed in flow and meaning and when to rise above it into autonomy.

The problem is that the book ends well short of articulating how exactly, on an everyday basis, the common citizen of the secular world—as distinct from the exemplary craftsman, philosopher or aesthete—can live the *meta-poietic* life. This is a problem not for the individual, but for society, since if there is no practical overhaul of our culture to be had, one would expect a combination of religious belief and nihilism to prevail. In this respect, Dreyfus and Kelly may be said to have fallen into the same trap as Nietzsche and Heidegger before them. They have set out a kind of aesthetic of alienation, but have not thought through a workable social doctrine.

There is a deeper critique of their work which might be offered, of course. It is that the modern sciences have made possible both an instrumental reckoning with an ever harsh and godless natural world and an unprecedented opening of the horizons of meaning and truth. This open horizon triggers nihilism, but also wonders far transcending Homer, Dante and Kant alike.

Ishmael's house and the origins of Israel

It's always disconcerting when you pick up a book by a reputable historian and stumble upon an error or incorrect citation in the first few pages. It is particularly disconcerting when the incorrect citation is from a famous source. At p. 3 of *In the House of Ishmael*, Martin Gilbert describes Josephus as having written about the Romans crushing a Jewish revolt in Cyrenaica in 115 CE and then deporting Jews from Judaea to Cyrenaica after the Bar Kokhba rebellion in the early 130s CE. Josephus died in 100 CE and his *The Jewish War* covers the war of 69-74 CE, in which Titus crushed the Jews and destroyed Jerusalem.

He did not live to see the rebellions of 115 or 132-35 CE. Yet Gilbert's footnotes refer to a secondary source supposedly quoting Josephus and to page 408 of the Penguin edition of *The Jewish War*. Inevitably, one wonders: if he got this wrong, what other errors has he made? Despite that inauspicious start, *In Ishmael's House* is a deeply engaging work of history. It provides a highly readable general account of the relations between Jews and Muslims since the beginnings of Islam. Three quarters of the book are devoted to the modern world and only a quarter to the thousand or so years between the life of Mohammed and the Enlightenment. Yet in that quarter of the book there is a great deal of important and fascinating history to be told.

One has the sense that Gilbert foreshortened it because he lacks the knowledge of languages and primary sources to delve much further into it. But his chief aim in writing the book seems to have been to draw attention to the manner in which Muslim societies in the twentieth century treated Jews. He devotes seven whole chapters to the expulsion of the Jews from Muslim lands after 1948. The earlier history, filled with remarkable characters and dramatic incidents, seems to have been related chiefly to provide depth of perspective for the more familiar twentieth century drama.

Gilbert's book is good to read alongside Jonathan Schneer's *The Balfour Declaration*. Schneer's is the more thorough book, better grounded in the primary sources of the subject and written in a more fine grained and analytical style. Yet it leaves virtually unexamined the historical background of anti-Semitism in the Muslim world against which the conflict over Palestine arose. One comes away from it with a sense that Arab grievances over having been misled by the British in the 1910s were, as he puts it, the 'dragon's teeth' that caused armed men to rise up out of the ground.

He goes to great lengths to show that the Grand Sharif Hussein and his sons in the Hejaz were made vague and perhaps deliberately dishonest promises by the British government in order to bring them into the war against the Ottoman Empire. He explains in detail the ambitious plans of Britain, France and Russia, before 1917, to partition the Ottoman Empire. He is correct to point out that all this was always bound to lead to trouble. What he does not do is duly note the extent to which future trouble was always likely given the nature of Islam and the nature of Arab politics.

Schneer makes an important contribution by describing in detail the differences of opinion among Jews themselves about Jewish nationalism as a solution to the widespread persecution of Jews. He also shows the Balfour Declaration was largely the product of a belief in high British circles in the mythical power of the Jews, more than it was the fruit of any such real power.

The efforts of Chaim Weizmann and his Zionist allies were tireless and nimble, but the crucial factor was the conviction on the part of a few influential British statesmen that the Jews were very powerful around the world and that support for a Jewish state in Palestine might bring them into the First World War on the Allied side. There is a fearful irony in this and its consequence. The Declaration has been widely represented as demonstrating both the power of Zionist influence and an alliance between Zionism and British imperialism. The 'alliance', as Schneer shows very clearly, was no more than a tenuous and limited alignment of interests between a few energetic Jews and a few opportunistic British imperialists at the height of a disastrous war.

Schneer appears to have rather more sympathy for Arab nationalism than for Jewish nationalism without ever explaining quite why. This is where Gilbert's work complements Schneer's most usefully. He shows that Islam had long been deeply problematic for the Jews, though in some times and places less hostile than Christianity.

He shows that the Jews had, nonetheless, often contributed much in Muslim societies and had generally fared better under the Ottomans than under many other Muslim states. By the 1930s and 1940s, there were compelling reasons for the Zionists to pursue their project and some grounds for them to hope that they could reach a constructive understanding with the Arabs in the Levant. The disappointment of that hope was less the legacy of the Balfour Declaration, than of many centuries of irrational and violent Muslim anti-Semitism.

Gilbert sets in this deep perspective the flight of over 500,000 Arabs from Palestine and over 600,000 Jews from Arab countries after 1948. The Jewish refugees have all been resettled in Israel or the Anglo-Saxon democracies. The Palestinian Arab refugees, never wanted by their Arab neighbours, have remained stateless and impoverished.

Can this be laid at the door of the Balfour Declaration? Perhaps, but only in the limited sense argued by Schneer: that the Zionists might never have got a chance to lay the foundations of the state of Israel had it not been for the workings of British diplomacy during the First World War. Yet, in the wide world opened up by the collapse of the Ottoman Empire, there was plenty of room for Arabs and Jews to prosper side by side.

Why did it not occur to Arab leaders to offer the Jews a safe haven from European and Christian persecution for the sake of economic development and social modernization in the Middle East? Gilbert's sweeping history goes far toward explaining why.

Jose Saramago's Cain mutiny

In *Why Translation Matters*, Edith Grossman remarked last year that 'translation asserts the possibility of a coherent, unified experience of literature in the world's multiplicity of languages.' An acclaimed translator of Cervantes, she made the point that the development of the modern novel in Europe "grew directly out of the model of *Don Quixote*, which was translated almost immediately after publication." Yet the art of translation, she argued, seems to be taken so much for granted that one would have thought either that it was unnecessary to bother translating books from other languages or that translation itself amounts to mere paraphrase.

Poignantly, she asked, 'What is the point of translating works of literature when we already have a huge surfeit of books in our own language and a diminishing number of readers?' The answer, of course, is to draw people out of their cultural shells. She cites the really hilarious bumper sticker in use among American campaigners against English/Spanish bilingualism which reads: 'If English was good enough for Jesus, it's good enough for me.' Peter Garrett should have that bumper sticker plastered on his forehead, after his recent declaration that language studies in this country are superfluous given that 'everyone speaks English now.'

Reading *Cain*, one is reminded of Grossman's argument at multiple points. Saramago, son of landless Portuguese peasants, poet, playwright and novelist, was a self-styled "libertarian communist" who delighted in writing works of acid satire and mordant literary revisions of historical events. His subversive take on the New Testament, *The Gospel According to Jesus Christ*, was ordered removed from the short list of candidates for the European Literary Prize, in 1992, on the grounds that it was offensive to the Catholic Church. Saramago left Portugal in protest. When he died last year, Harold Bloom declared that his books—which have sold two million copies in Portugal alone and been translated into twenty five languages - should be a considered a permanent part of the Western canon.

The Western canon? Is there still such a thing? Bloom himself, famously, titled the opening chapter of his 1994 polemic *The Western Canon: The Books and School of the Ages*, 'An Elegy for the Canon'; believing that the habit of reading well has been dying out in Western society for some time. Any such canon includes the Bible—read or unread. And the case of Saramago is a rich study in what canonical writers themselves *do* with the canon; for both his Jesus book and *Cain* are relentlessly subversive of religious belief, but based on a witty and morally serious response to the canonical stories in the Bible.

To bring Grossman and Bloom together here, Saramago's account of the famous tale of the Tower of Babel pivots, characteristically, on the irrationality of Yahweh's decision to bring about the confusion, the babel of tongues merely because human beings were seeking to build a great edifice. The author remarks that his peripatetic Cain:

> *was fortunate enough to meet a man who spoke hebrew, the language that had fallen to him to speak in the midst of all that deliberately created confusion, the scale of which cain was just beginning to grasp, with people talking without the aid of dictionaries or interpreters in english, german, french, spanish, italian, basque, some in latin and greek, and even, who would have thought it, in portuguese*

The lack of the upper case is one of Saramago's casually anarchic orthographic tendencies. Punctuation is idiosyncratic; inverted commas are omitted entirely; one has to parse conversations much as one would have had to parse the distinction between words in ancient manuscripts, which placed no breaks between them.

Cain is Saramago's common man, stumbling back and forth around the Pentateuch in growing horror at the atrocities of the lord god—like burning alive the men, women and children of sodom and gomorrah or prompting the hebrews to genocidal massacres in canaan—until, finally, he subverts the divine plan for renewal of the human race through Noah and his sons by means of a mutiny aboard the ark: he throws the whole family overboard into the flood. This was well worth translating. It is every bit as biting as Rushdie's *Satanic Verses*. An inspired teacher could use it to provoke students into both reading the five books of Moses and thinking freely about what they find there.

In the wry prose and self-parodying narrative style of *Cain*, one can still hear the humour and irony of Cervantes that have inspired centuries of Iberian literature. This is inimitably represented by Saramago's remark, just over half way through the book:

> *For reasons it is not in our power to explain, mere repeaters as we are of ancient stories, constantly wavering between the most ingenuous credulity and the most resolute scepticism, cain found himself plunged into what we can, without exaggeration, call a tempest, a calendric cyclone, a temporal hurricane.*

The first person plural here is inclusive, but Saramago is far from merely repeating ancient stories. He is translating those stories into a very new, biting idiom and, in the process, inviting his readers—whether in English or (who would have thought it, in Portuguese)—to reimagine those stories, the nature of stories as such and the extent of their own credulity. Those are the marks of a free spirit and a literary master. *Cain* is a fine little tempest.

Efraim's Karsh's tour de force on Palestine

In four decades of reading about international affairs and Middle Eastern geopolitics, I do not think I have come across a work of history that more fully illuminated the true sources of Palestinian terrorism and irresolvable conflict with the realities of Israel than does Efraim Karsh's *Palestine Betrayed*. If ever a book merited the description *tour de force*, this is it. The pity of it is that only those who are already favourably disposed to the state of Israel are likely to so much as read it—and most of those will probably skim it, not really absorbing the subtle power of its detailed argument.

Unless one starts from the groundless assumption that Palestine naturally belongs exclusively to Arabs (and Muslim Arabs at that), there can be no basis for the consistent and violent rejection by the Arabs of the idea of a Jewish state in Palestine. Yet such rejection has been the response of the Arab world and of the reactionary leaders of the Palestinian Arabs to the Balfour Declaration (1917), the League of Nations mandate (1920) and the United Nations Partition Resolution (29 November 1947); to say nothing of the tireless efforts of the Zionist movement, from the late nineteenth century all the way through to the 1940s and even beyond to persuade the Arab leaders to form a cooperative and constructive partnership with the Jewish state for the greater good of the Middle East. Karsh's book demonstrates all of this with what can only be called—looking at Arab behaviour—damning lucidity.

The first and most fundamental historical fact that Karsh establishes is that Zionism was in no sense predatory and was by no means the tool of 'Crusaders' or Western imperialists intent on colonizing the Arab world. Indeed, the irony of claims to the contrary is that the British, who exercised the League of Nations mandate in Palestine between 1920 and 1948, were decidedly inclined to favour the Arabs, not the Jews in the conflict over land in Palestine. Nor was this for any honourable or principled reason, but purely for reasons of perceived expediency. This, also, Karsh shows with meticulous attention to detail. In the pursuit of their muddled geopolitical aims, the British authorities succeeded only in making a mess in the Middle East, as they had at the same time in the Indian sub-continent, with another scheme for partition.

The real predators, Karsh shows, were the Arab states themselves, not least among them the Hashemites, in both Transjordan and Iraq, who scarcely had any historical claim to the lands of Palestine, but nourished overweening ambitions to build a pan-Arab empire where the Ottomans had ruled for centuries. The Syrians and Egyptians, similarly, harboured ambitions for grabbing pieces of Palestine as the League of Nations mandate expired and the British withdrew and none of them exhibited the least intelligence or humanity as regards the likely fate of the Palestinian Arabs in the event of a war to the death with the Jews. This is the thrust of Karsh's title—Palestine was betrayed, not by the British (though they did badly), not by the United Nations, not by the Zionists, but by the Arab leaders and especially the leaders of the Palestinian Arabs.

When the United Nations Partition Resolution was passed, on 29 November 1947, Jews danced in the streets throughout Palestine and Golda Meir, a prominent Zionist official who was to later become prime minister of Israel, declared to thousands of them in Jerusalem, 'Our hands are extended in peace to our neighbours. Both States can live in peace with one another and cooperate for the welfare of their inhabitants.' That this did not happen is exclusively the responsibility of the Arab leaders, whose response to the UN Resolution was to launch all-out war on the nascent and very small state of Israel. Meir knew, as did the other Zionist leaders, that neither the Palestinian leaders nor the Hashemites, nor the Egyptian and Syrian leaders, intended to accept the hand of peace; but it did not stop them from extending it. Perhaps the greatest service Karsh renders as an historian, is patiently documenting the record of their attempts, over decades, to gain Arab acceptance of Jewish autonomy on peaceful terms.

But perhaps the most insidious myth propagated by anti-Zionist and anti-Semitic sources for decades since 1948 has been the notion that the Jews engaged in systematic and premeditated ethnic cleansing in 1948, driving out hundreds of thousands of Palestinian Arabs to make way for a pure Jewish state on Arab lands. I had, until I read Karsh's book, given a degree of credence to this tale, though tending still, in all the circumstances, to feel sympathy for the Jewish cause.[267]

The single most potent piece of evidence in this version of events has long been the massacre at Deir Yasin carried out by the Irgun, on 9 April 1948. Karsh shows, however, that Deir Yasin was altogether the exception and was not an act of official Zionist policy at all. Elsewhere, the premeditated and systematic policy was an effort to encourage the Arabs to (1) accept the partition plan; (2) remain within the borders of the Jewish state if they so desired and on equal terms with its Jewish citizens; and (3) to urge the Arabs to stay especially in their own villages and cities as the conflict began, while withholding support from those who were truly intent on ethnic cleansing—the Arab Higher Committee and the Arab Legion.

One of the beauties of Karsh's book is that he provides a set of five maps which show the successive evolutions of the territorial division of Palestine. These maps show: the British

---

267 For a fresh take on the struggles for Palestine in the years before the state of Israel was created, see Bruce Hoffman *Anonymous Soldiers: The Struggle for Israel, 1917-1947* (Alfred A. Knopf, New York, 2015).

administrative divisions of Palestine under the League of Nations mandate; the administrative divisions of the Levant under late Ottoman rule; the Peel Commission Plan for the partition of Palestine, of July 1937; the United Nations Partition Plan of 1947; and the armistice lines in Palestine at the end of the Arab war to destroy Israel in 1948-49.

The final three of these maps show that, had the Palestinians—or their reckless and territorially ambitious Arab overlords—accepted partition in 1937, Israel would have been a tiny state extending only about 25 miles to the south of Tel Aviv, excluding Jaffa and confined to the old Galilee, Haifa and Lydda Districts and the Tulkarm Sub-District of the Samaria District of the old British mandate. The Arab state would have included the whole of the present West Bank, most of the Jerusalem District, the Beersheba Sub-District, the Gaza District and the Negev. Had they accepted partition in 1947, they would have no longer had the Beersheba Sub-District or the Negev, but would have gained a good deal of the Galilee District. Having been goaded and led to war, they ended up with only the West Bank, excluding Jerusalem and the Gaza Strip.

The tragedy of the Palestinian Arabs is not that Israel was established, but that their benighted leaders insisted on refusing any accommodation with Israel and betrayed them to defeat and dispossession. As Karsh shows, the Palestinians fled because the Arab leaders either fled, or urged them to leave or cleared them out of the way in anticipation of a genocidal pan-Arab onslaught against the Jews. His accounts of how all this unfolded in Haifa and Jaffa are particularly detailed and impressive. The result was that hundreds of thousands fled and the obdurate refusal of the Arab leaders to come to terms with the legitimacy of the state of Israel made it entirely impossible for Israel to allow a "right of return" after the armistice.

Showing a criminal disregard for the well-being of the Palestinian Arabs, Arab leaders treated them as expendable pawns in an irrational campaign to annihilate Israel. The execrable Secretary General of the Arab League, Abdel Rahman Azzam, irresponsibly declared in the midst of negotiations over a settlement to the 1948 war that sooner or later the state of Israel would be destroyed and that, in the event of repatriation, Israel would, fortunately, be placed in an impossible situation by the sabotage its Arab inhabitants would be well-placed to carry out against it.

Until I read this book, I was inclined, while partisan to the cause of the democratic state of Israel, to see the long conflict between it and the Palestinians as a tragedy of irreconcilable territorial claims. That is no longer the case. Karsh has caused the scales to fall from my eyes. I no longer see any excuse whatsoever for the violence of the Palestinian 'militants' or the anti-Israeli rhetoric of the Arab states and their allies elsewhere in the world. These things are nothing but the stubborn continuation of irrational and counter-productive strategies that have long since betrayed the best hopes of Palestinian Arabs and forced Israel to adopt often condign measures for self-defence. Until or unless the Arab leaders finally renounce their avowed aim to annihilate the state of Israel and embrace it as a partner for peace and development in the Levant, there cannot be a peaceful settlement of the conflict. And the responsibility for this lies squarely on the shoulders of the Arab leaders; nowhere else.

The end is NIE: divergent assessments of the nuclear peril

There is a famous story about US President John F. Kennedy sending two advisers to South Vietnam to assess the situation there and report back to him. One was a civilian from the State Department, Joseph Mendenhall. The other was a Marine officer from the Pentagon, Victor Krulak. They went separately and gave JFK such divergent assessments on their return that he quipped, 'The two of you did visit the same country, didn't you?' Reading Mohammed El Baradei's *The Age of Deception: Nuclear Diplomacy in Treacherous Times* and Ron Rosenbaum's *How the End Begins: The Road to a Nuclear World War III* brought this anecdote back to me.

El Baradei depicts the United States and Israel as aggressive and hypocritical. The decision by Nuclear Non-Proliferation Treaty (NPT) signatories such as Iraq (before 1991), North Korea (until it withdrew from the NPT) and Iran (up to the present) to deceptively develop nuclear weapons under the cover of the NPT he views with comparative equanimity. Rosenbaum is not at ease with anyone having nuclear weapons, but is especially concerned about Iran's nuclear weapons program as an existential threat to Israel and a probable trigger for catastrophic war in the Middle East.

A very well informed European friend remarked to me that Rosenbaum is 'a shrill alarmist' and El Baradei 'a vulgar apologist'. But it is too easy to just say that the truth lies 'somewhere in the middle'. For one thing, that merely begs the question, 'Where, exactly, then, does the truth lie?' But more importantly, it encourages evasion of the disturbing questions raised by each of these books and also by the fact that it is possible for two intelligent and well-informed observers of this terrifying subject to hold such divergent views.

How the End Begins is an apocalyptic book, but it isn't a hysterical one and it certainly is not a hawkish one. Ron Rosenbaum is a denizen of New York, born in Manhattan and raised on Long Island, who having graduated from Yale with a degree in English literature, dropped out of graduate school to become a full time writer. His first book was about Shakespeare. His bold attempt to reckon with the stark issue of nuclear weapons is not that of an international relations or strategic affairs specialist. It is that of an intelligent, articulate and Jewish citizen of the West trying to grapple with a desperately alarming subject to which far too many of us continue to be rather anaesthetized.

Mohammed El Baradei served as Director General of the International Atomic Energy Agency (IAEA) from 1997 until 2009. *The Age of Deception* is his account of this extraordinary experience. It covers the dramatic subjects of Iraq, North Korea and Iran and is an eye-opening account of how the IAEA works. El Baradei and the IAEA were jointly awarded the

Nobel Prize for Peace in 2005. After completing his work at the IAEA, the Nobel laureate returned to Cairo and played a leadership role in the Egyptian opposition movement which, earlier this year, overthrew Hosni Mubarak. His refrain throughout the book is that diplomacy and dialogue, not pre-emptive use of military force, are the ways to deal with the nuclear weapons problem.

The New York Jew is far edgier than the Egyptian Nobel laureate. He follows in the footsteps of Jonathan Schell's *The Fate of the Earth* (1982), *The Gift of Time: The Case for Abolishing Nuclear Weapons Now* (1998) and *The Unfinished Twentieth Century: The Crisis of Weapons of Mass Destruction* (2001), in arguing that we must *abolish* nuclear weapons, reversing the fateful steps taken from the Manhattan Project through the Cold War nuclear arms race. He introduces us to the Russian counterparts of those in the United States who have long seen the perilous fragility of the nuclear command and control system. He thinks through the moral logic of nuclear retaliation by Israel in the event it should suffer nuclear assault by Iran. He ponders the call for abolition of nuclear weapons, in the *Wall Street Journal* in 2007, by Henry Kissinger, George Schultz, William Perry and Sam Nunn: and concludes that the idea is right, but that it seems dismally improbable that it can be accomplished.

He does these things lucidly. His outlook is not shrill, but sombre. It is informed by a sense that the matter was always more dangerous and command and control systems always less reliable even during the Cold War than we have been assured (when we have been told anything at all); that the nuclear balance is fast becoming even more fragile and dangerous than it was during the Cold War; and that we delude ourselves if we think that any state is making very rational decisions about these matters. As Peter Bergen has expressed it, Rosenbaum fears that Armageddon might come simply because of 'the endemic incompetence of the human species'. That incompetence covers the technical, political, cognitive and moral domains.

Rosenbaum's dark view of the nuclear prospect is nowhere more evident than in the two chapters he devotes to the profound concern in Israel about the possibility of nuclear weapons in Iranian hands—chapter seven '"The Ashes are Still Warm": The Second Holocaust, Israel and the Morality of Nuclear Retaliation' and chapter eight 'Iran: The 'Enigmatic Box' and the NIE'. These chapters make the book worth reading even on their own. El Baradei devotes four whole chapters to the question of Iran. The alarming thing is that their two accounts barely overlap at all. It seems extraordinary that this could be the case.

El Baradei makes the astonishing claim that there is 'not a whiff of evidence' that Iran is intent on developing nuclear weapons. He argues that it has only developed its nuclear facilities in secret for fear that the West would seek to prevent it from developing nuclear energy at all; and that the dictatorial leaders of Iran, Ayatollah Khamenei and Mahmoud Ahmadinejad, are both eminently reasonable and pleasant gentlemen, much misunderstood by the West and slandered by Israel. He records that at one point he privately admonished them that their remarks about there not having been a Holocaust and about wiping Israel off the map were not helping their cause. Astonishingly, he nowhere states that he regards such remarks as deplorable in themselves.

That a Director General of the IAEA should have held the views that El Baradei expresses about Iran seems to me deeply troubling. The general tone of his book comes across as that of a dedicated, dispassionate international civil servant, resistant to Western pressure and determined, to the best of his ability, to fulfil his mandate under the NPT. This and his frequent broadsides at the United States and Israel (not least over the bombing of Iraq's Osirak nuclear reactor in 1981 and Syria's Dair Alzour nuclear plant in 2007) will appeal to many readers, while alienating others. But his argument in regard to Iran is so systematically at odds with that of mainstream strategic opinion that one wonders how he feels able to sustain it. If only he were right. Read him. Understand his point of view. Then read Rosenbaum.

Is China an autistic dragon?

In a fascinating interview on *Lateline* recently, Edward Luttwak, remarked that China is an 'autistic' nation and has always been bad at strategy. Luttwak, a prolific American public intellectual, a Romanian Jew and Holocaust survivor by origin, fluent in at least five languages; is the author of controversial books on the grand strategy of the Roman and Byzantine empires. His latest book, *The Rise of China and the Logic of Grand Strategy* is about to be released. It, also, is quite controversial, but his claim that China is strategically autistic is a provocation to clear thinking about China's grand strategy.[268]

We are urged by Hugh White, Malcolm Fraser, Twiggy Forrest, Kerry Stokes and others to understand China's legitimate interests and rising power and to avoid provoking it or trying to contain it. Luttwak's contrarian voice cuts through this sedative rhetoric. His argument is not that China is a direct threat to Australia, or that it has a deliberate strategy to dominate the region, but that it has *no coherent strategy at all*—and that this is an increasingly serious problem both for China and for the rest of us. His use of the word 'autistic' in this context seems to be intended as clinical rather than deliberately offensive and is refreshingly counter-intuitive.

Those who subscribe to the Middle Kingdom mystique see China as a collective Sun Tzu, with an ancient, intelligent and non-expansionist strategic culture. Those who fear China's rise see it as a dictatorship with overweening ambitions, which is getting more and more assertive as its power grows. It is seen as having hegemonic designs. That its recent assertiveness might be due more to incoherence or autism than to a hegemonic design is not an idea that has had any currency. That it might be harder to deal with a strategically incoherent China than with a deliberately aggressive one is a troubling thought and worth pondering.

The idea that China is autistic might seem offensive; even absurd. But that should not lead

---

[268] It was in response to this piece, writing in his diary, in Sydney, on Sunday 7 October 2012, that then Foreign Minister Bob Carr remarked:

> *Paul Monk's article on China in* The Australian *on October 1 takes up Luttwak's view that China is an autistic nation and has been bad at strategy, locked up as it has been in its own Middle Kingdom mystique and totally unused to dealing with other powers as equals. Luttwak had said, 'Constructive dialogue with China is important ... the problem is that China is tone deaf in strategic matters.' Paul Monk, I think, is one of Australia's best intellectuals—no, the best; this is another case of him leaping over the various divides and factional camps, the culture wars. He says, 'China has never broken the centralist, authoritarian, repressive mould of politics dating back to the Shang dynasty ... it has never developed an open, pluralist politics of the kind that dates back to classical Greece in the West.'*

Bob Carr *Diary of a Foreign Minister* (Newsouth Publishing, Sydney, 2014), p. 184.

us to dismiss Luttwak's provocative thesis, any more than we should avoid or suppress criticism of Islam in order to avoid offending Muslim fanatics. The whole idea of a culture of critical analysis and freedom of expression is that unorthodox, provocative and iconoclastic ideas are to be encouraged and examined, not dismissed as politically incorrect, blasphemous or "unhelpful". In fact, Luttwak's assertion could be really helpful in forcing out into the open a number of deeply embedded and largely unexamined assumptions about Chinese strategic culture and intentions

China has a wonderful material and cultural tradition, Luttwak says, but it spent millennia isolated from most of the outside world by the ocean on one aside and the Central Asian deserts on the other. Consequently, it has never learned to deal on equal or deeply engaged terms with others. It has long suffered from the conceit that it is the only 'serious' culture going around. This served it badly and made it poor at grand strategy, with the result that it was conquered by barbarians from the north and ruled by them for centuries at a time. One might add another result: the decrepitude of late Manchu China and its incapacity to deal intelligently or successfully with the Europeans in the nineteenth century or the Japanese in the twentieth.

The problem we have now, Luttwak suggests, is that China has learned very little about how to get on with its neighbours and is picking fights with many of them when it is not well placed to prevail and is likely to trigger coalitions of resistance by its actions. Australia, he thinks, has been doing constructive and intelligent things by trying to develop strategic dialogue around the Asian region; enabling China's increasingly uncomfortable neighbours to believe that they will not be left alone to face it down. Constructive dialogue with China is important, Luttwak argues, but the problem is that China is tone deaf in strategic matters.

There is a rich literature on China's strategic outlook. Two of the modern classics are John Wilson Lewis and Xue Litai's *Imagined Enemies* and Alastair Iain Johnston's *Cultural Realism*. Johnston's book, especially, is a handy foil to Luttwak. He argued that, contrary to the widespread perception that Chinese strategic culture is largely passive, adroit and sophisticated, it has in reality been characterized by use of force when China felt strong and appeasement of the barbarians when it felt weak. China is getting strong again.

To the extent that Johnston is correct, this must be cause for watchful concern on the part of China's neighbours. If Luttwak is correct, that concern would be difficult to translate into constructive dialogue with China. And, as it happens, such dialogue has been proving difficult—for most of China's neighbours.

China has never broken the centralist, authoritarian, repressive mould of politics dating back to the Shang dynasty and apotheosized under the First August Emperor, Qin Shi

Huangdi, in the third century BCE. It has never developed an open, pluralistic politics of the kind that dates back to classical Greece in the West. It has what political scientist and dissident Yan Jiaqi described, in 1988, as a 'dragon culture'. He declared that China needed to put this behind it, if it was to become a fully modern, cosmopolitan and law-governed state.

Yan Jiaqi has lived in exile since 1989. China remains a dragon culture. And Edward Luttwak suggests that the dragon is autistic. With autistic children, we tend to compassion, therapy and empathy. But what do you do with an autistic dragon, whose reflexive approach to being strong is to throw its weight around? Behaving in a similar manner is not recommended. But fire-proofing the neighbourhood might be wise. At the very least, looking at China's behaviour through the Luttwak lens makes it possible to see things differently and shake off the complacency which comes from basing our thinking on lazy assumptions. That would be a healthy development and wiser than feeling overawed or enthusiastic.

If current trends continue ...

The literature on China's economic growth and geopolitical rise is now too vast for even a specialist to keep up with. One has, therefore, to be selective in one's reading. For the generalist or common citizen this is even more so. Given those constraints, if you are seriously interested in China's global role and its relationship with the United States—especially as an Australian—then you should definitely read Aaron Friedberg's *A Contest for Supremacy*. It has several things to commend it. It is a compact reflection on the full scope of the rise of China; it is a work of genuine and profound scholarship; and it specifically addresses both the complex history and the various possible futures of Sino-American relations. Few other books on the subject have this combination of qualities.

Aaron Friedberg is a classic product of America's Ivy League institutions, Harvard and Princeton; and among the finest exponents of what might be called a conservative realism in geopolitics. Currently at the Woodrow Wilson School at Princeton University, he has worked in the White House on national security affairs and is the author two previous books which plainly helped prepare him for the systematic thinking embodied in this latest one. In *The Weary Titan: Britain and the Experience of Relative Decline, 1895-1905* (1988), he anticipated, even as the Cold War was ending, something of the challenge the United States now faces. Then, in 2000, came *In the Shadow of the Garrison State: America's Anti-Statism and Its Cold War Grand Strategy*. This was an excellent grounding for thinking about an American grand strategy for absorbing the extraordinary ascent of China.

In September 2001, coincident with the dramatic al Qaeda assault on America that month, he undertook a nine month fellowship as the first Henry Alfred Kissinger Scholar at the Library of Congress. He used that privileged time to commence research on the rise of Asia and its implications for America. Prior to that appointment, he had been invited to participate in a Clinton administration "review of the intelligence community's assessments of China's economic performance, political stability, strategic intentions and military power." He doesn't divulge much about the review itself, but it is clear from the content of his book that he has acquainted himself with the full spectrum of issues that such a review—if well done—would have had to consider.

It was the review that seems to have prompted him to embark on the present book. The experience, he writes:

> left me deeply troubled about where China was headed and about the future direction of relations between that country and my own. I also found myself puzzled and frustrated by what struck me as a wilful, blinkered optimism on these matters prevalent at th354e time in the academic and business communities and across significant portions of the US government.

A major theme and strength of his book is that he interrogates such optimism without lurching too far in the direction of pessimism or polemic. Indeed, the judicious way in which he thinks through the possible scenarios for the decade or two ahead of us is one of the chief reasons why his book should be widely and closely read.

Another is his uncommonly sensitive understanding of the way America's various regional allies see the Sino-American rivalry. Immediately after his Kissinger Scholar stint at the Library of Congress, he spent six weeks in the Australia winter of 2002, at the Australian Strategic Policy Institute, as a guest of Hugh White and Alan Dupont. It was good for Australia that he had been invited to spend those six weeks in Canberra (and that he accepted), since it gave him a lucid appreciation of Australia's outlook and dilemmas in the context of the rise and rise of China. His remarks on this head, as on the outlook of other regional American allies such as South Korea and Japan, exhibit an uncommonly nuanced and perceptive appreciation of the strategic circumstances facing each of these key allies of the United States.

For precisely this reason, Australian readers of *A Contest for Supremacy* should take note of a key observation Friedberg makes early in the book and which he carries through in a temperate and deeply informed manner. On the one hand, he remarks, the emerging Sino-American rivalry is not something grounded simply in 'easily erased misperceptions or readily correctible policy errors', but is structural and serious; something vitally important for which, however, the United States is not especially well prepared.

On the other hand, 'it has become virtually impossible to discuss China in a measured and dispassionate way'. That holds true also in this country and it is most important that the impediment be overcome. The irony of the situation is that the possibility of the rivalry lapsing into confrontation is so disturbing that a wide spectrum of 'informed and responsible opinion' simply does not want to "face unpleasant facts" and therefore discourages dissent and debate on the grounds that 'alarmists' risk 'creating problems where none need otherwise exist.'

This is where the richness and value of the book centre. We must have a dispassionate debate about future possibilities, he argues, because '*if current trends continue, we are on track to lose our geopolitical contest with China.*' There are two key factors in this calculation: the relentless build-up of Chinese military capabilities with the explicit strategic aim of excluding the United States from East Asia and denying it the dominance in the Western Pacific that it has enjoyed since 1945; and the parlous fiscal condition of the United States.

What is at risk over the next decade is that the United States will forfeit the 'pivotal axiom' of its strategic policy over the past hundred years: to prevent the domination of either end of the Eurasian land mass by a potentially hostile power or coalition. America needs to exert itself to 'stay in the game'. This means addressing both of the factors just mentioned. That is the challenge that lies ahead in this decade. Read and understand.

Section 4: 2010-11

Love among the ruins of Stalinism

In *The Novel: An Alternative History—Beginnings to 1600* (2010), Steven Moore remarks that, from its pre-classical beginnings, the novel was a highly elastic literary form, in which 'the plot was a mere convenience that allowed the author to engage in rhetorical display, literary criticism, socio-political commentary, digressions and so on.' He wrote his book in outrage at the tendency of a certain kind of contemporary critic to deplore the narrative styles and rhetorical excesses of modern authors such as James Joyce, William Faulkner, Vladimir Nabokov, Thomas Pynchon and Don De Lillo.

It is a fascinating thesis. Moore concluded (in 2010) with the observation that, had anyone in 1600 read all the novels written up to that point, she might have deduced that the future of the genre lay in China. But she would have been in error. Its future was shaped in Spain. There the 'failed writer', Miguel de Cervantes, created a work of genius when he 'imagined a man of La Mancha who had been driven loco by reading too many novels.' That Don Quixote was loco is proverbial. But Cervantes had far more in mind than that. However, only the close reader who is also attuned to Spanish history in the century and more before Cervantes will perceive what else Cervantes had in mind and was pointing to, through the Knight of Sorrowful Countenance.

All this came to mind as I read Elena Chizhova's 2009 Russian Booker Prize winning novel *The Time of Women*. It's narrative structure and literary style appear disorganized and even incompetent to the impatient eye. The narrative shifts, sometimes bewilderingly, between a variety of first person voices, with occasional passages in italics which are not always continuous with the preceding voice or even context. The syntax is often disjointed and where prepositions seem wrong or the verb tense alters within one sentence in an incoherent way, it's hard to know whether this results from poor translation, bad writing or some baffling artifice on the author's part.

Yet there is a story here with many strands. At the level of plot, it is a story about three generations of Russian women struggling to live dignified lives in the 1960s, in Leningrad. There are three elderly women (Yevdokia, Ariadna and Glykeria), a younger woman, who is a single mother (Antonina) and her mute child (Sophia, or Suzannochka). The five share a small apartment, where the elderly women, living on meagre pensions, look after Suzannochka, while Antonina works a dreary double shift at a factory. This 'plot story' is communicated with an eye for detail and a feel for common humanity which are both striking and memorable at many points. But the 'real' story behind the plot is the point of Chizhova's unusual and apparently stilted rhetorical display.

That real story is at once the appalling twentieth century history of Russia under Communist rule and Nazi assault; and the amnesiac and muted condition to which Russians had been reduced in the decades after Stalin. Not only the digressions or conversations in the book, but the very disjointed language used by the voices and the actual muteness of the little girl reflect this legacy of trauma and damage. Chizhova surely intended not only to depict Russian society in the 1960s, but to hold a mirror up to Russian society now. It is the beauty of literary art that it can throw light on our present dilemmas or shortcomings by getting us to look at other times and places. There are no inspiring or charismatic figures in the story; only ordinary, suffering human beings. The central figure, Antonina, dies of uterine cancer at the end of the story and her mute daughter seems to live on with difficulty as a struggling artist, consoled by remnants of Christian mysticism. She would appear to stand for Russia as a whole in the time of Putin.

There is something about *The Time of Women* redolent of Beckett, as well as Chekhov. Yet Chizhova does not see her characters as either absurd or anachronistic. She sympathizes with them and seems to endorse both the nostalgia of the old women for the culture of pre-Communist Russia and the recourse to residual religious belief. She appears to see herself as writing not *avant garde* literature, but a stuttering and loving reflection on Russian humanity amid the ruins left by the disasters of the twentieth century. The old women can remember the world of Tolstoy, but have lived through that of Bulgakov's *The White Guard* and Platonov's *The Foundation Pit*. Perhaps the illness and death of Antonina are also an inflection of Solzhenitsyn's *Cancer Ward*.

It's striking that this book has won a prestigious literary prize. I don't know what criteria the judges used in finding distinguished merit in it. But apart from those echoes and characteristics to which I have referred, it brings a notable range of quite distinct voices to life, as genuine personalities. This gives the novel that quality which the great Russian literary critic Mikhail Bakhtin argued sets literature apart from pulp fiction: its 'dialogical character'; the sense that authentically different voices and points of view are given expression. Though Chizhova came relatively late to literature, after a career as an economist, teacher and entrepreneur; all the Russian writers to whom I have referred have surely long been familiar to her; perhaps including Bakhtin.

You might choose to read *The Time of Women* because it won the Russian Booker Prize; or because it was written in contemporary Russia; or because it is about three generations of women finding ways to survive by supporting one another in a rather bleak world. But my recommendation would be that you read it in order to grapple with Chizhova's jarring and challenging narrative and rhetorical style. And also because her struggling and verbally inhibited characters are not representative only of Russia's tragic history; but stand, also, for certain aspects of our common humanity and certain aspects of the lives even of those of us in the relatively untroubled and pampered West.

Constraining Iran's nuclear ambitions

There has been a renewed debate of late as to whether Israel or the United States should bomb Iran's nuclear facilities in order to head off Iran's quest for a nuclear weapons capability. The prior question that commands attention is: should Iran be *permitted* to acquire a nuclear weapons capability? I do not say 'acquire nuclear *weapons*'. Once the capability is in place, weaponization is a mere technicality. And Iran is working relentlessly to develop the capability.

The answer has to be: No. This is premised less on a judgment about the proclivity of Tehran to use nuclear weapons; much less on any kind of 'racist' prejudice against Iranians, than on the fact that Iran, as a voluntary signatory to the Nuclear Non-Proliferation Treaty, has a standing commitment not to develop a nuclear weapons capability and is refusing to abide by its safeguards agreement with the IAEA, designed to ensure that it honours this fundamental commitment. In short, the regime in Tehran is breaking an international covenant. If the international order is not upheld against this violation of a crucial collective security regime, then the NPT itself, already troubled, will become pretty much an empty letter.

There are those who argue that Iran cannot now be prevented from acquiring a nuclear weapons capability and an arsenal of nuclear weapons and, therefore, we need to abandon the idea of denying it these things and work on deterring and containing a nuclear armed Iran. The word "cannot" here is too strong. Rather, the putative *costs* of attempting to deny Iran such a capability are deemed high and therefore, it is argued, they should not be incurred. Yet if the costs of *facing* a nuclear armed Iran would be greater, the argument ought to be, in a strictly logical sense, that pre-emptive action be taken. And there should be no ducking the fact that the costs of having a nuclear armed Iran could be very high.

To begin with, Iran openly aspires to a kind of regional hegemony. This has less to do with Islam, than with nostalgia for the days of the Persian Empire; rather like Mussolini aspiring fecklessly to recreate the Roman Empire. Its Sunni Arab neighbours are so clearly alarmed at its ambitions that they are likely to approve destruction of Iranian nuclear facilities. Failing such pre-emption, it is entirely possible that several of them, not least Saudi Arabia and Egypt, would seek nuclear weapons for themselves. Such a development alone would surely be profoundly undesirable. But short of it, the world would face a prolonged nuclear balance of terror in the Middle East, as Israel and the United States sought to deter Iran (or Arab nuclear powers) from using nuclear weapons not just in a first strike, but in dangerous regional brinksmanship.

Here is where the greatest danger lies. Assuming, for the sake of argument, that even the chiliastic revolutionaries in command of Tehran's Shi'ite regime could be deterred from first use of a nuclear weapon; they might well calculate that they could up the ante in their avowed campaign to destroy Israel, by arming Hezbollah and Islamic Jihad and prompting greater and greater provocations, while threatening Israel against "disproportionate" responses to them. What has long been an unsatisfactory battle of nerves with Tehran regarding its support for international terrorism would become even more fraught once it acquired nuclear weapons. All the more so because it would have done this despite repeated international calls for it to desist and American and Israeli insistence that they would *not allow* such a development.

So, Iran should not be permitted to acquire a nuclear weapons capability. But how is this non-permission to be enforced? For many years now, dialogue has been held with Iran. But to what end? First of all, there should be no dialogue premised on the insistence by Iran of refusing to honours its own safeguards agreement and open facilities to IAEA inspection. Secondly, Iran has not frozen its nuclear program while this dialogue has proceeded. Rather, it has used the extended and fruitless dialogue as a cover for pushing forward ever closer to having the capability in question, all the while refusing to either acknowledge its bad faith or allow the IAEA to test its claims on the grounds.

Sanctions have been both proposed and applied; never more seriously than now. Yet still Iran thumbs its nose at the international order and proceeds with its plans. It is now a race against time: can sanctions work before Iran crosses the nuclear capability threshold? Unconditional honouring of its IAEA obligations is not being insisted upon, because no-one wants to incur the costs of taking action. But at what point do those with the greatest stake in the matter reasonably decide that diplomacy and sanctions have not availed? Those who refuse to see such a point surely abandon any responsibility for collective security. They allow that no red line or warning should mean anything or be enforced. That is a parlous condition in which to place what still passes for international collective security.

The interim step would surely be for the United States to at least place several aircraft carrier battle groups and submarines in the Persian Gulf area, to give teeth to its declaratory position that all options are on the table and that Iran must open up unconditionally to IAEA inspections. Anything less inevitably sends a signal to Iran that, when it comes right down to it, no-one will stand up against it. Except, perhaps, Israel. Israel has taken down both Iraqi nuclear facilities (1981) and Syrian ones (2007). This, however, would be a supreme test of its audacity and its capabilities. One thing ought to be clear, though: if Israel has to act alone and if it does act, it will have done so because of the cowardice and irresolution that prevail in the West; to say nothing of the obstructionism at the UNSC that has always characterized Russia and China.

Daniel Kahneman on thinking, fast and slow

Daniel Kahneman's *Thinking, fast and slow* should be required reading for everyone this summer. Not because it is entertaining or a mere diversion, but because it is a subtle and beautifully scientific guide for the perplexed. If you see yourself as a citizen in a democratic polity, read this book. Self-indulgent cynics and self-important ideologues probably won't read it, but they are the ones most in need of what it has to teach. Do yourself a favour, whoever you are: rush out, buy this book and read it quietly and thoughtfully, absorbing its highly readable insights.

Kahneman was awarded the Nobel Memorial Prize in Economic Sciences in 2002 for his work on prospect theory. To understand what is meant by this, how Kahneman got into thinking about it and what his key insights were—in collaboration with his long-time research partner Amos Tversky - go straight to chapter 26 'Prospect Theory'. It's a fascinating excursion into clear thinking all on its own. Prospect theory is about gambling, risk-taking and expected returns. It's a body of theory with considerable practical relevance to the king-sized mess both welfare economics and financial markets got themselves into by the late 2000s.

Kahneman re-examined the fundamentals of utility theory, articulated by Daniel Bernoulli, almost three hundred years ago. He did this long before the past decade or two's extravagant follies came close to wrecking economies from California to Greece. Utility theory lies at the foundation of modern economics and there is a rather urgent need right now to *understand* what has gone so awfully wrong in so many economies. Falling back on Marxism or some kind of self-satisfied ideological cliché does not amount to such understanding. Kahneman confers considerable understanding. That's why he deserved his Nobel Prize.

Thinking, fast and slow has five parts: Two Systems, Heuristics and Biases, Overconfidence, Choices and Two Selves. It also contains, as appendices, two of the classic papers for which Kahneman won his Nobel: 'Judgment under Uncertainty' and 'Choices, Values and Frames'. Part I sets cognitive science in an easy to understand frame of reference which acts both as a disciplined corrective to a good deal of pop psychology and a lucid introduction to the theoretical work in the following four parts of the book.

He suggests that we think of our brain—our 'machine' for making judgments—as consisting of two basic systems; which he calls System 1 and System 2. He describes the characteristics of each and explains how their faults and standard ways of interacting result in many kinds of error, bias and illusion—universally and predictably, not in merely unusual or idiosyncratic cases. System 1 is the intuitive, unconscious, fast reaction part of the brain. It is emotional, holistic and instinctual. It is, as he expresses it, "a machine for jumping to conclusions".

In certain circumstances and often in everyday life, its functions are reliable, rapid and even remarkable. But when it comes to matters that require complex, abstract thinking it is in deep trouble. System 2 is better equipped—if trained and switched on—to handle such matters. The problem with System 2 is that it is lazy and highly inclined to rationalize rather than critically examine the intuitive judgments of System 1.

In Parts II, III and IV of the book, drawing upon the work of many psychologists and cognitive scientists, Kahneman offers an endlessly fascinating dissection of the brain of *Homo sap*. The chapters include 'The Law of Small Numbers', 'Anchors', 'The Science of Availability', 'Availability, Emotion and Risk', 'Causes Trump Statistics', 'Intuitions vs Formulas', 'Risk Policies' and 'Frames and Reality'. And at every point Kahneman exhibits a demeanour at once keenly curious, meticulously scientific and utterly unpretentious. The implications of what he imparts are enormous and need to be digested by our education systems (not least all business administration courses), our public policy systems and our methods for public debate.

An indication of the ways in which such insights can be applied was offered several years ago, in Richard Thaler and Cass Sunstein's *Nudge: Improving Decisions About Health, Wealth and Happiness*. Originally completed in 2007, it was reissued in 2008 with a Postscript titled 'The Financial Crisis of 2008'. They drew attention to the alarming reality that almost no economists or financial analysts had foreseen the crisis, or issued public warnings as it approached. They praised the behavioural economist Robert Shiller for having done so.

Shiller's warning in 2005 had been that "social contagion" was creating a massive housing market bubble that would inevitably burst. Shiller's books, *Irrational Exuberance* (2000) and *The New Financial Order: Risk in the 21st Century* (2003) are recommended reading. Thaler and Sunstein's own observation is that sound public policy, informed by the insights of cognitive science and behavioural economics, needs to invent ways (they suggest a number) to prevent or defuse such outbreaks of social contagion, or what Charles Mackay long ago called 'extraordinary popular delusions and the madness of crowds.'

As Michael Lewis's peerless writing shows, a little thoughtful analysis can reap enormous dividends. If markets and capitalism are to flourish and the costs of human stupidity are to be contained in future, then many things will need to be rethought and reformed. Lewis's latest book, *Boomerang: The Meltdown Tour*, a characteristic *tour de force* shows this from Iceland and Ireland to Greece, Germany and California. If you don't read Kahneman this summer, you simply must read Lewis.

Kahneman, meanwhile, is hard at work trying to engineer better thinking in the marketplace, or at least to nudge the unwilling and unwitting in that direction. He is a partner in a firm called

Greatest Good, committed to applying cutting-edge data analysis and the insights of behavioural economics to real business challenges. His associates are a highly impressive group of people, including Steven Levitt (of *Freakonomics* fame), innovative economists Gary Becker and John List, the checklist manifesto man Atul Gawande and the brilliant theoretical physicist Lisa Randall. Now that, to paraphrase Groucho Marx, is a club of which I'd *like* to be a member.

Roman Krznaric's wonder box

Roman Krznaric's grandmother, Naomi, he tells us, was born the daughter of a Moldovan rabbi, fled across Eurasia to Manchuria, begged her way to Shanghai, took ship to Australia and lived out her life in Sydney a fervent Communist, a nudist and a vegetarian. Heterodoxy, you might say, was his inheritance. In *The Wonder Box*, he has distilled this inheritance in a beautiful and generous way.

It is a delightfully lucid book of provocations to freedom of mind and spirit. Unlike the mass of self-help, psychology or spirituality books, it is based on history, rather than abstract or new-fangled ideas. It offers practical examples of what has been done before and is being done now to make life more hands-on, creative and adventurous.

Moreover, the author has lived his wisdom. He has learned handicrafts, worked and researched among the poor and downtrodden, lived in different countries and helped found the School of Life in London. And he writes in a most engaging, down to earth manner, without fear or favour; but also without humbug or pretension.

His keynote is a call to be bold. One could be reading Kant (*To be wise, be bold*), Emerson (*Do not be too timid and squeamish about your actions. All life is an experiment*), or Nietzsche (*Live dangerously!*). But Krznaric is both more accessible and more practical than those writers. His is a handbook for the common citizen, more than a clarion call for heroes.

Indeed, quite often he argues that the cults of genius and celebrity are destructive of our common humanity and that we would be well advised to lay them aside and cultivate our skills and aspirations without much regard to them. The idea is not to be overawed and thus, perhaps, paralysed by a sense of inadequacy or fate; but to be active and engaged and free-spirited.

The book is neatly structured and covers so much everyday ground so thoughtfully, that one could almost urge: 'Read this book a chapter at a time, a week at a time and let its reflective observations slowly fertilize the way you see your life. Above all, don't rush through it.'

The Preface and Epilogue, bookending the work, are transparent and concise. In between, the book has four parts, each with three chapters: Nurturing Relationships (Love, Family, Empathy), Making a Living (Work, Time, Money), Discovering the World (Senses, Travel, Nature), Breaking Conventions (Belief, Creativity, Deathstyle).

Almost like an opera, it begins with love and ends with death. But it isn't operatic in style. It is both earthy and literate in a kind of old-fashioned style; both iconoclastic and realistic. It both throws light into the world of personal fulfilment and issues a call to empathy and ethical action in a global context.

Above all, Krznaric counsels: free yourself of idols, dogmas, unexamined prejudices and timid conformity. He holds up a refreshing diversity of human beings as examples, rather than pushing an ideological line that many of us would have found hectoring and tiresome. He certainly holds up Galileo as a champion of liberating iconoclasm, but his use of Galileo's exploration of the starry sky as a metaphor is the key to his appreciation of the matter:

> *What does Galileo's story mean for the art of living today? Unlike Galileo, most of us never even raise the telescope. We do not turn our gaze towards that which might challenge our long held beliefs or lifestyle choices ... But if we want to have a Galilean revolution in our own lives, we need to decide where to point the telescope.*

I love his reflections on Jiddu Krishnamurti, Leo Tolstoy, Albert Schweitzer and so many others, but no example of imagination and daring in the book made a deeper impression on me than that of Philippe Petit, the juggler and high wire artist, who walked, ran and even danced on a high wire between the twin towers of the new World Trade Center, on 7 August 1974.

Asked why he had done it, Petit told police, 'When I see three oranges, I juggle; when I see two towers, I walk'. What an extraordinary and side-splitting bon mot—and how intimidating to those of us who lack the skill and courage to do such things, literally or metaphorically! Fortunately, most of what Roman Krznaric offers is not quite so hair-raising as tightrope walking without any harness or safety net hundreds of metres above the ground.

He shows how we can think far more freely about love and family, our place in nature, our hands and creative abilities, our diets and entertainment habits, our conversation with others and our attitudes to authority, genius, technology, consumer goods and death. He calls us to converse and to act, freely and imaginatively, for the sake of a better life and a better world. His is a very sane voice, I think. Have a listen.

The soloist and the chorus

Five realities frame debate within Australia over its relationship with China: the immense increase in bilateral trade between the two countries, especially in the past decade; the way our commodities trade with China is warping the domestic economic balance we sought to create with the reforms of the 1980s and 1990s; the fact that China is the first country in our history to be our largest trading partner without being a member of the strategic alliance that guarantees our security; growing regional concern at the relentless expansion of Chinese military capabilities and the economic difficulties of the United States since 2008.

Everyone is aware that these realities have created substantial policy challenges for Australia. Many argue that the present Government is not handling those challenges with distinction. Regrettably, the Opposition isn't offering any great insights either, although it is widely conceded that the Howard government, following a shaky start, got the relationship with China pretty much right.

But the current climate of debate is shaped by the implications of two post-Howard phenomena: the massive 2008 financial debacle centring on Wall Street and the important role of our exports to China in enabling Australia to avoid the crunch that hit so many other countries since 2008. Exacerbating those problems has been the fact that China's diplomatic and military behaviour has become discernibly more assertive since 2008.

In short, there is a great need for informed debate about all this. If you are a non-specialist wondering how to get your mind around the challenges in question and perhaps wanting to become a better informed participant in the conversation, both David Uren's *The Kingdom and the Quarry* and James Reilly and Jingdong Yuan *Australia and China at 40* will be very useful resources. Uren's is a cohesive and well-informed analysis of the economic relationship and its wider ramifications.

Reilly and Yuan have put together a collection of essays by a variety of Australian and Chinese scholars that is notable for its divergent perspectives and includes several quite fine pieces that deserve to be read not only by the wider public but by specialists in government and industry. If you are pressed for time and have to choose between them, go for Uren's book. Its strengths as a solo act make it a better briefing on the big picture than the sometimes discordant chorus of voices in the Reilly and Yuan book.

Ross Garnaut, our ambassador to China back in the 1980s, when both China and Australia were going through major economic reforms; and subsequently the main author of the groundbreaking 1990 report *Australia and the East Asian Ascendancy*, is quoted on the front cover of

The Kingdom and the Quarry as saying that the book is "entertaining and informative." I think this sells the book a little short.

I wouldn't describe it as 'entertaining' and while it is informative, especially for a non-specialist readership, its chief virtue is its consistently good sense. At a time when both enthusiasm about and fear of China can be overhyped in Australia, Uren has done an impressive job of analysing the relationship between economics and security cohesively and intelligently. I hope many thousands read his book and profit from what it has to say.

Indeed, I would go so far as to say that Garnaut himself might reasonably have described it as a judicious and highly readable assessment of what has unfolded over the twenty two years since his 1990 report was published by the Australian Government.

Australia and China at 40 is less consistently impressive than *The Kingdom and the Quarry*. There are, however, a number of striking contributions: the data-rich essay by Ding Dou on 'China's resources trade and investment with Australia', Nick Bisley's 'Never having to choose: China's rise and Australian security', Fergus Hanson's 'How your attitudes help shape relations with China', John Lee's 'Divergence in Australia's economic and security interests?' and Michael Wesley's concluding reflection 'Australia and the China boom'.

These are the pick of the bunch. The essays in the book haven't been fully reconciled. They express occasionally divergent opinions at times. But this provides stimulus to thoughtful debate and it could be that this is in its own way a more useful contribution than Uren's individually articulate and well-balanced contribution. But the weaknesses in some of the essays mar the Reilly/Yuan book and make Uren's the higher quality offering overall.

James Curran's essay 'The World Changes: Australia's China Policy in the Wake of Empire', for example, gets the Reilly/Yuan book off to a poor start. He refers to Malcolm Fraser as once having been 'a hard-line cold warrior prone to foaming at the mouth about the evils of Chinese communism'; to the 'Menzian dark age' in Australian foreign policy; to America having, in the 1950s and 1960s, 'denied itself access to the great China market'; and to Harold Holt deciding, in 1966 'to establish an Australian diplomatic mission in the province of Taiwan.'

Language of the kind Curran uses is neither sophisticated nor accurate and detracts from the quality of the book in which it is used. There are solecisms elsewhere in the book, but these irked me. It is quite astonishing that Malcolm Fraser should be described as having foamed at the mouth; especially given that the evils of Chinese communism in the 1960s were absolutely real. The Menzies era was no dark age like the Mao era and as for the US denying itself access to the 'great China market', there was no such market before the 1980s.

Finally, Taiwan was not and is not a 'province' of the People's Republic of China. Diplomatic recognition was accorded it as the Republic of China on Taiwan, at the height of the Cold War and the Cultural Revolution. Resolution of the conflicting claims of the governments of the PRC and Taiwan remains to be accomplished. Curran, in short, is full of nonsense. Uren's work, by contrast, is refreshingly free of such cant and deserves to be read widely and seriously both here and in China.

Mississippi Burning in Tibet

In Tibet, people are being shot out of hand by Chinese security forces and monks and nuns are setting themselves on fire in grim protest at the relentless repression of any meaningful autonomy in that vast and ancient country. There are those in Australia who say we should "stop lecturing the Chinese about human rights", but at the very least we need to be able to put the ongoing violence in Tibet into a thoughtful perspective. The EU-China Summit is underway in Beijing and the next president of China, Xi Jinping, who will not be elected, but has been selected, is in the United States, meeting with President Obama. Conscientious activists have been urging both the EU leaders and official Washington to raise concerns about Tibet during these meetings. That's a good context for all of us to get some perspective.

The Communist regime in Beijing has ruled Tibet with an iron fist since crushing a rebellion, in 1959, against its occupation of the country. It insists that Tibet has always been and must remain an inalienable part of China. The claim is flatly false. Tibet has a very long history as a state and culture entirely independent of China. It only became part of the Chinese empire under the non-Chinese Manchu dynasty, in the eighteenth century. Yet the republican revolutionaries in early twentieth century China—Nationalist and Communist alike—claimed that both it and other vast areas of non-Han territory, such as Xinjiang, Manchuria and Mongolia, were integral parts of the new Chinese republic. This is the source of the conflicts that plague the Communist state at the beginning of the twenty first century.

Mongolia, of course, is independent. Manchuria is fully integrated. Xinjiang and Tibet remain highly restive. Had the Communist Party been better at basic governance and able to establish a viable constitution, there might be more resilience in their sway over these immense outlying territories. The problem, as Liu Xiaobo pointed out in April 2008, during the violent uprising in Tibet in the lead up to the Olympic Games, is that the Communist dictatorship will brook no authentic autonomy and rides roughshod over any kind of civil association that seeks to exercise it. Liu, who is now in prison for having helped author and circulate the visionary Charter 08, calling for political reform in China, summed things up succinctly by stating, 'We must be clear that the roots of the crisis in Tibet are the same as the roots of the crisis in all of China. The conflict between central rule and the 'high level of autonomy' that Tibet is seeking is in essence a conflict between dictatorship and freedom.'

Here are five Tibetan names to remember: Yeshi Rigsel, Yeshi Samdup, Sonam Rabyang, Rigzin Dorje and Tenzin Choedrun. All died last week in Tibet. The first two were brothers. Yeshi Rigsel was shot and wounded by Chinese security forces during a peaceful protest, then hunted down in the mountains and shot dead on 9 February; along with his brother Yeshi Samdup, who was caring for him. The other three immolated themselves by fire in a terrible Buddhist tradition of protest on 10 and 11 February. Think about these people, all young, the last three very young, as the moral equivalent of freedom riders lynched and buried in shallow graves in the old racist South in the 1960s and you will have the beginnings of a sense of perspective. Think *Mississippi Burning*.

But that is, of course, only a beginning; because these people are the victims not of lawless vigilantes, but of a lawless state. It is as if the FBI had been hunting down and shooting the freedom riders. To be sure, the FBI under J. Edgar Hoover was not exactly pro-active in protecting such people, but the Communist Party's security forces are in the present case directly responsible for the desperation and violence. Unlike the United States in the 1960s, there is no central government pushing against regional resistance for civil rights reform; there is no free press reporting on the atrocities; there is no freedom for civil rights protestors to march in Beijing or anywhere else and accuse the government of abuses; there is no serious debate in the one-party state's rubber stamp parliament about the actions of the security forces; nor is there an even notionally independent judiciary that might, in principle or in time, bring the violators of human rights norms to trial. It is as if George Wallace had become dictator of the United States in about 1964 and was using the FBI and the National Guard to enforce racist norms.

So how should we, in Australia, think about this situation? Surely with moral concern. If we look back on the American civil rights struggle and the remarkable 'I have a dream' speech of Martin Luther King Jr, in August 1963, as beacons of democratic human rights reform; then we should look upon the Dalai Lama and the problems in Tibet in a similar light. That does not entail being anti-Chinese or wanting to see China weakened, any more than moral support for civil rights in the 1950s and 1960s entailed being anti-American or wanting to see the United States weakened. We need to be very clear about these things.

The Communist Party is not China. It is an incubus on the back of a China that has for a hundred years sought to throw off the shackles of dictatorial rule and find its way to a modern, democratic form of governance. Now is the time, as Martin Luther King might have expressed it, for that promise to be fulfilled. Now is the time and Tibet is the place where democratic norms and the rule of law should at long last be honoured.[269] And we should care, because a China

---

269   For an introduction to the Tibetan cause see Tsering Shakya *The Dragon in the Land of Snows: A History of Modern Tibet Since 1947* (Pimlico, London, 1999) and John B. Roberts II and Elizabeth A. Roberts *Freeing Tibet: 50 Years of Struggle, Resilience and Hope* (Amacom, New York, 2009). The Chinese Communist Party and its Foreign Ministry like to assert that Tibet has 'always been part of China'. This

that remains a truculent and mendacious dictatorship cannot be the friend to Australia that all sensible people would like to see it become.

---

　　　　　is not true. It was not a part even of the Chinese Empire until the foreign and imperialistic Manchus conquered it in the 18th century. In the decrepitude of the Manchu Empire, during the late 19th century, Tibet slipped from Beijing's control. For strategic reasons, the late Empire, the Nationalist government and the Communists have always claimed it, but the Communists were the ones who reconquered it, in the 1950s. They have since colonized and suppressed it, expressing unwavering determination to keep their grip on it. It may prove impossible to weaken or even moderate the Han/Communist domination of Tibet, but historical claims to legitimacy are not credible and should not be acknowledged.

Two funerals and an anniversary

By coincidence, one of the greatest heroes of resistance to Communist tyranny, Vaclav Havel, and one of the most odious of Communist tyrants, Kim Jong Il, died this past week within about twenty four hours of one another. The first was a shining example of everything we should seek in 21st century political leadership. The second embodied the very worst of 20th century totalitarianism.

Havel led the cause of human rights in Czechoslovakia and the great human rights manifesto, Charter 77, which paved the way to the 'velvet revolution' of 1989, in which Communist rule was brought to an end peacefully. Kim succeeded his father in 1994 and carried his father's horrendous rule forward to his dying day, presiding over a regime of mass starvation, concentration camps and stultifying propaganda.

By further coincidence, Havel's funeral in Prague today (23 December) coincides exactly with the second anniversary of the 2009 trial of the great Chinese human rights and political reform activist, Liu Xiaobo. One of the very last things written by Havel was a brief Foreword to a newly published collection of Liu's essays and poems. In that Foreword, Havel explicitly drew the obvious parallel between Charter 77 and the path breaking manifesto co-authored by Liu, Charter 08.

Havel recalled how, after Charter 77 was published by 242 private citizens, four of the signatories, including him, were detained and then jailed; while the others were subjected to surveillance, harassment and a barrage of malicious press attacks intended to discredit them. Charter 08, needless to say, met with the same response from the Communist dictatorship in China.[270]

This was no surprise, of course. Under first Jiang Zemin and then Hu Jintao, human rights have been grossly abused in China and have, if anything, got worse in recent years. Hu has expressed his condolences to the North Korean regime at the death of Kim. Not so long ago, he remarked that Kim had got his economics wrong, but his politics right. It was just such a political attitude that led Hu and his Party to arrest Liu Xiaobo in the wake of Charter 08's calls for constitutional reform, the rule of law and respect for basic human rights in China..

---

270 As Havel remarked:

> Despite Liu's imprisonment, his ideas cannot be shackled. Charter 08 has articulated an alternative vision of China, challenging the official line that any decisions on reforms are the exclusive province of the state. It has encouraged young Chinese to become politically active and boldly made the case for rule of law and constitutional multi-party democracy. And it has served as a jumping off point for a series of conversations and essays on how to get there.

Charter 08 was initially signed by 303 Chinese human rights activists, lawyers, intellectuals, academics, retired government officials, industrial worker activists and peasant association leaders, which is to say courageous and imaginative members of China's nascent civil society. It was then circulated on the Internet.

Although the Communist Party exerts extraordinary energies in trying to censor the Internet, the charter was shortly signed by another ten thousand people. The Party's alarm was such that many of the signatories were detained, called in for questioning, harassed or blacklisted. Liu Xiaobo was among the first and most prominent of those arrested.

Liu Xiaobo: No Enemies, No Hatred—Selected Essays and Poems edited by notable American China scholar and democratic reform activist Perry Link, Tienchi Martin-Liao and Liu Xiaobo's wife and companion in activism Liu Xia, which has just been released by the Belknap Press of Harvard University for 2012, makes abundantly clear both why Hu and his henchmen have tried to silence Liu; and why he is in fact an admirable figure.[271]

This is a book you must read, as an Australian citizen and as a human being, because our national stake in what happens in China has become enormous and our human engagement with it must take the side of those who, like Liu, have the greatest integrity and the most generous vision of their country's future. Whether from a scenario planning or moral point of view, this man's ideas need to be a key part of how you see China.

The book includes reflections such as 'To Change a Regime by Changing a Society', 'The Land Manifestos of Chinese Farmers', 'The Spiritual Landscape of the Urban Young in Post-Totalitarian China', 'On Living with Dignity in China', 'Long Live the Internet', 'Imprisoning People for Words and the Power of Public Opinion' and 'Behind the 'China Miracle'. The poems include such titles as 'What One Can Bear', 'Alone in Winter', 'My Puppy's Death' and 'Hats off to Kant'. It's a brilliant collection and belongs in the great tradition going back to the *Apology of Socrates* and Boethius's *The Consolation of Philosophy*.

When Liu was tried on 23 December 2009, the keynote of his defence was the observation that Article 35 of China's own constitution guarantees freedom of speech as a fundamental right of Chinese citizens, but that Article 105, section 2 of the criminal code, under which he

---

271 Liu Xiaobo: *No Enemies, No Hatred—Selected Essays and Poems* (ed. Perry Link, Tienchi Martin-Liao and Liu Xia, Belknap Press of Harvard University, 2012). It is just over five years since Liu was imprisoned, yet the Communist Party seems to have succeeded in closing him off from the world and even in quelling protests on his behalf. If ever there was a prisoner of conscience whose incarceration warranted an unrelenting campaign by Amnesty International, this is surely it. Yet there seems to be no sign of any such campaign. Perry Link's Introduction to the book is excellent and conveys very crisply both Liu Xiaobo's character and the evolution of his thinking about politics and law in China.

was indicted, patently contravenes this article of the constitution and 'should be referred to the National People's Congress for a review of its constitutionality.' This was, as it happens, virtually the same defence made by Wei Jingsheng at his trial under Deng Xiaoping, in 1979.

The NPC being a rubber stamp body, of course, Liu's point was purely rhetorical. The court being a Communist Party instrument, he was sentenced to eleven years in prison, just as Wei was imprisoned for fourteen years in 1979. To the Party's anger and frustration, Liu was then hailed by the international human rights fraternity and awarded the 2010 Nobel Peace Prize.

The reaction of the Communist Party was venomous. Its mouthpieces denounced the award as 'an obscenity' and refused permission for Liu or any of his relatives to attend the ceremony in Stockholm. Beautifully and unforgettably, the committee conducted the award ceremony with an empty chair for where Liu would have sat. The Party promptly banned Internet use of the term 'empty chair' in China. Now there is a regime paranoid to its rotten back teeth. But of course, all this has only served to lend lustre to Liu's stature. Remember him as you read about the two funerals in Prague and Pyongyang this Christmas. And, in the new year, buy and read his book. He is the Chinese Havel and a far greater man than Hu Jintao.

The epic life of Ariel Sharon[272]

On 4 January 2006, Ariel Sharon suffered a crippling stroke, which truncated his prime ministership without ending his life.[273] He lingers still in a persistent vegetative state, beyond hope of recovery. This is a mournful last stage in the life of so active a man; one of the true giants in the modern history of Israel. He was the protégé of David Ben Gurion, who gave the young Ariel Scheinermann the Hebraic name 'Sharon'. He fought or led in every one of Israel's wars: 1948, 1956, 1967, 1973, 1982, right up to the second intifada of 2000, which catapulted him into the prime ministership. And he arranged the strategic withdrawal from Gaza in 2005, in a fruitless quest for peace.

The picture his son, Gilad, paints of his father in this new biography will be treated with scepticism or even hostility by some, but no-one should be deterred from reading it. While unapologetically partisan, it is not obviously inaccurate. Sharon has always had his detractors; and for most of his career he has been dogged by accusations that he was ruthless and disdainful of the lives of Arabs. Gilad Sharon takes on all this without fear or favour. Neither his father's political rivals, nor partisans of the Palestinian cause will take kindly to his unsparing commentary, but his candour is bracing and his trenchant defence of his father fascinating.

'Even at a young age my father had a strongly developed sense of history', he writes. 'Over the years, he meticulously kept material, including letters, notes, maps, records of conversations, articles, speeches and detailed notebooks.' This paternal archive deeply informs the passionate biography the son has written. It is rich in photographs, hand drawn maps (as well as standard printed ones) and personal letters. Combining his personal knowledge with this unique family resource and public documents, the filial biographer weaves together his father's public life and private loves in a manner that even the finest of dispassionate biographers will find it difficult to match. Others may write more critically about Ariel Sharon; but anyone setting out to draw a more intimate and moving portrait of him will face a daunting task.

One aspect of the book to savour is the depiction of the Sharon family, especially Ariel's mother Vera Scheinermann and his two wives, Margalit (Gali), the mother of his first son, Gur, who was killed in a shooting accident in 1967; five years after his mother was killed in a car accident; and Lily (Gali's younger sister and mother of Omri and Gilad). Vera comes across as a formidable woman; Lily as an utterly charming and complete one. Gali was a woman Gilad

---

272   This piece was first published in the *Australia Israel Review*, in 2012.
273   He died almost exactly eight years later, on 11 January 2014, without ever recovering consciousness.

never knew. The family's background, from ancestral Hungary and Russia to pioneer farming in Palestine before the Holocaust and down through Gilad's life with his parents, is beautifully drawn. The multi-lingual, multi-talented, warm hearted and sharp witted Lily was a wonderful cook especially of Hungarian cuisine; while Ariel inherited from his parents both fluency in Russian and a love of Russian culture.

The author's analytical assessment of his father's military campaigns is no less well drawn than the portrait of his family life. The dissection of Israeli domestic politics is something that could only take place in Israel's remarkably open and liberal society. The son tackles head on the alleged sins of the father, of which the two most important are the Qibiya incident in late 1953 and the massacre of Palestinians in the Sabra and Shatila districts of Beirut in 1982. Ariel Sharon was the chosen commander of Unit 101, the special force for retribution against Arab terror set up by David Ben-Gurion in 1952 and Minister of Defence in 1982. But anyone who believes that he was a heartless killer must read the account of these matters in his son's book.[274]

Sharon was a redoubtable enemy of Arab armies and terrorists; but not a killer of innocents. He never sought to perpetrate terror; only swift retribution on those who did. The unintended deaths of 69 innocent civilians at Qibiya, and even of Egyptian soldiers in the 1967 and 1973 wars, pained him deeply. As for Sabra and Shatila, Gilad reminds us that his father successfully sued *Time* magazine for what a New York jury concluded were false and defamatory assertions about his responsibility for the massacre of perhaps several thousand Palestinians by Christian Phalangist militia.

The Kahan Commission, investigating the matter for the state of Israel, recommended that he be stood down as Minister of Defence not for inciting or endorsing the massacres but simply for not having foreseen the possibility of them and kept the Christian militia on a tighter leash. Given that Palestinian and other Arab leaders constantly incite their benighted

---

[274] There is an instructive comparison, which appeared in *The Australian* just a few days before I edited this piece. It was about Rainer Hoess, the grandson of Rudolph Hoess, Nazi commandant of Auschwitz, and very much a heartless killer. Under his grandfather's direction, Auschwitz was the leading Nazi extermination camp, where an estimated one million people were killed and cremated. Rainer Hoess is now 49, meaning that he was not even born until twenty years after the Second World War. He was told nothing by his parents about what his grandfather had done, until he was 15 years old, when he had a long conversation with the former driver of his grandfather, 'a Nazi through and through' who remained a family friend and who told him about the past. Yet within the family, the Holocaust was 'walled off from the memory' of Rudolph Hoess as a supposed war hero and 'good commandant'. Rainer's father was a coarse and brutal man and the boy left home at 16 to make his own life. The stress of the family past and family name, however, radically undermined his health, precipitating a decision, in 2004, to actively campaign against Nazism and Neo-Nazism and to reach out to survivors of Auschwitz. It is a remarkable story. Gilad Sharon's story is utterly different.

peoples to genocidal massacre of Jews, this is a vital benchmark for any assessment of both Ariel Sharon and the state of Israel.

A striking testimony to the character of Sharon is that of Marit Danon, chief secretary in the Israeli prime minister's office. She had served several previous prime ministers before Sharon was elected in February 2001. She told the outgoing Ehud Barak 'with that man I will not work'. 'She, like many others,' Gilad comments, 'had a very low opinion of my father. Barak got angry and slammed his hand down on the table. 'That man is not who you think he is. He is a sensitive man, well read, a lover of music; you'll see that he's not what you think," he said. 'You must stay on."

She did so. Five years later, with Sharon incapacitated, she did resign, saying that she did not want to work with anyone *else*. I suspect that, if you read *Sharon: The Life of a Leader* you will undergo a similar shift in perspective, as you get to know him through the eyes of his son. Even if you remain somewhat sceptical, you will have read an epic account of an extraordinary life that merits pondering right down to its intimate details.

The task in front of Barack Obama

Barack Obama, having won re-election, declared 'we still have work to do'. Too right he does. Unfortunately, it seems unlikely that his team will be able to make the policy adjustments required. Disturbingly, the alternative touted by the Republicans appears just as unlikely to have worked. The structural problems into which the United States has got itself require changes that are, at present, nowhere in sight on the political horizon in America.[275]

That, at least, is the verdict of a number of astute observers. In *The Betrayal of American Prosperity* (2010), veteran trade negotiator and economic analyst Clyde Prestowitz argued trenchantly that the United States had grown rich between 1790 and 1945 as a mercantilist state and has been running itself into the ground since 1945 by embracing free trade in the face of persistent mercantilism among its key competitors, especially in East Asia. His book repays a close reading.

Edward Luce of the London *Financial Times* has followed Prestowitz in articulating this case. Luce, a graduate of Oxford in philosophy, politics and economics; has been a *Financial Times* journalist for many years; serving as bureau chief in New Delhi and Washington. He spent a year as speech writer for US Treasury Secretary, Larry Summers, in 2000. That gave him an inside view of the workings of the Washington Consensus. *Time to Start Thinking: America and the Spectre of Decline* sets out his slowly developed judgment that America is in serious trouble.

Luce borrows his title from a remark by Ernest Rutherford: 'Gentlemen, we have run out of money. It is time to start thinking.' He derives his theme from a remark by Alexis de Tocqueville: 'The greatness of America lies not in being more enlightened than any other nation, but rather in her ability to repair her faults.' What concerns Luce is whether America will be able to repair the many faults that now plague its political system, economy and society. Far from anti-American, he is also far from optimistic.

Early on, he quotes Mitt Romney's *No Apology: Believe in America*, as declaring that the Founding

---

[275] In the short period since this piece was written, the shale gas revolution has taken place, oil prices have plummeted, US manufacturing has begun to revive and President Obama has given a State of the Nation address to a Republican dominated Congress, in January 2014, in which he has declared that no nation in the world has a better possibility in present circumstances of remaking itself as freely and creatively as does the United States of America. He may be correct. Certainly, it is to be hoped that renovation will occur on a large scale and in a sustainable manner. There is, however, a great deal to be done and it is by no means self-evident that it will get done, whether in the last two years of Obama's presidency or in what may well become a new Republican presidency from 2017. Obama's insistence on increasing both taxation and spending before the national debt has even been brought under control is not a promising sign.

Fathers were committed to 'free enterprise, free markets and free trade.' Luce comments wryly:

> *America's Founding Fathers disagreed sharply among themselves on many subjects, including the economy. So it is always enjoyable to speculate which of the founders a politician has in mind when he or she cites them in support of an argument (or whether, in Sarah Palin's case, she struggles to remember the name of any).*
>
> *'It is unclear whether Romney had a specific one in mind. But if it was Alexander Hamilton, America's first treasury secretary who viewed free trade as a luxury the young Republic could not afford, then Romney would have been mistaken. It was Hamilton who led the way in devising the pragmatic ideology that propelled America from an agricultural backwater in the 1790s to the world's foremost industrial power by 1900. Today, anyone looking at the main details of what was widely known in the nineteenth century as the 'American system' could mistake it for China's industrial policies in the early twenty first century.*

Hamilton learned from the way England had pulled itself up by its mercantilist bootstraps. He created a strategically protectionist America, not a free trade one. In the early 1860s, Abraham Lincoln raised average tariffs up to between 40 and 50%, a level around which they would fluctuate until the middle of the twentieth century. Britain, conversely, championed free trade from the repeal of the Corn Laws in the 1840s and saw its industrial ascendancy relentlessly eroded by its mercantilist competitors in the late nineteenth century.

America, also, has seen its industrial ascendancy relentlessly eroded by mercantilist competitors since the Second World War. Here Prestowitz is a better guide than Luce, but the message is the same. Luce quotes a range of American CEOs as saying that America has a delusional macro-economic policy. 'This debate is too important to leave to the economists', declares the highly regarded Andy Grove of Intel. 'We are in the middle of a titanic war for global supremacy. We shouldn't be carrying on as though it's business as usual'.

What concerns Luce most is that:

> *America has not yet begun to think seriously about the consequences of where it is headed. Nowhere is this deficit more apparent than in American politics. If America is to restore its competitiveness it will need to do many things, few of which will be possible without a much more effective federal government.*

But how is that to be accomplished? He doesn't say. Here, a better source is Lawrence Lessig's *Republic, Lost: How Money Corrupts Congress—and a Plan to Stop It* (2011).

Luce is an admirer of the great institutional economist Mancur Olson. He believes that institutions are vital to prosperity—especially political institutions. He expresses an ominous sense that America's core institutions are failing it and that there may be no way out. A charming 'global cartoon' reprinted in *The Australian* on 13 November, showed a pensive Obama looking at a map which declared helpfully, with an arrow pointing to the heart of the maze in which he stands, 'Congratulations! You are here.'

America is in need of genuine renovation and it is, indeed, time to start thinking. The acute structural challenges confronting the great republic bring to mind Theodor Mommsen's grim reflection, over a century ago, on the symptoms of decline in the late Roman republic: the 'fearful moaning and cracking that foretold the mighty breaking up that was at hand.' 'This much is certain,' wrote Mommsen, the greatest historian of his age, 'that a thorough amendment of the state in all its departments, was urgently required, and that in no quarter was any serious attempt made to accomplish it.' A great deal is at stake in all this—and shale gas alone will not provide a solution; nor will further 'quantitative easing'. Read Luce (or Prestowitz) and start getting some perspective on all this.

Neuroscience and the new atheism

Sam Harris, an outspoken member of the New Atheists club, while still studying for his PhD in California, wrote a book called *The End of Faith*, in which he called for the abolition of the great religions and expressed the hope that the words God and Allah would soon sound as dated as Apollo and Baal. He has just written a new book, drawing upon his doctoral research in neuroscience.

It is called *The Moral Landscape* and it is, like his earlier book, a polemic directed at organized religion, especially American Christianity and the Catholic Church. As polemic, it stands in the Enlightenment tradition. It has something in it of the flavour of Voltaire's *Philosophical Dictionary*, Hume's *Dialogues Concerning Natural Religion* or Paine's *Common Sense*. As a piece of argument, it suffers from its author's rather Jacobin temperament and his apparent unwillingness to see religion in any but the most invidious light.

The book has six parts: an Introduction with the title 'The Moral Landscape' and five chapters—Moral Truth, Good and Evil, Belief, Religion and the Future of Happiness - and all this in fewer than 200 pages. In his Introduction, he argues that 'Just as there is no such thing as Christian physics or Muslim algebra, we will see that there is no such thing as Christian or Muslim morality.' In reality, he argues, 'morality should be considered an undeveloped branch of science'

Religious conservatives, he declares, have come to accept that the physical world is best understood through natural science, 'but they believe that values must come from a voice in a whirlwind. Secular liberals, on the other hand, tend to imagine that no objective answers to moral questions exist.'

He describes multiculturalism, moral relativism, political correctness, tolerance even of intolerance as leaving secular society 'supine before the unreasoning zeal of old-time religion', because the belief that there is no objective way to decide what is truly right 'often leads secular liberals to surrender their intellectual standards and political freedoms with both hands.'

In taking this line, Harris is not only assailing the major religions, but also a wide cross-section of secular opinion, which in some form of words or other has come to accept the idea that science and religion 'cannot be in conflict because they constitute different domains of expertise.' With his characteristic forthrightness, he states 'I hope to persuade you that this is not only untrue, it could not possibly be true.'

Since, statistically speaking, you as a reader are rather likely to fall into either the religious believer or the secular liberal category, Harris has a challenging bill of claims to make against your outlook. You should hasten to read this book in order to test your own thinking. Conversely, if you happen to believe already that somehow or other natural science can lead us to better judgments about morality than can religion, you will find Harris's distinctive argument interesting.

The Moral Landscape is brief and attempts to cover a remarkable amount of ground, but perhaps Harris is aware of Voltaire's remark, in 1762, 'Twenty folio volumes will never make a revolution. It is the little portable volumes of thirty *sous* that are to be feared. Had the gospel cost twelve hundred *sesterces*, the Christian religion would never have been established.'

Pivotal to Harris's argument are three claims:
1. the famous is/ought distinction enunciated by David Hume, dubbed the 'naturalistic fallacy' by G. E. Moore and repeated by philosophers and natural scientists endlessly in the modern era, is false—we cannot draw our values from anywhere *other* than facts;
2. drawing upon neuroscience —the science of the human brain and its way of being in the world - we are increasingly able to see what does and does not make for the well-being of conscious creatures; and
3. the well-being of conscious creatures must by definition be the foundation of moral judgments regarding what is good and right.

Whatever the polemical edge to Harris's writing, these are interesting and productive claims and he proceeds to support each of them by reasoned argument. They undergird a renewal of Enlightenment claims to universal understanding and a science of well-being. It has become so uncommon to see anyone try to make such a case in recent times that the endeavour alone is bracing and, like Voltaire's dictionary, it is likely to be condemned by all established religions

One cannot help but admire a young scholar who is prepared boldly to take on so many enemies at once. And Harris is perfectly aware of the extent to which he is flying in the face of conventional wisdom in making the argument that he does. In the northern autumn of 2006, he writes, he attended a conference at the Salk Institute under the rubric Beyond Belief: Science, Religion, Reason and Survival.

'It was a room full of highly intelligent, scientifically literate people—molecular biologists, anthropologists, physicists and engineers—and yet, to my amazement, three days were insufficient to force agreement on the simple question of whether there is any conflict at all between religion and science. Imagine a meeting of mountaineers unable to agree about whether their sport ever entails walking uphill, and you will get a sense of how bizarre our deliberations began to seem.'

It's hard to not to feel a certain sympathy with Harris in his bewilderment here. Yet had he paused to place the Salk conference in a somewhat broader context, he might have reflected that what he was witnessing was the unease of highly intelligent human beings, with widely differing areas of expertise, in seeking to address a question with quite profound consequences for human civilization.

The actual task confronting both that gathering and the rest of us is surely not to reach a simple judgment about whether there is any uphill climb involved in building a civilization and possibly a religion for the 21st century, but how to tackle the Mount Everest that this task actually represents. In this respect, Evan Thompson's *Mind in Life: Biology, Phenomenology and the Sciences of Mind* (Belknap Press, Harvard, 2007) and the ruminations on science, poetry and human freedom penned by Boris Pasternak in *Doctor Zhivago* offer a surer and richer guide than Sam Harris's enthusiastic polemic. But read his book. It is a great provocation to thinking well.[276]

---

276 In late 2014, Sam Harris produced yet another compact book called *Waking Up: A Guide to Spirituality Without Religion* (Bantam Press, London, 2014). Its chapters have the alluring titles: 'Spirituality', 'The Mystery of Consciousness', 'The Riddle of the Self', 'Meditation' and 'Gurus, Death, Drugs and Other Puzzles'. Interestingly, he remarks, towards the end of this new book:

> *Spirituality remains the great hole in secularism, humanism, rationalism, atheism and all the other defensive postures men and women strike in the presence of unreasonable faith. People on both sides of this divide imagine that visionary experience has no place within the context of science—apart from the corridors of a mental hospital. Until we can talk about spirituality in rational terms—acknowledging the validity of self-transcendence—our world will remain shattered by dogmatism. This book has been my attempt to begin such a conversation.*

Harris has worked closely with some of the leading secular philosophers of our time, such as Daniel Dennett, Paul Churchland and Steven Pinker is developing his ideas. Working on closely related problems, but from a broader point of view, Evan Thompson has recently produced a fascinating book called *Waking, Dreaming, Being: Self-Consciousness in Neuroscience, Meditation and Philosophy* (Columbia University Press, New York, 2015) which will repay a close reading alongside Harris's work.

Section 5: 2012-13

Massive Chinese espionage afoot

A report just released by Bloomberg makes clear that Chinese espionage, especially cyber-espionage, has reached extraordinary levels. According to Mike Rogers, chairman of the Permanent Select Committee on Intelligence, 'They're stealing everything that isn't bolted down and it's getting exponentially worse,' Says Richard Clarke, former special adviser on cyber security to the White House, China has been 'hacking its ways into every corporation it can find listed in Dun and Bradstreet.' Scott Borg, an economist and director of the US Cyber Consequences Unit, says that the theft of commercial intellectual property involved constitutes the greatest illegal transfer of wealth in history.

We should be taking note of this in Australia for all sorts of reasons. Chinese hacking is certainly targeting this country as well as the United States, but there are national security as well as economic implications. Moreover, it is not only cyber espionage of which we need to be wary. High level Soviet moles operated in this country during the Cold War and have yet to be exposed. And we are even more vulnerable to Chinese espionage now than we were to Soviet espionage then. It's high time this hidden history was made public, if only in order to put the problem of Chinese (and revitalized Russian) espionage in sober perspective for an Australian public rather too given to complacency or cynicism in such matters.

Thirty years ago, in *The National Times*, Brian Toohey wrote a full page piece on Soviet operations in Australia, based on an extended interview with CIA operations veteran Ted Shackley. His opening paragraph was stunning in its implications:

> The Soviet intelligence service, the KGB, has been more successful in its penetration operations in Australia than in any other country, according to hard evidence available to the American Central Intelligence Agency. The long standing CIA assessment is that the KGB has planted a mole in a key position in Canberra—probably high in Foreign Affairs, Defence or the Prime Minister's Department.

The CIA's hard evidence, Toohey wrote, had been built up over many years from both human and electronic sources. It demonstrated that the KGB had for years 'been able to obtain a much higher level of classified information from Canberra than anywhere else.' This was especially significant because much of what was obtained was sensitive intelligence shared with Australia by the United States. Yet, as of 1981, the CIA had been baffled in trying to establish who exactly the Soviet mole or moles in Canberra were. Between 1993 and 1995, two highly secretive investigations, Operation LIVER and the Cook inquiry, were conducted for the Keating government. They concluded that there had, indeed, been high level, long-term penetration by Soviet intelligence;

but the Federal government has ever since kept their findings under lock and key.

It's high time they were unlocked, because they provide a key to the danger now presented by China, which is far better placed than the Soviet Union was to place moles and agents in Australia. It is a huge trading partner of Australia, which the Soviet Union never was. It is ascendant at a time when the United States is floundering in economic and strategic terms, which has already tempted a number of Australian strategic analysts to suggest we should edge closer to it and distance ourselves somewhat from the United States. And, despite its sinister Communist past and the ongoing ruthlessness of the Communist regime there, it cultivates a "Middle Kingdom" mystique that all too many find seductive. Only a few need be seduced, if they are well-placed, for very serious damage to be done to our national security.

David Wise's newly published *Tiger Trap: America's Secret Spy War with China* (2011) fills in the deeper background behind the Bloomberg report. It places recent developments in the context of ancient Chinese traditions of espionage going back to Sun Tzu. It shows that Chinese espionage has grown relentlessly in the past few decades, even as many of us came to see China as a reformed totalitarian state with a market economy and a growing stake in global order. It describes the structure of the Chinese intelligence agencies; their *modus operandi* and their recent strategic successes against the United States.

Wise tells, for example, of Chinese acquisition of the top secret technology for the W-88 nuclear warhead for the missiles carried by the Trident submarine; stealth technology for fighters, bombers and perhaps now helicopters; and a great deal more from the high tech sectors of the American economy and defence sector. Even more disturbing is that the spies who are supplying this technology to China remain mostly undetected. A four year investigation, from 1999 to 2003, by a veteran counter-intelligence officer, Stephen Dillard, was unable to pinpoint the source of the W-88 breach. As Wise remarks, 'The answer remains locked up in Beijing.'

As with China's relentless military build-up, there will be those who'll say, 'Well, they're not doing anything the Americans aren't doing, so who are we to complain?' That is to forget where we stand in the world and where our interests lie. We are a key ally of the United States; it is the bastion of our own strategic security; we depend on it for cutting edge military technology; we house major joint facilities on our soil; we have a new agreement for increased US presence here; and China's rising power and aspirations are, by regional agreement, the major uncertainty in Asia Pacific stability for as far ahead as we can currently see.

Don't cry for me, Venezuela: the death of Hugo Chavez

Hugo Chavez aspired to emulate Fidel Castro and become dictator of his country for life. He is dead, at 58. His funeral will be held this Friday—the Ides of March. Much of the commentary on his fortuitously early demise has been polemical. Some heap extravagant praise on him for throwing tens of billions of dollars into social programs. Others accuse him of leading his country to ruin through waste, arbitrary expropriations and destructive manipulation of the economy and constitution. A thorough economic and political balance sheet of his rule will require book length treatment. But the funeral extravaganza demands at least a basic reality check.[277]

---

277 Things have continued to get worse since this piece was written only a few years ago and the analysis is not far behind. Venezuela's credit rating has dropped to CAA3, just one step away from default on its national debt. Writing in *Forbes*, on 15 January 2015, Francis Coppola commented: '

> *What we are witnessing is the destruction of Venezuela's economy. And that destruction is not, fundamentally, because of external factors. It is a direct consequence of the economic policies pursued by the Chavez and Maduro regimes. Over the last fifteen years, the Venezuelan government has nationalized hundreds of companies and seized assets on a massive scale. Many of those seizures have been the subject of expensive litigation in international courts: the most recent case was Exxon's award of $1.6bn in compensation for expropriation of its Venezuelan oil projects. Often, these nationalizations have come in response to falling production due to government price and exchange controls. For example, production in Venezuela's car industry dropped by 85% between January 2013 and January 2014: in February 2014, Toyota suspended production for six weeks citing inability to import parts, resulting in calls from trade unions for the industry to be nationalized. All too often, the Venezuelan government has given in to such calls, rather than addressing the underlying problems.*
>
> *Widespread nationalization of private enterprises and seizure of assets discourages both domestic entrepreneurialism and foreign investment, and nationalized companies too often end up less efficient and less productive than they were when in private hands. The Venezuelan government has mismanaged its nationalized oil industry, resulting in revenues far below what would reasonably be expected from its vast oil reserves, and misallocated those disappointing revenues into the bargain: instead of using the revenues to diversify its economy and develop domestic production in other sectors, it has diverted them into politically popular but unproductive social programs and distortionary price controls and subsidies. Consequently, Venezuela has become far too dependent on oil revenues, its fiscal finances are in a parlous state and its industry is highly inefficient. It was in a mess long before the present fall in oil prices. The deprivation that awaits the Venezuelan people is far, far worse than anything they are experiencing at the moment. Attracted by the lure of socialism and promised equality and prosperity, they have walked an all too well-trodden path—the road to hell.*

In the next six to twelve months, we may well see the political crisis finally break things open in Venezuela.

Those paying any attention to Friday's obsequies, if they know little of Venezuela, are likely to be disproportionately affected by the huge outpouring of popular emotion. What to make of it? There is a famous Latin American precedent for it: the funeral rites for Eva Peron, in 1952. Listen to Andrew Lloyd Webber's 'Oh, What a Circus' from *Evita* and you'll get the basic idea. An updated version would begin:

> *Oh what a circus,*
> *Oh, what a show,*
> *Venezuela has gone to town*
> *Over the death of an actor*
> *Named Hugo Chavez.*

The political partisans of the man are seeking to enshrine him, literally, as the 'Pater Misericordiae' of his people; and the wry lyrics of *Evita* are a delightful corrective.

If Venezuela was politically healthy, this wouldn't be happening. It isn't healthy, so it *shouldn't* be happening. It's important not to give the cult oxygen. Serious attention should focus on the quotidian realities of Venezuela and its possibilities for improved health. A key reality is the country's horrendous homicide rate. Its possibilities, conversely, might best be symbolized by the musical culture that has flourished there over the past thirty years. That musical culture, not Chavez's military fatigues and soak the bourgeoisie ideology, embodies what is best and most beautiful in Venezuela.

Let's start with the murder rate. We read with horror of regular mass shootings in the United States; less frequently of the drug war mayhem in Mexico. We *never* read about the appalling surge of violence in Venezuela. Global homicide rates are measured in annual murders per 100,000 inhabitants, country by country. The global average is currently just under 7. In the United States it is has more than halved since 1980 and is now 4.8. In Australia it is 1.2. In Venezuela, it was 18.2 when Chavez first took office. By 2006, it was 48. By 2011, it was 67. Last year, it hit 73. In Caracas, Venezuela's capital, it hit 200.

The homicide rate in Venezuela, with no insurgency or drug war, is four times greater than in Mexico and *seventeen times* that of the United States. The raw number of homicides in Australia declined from 385 in 1999 to 229 in 2011. In Venezuela, with a similar population size (29 million in 2012, compared with Australia's 23 million), it soared from 4,550 in 1999 to 19,336 in 2011. These figures are a terrible indictment of governance in Venezuela. Along with abuses of political power by Chavez, they inspired the brilliant Venezuelan pianist Gabriela Montero to compose a passionate tone poem called 'Ex Patria' to express her dismay and anger at the condition of her country. Born in 1970, Montero was a child prodigy. At the age of eight, she made her international concert debut, performing the whole of Haydn's Piano Concerto in D

Major, accompanied by the National Youth Orchestra of Venezuela. Her career took off even as her country's prosperity deteriorated in the 1980s and 1990s. Under Chavez, she says, she feels as though she has lost her country.

Jose Antonio Abreu conducted the orchestra for Montero's debut. An oil economist and gifted musician, he has created, since 1975, a remarkable musical education program called El Sistema[278]. It has brought musical education to hundreds of thousands of disadvantaged Venezuelan children and generated a galaxy of youth orchestras that exude an internationally acclaimed freshness and vitality. He has long argued that learning how to play an instrument in an orchestra is character forming as few other things can be. His work has been an inspirational triumph.

Yet, though El Sistema has flourished, Venezuelan society has descended into political polarization and rampant violence. El Sistema has *not* transformed the polity; whatever else it has achieved. Moreover, Abreu made his peace with Chavez and accepted his patronage of El Sistema. This is as troubling, in its own way, as the escalation in homicides. What is the alignment between the youth orchestras and the regime?

Abreu's protégé, Gustavo Dudamel, will conduct the orchestra at Chavez's funeral. Will the dissonance between the vision of El Sistema and the realities of contemporary Venezuela be on his mind, as he flies into the seething cauldron of Caracas? In Los Angeles, he has been conducting the premiere of the new John Adams opera, *The Gospel According to the Other Mary*. In Caracas, he will literally help orchestrate the cult of Chavez as a latter day Jesus Christ. Venezuela deserves better—as Gabriela Montero knows.[279]

---

278 José Antonio Abreu is a man of many parts: orchestra conductor, pianist, economist, educator, activist, and politician. He is Catholic, with an understanding of the philosophy of Martin Heidegger. He is highly intelligent, visionary and extremely well connected internationally. He also has all the knowledge he needs in order to have spoken out about waste, irresponsibility, abuse of power and corruption in Venezuela, but has not done so. This is a moral disgrace and detracts appreciably from his accomplishments in other respects as a citizen of Venezuela.

279 In early 2015, the former head of Chavez's security team, Leamsy Salazar, having defected to the United States, declared that Chavez had been dead for more than two months before the Venezuelan government, under his successor Nicolas Maduro, announced that he was dead. This meant both that he could not be embalmed, because the decay of his corpse was too far advanced by the time his death was actually admitted; but more importantly that dozens of pieces of legislation supposedly signed by him were in fact fraudulently signed and are unconstitutional.

Zionism, peace and illusion

Patrick Tyler is a veteran American journalist who has worked for *The New York Times* since 1990, serving as a military analyst and as a foreign correspondent in Beijing, Moscow, Baghdad and London. In *Fortress Israel*, he has given us a massively researched and passionately argued polemic against the secular sabra elite who founded and have led Israel over the past sixty five years. It is an intriguing, deeply thought-provoking book; but it is flawed in several ways.

Tyler gained remarkable access. He was able to draw upon numerous very high level interviews, as well as public documents, critical analysis in Israeli newspapers, criticism of Israel by both Jewish diaspora and non-Jewish analysts, debates in the Knesset and the memoirs and histories written over the decades he covers. This gives him immensely rich and nuanced material for his argument.

But at no point in his book does he pause and ponder the fact that all this is available within and around Israel, while no such rich or open debate is available in or from the Arab or other Muslim countries around Israel who have besieged it since its inception. He expresses no appreciation of the fact that this rich and vital Israel has risen from almost nothing while the Arab world around it has remained mired in despotism, poverty and bigotry. This is the book's most obvious flaw.

The second is that he writes as if the Israeli elite were at any given point since 1948 in a position to make peace with the Arab enemies of Israel if only they wished to do so. Yet at no point does he attempt to lay out a blueprint for a settlement with its Arab neighbours that Israel could actually have made.

Even his analysis of the peace between Sadat and Begin suggests that Sadat was magnanimous, Begin grudging and opportunistic and the whole episode an illustration of the lost possibilities for Israel to make peace more generally with its neighbours. But it was the initiative of an Egyptian leader who had seen his country soundly defeated in four wars[280] by the Israelis, acknowledged his own country's need for peace and defied anti-Israeli sentiment among his countrymen to make it. For that bold initiative, of course, he paid with his life.

The third flaw is Tyler's implicit assumption that the situation of Israel has deteriorated since

---

280 Those four wars were fought in 1948, 1956, 1967 and 1973. In the first and fourth, the Arabs launched war against Israel and were routed after initial tough fighting. In the second and third, the Israelis took the initiative. In 1967, this was because they had good reason to believe that the Arab states were preparing to launch a coordinated attack on them.

1967 because of the lack of peace. By his own account, for a long time now, numerous generals and intelligence chiefs, sabras all, have actively and publicly lobbied for peace initiatives and diplomacy and been openly critical of some of the country's recent military interventions against Hamas and Hezbollah.

They have, admittedly, run into entrenched opposition within Israel to the central idea of handing back the West Bank; but the unwillingness of their Arab enemies to accept the very existence of Israel has been at least as important. Yet nowhere does Tyler consider the possibility that, despite the unresolved confrontation with the Arabs, Israel has actually flourished and is, today, a remarkably prosperous and secure state; far better off than any of its Arab neighbours.

Diana Pinto, like Tyler, is concerned with the changes Israel has undergone since the secular Zionist humanism of its early years. She would like to see it return to those roots. But her book is not a polemic. It is, rather, the kind of incisive and erudite little book on Israel that one might have expected from, say, Hannah Arendt, were she alive today. Pinto is Jewish, but lives in Paris.[281] She plainly loves and is deeply immersed in her Jewish identity, but she is an Enlightenment European Jew, the Holocaust notwithstanding.

She is bemused and a little troubled by the robust revival of ultra-orthodox and ethnically Hebraic identities in Israel. Perhaps nothing symbolises this more strangely for her than the project of the Temple Institute - a tiny, fringe group to which she devotes much attention - to reclaim the Temple Mount from the Muslims, destroy the Dome of the Rock and rebuild the Second Temple. The Institute even plans to take Judaism back to pre-rabbinical times by reviving the animal sacrifices still practised until the Romans sacked the Temple in 70 CE.

Israel, Pinto argues, has begun to cut its umbilical cord to the European Enlightenment and create its own 'post-modern' identity. With a rate of economic growth comparable to the most dynamic economies in Asia and grounded in scientific and commercial fertility in numerous cutting edge fields, it no longer feels a need to cling to the stagnant West, she suggests. In those respects, it is becoming ever more cosmopolitan.

Yet as it builds a new, Hebrew-speaking, Bible and Talmud and Kabbala-fixated identity, it is becoming culturally 'autistic' and even schizophrenic, enclosed not only behind security walls, but behind newly strengthened linguistic, cultural and religious walls. These, she emphasises, are not eccentric or polemical observations of her own. They were remarks made to her in Israel by

---

281 I have not seen a comment from Diana Pinto on the *Charlie Hebdo* affair and the growing unease among French Jews about violent anti-Semitism. Yet being a Jewish public intellectual in Paris, she must have considered views of these latest atrocities. It would be interesting to know exactly what they are. What a development it would be if she, like thousands of others, decided to leave France and become an Israeli citizen.

Israelis young and old, secular and ultra-orthodox 'as so many self-evident truths.'

Of the two books, I find Pinto's the more original and eye-opening. Tyler's preoccupations are those of J Street and the Israeli revisionist historians. He is out to prove a point. Pinto looks at Israel through multiple, often unfamiliar lenses and is rich in humane sympathies. Tyler finds excuses again and again for Arab terrorism, while excoriating Israeli counter-measures as 'brutal.' This is nicely illustrated in his double standard over the *Karine A* affair.

He accepts that Ben-Gurion seized the *Altalena* from the Irgun in June 1948 to demonstrate that the Zionists were not terrorists and that the government of the new state of Israel would exercise a monopoly of the use of force. He then writes of Yitzhak Rabin, more than forty years later, looking for the nascent Palestinian Authority to have its '*Altalena* moment'. Poignantly, it had been the young Rabin who had carried out Ben-Gurion's orders in the first place.

Famously, Rabin was murdered by an Israeli fanatic, Yigal Amir, and attempts to negotiate peace with the Palestinian Authority ran aground. But in 2002, as Shimon Peres called for another effort at peace talks with Yasser Arafat, then-Prime Minister Ariel Sharon showed that Arafat was no Ben-Gurion. Israeli security forces boarded the cargo ship *Karine A* in the Red Sea and found it loaded with machine guns, rocket propelled grenades and enough C-4 explosive for 300 suicide vests—all coming from Iran and destined for Arafat's armouries. Tyler remarks, 'Arafat denied any connection with the ship. Israeli intelligence, however, had documents to prove Arafat was involved and the CIA seemed to agree. Arafat had arranged the shipment through Hezbollah intermediaries.'

Yet Tyler bitterly denounces Sharon's head of military intelligence, Aaron Ze'evi Farkash, for declaring that the *Karine A* proved Arafat was a terrorist and not someone with whom it would be possible to come to a workable peace agreement. He writes heatedly, 'Farkash's language was not the neutral syntax of professional intelligence but rather the didactic cant of a military elite straining to declare the political track bankrupt.' I would have thought that *syntax* was inherently neutral and that vocabulary or semantics were the issue. But let that pass. What conclusion was Farkash to have drawn other than the one he did? He was not straining to make a point. He would have had to strain to make any other, in the circumstances.

Of course, mention of the *Altalena* in juxtaposition with the *Karine A* takes one into current controversies in Israel about the Likud's plan to find the wreck of the *Altalena* and integrate it into a monument to Begin and Irgun. That, perhaps, is occurring because the Likud under Netanyahu has drawn the conclusion that Ze'ev Jabotinsky (and thus the Irgun) has been vindicated. Pinto worries that this is so. Tyler is apparently irritated that it is so and refuses to accept it. Both seem to believe that it would be highly desirable for Israel to find a way to establish a peaceful settlement with the Palestinian Arabs; but neither offers a persuasive formula for how this is to be done. Pinto remarks almost wistfully that the minuscule state of Israel created in 1948 is something the Arabs 'should have accepted early on.' Tyler, strangely, writes as if the only party to blame for this not happening was Israel itself. Everyone is likely to find Pinto's book illuminating. Most will find Tyler's polarizing.

Miscavige of justice: indicting the Church of Scientology[282]

Paul Thomas Anderson's recent film *The Master* is transparently a critical portrait of the early years of the Church of Scientology under its strange founder Lafayette Ron Hubbard. It is 1950, the year Hubbard published his signature book *Dianetics*. Philip Seymour Hoffmann plays Lancaster Dodd, who sails around in a boat called *Aletheia*, practising a new form of talking cure called 'processing' and recruiting volunteers on billion-year contracts, while bullying and abusing critics or questioners.

Hubbard sailed around in a ship called *Apollo* and did all these things. He called his talking cure 'auditing'. Anderson's use of the name *Aletheia*, a Greek word meaning 'truth' or 'disclosure' is presumably ironical. It was the word Martin Heidegger used in *Being and Time* (1927) to define what he meant by 'truth', or what he called 'unconcealment'.

Does Anderson mean us to understand that his film discloses the truth about Scientology? Or merely that the charlatan Dodd has the vast pretentiousness to proclaim, like many another religious figure or snake oil salesman, that he knows the truth about life, the universe and everything?

If you know only a little about Scientology, *Beyond Belief* will be an eye-opener. It is the memoir of Jenna Miscavige Hill, niece of David Miscavige, the maestro who usurped power over the Church of Scientology after Hubbard died (or 'dropped his body', as Scientologists put it), in January 1986.

The manner in which Miscavige climbed through the ranks of Scientology and took over in the late 1980s bears an eerie similarity to the way in which Stalin rose as Lenin's lieutenant

---

282 This piece first appeared in *The Australian's* Weekend Review on 23-24 March 2013. The documentary *Going Clear: Scientology and the Prison of Belief*, based on Lawrence Wright's book, reviewed here, opened in Australian cinemas in mid-June 2015. This is the only piece in this book for which the publisher felt it necessary to consult lawyers before going into print. In order to provide the Church of Scientology with no pretext for legal action, I reworded the draft to make it clear that claims about it were strictly derived from the two books under review and were not gratuitous or unsourced comments by the reviewer. There was no legal action or other form of harassment. However, I was contacted by members of the public relations staff of the Church here in Australia. They expressed regret that I had chosen to lend credence to what they described as the misleading or ill-informed claims by both Jenna Miscavige and Larry Wright. I was then invited to meet for a drink with two women from a kind of ladies auxiliary arm of the Church. They offered me a pile of reading material about the Church produced by it to advance its cause. I politely declined the offer on the perfectly honest grounds that I had too much else to read and would never get around to reading such things.

and then took over after Lenin had a fatal stroke and died. Hubbard also died of a stroke. Miscavige ousted Hubbard's presumptive heir, purged his lieutenants and declared his opponents Suppressive Persons (think 'counter-revolutionaries').

Jenna Miscavige was in infancy at that point. Born into a family of Scientologists in 1984, she grew up indoctrinated into and totally controlled by the cult. She remained in its thrall until a few years ago. She finally fled from it and made common cause with many others who had done so. She now seeks to expose it for what she claims it is: in the words of Cynthia Kisser of the defunct Cult Awareness Network, 'the most ruthless, the most classically terroristic, the most litigious and the most lucrative cult' in modern America.

I write of the Cult Awareness Network being 'defunct' because, in the early 1990s, a barrage of law suits drove it into bankruptcy. David Miscavige's Church of Scientology led the charge. The network's name and assets were then bought by a Scientologist and used to issue a brochure praising Scientology for its 'good work'.

Having produced *The Master*, thinly fictionalising Hubbard, Hollywood should now make a major motion picture of Jenna Miscavige's story, because it is astounding. Again and again, reading it closely, I found myself appalled and fascinated by her first-hand account of the way Scientology entraps and manipulates its adherents. Also how very difficult they find it to escape the church's coercive machinations and the totalistic belief system it instils in them.

Exhibiting remarkable resilience and independence of moral judgment, the 18-year-old old Jenna finally rebelled against all that she claims to have experienced: mindless and unjust punishment, sleep deprivation, hard labour, isolation from her family, invasive interrogation and denial of the rights to date, marry or reproduce.

Only after she had escaped the clutches of Scientology did she learn to associate with people altogether independent of the organization, whom Scientologists call 'Wogs'. 'Through their eyes,' she writes, 'I slowly learned how weird my upbringing had been.' She gained 'an outsider's perspective on the Church' and came to see doctrines she had been taught all her life as 'nothing but a complete suppression of free thought'.

She claims that her own experience was part of a systemic pattern. 'To me,' she writes, 'the Church is a dangerous organization whose beliefs allow it to commit crimes against humanity and violate basic human rights. It remains a mystery to me how, in our current society, this can go unchecked.' Once this became clear to her, she declares, 'I felt an overwhelming need to do something.' That was the origin of her book.

But moving and damning as Jenna Miscavige Hill's memoir is, Lawrence Wright's forensic investigation and clinical dissection of the cult, *Going Clear: Scientology, Hollywood and the*

Prison of Belief, is vastly more informative. He tells from its beginnings the story of the crank Hubbard who, having been a prolific writer of science fiction, decided to declare his fantasies true, in the early 1950s and founded a 'religion'.

Jenna Miscavige gets only a single, passing mention in Wright's book. He shows, in ways to which she was completely oblivious while a member of the organisation, that it was already out of control long before she was born. It should have been hounded out of existence in the 1970s, but it has exhibited a disturbing tenacity. Wright shows us how it has fought to survive.

In 1971, Paulette Cooper, a student of comparative religion at Harvard and the daughter of Jewish parents who had perished in the Holocaust, published a book called *The Scandal of Scientology*. According to Wright, Cooper's book attacked the absurd cosmology of Hubbard and quoting refugees from Scientology who testified to having been 'financially defrauded and then harassed when they tried to speak out.'

Wright relates that Cooper received death threats, was stalked, had her phone tapped, was sued 19 times, was defamed and harassed. She was financially ruined, depressed and professionally destroyed. She came close to committing suicide.

Paranoid and convinced that governments were out to get him, Hubbard in 1973 created a scheme for infiltrating government agencies, in the US and other countries. He called it Operation Snow White. Evidence of the extent of it was unearthed in 1977, when the FBI raided key Scientology buildings, seizing tens of thousands of documents. They discovered that 5000 Scientology agents had penetrated 136 government institutions around the world as spies for Hubbard. They also found a file labelled Operation Freakout, detailing the plot to destroy the unfortunate and courageous Paulette Cooper.

Having consolidated his totalitarian grip on Scientology by 1990, David Miscavige launched an all-out campaign to buttress the cult's defences. He engaged the public relations firm Hill and Knowlton to help disseminate his propaganda. He launched a huge campaign against the Cult Awareness Network and against *Time* magazine, which had published a cover story denouncing Scientology as a 'cult of greed and power'.

Above all, Miscavige went to war with the Internal Revenue Service and won a stunning and disturbing victory. Hubbard's organisation had lost tax exempt status in 1967, when declared a commercial enterprise, not a religion. But it still refused to pay taxes and the bill accumulated, Wright tells us, to $US1 billion. Had it been collected, it might have broken Scientology's back. But this didn't happen.

Instead, Miscavige launched 200 law suits against the IRS in the name of Scientology's subsidiaries and another 2,300 in the name of individual Scientologists. This overwhelmed the

IRS. It capitulated; settling for a mere $12.5 million in back taxes and the cessation of hostile litigation. It also conceded tax exempt status to all Scientology's subsidiary organisations. This gave the Church of Scientology financial advantages that Wright describes as perhaps 'unique among religions in the United States'. Miscavige declared to his core staff, 'The future is ours!'

Reading these books, I was reminded of the famous experiments by Stanley Milgram half a century ago, showing the disturbing extent to which many people will obey those they perceive to be authority figures. I was reminded of disturbing scenes of human submission to abuse in Nazi concentration camps recounted by Bruno Bettelheim in *The Informed Heart*. The problem of Scientology, I think, demonstrates that we need to rethink the rules governing religious freedom, in the name of basic civic order and human rights.

What Scientology has done in secrecy for decades is disturbingly comparable to what totalitarian regimes have done on a far larger and more violent scale. Its secret and fortified compound Gold Base in California embodies this disturbing character. Its own former head of security, Gary Morehead, told Wright that about a hundred people try to "escape" each year. Fortunately, as Jenna found, Scientology exists within a wider, freer society in which there are sources of refuge and redress. These two bracing books are proof of that. Read them and join the awareness network.

A calm and humane eye cast over China

Reading *Party Time: Who Runs China and How*, one gets the impression that Rowan Callick, a senior and decorated journalist, did not waste a minute when he was in China as a foreign correspondent. He travelled widely, met a remarkable range of people and kept an admirably open mind regarding what is happening and what it means for the outside world. Political leaders, diplomats and business people who work in China or travel there are unlikely, for the most part, to have such a wide range of encounters. Nor are they likely to be able to ponder them in print with the dispassionate candour Callick brings to his task. For this reason, such professionals are likely to find his book almost as valuable as are the far larger number of readers who lack such exposure to China.

There have been several fine recent books by senior Australian journalists that have risen above the old derogatory cliché 'journalistic' to offer genuinely informative and richly reflective insights into the changes going on in China, or in our relations with it. Richard McGregor's *The Party: The Secret World of China's Communist Rulers* (2010), David Uren's *The Kingdom and the Quarry* (2012) and John Garnaut's *The Rise and Fall of the House of Bo* (2012) all fit this description.

This new book by Rowan Callick, several years in preparation, is right up with the best of them. If anything, it is better than the others in at least one crucial respect: it provides a more fascinatingly diverse portrait gallery of contemporary individuals in China than any of the others. Moreover, Callick has a notably calm and humane eye. His encounters do not reduce individuals to mere evidence for a reductive argument. He brings them all alive. He allows us to hear these diverse voices.

Callick, plainly, has not set out to write either a polemic against the Communist Party or an apologia for it. He is fascinated by the complexity of the picture with which China and Party rule in China now present us. He draws attention to this at the outset, writing that:

> *perceptions can, of course, be misleading. They can even be designed to that effect. Trompe l-oeil was not unique to the French gardeners who devised the term. Virtually every Chinese garden features the clever device called zhang jing—'blocked view' or 'screened scenery'—by which, even in a comparatively confined space, the stroller keeps encountering fresh, formerly hidden vistas.*

He made it his business to explore the vast 'garden' of the Chinese world, recording and reflecting upon many of its blocked views; and he has succeeded admirably. Regardless of your starting point, if you are looking for a refreshingly up to date and candid introduction to how China works in our time, you will both enjoy and learn from his account of the garden.

One particularly striking interview, recounted very early in the book, was with Wang

Xiaodong, an influential and outspoken figure at the China Youth and Juvenile Research Centre (affiliated with the Communist Party's Youth League). He quotes Wang, whom he describes as 'brooding and intense' with 'no time for small talk', as stating that China's youth today reject Mao's socialism, but embrace his nationalism.

As they replace the current generation of leaders, he declared to Callick:

> *China will globalise its national interests and this will affect not just our close neighbours, but the whole world. We must gain the capacity to protect those interests.*

Callick comments of Wang and his nationalistic and ambitious cohort:

> *Tomorrow, they feel, assuredly belongs to them. They are impatient for China to assume global leadership and most cannot conceive of this happening without the Party.*

When I read this passage, I was at once reminded of a scene from Bob Fosse's classic film *Cabaret* in which Michael York (a young Englishman teaching English in Berlin in 1931) and Helmut Griem (a wealthy and complacent Junker) drive out to a country beer garden for a quiet drink, only to witness a group of Hitler Youth stand and sing a rousing nationalistic song with the stirring refrain:

> *Now Fatherland, Fatherland, show us the sign*
> *Your children have waited to see*
> *The morning will come*
> *When the world is mine*
> *Tomorrow belongs to me*

Fortunately, as Callick shows, there are a great many other moods and voices in contemporary China, though this nationalistic feeling is one we are coming to realize could become disturbingly dominant. This is especially so, given the Party's insistence on its political authority and its use of nationalism to reinforce it. Xia Chuntao, a historian at the Deng Xiaoping Thought Research Centre told Callick 'there is only one correct and accurate interpretation of history and only one explanation that is closest to the truth. There is a pool of clear water and there's no need to stir up this water. Doing so can only cause disturbance in people's minds.'

The richness of Callick's book is that it gives us these voices, but not in a polemic narrative or ideological argument. They are simply juxtaposed with many others, allowing us to see different aspects of the Chinese garden and discouraging us from drawing hasty conclusions about what "the people of China" or even the Party thinks. Actually, the Party's attempt to monopolize political information and history is both grotesque and in trouble.

Callick quotes one Zhang Yaojie, a writer with a strong following, as remarking:

> *China introduced a democratic system after the Qing Empire was overthrown in 1911. But then the leader of the Kuomintang, Sun Yatsen, overthrew the democratic system. Then the Communist Party overthrew the KMT. For now the Chinese people are not strong enough to claim the country back.*

So much, right there, for the Party's propaganda and monopoly on the interpretation of history. Yet the path from here is quite uncertain. Callick's great merit is not to pretend or assert otherwise. Indeed, his great weave of scenes and voices shows there is no single predictable path.

The puzzle of why nations fail

Many formidable scholars have acclaimed Daron Acemoglu and James Robinson's *Why Nations Fail: The Origins of Power, Prosperity and Poverty*. The book is not as impressive, however, as their accolades suggest. Nobel laureates in economics Kenneth Arrow, Gary Becker, Robert Solow and Michael Spence have all given the book their seal of approval; as have such academic luminaries as Joel Mokyr, Niall Ferguson, Jared Diamond and Steven Levitt, among others.

Yet it is marred by sometimes astonishing errors of detail and advances a theory which, though it begins promisingly, becomes progressively vaguer and more platitudinous as the authors proceed. In the end, I was left wondering whether those who had praised it so highly had actually read it attentively, or merely skimmed it, liked its sweep and originality, but didn't pause to really think systematically about its argument.

Acemoglu and Robinson have certainly tackled an important problem. By their own account, they spent fifteen years researching and writing their book. They begin well, observing that there are a number of widely held hypotheses about why some nations prosper while others flounder in poverty, but that none of these hypotheses stands up well to critical scrutiny. They are at their best in producing diagnostic evidence which refutes each of these hypotheses. Their evidence is well chosen and very telling.

The hypotheses they refute are the geography hypothesis (that climate and natural endowment determine wealth and prosperity), the culture hypothesis (that religious beliefs and ethical values determine wealth and poverty) and the ignorance hypothesis (those who are poor are so because they don't know how to create wealth). In all probability, it is these early chapters which captivated those who have praised the book.

However, the authors then proceed to advance their own hypothesis and here they gradually get themselves mired in a conceptual quicksand. Their hypothesis is that it is *institutions*—political and economic—which determine the wealth and poverty of nations; specifically that 'inclusive' institutions generate wealth, while 'extractive' ones produce poverty. Unfortunately, these terms are only vaguely defined. And, having set up an overly vague hypothesis, they then set about presenting evidence in support of it, rather than seeking to test it as they had the competing hypotheses.

The consequence is that 'extractive' and 'inclusive' get stretched to fit societies that happen to have been (more or less) poor and (more or less) wealthy to the point where meaningful distinctions get lost and prognoses proceed by tautology. For example, we are told (by authors who betray an exceedingly weak grasp of classical history) that the Roman Republic was 'inclusive', but the Roman Empire 'extractive', so that the latter was bound to fall. Never mind that the Republic looted the Mediterranean basin and then fell, while the Empire extended Roman citizenship around that basin and lasted for five hundred years.

They write that Robert Mugabe has run a regime in Zimbabwe that is 'no less extractive' than that of the preceding white colonial regime under Ian Smith and that 'its economic performance has been even worse (sic) than before independence.' But it has been a good deal more 'extractive' than the Smith regime and before 'independence' Zimbabwe's economic performance was actually very respectable; so much so that Mugabe was told by Julius Nyerere and Kenneth Kaunda in 1980 that he had inherited 'the jewel of Africa' and should take care not to tarnish it.

Similarly, they allow that a great deal of wealth has been generated by an 'extractive' regime in China in recent years, but assert that this cannot last, because extractive institutions can't sustainably create wealth. Now there are various reasons why China's existing institutions might hit the wall in the foreseeable future, but it's not theoretically satisfying or pragmatically very useful merely to assert that this is true *by definition* and that an end to China's 'extractive' growth is bound to come in 'the long run.' Moreover, they draw upon a distressingly thin set of sources in their reflections on China.

These shortcomings in the book are troubling at a time when it is precisely the 'inclusive' institutions of the US, the EU and Japan that have all but stopped creating more wealth, have got themselves buried under mountains of debt and are making very heavy institutional weather of trying to find a way through their economic and political dilemmas. There is no hint of this in *Why Nations Fail*. Arguably, the EU is floundering because it has been altogether too 'inclusive' and is now reaping the rewards of its inclusive fecklessness.

Finally, at a time when there is mounting concern about the sustainability of humanity's vast extraction of natural resources, it seems odd to find these two authors differentiating between 'extractive' and 'inclusive' institutions without even mentioning ecological challenges. Isn't it the case that the very effort to make the global economy more 'inclusive' in the sense of facilitating the rapid rise of standards of consumption among billions of Asians and now Africans is placing acute strain upon the world's material resources? The authors are clearly acquainted with Jared Diamond's work. How can they not have pondered this ecological aspect of the future prospects for human wealth and poverty?

Beyond Benedict: the possibilities of bridge-building

The announcement that Pope Benedict XVI was retiring prompted an outpouring of commentary on his decision. But almost all of it seems to have concentrated on relatively banal topics, such as what he will do in retirement, who will succeed him and what prompted him to become the first Pope in six hundred years to lay down his office rather than wait for death to take him. Today he actually steps down. His departure should lead us to reflect on two larger questions: the nature of the Papacy itself and the role of religion in the 21st century world.

Large numbers of people who call themselves Christians in our time are Protestants or evangelicals of various kinds. All these sects and curious congregations reject Papal authority for historical reasons. They all in their different, often strangely literal ways appeal to the Bible as authority. Large numbers of people who more or less still call themselves Catholics also, now, repudiate the Pope, because they regard his office as 'medieval', out of touch with contemporary society and unacceptably authoritarian. Few such people will regret the retirement of Benedict XVI, Joseph Ratzinger. He has long been regarded as a reactionary figure, trying to hold the Catholic Church back from heading down the liberal and even 'new age' direction they think it should take.

Yet the challenge facing Cardinal Ratzinger when he became Pope eight years ago was formidable. It was to hold a besieged Catholic Church together. It's worth putting aside our prejudices and judgments for a while to consider the nature and possibilities of the Papacy. One way to do that is to consider that the Pope is the 'Pontifex Maximus' and not just St Peter's heir. The title is Latin, of course, and literally means 'Greatest Bridge-Builder' - from the words *pons* (bridge), *facere* (to make or build) and *maximus* (greatest). That is worth pondering, because it is a title taken over by the Papacy from ancient Rome; much as the titles of Mary such as 'Star of the Sea' were taken over from Isis and Venus. It has great potential symbolism now.

The office of Pontifex Maximus dates back to the 8th century BCE and was, for over a thousand years, the title of the leading religious figure in Rome, head of the College of Pontiffs (of whom there were originally five). Their role was to form a bridge between the gods and humanity and to tend the *pax deorum*, the peace of the gods. It was only as or even after the Roman Empire fell that the bishops of Rome took over the title.[283] By some

---

283 The Emperors had preceded them in doing so. The title was conferred on Julius Caesar and it came to seem a sound political move, thereafter, for the chief citizen and master of the state to hold it. That the

accounts it was Pope Leo the Great (440-61), by others Pope Gregory the Great (590-604) who first officially took the title Pontifex Maximus. But this gathered into the hands of the Papacy the prestige and public role originally vested in the head of the Roman College of Pontiffs.

From a Protestant or sceptical secular point of view, of course, this is precisely where the mischief started. The Popes became semi-pagan figures mingling religious charisma with political authority, the gospels with older superstitions. They assumed the imperial aura of Rome itself, the Eternal City, and claimed that they had authority on Earth as the representatives of the messiah. There is some truth in this. The medieval Papacy was, at many points, a corrupt and much-abused institution. Just ask Dante. The rebellion against Papal authority during the Reformation was, on moral and theological grounds, entirely understandable.

And yet there is something about the heritage of Rome and the idea of the Pontifex Maximus which, mingled with the Biblical heritage, can lend immense symbolic and moral significance to the gestures and utterances of Popes in our time. If we put to one side the merely dogmatic insistence of true believers that this is because the Pope 'really is' the 'Vicar of Christ on Earth' and think simply of the capacity of the holder of that office to play the role of Greatest Bridge-Builder, we can appreciate, without being believers at all, the possibilities of the Papacy even in the 21st century. No other religious figure in the world comes close; not the Dalai Lama, not any Muslim cleric and certainly no Protestant one.

The question is: what can be asked of the Pontifex Maximus in the 21st century? Surely, the single most important role, apart from revitalizing the Catholic Church itself, is to further develop the art of bridge building in an era when divisions among religions and states are grave and when coordination and cooperation around the planet for the common good are both urgent and challenging. But if the building and care of new bridges is to be undertaken by whoever holds the ancient office of Pontifex Maximus in Rome, he will surely need to find a better balance between the emphasis on religious dogmas and rituals that goes with being the Pope and the broader and ultimately higher office of exemplary leadership and moral integrity that the world as a whole respects.

Popes took it over was not, therefore, only a religious move, but a political one. Until the abolition of the Papal State with the modern unification of Italy, in the second half of the 19th century, the Popes were distinctly political as well as religious figures. We talk and write rather loosely about the Western tradition of the separation of Church and State, without sufficiently acknowledging that this was not the preference of the Papacy and was expressly repudiated as an idea by Pope Pius IX in his *Syllabus of Errors* in 1848.

The new atheists, such as Richard Dawkins[284], have called for the abolition of monotheistic religion for the sake of humanity. A more plausible and surely more attractive scenario would be the transformation of monotheistic religion (not just Catholicism or even Christianity) and the healing of schisms and bitter discords that have so discredited it throughout the past two millennia. For historical reasons, this is a difficult role for the Popes to play; but for symbolic reasons it is a role that the Pontifex Maximus is better placed to play than any other religious or for that matter political leader. This is not because of the 'truth' of Catholic claims. It is, as Dietrich Bonhoeffer understood, visiting Rome in 1924, because of the potential for profound universalism that Rome embodies. Bonhoeffer didn't convert to Catholicism. He simply admired its possibilities. They remain to be fulfilled. There's the great challenge confronting the next Pontifex Maximus.[285]

---

284   Richard Dawkins is justly famous as a biologist, but has become rather notorious for his polemical and somewhat ham-fisted attacks on religion, especially for his absurd claim that religion is 'the root of all evil'. The quality of his writing on evolutionary biology can be seen at its best in *Climbing Mount Improbable* (Viking, 1996) and *The Ancestor's Tale: A Pilgrimage to the Dawn of Life* (Penguin, 2004). Where he goes astray in his critique of religion is in his complete failure to grasp human cultural evolution and the role in it of myth, ritual and cosmogony. That all this has been 'evil' is a preposterous assertion, however clear it may be that so much of it has now lost its grip on reality. He should, at the very least, before launching into his crude polemics, have read a little of Weber and Durkheim on the sociology and functions of religion in human history.

285   This piece was written shortly before the surprising and refreshing election of Pope Francis I, an Argentinian of Italian background who has been a Jesuit throughout his religious career.

Keating's confusion in regard to Indonesia

Paul Keating tells us his prime ministership was that one brief, shining moment in which Australia had something like a 'real foreign policy'; 'a get it done foreign policy'. Before him there was only 'alliance management'. Since his tragically premature departure from power, 'Australia has rolled back into easy accommodation of the foreign policy objectives of the United States'. That, at least, was the thrust of his Keith Murdoch Oration recently.

But there was more to the Oration than this claim to pre-eminence. Keating has always been given to 'the vision thing'. At the onset of what he and others herald as 'the Asian century', he urges that we do three things in the immediate future:

1. distance ourselves without regret from the relatively declining United States;
2. concentrate on South East Asia as our primary strategic concern; and
3. form a mutual security pact with Indonesia, making it our greatest strategic partner.

This last suggestion is highly original. Unfortunately, the way Keating pitched it had as little practical substance or plausibility as the Asia Century white paper.

Allow, for the sake of argument, that the idea is interesting. After all, as Keating declared, Indonesia is one of the largest countries in the world; it is a gigantic archipelago to our north west, sitting athwart all the vital straits through which much of the 21st century's trade flows; it is a secular democracy, even though the world's largest Muslim country and, by 2030, it may have a GDP twice the size of our own and growing military capabilities to match. Friendship with such a state would have a lot to recommend it.

But there are a few things Keating doesn't appear to have thought through. Firstly, even assuming that Indonesia's economy grows to two or three times the size of our own GDP, that will still leave it a relatively poor country, with a per capita GDP a fraction of ours (between 20 and 30%). Even if it invests in greater military capabilities, there is no possibility of it being able to play the role that the United States plays as our greatest strategic partner: supplying strategic intelligence, advanced weapons platforms, global security reassurance, (including nuclear deterrence of major or rogue powers) and diplomatic access. How, therefore, is Indonesia supposed to become 'our most important strategic partner'?

Secondly, Keating declares that we spent the whole of the Cold War doing little more than 'alliance management'; but he now urges upon us a new alliance, which would plainly require a great deal of management; not least because of the very proximity of Indonesia to our shores. There are numerous complexities inherent in being a close ally of Indonesia. How does he square this circle? Surely, if sound and adroit alliance management is to be our game, we would do better to practice first with the culturally and strategically familiar and geographically distant United States, before having a crack at doing so with Indonesia.

Thirdly, critics of our alliance with the United States have always griped that 'paying our dues' has involved us in dubious foreign wars. The Vietnam War, Keating says, was a war in which we should never have participated. Likewise, it seems, the wars in Afghanistan and Iraq. There are plenty who will agree with him. But surely if we build a mutual defence pact with Indonesia, we risk embroiling ourselves in every squabble that might occur from the South China Sea to the Bay of Bengal as Asian powers rise and flex their muscles. The wealthier and more confident Indonesia became the more probable this would be. Why substitute a symbolic role in distant wars for an inextricable entanglement in much closer ones?

China currently resents what it sees as our backing for America's pivot to Asia, because it might mean 'containing' Chinese ambitions. Wouldn't China see a mutual defence pact between ourselves and Indonesia in similar terms? If not directed at China, at whom, pray, would it be directed? Presumably not the other ASEAN states. Given the stakes, why would we not adjust our sound relationship with the United States and quietly foster our relations with both Indonesia and China? This would surely be a more practical proposition than Keating's.

Fourthly, Keating is somewhat erratic about our role in the Anglosphere—first declaring that he has always been struck by how influential we were in the counsels of the great powers across the 20th century; then declaring that we have always been scammers in the temples of those powers. He craves 'natural' alliances, but nothing could have been more natural than our alliances with Britain and the United States. He asserts that integration into ASEAN would be natural because of our geography, but in sober fact it would be exceptionally challenging.

Fifth, Keating talks glibly of us cutting loose and 'striking out on our own', in the same breath as calling for a close alliance with Indonesia. He fails to mention that to do so we would need to invest far more resources than we are accustomed to in national security. It's far from obvious that Indonesia or the rest of ASEAN (or China) would welcome this. Indeed, it would be a very hard sell domestically. Given the shambles the Gillard government has just made of the defence budget, what case would Keating put to the electorate for doubling or even trebling defence expenditure in the name of independence from America?

There is a lot to be said for the ebullience Paul Keating brings to the large questions about Australia's future. But the man who loves Mahler and Second Empire clocks should slow down a little. Australia's geography and lineage have always meant we faced peculiar strategic dilemmas to which there are no quick fixes. If we are to build a better strategic relationship with Indonesia—

which is a fine and even necessary undertaking—it needs to proceed thoughtfully, rather than being based on extravagant and fanciful premises. And, to the extent that Asian powers rise, we should seek first and foremost to ensure that the tide lifts our boat; rather than hastening to moor it in any given Asian port.

Abraham Lincoln and the great task remaining before us

Stephen Spielberg's *Lincoln* opens in our cinemas today. Make sure you see it. It isn't only fine historical drama. It is a beautifully calibrated piece of theatre for our own time. Purists and pompous critics will carp about its imperfections. In almost every respect, however, it is excellent: poignant, stirring, sombre, eloquent. See it for that reason. But more importantly, see *Lincoln* because it addresses us in the language Lincoln learned from Shakespeare, the King James Bible and the Greek classics about the resonance in our time of the political upheaval and moral conflict through which the first Republican president steered America.

Perhaps John Williams' musical score is, at times, a little sentimental. Perhaps the drama is not at every point faithful to the historical record. Perhaps we could have been told a little more—even if in notes at the film's end - about the two remarkable women of mixed race, Elizabeth Keckley and Lydia Hamilton Smith, who were so close to the Lincolns and Thaddeus Stevens. The Lincolns had lost two young sons to illness by 1865, not one. And why was the attempt on William Seward's life at the same time as the assassination of Abraham Lincoln omitted? But these are quibbles.

There is so much to admire. That begins with the striking piece of poetic licence with which Spielberg opens his play. Four young soldiers, two black, two white, recite the Gettysburg address to Lincoln's face. The younger of the black ones challenges him over inequality between blacks and whites even in the Union army. As he walks away from the president, he completes the oration:

> we here highly resolve that these dead shall not have died in vain; that this nation, under God, shall have a new birth of freedom; and that government of the people, by the people, for the people, shall not perish from the earth.

This was almost one hundred years before the Civil Rights Act of 1964.

Spielberg surely created this Shakespearean opening, because he wants to lift our gaze *above* what is about to unfold on the screen. He subtly invites us to ponder the challenges we face in sustaining and enlarging the democratic project now. He is saying to us, as plainly as he can, playing Lincoln's words back to Lincoln and to all of us, in the words of the famous address:

> in a larger sense, we cannot dedicate, we cannot consecrate, we cannot hallow this ground. The brave men, living and dead, who struggled here, have consecrated it, far above our poor power to add or detract ... It is for us the living, rather, to be dedicated here to the unfinished work which they who fought here have thus far so nobly advanced. It is rather for us to be here dedicated to the great task remaining before us ...

He then presents us with the drama of the last, bitter months of the American civil war and the harrowing passage, through great difficulties and by the narrowest of legislative margins, of the Thirteenth Amendment to the US Constitution—finally abolishing slavery. We are intended to take away from the film, I believe, not only the injunction that that work—ending slavery and racism—remains unfinished, but that the even larger project of human emancipation and effective democratic government is 'the great task remaining before us'.

It's fitting that this film has happened to come out at the very point in history at which Barack Obama was re-elected, confirming the 2008 fulfilment of the dream of Martin Luther King. Like Lincoln in early 1865, he faces daunting second term challenges. But whatever one's political persuasion, this film transcends racial issues and narrowly partisan agendas. Lincoln was a Republican. The Democrats were not an anti-slavery party. Spielberg calls upon all of us to think more deeply than we normally do about politics, principle and processes.

This is vividly dramatized in a dialogue without witnesses between Lincoln and his radical Republican critic, Thaddeus Stevens in a White House scullery. This scene is as much the creation of Spielberg and his screen writer, Tony Kushner, as the film's opening, though faithful to the outlooks of Lincoln and Stevens.

Thaddeus Stevens, a battle-hardened reformer, was impatient—like many zealots—with political processes. He tells Lincoln:

> *I don't give a damn about the people and what they want. This is the face of someone who has fought long and hard for the good of the people without caring much for any of them ... You claim to trust them, but you know what the people are. You know that the inner compass which should direct the soul towards justice has ossified in white men and women, north and south, through tolerating the evil of slavery.*

'I admire your zeal, Mr Stevens,' Lincoln responds, 'and I have tried to profit from your example, but if I listened to you ... the border states would have gone over to the Confederacy, the war would have been lost and the Union with it ... '. He adds, 'A compass ... will point you true north from where you are standing, but it's got no advice about the swamps and deserts and chasms that you'll encounter along the way. If, in pursuit of your destination, you plunge ahead heedless of obstacles and achieve nothing more than to sink in a swamp, what's the use of knowing true north?'

Later, Elizabeth Keckley tells Lincoln that God will shepherd the Thirteenth Amendment through Congress. He responds that God might have chosen a more wieldy instrument than the US House of Representatives. This wry humanity on Lincoln's part amid severe difficulties and passionate opposition is what Spielberg chiefly offers for our consideration. Not 'true north' according to our own inner compasses; but what it takes to make our way across swamps, deserts and chasms. Yet we clearly do need to devise more wieldy instruments to meet the challenges facing humanity. That's our most fundamental challenge in the great task remaining before us.

Making democracy work

As we await the Federal election[286], Egypt is in the throes of an upheaval and is struggling to produce 'democracy'. The *Time* cover story this week is headed 'Egypt: World's Best Protesters, World's Worst Democrats: The Street Rules'. Protests, democracy, street rule are vital distinctions in the Twitter and occupy era. We need to think about it here, as much as they do in Egypt. Protest is one thing. Workable and rational consensus is another thing entirely.

Let's start with Egypt. I was there in April. The Muslim Brotherhood was not governing well. It did not know how to govern for all Egyptians. No-one else appeared organized enough to do much about this, least of all the Army. It had apparently chosen to step back from politics and acquiesce in the Brotherhood's attempt to take Egypt down the Turkish, if not the Iranian path.

In fact, it was preparing to step in and was encouraging the opposition to come out into the streets. The Army chief, General Sisi arrested an incredulous Mohammed Morsi and the country is again faced with a constitutional crisis. The question is: what kind of constitutional rules will confer progressive stability on Egypt; and after the coup, what rules can the Brotherhood now be persuaded to accept?

On the one hand, there may well *not* be an agreed set of rules any time soon; so constructive reform will be hard for Egypt to achieve. Like Syria, it may find itself spiralling into internal conflict. The grim reality is that 'spring' is not coming easily to the Arab world. Its reactionary monarchies and repressive dictatorships, its Muslim fanatics and military elites are none of them good material out of which to build constitutions based on the principles of legitimate elections, bipartisan consensus on fundamentals, civil liberties and an independent, enlightened judiciary.

On the other hand, much of the ferment in 'the street' has taken the form of a demand for at least *some version* of these things. What is necessary, therefore, is to step back from the immediate inclination to react and reflect on what could really make democracy work for countries like Egypt. As soon as this question is posed, the situation there should serve as a sobering reminder that the answer cannot be simply the holding of elections, if elections result in the formation of a government intent on systematic gerrymander and the imposition of what amounts to one party rule or even theocratic tyranny on the Iranian model.

Nor, however, can it be the rule of 'the street'. The aim has to be a system of government

---

286 This was, of course, the 2013 Federal election, in which the reinstated Kevin Rudd ran a ramshackle campaign, disconnected from ALP campaign headquarters, and went down to terminal defeat.

in which policies are debated and reformulated through a set of institutions which respect 'Marquis of Queensberry Rules' when it comes to politics and the exercise of power. This requires genuinely independent 'referees' and 'judges' and willingness on the part of contestants for office or advocates of public policy to accept the rules and to compete within their constraints. This is what constitutions are all about. But they don't come about easily. England's took centuries to hammer out. France took a hundred years after 1789 and multiple upheavals to get anything like constitutional stability. The United States took a hundred years after its bloody civil war to get a Civil Rights Bill through Congress.

So spare a thought for the Egyptians, but keep your eyes on the prize. Don't be distracted by feckless talk of Islamic cultures pro and con. The religious and aristocratic orders of old Europe in the seventeenth and eighteenth centuries took a lot of changing. The slave system in the Southern United States took a lot of changing. Things certainly need to change in the Arab world and there is no substitute for vigorous debate about how to change them. We should, however, take a keen interest in all this while keeping it in judicious perspective.

But most of all, we should make our own democracies work better. This would set a practical example to others—as Australia did a century and more ago. It's increasingly clear, as Lindsay Tanner pointed out in his troubled 2011 political memoir, *Sideshow*, that doing this is going to require really thoughtful innovation in the ways we debate public policy, discern the collective wisdom of the electorate and reshape our political parties to render them more fit to govern.

The single greatest vice of 'democratic' government, ever since its first variants in the classical world, has been the drift into a downward spiral of demagoguery and 'mob' rule—the rule of 'the street'—as constitutional procedures for deliberation and careful making of public policy decay. It can't be emphasized too strongly that what makes good government work, whether under a 'democracy', an 'oligarchy' or a 'benign dictatorship' is a well-honed capacity for deliberation and the arrival at a rational consensus.

Elections and opinion polls aren't enough and the way we conduct and use them often now seems unsatisfactory. This is widely felt. The answer has to lie in better means for engaging citizens in deliberative processes. Twitter and Facebook are not the answer. Mobilization, while it can provide a 'sugar hit' of participation, is not the point. Citizens need to be able to see what the issues are, to have unobstructed access to the claims on either side and be able to express opinions individually based on these things. Those individual opinions then need to be sifted and aggregated to arrive at the collective wisdom and that collective wisdom needs to be seen as the basis for shaping public policy.

Streams of blogospherical opinion, occupy movements, web-based mobilization a la Avaaz, are the equivalent of rallies in the street. As we can see in Egypt, the effect they have isn't constitutional reform and does not produce sound rules or workable policies. As the Egyptians struggle for a constitution, we should be working for deliberative innovation and political renovation as a public good. It has begun. Let's take it further during the forthcoming Federal election.

Section 6: 2013-14

You call that a leaders' debate?

Sunday night's televised debate between the prime minister and the leader of the opposition was empty and flat. All manner of polls, differing enormously in their findings, report on who 'won' the debate; but it was all posturing and evasion. We need serious debate about key issues, not this kind of political pantomime of slogans and artful dodging.

A defining moment in the proceedings was when Fairfax journalist Peter Hartcher asked both candidates a very clear question. He began by stating that Ken Henry, former Secretary of the Treasury and lead author of the 2008-10 report *Australia's Future Tax System*, has declared that 'Australia is failing to meet the immense challenge of paying for its future needs. Whoever governs will either have to raise taxes or cut expenditures.'

'What specific expenditures will you cut?' he asked the candidates, 'Or what taxes will you increase?' Excellent question. No room for ducking and weaving, you might have thought. But neither candidate rose to the challenge. Either might have responded that Ken Henry was in error. Or that he was correct and that tough decisions would need to be taken, with clear explanations being provided to the Australian people. They could have offered competing and informed visions. Instead, both of them waffled and totally flubbed the test of credible economic leadership.

A week ago, in this newspaper, Hartcher had a small column drawing attention to Ken Henry's analysis. He quoted Henry as stating, 'Whoever wins the election has to commit to tax reform to improve the tax system so it's capable of producing more revenue with minimal economic damage.' The column was enlivened by a poignant little Tandberg cartoon, showing a forlorn figure standing at a podium beneath a banner reading 'I'll increase taxes'. The caption read '... the loneliness of the honest politician.'

Sunday night's televised debate was an opportunity for the candidates to exhibit both integrity and leadership on this issue. The prime minister might have declared, 'I commissioned the Henry Review and it has provided a blueprint for taxation reform. We will be acting on that blueprint with decisiveness if we are re-elected.'

The leader of the opposition might have retorted:

> Yes, you commissioned the Henry Tax Review in 2008. It was published in 2010 and the only one of its recommendations that the Labour government adopted was a botched and politicized version of a resources tax. You've had six years to get this right and what have we seen? We've seen relentlessly rising expenditures, failure to implement tax reforms and endless internal backbiting and factional strife within the Labour Party. And you expect the Australian people to give you another three years based on that record?

It's worth recalling that the Henry Review called for a sweeping series of clarifying reforms of the national taxation system. You'd never guess this from Sunday night's 'leadership' debate. The Review called for revenue-raising from four efficient tax bases: personal income, business income, consumption and economic rents from natural resources. It called for an equitable, transparent and simplified personal income tax, with a much higher tax-free threshold, only two tax brackets and a simplification of superannuation, deductions and offsets.

It called for efficient land and resources taxation, retirement income reform and, more generally, an open, understandable and responsive tax system. Where was the debate on any of this on Sunday evening? AWOL. Absent Without Leave—and also without excuse. The Henry Review has been in the public domain for three years. Are we, the citizens and voters of this country, seriously expected to vote for either of these candidates, who, when asked a direct question about one of the most fundamental aspects of responsible government, completely fail to address its terms?

We have to do better than this. We need, in this field, as in others, for the key proposals of thoughtful specialists like Ken Henry to be openly and publicly debated in such a way that large numbers of citizens—anyone, in principle—can see the arguments, consider the reasoning and the evidence and vote on the substantive issues. So long as, instead, we have politicians driven by perverse incentives to avoid scaring the horses by owning up to elementary fiscal realities, we undermine democracy and our common wealth.

When the taxation review was a work in progress, in 2008-09, there were 1,500 submissions to it and a conference, in June 2009, at which leading international experts and a range of academics and stakeholders debated ideas for tax and transfer reforms. A more widely disseminated version of this process is what we surely need—and not just with regard to taxation reform. The disgrace of Sunday night's debate was that you would never have known that all that inquiry and debate on taxation reform had occurred at all.

Syria and the next white paper

While we have been going through an uninspired election campaign, Syria has been in the throes of a calamitous civil war. Appalled by what is happening there—100,000 dead, two million refugees and the apparent use of chemical weapons against civilians—there are cries of 'Do something!' But there are no easy or effective things to do. And who should do this 'something'?

Our election tomorrow will be peaceful. No such peaceful change is coming to Syria. If there was an open and free election there, Bashar al-Assad would be defeated by a Sunni and increasingly Islamist majority, which would be vengeful and illiberal. It would be like Hamas winning the election in Gaza: one man, one vote, one time

Neither Assad and his Alawite fascist regime, nor the Christian and Druze minorities want a Sunni Islamist government. Nor do the Russians, the Shiite Iranians or Hezbollah want to see Assad overthrown. They are all arming Assad. Therefore, there will be neither elections nor peace. Those are the realities.

Who should step in to sort this out? No-one? Then the suffering will continue. The United Nations? It is anything but united. The Security Council has almost never worked effectively. Russia and China have again blocked any kind of effective sanction against Assad. The Anglosphere? Not us, the British Parliament has declared resoundingly. Uncle Sam? 'Not again!' groans Barack Obama, having painstakingly pulled back from costly wars in Afghanistan and Iraq. One can surely understand his reluctance. Yet the world continues to turn.

Syria may be on the on other side of the world, but the chaos there and the failure of all international collective security institutions to do anything about it point to why the next government—which looks likely to be a Coalition government - must put the Defence portfolio in better order and condition. It has promised a new Defence White Paper. That White Paper has some serious work to do.

Sitting here in Australia, the worst we have to fear right now is a conservative government that many on the left of politics think will be reactionary, while more ambitious liberals fear it will be too complacent. It's all too easy to sit here and bleat 'Something should be done.' That means by someone else—somehow.

The next White Paper must be premised on the axiom that, if anything is to be done in cases like Syria, both the collective security mechanisms and well-drilled and well-equipped military capabilities need to be in place already. They cannot be summoned into being at a moment's notice when a crisis breaks. Having them in place requires sustained diplomacy and sustained investment in readiness and capability.

Syria in 2012-13 is a larger version of what we saw in East Timor in 1998-99. In that situation, too, there were calls for the United Nations and the Australian government to 'do something'. Reluctantly, the Howard government decided to intervene. But it discovered that it had barely any capacity to do so—just off-shore and well within the so-called 'air-sea gap' we had long been told was our region of primary strategic interest.

In that case, there were voices right across the political spectrum calling for Australia to step in. Yet there had not been sufficient investment in logistical and military capabilities for many years beforehand to make that a ready option. Had there been Indonesian resistance and no US support, we would have been in very serious difficulties.

We lucked out, because there was no fighting. But the Howard government was alarmed at what it had found and set about trying to remedy twenty years of neglect of Australia's military, especially the Army and amphibious lift capabilities.

Over the past six years, what had begun to look like a more or less serious and sustained refurbishment of the Australian Defence Force has been allowed to fall into serious disarray. The consequences, looking ahead, are that we will not have the capabilities to participate meaningfully in collective security actions, whether near at hand or in the further abroad, in the remainder of this decade or in the 2020s and 2030s.

We cannot do anything about Syria. It could be that no-one can now.[287] But we can, once a new government is in office in Canberra, set about putting our foreign and security affairs in good order and condition. That will require a focus on three things: bringing coherence to our diplomacy and national security strategy; reassessing our alliance and collective security commitments; and creating a sustainable, bipartisan consensus on what level of investment we are prepared to make in realistic military capability.

Pity the poor Syrian people. But if you are concerned about the mayhem there and think something should be done about it; then start to get serious about what doing anything meaningful or effective in such cases requires. Start to acknowledge that it entails readiness in place. And put your money where your mouth is.

---

287   This was written before the 2013 Federal election, as is clear from its wording; and well before the irruption of ISIL in Iraq and Syria in 2014. That subject is addressed later in the book.

Edward Snowden: peering into the stateroom[288]

Yesterday morning, the front page of this newspaper[289] carried a report headed 'Revealed: How Australia Spies on its Neighbours', by Philip Dorling. His sources, he wrote, were 'new information disclosed by intelligence whistle-blower Edward Snowden and a former Australian intelligence officer.' It might come as a surprise to some naïve citizens to learn that we have been spying on our neighbours; but anyone who is serious and has been paying even a modicum of attention knows that we have been doing so for many decades. What is news in this particular report, therefore, and what should responsible citizens make of it?

It claims that the Anglo-American 'Five Eyes' intelligence alliance has been running a collection program called STATEROOM that has been intercepting the communications of high ranking officials in other countries. It alleges that our own services have been contributing to this program by running surveillance facilities inside our embassies in Jakarta, Beijing, Tokyo, Hanoi, Kuala Lumpur, Dili and, by implication, elsewhere.

Those facilities, it states, are so secret as to be unknown even to our own diplomatic personnel. It allows that the intelligence collected in this manner can be very useful. It makes no comment on the question of whether revealing the program's existence was a good or a bad thing. It is this question we most need to think about, however.

We can dismiss at once, of course, the idea that Philip Dorling and *The Age* have given anything away by printing this report. What gave the program away was Edward Snowden's leak of highly classified information. Once Snowden leaked this material, the intelligence services

---

288 As I edit these pages, the documentary about Edward Snowden, *Citizen Four*, has just been released in Australian cinemas. It is being highly acclaimed, even as 'the film of the century'. It is surely no such thing. Snowden comes across as articulate and well-informed, but there is no balance or sense of proportion in his assessment of what the American government is doing or why. Nor does the film-maker, Laura Poitras, correct this in any way. The film concludes with *The Guardian's* Glenn Greenwald interviewing Snowden in his comfortable Moscow apartment, without the slightest touch of irony.

Given that the Putin government is made up of former KGB totalitarians, deeply corrupt, a practitioner of surveillance and repression, censorship and cyber-warfare transparently more insidious than anything happening in the United States, it is bemusing to see Snowden taking refuge there—as Julian Assange has done in the Ecuadorean Embassy in London—rather than having stayed in the United States and begun a civil disobedience and public intellectual campaign against the uses of surveillance under the Obama administration. He could have done so without serious danger of arrest, whereas his Russian counterparts face not only the danger of arrest, but beatings and even murder. You would never guess this from watching *Citizen Four*, which makes the US government seem sinister and 'Orwellian'.

289 *The Age*, in Melbourne.

of other countries, especially those of China (and Russia, where Snowden has found asylum) will have been onto it even more quickly than our own press. There was no point, from there, in keeping the matter secret from the mass of Australia's citizens. But Dorling's commentary on the facts left something to be desired.

The fact that such a program—if not already known to the foreign governments at which it was directed—should be exposed at all ought to give us pause. For one thing, Edward Snowden claims to be operating from the high moral ground in exposing such programs, but he has taken refuge with a government that has always conducted them itself, is far more arbitrary and dictatorial in its treatment of dissent than any of the Anglo-American countries and is run by a clique of former secret policemen, headed by Vladimir Putin. How does this add up?

Snowden has revealed that we keep tabs on the leadership in China to the best of our ability. Should we not do so? Does he think that our targets in that country are naïve and ingenuous and that they are being preyed upon by a malicious Anglo-American intelligence cartel? China has a massive intelligence apparatus itself; it is a very unpleasant and deeply corrupt one party state; its military capabilities are growing at remarkable and indeed alarming speed; it is our largest trading partner, but runs a highly and disingenuously mercantilist economic policy. Are we seriously supposed to take its pronouncements on trust and not try to get behind the veil?

Snowden has shown that we have long been collecting high level intelligence in Indonesia and on East Timor. Well, our relationship with Indonesia is very complex and has had a troubled history. Is it foolish or immoral for us to try to obtain clear, inside information about what its military and civilian leaders are thinking? Is it not possible that doing so will help us to avoid serious misunderstandings and collisions with Indonesia? Is it not possible that it might enable our government to manoeuvre more adroitly in negotiating with Indonesia over such vexed matters as people smuggling, human rights abuses in Irian Jaya, deforestation in Kalimantan and Sumatra or regional security issues further afield?

The world is, unfortunately, a place full of machinations, confusion and mistrust. We cannot alter that by avoiding the collection of intelligence. What we can do is expose ourselves to being seriously mislead or blind-sided if we do *not* have such intelligence. And we cannot obtain it, especially where it is most required, without doing so clandestinely. That is the nature of the case and there is no way around it.

This is an old, harsh lesson and one that the enthusiasts for wholesale leaking appear not to have grasped. Certainly there are times when we—like Snowden—have reason to mistrust the secrecy of our own governments, but it is a very strange inference from this to the supposition that other, less democratic governments should not be spied upon for strategic reasons. And, once it is agreed that we need such intelligence—the world being the way it actually is—there is no option but to conduct our collection of intelligence under the shroud of secrecy. It simply cannot be collected any other way.

Many years ago, before the crisis of the 1930s which led to the Second World War, the US Secretary for War Henry Stimson, abolished the US government's fledgling signals and codes intelligence capability, the so-called Black Chamber, with the admonition 'Gentlemen do not open each other's mail.' The US learned to its cost that if you do not do so you can pay a very high price. Part of that cost was the Japanese surprise attack on Pearl Harbor on 7 December 1941.

Conversely, signals intelligence collection, developed in the very nick of time, played a decisive role in enabling the Western Allies to defeat Germany and Japan, after 1941.[290] It was also the origin of the National Security Agency and of the 1947 Anglo-American (UKUSA) 'Five Eyes' agreement to collect and share such intelligence on a global basis. Edward Snowden and those who think like him would appear to want to make this secret work impossible. Those who have given him shelter must certainly regard him as what Lenin used to call a 'useful idiot'.[291] The rest of us should be alert to how he has deeply compromised a useful program.

---

[290] The recent film *The Imitation Game*, starring Benedict Cumberbatch as Alan Turing, rather nicely dramatized the breaking of Germany's ENIGMA code in the early 1940s; a feat which, as the film's makers state at the end of the film, is estimated to have shortened the war by two years and saved 14 million lives. It was, however, seriously inaccurate in a number of ways, regarding both the decoding work at Bletchley Park, the relationship between John Cairncross and MI6 and the death of Turing

[291] Lenin himself, of course, was a more or less complete idiot—not so much in instrumental terms, but in economic and political ones. His illegitimate seizure of power not once but twice over in November 1917 from the Provisional Revolutionary Government and in January 1918 from the democratically elected Constituent Assembly, followed by his utterly incompetent economic policies thoroughly wrecked the Russian world in the years after 1917, causing the collapse of the monetary and financial system, a famine that claimed millions of lives and a brutal civil war in which far more Russians perished than had died in the First World War, while many of Russia's educated and indispensable people fled abroad, never to return. The most systematic account of his failures is Richard Pipes *Russia Under the Bolshevik Regime 1919-1924* (Harvill Harper Collins, London, 1994). For a devastating account of the depredations of the Bolsheviks in the first year of their rule, see Sean McMeekin *History's Greatest Heist: The Looting of Russia by the Bolsheviks* (Yale University Press, 2009).

'Suzie' and the fate of China

Jung Chang, now 61, is still best known for her best-selling memoir, *Wild Swans* (1991). Eight years ago, her controversial biography of Mao Zedong was published. Now she has written a biography of the last effective dynastic ruler of China, *Empress Dowager Cixi: The Concubine Who Launched Modern China*. By her account, Mao Zedong was a psychopath and the greatest mass killer in history. The much-maligned Cixi, by contrast, she lauds as an "amazing stateswoman" and the true architect of China's modernization.

Reviewing *Mao: The Unknown Story* in August 2005, I remarked that the book read too much like a rather hastily drafted polemic. It was deficient psychologically, sociologically and statistically. I have fewer reservations about this new book, but I still think that it reads as a kind of 'popular' history. The chief difference between the two books is that Mao was damned, while Cixi is praised. The juxtaposition is vital. Both verdicts challenge widely held views: the first that Mao was a great 20th century statesman who made a few costly errors; the second that Cixi was a 19th century despot who held back reform.

If you are not a Sinologist, you may be wondering how to pronounce the unfamiliar name Cixi. It is sometimes spelt Tzu Hsi. For convenience, without too much distortion, you can pronounce it 'Suzie'. That little bit of indulgence might be serviceable, actually, in making a distant and long-reviled figure sound and seem a bit more familiar and *simpatico*. And that is clearly the aim that Jung Chang had in writing the book. She argues that this woman, against enormous odds and in exceptionally trying circumstances, set out successfully to modernize China and to avoid civil war in the process.

Certainly, this book can be recommended to the general reader. It is highly readable and it tells an intrinsically fascinating tale. It is, in many ways, the tale of a woman who should be a feminist icon as much as a study in statecraft. Born in 1835, just before the Opium War, she was raised under challenging circumstances and never became more than semi-literate. In 1852, she was selected as a concubine for the feeble nineteen year old Emperor Xianfeng. She bore him a son in 1856 and when Xianfeng died young, in 1861, she formed an alliance with his chief consort, the Empress Zhen, and through extraordinary acumen came to dominate the Imperial Court for the next forty seven years.

Those forty seven years have long been depicted as a half century of the disintegration of the Chinese Empire and the Manchu dynasty, culminating in the Republican revolution of 1911 and the serious struggle to bring modernization and economic revitalization to China. Jung Chang tells a different story. She shows us a remarkable, imaginative, tenacious, perceptive and magnanimous woman who, surrounded by conservative or treacherous males, won loyalty, defeated conspiracies and set a course for preserving and reforming a vast empire, even as foreign powers preyed upon it. The 'Suzie' that emerges from her pages is a far more nuanced and interesting figure than the Empress Dowager of anti-Manchu and Communist propaganda.

The two key judgements in the book come in chapter 28 'Cixi's Revolution (1902-8)'. The first has to do with the scale and importance of Cixi's reforms. Jung Chang writes:

> *The reforms in these years were radical, progressive and humane, designed to improve people's lives and to eradicate medieval savagery. Under her measured stewardship, Chinese society was fundamentally transformed, thoughtfully and bloodlessly for the better, while its roots were carefully preserved and suffered minimum trauma.*

It was the absence of such measured and humane reform in the French Revolution that Edmund Burke deplored in the 1790s and Alexis de Tocqueville lamented looking back in *The Old Regime and the French Revolution*.

The second judgment, a few pages later is this:

> *Cixi's tolerance of attacks on her government—and on herself—as well as her willingness to permit a diversity of viewpoints were unmatched by any of her predecessors—or, indeed, her successors.*

This is a crucial judgment because it throws into relief the ruthless repression of critics and diverse viewpoints by the Communist Party throughout its history and challenges the common Leftist notion that revolutionaries simply suppress different people than do 'reactionaries' and for a better cause. This remains an important lesson of history in our time and one highly pertinent for China, where the suppression of dissent now is much worse than it was in the last years of Cixi.

If you are curious about China's past and struggling to think through the complex politics of contemporary China, this book will be a useful stimulus. It will break up any crassly ideological view of China's history that you may have imbibed over the years and provide you with much food for fresher thinking. For this reason, it is well worth reading.

Stuffing up a conspiracy theory[292]

Did you watch *JFK: The Smoking Gun* last Sunday night on TV? Or buy the book, by retired Melbourne detective Colin McLaren? If you haven't bought the book, don't bother. Everyone seems to love a good conspiracy theory and the JFK assassination is the mother of them all.[293] It's a terrific case study in how people get muddled by portentous claims and believe the most absurd things. This latest addition to the genre is a textbook case of muddle.

It's argument is that JFK was killed not by a bunch of nefarious conspirators (the Grassy Knoll, the Magic Bullet and all that) and not by Lee Harvey Oswald acting alone, but by Oswald acting independently and a Secret Service agent accidentally firing the fatal shot from his AR-15 automatic rifle as he fell backwards inside the Secret Service vehicle behind the car in which Kennedy was seated.[294] And, naturally, it has been covered up ever since by that fortress of conspiracies and secrets the Federal government of the United States.

This is not a new idea. It was advanced twenty one years ago by Bonar Menninger in *Mortal Error*. It has been ridiculed by every serious analyst ever since, when they bothered to address it at all. When its original proponent, Howard Donahue, phoned Secret Service agent Winston Lawson to interview him about the matter, Lawson retorted, 'That's about the biggest bunch of bull I have ever heard in my life. That's absolutely ridiculous. That's all I've got to say. Thank you for calling. Goodbye.'

Yet I keep hearing people declare—like Graeme Blundell in the *Australian's Weekend Review* last Saturday - that McLaren makes 'a compelling case'. In fact, McLaren's argument is nonsense

---

292 This piece first appeared in *The Age* on 7 November 2013, close to the fiftieth anniversary of the killing of President Kennedy. It has been revised and expanded for this book. By then, my colleagues and I at Austhink Consulting had been running a three day workshop on the JFK assassination for over a decade.

293 On the pivotal role of the JFK case in fostering a paranoid conspiracy mentality in recent decades, both in the United States and further afield, see David Aaronovitch *Voodoo Histories: The Role of the Conspiracy Theory in Shaping Modern History* (Riverhead Books, New York, 2010); Peter Knight *Conspiracy Culture: From Kennedy to the X Files* (Routledge, London and New York, 2000); and Emma A. Jane and Chris Fleming *Modern Conspiracy: The Importance of Being Paranoid* (Bloomsbury, London, 2014).

294 This vehicle had ten people either in it or on the running boards on either side. Eight of them were Secret Service agents. Two of those, George Hickey and Glen Bennett, sat in the rearmost seats; with Hickey on the left, Bennett on the right. Between them and the agents at the front of the vehicle sat Dave Powers and Kenny O'Donnell, JFK's close friends and personal advisers. Vincent Bugliosi *Reclaiming History: The Assassination of President John F. Kennedy* (W.W. Norton & Co., New York and London, 2007).

and is based on truly shoddy research and thinking. McLaren complains that the Warren Commission's 1964 Report was 'poorly indexed' and dismisses other conspiracy theories as ridiculous, but fails to provide citations in his own book at all and boldly advances a perfectly ridiculous and long since discredited theory. He claims to have read 'all the available evidence and testimony', but there is not a single endnote or precise citation in his book and there is no bibliography.

Frankly, his claim about all the reading he did is not credible, both because of the sheer volume of material in question (literally millions of pages) and because the glaring omissions in his little book strongly suggest he has done nothing close to what he claims. He bangs on about what a great detective he was, but shows himself to be a poor a forensic analyst by declaring that 'the problem with science is that it is often contradictory' and 'comes down to interpretation' (pp. 133 and 135), so he prefers to rely on 'the purity of witness evidence' (p. 6).

Belief in the 'purity of witness evidence' should have been drummed out of his head a long time ago. Both eye and ear witness testimony are highly unreliable and have to be very carefully sifted and collated to get even an approximation to the truth. This is one of the most glaring features of the JFK case, in which, again and again, witness testimony was clearly confused, contradictory or based on distortions of memory years after the event, because of the drama that had surrounded the killing and its aftermath.

But even if witness testimony as such could be relied upon implicitly, his use of it in this case is both extraordinarily selective and ham-fisted. He ignores an overwhelming body of testimony from Dealey Plaza that contradicts his case and puts down to government cover-up the fact that not one of the people in the Secret Service vehicle behind Kennedy's limousine testified that agent George Hickey (the alleged culprit) either fell backwards or fired his rifle. It is especially telling that neither Dave Powers nor Kenny O'Donnell did so, given their personal closeness to JFK. But McLaren's does not even mention them. Hickey's own account was that he did not pick up his rifle until after all three shots had been fired (by Oswald) and the motorcade was already going under the overpass out of Dealey Plaza.

McLaren's theory depends on Oswald firing only *two* shots, not three; since he accepts that only three shots were fired; all from behind the Presidential vehicle. Unfortunately for him, there is both material and ear witness testimony that *three* shots were fired from Oswald's sniper's perch. Three employees of the Texas School Book Depository were standing in the windows immediately below the sniper's perch at the time of the assassination and testified that they all heard three shots fired and three shells falling onto the wooden floor overhead. Was this pure or impure testimony? McLaren doesn't even refer to it. This kind confusion or omission is, unhappily, par for the course in the voluminous conspiracy literature on the JFK case. *JFK: The Smoking Gun* is riddled with it. But it's central claim so beguiles the brains of all too many people that he was able to get a book published and a film made.

Rather interestingly, McLaren dismisses all *other* conspiracy theories out of hand as 'ridiculous' without any argument, yet better than 97% of the 1,000 books that have been published on the matter advance conspiracy theories of one kind or another and only one of them agrees with him. Indeed, he gets his theory from that book, Bonar Menninger's *Mortal Error* (1992). It would have been rather more impressive had he identified precisely *why* so many people have spent years writing such books—just as he has—only to come out with ridiculous theories. Had he taken the trouble to lay out the flaws in other conspiracy theories, he might just possibly have been able to avoid constructing a ridiculous theory of his own. But that was, perhaps, too much like hard work. There was gripping fun to be had in just putting together what he thought was a highly original 'solution' to a supposedly unsolved murder.

Had he done the hard yards, he might have pinpointed the crucial misperceptions and errors that have bedevilled the case since 1963 and still lead huge numbers of people to swallow one or another conspiracy theory as compelling. Instead, he proceeded to do pretty much what other conspiracy theorists have done for fifty years:

1. Begin with a hunch (in his case, fascination with the Donahue/Menninger claim) then look for evidence to confirm it;
2. Interpret witness evidence to fit his preconceived theory, even when that evidence is clearly confused or demonstrably in error, e.g. regarding the number or direction of shots;
3. Complain of material witnesses not being asked to testify when the only reason to ask them to do so would have been if his own hypothesis was under examination, which it wasn't;
4. See conspiracy at every step without ever asking whether there could be alternative explanations, especially with regard to (a) the autopsy and (b) the Warren Commission. Thus, for example, he implies that the Secret Service imperiously controlled the autopsy, despite the presence of Army, Navy and FBI personnel, the president's personal physician and members of the Kennedy family; but he never attempts to explain how this was conceivable. What does he think the mandate of the Secret Service actually is?
5. Ask rhetorical questions again and again that presuppose the conclusion he has already drawn and point to supposed intentions or even facts that he does not demonstrate. This sits oddly with his complaint that Warren Commission lawyers too often led witnesses

With one trivial exception, embedded in the text itself (a page reference to Jim Bishop's book *The Day Kennedy Was Shot*), he provides no endnotes, footnotes, bibliography or other direct citations to pinpoint where he got his evidence from. He is extraordinarily cocksure in his assumption that he has it right and that readers will simply be taken along for the ride—like his editors.

He organizes his argument poorly, telling a story laden with personal chatter and rhetorical questions. He would have done better to have written that it has, of course, long been suspected that there was a conspiracy in the JFK case; that the core considerations need to be understood; that he believes they have not been sufficiently understood and, therefore, the wrong *kinds* of conspiracy have been suspected by everyone except him, Howard Donahue and Bonar Menninger; that he cannot readily expect us to believe him (even though he was such a splendid detective) in so extraordinary a matter and he will, therefore, set out his argument as clearly and dispassionately as possible.

That argument would then be that the key to the whole matter is that the fatal shot was a frangible bullet, which, therefore, could not have come from Oswald's rifle, but from only one source in Dealey Plaza that day. This would be the first part of the case, which would have had to be set out very carefully. The second part would have had to be that this 'mortal error' was immediately and successfully *concealed*, on a totally improvised basis, by a Secret Service that had been asleep at the wheel all along and was caught up in chaos and surrounded by other government and state officials. This, of course, is considerably harder to believe than the first part of the argument, but it is an inescapable part of the case he wants to make.

There is a third part: that the Secret Service was then subsequently *supported* in its cover-up over months and years by the Dallas Police, the FBI, the LBJ White House, the Warren Commission, the Kennedy family and their loyalists, senior Army and Navy officials and so on and so forth. The problem here, of course, is that we are in Oliver Stone territory all over again, with a conspiracy that has a cast bigger than *Ben Hur*. This is something that McLaren seems never to have contemplated. Yet it raises surely insuperable objections to his argument and should have led him back to the drawing board to discover what he had missed. It didn't; with the result that he has written a book which is an embarrassment to the name 'detective', unless we think of it simply as detective *fiction*.

In short, even if he could come up with a *plausible* case that Oswald did *not* fire three shots and that the fatal bullet *was* a frangible one (a task in which he failed), he would then have run into insuperable obstacles in making the second and third parts of his argument. A truly rational mind would see this and pause to ask: Could it not be that the solution is much simpler: that Oswald *did* fire three shots (something for which there is overwhelming evidence) and the third of them, when it penetrated JFK's skull caused a massive exit wound (not the total explosion of the skull McLaren alleges), just as the Warren Commission concluded?

The source of his complete muddle about the bullets is his uncritical acceptance of the old cliché that all the shooting took place within 5.6 or 6 seconds. In fact, the Zapruder film and careful examination of witness testimony show that the first shot (which missed the motorcade) was fired more than 8 seconds before the fatal shot. It came at about Zapruder film frame 160 to 165. The fatal shot came at frame 314. The film moves at 18.3 frames per second. You do the arithmetic. What McLaren should have done, as official inquiries and the best analysis have done, is use the Zapruder film as a chronometer. He would then have realized that you only get 5.6 to 6 seconds total shooting time if you assume that the neck shot was the first shot. In fact, it was the second shot, somewhere between film frames 210 and 222.

The first shot was fired well before the neck shot. As Governor Connally pointed out to the Warren Commission, he heard the first shot shortly after the motorcade turned into Elm St and turned around to his right rear to try to see where the shot had come from, since as a hunter he recognized it as a rifle shot. He could not discern anything and was turning back around to look in another direction when the second shot hit JFK in the back of the neck, came out through his throat and then passed through Connally in the back and chest, fracturing a rib, before hitting his thigh and wrist.

McLaren puts a lot of weight on Jim Bishop's attribution to Clint Hill of the statement to Bobby Kennedy, from Parkland Hospital, that 'There's been an accident.' Given his belief that the 'accident' was Hickey killing JFK by mistake, this is unsurprising. But he does not pause to ask what JFK's very close brother, who was the US Attorney General, made of that line. Nothing? Why would that be? We know, in fact, that Bobby Kennedy believed to his dying day that there had been a conspiracy in the matter of JFK's assassination[295], but there is not a scintilla of evidence

---

295 The best book on this subject is David Talbot *Brothers: The Hidden History of the Kennedy Years* (Free Press, New York, 2007). He remarks in an Author's Note at the beginning of his book:

> *Bobby Kennedy was the president's devoted partner, as well as the nation's top lawman. It has long been a mystery why he apparently did nothing to investigate his brother's shocking death on November 22, 1963. I have sought to understand this enduring mystery by not only immersing myself in the deep well of Kennedy scholarship, but by poring over newly released government documents and, most important, by reliving these years with the Kennedys' 'band of brothers', as Bobby called them—the living links to the New Frontier—before this political generation disappears entirely.*
>
> *What I discovered is that Robert Kennedy did not resign himself to the lone gunman theory, the official version of his brother's death. On the contrary, he immediately suspected that President Kennedy was the victim of a powerful conspiracy. And he spent the rest of his life secretly searching for the truth about his brother's murder. This book will not only shine a light on Robert Kennedy's hidden quest; it will seek to explain why he came to such a dark understanding of JFK's death.*

Unfortunately, at the end of his book, he succumbs to the old lure of discovering dubious 'confessions' pointing to CIA involvement in the assassination, believes them, but then fails completely to drive home an inquiry into whether they line up with the known realities of the assassination. He indulges in all the old conspiracy theory language about CIA agents and Mafia hit men without making any

that I am aware of—and McLaren does not cite any—to suggest that he thought the conspiracy in question was a Secret Service cover-up of a huge and fatal blunder. He suspected the Mafia and the Teamsters or Castro—but by McLaren's account such notions were and are 'ridiculous'.

He claims that Hickey fired a shot from the AR-15, but provides no direct evidence that such a shot was fired; only evidence that Hickey picked up the rifle and then fell backwards. When exactly he did this remains unclear, even going by the confused witness testimony McLaren cites. Moreover, he makes no attempt to demonstrate that the angle of Hickey's rifle at the critical moment was such that a shot, if fired, *could* have hit JFK in the back of the head. He simply assumes that it *must* have done, because he has already decided (for other reasons) that the bullet in question was a frangible one and ergo came from Hickey's AR-15.

A great deal depends, therefore, on his claim that the fatal bullet *was* a frangible one. In fact, this is the pivotal claim in his case. He goes to considerable lengths to demonstrate that it was, but by his own account the science is inconclusive and he relies on what he calls 'the purity of witness testimony'. But the scientific tests are only part of the picture. Given that, by his own account, only three shots were fired, all from behind, the conceptual space for a frangible bullet would only have opened up had he been able to establish that Oswald fired only two bullets. He fails totally in that critical part of his argument. Case closed.

If you want to read a good (but still errant) 'conspiracy theory' about the JFK assassination, your best bet is either of two novels: Charles McCarry's *The Tears of Autumn* (1974) or Don De Lillo's *Libra* (1988). Each is much tighter, better researched and far better written than McLaren's book. If, on the other hand, you seriously want to get your mind around the whole JFK conspiracy debate, you must read Vincent Bugliosi's *Reclaiming History: The Assassination of President John F. Kennedy* (2007). Above all, if you want to do yourself a favour on the party circuit, don't, for heaven's sake, go around chattering about how 'compelling' McLaren's book is. He thinks he finally found the proverbial 'smoking gun'. His book is a pile of smoking something, but it's author is no gun.

---

attempt to establish that anyone other than Lee Harvey Oswald was involved in firing shots; or that Oswald was in any way a credible hit man for such a high level conspiracy.

A Young Hazara Woman Off a Boat[296]

Last year[297] I befriended a young Hazara woman who had arrived in Australia by boat via Indonesia and been detained, first on Christmas Island, then in Melbourne. She and her ailing mother had fled persecution and harassment in Iran, as her mother's and father's families had both fled persecution in Afghanistan, a generation before.

She is an extraordinarily dignified, highly intelligent and principled young woman; the kind of refugee we should be welcoming with open arms. But she is on a temporary bridging visa and faces a highly uncertain future. Getting to know her and learning her story has humanized the asylum seeker debate for me as never before.

I read Paul Toohey's Quarterly Essay against this background, with both personal engagement and intense intellectual interest. At just 94 pages, it is a valuable resource for anyone who is both flummoxed by the state of the debate and time poor in terms of coming to grips with it. In that sense, it is a fine contribution and perhaps one of the most useful and important of Black Inc.'s long series of Quarterly Essays.

It is at its best in bringing the specifically human side of the matter vividly to life. It both begins and ends with the story of an enraged Afghan refugee, Ali Reza Bahrami, whose personal story (of persecution as a Hazara in eastern Iran) is stunningly similar to that of my young friend. In between, there are many more touching stories of women and children and deaths at sea that, in a quite classic manner, should find a place at the centre of our moral reflections on this vexed subject.

Toohey has done strenuous and wrenching field work in Java and tells heart-rending tales of exploitation, tragic bereavement, bewilderment and longing. Everyone who has come to see the matter in abstract or merely political terms should read these tales. Their moral implications and emotional resonance are inescapable.

Moreover, Toohey embeds these tales within a coherent narrative of how the people smugglers work, how those who make their way to Indonesia in the hope of reaching Australia

---

296 Paul Toohey *That Sinking Feeling: Asylum Seekers and the Search for the Indonesian Solution* Quarterly Essay, Issue 53, 2014. This piece was first published in *The Australian's* weekend review.

297 This means in 2013, the year that Elnaz Tavancheh and her mother arrived in Australia. They reached Christmas Island on her 21st birthday, after considerable drama in Indonesia and at sea. Elnaz has since attended Parade College, Bundoora, in 2014 to undertake her Year 12 studies (the only female student ever to attend the College). She achieved an outstanding ATAR score of 89 and is now a student at Latrobe University, studying biomedical technology and again achieving outstanding grades. The university created a new scholarship for people in her situation, of which she has become the first recipient.

by boat actually live while still in Indonesia (chiefly in the town of Cisarua, which has become asylum-seeker central) and the impact on those of them who fell victim to the belated reversal of Labour policy under Kevin Rudd last year and were shunted off to Manus Island.

He also exhibits enough hard-headedness to make a couple of points that too often get lost in the heat of the political debate. The first is that those arriving by boat are, in fact, illegal arrivals under both the United Nations people smuggling protocol and the 1951 Refugee Convention, even though, as he expresses it 'they have not committed any crime or broken any international law.'

The second is that a good many of those arriving by boat, especially from Iran, are in fact not refugees, but simply people determined to get away from regimes and economic circumstances that weary them (such as the theocratic regime of the Shiite mullahs in Iran). Here the statistics are telling. He observes:

> ... *from June 2012 to June 2013 ... when 25,126 people came by boat ... Sri Lankans led the numbers with 6862 boat arrivals, followed by 6579 Iranians. And these Iranians had come out of nowhere, suddenly and easily overtaking the Hazaras, most of whom could readily prove they were suffering persecution, whether they'd come directly from Afghanistan or were living as exiles in Iran or Pakistan—where, in the city of Quetta, there was a program afoot to suicide bomb them from the face of the earth.*

He doesn't draw any hard or fast conclusion from all this about whether the Iranians should be accepted. What he does do is point out that, too often, Australians fail to make any meaningful distinction between Iranians, Afghans, Iraqis, Sunni and Shia, Hazaras, Tamil Sri Lankans or Burmese Rohingyas, due to a combination of ignorance, fear and resentment. Lamentably, he reminds us, the political rhetoric from the major parties has only exacerbated these deficiencies in popular understanding.

The least satisfying characteristic of the essay, however, is precisely Toohey's plainly frustrated but unsystematic treatment of the political debate. Perhaps his finest moment is when he fires a broadside at Kevin Rudd for his shameless moral backflip on the matter. In a 2006 essay in *The Monthly*, Rudd invoked Dietrich Bonhoeffer, Christian compassion and the 'Biblical injunction to care for the stranger in our midst'. But in 2013, Toohey remarks savagely, 'Rudd was, to borrow one of his own terms, rat-fucking asylum seekers to win himself another term.'

Toohey makes many another barbed remark about the politics of the matter. What he doesn't do is make any kind of clear argument about what should be done to turn the situation around. He does a lot of hand-waving about Australia needing to work for an Indonesian solution, but he is singularly vague about how exactly this would work.

It would have been bracing had he, instead, concisely set forth a proposal for change, including legislation and new quotas, onshore processing of a practical and humane kind and public diplomacy about Australia being a land of opportunity rather than an island fortress. But one cannot do everything in a single essay, I suppose.[298]

---

298 In late May 2015, as this book was in press, Social Services Minister Scott Morrison 'warned that Australia risks creating an underclass of migrants unless urgent action is taken to equip these new arrivals with the skills necessary to participate in mainstream Australian life. These migrants, many of them Muslim, would be vulnerable to the predations of criminals and extremists without help, Mr Morrison said.' *The Weekend Australian*, 23-24 May 2015 p. 1. The case of Elnaz Tavancheh makes clear that integration can be an outstanding success – at least where there is 'promising material'. What, then, will be the program of integration, after the long delay in recognizing the need for it?

Stan Wawrinka at the Australian Open[299]

This year's Australian Open has already been engrossing and is building to a climax. Tonight Stanislas Wawrinka plays off in one of the Australian Open semi-finals against Czech seventh seed Thomas Berdych. It should be a terrific match, going by Wawrinka's unforgettable quarter-final match against his long-time nemesis Novak Djokovic. That was an epic battle, with numerous fantastic rallies and many spectacular strokes; Wawrinka finally winning the fifth set 9-7.

Two things stood out about it, apart from the quality of the tennis and the fact that Wawrinka had finally defeated the brilliant and ascending Joker. The first was the extraordinary graciousness of the loser; the second was the discovery that the winner has a tattoo on his arm which, perhaps, we could all take to heart—especially after Wawrinka's win.

After a fiercely competitive match, throughout which he several times roared with satisfaction at winning key points and consistently avoided eye contact with his rival when they went to their chairs for breaks between sets, Novak Djokovic exhibited almost tenderness towards an equally humble and friendly Wawrinka at the net when the match was over.

The picture should be framed. It was an enormous credit to the character of both individuals and put tennis itself in a very good light. There was a similar moment at the net after the superb Rafael Nadal defeated the talented youngster Thanasi Kokkinakis. In that case, the encounter was different, though. It was almost like a father and son, a man and a boy, a master and an apprentice.

With Djokovic and Wawrinka, on the other hand, it was two rivals who have met many times, with Djokovic invariably winning. There was no asymmetry in physique or age, only in achievement. And this is where Wawrinka's tattoo comes in. It is an epigram from the writings of Samuel Beckett and reads:

> *Ever tried? Ever failed? No matter. Try Again. Fail again. Fail better.*

That is a great epigram and one we might all do well to learn by heart. Human life is about striving

---

299 As I edited this manuscript, the Australian Open was again under way for 2015 and Stanislas Wawrinka again won through to a semi-final—where, as it happens, he faced Novak Djokovic; while Tomas Berdych faced off against Andy Murray in the other semi-final. But the big news was that he actually *won* the Australian Open in January 2014. He defeated Tomas Berdych in the semi-final and went on to defeat the great and tenacious Rafael Nadal in the final. In 2015, he went down to Djokovic in a five set epic, collapsing in the final set to go down 0-6, very much to my disappointment and, I'm sure, that of many other spectators, who hoped to see the match go right down to the proverbial wire. Murray overwhelmed Berdych in the other semi-final, stood toe to toe against Djokovic in the final for two magnificent sets, but then also capitulated or was himself overwhelmed, losing twelve of the last thirteen games, to bow out 6-7, 7-6, 3-6, 0-6; giving the remarkable and resilient Djokovic his fifth Australian Open cup and his eighth Grand Slam trophy.

and almost always falling short of the goals, hopes or standards we set ourselves. Winning, it has been said, comes from getting up off the floor just one more time. In Wawrinka's case, this came true last night. In fact, it came true several times within the match, not just in this match compared with fourteen previous losses to the great Djokovic.

But note that the epigram does not say, Try again and you are sure to win. It says, Fail again. Fail better. Fail better! Magnificent words! And Wawrinka will carry them with him now into a semi-final and, who knows, perhaps a final, in which he will have to face new and formidable opponents. Perhaps he will win, but his record, his tattoo, the human challenge is not to win at all costs, it is to strive and, given the probability of failure, to *fail better*.

Today, Wawrinka will confront Tomas Berdych in a semi-final. As he put it on Tuesday night, 'I'm still far from winning the tournament'. He still has two difficult matches to go if he is to win the title. But he added:

> *I'm not thinking at all about that, to be honest. I'm thinking match by match. Tonight I'm going to enjoy the victory of today because I think it's important. That's why I've played well over the last year, because I'm enjoying my life, I'm enjoying the tennis.*

Isn't that both important and refreshing? Isn't all this what each of would do well to bear in mind as we go: to strive with integrity, to win if we can, but to fail better if we cannot win; to be both gracious and resilient in defeat and to enjoy and savour our victories with a sense of proportion and a sense of humility? I think Stanislas Wawrinka is admirable and set a wonderful example to us all on Tuesday evening.

This is worth dwelling on for another reason. Sport in general and elite sport in particular have suffered in recent years from several corruptions: the insidious mantra that winning is everything and there are 'no prizes for second place'; the immense amounts of money that now accrue to stars and sporting associations; and the taint of cheating, whether with performance enhancing drugs or through betting and match-fixing.

We have seen wonderful upset victories in the Australian Open, fine athletes 'failing better', but above all a pretty consistent exhibition of authentic sporting spirit. So far, I think Stanislas 'Stan the Man' Wawrinka's performance has, in every sense, set the bar highest and merited the greatest accolades. Let's remember him for that and hope that not only the rest of the Australian Open, but other sporting competitions in 2014 rise to something like his standards.

Dog days punditry and the mining boom

Ross Garnaut's recent book *Dog Days* has warned that we feckless Australians wasted the resources boom and could now pay a stiff price for our profligacy. Andrew Charlton's new Quarterly Essay, *Dragon's Tail: The Lucky Country after the China Boom* sits squarely within this school of thought. John Edwards, who sits on the Board of the Reserve Bank and who played a key role in the reforms of the Keating era, pointedly disagrees with it.

In a ringing passage in *Beyond the Boom*, he states:

> *In all important respects—savings, investment in physical assets and in human capital, workforce participation, moderation in both household consumption and house spending—Australians during the resources boom have been more frugal, hardworking and attentive to the future than they were during the two previous decades, though those two decades are often recalled as models of exemplary behaviour compared to our later fecklessness.*

If you want to grapple with the debate about the structure, dynamics and future of our economy, Edwards' little book is an ideal counterpart to Ross Garnaut's indispensable and challenging book. Taken together, they will provide you with a clear set of parameters for understanding the policy dilemmas we face and developing an informed opinion about them.

Dragon's Tail, like many of the Quarterly Essays, is also highly readable; but it is more literary than analytical, when compared with *Dog Days* or *Beyond the Boom*. It paints a picture of the mining boom's impact on Australia and of how the dizzying rise of China has transformed our economy and our neighbourhood. It points out that the boom is ending not because of anything we did, but because China's growth model has reached a crucial turning point, requiring institutional and political reforms. Understand that.

Charlton's discussion of China's internal challenges is quite well informed. He hedges his bets, however, on the chances of institutional reform in China, especially financial sector reform; and refrains from comment on the political implications of a massive shift from investment to consumption driven growth. This softens and diminishes the essay. Edwards doesn't attempt a survey of China. He confines himself to an analysis of Australia's fiscal policies and trade balances. He argues that the mining boom, in terms of commodity exports is really not over, only the investment boom and that LNG could soon make Japan, not China, our largest export market again.

Pivotal to Charlton's overall position are two claims that Edwards challenges. The first is that Australia's economic history has been marked by resource booms bringing windfall gains, complacency about macro-economic policy given such gains and a long decline in economic performance (between 1890 and 1990) from which only the reforms of the 1980s and 1990s rescued us. The second is that we had another great period of windfall gains in the 2000s and were just as profligate and lacking in foresight this time as in the gold rush era before 1890; so that we could, unless we are disciplined and pro-active, again start sliding down the economic league tables.

He provides two graphs, showing that in statistical terms, Australians were the richest people in the world by the 1880s, slid gradually down the league tables to a nadir of number 21 by 1990 (the era when Lee Kuan Yew declared that we were becoming the 'poor white trash of Asia'); then climbed back to number 7 by 2012. Yet he declares that 'the end of the China boom has brought Australia to a point of vulnerability all of our own making.'

The indictment is unsparing and fairly familiar:

> *We have allowed temporary wealth to wash through the economy, eroding the competitiveness of industries other than mining. Governments on both sides of politics have used the temporary revenues of the boom to fund permanent tax cuts and spending increases. We have failed to prepare our economy and our people for life after the boom.*

Edwards, drawing on Ian McLean's path-breaking 2012 book, *Why Australia Prospered*, rejects the historical claim as the 'black armband' school of Australian economic history. McLean argues that, over the long haul, Australia has managed its economy remarkably well. Drawing on contemporary data, Edwards shows that claims of feckless complacency during the boom are greatly exaggerated. Both the windfall gains and their impact on the economy, he argues, have been overestimated.

The message of *Beyond the Boom* is that 'Australia comes from a position of strength rather than weakness, and achievement rather than failure' in looking ahead at the next set of challenges and opportunities:

> *For all the hype, the mining boom has been but one more episode in Australia's uninterrupted expansion over more than two decades, and in some respects not the most important one. Australian output grew faster in the ten years before the mining boom began than it has since. Incomes and employment rose just as much before as after ... Nor, for all the indignant scolding, can it reasonably be said that Australians have been merely the lucky beneficiaries of China's explosive growth, or that they have complacently dozed through an unparalleled opportunity to reshape their nation and prepare for the challenges ahead. Australians have been saving more, investing more, working more and learning more.*

The chief weakness of his book is that, in contrast with Garnaut, he does not set out a policy agenda for meeting the challenges ahead. They are in agreement that the reforms of the 1980s and 1990s gave Australia a much more flexible and open economy and ignited the long growth surge that has had us called a miracle economy within the OECD. They also agree that the export of agricultural commodities and services, rather than manufactures, will have to make up for the slowing of commodity exports in future, if our growth is to be sustained. They disagree on the handling of the mining boom and its implications. Edwards is both more sanguine and, correspondingly, less prescriptive than is Garnaut.

No chapter of *Beyond the Boom* better exhibits Edwards' position than 'Did the Australian government waste the boom?'. He pinpoints the precipitous budgetary fall into a deficit of proportions dwarfing any previous Australian experience, including the Great Depression. He points out, however, that 'tax revenue as a share of GDP fell by nearly *ten times as much as spending increased* as a share of GDP' between 2007 and 2013. That was the root of the problem.

Income tax cuts, not lack of mining taxes were decisive. Annual company tax revenue grew from $40 billion in 2003 to $61 billion in 2009. Mining company tax soared from $2.8 to $13.4 billion. Budgetary surpluses rose from $8 billion to $20 billion. The Howard government decided to dispense 'lower personal income tax rates, flatten tax scales and extend superannuation tax concessions'. Just as these kicked in, the situation changed and structural deficits suddenly loomed large.

Even so, Edwards believes that a steady fiscal hand for a few years and ordinary bracket creep can solve the problem. Garnaut believes much more than that is needed if we are to avoid a prolonged recession. Don't read one; read both and join what Garnaut calls the 'independent centre' committed to public interest policy.

Cancer as a cellular atavism

In 1971, President Nixon declared that the United States would 'conquer cancer within five years'. It was a clarion call, much like JFK's call to put a man on the moon by the end of the 1960s. *That* goal was achieved. Not so the conquest of cancer. We're not even close to doing so now. That doesn't mean, of course, that we should abandon science and rush off into nutty fads. On the contrary, it clearly means the problem is exceptionally challenging and any new thinking must pass very rigorous tests to be taken seriously.

That's the context in which astrobiologist Paul Davies and a team of inter-disciplinary investigators have been looking afresh at the problem. As he expressed it recently at the Adelaide Festival of Ideas, broadcast on Robyn Williams' Science Show on the ABC, after decades and hundreds of billions of dollars, cancer is very much unconquered. The US government spends more annually on cancer research than on space exploration. Yet cancer incidence is increasing and the cost of cancer care is ballooning. This isn't just a health crisis. It's a budgetary crisis. It's also a scientific one.

We've taken huge strides in the suppression of infectious diseases globally, Davies observes. What's so intractable about cancer? Good question. He related that he had been called a few years ago by the deputy director of the US National Cancer Institute, Anna Barker, and asked to help assemble a team to *rethink cancer* from the ground up. He exclaimed to her, 'I know nothing about cancer'. To which she responded, 'That's perfect'. She wanted a first rate scientific mind free of the embedded assumptions of cancer orthodoxy.[300]

She sought critical thinking about assumptions and an inter-disciplinary inquiry about realities. They set up a number of Centres for Physical Science and Oncology to 'change the culture of thinking, the culture of research in cancer biology'. They began by asking 'What *is* cancer? Why does it exist?' They discovered that there is actually *no* well-defined theory of cancer and that current attempts to 'conquer' it are based on a number of dubious assumptions.

---

300   Cancer orthodoxy has been challenged again and again over the past century and more, as doctors and researchers grappled with the proliferating and multi-faceted disease (or family of diseases). See Siddhartha Mukherjee *The Emperor of All Maladies: A Biography of Cancer* (Scribner, New York, 2010). The inquiry into cancer is, of course, but one of the many, many areas in which, largely since the 18th century, but especially since the early 20th century, our sciences have tackled the myriad material complexities of the world of microbes, infections and morbidities within which our species lives and dies. Two excellent introductions to this larger story are Roy Porter *Flesh in the Age of Reason* (Allen Land, London, 2003) and Daniel E. Lieberman *The Story of the Human Body: Evolution, Health and Disease* (Pantheon Books, New York, 2013).

Physicians have a lot of details, a lot of facts, but no real understanding of why cancer happens in the first place, Davies says.

The standard theory or *dogma* (Davies' word) is that cancer is due to molecular damage at the genetic level, a harmful mutation of some kind. This leads to the current battery of attempts to destroy the cancerous growths by cutting them out, burning them, poisoning them or cutting off their growth paths. If this sounds like violent counter-insurgency or counter-terrorism, that's because it is. Current cancer care is like the Vietnam War or the wars in Iraq and Afghanistan. It's going about as well—and I speak as something of a specialist on the history of counterinsurgency.

The alternative view or *heresy* advanced by Davies and his colleagues is that cancer is an *atavism*—an evolutionary regression. It is 'an accident waiting to happen' because of a pre-programmed sub-routine embedded in *all* cells that dates back billions of years to when cells were prokaryotic and reproduced by self-replication. Cancer, in other words, is evolution going into reverse gear at high speed for fortuitous reasons. It isn't a disease, but a breakdown of the implicit inter-cellular bargain that makes multicellular organisms possible—from sponges to human beings.

According to the heretics, *all* cells have the potential to become cancer cells, but even when they do so many regulatory mechanisms generally keep them in check. For this reason, cancer cells and even tumorous growths can be dormant for years or can go into remission for reasons that *do not show up* in the orthodox dogmatic view. It is not the case that people either have or do not have cancer, it's latent in everyone and only more or less under control.

Is this heresy scientifically accurate? Davies declares that no theory is of any use unless it is testable and the teams are busy testing it in a number of ways. But the implications are surely very interesting. As he remarks, if the heretics are on the right biological track, huge efforts and vast sums of money have been expended in attacking the *wrong targets*. Not understanding what cancer is, the counterinsurgency teams have been attacking its strengths, instead of its weaknesses. Think of Robert McNamara and the Ho Chi Minh trail.

Cancer, Davies points out, is common to all multi-cellular organisms. It didn't begin with tobacco or sunbaking. This is a vital clue. The beginnings of such organisms take us back one and a half billion years. The heretics are now busy tracing the genetic pathways back to their origin and exploring the weaknesses of self-replicating cells. Cell biology is clearly crucial in any case; but perhaps cellular evolution is the real key.

Three candidate weaknesses have been identified. The cell behaviour of cancer evolved in an oxygen depleted environment. We might, therefore, attack cancer with high doses of *oxygen*.

Adaptive immunity evolved only 400 million years ago—which happens to be around the time when life forms first emerged from the oceans and began to colonize the land environment. We might, therefore, attack cancer with infectious germs. The body's immune system, suitably inoculated, would protect the patient, while the germs killed the cancer cells. Or we might deprive the cancer of glucose, which it feeds on.

Are Davies and his inter-disciplinary teams on the right track? They might not be. But three things are notable about their undertaking: it is only occurring because the existing science and cancer care system is floundering;[301] it is based on critical thinking at the most fundamental level about what cancer is and how to understand its behaviour; and it is grounded in both solid biological science and systematic scientific method. All these things make it important, fascinating and exemplary. Similar critical thinking is called for in many other domains.

---

301 It is only fair to add that the rate of innovation in medical means for attacking or blocking cancer is very rapid in this decade. I am closely attuned to it, since I face a life-threatening metastatic melanoma. Since March 2014, I have been provided with a series of medical interventions designed not, like old fashioned chemotherapy, to simply poison the cancer cells; but to block the pathways that make their proliferation possible genetically (Dabrafenib and Trametinib) or to mobilize the immune system to attack the melanoma as if it was an infectious disease, which is to say to recognize it as dangerous and seek to destroy it by natural means (Ipilimumab and Nivolumab). These treatments are ferociously expensive and their success rate is, in every case, less than 50%, which means less than the odds in a coin toss. Nonetheless, they are scientifically fascinating and at the cutting edge of the current understanding of what cancer (or at least melanoma) is and how to check it.

Duty: the Pentagon memoirs of Robert Gates[302]

When the memoirs of Robert Gates were released in Australia, in mid-January, much was made of his alleged criticisms of Barack Obama. Gates was a holdover from the Bush administration and is a lifelong Republican, as well as the former head of the CIA; so those already inclined to be critical of Obama—or for that matter those more inclined to leap to his defence—might be expected to jump on any criticism of the President by his former Secretary of Defence.

Yet what emerges unequivocally from the memoir is not Gates's *criticism* of Obama, but his lavish *praise* of the man. This needs to be registered forcefully, if the criticisms (which have to do chiefly with the Defence budget and the withdrawal from Afghanistan) are to be kept in perspective.

It's important to remember that Gates had been a career CIA man between 1968 and 1993, rising through its ranks and working, for a while, also on the National Security Council. He worked under Presidents Johnson, Nixon, Ford, Carter, Reagan, George H. W. Bush and Clinton. He then retired, in 1993, writing a memoir - *From the Shadows* - published in 1996. For a decade he enjoyed a different life, becoming president of Texas A&M University in 2002, but was called back into the civil service by President George W. Bush, in late 2006.

Against this background and his Wichita Kansas Republican upbringing, it is striking to find Gates writing what he did about Obama as a man and as a decision-maker, on pp. 299-300:

> *Obama was the most deliberative president I worked for. His approach to problem solving reminded me of Lincoln's comment on his approach to decision-making: 'I am never easy when I am handling a thought, till I have bounded it north, and bounded it south, and bounded it east and bounded it west.'*
> *... I rarely saw him rush to a decision when circumstances allowed him time to gather information, analyze and reflect. He would sometimes be criticized for his 'dilatory' decision-making, but I found it refreshing and reassuring ... When the occasion demanded it, though, Obama could make a big decision—a life and death decision—very fast ... .I never saw anyone who had not previously been an executive—and especially someone who had been a legislator—take so quickly and easily to making decisions and so relish exercising authority ...*
>
> *I always thought Obama was 'presidential'. He treated the office of the presidency with respect ... He was a man of personal integrity and, in his personal behavior—at least to the extent that I could observe it—he was an excellent role model ... I often wished both Bush and Obama would be less partisan, but clearly the political world had changed since I retired the first time, in 1993. I thought Obama was first rate in both intellect and temperament. You didn't have to agree with all of his policies to acknowledge that.*

---

302 This essay was published in *Quadrant* in mid-2014 under the title 'The civil servant and the insurgents'. An edited version of it was also published in the *Australia Israel Review* shortly afterwards.

That is a long quotation for a review, however it demonstrates not only that Gates was not a partisan Republican sniping at Obama; but also his more general commitment to non-partisan thinking, judgment and service to country. The relentless personal attacks on successive US presidents in recent decades, from both sides of politics, have not served America well. Gates, however, *did* serve America well and his memoir is a study in what that means.

Duty is one of those books which needs to be read alongside of or in the context of several others in the effort to gain clear perspective. One thinks of the memoirs of his predecessor, Donald Rumsfeld, *Known and Unknown: A Memoir* (2011) and of President George W. Bush *Decision Points* (2010); or Bob Woodward's books on Bush at war and Obama at war.

But the book that seems to me to best complement *Duty* is Fred Kaplan's *The Insurgents: David Petraeus and the Plot to Change the American Way of War* - primarily because, by Kaplan's account, Gates became 'the insurgent in the Pentagon' as Secretary of Defence.

The 'insurgents' were a small number of military officers, chiefly graduates of West Point's social sciences and humanities department (SOSH) who took an interest in the theory of counter-insurgency in the 1980s and 1990s, then revived it—against strenuous mainstream resistance—for application in Iraq and Afghanistan from 2006-07.

This intersects with Gates's memoir because Gates is incomparably more critical of the Pentagon, White House staffers and the Congress than he ever is of Barack Obama. He took over from Rumsfeld at a time when the war in Iraq had become a debacle, while the one in Afghanistan had become neglected. He was stunned to find that senior echelons of the military and many others in the Pentagon regarded these wars as ephemeral sideshows, with the consequence that they were not paying attention to what was required to fight them effectively.

Currently, the Abbott government here in Australia is uncertain how to go about reviewing, reforming and running the Department of Defence, with a mere 100,000 military and civilian personnel amidst a peace-time environment. Imagine the task which confronted Gates in 2006: a gargantuan organization with three million personnel, a budget in the many hundreds of billions, two prolonged, increasingly costly and controversial wars and enormous Congressional inertia and pork-barreling around defence procurement.

It is his impressively candid account of these matters that chiefly gives *Duty* its weight and its considerable value. All the more so because Gates had not been a career Defence bureaucrat or military man and had not sought the job as Secretary of Defence. He accepted it and stayed on solely out of a sense of—duty. There is an air of civic virtue of a quite classical kind about his attitude to public service and his cherishing of private life.

There are countless matters of detail in the book's six hundred or so pages, but the most striking thing about it as a whole is the manner in which Gates so consistently exhibits a trenchant commitment to the public good. As I read the book, I found myself thinking at times that it could almost be made required reading for anyone setting out to become a serious civil servant.

Inevitably, the Iraq war bulked largest in his preoccupations throughout his time at the Pentagon. His second chapter is titled 'Iraq, Iraq, Iraq'. His judgment of the matter is lucidly set out early:

> *I knew for sure that whatever people had thought about the decision to go to war in Iraq, at this point (late 2006) we could not fail. A defeat of the US military and an Iraqi descent into a vicious civil war that likely would engage other countries in the region would be disastrous, destabilizing the region and dramatically boosting Iran's power and prestige. In the months of furious criticism of Bush's surge that would follow, I never heard the critics address the risk that their preferred approach of a precipitous withdrawal would, in fact, lead to these very consequences.*

He adds that, with a view to retrieving the situation, he not only approved the surge itself, but recommended that General George Casey, the commander in Iraq, be replaced by General David Petraeus, as 'the right man' for the job.

This is where *Duty* intersects with *The Insurgents*. The latter tells in gripping detail the story of those military officers, foremost among them David Petraeus, who had spent their professional careers thinking about and arguing for a US capacity for 'stabilization operations' or 'COIN' of the kind that was crucial to the considerable success of the surge in turning the situation in Iraq around in 2007.

My own doctorate in International Relations, written in the mid-1980s, centered on US counter-insurgency operations throughout the Cold War—in the Philippines, Vietnam and El Salvador, in particular. *The Insurgents* shows that the young David Petraeus and a number of others were immersing themselves in the same topic at the same time. Had I found my way to the United States in the late 1980s to do a post-doc, I might well have found myself networked with this circle of thinkers—as Australia's own Lieutenant Colonel David Kilcullen did twenty years later.

I didn't do that, but reading *The Insurgents* alongside *Duty* brought back countless insights and interests of my own from the 1980s and threw into high relief the importance of critical thinking about force structure, strategy, tactics, policy and operational planning at every level—and how it is, again and again, subverted by institutional inertia, institutional amnesia and perverse incentives.

The two books, taken together, are a wonderful study of all this. Gates's memoir is a reminder that it is still possible to be a genuine, professional, non-partisan civil servant. His praise of Obama's qualities of deliberation is a reminder that such qualities are vital - not only in a chief executive, but right down the chain of command. The story of *The Insurgents* shows some of

America's best and brightest military officers exhibiting those qualities in the schools, training grounds and combat zones to which they were assigned.

Reading the two books left me with the belief that as many people in our own national security institutions as possible should read both books. Indeed, I briefly entertained the fantasy of running an intellectual retreat for senior Defence officials and military officers in which the two books would be thoroughly discussed and their relevance to Australian experience explored. But that was only a fantasy. My days with Defence are long over and, like Gates, I cherish the freedoms of private life too much to wade back in.

Section 7: 2014-15

Noah: a fatuous cartoon

By seeming coincidence, Darren Aronofsky's film *Noah* has come out at the same time as the IPCC's Fifth Assessment Report (AR5). It reportedly grossed $US44 million on its opening weekend, so it seems certain to make a wider and deeper impact than AR5. But *Noah* is a thoroughly silly film. As a few religious purists have pointed out, it makes very free with the original fable in chapters 5 to 8 of *Genesis*; but that is the least of its problems. From an ecological, historical and moral point of view, *Noah* is confused, misleading and nonsensical from start to finish. When we should all be debating the merits of AR5, it is an absurd take on ecological reality.

I don't recommend it, but should you decide to go and see the film (starring Russell Crowe, Jennifer Connolly and Anthony Hopkins), read the Biblical text first, to refresh on the old tale. Robert Alter's splendid translation (with commentary) of *The Five Books of Moses* provides the best version of the matter, but the King James Bible will do almost as well. Reading or re-reading the story will give you a point of reference against which to consider Aronofsky's ahistorical, anti-scientific and technologically delusional fable.

Noah (Crowe) and his family are shown as the only virtuous human beings left on Earth. They are depicted as vegetarian (perhaps even vegan) though, oddly, they live in a barren, stony landscape with no sign of greenery to sustain their gentle lifestyle. They abhor the hunting of animals and the eating of meat. We are told, through the mouths of a stone giant ('fallen angel') and Noah himself, that until the 'fall' of man and his lapse into evil, nature was peaceful and harmonious and 'everything had its place'. But then the fallen angels helped the children of Cain to develop an 'industrial civilization' that utterly denuded the Earth, making it a wasteland.

Noah becomes a complete misanthrope, concluding, based on his dreams, that God intends to wipe out the entire human species. Only he and his family will be (temporarily) spared, so that they can save breeding pairs of every species of animal (and presumably plant, though that is left unclear in the film) by taking them into the Ark—a huge shipping crate made of logs and tar. After the extermination of humanity, God will recreate Eden, as the animals resume their harmonious existence. Noah's wife (Connolly), however, persuades him that this is too harsh a judgement and that God surely intends their family to replenish humanity also; through their two infant granddaughters. Never mind that it would only be through incest that those granddaughters could reproduce. Perhaps parthenogenesis or virgin births are presumed?

What Earthly purpose is served by projecting all this nonsense on the cinema screen? It has been called 'the least Biblical of Biblical films', but in many respects it is all too Biblical and in any case the Bible is actually beside the point. *Reality* is the point and the Bible itself has only ever had a very tenuous grip on reality. Even if Aronofsky intended only to offer a simple-minded children's story he is off-beam. One suspects, however, that he and his collaborators believe they have presented us with a serious parable for our time. If that is their belief, they have got it terribly wrong.

Parables are all very well, but Biblical tales have a tendency to be taken rather literally and, given what is at stake in this case, all audiences need to be reminded that, in reality, the world was *not created* by a confused and vengeful deity (male or female); our species did *not* arrive full-blown 'in God's image' in an Eden of peace and harmony; we did *not* 'fall from grace' and lapse into evil and we did not learn our technology from 'fallen angels'. Our history, while marred by violence, greed and stupidity, has nonetheless been an *ascent* to extraordinary collective accomplishment and the creative transformation of what it *means* to be human.

Shared recognition of these things should frame any *instructive* fable we might use to bring alive the public imagination. For the reality is that the Earth is 4.5 billion years old, not a few thousand. Life has evolved over 3.8 billion of those years. Our own biological ancestry goes all the way back and is still encoded in our cells. Natural catastrophes, mass extinctions, predation and danger, parasitism, disease, famine and monstrosity have *always* characterized life on Earth, especially since the Cambrian explosion of complex life forms more than half a billion years ago. A serious parable for our time would situate our dilemmas in this vast and turbulent context.

I left the cinema after watching *Noah* not quite sure whether to feel bemused, annoyed or merely dismissive. I returned to my study in the world of AR5 and the debates over what kind of energy mix is most likely to prove viable for the 21st century; what manner of macro-economic policy is most likely to prove conducive to intelligent adjustments in resource use; and what the accelerating revolutions in the material sciences imply for radical new approaches to the challenges of the 21st century world.

I reflected gloomily that billions of human beings still profess belief in religious faiths or various kinds of quackery no more soundly based than Aronofsky's *Noah* and that this is the world in which AR5 has to find its readership and be debated. What hope is there, then, of rational agreement or cohesive action? Little enough; but then it was ever thus and less because of human evil than because of human simplicity, confusion and compound error. All this might induce despondency, but it should not give rise to an ante-diluvian misanthropy and it would certainly not justify a deranged Deity in unleashing the Apocalypse. We have to muddle through as best we can, relying on patience, compassion, ingenuity and as much cooperation as we can contrive.

Malcolm Fraser's rejection of the US alliance

As this piece goes to press, the prime minister, Tony Abbott, is in Washington where he will meet with President Obama. China and its pushiness in Asia are certain to be high on the list of things they will talk about. As Hugh White pointed out in Tuesday's paper, China is testing American resolve and commitment to its allies. We are one of those allies and the question Obama and his national security team will put to Tony Abbott may well be, 'If push comes to shove, what will Australia contribute in the East and South China Seas?'

The honest answer to this would have to be:

> With the best will in the world, we would be able to contribute very little; because right now and for years to come we have very little operational capability to offer. Our defence budget was cut to the lowest percentage of GDP since before the Second World War by my predecessor and right now we are not well placed to restore spending to a credible level.

This has been an issue in our exchanges with Washington for many years, of course. We make token contributions to alliance operations, but basically freeload on America's vast expenditure and global security shield.

But the prime minister might also be asked, quite directly, what he makes of recent calls for Australia to go further than freeloading tokenism and withdraw from the alliance altogether. In his new book *Dangerous Allies* Malcolm Fraser urges exactly this. He argues that Australia should quit ANZUS, close Pine Gap, dismantle the Marine Air-Ground Task Force base at Darwin and, as Paul Keating, expressed it last year, 'go our own way'. Gareth Evans hails Fraser's book as 'a major contribution to a debate Australia has to have'. Fraser himself hails Hugh White's *The China Choice* as a 'substantial contribution to this debate'. Mining magnate Twiggy Forrest called the Darwin base a bad idea. There is a trend forming here and it needs to be carefully attended to.

It's unlikely that the current government, whose National Security Adviser is reportedly keen to be our next ambassador to Washington, will contemplate what Fraser urges. It would be surprising if the next Defence White Paper even hinted at such a possibility. But Gareth Evans is right that we now need to have this debate, if only because so many Australians, including two former prime ministers, are pressing one side of it unequivocally. It's good that the proponents of cutting loose from America have stated their case clearly. That makes for productive debate. Now the other side of it needs spelling out.

Fraser argues that we have three options: to continue in our current close relationship with America (what he calls strategic dependency); to carve out a more independent role within the alliance; or make a clean break, end the alliance, close the American bases and rely upon good will and diplomacy in Asia to safeguard our interests and the general peace. He concurs with White that we should 'drive America' (Fraser's words) off its present course of seeking to maintain global primacy and induce it to cede primacy in Asia to China as a strategic peer.

However, he argues that the second option is 'no option at all'. In short, he doesn't proffer three options. He rejects the first, dismisses as impossible the idea of exerting greater independence within the alliance (like Canada, Britain or France) and declares that we '*must*, therefore, turn to the third option' of strategic independence to avoid 'complicity (sic) in America's future military operations'. This looks like a classic, loaded three-option paper for a minister: one you know she rejects, another that she will see is impossible and the one you know she favours'

Fraser declares that the United States is run by 'neo-cons', which is odd when Barack Obama has withdrawn from Iraq and Afghanistan and declared that America does not wish to be the world's policeman. His knowledge of Chinese history and motives is thoroughly muddled and he makes no allowance for the likelihood that an Australia disconnected from Washington would be vulnerable to bullying by China to a far greater extent than it currently is.

The China he sees as more benign than America is a relentlessly repressive, deeply corrupt one party state, which is increasing its defence expenditure at a compound rate of around 10 to 12% per annum, as that of America shrinks. It asserts claims to maritime (and other territories) on the absurd basis that they used (allegedly) be part of the Chinese or even the foreign Manchu Empire (as if any empire is sacrosanct and should hold all its territories forever). It has for many years run a xenophobic propaganda line domestically about the West (America in particular) and Japan being China's enemies. Its neighbours are begging America to hold the line.

Yet in this situation, Fraser urges us to cut our ties with America—for 'safety's' sake. Gareth Evans is right. We have to have this debate. If we ditched America as Fraser suggests, it would transform our security policy more radically and dangerously than anything in our history. Unless we opted for *unarmed* neutrality, we would have to double or even treble defence expenditure. And if the Sino-American confrontation Fraser, White and others dread *does* take place, we stand to lose whatever the outcome. Should America prevail it would look coldly on our neutrality. Should China do so, it would presume it could push us in almost any direction it chose.

August 1914 and war in our time

There has been an outpouring of reflections this year, both here and abroad, on the centenary of the start of the First World War. Much of it recycles old clichés about the war or dwells on the merits and consequences of Australian involvement on the side of the British Empire. At a time when there is growing debate about the rise of China, the wisdom or otherwise of attempting to 'contain' it and the merits and possible consequences of Australia's alliance with the United States, we would do well to ponder the beginnings of the First World War in at least three respects.

First, we should reflect on Germany's sense of being hemmed in by the Triple Entente (England, France and Russia) compared with China's concerns about being hemmed in by America and its allies.[303] Second, it took decades of painstaking scholarly inquiry to reach any kind of clarity as to who was to blame for war starting in 1914. In our time, we cannot afford such a luxury. We need much greater clarity in advance, in order to head off destructive conflict. Third, the cream of German society in 1914, though neither militaristic nor in any way barbarous, tended, on the whole, to see the war from their own government's point of view. This may seem unsurprising, but it has important implications for our time.

Germany was an ascendant military and economic power in the decades before 1914. It wanted and felt it was entitled to a more dominant and acknowledged position on the European continent and around the world. Does this sound familiar? It should. Its major neighbours were, for differing reasons, uneasy about this and formed an alliance which grew firmer as Germany grew stronger and more assertive. France felt threatened directly by Germany's rising power. Russia feared German territorial ambitions in Eastern Europe. Britain had always been concerned to prevent the domination of the European continent by a single power and saw the protection of Belgium, directly across the North Sea from its own shores, as a trigger point for intervention. In all these respects, we might readily draw parallels with aspects of the current situation in Asia and ponder these thoughtfully.

When the July crisis came, in 1914, after the famous assassination in Sarajevo of the Austro-Hungarian Archduke Franz Ferdinand, the Germany of the Kaiser overplayed its hand and

---

303   For a magisterial study of this issue and how it played out during the Great War, see Alexander Watson *Ring of Steel: Germany and Austria-Hungary at War 1914-1918* (Allen Lane, Penguin, 2014). The keynote, in regard to analogies for our time, is struck at p. 257, where Watson observes that 'leaders in Germany and Austria-Hungary were careful to emphasize that the war was 'purely defensive''. Yet Germany's war aims were extraordinarily ambitious. China, similarly, insists that its territorial claims in the East and South China Seas, in Arunachal Pradesh and over Taiwan are purely defensive, because these territories allegedly belonged, in some imperial past, to the Manchu Empire.

brought on continental war in a fit of misplaced hubris. A generation earlier, under Bismarck, it would almost certainly have played a more cautious hand and averted such a war. But the Kaiser and those around him lacked Bismarck's canniness and sense of proportion. This is a crucial consideration for our time. Deng Xiaoping, while he lived, counselled canniness and restraint in Chinese foreign and security policy. Under China's post-Deng leadership, that restraint has been ebbing away as Chinese military power has grown.

For decades after 1919 the question of who had been most responsible for 'causing' the outbreak of war was endlessly debated. The most telling contributions did not come until after the Second World War. It then emerged, from German and other diplomatic archives that the circle around the Kaiser and in the German high command had conceived dangerously ambitious war aims by July 1914. When the crisis came they opted for confrontation rather than for restraint. That, more than any other element in the situation, precipitated the 'Great War' in August 1914. Their aims at that point and right into 1918 were to exert control over Eastern Europe at Russia's expense, crush the power of France 'for all time' and reduce Belgium to the status of a German protectorate.

Though it may sound unduly alarmist to make this point in 2014, there are those in China now whose outlook warrants comparison with such German aims a century ago. In place of France read Japan. In place of Russia in Eastern Europe read the United States in East Asia and the Western Pacific. In place of Belgium read the littoral states around the South China Sea. Yet there is nothing foreordained about the coming of war. And while we ponder the dangers and dilemmas we face and the lessons of history, we need always to bear in mind the third point I noted above: the humanity of the other side. In the case of Germany, in the summer of 1914, many deeply civilized and educated people neither wanted nor expected a war. Yet, when it came, they were patriots who saw the war through distinctly German eyes.

My own favourite example is the Bonhoeffer family, the parents and siblings of the famous Dietrich Bonhoeffer, the dissenting theologian executed by the Nazis in the last days of the Second World War. Karl and Paula Bonhoeffer and their eight children were rooted in the finest traditions of the German Enlightenment and liberal-minded pietism. They were model citizens and human beings.

Karl was professor of psychiatry and neurology at Berlin University and an active member of a remarkable inter-disciplinary circle of intellectuals. Their son Walter was killed on the Western front in April 1918, during Ludendorff's massive offensive in the Ypres salient. Several nephews had been killed or wounded earlier in the war. The Bonhoeffers never lost their sense of balance during or after the war, though Paula suffered a nervous breakdown as a result of Walter's death.

She recovered and the couple, as well as their extended family, went on to oppose Nazism. As a consequence, two more of their sons and two of their sons in law were executed, along with Paula's first cousin, Paul von Hase, who had been the commandant of the Berlin garrison and a member of the anti-Hitler underground.

In short, the Bonhoeffers paid a terrible price for Germany's 20th century war-making, without ever subscribing to German imperial or racial supremacism. They were far from being alone. The problem was that such people could not govern the rip tides of public affairs and were swept along and away by them. Right now, there are very many people in China who meet the description I have applied to the Bonhoeffers. They are deeply civilized, highly educated, thoroughly decent; but also, under most circumstances, patriotic. Our caution and concern about the strategic intentions of the Chinese government are warranted. But we must never lose sight of the basic humanity and natural outlook of the core citizenry of China. It is with their hopes and values that we must strive to connect, if conflict is to be avoided in the years ahead. It is others in China who are the problem.

Getting perspective on Gaza and Hamas

If we are to make balanced judgements about the Israeli incursion into Gaza, we must be able to put it in sober perspective. Three things make that very difficult: pictures of the death and injury of women and children; evidence of the overwhelming superiority of Israeli arms compared with those available to Hamas; and the belief that the Arab population of Gaza (and for that matter on the West Bank of the Jordan) are refugees, deprived of their homes, oppressed and bullied by Israel.

If you start simply from one or more of these premises, without putting the situation in deeper perspective, you will not be able to think your way through it in a responsible manner. I cannot here and now offer a 'solution' to the confrontation between Israel and its Arab enemies. I do believe, however, that the following five considerations are indispensable to thinking clearly about it. They are not partisan positions, but bedrock facts, easily checked.

First, the death and injury of women and children is almost invariably one tragic consequence of war. That's one of the reasons most of us find war abhorrent. Yet during the Allied invasion of Normandy in 1944, to liberate France from the Nazis, tens of thousands of French civilians were killed by Allied bombs. That's a mind-numbing figure and it isn't anyone's propaganda.

Should the bombing, therefore, not have been carried out? Was the invasion the wrong thing for the Allies to do? Given the technology of the time, precision strikes were impossible. Eisenhower and the Allied high command were not trying to kill French civilians, but to defeat the Nazi war machine. They were unable to accomplish the second without doing the first. Far greater precision is possible these days and, in general, civilian casualties from bombing are far fewer.

Second, when Israel withdrew from Gaza in 2005, it offered the Fatah leaders a deal: make your peace with us and we will help you develop Gaza into a thriving entrepôt. Infrastructure was left in place and investment offered. What happened? Fatah was ousted by Hamas in a brutal coup, the Israeli offer was spurned, the infrastructure torn up because it was Jewish and the metal from torn up pipes used to make rockets to fire into Israel. Hamas is not in the business of negotiating for any kind of viable settlement with Israel. Its agenda is the destruction of Israel by any means available.

Third, the so-called 'peace process' in regard to Israel and the Palestinian Arabs centres on calls for a 'two state solution'. Yet the Peel Commission, in 1937, proposed a two state solution under which two thirds of what is now Israel would have formed an Arab state and the Jews would not have had control of Jerusalem. The Jewish leaders reluctantly accepted the plan. The Arab leaders flatly rejected it. There would be no Jewish state in Palestine, they insisted.

Further Jewish proposals were rejected. The Second World War and the Holocaust exacerbated the Jewish situation. In the wake of those colossal upheavals, the United Nations again proposed a two state settlement in Palestine. It would, once more, have given the Arabs a more than equitable share of the territory. The Jewish leadership again accepted the offer. The Arab leaders again flatly rejected it. They then launched a three-pronged attack on the nascent state of Israel, to destroy it in its cradle. To almost everyone's surprise, they were roundly defeated.

Fourth, the Palestinian Arabs in Gaza and the West Bank are deemed refugees, because half a million Arabs fled their homes during the Arab war against Israel in 1948. Yet in the years after 1948, some 600,000 Jews were expelled from Arab lands, from Morocco to Yemen and Iraq, and their property confiscated. None of them, nor any of their descendants is considered a refugee now; nor do they claim a right of return and they have certainly not been compensated for their property. Yet the Arabs claim such things from Israel.

Fifth, in the mid-1990s, Israeli elder statesman Shimon Peres wrote a book called *The New Middle East*, proposing that Arabs and Jews cooperate to develop the Middle East free of the trammels and polarities of the Cold War. He reiterated what Zionists had proposed to the Arab leaders long before Israel had ever been formed: we Jews are Semites just like you; we are brothers and can bring science, education and finance to the table. What happened? His book was translated into Arabic in Cairo, but published with a preface denouncing it as proof positive of the Jewish conspiracy to take over the whole of the Middle East and dominate the Arabs.

The situation in Gaza is so intractable for these kinds of reasons. Had the Arab states around Israel and across the Middle East been better governed, more open, more prosperous than they are, the whole Gaza problem need never have arisen. Israel could have been welcomed, to the region's immense and cumulative benefit. As things now stand, there is no concession that Israel can make to Hamas that would mollify it. And there is no way to punish Hamas for its relentless provocations without inflicting at least some harm on Arab civilians. Those are the harsh realities of the situation. If you do not take them into account, you will not be able to hold an informed or responsible conversation on the subject. Pity, partisan anger and frustration don't suffice.

Eichmann and the caliphate: grappling with evil

We are sending forces to Iraq to contribute to a military effort to suppress ISIS. We are doing so for three reasons: that ISIS is committing barbarous acts of genocide and butchery; that it openly seeks to overturn the existing political order in the Middle East; and that it is recruiting foot soldiers from our own country, who declare they will bring violent jihad back here in due course.[304]

Should we be making such a military contribution? Or should we just police our own shores; detaining would-be terrorists if they cause problems here? One could make a utilitarian calculation that our strictly military concerns should be in our own neighbourhood. China, for example, is building artificial islands in the South China Sea to buttress its highly dubious territorial claims there.

Is that of military concern? Not for the time being, anyway. Once we have Japanese submarines, we'll see. It is the nascent caliphate, not the rise of China that is drawing our fire. It's doing so not on utilitarian or strategic grounds, but on *moral* ones. ISIS is openly described as *evil* and that is why we are lining up to fight it. Whatever one thinks of China's claims, no one is denouncing them as evil.

Foreign Minister, Julie Bishop, came closest to defining the ISIS challenge when she observed last week that the would-be caliphate cannot be defeated by purely military means, but has to be defeated on the *ideological* battlefield. ISIS embodies a fanatical idea, which in turn motivates its savagery and it's (one would certainly like to think) delusional ambitions.

If we are to comprehend ISIS, we need to grapple with that fanatical idea. The fanatical

---

[304] Since this piece was written, ISIS has committed a series of further barbarities, including the beheading of two Japanese civilians and the burning alive of a captured Jordanian pilot. The *Charlie Hebdo* massacre has also occurred in Paris and the Lindt siege in Sydney. Moreover, the dangers from terrorism, especially Islamic terrorism, appear to be growing rather than diminishing and the kinds of destruction that might be committed by such unscrupulous nihilists seem to be growing rather than being eliminated. The danger of disabling cyber-attacks has recently been warned against in the gravest terms, while the use of WMD seems, on the balance of probabilities, to be a continuing and ominous possibility. Again and again, as recent events have unfolded, I have found myself drawn back to the two seminal works on security and terrorism in the 21st century by my friend Philip Bobbitt: *The Shield of Achilles* (Alfred A. Knopf, New York, 2002) and *Terror and Consent* (Alfred A. Knopf, New York, 2008). I have read each of them, pencil in hand, more than once and can think of no more thought-provoking reflections on the challenge of contemporary terror to the legitimacy and functionality of the constitutional democracies than these two books and will almost certainly re-read them this year by way of continuing to grapple conceptually with the realities of terrorism and the strategic responses they call for.

idea is that once there was a glorious Muslim caliphate in which the purity of Koranic revelation provided the basis for the only possible true social order. Then history went horribly wrong, because Mongols and Western Crusaders and Turks and then Western imperialists invaded the blessed Umma and upset the applecart of Allah's plan for history. Since then, craven and apostate Muslims have ruled the Arab world and led it into poverty and corruption.

The only hope for the restoration of Allah's divine order is jihad to overthrow all this and restore the caliphate. That should be done by the traditional Koranic means of killing unbelievers and imposing true Islam on those who submit. That's how the original caliphate was created—at the point of a sword, when Mohammed and his heirs conquered the gravely weakened Roman and Persian Empires (which had fought each other to a standstill over the preceding half century), reaching the shores of the Bosporus and the mountains of Afghanistan.

If we put aside our horror at the specific deeds of ISIS and ponder their idea, we will appreciate the nature of the ideological problem we have. It is very like confronting committed Nazis—let's take Adolf Eichmann as an example—and coming to realize that they really believe their anti-Semitic conspiracy theories and actually think that 'world Jewry' is out to get them and has to be destroyed by any means possible.

I use the example of Eichmann, the key engineer of the Holocaust, for a number of reasons. The first is that once Nazism was on a roll, the ideological battle could not be won short of the overwhelming use of force to crush it and reopen the space for democratic order in Germany. The battle against Hitler's Germany could not be won by ideological means, in other words. It had to be eviscerated by fire and steel, as it was.

The second is that there was in the 1930s and 1940s and afterwards a disastrous blending of Nazi with Muslim anti-Semitism, the consequences of which we are still dealing with now. Many Arab leaders, not least among them the Grand Mufti of Jerusalem, openly took Hitler's side in the Second World War and enthusiastically encouraged his attempt to exterminate the Jews. The third is that Eichmann, on trial for his crimes in Jerusalem in 1961, was famously described by Hannah Arendt as a 'banal' individual unable to morally grasp the enormity of what he had done.

Yet a splendid new work of scholarship by Bettina Stangneth, *Eichmann Before Jerusalem: The Unexamined Life of a Mass Murderer* (2014) demonstrates that Eichmann knew exactly what he had done and was completely unrepentant, but worked for years before he was captured and put on trial, to develop an alibi, so that he could avoid becoming a scapegoat for those thousands of other Nazis who had got away scot free with mass murder.

The leaders and foot soldiers of ISIS, who are now shooting, crucifying, beheading, raping and enslaving their perceived enemies in northern Iraq and north eastern Syria are best seen as little Eichmanns in all the ways I have enumerated. They will not be halted by sweet reason, they are authentic and brutal fanatics, they are 'banal' in that they seriously lack moral imagination; but they know very well what they are doing. Regrettably, they need to be constrained and as good international citizens it is appropriate that we play at least a modest part in this work. But if their ideology is to be displaced—both there and around the world—a new vision for the Islamic world and for the wretched Arab world in particular, is badly needed.

The common foundation on which such a vision ought to be developed is that when the Arabs broke out of the Arabian peninsula and conquered the Roman and Persian Empires in the 7th century they took over the classical Greek heritage in philosophy and science. That heritage, not the Koran, was the fountainhead of Islamic scholarship and science over the five centuries that followed. That was the chief glory of the caliphate, from Baghdad to Cordoba. That heritage returned to the West from Muslim Arab sources (often via Jewish translators) only a century or so before the Mongols sacked Baghdad. Things went steadily downhill from there for the Arab world. The question is how to revitalize that world in the 21st century. ISIS and their ilk cry 'The Koran!' That's a battle cry, but it's not a solution.

The revitalization of the Arab world needs to draw upon this history in a non-fanatical and constructive manner. There is no end to the scope for dialogue about science, civilization and the future of the Arabic world. That is the ideological challenge before us. Only when it is addressed will the evil that now looms recede. In the meantime we have to deal strategically with the Eichmanns of Islam. While the ideological battle must be fought—and far more overtly and strenuously than it has been to date—the fanatics are not, themselves the target of suasion. They must be crushed, lest they inflict their delusional barbarism on millions more in Africa and the Middle East and bring their savage jihad ever more deeply into the Western world.

Israel as an occupying power: victory and frustration

'Rarely in modern times has so short and localized a conflict had such prolonged, global consequences', wrote Michael B. Oren in the opening paragraph of *Six Days of War* (2002), his compelling history of the June 1967 conflict, in which Israel crushed its Arab neighbours and seized control of the Sinai, Gaza, the West Bank and the Golan Heights. He listed some of those consequences: the Black September incident in Jordan (1970), the Munich massacre of Israeli athletes (1972), the Yom Kippur War (1973), the Lebanon War (1982), the controversy over Jewish settlements and the future of Jerusalem (1967 to the present), the Oslo Accords (1993), the Camp David Accords (2000), and the *intifada* beginning in 2000.

The most protracted and intractable of these consequences has been the controversy over the occupation of Gaza and the West Bank (Judaea and Samaria), with its attendant controversies over Jewish settlements in those areas; and the status of Jerusalem. Those issues are commonly seen as the crucial obstacle to a two-state solution to the territorial stand-off between Israel and the Palestinian Arabs, although the divisions among the Palestinian Arabs are at least as serious an obstacle.

Ahron Bregman's *Cursed Victory: A History of Israel and the Occupied Territories* (2014) is an attempt by a self-exiled and revisionist Israeli historian to get these matters into historical and conceptual perspective. It is a well-researched, probing book. It is the work of a man troubled by his country's policies and the dilemmas with which those policies have saddled the people of Israel. The detail he has gleaned from often highly classified sources is fascinating and thought-provoking. His argument, however, is flawed at a fundamental level.

Bregman was born in Israel in 1958 and grew up there. He left it in the late 1980s for England, because of the occupation, which he could not accept or justify. He has written several books on the history of Israeli/Palestinian Arab relations since then. Like a number of well-known Israeli revisionists, he is chiefly concerned with re-examining the Zionist project and asking, 'Where did we go wrong?'

His argument is that Israel went wrong when, at the moment of victory, in June 1967, it chose to occupy not only the Egyptian territories of the Sinai and Gaza and the Syrian territory of the Golan Heights, but the Jordanian territory of Judaea and Samaria. The Sinai has been returned to Egypt, as part of a comprehensive peace settlement. The Golan has been retained because Israel and Syria could not agree on a settlement while Hafez Assad lived and have not seriously attempted a negotiated settlement since his son, Bashar Assad took power.

Gaza was finally handed over the Palestinians in August and September 2005, but settlement has been elusive. The West Bank, however, is the big one, from the point of view of any rapprochement between Israel and the Palestinian Arabs. And, in that case, no solution is currently in sight. The Arab population grows and so do the numbers of Israeli settlers. The right-wing Zionists would like to annex Judaea and Samaria into the state of Israel and Likud is sympathetic to this goal. Neither, however, want the Arab population within the borders of Israel. Yet they cannot bring themselves to engage in outright ethnic cleansing and simply expel the Arabs from the West Bank.

The Arabs, for their part, cannot bring themselves to accept the predominance of Israel and cannot even maintain a common front or a coherent approach to negotiations with it. They want their own state and this is generally taken to mean a state incorporating Gaza, the West Bank and at least part of Jerusalem. That might have been possible had it not been for the Jewish settlements, which have certainly complicated the matter. The more fundamental problem is that Hamas is set on trying to destroy Israel and even Fatah has shown an inability to accept any deal which provides unambiguous recognition of Israel's right to exist and its security concerns.

Bregman argues that Israel's occupation policy has 'failed' and that it must now seek a two state solution, withdrawing as many of its West Bank settlers as possible in order to achieve this. One can quite see why he wants to argue that the occupation has failed, but he overlooks the fact that the Palestinian campaign of violence directed against Israel has *also* failed. After all, Israel is still the occupying power and in no danger of being expelled from the West Bank.

The bulk of *Cursed Victory* is devoted to arguing that Israel has failed in three respects. It has failed to induce the Arabs to leave, which would make annexation of Judaea and Samaria conceivable. It has failed to subdue the Arab population and persuade it to accept Israeli occupation. And it has failed to find a negotiating partner on the Arab side willing and able to come to a settlement on terms attractive to the Israelis.

Bregman's book, in these respects, compliments Dror Moreh's remarkable documentary *The Gatekeepers* (2013), in which six former heads of Shabak, the Israeli internal security and counter-terrorism organization (it's ASIO) were interviewed about the occupation and its consequences. In its close documentation of fraught internal debates and 'lost opportunities' for pulling back or reaching out, *Cursed Victory* contains much food for thought.

Bregman does not, however, ask himself whether things would truly have been better had Israel either *not won* the 1967 war or chosen not to occupy new territories after its victory. He writes as if the occupations of 1967 were the chief cause of Arab hostility to Israel. This is patently untrue. That hostility had been intractable before Israel was first created in 1948. It led to both the rejection by the Arab leaders of any 'two state solution' in the 1930s and 1940s; and the attempt to destroy the nascent state of Israel in 1948. It has not changed, with the exception of Egypt since Sadat, which has run a more realistic foreign policy; but whose Muslim majority still seethe with irrational hatred of Israel.

Had Israel withdrawn from Judaea and Samaria and even Jerusalem in 1967, Jordan, not the Palestinian Arabs, would have become again, as it had been before the 1967 war, the occupying power. What right did the King of Jordan have to Judaea and Samaria? Would he have granted the Palestinian Arabs a state of their own there? Or would they have joined with their brethren in the attempt to overthrow him in 1970 and make Jordan a 'Palestinian Arab' state? In either case, would such a state have kept its peace with Israel? And had it made war on Israel and been roundly defeated, would Israel then have been justified in driving the Arabs out and annexing Judaea and Samaria?

Bregman ponders none of these counterfactuals of history. Nor does he pause to reflect that the kind of critical, revisionist history he is writing appears only on the Israeli side. Where are the Palestinian or more broadly the Arab revisionist historians, lamenting the opportunities that the Arabs have let slip since the 1930s; or roundly condemning the resort to terrorism and incitement to genocidal anti-Semitism among the Arabs? The Iraqi dissident and exile Kanan Makiya's work, notably *Cruelty and Silence* (1993) raised this concern trenchantly with regard to the Arab world as a whole. It's notably true of the Palestinian world.

Not least among the virtues of Israel is the deeply informed and hard hitting debates that take place, both within Israel and throughout the diaspora, about the humanity, legality and viability of Israeli national security and settlement policies. ' ... the true tragedy of Arab-Israeli conflict is one of lost opportunities ... ', Bregman insists from the diaspora. Perhaps, but this goes back before 1948 and unless the Arabs agree that having a Jewish state in Palestine is *itself* an opportunity, it's not clear that the much lamented 'lost opportunities' are anything but an illusion.

'I regard *Cursed Victory* as a work in progress', Bregman concludes, 'and hope to add to it as the story of Israel's occupation continues to unfold and, I trust, comes to an end in the not-too-distant future.' Yet it is far from clear what grounds he has for optimism in this regard, especially given the things that have occurred in the last half dozen years. Moreover, his account ends in 2007, which seems rather odd for a book published in 2014. It leaves out Israel's conflict with Hamas in Gaza, the 'Arab spring', the disintegration of Syria and the growing Sunni vs Shiite clash across the Middle East, as well as the irruption if ISIS in Syria and Iraq.

Surely all these things have altered the situation very considerably—and not for the better.

Yet there is no mention of any of them in Bregman's concluding reflections. He simply ends with the summary judgement that 'Israel's attempt to swallow the occupied territories over the past four decades has failed'. That conclusion goes well beyond the evidence that he brings to the table. It omits to take into account the failure, on the other side, not only to oust Israel from those territories, but to come to terms in an intelligent, multilateral way with the existence of Israel. Until the Muslim Arab world does that, there is most unlikely to be a solution to the Palestinian Arab travail. And the condition of the Muslim Arab world in 2014 does not suggest that any such development is imminent.

Euthanasia: give us good choices, not fearful bans

In May this year, in these pages, Peter Short wrote a forthright opinion piece declaring that he was dying of oesophageal cancer, had a supply of Nembutal and would end his own life at a time of his choosing.[305] In January this year (2014), his doctors gave him six months to live. He is still very much alive and is campaigning vigorously for the passage of legislation that would make it easier for people to do what he declares he will do: choose the manner and timing of their own deaths over medically protracted indignity and suffering.

I am writing to add my voice to the chorus calling for this serious matter to be addressed in such a way that we can create a new and better code of civilized norms around suffering, medicine and death. I am not terminally ill and I do not have a supply of Nembutal. I do, on the other hand, have metastatic melanoma. That means that my health and general viability are an ongoing experiment, at the cutting edge of current medical science. The debate about euthanasia hovers—and must be conducted—at the cutting edge of moral philosophy.

We dwell, I think, more in stories than in systematic arguments when it comes to death and dying. When I contemplate the possibility of freely embracing and actively triggering my own demise, three stories are foremost in my mind. Two of them are historical and of those one far better known than the other. The third is from a highly popular work of fiction by a devout Catholic writer and all the more remarkable for that reason.

The first story is that of the death of Socrates, in 399 BCE. (I write BCE, Before the Common Era, not BC, Before Christ, since this is a moral dialogue in which only *some* of us are Christians). He was condemned to death by the state for corrupting the youth and encouraging atheism. His friends urged him to escape and flee Athens. He chose instead to take his hemlock and pass away. Was he wrong to do so? He famously remarked, as his vitality ebbed away, that he owed a cock to Asclepius—as if his death had cured him of an illness. Certainly, he died with lucid dignity. Bettany Hughes provides a fine account of both his life and death in her 2010 book *The Hemlock Cup: Socrates, Athens and the Search for the Good Life*.

The second story is one related by the Roman historian Tacitus in Book XI of his *Annals of Imperial Rome*. It concerns the death of a wealthy Gallo-Roman aristocrat, Valerius Asiaticus,

---

305 Peter Short and I met in September 2014, in the Cricketer's Bar, at The Windsor. We spoke for a couple of hours about terminal illness, freedom to choose and euthanasia. We remained in touch after that and met with Rodney Syme, author of *A Good Death: An argument for voluntary euthanasia* (Melbourne University Press, 2008), who has been a campaigner for euthanasia reform for twenty years. Peter died shortly after new year 2015. He died under palliative care and did not take his Nembutal.

whose opulent villa and gardens were coveted by the dissolute Messalina, mistress of the Emperor Claudius. She had false charges of treason brought against him and he was condemned to death, but was permitted to choose the means of his own demise. The historian recounts that 'he took his usual exercise, then bathed and dined cheerfully and ... opened his veins, but not until he had inspected his funeral pyre and directed its removal to another spot, lest the smoke should hurt the thick foliage of the trees. So complete was his calmness even to the last.'

The third story is buried in Appendix A to J. R. R. Tolkien's *The Lord of the Rings*. It concerns the voluntary suicide of Aragorn, 120 years after the fable ends. Having lived a long life, he announces to his beloved Arwen that the time has come to lay down the gift of life and leave the throne to their son. She begs him to linger with her and not go before his time. His response is remarkable. He answered:

> *Not before my time. For if I will not go now then I must soon go perforce ... Take counsel with yourself, beloved, and ask whether you would indeed have me wait until I wither and fall from my high seat, unmanned and witless. Nay, lady, I am the last of the Numenoreans and the latest King of the Elder Days; and to me has been given not only a span thrice that of Men of Middle-earth, but also the grace to go at my will and give back the gift. Now, therefore, I will sleep.*

That phrasing is worth dwelling upon: 'the grace to go at my will and give back the gift'. That, I suggest, is the tone in which to think about our ends—not a tone or language of fear, anxiety and a ban on choice. But all three stories inform my sense of what it could mean to voluntarily bring an end to one's own life and to do so in a dignified manner. Should I reach the point where ending seemed more dignified than enduring, it is stories such as these that I would bear in mind.

The chief source of our ban on voluntary euthanasia derives from the Catholic tradition, dating back not to Scripture, but to St Augustine. He rejected the Stoic and the Epicurean approach to free death. Yet Tolkien, a deeply moral Catholic, had one of his most exalted figures choose to lay down the gift of life simply in order to avoid the infirmities of old age. He was being neither frivolous nor sinister. He plainly conveys, in his telling of the story, the sense that this was a lofty freedom available to the 'latest King of the Elder Days' and that it made good sense.

The need, in whatever set of laws we frame around medicine and mortality, is for civilized norms. All three of these stories, I believe, show that voluntary death can be experienced and conducted according to civilized norms. At the very least, they exhibit norms in which the emphasis is on choice and dignity, not a fearful ban on freedom of action. That is the spirit in which we should frame our laws. That is the calmness and dignity we need.

Xi Jinping and the denial of historical facts

The Chinese Communist Party again and again accuses Japan of being in denial about its World War Two history and being insufficiently repentant about its crimes of that by-gone era. In a speech at Nanjing recently, Chinese president Xi Jinping was at it again, attacking Japan for atrocities committed 77 years ago and charging that it continues to fudge or deny the facts of the matter. 'History will not be altered as time changes and facts will not disappear because of any chicanery or denials,' he declared to an audience of thousands.

He was referring specifically, in his speech, to the famous atrocities by Japanese forces after the fall of the Chinese Nationalist capital, Nanjing, in 1937. All informed sources agree that very large numbers of people were killed, often with appalling barbarity. Estimates range from about 140,000 up to 300,000. It was the largest single atrocity committed by the Japanese in a long and brutal war. It is quite natural, therefore, that it would be remembered and deplored in China and that perceived Japanese denial would be resented.

But the Chinese Communist Party has been responsible for vastly more killing and death in China than the Japanese invaders ever committed; and it continues to this day to seal archives, suppress documentation, discourage and even punish inquiry, ignore and denounce scholarship which exposes the truth. When it comes to accusations of trying to make facts disappear through chicanery and denial, the Communist Party doesn't have a leg to stand on.

Chicanery and denial have been standard Party practice throughout its brutal history. Atrocities every bit as savage and far larger in number than those committed by the Japanese are sealed up in Party archives and all inquiry into them discouraged. The surest way for Xi to encourage a more open and confessional stance on Japan's part would be to set a good example by opening up the huge can of worms that is the history of his own dictatorial Party. There is no sign that he has any intention of doing so.

When the Communist armies besieged Changchun, in central Manchuria, in 1948, their commander, Lin Biao, ordered that it be turned into 'a city of death'. An estimated 160,000 people died from hunger and disease during his blockade of the city, as he prevented the escape of any civilians in order to keep pressure on the defending garrison. The Party has never countenanced any open inquiry into this matter, much less admitted that it constituted an atrocity on an immense scale. Officially, it never happened.

At a conservative estimate, some 2,000,000 'landlords' or 'rich peasants' were killed in a revolutionary agrarian terror in the late 1940s. They were buried alive, tied up and dismembered, strangled or shot. In a wave of terror directed against 'bad elements' and 'counter-revolutionaries' in 1950-52, in which Mao Zedong issued 'quotas' for killings by general categories of people, another 2,000,000 people were executed, perhaps more. There were purges, confiscations and imprisonments on a vast scale, in the name of 'liberation'. The scale of it all and the details remain sealed up in Party archives.

In 1957, the Party attacked the intelligentsia in an extraordinary manner and confined an estimated half a million of them to Mao's mushrooming GULAG. The lack of intelligence in his national development policies was then revealed when he imposed and the Party enforced the so-called 'Great Leap Forward', causing a famine in which at least 35 million people died of starvation, between 1959 and 1961[306]. To this day, the Party discourages either inquiry into or discussion of this monumental catastrophe, which was wholly its fault. Only non-Party scholarship has established the reality of the matter. Mao Zedong, meanwhile, remains an icon and his portrait sits above Tiananmen Square; his embalmed body lies in a mausoleum in that same public space.

You would think that someone who causes tens of millions of deaths by starvation would, at the very least, lose his job. But Mao remained the head of state and proceeded to inflict the Cultural Revolution on the country, in the mid-1960s, in which far more people were killed than by the Japanese at Nanjing. By Deng Xiaoping's later estimate, some 100 million lives were severely disrupted. Is any of this a matter of open and critical inquiry today? Not remotely.

History will not be altered as time changes and facts will not disappear because of any chicanery or denials, the Chinese leader declares. Very well, then; let us have an unexpurgated history of the Party, Master Xi; cleansed of chicanery and denials. That would be something to behold. Of course we can't expect anything of the sort from the dictatorial and propagandist machinery of the Party; but we should all scoff at the rank hypocrisy of its demands on Japan.

---

306 There are a number of first class books on the great famine. Two of the best and most recent are Yang Jisheng *Tombstone: The Great Chinese Famine 1958-1962* (Farrar, Straus and Giroux, New York, 2012) and Frank Dikotter *Mao's Great Famine: The History of China's Most Devastating Catastrophe 1958-62* (Bloomsbury, 2010).

Cosmology and intelligent design

Just before New Year, this newspaper reprinted a column from *The Wall Street Journal* headed 'Science turns to God as universe appears to be ultimate miracle'. The author was one Eric Metaxas, an American religious writer, who has written a biography of Dietrich Bonhoeffer. He argued that there is increasing evidence that the probability of the universe existing at all and in such a way that intelligent life can have evolved is so astronomically small that these things cannot have happened by chance, but must be the work of an intelligent designer—'God'.

Clearly, Metaxas badly wants to believe that something he calls 'God' both exists and is responsible for creating the universe and the conditions for intelligent life. His argument is flawed in several quite fundamental ways, however, like all older arguments from intelligent design. If he had not been so eager to find support for his belief in God, he might have paused to think things through a little more clearly, both in terms of the available evidence and the inference he wants to draw from it.

He claims that in very recent years, as the number of factors needed to make life (never mind intelligent life) possible kept growing 'the odds turned against any planet in the universe supporting life, including this one'. He adds that if the value of any one of the four fundamental forces that govern the physical cosmos was only slightly different, then the universe as we know it could not have come into existence and that the odds of them all having exactly the right value are so enormous that only the presence of an intentional designer (God) can have made it possible.

The search for extra-terrestrial life has made for fascinating debates, of course, and there has been a very wide spectrum of opinions or estimates about the probability of finding it. Amir Aczel's *Probability 1: Why There Must Be Intelligent Life in the Universe* (1998), Peter Ward and Donald Brownlee's *Rare Earth: Why Complex Life is Uncommon in the Universe* (2000) and Paul Davies' *The Eerie Silence: Are We Alone in the Universe?* (2010) are indicative of that spectrum of opinion. Only in the past decade or so, however, have our instruments begun to actually detect significant numbers of planets elsewhere even in our own galaxy and the real search, therefore, has only just begun.

In the January 2015 issue of *Scientific American*, Canadian astrobiologist Rene Heller points out that there is growing evidence for large numbers of habitable planets in the Milky Way and that our Earth 'may not be anywhere close to the pinnacle of habitability'. Our Sun is a perfectly ordinary, mid-range yellow star and our proximity to it places us, for the time being, in a 'Goldilocks Zone' in terms of heat and habitability. But there are many candidates for what Heller calls 'super-habitability'. These are planets larger than the Earth orbiting what are called K dwarf stars, which are more stable and burn longer without exhausting their hydrogen fuel than our Sun will do. It turns out that we are finding more and more such stars and most of the planets we have started detecting are of the 'super-Earth' kind. In other words, it is far from clear that the odds are against the existence of extra-terrestrial life.

Suppose, however, for the sake of argument, that Metaxas was right about the odds being overwhelmingly against the existence of the 'fine-tuned' cosmos and the existence of life anywhere. Would it follow from this that we must infer the existence of 'God'? It would not, actually. As Steven Weinberg, a Nobel Prize winner in the field, put it at the turn of the century, the more plausible, if daunting, hypothesis is that we are part not of a 'universe', but of a 'multiverse', in which universes come and go with infinite variations. We just happen to be in one in which things worked out this particular way.[307]

Metaxas makes no mention of the multiverse hypothesis and one suspects it is because he is so eager to embrace the old theological 'answer' to the conundrum of existence. Yet suppose—also for the sake of argument—that it made sense to infer the existence of a 'designer' of the cosmos and a 'creator' of life. We would then be left with more questions than we started with. For one thing, if 'God' had wanted to create a universe with intelligent life in it, why would he have created a universe in which the odds were still overwhelmingly against life and immense stretches of space consisted of superfluous and sterile stars and dark matter?

Why would he have made life struggle through billions of years of biological evolution and have had intelligence emerge through the brain of a primate with many flaws, instead

---

307 Even as I was writing this piece, in December 2014, a new book was coming off the press offering a radical new theory of evolutionary cosmology. Roberto Mangabeira Unger and Lee Smolin, in *The Singular Universe and the Reality of Time* (Cambridge University Press, 2015), argue against the multiverse hypothesis, but do not suggest that the singular universe requires the hypothesis of a creator deity. They argue that contemporary cosmology has got itself into a set of conceptual difficulties from which it has attempted to extricate itself through the multiverse hypothesis, but that the more scientific approach is to rethink 'the metaphysical commitments for which the findings of science are often mistaken.' They go so far as to argue that the laws of nature evolve and have not been constant, that time is real and that mathematics is a human invention which, despite its 'vast power and prestige' does not provide a 'shortcut to timeless truth either about nature or about some special realm of mathematical objects outside nature.' This line of argument is squarely within the Popperian tradition of cosmology and surely fresher and more thought-provoking than falling back on a rather tired theological 'answer' to the enigma of the existence of things.

of simply—like his Biblical avatar Yahweh—just plonking a more ideal form of intelligent life into an ideally formed biosphere? Why would he, as David Hume famously asked two centuries ago, have created mosquitoes—or, one might add, infectious microbes or ferocious predatory beasts? All these things make sense within an evolutionary frame of reference, but the notion of an 'intelligent designer' makes them quite inexplicable.

Finally, although, like most 'intelligent design' advocates, he does not own up to this in his article, Metaxas almost certainly wants to be able to infer from his argument about probability that not only is there a 'God', but that it is *his* God. That is to say, a God he and others can pray to, who meddles in his creation in arbitrary ways. *That* God sent his only begotten son to 'save' from their 'sins' a species of intelligent primates that had evolved over billions of years on a remote planet way out on the periphery of an ordinary galaxy in the middle of nowhere. None of that, however, has the slightest connection with scientific fact or the new cosmology.[308]

---

308 After I had written this piece, I had the good fortune to discover Mary-Jane Rubenstein's *Worlds Without End: The Many Lives of the Multiverse* (Columbia University Press, New York, 2014), which is a splendid account of the debates about cosmology and religion going back to the Pre-Socratics and forward to the most current and arcane speculations. Those interested in serious reading on the subject will also find it worthwhile to look for Jeremiah P. Ostriker and Simon Mitton *Heart of Darkness: Unravelling the Mysteries of the Invisible Universe* (Princeton University Press, 2013); Lisa Randall *Knocking on Heaven's Door: How Physics and Scientific Thinking Illuminate the Universe and the Modern World* (Bodley Head, London, 2011); John D. Barrow *The Book of Universes: Exploring the Limits of the Cosmos* (W. W. Norton & Co., New York and London, 2011) and Lawrence Lipking *What Galileo Saw: Imagining the Scientific Revolution* (Cornell University Press, Ithaca and London, 2014).

Palmyra, ISIS and the crisis of Islam

As I write, the marauding forces of ISIS have descended on the ruins of ancient Palmyra, one of the archaeological jewels of Syria[309]. There is no reason to believe that they will spare it their destructive iconoclasm should they take it[310]. They have—like the Taliban in Afghanistan—shown a manic wilfulness in destroying the treasures of a complex past. The prospect should, more than ever, concentrate our minds regarding what ISIS embodies and how to address the dangers that it poses both to the Middle East and the world at large.

Let's begin with Palmyra. It is an extremely ancient human settlement, dating back to the eighth millennium BCE. It has featured as a trading post and caravan watering hole on the ancient high roads of trade between the Levant and Asia since the third millennium BCE. It flourished as a great commercial city under the Roman Empire for some three hundred years. Then, during the 3rd century CE crisis of the Roman Empire, it sought to replace Roman rule in the East, under its colourful leaders Odenathus and Zenobia—the Antony and Cleopatra of Palmyra. They overran Syria, Roman Arabia, Judaea and Egypt before being brought to heel by the Roman Emperor Aurelian.

ISIS threatens to ransack and demolish an archaeological site. Aurelian razed Palmyra to the ground, in 273 CE, for its rebellion against the Empire. It has never recovered. As Edward Gibbon remarked, in the first volume of his famous history of the decline and fall of the Roman Empire: 'The seat of commerce, of arts and of Zenobia gradually sank into an obscure town, a trifling fortress and, at length, a miserable village. The present citizens of Palmyra, consisting of thirty or forty families, have erected their mud cottages within the spacious court of a magnificent temple.'

Gibbon was writing in the late 18th century. Palmyra had only under the Ottomans declined into a village. It had still been a town under the early caliphs—who had not done to it what ISIS now threatens to do—but had been destroyed a second time, in 1400 by the self-proclaimed hero of Islam, Tamerlane, the genocidal Mongol conqueror. That had precipitated its final decline. Under the French mandate, in the early 1930s, it was finally abandoned and became the archaeological relic that it is in our time.

---

309 Within hours of this piece appearing in print, in *The Age*, on Thursday 21 May 2015, Palmyra fell to ISIS foforces.

310 Some days after the fall of the archaeological site, the ISIS commander in charge of the occupation of Palmyra, a Saudi named Abu Laith al-Saoudi, stated on radio that ISIS would not destroy the monumental ruins in Palmyra, but would pulverize statues of pagan gods 'that the miscreants used to pray to.' *The Australian* 30-31 May 2015 p. 14

The motives of Aurelian and of Tamerlane are matters of history. The motives of ISIS are a contemporary challenge. The ISIS forces seek to restore, as they see it, the 'glories' of the Umayyad caliphate of the 7th century, based on the fiercest and most literal interpretation of the Quran and of the sayings of Muhammed. They are, among other things, extreme iconoclasts, who assert that all remnants of non-Islamic religion should be erased, especially images of buildings associated with pagan cults. But they are also destroying Shiite mosques and Christian churches.

The prime minister refers to ISIS as 'a death cult'. He and the foreign minister also refer to it as Daesh on the grounds that this denies it the status it claims as an Islamic organization. Yet that is what it is; just as the Taliban is Islamic and Boko Haram is Islamic and the killers of the staff at *Charlie Hebdo* were Islamic. There can be no ducking this out of a desire to avoid offending less violent Muslims. The challenge is to understand where such violence comes from within Islam, because it is now endemic and by no means confined to ISIS.

The Somalian refugee from Islam, Ayaan Hirsi Ali, now living under armed guard in America because of death threats, has just published a splendidly polemical and thought provoking book called *Heretic: Why Islam Needs a Reformation Now* (Fourth Estate, 2015). It is a cry from the heart by a highly intelligent woman for fundamental changes within Islam—the kind of 'revolution' that the Egyptian president Abdel Fattah el-Sisi called for at Al-Azhar University in Cairo so very recently. Hers is a stirring clarion call and deserves to be very widely read and discussed. She stands up for the numerous dissidents within Islam (not least women calling for change) and makes no bones about the fact that the problem isn't only a few 'death cults', but deeply rooted beliefs and long established practices within Islam.

She asks for a Reformation, but here is where the current crisis within Islam really strikes home. The Muslim Brotherhood and its violent off-spring, the theocratic mullahs in Tehran and the rampant Islamists in Africa *are* the Islamic Reformation. That, precisely, is the problem. Just as Luther, Zwingli and Calvin (the last two of whom were noted iconoclasts and strippers of the altars) called for a return to the 'purity' of Biblical scripture, the Muslim Brotherhood's Sayyid Qutb and the Ayatollah Khomeini's followers demand a restoration of 'pure', Quranic Islam and a renunciation of half-secularized, lax Islam, as well as the suppression of infidels and sinners.

What threatens Palmyra right now is only one manifestation of the religious wars unleashed by the Muslim 'Reformation'. The wrecking ball that is purist Islam is triggering the Islamic equivalent of Europe's 16th and 17th century wars of religion. In Europe, these wars triggered the Enlightenment reaction *against* organized religion. What Ayaan Hirsi Ali is actually hoping for is something similar within Islam. Her true heroes are Locke and Voltaire whom she quotes whenever she explicitly calls for tolerance and pluralism in a modernized 'Islamic' society..

We should, also, work for and support Enlightenment values in the Islamic world. But that is a tall order and will face massive resistance. It will require a sustained war of ideas over the status of Muhammed and the Quran, as well as the reactionary, misogynist practices in much of the Muslim world. It will be a long war, whatever happens to Palmyra; but for the sake of the Muslim world and the world at large it must be won—and Palmyra remembered. The cost of avoiding these issues has already become too high. The costs of giving up would be incalculable.

Acknowledgements

I owe many people thanks for this book being possible at all, beginning with the editors of magazines and the opinion or literary editors of newspapers who have shepherded me into print over so many years. This began with Jack Waterford, Robert Hefner and their colleagues at *The Canberra Times*, in the early 1990s. Little by little, it grew from there, as editors at *The Age*, *The Sydney Morning Herald*, *The Australian*, *Quadrant*, *The Australian Financial Review*, the *Australia Israel Review* and *Critical Asian Studies* saw value in what I had to say and how I wrote and gave me access to their pages. I owe thanks at various points along the way, most particularly, to Rowan Callick, Ben Potter, Hugh Lamberton, Rebecca Weisser, Sushi Das, Robert Manne, Paddy McGuiness, Colin Rubenstein, Tzvi Fleischer, Stephen Romei and my tireless advocate and great friend John Spooner. Though I have never become a columnist for any of the newspapers, working with such a variety of editors over the years has been educational and enriching. There have, over that time, been a few editors with whom I found I could not work, but they shall remain unnamed.

I owe a big vote of thanks, also, to the countless scholars whose work I have devoured over the years and have commented upon or drawn upon in order to throw these many subjects into the clearest perspective that my own abilities allowed. I am, as the reader will have quickly realized, an omnivorous reader and my eye roves constantly over the new releases shelves of my favourite bookshop, Readings, in Lygon St, Carlton; and the Hill of Content in Bourke St, Melbourne, for the best and most instructive scholarship. They are such well-stocked and alluring bookshops and the world's best universities, many of them in the much-maligned United States, keep producing the most stunning range of new books on almost every conceivable subject. Having easy access to them and then an outlet for reflecting on what they reveal or argue are the greatest benefits of my liminal condition as a writer and public intellectual.

Over many years, also, I have gradually realized that there is a readership out there for my thinking; though overwhelmingly of people I never meet. Over the years, however, I have been struck by the number of people I have met who have declared spontaneously that they have been avid readers of my writings. Among them have been Kim Beazley, when he was still leader of the Opposition, some years ago; Geoff Raby, when he was ambassador designate to China; and the China scholar and translator of the Nobel Prize winning novels of Gao Xingjian, Mabel Lee, who surprised me a decade ago by approaching me at a Sydney conference and declaring 'We all read your wonderful essays'. To know that one has such readers is a strong inducement to serious thinking and the effort to keep one's standards up.

As with three previous books (*Sonnets to a Promiscuous Beauty*, *The West in a Nutshell* and *Darkness Over Love: A Writer's Workbook*, I owe a vote of thanks to Ian Gordon and his small team at Barrallier Books for making possible the creation of a beautiful volume, with hard covers, fine art work, high quality paper and, in all, aesthetic distinction. They are, as I put it to Ian recently, my Aldine Press, in an age of commercialism and social media. I treasure the physical beauty of the books they produce and look forward to adding a couple more to my shelves in the course of the next year or two. We have lost the wonderful Jorg Schmeisser, but his legacy of art has survived and it has been a privilege to have been able to draw upon it, so to speak, in order to grace a succession of books since 2006. Perhaps, in time, my series of books, with his etchings on them and in them, will come to be regarded, among other things, as a repository of some of his best work.

I must, as ever, acknowledge the work of David Speakman, Ben Brady and the rest of the team at Peter Mac, who continue to provide the medical advice and professional intervention required to keep me from being overwhelmed by what I call 'my inner ISIL (or ISIS)': the metastatic melanoma that has been seeking to overwhelm my health since the winter of 2013, but which so far we have kept at bay. I have several more books awaiting completion and hope that we can keep the 'terrorists' bottled up in their relatively small enclaves long enough for me to finish these and see them into print; or even exterminate the enemy and go onto a longer and brighter future. Both the history and theory of counterinsurgency, going back to my PhD days, as well as the realities of current geopolitics, continually spring to mind in the context of this existential struggle.

Finally, I must acknowledge my beloved partner and muse, Claudia Maria Alvarez Ortiz. She requested this book and, when I sent her an early draft of it, responded with great warmth and enthusiasm. It is, primarily, a gift for her, but one which I hope will come to appeal to a far wider readership. She is Venezuelan and has been fighting the good fight for many years for both freedom of expression and critical thinking in her troubled and misgoverned country. It is against that background that her appreciation of this book arises. It would be wonderful to think that it could find its way into Spanish and serve both her and her countrymen well, starting with the disorganized and somewhat demoralized opposition and perhaps—who knows?—even the more thoughtful members of the Chavista *nomenklatura*. Short of that, I hope it will at least hearten her in the struggle she has undertaken.

Index

A

Abbott, Tony, 296, 441, 448
Abreu, Jose Antonio, 386
Adams, John (composer), 386
Adaptive immunity, 439
Aegean Hypothesis, 212, 213, 215
Ai Wei Wei, 326
Altalena, 389
Angleton, James Jesus, 29-33
Angleton, Carmen, 254
Anthropogenic Global Warming (AGW), 298, 300, 319, 321
Anti-Semitism, xii, 24, 59-61, 157, 159, 294, 336, 337, 388, 456, 460,
Arab League, 342
Archaeology, xxi, 196-97, 199-201, 205-06, 208-09, 214, 218, 302
Arendt, Hannah, xviii, 7, 36, 59, 92, 104, 146-48, 253, 257, 388, 456
Argentina, economic follies of, 312-15
Aron, Raymond, xxiii, 147-48, 176
Aronofsky, David, xvi, 446-47
Arriens, Jan, 228-31, 235, 237-38, 245, 247, 249-51
ASIO, 32, 86-87, 277-78, 459
Assange, Julian, 42, 317-18, 418
Atlantis, 208-18 (*passim*)
Atlantean Hall of Records, 209
Augustine of Hippo, 176, 206-07, 334, 463
Aurelian (Roman emperor), 469-70
Auschwitz, 34, 145, 158-59, 373
Australian Defence Force, 417
Australian mining boom, 434-36
Australian Open, 432-33
Ayaan Hirsi Ali, 470

B

Bacon, Francis, 208, 212
Balfour Declaration, 294-95, 336-37, 340
Balibo, 219, 237, 241, 245, 291, 293
Bar Kokhba rebellion, 205, 336
Barwick, Garfield, 222-24, 226-28, 230, 234, 247, 250, 292
Beaufre, Andre, 149, 151
Beauvoir, Simone de, 147, 257
Beijing Consensus, 312
Ben Gurion, David, 23, 46, 372-73, 389
Bettelheim, Bruno, 394
Blackbird SR-71, 42
Blok, Alexander, 66-67
Bloom, Allan, 81, 116-18
Bloom, Harold, 204, 206, 338
Blundell, Graeme, 423
Bonhoeffer, Dietrich, 206, 402, 430, 451, 466
Bonhoeffer, Karl, 451
Bonhoeffer, Paula, 451
Brahms, Johannes, 13
Broecker, Wallace, 304
Bruno, Giordano, 194, 322
Buñuel, Luis, 209
Bush, George H. W., 46, 79, 81, 95, 97, 440
Bush, George W., 42, 220, 266, 269, 270, 440-42
Butler, George Lee, 35, 268-69
Brzezinski, Zbigniew, 105-06, 126

C

Cabaret (film), 396
Calasso, Roberto, 187
Callick, Rowan, 395-97, 473
Calvin, John, 470

Calvin, William, 153
Cambodia, 102-04, 131, 157, 266, 292
Cancer, 8, 35, 100, 154-55, 268, 303, 309, 355, 437-39, 462
Castleden, Rodney, 208-18 (*passim*)
Cervantes, Miguel de, 338, 339, 354
Changchun (as 'city of death'), 464
Charlie Hebdo (terrorist attack), xii, 157, 388, 455, 470
Charter 08, xvii, 366, 369-70
Chauvet Cave, 202
Chavez, Hugo, 270-72, 312, 315-16, 384-86
Chile, economic reform in, xviii-xix, 109, 132, 270-71, 313-16
China Development Brief, 264
Chinese Communist Party, xvii, 6, 264, 288, 290, 297, 326, 330, 367, 464
China Youth and Juvenile Research Centre, 396
Chomsky, Noam, xi, 42-44, 92-93, 102, 109, 154
Churchill, Winston, 20, 21, 69, 111,
CIA, 29, 182, 382
Civil rights, 126, 288, 332, 367
Civil Rights Act 1964 (US), 406, 409
Cixi (Tzu Hsi), Chinese empress, 421-22
Clarke, Arthur C., 123
Clarke, Richard, 382
Clarridge, Duane 'Dewey', 270-71
Clausewitz, Carl von, 121-23
Climate change debate, xii, 107, 153, 298-306, 319-21, 363
Cohn, Norman, 59
Cohn-Bendit, Daniel, 173
College of Pontiffs, 400-01

Conspiracy theory, 49, 52, 55, 317, 423, 425, 427-28
Cook, Michael, 87, 242-43, 246, 248, 277-78, 292, 382
Cooper, Paulette, 393
Copernicus, Nicolaus, 320, 322
Crowe, Russell, 446
Cult Awareness Network, 392-93

D

Dalai Lama, 367, 401
Dante, 61, 78, 176, 183-84, 334-35, 401
Darwin, Charles, 154, 198, 256
Davies, Paul, 155, 437-39, 466
Dawkins, Richard, 196, 402
Dead Sea Scrolls, 205-06
De Gaulle, Charles, xxiii, 18-21, 52, 54, 71-73
Deir Yasin, 341
Deng Xiaoping, xvii, 97, 113, 115, 126-27, 139, 276, 371, 451, 465
Deng Xiaoping Thought Research Centre, 396
Diamond, Jared, 398-99
Doctor Strangelove, 35, 36, 126
Dorling, Philip, 418-19
Dreyfus, Hubert, 333-34
Dudamel, Gustavo, 386

E

East Timor, 163, 219-22, 224-28, 231, 233-34, 237-41, 243, 245-51, 274, 291, 417, 419
Edwards, John (economist), 434-36
Edwards, Peter (historian), 84-88, 224
Edwards, Sebastian, 312-15
Egypt, 132, 207, 210, 212-14, 216, 356, 408-410, 458-60, 469

Eichmann, Adolf, 36, 104, 141, 455-56, 456-57
Einstein, Albert, 111, 124, 155, 299
El-Baradei, Mohammed, 344
El Sistema, 386
Ellsberg, Daniel, xxvi-xxvii, xxix, 34, 87, 149, 151, 177, 179-82, 317-18
Empty chair, 371
EP-3 incident, 275
Euthanasia, xii, xvi, 311, 462-63
Evita, 385

F

Fagan, Brian, 197, 202
Faulkner, John, 87, 277-78
Federation of American Scientists, 275
Fitzgibbon, Joel, 277
Fraser, Malcolm, 246, 265, 274, 347, 364, 448-49
Free trade (critique of), 113, 314, 375-76
Friedberg, Aaron, 350-51
Friedman, George, 38-40
Friedman. Milton, 314
Fukuyama, Francis, 5, 146
Furlonger, Robert, 224, 229-37, 239-40, 249-50

G

Galileo Galilei, 289, 322-23, 362, 468
Garden of Eden, 141, 202, 207
Garnaut, Ross, 80, 363-64, 395, 434-36
Gates, Robert, 318, 440-43
Genesis (book of), 446
Genocide, xii, 22, 35, 102, 105, 131, 142, 157, 159, 189, 266, 281, 288, 455
Gettysburg address, 406
Gatekeepers, The (documentary film), 22, 459

Gaza (conflict in), 22, 342, 372, 416, 453-54, 458-60
GFC (Global Financial Crisis), 288, 312
Gibbon, Edward, xxi, 61, 194, 469
Gorbachev, Mikhail, 5-6, 29, 64-67, 126, 146, 148, 189, 192
Gould, Stephen Jay, 154-55
Graves, Robert, 204, 206
Great Leap Forward (famine caused by), xxvii, 104-05, 145, 465
Great Terror, xxi, 48, 145, 282-84, 309
Green, Marshall, 25-28,
GRU, 29, 32, 48-50, 86, 278
GULAG, 7-8, 48, 145-46, 281-82, 306, 309, 311, 465
Guo Guoding, 264-65

H

Hamas (terrorist organization), xvi, 22, 388, 416, 453-54, 459-60
Hamilton, Alexander, 376
Hansen, James, 302-04
Harris, Sam, 378-80
Hartcher, Peter, 414
Havel, Vaclav, 185, 369-71
Heidegger, Martin, 74-75, 77-78, 333-34, 386, 391
Heisbourg, Francois, 63-67
Heisenberg, Werner, 109-112, 299-300
Henry, Ken, 414-15
Henry Tax Review (2008), 414
Hersh, Seymour, 45-47, 56, 132
Himmler, Heinrich, 141, 143
Hitler, Adolf, 14, 20, 48-49, 67, 110-12, 120, 131, 141, 143, 145-46, 148, 159, 255, 281, 396, 452

Hitler Youth, 396
Ho Chi Minh, 19, 149-52, 438
Hoffmann, Abbie, 175, 177
Hoffmann, Philip Seymour, 391
Hollander, Paul, 92-95
Holocaust, 7, 34, 37, 46, 61, 141, 157-59, 298, 345-46, 347, 373, 388, 393, 454, 456
Hong Kong, xvii, xxx, 96, 98, 113-15, 125-26, 128, 133-36, 138, 215, 265
Hope Royal Commission on intelligence and security, 277
Hopkins, Anthony, 446
How Old is the Universe? (book), 319
Hubbard, L. Ron, xiii, 391-93
Hubble, Edwin, 320
Hume, David, 194, 378-79, 468
Humes, James, 57

I

IAEA, 344-46, 356-57
Indonesia, 25-28, 86, 105, 219-52 (*passim*), 273-74, 291-92, 403-04, 417, 419, 429-30
Intelligent design, 466, 468
IPCC, 301-02, 305, 446
Iran, xi, xv-xvi, xxvi, 35, 45, 47, 62, 64, 84, 186, 205, 266, 268-69, 279-80, 318, 344-46, 356-57, 389, 429-30, 442
Iranian nuclear program, 279
Irving, David, 141, 157
ISIS (ISIL) (Islamic terrorist organization), 455-57, 460, 469-70, 474
Israel, xii, 22-24, 35, 45-47, 59, 61, 92, 157, 205, 269, 279-80, 294, 336-37, 340-43, 344-46, 356-57, 372-74, 387-90, 453-54, 458-61

J

Jane, Frederick, 69
Japan, xxv, 29, 38-40, 46, 64, 66, 68, 70, 79-80, 82, 96, 98, 110, 125-26, 132, 139, 151, 276, 351, 399, 420, 434, 449, 451, 464-65
Jardine Matheson, 115
Jockel, Gordon, 224-28, 230, 232, 234-36, 238-43, 248-50, 274, 292
Jung Chang, 421-22

K

Kadeer, Rebiya, 288
Kahan Commission, 373
Kahn, Herman, 36, 125-26
KAL-007, 45-46
Kahneman, Daniel, 358-59
Kant, Immanuel, 194, 319-20, 334-35, 361, 370
Karine A (affair), 389
Kaunda, Kenneth, 399
Keating, Paul, 80, 87, 277, 312, 382, 403-04, 434, 448
Keegan, John, 120-23
Keeling, Charles David, 304
Kennan, George Frost, 99-101
Kennedy, John Fitzgerald, 52-58, 72, 92, 128, 223, 273, 344, 423-25, 427-28
Kennedy, Paul, 105-08
Kennedy, Robert (Bobby), 172, 427
Kessing, Allan Robert, 263
Keynes, John Maynard, 12, 15
Khlevniuk, Oleg, 282
Khmer Rouge, xxii, 102-04, 131, 266
Kilcullen, David, 442
Kim Il-Sung, 165-69 (*passim*)

Kim Jong-Il, 96, 163, 166-68
Kim Dae-Jung, 171
King George III, 134
King, Martin Luther, 367, 407
Kissinger, Henry, xviii, 31, 45-46, 129-32, 221, 317, 345
KGB, 29, 31-32, 48, 50-51, 54-55, 86, 145, 173, 277-78, 281, 318, 382, 418
Klimt, Gustav, 13
Knopfelmacher, Frank, xxvi, 7-8, 94-95, 146, 175, 182
Knossos (Crete), 212, 215-16
Koestler, Arthur, 145, 306-07, 309-11
Komer, Robert, 178
Kraus, Karl, 13
Krivitsky, Walter, 48-49
Kubrick, Stanley, 126

L

Langer, Albert, 174-75
Lavarch, Michael, 87, 277
Lean, David, 89
Lebensborn Experiment, 141-43
Le Carré, John, 23, 29, 51
Lee Kuan Yew, 125, 435
Lehrer, Tom, 196
Lessig, Lawrence, 94, 376
Levi, Primo, 34
Levitt, Stephen D., 360, 398
Levy Bernard-Henri, 92, 103
Lewis, Michael, 359
Lincoln, Abraham, 54, 376, 406
Liu Xiaobo, xvii, 326, 330, 366, 369-70
Lives of Others, The, 262
Luther, Martin, 470
Luttwak, Edward, 347-49

M

Mahler, Gustav, 13
Mandela, Nelson, 6
Mann, Thomas, 13, 204, 207
Manne, Robert, 157, 163, 473
McCarthy, Joseph, 257
McCarthy, Mary, 253, 257, 262
McNamara, Robert S., xxvi, 22, 34, 87, 178, 268, 317-18, 438
Mao Zedong, xv, xxii, xxvii, 18, 25, 97, 104-05, 115, 145, 281, 326, 328-29, 421, 465
Markwell, Donald, 208
Menzies, Robert Gordon, 223-24, 234, 245, 250, 273-74, 291, 364
Metaxas, Eric, 466-68
Mexico, 272, 313-15, 385
Milgram, Stanley, 36, 394
Milky Way, 319-20, 466
Miscavige, David, 391-94
Miscavige Hill, Jenna, 391-93
Mitrokhin, Vasili (archive), 277-78
Mommsen, Theodor, xxi, 39, 377
Monbiot, Georges, 305
Montaigne, 117, 194, 289
Montero, Gabriela, 385-86
Moore, Steven, 354
More, Thomas, 212
Morsi, Mohammed, 408
Mossad, 22-23
Mugabe, Robert, 399
Muslim Brotherhood, 408, 470
Mussolini, Benito, 146, 148, 356

N

Nabokov, Vladimir, 172, 307, 354
Naim, Moises, 271
Nanjing (1937 atrocities in), 464-65
Nembutal, 462
Newman, John Henry, 191-92, 205
Nguyen Ngoc Loan, 177
Nietzsche, Friedrich, xiii, 14, 17, 33, 131, 174, 185, 187-88, 195, 203, 205, 333, 334, 361
Nitze, Paul H., 268-69
North, Oliver, 44
Nuclear Non-Proliferation Treaty (NPT)
Nyerere, Julius, 399

O

Obama, Barack, 127, 269, 280, 289, 366, 375-76, 407, 416, 418, 440-42, 448-49
Olson, Mancur, 376
Operation Freakout, 393
Operation Liver, 277, 382
Opium Wars, 134-35
Oppenheimer, J. Robert, 12, 110, 111
Origen, 194
Orwell, George, 5, 145, 253, 285, 289
Oswald, Lee Harvey, 52-56, 58, 423-24, 426, 428
Ottolenghi, Emanuele, 279-80
Overholt, William, 125-28

P

Pacific Asian policy package, 127
Palestine, 24, 158, 175, 294-95, 307, 336-37, 340-42, 373, 453-54, 460
Palmyra, 469-71
Pasternak, Boris, 308, 380
Peel Commission Plan 1937, 342, 453

Pell, George (Cardinal), 331
Pentagon, xxvi, 22, 34, 63, 85, 87, 92, 126, 179, 317, 344, 440-42
Pentagon Papers, xxix, 84, 87, 173, 179, 317
Peres, Shimon, 23, 389, 454
Petit, Philippe, 362
Petraeus, David, 267, 441-42
Philby, Kim, 30, 48-51, 278
Pilger, John, 270
Plato, 58, 74, 81, 116-18, 194, 208-18
Platonov, Andrei, 308, 355
Plimer, Ian, 302
Pollard, Jonathan, 23
Pol Pot, 102-04, 145
Pontifex Maximus, 400-02
Pope Benedict XVI, 187, 302, 400
Pope Gregory the Great, 401
Pope John Paul II, 183-85, 187, 189-90, 192-95, 323
Pope Leo the Great, 185, 401
Pope Pius IX, 185, 401
Pope Urban VIII, 323
Popper, Karl, 211, 218, 299, 302, 467
Port Huron Statement, 180-81
Prestowitz, Clyde, 375-77,
Putin, Vladimir, xi, 31, 63, 67, 281, 318, 355, 418-19

Q

Qianlong, Emperor, 134
Qutb, Sayyid, 470

R

Rabin, Yitzhak, 389
RAND Corporation, xxvi, 34, 178, 317
Reagan, Ronald, 46, 79-80, 94, 129, 173, 178,

189-90, 440

Reformation, xx, 193, 401, 470

Roman Empire, xxi, 59, 61-62, 173, 194, 212, 356, 399-400, 469

Roosevelt, Franklin Delano, 20-21, 110-11, 130, 283

Rudd, Kevin, 264, 270, 296-97, 312, 327, 408, 430

Russell, Bertrand, 12-13

Russo, Lucio, 323

S

Salk Institute, 379

Sanger, Larry, 318

Santamaria, Bob, 172

Santorini, 210, 212-15, 217

Sanya, Chinese naval base, 275-76

Sartre, Jean-Paul, 104, 147-48, 190, 281, 333-34

Schell, Jonathan, 35, 153, 268, 345

Schoenberg, Arnold, 13

School of Life, 361

Scientology, Church of, 391-94

Sharon, Ariel, 372-74, 389

Shawcross, William, 103, 266

Shentalinsky, Vitaly, 308-09

Shiller, Robert, 359

Shirer, William L., 141

Short, Peter, 462

Snowden, Edward, 42, 418-20

Socrates, xiv, xix, 208, 289, 370, 462

Solvay conferences, 111, 299-301, 305

Solzhenitsyn, Alexander, 145, 281-82, 306-11 (*passim*), 355

Sontag, Susan, 255-56

SOSH (Westpoint), 441

Spence, Jonathan, 128

Spielberg, Stephen, 406-07

Stalin, Joseph, xxi-xxiii, 6-8, 18-20, 29, 34, 36, 48-51, 63, 67, 72, 99, 104-05, 130-31, 145-46, 165-67, 173, 183, 255, 281-85 (*passim*), 306-09, 355, 391

Stalin's Police (Hagenloh), 281, 283-84

Stangneth, Bettina, 141, 456

Stasi, 262-63

Steiner, George, 17, 74-78, 194, 199

Stevens, Thaddeus, 406-07

Stone, Oliver, 52, 56-58, 426

Students for a Democratic Society (SDS), 180

Suharto, 26-28, 219-21, 226-27, 229-30, 232-39, 243, 245-50, 273-74, 291-92

Sukarno, 25-28, 220, 223, 227, 229, 242, 250, 273-74, 291

Sunstein, Cass, 359

Syria (civil war in), xi, 23, 62, 346, 357, 408, 416-17, 457-58, 460, 469

T

Tacitus (Roman historian), xxi, 222, 289, 462

Tamerlane, 62, 469-70

Tange, Arthur, 224, 226-28, 234, 274, 292

Tanner, Lindsay, 409

Temple Institute, 388

Thucydides, xiv, 39, 78, 84, 177, 211

Thurow, Lester C., 79-82

Tiananmen Square, 6, 97, 126, 134, 182, 264-65, 329, 465

Tibet, 114, 330, 366-68

Tjan, Harry, 228-40, 242-45, 247-50

Toffler, Alvin, 120, 123-24

Tolkien, J. R. R., 74-78, 173, 463

Tolstoy, Leo, 14, 117-18, 188-90, 307-08, 310, 355, 362
Totalitarianism, 43, 50, 59, 99, 145-48, 369
Trotsky, Leo, 18-19, 48-49, 147, 281, 284-85
Tyler, Patrick, 387-90

U

UKUSA intelligence alliance, 240, 420
Unauthorized surveys, 264
United Nations Security Council, 35-36, 126, 179, 269, 279, 416

V

Venezuela, xi, xvi, 270-72, 312-16, 384-86
Venezuelan homicide rate, 385
Vietnam War, xxiv, 8, 16, 25, 84-88, 92, 94, 105, 120, 126, 130, 132, 149, 177, 179-80, 257, 266-67, 317, 404, 438
Voltaire, 194-95, 289, 378-79, 470

W

Walesa, Lech, 176
Wallace, David Foster, 333
Wallace, George, 367
Walter, Bruno, 13
Warfare, 19-20, 106, 121-24, 142, 145, 198, 213, 418
Warren Commission, 52-53, 55-57, 424-27
Washington Consensus, 312-13, 315, 375
Wawrinka, Stanislas, 432-33
Webber, Andrew Lloyd, 385
Weber, Max, xxvi, xxviii, 11, 333
Weil, Simone, xxiii, 176
Weinberg, Steven, 467
Weizmann, Chaim, 337
Wells, H. G., 143
West Bank, the, 22, 342, 388, 453-54, 458-59
West Papua (Irian Jaya), 219, 242, 251, 274, 291

Whitlam, Edward Gough, 174, 219, 221, 224-30, 232-39, 242-51, 274, 292
Why Australia Prospered (book), 435
Why Translation Matters (book), 338
WikiLeaks, 317, 327
Winchester, Simon, xvi, 96-98
Wise, David, 383
Wittgenstein, Ludwig, xx, 12-15, 74, 299
Woodward, Bob, 441
Woolcott, Richard, 219, 233, 239, 241, 243, 245-49, 252, 292-93
Wright, Lawrence, 391-94
Wright, Peter, 30, 48, 51

X

Xi Jinping, xi, 366, 464

Y

Yamamoto, Isoroku, 70
Yan Jiaqi, 330, 349
Young, Nick, 264-65

Z

Zenobia, 469
Zionism, xii, 24, 294-95, 307, 337, 340, 387
Zwingli, Huldrych, 470